"This *Handbook* undertakes a crucial reboot of media studies in light of the global climate crisis, reckoning with an array of urgent planetary matters. Assembling the most lucid thinkers in ecomedia studies, the book confronts the entanglement of media and ecology and unfurls vital forms of research and action."

Lisa Parks, *Distinguished Professor of Media Studies, UC Santa Barbara*

"Media Studies should always have been Ecomedia Studies, but it wasn't. A generation of pioneer scholars worked to change that, and most of them have written chapters for this absolutely essential collection. This book will from now on be a key reference-point."

Nick Couldry, *London School of Economics and Political Science*

"This collection is extremely useful in both being aware of the earlier waves of eco-criticism while stating out clearly and in depth that the only way forward for media studies is with ecology at its core – not just as one 'theme' but as the very essence of how politics and planetary futures unfold. The *Handbook* will become essential reading."

Jussi Parikka, *Aarhus University, author of* Insect Media *and* A Geology of Media

"*The Routledge Handbook of Ecomedia Studies* is a timely constellation of essays that whirls into the elements, borderlands, digital worlds, energetics, and spheres of affect—addressing how media not only represent the environment but are fundamentally *of* the environment. This book will be a valuable reference for years to come."

Melody Jue, *Associate Professor of English, UC Santa Barbara, author of* Wild Blue Media

THE ROUTLEDGE HANDBOOK OF ECOMEDIA STUDIES

The Routledge Handbook of Ecomedia Studies gathers leading work by critical scholars in this burgeoning field. Redressing the lack of environmental perspectives in the study of media, ecomedia studies asserts that media are in and about the environment, and environments are socially and materially mediated.

The book gives form to this new area of study and brings together diverse scholarly contributions to explore and give definition to the field. The *Handbook* highlights five critical areas of ecomedia scholarship: ecomedia theory, ecomateriality, political ecology, ecocultures, and eco-affects. Within these areas, authors navigate a range of different topics including infrastructures, supply and manufacturing chains, energy, e-waste, labor, ecofeminism, African and Indigenous ecomedia, environmental justice, environmental media governance, ecopolitical satire, and digital ecologies. The result is a holistic volume that provides an in-depth and comprehensive overview of the current state of the field, as well as future developments.

This volume will be an essential resource for students, educators, and scholars of media studies, cultural studies, film, environmental communication, political ecology, science and technology studies, and the environmental humanities.

Antonio López is Professor of Communications and Media Studies at John Cabot University in Rome, Italy. He has a research focus on bridging ecojustice with media education and is a founding theorist and architect of ecomedia literacy. He created the website ecomedialiteracy.org to provide resources for students and educators. His monographs are *Ecomedia Literacy: Integrating Ecology into Media Education* (2021), *Greening Media Education: Bridging Media Literacy with Green Cultural Citizenship* (2014), *The Media Ecosystem: What Ecology Can Teach Us About Responsible Media Practice* (2012), and *Mediacology: A Multicultural Approach to Media Literacy in the 21st Century* (2008).

Adrian Ivakhiv is Professor of Environmental Thought and Culture, and Steven Rubenstein Professor of Environment and Natural Resources, at the University of Vermont. From 2024 he will be J. S. Woodsworth Chair in the Humanities at Simon Fraser University, Vancouver. His books include *Ecologies of the Moving Image: Cinema, Affect, Nature* (2013), *Shadowing the Anthropocene: Eco-Realism for Turbulent Times* (2018), and the forthcoming *The New Lives of*

Images: Digital Ecologies and Anthropocene Imaginaries in More-than-Human Worlds. He is Research Fellow of the Cinepoetics Centre for Advanced Film Studies at Freie Universität Berlin, co-edits the *Media+Environment* journal, and blogs at Immanence: Ecoculture, Geophilosophy, MediaPolitics.

Stephen Rust teaches Cinema Studies and Writing at the University of Oregon and Oregon State University. He is co-editor of *Ecocinema Theory and Practice* (2013), *Ecomedia: Key Issues* (2016), and *Ecocinema Theory and Practice 2* (2023), and is a founding advisory board member of *Media+Environment* and the *Journal of Environmental Media*.

Miriam Tola is Assistant Professor at John Cabot University in Rome, Italy. Her work explores the intersections between gender, race, species, and the cultural politics of the environmental crisis. Her articles have appeared in journals including *South Atlantic Quarterly*, *Feminist Review*, *Environmental Humanities*, and *Feminist Studies*. She is the co-editor of the book *Ecologie della cura* and co-edits Living Lexicon for the *Environmental Humanities* journal.

Alenda Y. Chang is Associate Professor of Film and Media Studies at the University of California, Santa Barbara. Her book, *Playing Nature: Ecology in Video Games*, develops environmentally informed frameworks for understanding and designing digital games. She is a founding co-editor of the open-access journal *Media+Environment* and co-directs Wireframe, a studio that fosters collaborative theory and creative media practice invested in global social and environmental justice.

Kiu-wai Chu is Assistant Professor of Environmental Humanities and Chinese Studies at Nanyang Technological University, Singapore. He is also Luce East Asia Fellow 2022–2023 at the National Humanities Center, USA. He is currently Executive Councillor of the Association for the Study of Literature and Environment (ASLE-US) and Living Lexicon co-editor of *Environmental Humanities*. His research focus includes ecocriticism, human–animal studies, and contemporary film and art in Chinese and global Asian contexts. His work has appeared in *Transnational Ecocinema*, *Ecomedia: Key Issues*, *Chinese Environmental Humanities*, *Journal of Chinese Cinemas*, *Asian Cinema*, *photographies*, and *Screen*.

THE ROUTLEDGE HANDBOOK OF ECOMEDIA STUDIES

*Edited by Antonio López, Adrian Ivakhiv, Stephen Rust,
Miriam Tola, Alenda Y. Chang and Kiu-wai Chu*

Designed cover image: Core Dump 'E-Revenant' (2018) by Francois Knoetze. Photo Zidan, Courtesy of the Execution Team of Cosmopolis 1.5. Chengdu (2018). Reproduced with permission of Francois Knoetze.

First published 2024
by Routledge
4 Park Square, Milton Park, Abingdon, Oxon OX14 4RN

and by Routledge
605 Third Avenue, New York, NY 10158

Routledge is an imprint of the Taylor & Francis Group, an informa business

© 2024 selection and editorial matter, of Antonio López, Adrian Ivakhiv, Stephen Rust, Miriam Tola, Alenda Y. Chang and Kiu-wai Chu; individual chapters, the contributors

The right of Antonio López, Adrian Ivakhiv, Stephen Rust, Miriam Tola, Alenda Y. Chang and Kiu-wai Chu to be identified as the authors of the editorial material, and of the authors for their individual chapters, has been asserted in accordance with sections 77 and 78 of the Copyright, Designs and Patents Act 1988.

The Open Access version of this book, available at www.taylorfrancis.com, has been made available under a Creative Commons Attribution-Non Commercial-No Derivatives (CC-BY-NC-ND) 4.0 license.
Funded by multiple funders.

Trademark notice: Product or corporate names may be trademarks or registered trademarks, and are used only for identification and explanation without intent to infringe.

British Library Cataloguing-in-Publication Data
A catalogue record for this book is available from the British Library

ISBN: 978-1-032-00942-1 (hbk)
ISBN: 978-1-032-00944-5 (pbk)
ISBN: 978-1-003-17649-7 (ebk)

DOI: 10.4324/9781003176497

Typeset in Times New Roman
by codeMantra

CONTENTS

List of figures   *xi*
List of contributors   *xiii*
Acknowledgments   *xxiii*

Introduction   1
Antonio López, Adrian Ivakhiv, Stephen Rust, Miriam Tola, Alenda Y. Chang, and Kiu-wai Chu

PART I
Ecomedia Theory   **17**

1 When Do Media Become *Eco*media?   19
  Adrian Ivakhiv and Antonio López

2 Three Ecologies: Ecomediality as Ontology   35
  Adrian Ivakhiv

3 Meaning, Matter, Ecomedia   43
  Christy Tidwell

4 Blue Media Ecologies: Swimming through the Mediascape with
  Sir David Attenborough   51
  Stephen Rust and Verena Wurth

5 Political and Apolitical Ecologies of Digital Media   59
  Sy Taffel

6   Centering Africa in Ecomedia Studies: Interview with Cajetan Iheka   67
    Miriam Tola, Kiu-wai Chu, and Stephen Rust

7   Ecomedia and Empire in the US–Mexico Borderlands, 1880–1912   73
    Carlos Alonso Nugent

8   Spatial Documentary Studies, *El Mar La Mar*, and Elemental
    Media Remediated   84
    Janet Walker

9   Ecomedia Literacy: Bringing Ecomedia Studies into the Classroom   99
    Antonio López

PART II
Ecomateriality   **109**

10 Disaggregated Footprints: An Infrastructural Literacy Approach to the
    Sustainable Internet   111
    Nicole Starosielski, Hunter Vaughan, Anne Pasek, and
    Nicholas R. Silcox

11 Collapse Informatics and the Environmental Impact of Information and
    Communication Technologies   119
    Laura U. Marks

12 Electronic Environmentalism: Monitoring and Making Ecological Crises   129
    Jennifer Gabrys

13 Radiant Energy and Media Infrastructures of the South   137
    Rahul Mukherjee

14 Micro/Climates of Play: On the Thermal Contexts of Games   145
    Alenda Y. Chang

15 Relational Ecologies of the Gramophone Disc   153
    Elodie A. Roy

16 *Core Dump*: The Global Aesthetics and Politics of E-Waste   160
    Mehita Iqani

PART III
Political Ecology   169

17 Carbon Capitalism, Communication, and Artificial Intelligence: Placing
   the Climate Emergency Center Stage   171
   Benedetta Brevini and Daisy Doctor

18 Environmental Media Management: Overcoming the Responsibility Deficit 179
   Pietari Kääpä and Hunter Vaughan

19 Property Rights Control in the Data-Driven Economy: The Media
   Ecology of Blockchain Registries   187
   Jannice Käll

20 Common Pool Resources, Communication, and the Global Media Commons   194
   Patrick D. Murphy and E. Septime Sessou

21 #NOLNG253! Media Use in Modern Environmental Justice Movements   203
   Ellen E. Moore and Anna Bean

22 Contesting Digital Colonial Power: Indigenous Australian Sovereignty
   and Self-Determination in Digital Worlds   212
   Corrinne Sullivan and Jessica McLean

23 Who Makes Our Smartphones? Four Moments in Their Lifecycle   220
   Richard Maxwell and Toby Miller

PART IV
Ecocultures   229

24 Media and Ecocultural Identity   231
   Tema Milstein, Gabi Mocatta, and José Castro-Sotomayor

25 Eco-Territorial Media Practices: Defending Bodies, Territories, and Life
   Itself in Latin America   244
   Diana Coryat

26 Mapping for Accountability: Decolonizing Land Acknowledgment Initiatives 252
   Salma Monani and Sarah Gilsoul

27 Black Media Philosophy and Visual Ecologies: A Conversation between
    Armond Towns and Jeremy Kamal   261
    Armond Towns and Jeremy Kamal

28 On the Ecological Futurabilities of Experimental Film Labs   271
    Noélie Martin and Jacopo Rasmi

29 Popular Music: Folk and Folk Rock as Green Cultural Production   278
    John Parham

30 Women in the Global Pandemic Media Imagination: Mimetic Desire,
    Scapegoating Buddhist Hermeneutic, and Beyond   286
    Chia-ju Chang

PART V
Eco-Affects   **295**

31 Ecomentia, from Televised Catastrophe to Performative Assembly:
    Collapsonaut Attention in a House on Fire   297
    Yves Citton

32 Feeling *Wild*: The Mediation of Embodied Experience   305
    Alexa Weik von Mossner

33 Social Realism and Environmental Crisis: Clio Barnard's *Dark River*   312
    David Ingram

34 Ecopolitical Satire in the Global North   319
    Nicole Seymour and Anthony Lioi

35 Fear and Loathing in Ecomedia: Channeling Fear through Horror Tropes
    in Invasive Species Outreach   327
    Katrina Maggiulli

36 Slow Media, Eco-Mindfulness, and the Lifeworld   337
    Jennifer Rauch

Afterword: Posthumous Ecomedia   *345*
Seán Cubitt
Further Reading   *350*
Index   *357*

FIGURES

7.1	Ben Wittick, *Acequia Madre, Albuquerque New Mexico* (1881a,b)	74
7.2	NMBI, *Illustrated New Mexico* (1883, 23)	76
7.3	NMBI, *Farming by Irrigation in New Mexico* (1897)	77
7.4	NMBI, *Farming by Irrigation in New Mexico* (1897)	78
7.5	NMBI, *Heart of the Well Country* (1912)	80
8.1	The border wall prior to its disappearance from *El Mar La Mar*. Image by Joshua Bonnetta and J.P. Sniadecki, included with permission	87
8.2	Shooting along the border wall, "changing focal length and … focus"	87
8.3	Image from *El Mar La Mar* by Joshua Bonnetta and J.P. Sniadecki	89
8.4	Grid infrastructure in the vicinity of the Arivaca Lake Reservoir. Image from *El Mar La Mar*	90
8.5	Shot-mapping *El Mar La Mar*	90
8.6	Baboquivari Peak. Image from *El Mar La Mar*	93
9.1	The ecomediasphere using fake climate news as the ecomedia object	102
10.1	Extinction Rebellion anti-data center protest	117
11.1	The infrastructure beyond the image	121
11.2	Coughing cat meme	125
16.1	Core Dump "E-Revenant" (2018) by Francois Knoetze	161
26.1	Two views of the Tammany Regiment monument on Hancock Avenue on the Gettysburg National Military Park—looking north, and looking south with the Pennsylvania monument in the background	254
27.1	*Mojo: Da Floods* (2019) is one of a series of animated vignettes that depict a world where the rituals of Black culture shape geological phenomena. Each vignette is a portal into speculative ecosystems, landscapes, atmospheres, and climates that synchronize with the movement of black bodies in space. In this animated vignette, a music producer/sound engineer utilizes a tactile interface in order to operate a gantry crane used to mix and master sound spatially	261

Figures

27.2	*Mojo: Da Floods* (2019); bass notes from amplified music vibrate large bodies of water held in cisterns. The vibrations register cymatic patterns on the water surface used to help tune and EQ sound. Excess spill-over irrigates surrounding soil and flora distributed by seed-dropping drones	265
27.3	*Mojo: Da Floods* (2019); the film reframes the historic narrative of the black body as a landscape technology for colonial profit. Distinctions between the body and the landscape are blurred as technological systems allow black creativity, expression, and spirituality to materialize on an ecological scale. Tundras, grasslands, and forests are now the sites of music studios, cookouts, and kickbacks. Hands that worked the land for labor now shape the land for leisure	265
30.1	The tubed-up mother in a building under construction is juxtaposed against the backdrop of the Mekong River in *The Che Brother* (2020)	291
30.2	Two stills from *The Che Brother* (2020). These are perspective shots from the mother's and the River's perspectives, showing Xe paying homage to both his mother and Mother Nature. The one on the left is Xe's semi-conscious, tube-ridden mother in bed looking up at her son who, after caressing her feet, touches his forehead. The one on the right is from the River's perspective, where Xe first touches the water and then his forehead	292
35.1	"Have We Met? I'm Your Worst Nightmare": USDA APHIS produced banner display for outreach featuring the Vin Vasive "Hungry Pests" mascot, 2012	332

CONTRIBUTORS

Georgianna Bean (Anna) was born on the Puyallup Reservation in Tacoma, Washington and is an enrolled member of the Puyallup Tribe of Indians. In 2017 she became actively involved with the grassroots efforts against the Puget Sound Energy Liquefied Gas Plant on the Tacoma tide flats. In that effort she became known as one of the Puyallup Tribal Water Warriors. In 2018, Anna was elected to the Puyallup Tribal Council, where she currently is serving her in her 2nd term. In her current capacity, she has been able to assist grassroots efforts through legislation and remains passionate about protecting, restoring, and fighting for mother earth.

Benedetta Brevini is Associate Professor of Political economy of Communication at the University of Sydney and Senior Visiting Research Fellow at London School of Economics. She worked as journalist in Milan, New York, and London for *CNBC*, *RAI*, and *The Guardian* and held tenured positions at City University London and Brunel University, London. She writes on *The Guardian*'s Comment is Free and contributes to a number of publications including *South China Morning Post*, *OpenDemocracy*, and *The Conversation*. She is the author of several books including *Amazon: Understanding a Global Communication Giant* (2020), *Public Service Broadcasting Online* (2013), *Beyond Wikileaks* (2013), *Carbon Capitalism and Communication: Confronting Climate Crisis* (2017), and *Climate Change and the Media* (2018). *Is AI Good for the Planet?* (2021) is her latest volume. She is currently working on a new book project on Murdoch and his global media empire.

José Castro-Sotomayor is Assistant Professor at California State University Channel Islands. His work investigates environmental and intercultural dynamics of human and more-than-human communication, agency, and dissent. He is co-editor of *The Routledge Handbook of Ecocultural Identity* (2020).

Alenda Y. Chang is Associate Professor of Film and Media Studies at the University of California, Santa Barbara. Her book, *Playing Nature: Ecology in Video Games*, develops environmentally informed frameworks for understanding and designing digital games. She is a founding co-editor of the open-access journal *Media+Environment* and co-directs Wireframe, a studio that fosters collaborative theory and creative media practice invested in global social and environmental justice.

Contributors

Chia-ju Chang is Professor and Chair of the Department of Modern Languages and Literatures at Brooklyn College (CUNY). Her research interests include Chinese and comparative ecocriticism, multispecies and critical animal studies, eco-cinema studies, and eco-Buddhist studies. She is the author of *The Global Imagination of the Ecological Communities: Western and Chinese Ecocritical Praxis* (2013; Chinese). She has edited an anthology *Chinese Environmental Humanities: Environing at the Margins* (2019) and co-edited *Ecocriticism in Taiwan: Identity, Environment, and the Arts* (2016; with Scott Slovic). Her articles have appeared in many peer-reviewed journals as well as scholarly collections.

Kiu-wai Chu is Assistant Professor of Environmental Humanities and Chinese Studies at Nanyang Technological University, Singapore. He is also Luce East Asia Fellow 2022–2023 at the National Humanities Center, USA. He is currently Executive Councilor of the ASLE-US and Living Lexicon co-editor of *Environmental Humanities*. His research focus includes ecocriticism, human-animal studies, and contemporary film and art in Chinese and global Asian contexts. His work has appeared in *Transnational Ecocinema*, *Ecomedia: Key Issues*, *Chinese Environmental Humanities*, *Journal of Chinese Cinemas*, *Asian Cinema*, *photographies*, and *Screen*.

Yves Citton is fortunate enough to be paid to study and teach Literature and Media at the University Paris 8 Vincennes-Saint Denis and to count as one of the co-editors of the quarterly journal *Multitudes*. He recently published *Mediarchy* (2019), *The Ecology of Attention* (2017), *Altermodernités des Lumières* (2022), *Faire avec. Conflits, coalitions, contagions* (2021), *Générations Collapsonautes. Naviguer en temps d'effondrements* (2020), *Contre-courants politiques* (2018), *Zazirocratie* (2011). His articles can be accessed online at www.yvescitton.net.

Diana Coryat is an educator, researcher, and community media practitioner. Her recent work is focused on audiovisual defense of territory and feminist community media. She collaborates with Ojo Semilla, a feminist community cinema collective in Ecuador, and co-produces MendoLatino, a Spanish-language public affairs program on KZYX public and community radio. She co-founded and directed Global Action Project (New York). She teaches at the Universidad Andina Simon Bolívar in Quito, Ecuador, and Mendocino College, California. Diana holds an MA and PhD in Communication from UMass Amherst and BFA from New York University.

Seán Cubitt is Professor of Screen Studies at the University of Melbourne. His publications include *The Cinema Effect* (2004), *Finite Media: Environmental Implications of Digital Technologies* (2016), and *Anecdotal Evidence: Ecocritique from Hollywood to the Mass Image* (2020). Co-editor of *Ecomedia: Key Issues* (2016) and series editor for Leonardo Books, he researches the history and philosophy of media, ecopolitical aesthetics, media arts and technologies, and media art history.

Daisy Doctor is a journalist, freelance writer, and postgraduate student currently doing research on sustainability and communications. She is passionate about grassroots activism and understanding the intersection of social media and climate change.

Jennifer Gabrys is Chair in Media, Culture and Environment in the Department of Sociology at the University of Cambridge. She leads the Planetary Praxis research group and is Principal Investigator on the ERC-funded project, Smart Forests: Transforming Environments into

Contributors

Social-Political Technologies. Her newest book, *Citizens of Worlds: Open-Air Toolkits for Environmental Struggle*, was published in November 2022 and is available on Manifold as an open-access publishing experiment. She co-edits the "Planetarities" short-monograph series published through Goldsmiths Press. Her work can be found at planetarypraxis.org and jennifergabrys.net.

Sarah Gilsoul, originally from Utah, moved to the east coast to pursue a Bachelor of Arts degree in Environmental Studies and a minor in Education at Gettysburg College. She has always had a strong dedication to and love for the natural world, but at Gettysburg, she discovered a passion for environmental justice and communication. After graduating in the spring of 2022, Sarah has continued to pursue her interest in environmental communication at the Association of Zoos and Aquariums.

Cajetan Iheka is Professor of English at Yale University. He specializes in African literature, ecocriticism, ecomedia, and postcolonial literature. Iheka is the author of the books *African Ecomedia* (2021) and *Naturalizing Africa: Ecological Violence, Agency, and Postcolonial Resistance in African Literature* (2018), and the editor of the MLA volume *Teaching Postcolonial Environmental Literature and Media* (2022).

David Ingram is the author of *Green Screen: Environmentalism and Hollywood Cinema* (2000) and *The Jukebox in the Garden: Ecocriticism and American Popular Music Since 1960* (2010), as well as several articles on ecocriticism in film, music, and literature. He taught Film and Television Studies at Brunel University, London, until his retirement in 2020.

Mehita Iqani is the South African Research Chair in Science Communication based at Stellenbosch University and funded by the National Research Foundation. She is the author and editor of several books on media, consumer culture, luxury, waste, and the global south, the most recent of which include *Garbage in Popular Culture* (2021), *Consumption Media and the Global South* (2016), *Media Studies: Critical African and Decolonial Approaches* (2019), and *African Luxury* (2019).

Adrian Ivakhiv is Professor of Environmental Thought and Culture, and Steven Rubenstein Professor of Environment and Natural Resources, at the University of Vermont. From 2024 he will be J. S. Woodsworth Chair in the Humanities at Simon Fraser University, Vancouver. His books include *Ecologies of the Moving Image: Cinema, Affect, Nature* (2013), *Shadowing the Anthropocene: Eco-Realism for Turbulent Times* (2018), and the forthcoming *The New Lives of Images: Digital Ecologies and Anthropocene Imaginaries in More-than-Human Worlds*. He is a research fellow of the Cinepoetics Centre for Advanced Film Studies at Freie Universität Berlin, co-edits the *Media+Environment* journal, and blogs at Immanence: Ecoculture, Geophilosophy, MediaPolitics.

Pietari Kääpä is Reader in Media and Communications at the University of Warwick. He has published widely in the field of environmental media studies, including *Transnational Ecocinemas* (2013), *Ecology and Contemporary Nordic Cinemas* (2014), *Environmental Management of the Media: Industry, Policy, Practice* (2018), and *Film and Television Production in the Age of Climate Change* (2022) (with Hunter Vaughan). He is Co-PI of the Global Green Media Network.

Contributors

Jannice Käll is Associate Professor in Sociology of Law in the Department for Sociology of Law, Lund University, Sweden. Käll researches critical socio-legal aspects of digitalization, including AI. Her 2022 monograph *Posthuman Property and Law* was published with Routledge and focuses on new materialist philosophies of law and property in the context of digitalization.

Jeremy Kamal is a visual artist teaching at the Southern California Institute of Architecture, who engages CGI storytelling as a way of exploring relationships between culture, space, and ecology. In 2019, he released an animated short, *Mojo: The Floods*, which has been featured in Dezeen, Archinect, and screened at the Guggenheim Museum NY's World Around Summit 2022. Using films, animations, game engines, music, and storytelling, Kamal is depicting relationships between cultural abstractions and geological phenomena.

Anthony Lioi is Professor of English at The Juilliard School in New York City, where he teaches contemporary literature, composition, and the environmental humanities. His work has been published in *ISLE, Feminist Studies, ImageTexT, MELUS, Acoma, Ecozon@*, and in a number of critical anthologies. He is a past president of ASLE and an editor of *Resilience: A Journal of the Environmental Humanities*. In 2016, he published *Nerd Ecology*, the first ecocritical study of nerd culture. He is at work on *Metahumanism and Media*, on fan cultures as agents of ecotopia.

Antonio López has a research focus on bridging ecojustice with media education. He is a founding theorist and architect of ecomedia literacy. He created the website ecomedialiteracy.org for providing resources for students and educators. He monographs are *Ecomedia Literacy: Integrating Ecology into Media Education* (2021); *Greening Media Education: Bridging Media Literacy with Green Cultural Citizenship* (2014); *The Media Ecosystem: What Ecology Can Teach Us About Responsible Media Practice* (2012); and *Mediacology: A Multicultural Approach to Media Literacy in the 21st Century* (2008). Currently, he is Professor of Communications and Media Studies at John Cabot University in Rome, Italy.

Katrina Maggiulli is Assistant Teaching Professor of Comparative Cultural Studies/Environmental Humanities at Northern Arizona University. Anchored in her prior field work as an environmental educator for the U.S. Fish & Wildlife Service and various non-profits, her research focuses on the ethical dynamics of conservation policy, practice, education, and outreach. Her first book project is tentatively titled "Managing Life's Future: Species Essentialism and Evolutionary Normativity in Conservation Policy, Practice, and Imaginaries."

Laura U. Marks works on media art and philosophy with an intercultural focus and an emphasis on appropriate technologies. Her fifth book, *The Fold: From Your Body to the Cosmos*, is forthcoming. A co-founder of the Substantial Motion Research Network, Marks founded the Small File Media Festival and leads the research group Tackling the Carbon Footprint of Streaming Media. She programs experimental media art for venues around the world. A Fellow of the Royal Society of Canada, Marks teaches in the School for the Contemporary Arts at Simon Fraser University in Vancouver.

Noélie Martin's interest in contemporary artistic approaches to analogue film started with her own creative practice. Her work focuses on the political significance (social and environmental) of the use of "obsolete" techniques by cinema artists and the reinvention of media. Her work has appeared in the journals *La Furia Umana* and *La Revue Documentaire*.

Contributors

Richard Maxwell is Professor of Media Studies at Queens College, City University of New York. His publications include *The Spectacle of Democracy*, *Culture Works: The Political Economy of Culture*, *Herbert Schiller*, *Global Hollywood* (co-author), *Greening the Media* (with Toby Miller), *The Routledge Companion to Labor and Media*, *Media and the Ecological Crisis* (co-editor), and *How Green is Your Smartphone?* (with Toby Miller).

Jessica McLean is a White settler scholar who grew up in Wiradjuri Country and now lives in Gadigal Country. She is Senior Lecturer at Macquarie University in the Discipline of Geography and Planning, School of Social Sciences. Her current research considers how humans, more-than-humans, environments, and technologies interact to produce geographies of change. Her interdisciplinary research focuses on digital technologies, water politics, climate action, and activism and involves collaborations in applied research settings.

Gabi Mocatta is an interdisciplinary academic who researches at the intersection of media, environment, and climate change. She is a former journalist and is currently Lecturer in Communication – Journalism at Deakin University in Melbourne, Victoria, Australia. She is also Research Fellow in Climate Change Communication with the Climate Futures program, University of Tasmania, Australia. Gabi's research and teaching interests are focused broadly on environmental and climate change communication, including the ways that environmental conflicts play out in the media. Her co-authored book, *Environmental Communication in a Time of Crisis,* is forthcoming with Routledge.

Toby Miller is Profesor Visitante at the Universidad Complutense de Madrid and Research Professor in the Graduate Division of the University of California, Riverside. The author and editor of over fifty books, his work has been translated into many languages. His most recent volumes are *Violence*, *The Persistence of Violence: Colombian Popular Culture*, and *How Green Is Your Smartphone?* (with Richard Maxwell).

Tema Milstein's work tends to ways culture and communication shape ecological understandings, identities, and actions. Her recent co-edited books, *The Routledge Handbook of Ecocultural Identity* (2020) and *Environmental Communication Pedagogy and Practice* (2017), examine the interlinkages of communication and media with environmental perceptions, practices, and change. Her research spans the globe, illustrating tensions between overarching and marginalized environmental meaning systems, examining nuances of environmental activism and ecotourism, and exploring methods of transformative ecopedagogy. She is Associate Professor of *Environment & Society* and Convenor of the Master of Environmental Management program at the University of New South Wales in Sydney, Australia.

Salma Monani is Professor at Gettysburg College's Environmental Studies Department. She is co-editor, with Stephen Rust and Seán Cubitt, of *Ecocinema Theory and Practice* (2013), *Ecomedia: Key Concepts* (2015), and *Ecocinema Theory and Practice 2* (2022), and lead editor (with Joni Adamson) on *Ecocriticism and Indigenous Studies* (2016). She has also extensively published on explorations of film and environmental justice, film festival studies, and Indigenous eco-activism and is currently working on a monograph: *Indigenous Ecocinema: Decolonizing Media Landscapes*.

Ellen E. Moore teaches and conducts research at the University of Washington, Tacoma, on environmental communication and media coverage of environmental justice. Her latest book – *Framing*

Injustice: U.S. Media Coverage of the Standing Rock Movement – focuses on Hall's "politics of representation" when it comes to environmental justice struggles through interviews with the Standing Rock Sioux Tribe. Her latest course – Ecology, Inequality, and Popular Culture – focuses on how the media and environment form a system that can be used to reinforce but also challenge power structures and the status quo.

Rahul Mukherjee is Dick Wolf Associate Professor of Television and New Media at the University of Pennsylvania. He is the author of *Radiant Infrastructures: Media, Environment, and Cultures of Uncertainty* (2020).

Patrick D. Murphy is Associate Dean for Academic Affairs at Temple Rome and Professor at the Klein College of Media and Communication at Temple University. His research interests include global media, environmental communication, ethnographic method, and Latin American media and cultural theory. Murphy is the author of *The Media Commons: Globalization and Environmental Discourses* (2017), is co-editor of *Negotiating Democracy: Media Transformation in Emerging Democracies* (2007) and *Global Media Studies* (2003), and his work has appeared in numerous journals and chapters in edited books.

Carlos Alonso Nugent is an Assistant Professor at Columbia University, where he offers courses on US literature and culture, Latinx literature and culture, critical race and ethnic studies, and the environmental humanities. At present, Nugent is completing a book on the "imagined environments" that have shaped the US–Mexico borderlands since the mid-19th century; his other work has appeared in American Literature, American Literary History, ISLE: Interdisciplinary Studies in Literature and Environment, and other journals. He grew up in Tucson, Arizona.

John Parham is Professor of Environmental Humanities at the University of Worcester, UK. He has authored or edited six books including *Green Media and Popular Culture* (2016) and the *Cambridge Companion to Literature and the Anthropocene* (2021). He was co-editor of the Routledge/ASLE-UKI journal *Green Letters: Studies in Ecocriticism* for almost 20 years. John has published widely in the area of ecomedia, including recent or forthcoming articles on digital cli-fi, documentary, Japanese TV anime, and punk and the Anthropocene.

Anne Pasek is Assistant Professor and Canada Research Chair (Tier II) in Media, Culture, and the Environment at Trent University. She researches the cultural politics of climate change, with an emphasis on how carbon is mobilized within the tech sector and arts. She directs the Low-Carbon Research Methods Group, a network examining the climate and equity impacts of decarbonizing academia, and the Experimental Methods & Media Lab, a research-creation hub focusing on climate tech.

Jacopo Rasmi has not been able to stop studying in the past 30 years. While studying, sometimes he teaches (at Jean Monnet University), sometimes he writes alone (*Le hors-champ est dedans. Michelangelo Frammartino, écologie, cinéma*, 2021) but also in company (*Générations collapsonautes. Naviguer par temps d'effondrements*, 2020, with Yves Citton), sometimes he seizes good occasions to program film screenings and doesn't forget to feed himself with the collective intelligence of the editorial teams of *Multitudes* and *La revue Documentaires*. His research focuses on documentary creation, media theories, and ecological issues.

Contributors

Jennifer Rauch is a writer, educator, and scholar whose work explores news audiences, alternative media, ritual communication, media abstention, and zines. She's fascinated by how people talk, think about, and adopt alternative approaches to media use and production, in juxtaposition with "mainstream" practices. Her publications include *Resisting the News: Engaged Audiences, Alternative Media & Popular Critique of Journalism* (2021) and *Slow Media: Why Slow is Satisfying, Sustainable & Smart* (2018). Rauch is Professor and Chair of Journalism & Media Studies at Linfield University in McMinnville, Oregon, USA.

Elodie A. Roy is a media and material culture theorist with a specialism in the socio-material history of recorded sound. She is the author of *Media, Materiality and Memory: Grounding the Groove* and *Shellac in Visual and Sonic Culture: Unsettled Matter*, as well as the co-editor, with Eva Moreda Rodríguez, of *Phonographic Encounters: Mapping Transnational Cultures of Sound, 1890–1945*. Roy notably held research and teaching position at the Glasgow School of Art, the University of Glasgow, Humboldt University of Berlin, and Newcastle University and is currently a Research Fellow at Northumbria University, Newcastle.

Stephen Rust teaches Cinema Studies and Writing at the University of Oregon and Oregon State University. He is co-editor of *Ecocinema Theory and Practice* (2013), *Ecomedia: Key Issues* (2016), and *Ecocinema Theory and Practice 2* (2023), and is a founding advisory board member of *Media+Environment* and *Journal of Environmental Media*.

Emmanuel Septime Sessou is Assistant Professor in the Department of Communication and Media at Merrimack College, Massachusetts. After working in Benin his country's government as Press Secretary of the Minister of Interior, Homeland Security, and Religion, Septime studied at Temple University before joining Merrimack College. His research focuses on global media, communication for development and social change, and environmental communication, especially in relation to sub-Saharan Africa.

Nicole Seymour's most recent book is *Glitter*, part of Bloomsbury's "Object Lessons" series. Her previous monographs include *Strange Natures: Futurity, Empathy, and the Queer Ecological Imagination*, which won the 2015 Ecocriticism Award from the Association for the Study of Literature and Environment, and *Bad Environmentalism: Irony and Irreverence in the Ecological Age*, which was listed in the *Chicago Review of Books*' "Best Nature Writing of 2018." She has held fellowships at the Rachel Carson Center in Munich and at the Institute for Advanced Studies in the Humanities in Edinburgh. She is currently Professor of English at Cal State Fullerton.

Nicholas R. Silcox is a PhD candidate in the Department of English at New York University. His research and writing interests revolve around environmental issues and media and technology. He is working on a dissertation on sensing and sensor technologies and environments.

Nicole Starosielski, Associate Professor of Media, Culture, and Communication at New York University, is the author or co-editor of over 30 articles and five books on media, infrastructure, and environments, including: *The Undersea Network* (2015), *Media Hot and Cold* (2021), *Signal Traffic: Critical Studies of Media Infrastructure* (2015), *Sustainable Media: Critical Approaches to Media and Environment* (2016), and *Assembly Codes: The Logistics of Media* (2021).

Contributors

Corrinne Sullivan is an Aboriginal scholar with direct links to the Wiradjuri Nation in Central-West New South Wales. She is Associate Dean (Indigenous Education) and Associate Professor of Geography at Western Sydney University. Her multi-disciplinary research interests focus on experiences and effects of body and identity in relation to Aboriginal and Torres Strait Islander peoples. Her current work explores Indigenous Australian sexuality and gender diversity through the perspectives of youth, older people, sex workers, and in online spaces.

Sy Taffel is Senior Lecturer of Media Studies and co-director of the Political Ecology Research Centre at Massey University, Aotearoa-New Zealand. His research focuses on the intersections of digital technologies, the environment, and social justice. He is the author of *Digital Media Ecologies* (2019), and an editor of *Plastic Legacies* (2021) and *Ecological Entanglement in the Anthropocene* (2016).

Christy Tidwell is Professor of English and Humanities at the South Dakota School of Mines and Technology. She works at the intersection of speculative fiction, environmental humanities, and gender studies. She co-organized A Clockwork Green: Ecomedia in the Anthropocene (2018), a virtual conference sponsored by the Association for the Study of Literature and Environment, and is co-editor of *Gender and Environment in Science Fiction* (2018), *Fear and Nature: Ecohorror Studies in the Anthropocene* (2021), and a special issue of *Science Fiction Film & Television* on creature features and the environment (2021).

Miriam Tola is Assistant Professor at John Cabot University in Rome, Italy. Her work explores the intersections between gender, race, species, and the cultural politics of the environmental crisis. Her articles have appeared in journals including *South Atlantic Quarterly*, *Feminist Review*, *Environmental Humanities*, and *Feminist Studies*. She is the co-editor of the book *Ecologie della cura* and co-edits Living Lexicon for the *Environmental Humanities* journal.

Armond R. Towns is Associate Professor of Communication and Media Studies at Carleton University. His work brings together black studies, cultural studies, and media philosophy. His book, *On Black Media Philosophy*, was published in 2022. He is also the cofounder and inaugural editor of *Communication and Race*, the newest journal of the National Communication Association.

Hunter Vaughan is Senior Research Associate at the Minderoo Centre for Technology and Democracy, University of Cambridge. Dr. Vaughan is the author of *Where Film Meets Philosophy* (2013) and, most recently, *Hollywood's Dirtiest Secret: The Hidden Environmental Costs of the Movies* (2019). He is founding Editor-in-Chief of the *Journal of Environmental Media*, Co-Principal Investigator on the Global Green Media Network and Sustainable Subsea Networks projects, and is a Convening Team Member for the UNFCCC Entertainment and Culture for Climate Action initiative.

Alexa Weik von Mossner is Associate Professor of American Studies at the University of Klagenfurt. Her research explores the intersections of cognitive narratology, ecocriticism, and empirical studies of literature and film. She is the author of *Cosmopolitan Minds: Literature, Emotion, and the Transnational Imagination* (2014) and *Affective Ecologies: Empathy, Emotion, and Environmental Narrative* (2017), and the editor of *Moving Environments: Affect, Emotion, Ecology and Film* (2014).

Contributors

Janet Walker is Professor of Film and Media Studies at the University of California, Santa Barbara, and a founding co-editor of the open-access journal *Media+Environment*. With research specializations in documentary film, trauma studies, and ecomedia, her six books and publications at this intersection include *Sustainable Media* (with Nicole Starosielski, 2016), journal articles in *Media Fields* (2018) and *NECSUS* (2018), and a chapter in *The Routledge Companion to Media and Risk* (2020). Initiatives on which she was honored to collaborate are *Water Is Life: Standing with Standing Rock* (videos available at UCTV) and the Mellon Sawyer Seminar and resulting special issue, Energy Justice in Global Perspective (mediaenviron.org).

Verena Wurth holds a graduate degree in Teaching English and History from the University of Cologne, Germany, and a Master's degree in Comparative Literature from the University of Rochester, NY. She has published an article entitled "Pains, Planes, and Automobiles" on Extractivist Nostalgia in the TV Series Mad Men and, since 2021, she has been working on her PhD thesis on Ecocrime in New Golden Age TV at the University of Cologne, where she is a research assistant and junior lecturer in American literature and culture.

ACKNOWLEDGMENTS

The editors are grateful for the help and service of our editorial assistant, Elisabetta Petrucci. We also want to acknowledge the support of our families, friends, and home institutions for assisting us and creating the space to edit this volume. We are indebted to all of our authors for contributing their time and energy to producing this *Handbook* and for their commitment to creating ecomedia studies. We are additionally thankful for the editorial guidance and support of Routledge's Annabelle Harris and Jyotsna Gurung. Deep gratitude for the generous support of those institutions that provided funding to enable this volume to be available simultaneously in print and open access: University of Oregon Libraries Open Access Publishing Award, Frank J. Guarini School of Business at John Cabot University, University of Vermont Humanities Center, University of California Santa Barbara, and University of Lausanne.

In memoriam of John Parham, who passed away while this volume was in production. We wish to thank this well-respected ecomedia scholar for his contribution to the book and the field.

INTRODUCTION

Antonio López, Adrian Ivakhiv, Stephen Rust, Miriam Tola, Alenda Y. Chang, and Kiu-wai Chu

We are in the midst of a global climate emergency, yet academic programs that follow traditional approaches to media studies, cultural studies, film, or communications continue to marginalize ecological approaches and issues. Evidence for this can be found by perusing any standard reader or textbook for courses in these fields. Regardless of the good intentions of many in media studies, the environment remains symbolically annihilated, notwithstanding a consensus in the field that there is "nothing 'outside' media anymore … all the experiences in everyday life are connected to media" (Deuze 2021, 6). Indeed, a precondition of globalization is the mediatization of everything, from our personal lives to the entire planet via remote sensing technologies and information communication technologies (ICTs). But as Adi Kunstman and Esperanza Miyake (2022) observe,

> Despite decades of critical voices from feminist, post-colonial, diasporic and "global South" scholars […,] mainstream digital communication studies have largely enjoyed – and continue to enjoy! – the luxury of ignoring the deeply material consequences of the digital since such consequences mostly impact those in the Global South and the disenfranchised, racialised and colonised communities in the Global North.
>
> (122)

Addressing this gap, ecomedia scholars propose what would effectively be an "ecological reboot" to media studies and cultural studies. This reboot means combining the material and affective turns with ecocritical and postcolonial projects; expanding the ethical, political, and aesthetic considerations underlying media scholarship to include the other-than-human world and its biotic communities; and acknowledging the legacies of Western colonial epistemology (such as the nature-culture binary) which continue to shape academe and its relations with the broader world.

For the purpose of this volume, ecomedia studies serves as an umbrella term for areas of scholarship that bridge media and environment. But the concept of ecomedia—a contraction of ecology and media—is on the surface not obviously defined or universally understood. As a starting point, ecomedia studies align with ecocriticism's "triple allegiance to the scientific study of nature, the scholarly analysis of cultural representations and the political struggle for more sustainable ways of inhabiting the natural world" (Brereton 2016, 215). This triple allegiance has enabled ecomedia studies to grow over the past decade, attracting a diverse array of scholars with a wide variety of

This chapter has been made available under a CC-BY-NC-ND license.

expertise and training. Across multiple disciplines, ecomedia studies bridges the epistemological divide between "technology and nature, human and nonhuman, material and immaterial, suggesting that such categories are relationally defined and materially intertwined" (Parks and Starosielski 2015a, 15).

In trying to define ecomedia, two broad areas of inquiry have emerged: (1) media that grapple(s) with ecological issues, frameworks, and approaches; and (2) ecology that grapples with media. The first approach stems from a recognition that ecomedia is commonly used as shorthand for a wide variety of ecologically oriented media texts and contexts, including environmental(ist) media and communications, nature/wildlife/science films, green popular culture, and so on. In practice, however, the term remains in flux, being used either as a genre descriptor or effort to claim certain media as ecological (while thus excluding others) based on content and form. The second concept entails the ecological impacts of media. (Chapter 1 in this volume explores our approach to defining media and ecomedia in more detail.)

The emergence of ecomedia studies roughly parallels the evolution of ecocriticism and ecocinema studies as a series of waves (see Christman Lavin and Kaplan 2017). The first wave of environmental theory (1960s-1970s) formed the basis of ecocriticism, environmental communication, and related fields that emerged in the 1980s. The second wave (1990s) included the application of ecocritical toolsets to popular culture and mass media by cultural studies scholars, and the convergence of science studies, animal studies, and posthumanist discourses to a burgeoning "environmental humanities" literature. Ross's (1994) formulation of the "ecology of images" and "images of ecology" represented an important marker that moved the study of ecomedia from nature photography and wildlife films to examining popular culture. A postcolonial critique of the Euro-American orientation of ecocriticism led to the development of postcolonial ecocriticism (Guha 2000; Huggan and Tiffin 2015).

The third wave (2000–2010s) saw the emergence of media and environment study groups in major academic associations such as the Society for Cinema and Media Studies (SCMS), the Modern Language Association (MLA), the Association for the Study of Literature and Environment (ASLE), and the establishment of the International Environmental Communication Association (IECA). Ecocinema emerged as an important convergence, highlighted by studies of wildlife films (Mitman 1999; Bousé 2000; Chris 2006), popular cinema (Ingram 2000; Brereton 2004; Murray and Heumann 2009), experimental cinema (MacDonald 2001), and Seán Cubitt's paradigm-defining *EcoMedia* (2005). Scholars around the world began to map out the contours of a "transnational" ecomedia and ecocinema "beyond the human" (Lu and Mi 2009; Kääpä and Gustafsson 2013; Pick and Narraway 2013). Important research, including Nadia Bozak's (2011) *Cinematic Footprint*, Hunter Vaughan's (2019) study of Hollywood and water use, and Susan Hayward's (2020) application of "doughnut economics" to film ecology, has made visible the natural resources that sustain the film industry. Ecophilosophers focused on ecology and film, such as Adrian Ivakhiv (2008, 2013), expanded upon Félix Guattari's "three ecologies" and the "circuit of culture" model by viewing materiality, sociality (and power), and perception (or experience) as dynamic, ecological systems engaging audiences with film-worlds within multiple layers of relationality. Working with Cubitt, Stephen Rust and Salma Monani (Rust, Monani, and Cubitt 2016, 2022) have produced two comprehensive collections that summarize the central and emerging themes within ecocinema studies.

We could finally identify a fourth and current wave of ecomedia studies in the establishment of journals and ongoing research featured in this *Handbook*. While there is no formal field designation or single scholarly association that defines this scholarship, the two important academic journals most closely aligned with the subject, *Media+Environment* and *Journal of Environmental Media*, have since 2019 and 2020 (respectively) provided much-needed venues for the outpouring of ecomedia studies. Other journals that have also published ecomedia scholarship include *Environmental Communication, Interdisciplinary Studies in Literature and Environment (ISLE), Representations, Resilience, JumpCut, Interactions: Studies in Communication and Culture, Environmental Humanities, Screen, Cultural Politics, Critical Inquiry,* and *Ecozon@*. Ecomedia scholars engage in diverse research activities about both the tangible and abstract ecological conditions of media, co-evolving with emerging disciplines concerned with making the environment an expanded subject of media research. Most notably, several major theoretical developments have been closely tied to the expanding agenda of ecomedia studies: these include technoscience studies, feminist new materialism, affect studies, the "ontological turn," postcolonial and Indigenous ecocriticism, queer ecologies, infrastructure studies, political ecology of data, and Black media theory.

Ecomedia studies today is more a "sphere" than a "field," enfolding various areas of exploration without enforced boundaries. As suggested by the title of one book, *Teaching Ecocriticism and Green Cultural Studies* (Garrard 2016), there is in ecomedia studies a natural affinity between different research interests, such as how ecocriticism is the result of interdisciplinary work between literature and cultural studies. Likewise, ecocinema could be categorized under the umbrella of environmental humanities, but it has its own unique interests and pursuits that are closer to its "natural" home of film/cinema studies. Ecolinguistics is situated in ecocriticism and environmental communication, which offer insights into ecomedia studies' exploration of environmental discourses and ecoculture. Related fields like ecomusicology, environmental sound studies, environmental visual culture studies, and "media ecology" and "media archaeology" are among the adjacent fields that tackle similar or analogous themes—for example, the cultural construction of nature/society and human/animal binaries, the political ecology of socio-environmental systems, the postcolonial and decolonial critiques of Western modernity, the technological embodiments of human relations with more-than-human ecologies, and the materiality of image and communication regimes—but whose work reflects different disciplinary emphases (Smith 2015; Demos 2016, 2017; Allen and Dawe 2016). As these areas of study continue to cross-pollinate, overlapping ecologies of thought and research open new possibilities and produce "edge effects" (Nixon 2011, 30). What unites all of these is an underlying sensibility that contributes to the larger political project of addressing local and global environmental crises (see Oppermann 2011). As Jennifer Gabrys notes in this volume, "The media ecologies discussed here are ecologies in crisis."

We purposely maintain a wide perspective to accommodate the transdisciplinary character of scholarship in the field of ecomedia studies. However, we can identify three main streams. The first follows Rust, Monani, and Cubitt (2013, 2016) in taking ecomedia as an umbrella term for media that are *of* and *about* the environment. The second reflects on the changing nature of media, seeing ecomedia as energetic and material exchanges that comprise, encompass, and produce environments, milieus, objects (texts, gadgets, platforms), and infrastructures. This conceptualization moves beyond conventional views of media as the province of texts, industries, and audiences, or narrowly defining media as technologies that record, store, and process information (in whatever form). Though media are associated with communicating meaning, there are also layers of media—such as infrastructures—that have meaning but "do not speak" (Peters 2015, 2). The third stream within ecomedia studies concerns the iterative circuits within which ecomedia take place and have their impacts—the circuits that, in this book, we identify under the rubrics of "ecomateriality," "political ecology," "ecocultures," and "eco-affects." Combining these three streams—(1) ecomedia are media *of* and *about* the environment; (2) ecomedia involve a revised and expanded definition of media; and (3) ecomedia works through iterative circuits—we can conceive ecomedia as an ensemble of technologies, mediating apparatuses, and critical interpretive approaches that activate, coordinate, and help us make sense of how media entangle the world.

Handbook Organization

The aim of *The Routledge Handbook of Ecomedia Studies* is to give form to diverse scholarly activities concerning media and the environment and to characterize the current state of the art. It is our desire that these chapters can expand interest and awareness of the issues raised by these contributors to a broader audience, in particular to aid those who are new to the field. By combining overviews of the topic with case studies, each chapter is deliberately self-contained, which means that in some cases, ideas and themes may repeat themselves across the book. We wanted to ensure that individual chapters can be assigned as supplementary materials in curricula that do not focus on ecomedia studies and to provide starting points for those studying or teaching media more generally. With the recommended readings at the end of each chapter, readers can investigate topics in more depth.

By featuring leading established scholars as well as emerging researchers from across disciplines, we sought cultural and geographical diversity, a clear recognition of crucial contributions from the South and the East, and the centering of Indigenous and anti-colonial perspectives often marginalized from debates in media studies. We highlight four critical areas of ecomedia scholarship: ecomateriality, political ecology, ecocultures, and eco-affects. Ecomateriality and eco-affects register the material and affective "turns" that, in some ways, distinguish ecomedia studies from media studies. Given the interdisciplinary nature of ecomedia scholarship, many of these chapters do not fit within a single section but straddle multiple perspectives. For example, in many cases, it is difficult to distinguish between political ecology and ecomateriality, since environmental impacts are closely connected to political and economic contexts. Likewise, themes developed by environmental communication—such as communicating climate concerns or investigating news and journalistic practices—are also important for ecomedia studies and fall under both political ecology and ecocultures. But given that *The Routledge Handbook of Environment and Communication* (Hansen and Cox 2015) and *The Routledge Handbook of Ecocultural Identity* (Milstein and Castro-Sotomayor 2020) already offer thorough overviews of these subjects, we are emphasizing other areas that remain underexplored, such as eco-affects and ecomateriality. In the spirit of cultural studies' circuit of culture, we keep in mind how all these different zones are interacting. In organizing the chapters for the sections, we selected for each section those scholars whose work best represents its overarching theme.

Ecomedia Theory

This introductory section offers broad conceptual, philosophical, and epistemological considerations for ecomedia studies. Building on several of the foundational works in ecomedia studies, such as the anthologies edited by Stephen Rust, Salma Monani, and Seán Cubitt (2013) and by Nicole Starosielski and Janet Walker (2016), Adrian Ivakhiv and Antonio López open with an overview of the key approaches that have gone into defining what is meant by ecology, media, and, in their combination, ecomedia. They enter into dialogue with key texts in ecomedia scholarship, such as *The Marvelous Clouds: Toward a Philosophy of Elemental Media* (Peters 2015), *Program Earth: Environmental Sensing technology and the Making of a Computational Planet* (Gabrys 2016), *Wild Blue Media: Thinking Through Seawater* (Jue 2020), *On Black Media Philosophy* (Towns 2022), and *African Ecomedia: Network Forms, Planetary Media* (Iheka 2021). Special attention is paid to the significant contributions of feminist theory, postcolonial studies, and Black media theory to ecomedia studies. In the process of critically engaging the metaphorical implications of media and ecomedia, these explorations grapple with the theorization of elemental media and infrastructure.

In the following chapter, Ivakhiv disentangles some of the historical uses of "ecology" and "environment" in order to prepare the ground for a metaphysical regrounding of ecomedia studies. Drawing on his work in process-relational philosophy, film, and image theory (Ivakhiv 2013, 2018), he builds on Félix Guattari's "three ecologies" proposal—with its distinction between material, social, and mental or perceptual ecologies—to think through both the "eco" and the "media" ontologically in terms of what they imply for media philosophy, materiality, politics, and perception. Next, Christy Tidwell unearths the relationship between ecomedia and new materialism, beginning with the premise that media's materiality matters as much as its message and that the two cannot be separated. The chapter explores how to think differently about our relationships to the nonhuman world and the media we use to understand it, while also acknowledging that new materialist concepts echo what has long been present in many Indigenous ontologies.

One of the primary tasks of ecomedia theory is reappraising and resetting the use of ecology and environment metaphors that are used liberally in the history of media studies. As Stephen Rust and Verena Wurth note in their chapter, "metaphors of media ecology are most effective when they further our understanding of both the way that media technologies operate and how such technologies impact the material world humanity exploits to produce them." They develop the method/framework/approach of "Blue Media Ecologies," which investigates the meanings and shortcomings of ecological, especially water-related, metaphors in media studies, using David Attenborough's films about the ocean world as a case study. They consider "blue" ecomateriality and milieu-specificity of oceanic filming and underwater representational strategies.

Building on his essential book, *Digital Media Ecologies: Entanglements of Content, Code and Hardware* (2019), Sy Taffel synthesizes a political ecology of ecomedia with the materialism of ecological science and ecophilosophies. While metaphorical digital ecologies typically discuss flows of information in a disembodied and decontextualized manner, Taffel examines how today's media systems form vast planetary assemblages that extract, purify, and transport millions of tons of matter, and burn vast quantities of fossil fuels to produce, maintain, and extend the domain of media. This chapter is followed by a conversation with Cajetan Iheka, author of the groundbreaking *African Ecomedia: Network Forms, Planetary Politics* (2021). By grounding ecomedia in the African context, Iheka further explores the various ways ecomedia are used both in the service of empire building and as a form of resistance. In discussing the research in his book, Iheka talks about the transformative agency of African visual media with a focus on the socioecological costs of media processes in different African settings.

Applying various theoretical ecomedia approaches to a historical case study, Carlos Nugent situates how "ecomedia of empire" helped remediate and shape the material, infrastructural, and imaginative US-Mexico borderlands to form the modern Southwestern United States. Expanding on the theory of petroleum media, Nugent develops the novel concept of "irrigation media" as a narrative template of Manifest Destiny's worldbuilding strategy to colonize the borderland territory. He also highlights how anti-imperialist ecomedia can counter European cartographies. Continuing an exploration of US-Mexico borderlands, Janet Walker develops spatial documentary studies by probing the weaponization of the Sonoran Desert. Drawing on critical environmental media justice studies, this chapter countermaps an Anthropo/scenic cartography being razed upon the desert. Crucially, it puts elemental media into dialogue with Kathryn Yusoff's (2018) theorization of the White Anthropocene, calling attention to questions of racial violence in the historical unfolding of media and of ecology.

Closing this section, Antonio López offers strategies for applying ecomedia studies in the classroom. Building on his work developing ecomedia literacy (2021), he offers prompts for learners to make sense of how ecomedia infrastructures and our engagement with them connect with ecojustice. Just as environmental communication is a "crisis discipline" that seeks to intervene into the status quo, the goal of ecomedia literacy is to promote a normative shift in eco-ethical cultural policies, practices, and attitudes to transform existing media practices, industry structures, and government regulations.

Ecomateriality

Ecomateriality describes a significant area of emerging scholarship that documents how media are materially embedded in and extracted from the environment in forms including the infrastructural (cables, satellites, electromagnetic energy, server farms) as well as the directly ecological (mining, manufacturing, energy consumption, waste production and disposal). As we move around with our cell phones, all of us have a piece of Africa, China, or South America in our pockets (Bratton 2015; Parikka 2015). The infrastructures that deliver electricity and the internet depend heavily on minerals and chemicals, and the sources of energy that power our information exchange—especially the server farms that make up the digital cloud used for our streaming services, data, and social networks—are largely powered by non-renewable fossil fuels like coal and fossil gas. Chip production and even packaging, which requires paper pulp, are resource and energy intensive, while shipping and manufacturing also add to greenhouse gas emissions. We also have to consider the end of our screen technologies' life cycles and e-waste. A toxic brew of chemicals, plastic, glass, and metal devastates the health of workers and local ecosystems as our electronic trash gets tossed away and shipped across the world. Additionally, the ecomaterial flows (i.e. material impacts) of filmmaking, TV production, video game manufacturing, and so on are significant. The aim of this section is to embrace the material turn in the study of media, covering the significant impacts of media on the physical environment.

Over the past decade, a growing number of ecomedia scholars, including the contributors to this section of the *Handbook*, have enhanced our understanding of media infrastructures and materiality. Jennifer Gabrys' examination of the environmental impacts of digital information and electronic waste in *Digital Rubbish* (2011) has led to such innovative research as Elodie A. Roy's (2020) look at recorded music and the logic of waste and Mehita Iqani's (2021) broader investigation of the role of waste in popular culture. Richard Maxwell and Toby Miller's *Greening the Media* (2012) has sparked a growing body of scholarship on the manufacturing and disposal of screen technologies, including Seán Cubitt's examination of extractive mining in the life cycle of media technologies in *Finite Media* (2017), and Laura U. Marks' research on the carbon footprint of streaming technologies (Marks et al. 2020) and her call for media producers to limit the file-size of media as a mitigation strategy (Marks et al. 2020). Lisa Parks and Nicole Starosielski's critical look at media infrastructures in *Signal Traffic* (2015b) has provoked scholars like Anne Pasek (2020) to creatively interrogate the role that energy infrastructures play in everyday life and Rahul Mukherjee (2020) to explore how media coverage of infrastructures impacts public opinion on environmental issues. Inspired by Nadia Bozak (2011) and Hunter Vaughan (2019), others have deepened our understanding of cinema's environmental impacts, while Alenda Y. Chang (2019), Benjamin Abraham (2022), and others are exploring the ecology of video games. The chapters in this section extend such efforts in hopes of inspiring the next wave of materialist ecomedia scholarship.

The section opens with a co-authored chapter by Nicole Starosielski, Hunter Vaughan, Anne Pasek, and Nicholas R. Silcox that develops an infrastructural literacy approach to studying the material impacts of the internet. The authors provide an overview of the various infrastructures that compose the internet to support their claim that if scholars peripheralize their current focus on data centers and other hubs of network infrastructure, it is possible to develop a more localized, relational approach to the study of internet infrastructures that may lead, in turn, to the development of a more sustainable global system.

Next, Laura U. Marks undertakes a frank reckoning with the environmental demands of ICTs and the need to scale down future expectations around technology's ubiquity and accessibility in order to address current inequities and ecological impacts. Extending this work, Jennifer Gabrys considers that while electronics consume energy, they are also used to manage energy consumption and monitor changing environments to achieve greater sustainability. By developing the concept of "electronic environmentalism," Gabrys considers how to account for the environmental impacts of electronics while analyzing how they also inform broader energy practices.

Extending his previous scholarship, Rahul Mukherjee's chapter moves beyond theorizing radiant infrastructures such as nuclear power plants, cellular towers, and solar energy panels to consider the wider environmental and health implications that stem from the radiation emitted from such infrastructures. Mukherjee further examines how the socio-material relations that emerge with the introduction of such radiant infrastructures in the Global South are imbricated in questions about energy transitions and media materialities that are also crucial for ecomedia and environmental justice.

The chapters by Alenda Y. Chang and Elodie A. Roy zoom in on specific media forms in order to enhance our understanding of distinct sites where media consumers engage in the impacts of materiality. Chang provides a look at both the micro- and macro-climatic contexts of digital and analog gameplay (from computer cases and man caves to mass sporting events) to consider what one of the paradigmatic media forms of the twenty-first century can teach us about the cultures, infrastructures, and atmospheres of media use. Roy explores the theoretical and practical implications of material history of shellac-based gramophone discs in relation to music history and media archeology. Rather than understanding the raw materials of music as neutral substances divorced from historical and political times, Roy's approach sheds light on the material entanglement of gramophone discs with colonial and postcolonial practices of extractivism. Roy's contention that media resources are relational and become activated through material, social, and historical processes of association and encounter aligns well with the approach taken by Starosielski, Vaughan, Pasek, and Silcox.

Concluding the section, Mehita Iqani examines the *Core Dump* art project as an effective lens through which to examine the aesthetics and materiality of e-waste. *Core Dump* deploys a site-specific creative process that parallels the geographical journey of technological waste from mining locations in Congo, to manufacturing sites in China, consumer markets in the USA, and e-waste recycling and dumps in Senegal. Iqani's chapter brings the discussion of media materiality full circle through a consideration of our personal aspirations to be digitally connected alongside awareness of the deeply problematic forms of toxic detritus and working conditions in the Global South that result from industry's drive to provide that connection at a profit.

Political Ecology

This section considers the entanglements between the undesirable environmental impacts of media production, consumption, and disposal, and larger dynamics of exploitation and dispossession. Early studies in media ecology (Postman 2000) distinguished between the natural environment consisting of land, air, and nonhuman beings, and media environments consisting of symbols, language, and technologies. By defining the media environment as exclusively anthropogenic, this perspective perpetuated the divide between society and nature. In contrast, the *Handbook of Ecomedia Studies* privileges a political ecology of media that examines the interdependencies between political economy, power, and environments.

This approach investigates the structural constraints influencing media processes as well as how the media circulate environmental ideologies that contribute to the reproduction of dominant socio-ecological relations. It contends that materiality and discourse are entangled rather than oppositional (Taffel 2019). Crucially, it also accounts for environmental justice responses to these dynamics, often illuminating the role of media in socio-environmental conflicts. In addition to analyzing system design and the socio-environmental costs of media processes, a political ecology of media draws attention to mainstream media's propagation of the ideology of unlimited economic growth and consumerism. This includes normalizing the design of screen technologies that cannot be upgraded or repaired so that consumers are compelled to continuously update (and discard) outdated gadgets in order to participate in social and economic life. By obscuring the environmental dimension of digital technologies, advertising and popular culture reinforce the belief that our digital lives are "immaterial" and disconnected from questions of resource appropriation, labor exploitation, and waste. Further, digital platforms drive climate disinformation and the news media adopt the rhetoric of sustainability echoing corporate narratives of ecological transition, while marginalizing a variety of alternative perspectives on environmental justice, just transition, and degrowth.

The authors in this section provide insights on the political ecology of global communication systems, explore questions of property ownership, labor exploitation, and environmental policies in the media industry. They provide a decidedly decolonial perspective by foregrounding Indigenous struggles that contest the violence of extractive economies and center Indigenous sovereignty and self-determination in ecomedia.

Drawing on critical political economy of communication and extending the theoretical framework developed in the book *Carbon Capitalism and Communication: Confronting Climate Crisis* (Brevini and Murdock 2017), Benedetta Brevini and Daisy Doctor examine communications systems as assemblages of material devices and infrastructures. Their chapter explores the nexus between the accelerating impact of human activities on the planet and the rapid expansion of communication and computational systems, including developments in artificial intelligence (AI).

Pietari Kääpä and Hunter Vaughan's chapter takes a deeper look at an issue Kääpä explored in his book *Environmental Management of the Media* (2020), namely the lack of coordination between media organizations, content creators, and regulators in establishing who has accountability over the environmental impacts of the screen media sector. The authors call ecomedia scholars to pay more attention to the complexities of media governance. In the following chapter, Jannice Käll extends her analysis of digitally mediated property developed in the book *Posthuman Property and Law* (2022). Here, Käll explores the ecology of blockchain technologies, such as NTFs (non-fungible tokens), in terms of property rights.

As with several other co-authored chapters in this volume, Patrick Murphy and Emmanuel Septime Sessou's essay is the result of a fruitful partnership between a well-established and an emerging scholar. Expanding on Murphy's (2017) past explorations of media commons and the environment, Murphy and Sessou revisit the distinction between hegemonic "global media commons" and alternative "communications commons." Building on this distinction, they analyze the divergent media treatment of two conflicts over common pool resources (CPR): the Grand Ethiopian Renaissance Dam project in Africa and the Dakota Access Pipeline in North America.

Introduction

In partnership with Puyallup tribal council member Anna Bean, Ellen E. Moore deploys the interview strategies she developed for her book *Journalism, Politics, and the Dakota Access Pipeline* (2019) in their co-authored chapter. Discussing Bean's role as a leader in the effort to block construction of a liquid natural gas facility in Tacoma, Washington, Bean and Moore address the strengths and challenges of using social media as a tool for environmental activism. Furthering this section's engagement with decolonial struggles and digital media, Corrinne Sullivan and Jessica McLean problematize the misrepresentation of Aboriginal Australian peoples in non-indigenous digital spaces while also highlighting the potential of digital worlds that affirm the sovereignty of such groups.

The concluding chapter in this section reunites Toby Miller and Richard Maxwell, whose book *Greening the Media* (2012) has deeply influenced ecomedia studies over the past decade. Here, Miller and Maxwell examine the key points in the cellphone supply chain at which workers face hazardous working conditions and inhumane treatment at the hands of corporations. Reinforcing their more recent research on smartphones (2020), they urge each of us as consumers to keep using our current devices as long as possible, encourage our workplaces and other institutions to do the same, and pressure governments to better regulate working conditions and environmental waste.

Taken together, these chapters invite us to grapple with the materialities of political economy and the ways in which the close attention to dynamics of exploitation and dispossession can advance ecomedia studies.

Ecocultures

The next section of the *Handbook* addresses the myriad ways in which ecomedia shape culture(s) and different cultural responses to the environmental crisis. The term "ecoculture" thus corresponds with meaning, values, lifestyles, identity formations, ways of knowing, and rituals and practices mediated through shared interpretations and sense-making practices. From the standpoint of systems of representation, this section of the book explores semiotics alongside a variety of languages, discourses, and narratives.

Speaking of ecocultures in their plurality recognizes that there are diverse ways that cultures shape and are shaped by ecomedia. Building on recent scholarly work on "provincializing" and "pluralizing" the often universalized Anthropocene discourse (DeLoughrey 2019; Mentz 2019), ecomedia as a cultural discourse, too, demands being provincialized and pluralized as a way to acknowledge the "eco-territorial turn," as Diana Coryat highlights in her chapter. The section begins with Tema Milstein, Gabi Mocatta, and José Castro-Sotomayor's follow-up to their *Routledge Handbook of Ecocultural Identity* (Milstein and Castro-Sotomayor 2020). Here, the authors examine media's role in shaping ecocultural identity across four international case studies, in which media contribute both to the reproduction of existing anthropocentric identities and catalyze more regenerative ecocentric identities. For these authors, media ultimately may be less helpful than embodied experiences of our new climate realities.

Recently, there has been a proliferation of books that explore diverse ecocultural traditions and practices within global media contexts. In addition to the vast number of publications on North America and Europe, growing attention toward the Global South has been reflected in books such as *The Latin American Ecocultural Reader* (French and Heffes 2021); *Pushing Past the Human in Latin American Cinema* (Fornoff and Heffes 2021); *African Ecomedia: Network Forms, Planetary Politics* (Iheka 2021); *Chinese Environmental Humanities* (C. Chang 2019); and *Environment, Media, and Popular Culture in Southeast Asia* (Telles, Ryan, and Dreisbach 2022). Such a global turn is reflected in Coryat's discussion of work by audiovisual media collectives in Ecuador that brings ecomedia scholarship into necessary conversation with social movement cultures and political ecologies of the Global South. Focusing on global pandemic films produced in Hong Kong and Laos, Chia-ju Chang turns to Buddhism and East and Southeast Asian traditional cultures as a way of thinking beyond the nature-culture binary and the tenaciousness of the "Othering" of women and minority groups in contemporary power structures.

Evidence that ecological worldviews are not normative can be found across many different kinds of media, ranging from "green popular culture" to ecocinema, from activist media to corporate board reports. This section therefore also gives diverse examples of how ecology is expressed through different platforms and genres of media (cinema, digital maps, music, CGI artworks, and so on). Using Ani DiFranco's experimental folk music as a case study, John Parham offers a multifaceted study of "green music" by considering its generic conventions (folk and rock); technical renditions (synthesis of studio-engineered sounds with natural and animal sounds); and eco-thematic concerns (climate change, pollution, and animal perspectives) in order to argue that folk rock's blending of popular appeal and grassroots commitments to the land and the local can reach a broader audience with environmental messages. Salma Monani and Sarah Gilsoul discuss their collaboration on an ongoing Indigenous Pennsylvania digital Storymap project as a means of going beyond land acknowledgment statements in North American contexts, and as an instance of what they call "d-ecomedia," a shorthand for ecomedia projects that foreground decolonial methodologies. They argue that in order to be sustainable, "d-ecomedia" digital mapping projects operate within a process-oriented and relational framework that in turn requires institutional and public commitment and support.

While the material and ideological impacts of media are major contributors to the global climate crisis, media also afford access to information, produce the network effect of spreading and sharing information, and generate "weird solidarity" when "new forms of sociality are formed [...] across unlikely alliances and with unexpected things, people, communities and institutions" (McLean 2020, 23). In their transcribed and edited conversation, scholar of Black media philosophy Armond R. Towns and visual artist Jeremy Kamal find surprising resonances between Kamal's speculative Afrofuturist computer-generated worlds and Towns's reinterpretation of classical theories of communication studies through the lens of Black Studies. Their lively and stimulating discussion delves into a broadened perspective of media ecology, exploring the colonial assumptions about nature, Black radical thinking, and reflections on artistic design and resistance. Jacopo Rasmi and Noélie Martin give us a glimpse into the practical workshops of experimental film lab networks, which in this case turned to plants and other unusual, "animistic" ingredients to reimagine cinematic materiality through the chemicals and emulsions used to produce images. The new ecologies created by these experimental film labs are in a sense "ecoculture" that is built upon the complex networks of human and nonhuman beings. Ecocultures, in other words, are never solely about human culture; they also, as the range of forms and communities in this section attest, invite transgressive or "improper" affiliations with the more-than-human (Chen 2012).

Eco-Affects

Finally, "Eco-affects" explores the ways in which humans, including media users and audiences, feel and experience being part of our environments in and through the use of media. This area of inquiry corresponds with the "affective" and "sensorial" turns in cultural and literary studies. As Alexa Weik von Mossner writes, "Both reading and watching are highly embodied activities not only in that we need our senses in order to be able to perceive things, but also in that our bodies act as sounding boards for our mental situations of storyworlds and of characters' perceptions, emotions, and actions within virtual worlds" (Weik von Mossner 2017, 3). Weik von Mossner's *Affective Ecologies: Empathy, Emotion, and Environmental Narrative* (2017) and her edited anthology *Moving Environments: Affect, Emotion, Ecology, and Film* (2014) are among the pioneering efforts to chart this area. Other important scholarship includes E. Ann Kaplan's work on climate trauma (2016), Simon Estok's writing on ecophobia (2016), Pat Brereton's (2004) and Adrian Ivakhiv's (2011) explorations of cinema's utopian and dystopian affects, and the work of Robin Murray and Joseph Heumann on environmental nostalgia in eco-disaster movies (2005) and on the "monstrous natures" of eco-horror films (2016).

More broadly, this work builds on studies of environmental emotions and media "effects" including "positive" emotions (such as wonder, awe, optimism, and desire for action) as well as "negative" emotions (especially guilt, grief, and melancholia) in environmental and climate communication, eco-rhetoric, and sustainability education (Rozelle 2006; Dobrin and Morey 2009; Schneider and Nocker 2014; Lockwood 2016; Albrecht 2019; Jensen 2019). It also dovetails with a growing interest in cinematic and media moods, atmospheres, ambience, "elementality," and eco-phenomenology (Sinnerbrink 2012; Hven 2019, 2022; Müller and Kappelhoff 2020).

The study of new media further highlights how our increased dependence on smartphones and related devices impacts our sense of place, space, and time. It affects our attention, wrapping us within perceptual and "attentional" ecologies, as well as our experience and implication within ecologies that encompass the more-than-human world. Sustainability educators argue that environmental responsibility and action start when humans learn to care about their habitats and develop a "sense of place" (Orr 1992; Thomashow 1995; Capra 2005; Blewitt 2006; Sterling 2009). Increasingly, travel and gadget usage has made many of us global citizens but also have increased a sense of alienation and disconnection from living systems (Louv 2005; Rauch 2018). The role of interactive media in shaping users' cognitive and affective preparedness for environmental action is an active topic of study within environmental communication (Bendor 2018) as well as ecomedia studies.

Taking its cue from the affective turn in media and cinema studies, this section explores the impacts of ecomedia on our mental health, our perception and reception of the natural world, and of characters contending with specific environmental situations. It opens with Yves Citton's critical discussion of our collective state of mind and attentional foci in a time of crisis ("a house on fire"), in relation to ecomedia studies. By drawing upon his previous discussion of ecology of attention and "mediarchies" (2017, 2019), Citton argues digital media today exacerbate our "ecomentia," the schizophrenic dementia reflected in the mediated experience in our collapsing ecological milieus. He calls instead for cultivating "collapsonaut attention" in order to correct the excesses and negligence of our dominant extractivist attention.

Chapters in the section also reflect the diverse manifestations of human affectivities to environments and nonhuman worlds according to conventions of different film genres. Through a cognitive ecocritical lens, Alexa Weik von Mossner shows how Jean-Marc Vallee's biopic movie *Wild* (2014) engages us in processes of embodied simulations (of the individual characters' experience of the environments) guided by a diverse range of sight and sound, which generate a complex interplay of attention, cognition, embodiment, and emotion. David Ingram approaches ecomedia in the form of a British social realist film, Clio Barnard's *Dark River* (2017), that addresses environmental issues in a scale differing from commercial blockbusters and their (frequently) network narratives. Ingram intentionally focuses on a small-budget family drama to show, with the aid of ecological psychologist James J. Gibson's concept of "affordances," how social realist cinema can provide a range of cognitive and affective experience for conveying thoughts about climate change and environmental crisis.

Surveying works of satire as both a mode and practice of ecomedia, Nicole Seymour and Anthony Lioi's study of *Sarah Cooper: Everything's Fine* (2020) and *Don't Look Up* (2021) shows how ecopolitical satire makes use of techniques such as exaggeration to push viewers to feel and think more openly about environmental issues in current political landscapes of the Global North. Eco-satires, they argue, allow us to adopt "a less strictly instrumental approach" to media and art that recognize the need for unimportant, frivolous, playful yet affective spaces that do not necessarily go anywhere or mean anything. Moving beyond fictional films, Katrina Maggiulli examines how American educational environmental media make use of tropes from the classical horror genre to cognitively frame "invasive species" with fear and disgust, villainizing them to draw public attention to environmental problems. As she shows, however, these tropes also risk misdirecting or overdirecting fear toward undeserving targets.

Affect is closely related to time in the sense that the duration and speed of mediated experience hugely shape one's affective and emotional responses toward the environment. Reminding us to consider ecomedia studies by slowing down our own experience, this section closes with Jennifer Rauch's examination of "slow media" and its transformative capacities through mindful media practices. Rauch argues that slow media cultivate an ecomedia perspective that stimulates our disengagement from digital media and encourages people to engage in more traditional forms of print and analog media in order to repair perceptions of physical reality.

***

Given the rapidly evolving state of ecomedia studies—made more elusive by the broad definitions we insist on for both the "eco" and the "media" (delineated further in the opening chapters of the "Ecomedia Theory" section)—any attempt to capture the field in a single handbook can only be considered partial and incomplete. Indeed, many important works either lie outside or freely intermingle the frames we have established here of materiality, affect, culture, and political ecology. Works like Jacob Smith's *Eco-Sonic Media* (2015), Paul Roquet's *Ambient Media: Japanese Atmospheres of Self* (2016), Marie-Luise Angerer's *Ecologies of Affect: Intensive Milieus and Contingent Encounters* (2017), Erin Manning and Sense Lab's *Immediations* project (Manning, Munster, and Stavning Thomsen 2019), and various contributions to ecocinematic animal studies (2011), with their proposed goal of a "non-anthropocentric cinema" (Lawrence and McMahon 2015), and to technoscience studies and media biopolitics (Da Costa and Philip 2010; Väliaho 2014), cross boundaries between several of these categories, even as they map out further dimensions for transdisciplinary study of media and environments. We can only imagine that as such work continues to flourish, media in general, as Adrian Ivakhiv and Antonio López propose in Chapter 1, will indeed become *eco*media.

Lest that sound pollyannish, we should note that media today are far from ecologically (or socially) benign in their aggregate impacts. Our planetary ICTs would not exist without conflict minerals, fossil fuel energy, exploited labor, and e-waste. In their present form, they parasitically extract our attention, enable increased surveillance to predict our behavior and monetize it, and create vast openings for disinformation entrepreneurs, conspiracy theorists, and propagandists, whose political impacts obstruct and curtail humanity's ability to respond to the many dimensions of the climate crisis. Many of those on the receiving end of the outsourced systemic violence have experienced it for centuries; it is the "slow violence" of colonialism and its capitalist variations that voices of Indigenous people, ecojustice activists, and the Global South have long identified and resisted.

What has changed is that our globally interconnected media systems ensure that few today are isolated or immune to these impacts. We share an interconnected world, and our media are at the core of that interconnection and of the ways in which we share it, equitably or otherwise. Our media today *are* necessarily ecomedia: the question is, what *kinds* of ecomedia are we shaping, to whose benefit, and at whose cost? These are the kinds of ethical and political concerns that animate the contributions of this volume and that we believe are shaping the field of ecomedia studies within the rapidly evolving, highly "mediatized" environments making up the contemporary world.

References

Abraham, Benjamin. 2022. *Digital Games after Climate Change*. Cham: Springer.
Albrecht, Glenn. 2019. *Earth Emotions: New Words for a New World*. Ithaca, NY: Cornell University Press.
Allen, Aaron S. and Kevin Dawe, eds. 2016. *Current Directions in Ecomusicology: Music, Culture, Nature*. London: Routledge.
Angerer, Marie-Luise. 2017. *Ecology of Affect: Intensive Milieus and Contingent Encounters*. Translated by Gerrit Jackson. Lüneburg: Meson Press. https://doi.org/10.14619/020.
Bendor, Roy. 2018. *Interactive Media for Sustainability*. Palgrave Studies in Media and Environmental Communication. Cham: Palgrave Macmillan. https://doi.org/10.1007/978-3-319-70383-1.
Blewitt, John. 2006. *The Ecology of Learning: Sustainability, Lifelong Learning, and Everyday Life*. Sterling, VA: Earthscan.
Bousé, Derek. 2000. *Wildlife Films*. Philadelphia: University of Pennsylvania Press.
Bozak, Nadia. 2011. *The Cinematic Footprint: Lights, Camera, Natural Resources*. Piscataway, NJ: Rutgers University Press.
Bratton, Benjamin H. 2015. *The Stack: On Software and Sovereignty*. Software Studies. Cambridge: MIT Press.
Brereton, Pat. 2016. *Environmental Ethics and Film*. London: Routledge.
Brereton, Patrick. 2004. *Hollywood Utopia: Ecology in Contemporary American Cinema*. Portland, OR: Intellect Books Ltd.
Brevini, Benedetta, and Graham Murdock, eds. 2017. *Carbon Capitalism and Communication: Confronting Climate Crisis*. New York: Palgrave Macmillan.
Capra, Fritjof. 2005. "Speaking Nature's Language: Principles for Sustainability." In *Ecological Literacy: Educating Our Children for a Sustainable World*, edited by Michael K. Stone and Zenobia Barlow, 18–29. San Francisco, CA; Berkeley, CA: Sierra Club Books.
Chang, Alenda Y. 2019. *Playing Nature: Ecology in Video Games*. Minneapolis: University of Minnesota Press.
Chang, Chia-ju, ed. 2019. *Chinese Environmental Humanities: Practices of Environing at the Margins*. Cham: Palgrave Macmillan.
Chen, Mel Y. 2012. *Animacies: Biopolitics, Racial Mattering, and Queer Affect*. Durham, NC: Duke University Press.
Chris, Cynthia. 2006. *Watching Wildlife*. Minneapolis: University of Minnesota Press.
Christman Lavin, Sophie, and Ann E. Kaplan. 2017. "The Climate of Ecocinema." In *Oxford Research Encyclopedia of Communication*. Oxford University Press. https://doi.org/10.1093/acrefore/9780190228613.013.121.
Citton, Yves. 2017. *The Ecology of Attention*. Cambridge: Polity.
———. 2019. *Mediarchy*. Cambridge; Medford, MA: Polity Press.
Cubitt, Sean. 2005. *EcoMedia*. Amsterdam; New York: Rodopi.
———. 2017. *Finite Media: Environmental Implications of Digital Technologies*. Durham, NC: Duke University Press.
Da Costa, Beatriz, and Kavita Philip, eds. 2010. *Tactical Biopolitics: Art, Activism, and Technoscience*. Cambridge; London: MIT Press.
DeLoughrey, Elizabeth M. 2019. *Allegories of the Anthropocene*. Durham, NC: Duke University Press.
Demos, T. J. 2016. *Decolonizing Nature: Contemporary Art and the Politics of Ecology*. London: Sternberg Press.
———. 2017. *Against the Anthropocene: Visual Culture and Environment Today*. London: Sternberg Press.
Deuze, Mark. 2021. "On the 'Grand Narrative' of Media and Mass Communication Theory and Research: A Review." *El Profesional de La Información*, January, e300105. https://doi.org/10.3145/epi.2021.ene.05.

Dobrin, Sidney I., and Sean Morey, eds. 2009. *Ecosee: Image, Rhetoric, Nature*. Albany, NY: SUNY Press.
Estok, Simon C. 2016. "Ecomedia and Ecophobia." *Neohelicon* 43 (1): 127–45. https://doi.org/10.1007/s11059-016-0335-z.
Fornoff, Carolyn, and Gisela Heffes, eds. 2021. *Pushing Past the Human in Latin American Cinema*. Albany: State University of New York Press.
French, Jennifer, and Gisela Heffes, eds. 2021. *The Latin American Ecocultural Reader*. Evanston, IL: Northwestern University Press.
Gabrys, Jennifer. 2011. *Digital Rubbish: A Natural History of Electronics*. Ann Arbor: Univ. of Michigan Press.
Gabrys, Jennifer. 2016. *Program Earth: Environmental Sensing Technology and the Making of a Computational Planet*. Minneapolis: University of Minnesota Press.
Garrard, Greg, ed. 2016. *Teaching Ecocriticism and Green Cultural Studies*. Cham: Palgrave Macmillan.
Guha, Ramachandra. 2000. *Environmentalism: A Global History*. New York: Longman.
Hansen, Anders, and Robert Cox, eds. 2015. *The Routledge Handbook of Environment and Communication*. London; New York: Routledge.
Hayward, Susan. 2020. *Film Ecology*. London; New York: Routledge.
Huggan, Graham, and Helen Tiffin. 2015. *Postcolonial Ecocriticism: Literature, Animals, Environment*. London; New York: Routledge.
Hven, Steffen. 2019. "The Affective Niches of Media." *NECSUS. European Journal of Media Studies* 8 (1): 105–23. https://doi.org/10.25969/MEDIAREP/4190.
———. 2022. *Enacting the Worlds of Cinema*. New York: Oxford University Press.
Iheka, Cajetan Nwabueze. 2021. *African Ecomedia: Network Forms, Planetary Politics*. Durham, NC: Duke University Press.
Ingram, David. 2000. *Green Screen: Environmentalism and Hollywood Cinema*. Exeter: University of Exeter Press.
Iqani, Mehita. 2021. *Garbage in Popular Culture: Consumption and the Aesthetics of Waste*. Albany, NY: SUNY Press.
Ivakhiv, Adrian. 2008. "Green Film Criticism and Its Futures." *Interdisciplinary Studies in Literature and Environment* 15 (2): 1–28.
———. 2011. "Cinema of the Not-Yet: The Utopian Promise of Film as Heterotopia." *Journal for the Study of Religion, Nature and Culture* 5 (2): 186–209. https://doi.org/10.1558/jsrnc.v5i2.186.
———. 2013. *Ecologies of the Moving Image: Cinema, Affect, Nature*. Waterloo: Wilfrid Laurier University Press.
———. 2018. *Shadowing the Anthropocene: Eco-Realism for Turbulent Times*. Goleta, CA. Punctum Books. https://doi.org/10.21983/P3.0211.1.00.
Jensen, Tim. 2019. *Ecologies of Guilt in Environmental Rhetorics*. Cham: Palgrave Macmillan.
Jue, Melody. 2020. *Wild Blue Media: Thinking Through Seawater*. Durham, NC: Duke University Press.
Kääpä, Pietari. 2020. *Environmental Management of the Media: Policy, Industry, Practice*. London; New York: Routledge.
Kääpä, Pietari, and Tommy Gustafsson, eds. 2013. *Transnational Ecocinema: Film Culture in an Era of Ecological Transformation*. Chicago, IL: Intellect.
Käll, Jannice. 2022. *Posthuman Property and Law: Commodification and Control Through Information, Smart Spaces and Artificial Intelligence*. Abingdon; New York: Routledge.
Kaplan, E. Ann. 2016. *Climate Trauma: Foreseeing the Future in Dystopian Film and Fiction*. New Brunswick, NJ: Rutgers University Press.
Kuntsman, Adi, and Esperanza Miyake. 2022. *Paradoxes of Digital Disengagement*. London: University of Westminster Press. https://doi.org/10.16997/book61.
Lawrence, Michael, and Laura McMahon, eds. 2015. *Animal Life and the Moving Image*. London: British Film Institute. https://doi.org/10.5040/9781838711467.
Lockwood, Alex. 2016. "Graphs of Grief and Other Green Feelings: The Uses of Affect in the Study of Environmental Communication." *Environmental Communication* 10 (6): 734–48. https://doi.org/10.1080/17524032.2016.1205642.
López, Antonio. 2021. *Ecomedia Literacy: Integrating Ecology into Media Education*. London: New York: Routledge.
Louv, Richard. 2005. *Last Child in the Woods: Saving Our Children from Nature-Deficit Disorder*. Chapel Hill, NC: Algonquin Books of Chapel Hill.

Lu, Sheldon H., and Jiayan Mi, eds. 2009. *Chinese Ecocinema*. Hong Kong University Press. https://doi.org/10.5790/hongkong/9789622090866.001.0001.

MacDonald, Scott. 2001. *The Garden in the Machine: A Field Guide to Independent Films about Place*. Berkeley: University of California Press.

Manning, Erin, Anna Munster, and Bodil Marie Stavning Thomsen, eds. 2019. *Immediation I*. Place of publication not identified: Open Humanities Press.

Marks, Laura U., Joseph Clark, Jason Livingston, Denise Oleksijczuk, and Lucas Hilderbrand. 2020. "Streaming Media's Environmental Impact." *Media+Environment* 2 (1). https://doi.org/10.1525/001c.17242.

Maxwell, Richard, and Toby Miller. 2012. *Greening the Media*. New York: Oxford University Press.

———. 2020. *How Green Is Your Smartphone?* Cambridge; Medford, MA: Polity.

McLean, Jessica. 2020. *Changing Digital Geographies: Technologies, Environments and People*. Cham: Palgrave Macmillan.

Mentz, Steve. 2019. *Break up the Anthropocene*. Minneapolis: University of Minnesota Press.

Milstein, Tema, and José Castro-Sotomayor, eds. 2020. *Routledge Handbook of Ecocultural Identity*. London; New York: Routledge.

Mitman, Gregg. 1999. *Reel Nature: America's Romance with Wildlife on Film*. Cambridge, MA: Harvard University Press.

Moore, Ellen. 2019. *Journalism, Politics, and the Dakota Access Pipeline: Standing Rock and the Framing of Injustice*. London; New York: Routledge.

Mukherjee, Rahul. 2020. *Radiant Infrastructures: Media, Environment, and Cultures of Uncertainty*. Durham, NC; London: Duke University Press.

Müller, Cornelia, and Hermann Kappelhoff. 2020. *Cinematic Metaphor: Experience – Affectivity – Temporality*. Berlin: De Gruyter.

Murphy, Patrick D. 2017. *The Media Commons: Globalization and Environmental Discourses*. Urbana; Chicago: University of Illinois Press.

Murray, Robin L., and Joseph K. Heumann. 2005. "Environmental Nostalgia in Eco-Disaster Movies of the Early 1970s." *CEA Critic* 67 (2): 15–28.

———. 2009. *Ecology and Popular Film: Cinema on the Edge*. Albany: State University of New York Press.

———. 2016. *Monstrous Nature: Environment and Horror on the Big Screen*. Lincoln: University of Nebraska Press.

Nixon, Rob. 2011. *Slow Violence and the Environmentalism of the Poor*. Cambridge, MA: Harvard University Press.

Oppermann, Serpil. 2011. "Ecocriticism's Theoretical Discontents." *Mosaic: A Journal for the Interdisciplinary Study of Literature* 44 (2): 153–69.

Orr, David W. 1992. *Ecological Literacy: Education and the Transition to a Postmodern World*. Albany: State University of New York Press.

Parikka, Jussi. 2015. *A Geology of Media*. Minneapolis: University of Minnesota Press.

Parks, Lisa, and Nicole Starosielski. 2015a. "Introduction." In *Signal Traffic: Critical Studies of Media Infrastructures*, edited by Lisa Parks and Nicole Starosielski, 1–28. Urbana: University of Illinois Press.

———, eds. 2015b. *Signal Traffic: Critical Studies of Media Infrastructures*. Urbana: University of Illinois Press.

Pasek, Anne. 2020. "Everyday Oil: Energy Infrastructures and Places That Have Yet to Become Strange." 14 September. Accessed 1 Feb. 2023. Heliotrope. https://www.heliotropejournal.net/helio/everyday-oil.

Peters, John Durham. 2015. *The Marvelous Clouds: Toward a Philosophy of Elemental Media*. Chicago, IL: University of Chicago Press.

Pick, Anat. 2011. *Creaturely Poetics: Animality and Vulnerability in Literature and Film*. New York: Columbia University Press.

Pick, Anat, and Guinevere Narraway, eds. 2013. *Screening Nature: Cinema beyond the Human*. New York; Oxford: Berghahn Books. https://doi.org/10.3167/9781782382263.

Postman, Neil. 2000. "The Humanism of Media Ecology." *Proceedings of the Media Ecology Association 1*, 10–16.

Rauch, Jennifer. 2018. *Slow Media: Toward a Sustainable Future*. Oxford: Oxford University Press.

Roquet, Paul. 2016. *Ambient Media: Japanese Atmospheres of Self*. Minneapolis: University of Minnesota Press.

Ross, Andrew. 1994. *The Chicago Gangster Theory of Life: Nature's Debt to Society*. London: Verso.

Roy, Elodie A. 2020. "'Total Trash'. Recorded Music and the Logic of Waste." *Popular Music* 39 (1): 88–107. https://doi.org/10.1017/S0261143019000576.

Rozelle, Lee. 2006. *Ecosublime: Environmental Awe and Terror from New World to Oddworld*. Tuscaloosa: University of Alabama Press.
Rust, Stephen, Salma Monani, and Sean Cubitt, eds. 2013. *Ecocinema Theory and Practice*. New York: Routledge.
———, eds. 2016. *Ecomedia: Key Issues*. London; New York: Routledge.
Rust, Stephen, Salma Monani, and Seán Cubitt. 2022. *Ecocinema Theory and Practice 2*. New York: Routledge. https://doi.org/10.4324/9781003246602.
Schneider, Birgit, and Thomas Nocker, eds. 2014. *Image Politics of Climate Change: Visualizations, Imaginations, Documentations*. Bielefeld: Transcript.
Sinnerbrink, R. 2012. "Stimmung: Exploring the Aesthetics of Mood." *Screen* 53 (2): 148–63. https://doi.org/10.1093/screen/hjs007.
Smith, Jacob. 2015. *Eco-Sonic Media*. Oakland: University of California Press.
Starosielski, Nicole and Janet Walker, eds. 2016. *Sustainable Media: Critical Approaches to Media and Environment*. New York; London: Routledge.
Sterling, Stephen. 2009. "Ecological Intelligence: Viewing the World Relationally." In *The Handbook of Sustainability Literacy: Skills for a Changing World*, edited by Arran Stibbe, 220–20. Totnes: Green Books.
Taffel, Sy. 2019. *Digital Media Ecologies: Entanglements of Content, Code and Hardware*. New York: Bloomsbury Academic.
Telles, Jason Paolo, John Ryan, and Jeconiah Louis Dreisbach, eds. 2022. *Environment, Media, and Popular Culture in Southeast Asia*. Singapore: Springer.
Thomashow, Mitchell. 1995. *Ecological Identity: Becoming a Reflective Environmentalist*. Cambridge, MA: MIT Press.
Towns, Armond R. 2022. *On Black Media Philosophy*. Oakland: University of California Press.
Väliaho, Pasi. 2014. *Biopolitical Screens: Image, Power, and the Neoliberal Brain*. Cambridge, MA: MIT Press. https://doi.org/10.7551/mitpress/9587.001.0001.
Vaughan, Hunter. 2019. *Hollywood's Dirtiest Secret: The Hidden Environmental Costs of the Movies*. New York: Columbia University Press.
Weik von Mossner, Alexa, ed. 2014. *Moving Environments: Affect, Emotion, Ecology, and Film*. Waterloo: Wilfrid Laurier University Press.
———. 2017. *Affective Ecologies: Empathy, Emotion, and Environmental Narrative*. Columbus: Ohio State University Press.
Yusoff, Kathryn. 2018. *A Billion Black Anthropocenes or None*. Minneapolis: University of Minnesota Press.

PART I

Ecomedia Theory

1
WHEN DO MEDIA BECOME *ECO*MEDIA?

Adrian Ivakhiv and Antonio López

If ecomedia studies is intended as an ecological reboot of the study of media, it is necessary to define what we mean by both media and ecomedia. But rather than asking, what are ecomedia?, it's more fruitful to probe, when are media *eco*media?[1] In common usage, "the media" seems self-evident, yet as a taken-for-granted metonym it often changes meaning according to context and usage. Such is the case when "the news" is often equated with "mass media." Vernacular use often defaults to old definitions that are no longer tenable, which is demonstrated in the way OpenAI's ChatGPT[2] chatbot reproduces a superficial description of media as the "means of communication that are used to transmit information, ideas, and messages to a large audience" (ChatGPT 2022). This narrow one-to-many characterization has long been recognized by media scholars as limited; ChatGPT's extracted datasets merely repeat an outdated view of media that persists in obsolete textbooks and routine thinking. Curiously absent in this designation is the tech industry itself. Under the guise of surveillance capitalism, the four biggest tech companies in the world—Alphabet (owner of Google and YouTube), Apple, Meta (owner of Facebook, WhatsApp, and Instagram), and Amazon—are not conventionally thought of as "media" companies, yet in 2022 The Walt Disney Co's revenue was only a third of Alphabet's total earnings. Adtech, a form of algorithmically based "surveillance advertising," in 2021 was a $763.2 billion industry that automates where ads are placed through microtargeting and generating revenue for websites (Cucchietti et al. 2022). In 2020, 97.9% of Facebook's and 80% of Google's revenue was generated from advertising. In 2022, 80%–90% of the ad market (excluding China) was accounted for by Facebook, Google, and Amazon. Microsoft, IBM, Netflix, and providers like the telecom giant AT&T and cable service Comcast in the United States, are the owners and distributors of media content. Videogames have overcome legacy media, propelled by the popularity of multiplayer online games and esports. The gaming industry grosses more income than Hollywood and the music industry combined, making it the most profitable entertainment business in the world (Richter 2022).

Though global media have evolved as a result of digitization, the "mass" of traditional analog media has not gone away; many legacy media organizations (publishers, film studios, radio networks, etc.) are larger and even more monopolized and remain an influential presence in our lives. But the emergence of networks, multitudes, mass self-mediation, filter bubbles, algorithms, and fragmented audiences means that media studies is in the midst of a shift from considering media solely as texts, industries, audiences, and medium, to investigating platforms, infrastructures,

This chapter has been made available under a CC-BY-NC-ND license.

computer networks, satellites, databases, and software that are integral to everyday life and the operation of the planetary system. A major characteristic of our era is one of rapid digitization and deep mediatization, "an advanced stage of the process in which all elements of our social world are intricately related to digital media and their underlying infrastructures" (Hepp 2019, 5). A problematic consequence of this trend is "digital solutionism," an optimistic belief that emerging technologies like artificial intelligence and "smart cities" will solve the environmental crisis, yet, "they contain very little critical meditation on the question of whether, and to what extent, the digital itself might be unsustainable" (Kuntsman and Miyake 2022, 120). And what is framed as "new" digital technologies is actually based on "old" exploitative materialities: "the natural resources that make the digital possible, their relationship to global social relations of production and the political and environmental consequences of these relations" (Emejulu and McGregor 2019).

In the study of media, there is a tension between exploring them as objects, messages/meaning, organizations, or ecosystems. For example, media archeology deals with artifacts of "dead" media; media literacy reads textual representations; critical political economy investigates systemic structures and "media logics"; and fields like media ecology examine media as environments. As a baseline, media facilitate "the production and reproduction of sociality, social relations, social structures, social systems, and society" (Fuchs 2020, 377). They contribute to the "sense-making process by which people organize their experience and comprehend their physical and social environment" (Kaplan 1990, 38). Denis McQuail's (2012) popular communications textbook broadly divides media scholarship between media-centric (the study of texts and meaning) and sociocentric (the study of social forces), and between radical/critical or functionalist approaches. These categories tend to distinguish between what people do with media and what media do to (and with) people. Moving beyond the essentialization of screen media, the materialist turn in media studies is less interested in what media *are* than in what media *do* as actors in a broader "ecology" that "includes human bodies, technologies, and the most basic elements of the world's environment, such as minerals and the many other raw materials used to manufacture our devises" (Bollmer 2019, 17). New materialists claim that media include "the agency, liveliness, and vitality of the nonhuman world," "the inseparability of human and nonhuman," and the necessity "for an ethical response to these relationships" (Tidwell, this volume).

Increasingly the study of media is incorporating political-ecological and anti-colonial perspectives that recognize how media logics are founded on a system of "five Es": enclosure, extraction, expendability, exploitation, and externalization. The dominant global economic system is predicated on *enclosure*, the process of converting the commons (air, water, forests, shared knowledge, stories, etc.) into private resources (minerals, materials, energy, data, intellectual property, etc.) that can be *extracted* to make and power our media and to form information regimes; this also entails an epistemic enclosure that seeks to replace diverse cosmologies with a universal rational modernity used to justify this system. In order to make this system possible, *expendability* relates to how ecosystems become sacrifice zones and populations are designated as disposable. *Exploitation* connects to how these practices depend on "cheap things" (labor, care, etc.) that result from negative *externalities* that are factored into standard business practices. As a result, our gadgets are "colonial technologies." But instead of demonstrating mastery of the world, "they merely show a particular rearrangement of the practices, forms of life, and life forms, often with unintended and unforeseen consequences" (Davis 2022, 19). An example of a decolonial media logic is the recognition that people who work to process e-waste should be considered part of "digital labor" and the "knowledge economy" (Iheka 2021). Likewise, gender dynamics at sites of extraction and assembly are crucial to consider.

From an ecocritical perspective, a fundamental problem is that media have been historically conceived of as something immaterial, reflecting Western culture's mind/body duality in which the realm of ideas is considered disconnected from the physical world. For example, when ChatGPT is questioned about the environmental impact of its queries, it states, "As an AI language model, I do not have any physical presence or environmental impact. I exist solely as a software program and do not consume resources or generate any waste or pollution" (ChatGPT 2022). But just as we cannot have thoughts without a body, we cannot have communication without a physical means to communicate and sensory experience to inform that communication. Light is composed of photons that stimulate the photoreceptors in our eyes, and our voices (produced by the solar plexus, lungs, throat, tongue, and mouth) make sound waves that physically touch eardrums. Our very atmosphere and Earth's surface are the primary media through which all communication must pass. As Jussi Parikka (2015, 13) asserts, "it is the earth that provides for media and enables it: the minerals, materials of(f) the ground, the affordances of its geophysical reality that make technical media happen." Earth is integrated into our gadgets and batteries, making the planet's geology and biosphere a necessary part of any medium. For if there is no clay, there are no tablets; no organic matter, no printing press; no coal, no steam press; no copper, no telegraph; no electromagnetic spectrum, no broadcast. To paraphrase Parikka, without mineral mining, there is no data mining.

Modernity's legacy of "nature" designated as something contrasted to culture, civilization, and the human makes it conceptually difficult to integrate an environmental understanding of media because they are normally thought of as only belonging to complex, depersonalized technological societies, and in this sense always somewhat intangible. Without a common vocabulary to describe the intersection between media and environment, these issues continue to be ignored. That's why media metaphors matter. A contraction of "ecology" and "media," renaming media as *ecomedia* addresses media's ecological opacity (in the sense of unseen, unrecognized, ephemeral, hiding in plain sight, and taken-for-granted). Ecomedia reframes media as ecological media; that is, media are a material reality that are in, and a part of, our environment in the broadest sense(s). Media are inseparable from their material conditions and the environment that produced them.

Ecomedia studies serves as a "historically situated, ideologically motivated, and ethically informed approach to the intersections of media, society, and the environment" (Rust, Monani, and Cubitt 2016, 87). But since it has not entered into common usage, "ecomedia" can also be perplexing. For example, *Keywords for Environmental Studies* describes ecomedia as "shorthand for representations of and communication about the human and natural environment in media beyond traditional print" (Ziser 2016, 75). This is close to ChatGPT's description of ecomedia:

> Ecomedia is a term used to describe media that focuses on environmental issues or ecological themes. It includes a range of media forms, such as film, television, journalism, and social media, that seek to educate, inform, and engage audiences about environmental concerns and promote sustainable living. Ecomedia may also aim to influence public opinion and policy on environmental issues, and to inspire individuals and communities to take action to protect the natural world. Ecomedia often incorporates elements of activism and advocacy, and may be produced by organizations or individuals with a mission to promote environmental awareness and conservation.
>
> (ChatGPT 2022)

Both Ziser and ChatGPT reinforce the notion that media work solely in the realm of ideas and representations, and in the case of ChatGPT, a normalized notion of the environment signaled by the use of "eco." Like legacy concepts of media, this definition doesn't account for their materiality or their affective characteristics. This is not to say that communicating about the environment is not an important aspect of ecomedia studies. Indeed, the insights of ecocriticism, environmental communication, and ecocinema regarding rhetoric, symbolic resources, and discourses are integral to ecomedia studies. But the aim is to balance our understanding of media between representations and their materiality. Media are finite, so media *matter* matters: "because they are inevitably tied to physics… [they] are finite resources in the closed system of planet Earth. Because they are finite, media not only cannot persist forever; they cannot proliferate without bounds" (Cubitt 2016, 7).

For our purpose, "ecomedia" is inherently reflexive in a way that "media" is not. Ecomedia is indexical of media's inherent ecological condition. This affords a decolonial perspective, such as grappling with how media

> make possible communication and sustenance, but they are equally tethered to social and ecological degradation in Africa from their production, distribution, consumption and disposal. […] Ecomedia studies is primarily positioned to scrutinize this contradiction – of the possibilities and problematics of media.
>
> (Iheka 2021, 5)

By countering the ideological milieu that constrains this awareness, ecomedia registers the interrelationship and materiality of media with the physical environment inhabited by humans and nonhumans alike. From this perspective, all media become ecomedia, but there is a difference between explicit and implicit expressions of ecomedia. Explicit forms would be those ecomedia openly portraying environmental themes, whereas implicit ecomedia are inherently ecological by their condition as materially embedded in the environment and global economic system. Explicit forms of ecomedia are cultural and ideological inscriptions of ecological meanings. They can also be implicit in the ways they frame out or decenter environmental concerns.

Ecomedia helps us resolve some conceptual roadblocks that inhibit our ability to attend to media's "double ground": the first being the content and text of whatever it is we are attending to, the second being the material itself in/on which the text is available—the book in your hands, the screen, the metals, plastics, electricity, and production circuits that undergird its creation, and so on (Citton 2017, 198). Nadia Bozak's (2011) term "resource image" enables us to think of both at once: the image as representation of material-ecological production and the image as material and ecological product. For example, iconic images of burning oil fields from the 1991 Gulf War communicate about human domination/destruction of the environment and the ideology of oil dependence and war. But in order to create, view, and retrieve those images, we require supply chains that make image technology possible, technological infrastructures, and materials containing images (newspapers, TVs, computers, etc.). Digital images in turn are data files that exist on servers, whose storage and use produces CO_2. Like household utilities, we take for granted how media images are piped into our homes. Bozak (2011, 2) asks, what would happen if an "end of oil" affects "not only the functioning of society and culture at large, and on a global level, but also, as a consequence, the way moving images are produced and received?" Cajetan Iheka (2021) reminds us that in an African context, "resource media constitute the middle relationship between the site of extraction and the point of consumption, between Africa and Euro-America in this context" (5).

Ultimately, rather than regarding ecomedia as having a closed definition, we propose it as a "sensitizing concept."[3] Following Eva Horn's (2007) theoretical approach, Nicole Starosielski and Janet Walker (2016) frame "sustainable media" by using an

> "anti-ontological" approach in media theory, rejecting fixed concepts of what "media" are – whether technologies, communications, platforms, or institutions – in favor of seeing media

as conditions of possibility for events and processes, "heterogeneous structures," that comprise practices and forms of knowledge.

(4–5)

"Ecomedia" in this sense is not a thing or a set of objects (despite what object-oriented ontology might suggest), for a world of things arguably reflects the mechanistic thinking that has reified the Earth, humans, and the more-than-human world, contributing ideologically to the current ecological crisis. Instead, ecomedia entail processes of activation, mediation, institutionalization, and materialization. Ecomedia *perform* and do things that are ecological. (On the objects-processes debate, see Ivakhiv 2014, 2018.)

The remainder of this chapter grapples with some of the ways in which prominent scholars have been engaging ecomedia in both its "eco" and its "media" aspects and suggests some pointers for studying ecomedia that are reflected in the essays in this volume.

The "Eco" of Ecomedia

Just as the meaning of "media" is routinely taken for granted, so too are the concepts of nature, environment, and ecology. Nature, as cultural historians like Raymond Williams (1980) have long shown, is among the most complex and ambiguous terms in the English language, its uses marked by Eurocentric and colonial assumptions (see Ivakhiv 2017). The conceptual separation of nature and culture underpins much of Western scholarship, including the very division between the sciences, with their presumed objectivity focused on the study of "nature," and the humanities, with their attempts to grapple with the "subjective" dimensions of "culture." Nature has traditionally been seen alternately as the generative (yet inferior) matrix from which human civilization has "risen," as a set of limits to be either bound by or to overcome, and as the ground of rejuvenation for romantic (and typically masculinist) quests for wholeness. Historians of ideas have studied the ways in which these ideas of nature have shaped ideas and discourses of "ecology," arising in the late nineteenth and early twentieth centuries, and of "environment" as these emerged in the mid twentieth century (see Ivakhiv, this volume).

Because these terms have a way of essentializing "the environment" as something separate from humans, scholars in the environmental humanities, including ecofeminists and theorists of postcolonial and queer ecology, have highlighted the cultural constructedness of these concepts, showing how they support and reproduce forms of colonial, patriarchal, ableist, and heteronormative discourse. For feminists like Val Plumwood and Karen Warren, the nature-culture dualism has traditionally supported a "logic of domination" whereby men and women, white and Black, European and non-European, and reason and emotion are asymmetrically constituted to privilege the first term over the second (Plumwood 1993; Warren 1993). Postcolonial and decolonial theorists have extended this critique to encompass histories of colonialism that continue today in hierarchical power relations encompassing the capitalist world system, legacies of racial domination, neoliberal governance, discourses of "development," and much more (e.g., Escobar 1995; Mignolo 2007; Quijano 2007; Sultana 2022).

In response to this critique of conceptual dualisms, numerous theorists have worked to articulate alternative understandings of ecology (as holistic and encompassing of society alongside the natural world), cosmology (as relational), and ontology (as primary and thus preceding any possible duality of "nature" and "culture"), drawing from multiple sources, including Indigenous or non-Western traditions of thought, "postmodern" or post-positivist conceptions of science, and other novel philosophies from Spinozist monism to post-Heideggerian phenomenology, Whiteheadian processualism, and Deleuzian "assemblage theory." Terms like actor-networks (Latour 2005), naturecultures (Haraway 2008), quasi-objects (Serres 1982), rhizomes (Deleuze and Guattari 1987), assemblages (Law 2004), social nature (Castree and Braun 2001), the more-than-human world (Abram 1996), humanature (Milstein 2016), humanimal (Mitchell 2003), and hyperobjects (Morton 2013) have been proposed to aid in the conceptual unraveling of inherited binaries (see Milstein et al. this volume). Others, including political ecologists, biocultural anthropologists, and critical realists, have sought a balanced and multi-leveled understanding that combines both the material-empirical and the discursive-cultural characteristics of environment, as in Michael Carolan's distinction between Nature (physicality, causality, and permanence-with-flux), nature (socio-biophysical phenomenon), and "nature" (discursive constructions) (cited in Büscher 2021, 19–20).

As metaphors, "environment," "ecology," and "ecosystem" have both informed and obfuscated the ecological conditions shaping and making media, to the point of leaving out the material conditions that make any medium possible (Rust and Wurth, this volume). Discursive formations of "environment" do ideological work when they are tied to the idea of "enclosed" surroundings. "The environment," as Patel and Moore (2018) note, is always the frontier of capitalist expansion to incorporate nature and people into markets: "capitalism grows through its frontiers" (2018, 37). The most generic definition of ecology is the interrelationship between organisms and their environments (for novel approaches to the concept, see Hörl and Burton 2017), but over time two distinct concepts of media ecology have emerged. In the case of Neil Postman's notion of *media ecology* and Henry Jenkins' use of *media ecosystem*, both signal a prescriptive orientation but have different situated meanings (Anderson 2016; Nadler 2018; Wahl-Jorgensen 2015). As reflected in the Postman tradition, media ecology is based on a normative concern with how a new medium (such as television or digital media) emerges to dominate an established medium environment (like print) to achieve some kind of "cybernetic balance" with the overall health and harmony of society. It is anthropocentric in the sense that it regards "media health" as something that can benefit or harm humans. The other is the rhizomatic approach which describes networks and complexity in the flow of information. This draws on the work of Gilles Deleuze and Félix Guattari (1987), refined later by Matthew Fuller (2005) and others. In the rhizomatic version, humans are not at the center but are a node in symbolic and material networks. Guattari (2008) later formalized a three-ecology approach that combines the physical, social, and mental environments (see Ivakhiv, this volume). While the ecosystem metaphor has been used both to support an organic (and hence beneficial) perspective or to justify market competition (as in the idea of "survival of the fittest" media technologies or platforms), Richard Maxwell and Toby Miller (2012, 93) assert that technological and political processes should not be equated with or translated as natural ecosystems because they behave differently. Ultimately, Anthony Nadler (2018) urges that the term ecosystem be "de-reified" in order to allow for flexibility of use.

Newer formulations of media ecology explore the "material-spatial conditions of media" (Gabrys 2016a). Concepts of "elemental media" also destabilize and reframe traditional notions of environment (see below). In a move beyond the essentialization of the environment, as commonly used in the English language, some scholars are exploring "milieu" as an alternative formation. In this perspective, environments are made up of multiple milieus, which have historically been described as "spaces of transfer, influence, and environmental inhabitation" (Gabrys 2016a, 12). For Jennifer Gabrys (2016a), a milieu arises when "environments and entities are formed across individuals (inner) and environments (exterior) through energetic and material exchanges that occur through the transversal field" (12). A milieu in this sense is a space mediating some form of communication. While this approach risks maintaining the traditional Western view of cognition as "internal," more recent theories of cognition as embodied, embedded, extended, enactive, and affective ("4EA cognition") help to situate it within broader networks of agency encompassing, for instance, the personal use of gadgets, attending concerts, participating in all-night rituals, outdoor picnics and dinner parties, and so on. Here we are moving beyond a definition of media and communication as transference of information, to one based on the experience of mediation and ritual. Milieus can be experienced by plants, animals, insects, and chemicals. However, according to Seán Cubitt (2016), not all mediations are communication, but all communications are mediated (and material). "When we speak of media, we tend to refer to the technological media of the last two hundred years; but everything that mediates is a medium–light, molecules, energy" (4).

The "Media" of Ecomedia

In Friedrich Kittler's (1993) influential take on the topic, media are defined by their capacity to record, store, and process information. This suggests an imperative to cache knowledge in some external capacity independent of oral traditions where memory is social. Media don't have memory, they *are* memory. As John Durham Peters writes, "Like 'new media,' ancient media such as registers, indexes, the census, calendars, and catalogs have always been in the business of recording, transmitting, and processing culture; of managing subjects, objects, and data; of organizing times, space, and power." He continues, "Media as entertainment machines that provide news and entertainment are rare in human history" (Peters 2015, 19). In complex societies, media are logistical in order "to manage time, space, and power," and "what is not in the documents is not in the world" (Peters 2015, 20). According to Harold Innis' (1999) investigations, the properties of a medium, such as stone or papyrus, that predominates in complex societies produce different spatial and temporal biases that, in turn, give rise to specific sociopolitical structures. Innis was concerned with how dominant media forms create knowledge monopolies and expert classes.

But this view that media are defined by their civilization-ordering processes arguably also reflects an inherently Western prejudice, with the result that "pre-literate" cultural practices are often excluded from definitions of media because they are not "civilized." Armond Towns' (2022) formulation of "Black media philosophy" critiques this kind of medium theory by arguing that its technologically determinist thinking generalizes from Western media experience. The result of this universalization is that "Black" equals "close to nature" (tribal, sensual, with little technological development), while "white" is "advanced," detribalized, sensually isolated, less emotional, and so on. What counts or doesn't count as "media" is a matter of control:

> Unlike the slave catchers who relied on media like maps, printed paper, and the phonetic alphabet, the Black enslaved person's media economy was structured around media not deemed media by white people, but often deemed natural, such as orality, star constellations, tree branches, and even their own bodies.
>
> (23–24)

Towns critiques Marshall McLuhan's media epistemology as tainted by white, male, heterosexual, able-bodied, middle-class, and cisgender assumptions: "the media that the West deployed," he writes,

> produced the West as the monopolizer of knowledge. McLuhan's argument assumed that we are all derivatives of white Euro-Americans, and all media served a Western, temporal,

epistemological function: to show white Euro-Americans how far behind them we as Black people were.

(8)

Bridging the "eco" examined above with a broadened conception of "media," Nicole Starosielski's (2019, 1) "elemental analysis" of media encompasses "minerals that comprise media technologies," "the harvesting of ecological matter for media of inscription," "light that sets conditions for vision," "infrastructures that support signal traffic," "atmospheric media," "plastic as the substrata, a medium, of advanced capitalism," and earth itself as a medium. Starosielski asserts that "working with elements provides a way to come at ecological issues from an oblique angle, to refuse boundaries between human and environment, and to recast the terms of the conversation in environmental media studies" (2). John Durham Peters (2015), whose scholarship in "elemental media" has been influential, argues that the original concept of media was in reference to the elements; this is retained when we think of gel as medium in petri dishes. Tree rings, ice cores, and geological strata are all forms of storage, but technologies are expressions of nature by and for humans. For Peters, media "are ensembles of natural elements and human craft" (3). African ecomedia theorist Cajetan Iheka (2021) adds that "elemental media are indigenous inhabitants of the ecomedia sphere. Elemental media precede the arrival of media devices, media arts, resource media, and other recent immigrant arrivals threatening the survival of native ecomedia and the rest of the planet" (6).

Melody Jue (2020) reframes Kittler's heuristic of media as interface, inscription, and database, which supports the infrastructural approach to ecomedia. According to Peters (2015), what most of us currently experience as media, different from experience in earlier epochs, is a proliferation of infrastructures, such that media are "fundamentally logistical": they compress time and space, "organize and orient," "coordinate and subordinate," and arrange "relationships among people and things" into "grids" (Peters, 2015, 37). But by their nature, infrastructures are concealed, ordinary, background, and unnoticed. Infrastructures of data and control determine what we know about whales, forests, and medicine, which makes them "infrastructures of being, the habitats and materials through which we act and are" (Peters 2015, 15). This "forgotten" infrastructure has world-leveraging power to shift ontologies, but according to Iheka, they are also worldbuilding in the sense that fossil fuels are a medium of modernity that determine the geopolitical position of nations like Nigeria. A civilizational shift to "green" energy that requires cobalt and lithium for batteries will certainly change and reconfigure the planet in new ways (on media' energy infrastructures, see Cubitt 2016).

The turn to media infrastructures is an important facet of ecomedia studies. "The goal" of this turn, in Jean-Christophe Plantin and Aswin Punathambekar's (2019) words,

is not simply to study the technological properties of a particular medium of communications, but rather to show that the material transport of information (the 'signal traffic') reframes traditional questions of media production, circulation, access, consumption, and policy and regulation.

(2019, 165)

An infrastructural approach engages power relations between stakeholders, social and labor practices, scale (from personal gadgets to networks of undersea cables), contingent and relational conditions resulting from preexisting media platforms, and "the *ideological* work involved in imagining, assembling, and maintaining media infrastructures" (emphasis original, 166–67). But Tung-Hui Hu (2016) challenges the idea that we can know the materiality of infrastructure—what he refers to as "the cloud"—because it is not medium-specific, but medium-agnostic: "not even the engineers who have built it typically know where the cloud is, and as a consequence, what part of the apparatus to examine" (xix). As a totality (or as a hyperobject, to use Timothy Morton's term), it is unavailable to our senses. The form of the cloud comprises abstract layers (from least to most abstract): physical links between fiber-optic cable and Ethernet copper wire constitute the bottom layer; protocols like Internet Protocol and Transmission Protocol, the middle layer; and application software built onto the protocols, like streaming media, the top layer (xxiv). The "toxic cloud" enacts slow violence across space and time as it causes a double displacement, "the displacement of place itself from sight but also a temporal displacement" (xxix).

If we consider the environmental studies truism that we change the environment and the environment changes us, what does it mean if we take into account how "sensor technologies are generating distinct ways of programming and concretizing environments and environmental relations" across the planet (Gabrys 2016a, 4)? "The drive to instrument the planet," Gabrys writes, "to make the earth programmable not primarily from outer space but from within the contours of earthly space, has translated into a situation where there are now more 'things' connected to the Internet than there are people." She continues, "People-to-people communication is becoming a smaller proportion of Internet and networked traffic in the complex array of machine-to-machine (M2M), machine-to-people (M2P), and people-to-people (P2P) circuits of communication" (Gabrys 2016a, 7). The emerging "Internet of Things" and Earth sensors forming an "electronic skin" across the Earth together generate new environmental conditions that affect our experience and understanding of the planet. For example, the production chain for technology—from microprocessors to solar panels—is meant to monitor and "sense" the environment, but their manufacture, production, and infrastructure also materially change ecosystems.

An updated high-tech, datafied version of Lewis Mumford's (1970) "megamachine," our mediated planet increasingly is linked to an emergent, giant computer, or what Benjamin Bratton (2015) calls "the stack." According to Gabrys (2016a, 16), ecologies of satellites and sensors are assembled into networks of code that produce information so that "[c]omputational technologies are constitutive of environments, have environmental effects, and also in-form environmental practices." Theorists of "environing media" like Adam Wickberg and Johan Gärdebo (2022, 6) describe how the "dialectics of feedback—between knowing and doing the environment through media—continues to present day, where we may speak about a fully mediated planet of data." Responding to concerns with the way "data eats the world," an emerging area of scholarship engages a political ecology of data that examines both the materiality of data infrastructures (hardware, software, institutions, and governance) and the social infrastructures by which decisions are made about data (for whom, to what end, etc.) (Goldstein and Nost 2022). As a process of ongoing ontogenesis, this goes well beyond the traditional notion of screen-based subjectivity. As Ivakhiv (2021, 11) asserts,

> The technological systems we call "media" are extensions and transformers of how we perceive and respond to the world, a world that already includes political actors, social understandings, economic incentives, contractual agreements, design principles, and much more. Those media are a subset of the broader category of media, which […] are the technical, perceptual, and bodily modalities by which all things interact with other things. "Media" is simply a word for "mediating apparatuses," which mediate via the shaping of perceptual and responsive capacities. Mediation is how things work.

Utilizing a multiperspectival approach, ecomedia addresses media as objects, element(al)s, infrastructures, and processes of mediation, with different heuristics aiding us in understanding when media are ecomedia. Any ecomedia "object" is an ecological artifact that becomes an event articulating its infrastructure at any given moment. As events, media are "assemblages or constellations of certain technologies, fields of knowledge, and social institutions" (Horn 2007, 8). According to Melody Jue, "to be articulated as a medium is not about a stable ontological entity (this is a medium, that is not) but about being enfolded into an assemblage such that something performs a function of a medium" (Jue 2020, 24–25). Media as "entities" should "not be approached as detached objects for our subjective sensing and contemplation, but rather as processes in and through which experience, environments, and subjects individuate, relate, and gain consistency" (Gabrys 2016a, 9).

In the inaugural 2020 issue of the *Journal of Environmental Media*, the journal's editors elected to constrain media to "the study of digital screen culture," defining the digital as "all that is created by the binary code of 0's and 1's and is transmitted electronically." They wrote,

> [O]ur use of the term "media" is limited so as to avoid a number of neologisms and analogical terms that, in our opinion, have the potential to obfuscate the objects of inquiry within environmental media studies; an example of this is "elemental media", which stretches the definition of "media" to include anything that mediates (animals, air, rivers, clouds), and in doing so baffles attempts at the kind of conceptual clarity that is necessary for interdisciplinary research.
>
> (Shriver-Rice and Vaughan 2020, 4)

Coming out at roughly the same time, the journal *Media+Environment* articulated its focus, by contrast, as encompassing what media do in the world: "media do not merely communicate, transmit, and transport; they also transform. […] [M]edia are active participants in the social construction and material production of the world" (Chang, Ivakhiv, and Walker 2019, para. 2). Synthesizing these approaches, the Environmental Media Lab states,

> Environmental Media means looking at 'the environment' as a kind of mediating agent (mediator/medium). Whether this be water, smoke, black holes or DNA (etc.), 'environmental media' complicates the boundary between what is thought of as 'natural' and what is constructed, and it differs significantly from scholarship that looks at the environment as a place or cause. 'Environmental media' is more of a critical framework than a discipline.
>
> ("Environmental Media Lab" n.d., para. 2)

In Iheka's (2022) account, ecomedia could include conventional media devices and media arts (film, photography, et al.), resource media (oil, uranium, etc.), and elemental media (fire, air, earth, water) whose "making, use, and disuse implicate them in ecological degradation and/or environmental transformation" (6). "Ecomedia processes," he writes, "catalyze ecological consequences in the form of environmental degradation and/or advocacy for environmental renewal, and sustainability, making this media genre an assemblage of natural elements and cultural attributes with apparent superstructures and implicit infrastructures" (6).

Fundamentally, then, ecomedia are infrastructures and milieus that envelop and orient us in space, time, place, and entanglements with/in the more-than-human world. They are not just about communication and transmission, but they constitute the world as an ensemble of technologies and activities that activate, coordinate, and help us make sense of the world.

Studying Ecomedia

The milieu specificity of dominant media scholarship up to now has relied on an epistemology that has been characterized (or caricatured) as "WEIRD," that is, a Western, educated, industrial, rich, and "democratic" knowledge system. The media ecology tradition, as we have seen, sits comfortably within this characterization. Challenging this approach, Melody Jue (2020) asks how working at a desk, sitting in a chair, and gazing at or through a screen (which is how most scholarship is produced) may direct a certain vantage point. How can we achieve the necessary unfamiliar perspective to see our own thinking and being about media and environment?

The editors of this *Handbook* are inspired by the cultural studies' "circuit of culture" approach, which uses a multiperspectival analytical method that enables the study of media from different standpoints. In this volume, we characterize those broadly as "ecocultures," "political ecology," "ecomateriality," and "eco-affects." Ecomedia literacy can be used to explore how all media have an environmental mind/footprint (see López, this volume). This follows from the basic premise that a holistic analysis of media requires examining their material, symbolic, and affective characteristics. "Ecocultures" refers to the shared beliefs and related practices that are conveyed through the multimodal languages of symbols and discourses. "Political ecology" is the study of how economic and power structures design systems and produce impacts on the environment, including the production of ideologies and material goods. "Ecomateriality," in turn, is the realm of the environmental and material conditions of media, be it the physical properties of a medium (e.g., paper in books or magazines) or of gadgets (chemicals, glass, plastic, metals, etc.). And "eco-affects" refers to the ecology of perception and sensemaking and how media affect our felt sense of place, space, time, embodiment, and relationality amidst a world of complex and always somewhat elusive others. All these standpoints are applied to the object of analysis, which can be a media text, gadget, platform, or hyperobject (a dispersed phenomenon such as infrastructure).

In her insightful analyses of the materiality of media infrastructures, Jennifer Gabrys (2016b) calls for "re-thingifying" media theory by "open[ing] up attention to how things come to be, what sustains things, and the effects that things have on the world" (188). This is consistent with the ontological calls, inspired by the process-relational philosophy of A. N. Whitehead, to rethink media in terms not of what media *are* but of what they *do* (Fuller 2005; Ivakhiv 2013; Manning, Munster, and Stavning Thomsen 2019). And since media involve us, they are also the ways they change us (and we in turn change them). Yves Citton (2017, 23) builds on this in his focus on the ecology of attention:

> The biophysical ecology of our environmental resources, the geopolitical ecology of our transnational relations, the socio-political ecology of our class relations and the psychic ecology of our mental resources all depend on the media ecology that conditions our modes of communication.

Ecomedia scholars can follow the lead of "maker media studies," which calls for being "more attentive to the social, cognitive, affective, biological, and other environments in which media technologies move and have their being" (O'Gorman 2020, 12).

Researching ecomedia is in some ways not unlike studying plastic, which is not bound to a particular location or discipline, but necessitates following "where it leads, attending to the various ways in which it is both reshaping our material surroundings and inviting critical reappraisal of how matter is understood in Western thought" (Davis 2022, 14). Similarly, Nicole Starosielski (2019) describes "elemental thinking" as connecting "media studies to a network of infrastructural and ecological phenomena: to mines, oceans, roads, and social worlds otherwise located beyond media studies." Elemental research is "a contact zone, one where scholars are pushing, experimenting with, and redrawing the boundaries of media studies" (3).

Lisa Parks (2016) encourages a phenomenological methodology to physically explore infrastructure. This opens the possibility of engaging in material phenomenology, the "understanding that, whatever its appearance of complexity and opacity, the social world remains accessible to interpretation and understanding by human actors. Indeed, it is a structure built up, in part, through those interpretations and understandings"; actors include "individual actors as single humans, corporative actors as organizations, companies and state agencies as well as collective actors as communities or social movements" (Hepp 2019, 10, emphasis in original). But it is also essential that ecomedia studies decenter humans, embedding them within larger networks of material as well as social and discursive relations.

The emerging paradigm of comparative media studies recognizes interdisciplinarity as key to exploring media from multiple standpoints to engage "juxtapositions, attentive to the materiality of media across a variety of incarnations" (Jue 2020, 26). To investigate the "cloud," Hu suggests we utilize methods like examining representations of it in popular culture; studying diagrams, terms, and metaphors in computer science; and analyzing games, photos, drawing, and videos: "what the cloud looks like on-screen; how we draw or map its shape; how the cloud grew out of TV/video networks" (Hu 2016, xxii). Empirical ecocriticism draws on social science techniques to test assumptions about textual meanings by engaging "empirically grounded" methods like interviews, focus groups, surveys, and controlled experiments, aided by interdisciplinary approaches that benefit from co-authorship (Schneider-Mayerson, Weik von Mossner, and Małecki 2020).

As is the case of this *Handbook*, many scholars engage the media arts (such as photography, video, film) as ecomedia objects to think with. Beyond artifacts of popular culture, Iheka (2021, 10) calls for the engagement of imperfect media, "low-carbon media practices and infrastructures of finitude that are critical for ameliorating ecological precarity in the future," such as the various Afrofuturist aesthetics practiced by African artists, or some of the "slow" (often analog) media discussed, in this volume, by Jennifer Rauch. By exploring citizen science, maker culture, and artistic practices, Gabrys's (2016a) methodology, especially in her study of environmental sensors, combines environmental studies, digital culture, and arts with the study of technology and science.

Ecomedia studies has as a prime directive to decolonize how we study and think about media. As a political project, this requires a rigorous focus on political ecology and ecojustice, for instance, on the ways in which media naturalize finance, corporate personhood, hydrocarbon energy, extractivism, sacrifice zones, and endless growth, all of which are extensions of currently hegemonic knowledge systems that govern global institutions. Going deeper into the milieu, what is called for is also a fundamental shift in how we see the universe and our place within it. The aim is to reclaim ecology, regardless of the various ways the term has been (mis)used, as a guiding "methodology of intersectionality, which insists on thinking being and becoming at the cross section of multiple fields of social, political, economic, and material determinations" (Demos 2016, 25).

In a digital economy that is indifferent to "truth" and fails to distinguish information from the mis- and disinformation driving the global climate crisis, we are grappling with what Bram Büscher (2021) identifies as "truth tensions" (as opposed to "truth wars"). Environmental knowledge, in this realm, is produced through a complex negotiation between science and other truth-making processes, with "facts" (or "factishes," as Latour [2010] called them) emerging out of a contestation of empirical data points, translations, beliefs, and social negotiations. Reclaiming ecology requires attending to the fundamental problem of the epistemic or "post-truth" crisis that is "an expression of power under platform capitalism" (170). As is the case with ChatGPT cited earlier in this chapter, "whether or not something is true or not does not matter for algorithms or the (commercial success) of the platforms" (171). Büscher calls for a political ecology of truth that dialectically engages not only the power structure of surveillance capitalism but also the everyday praxis of lived realities, which are "messy, contingent, and contentious, and only can be studied as such" (27). In this way, ecomedia studies aligns with ecocriticism's commitment to combine science, cultural analysis, and ecological politics.

Conclusion

By asking when media become ecomedia, we are asking how media are to be rethought in the context of the climate emergency—that is, in the aftermath of the industrialization that gave rise not only to rapid carbonization of the atmosphere, but to mass media and electronic media as we know (or knew) them. This shift in how we define media is not just a philosophical or intellectual exercise; it is a cultural, ethical, and political—indeed, geopolitical—one as well. For at the basis of planetary geopolitics is a racially unjust, neo-colonial structure predicated on the extraction of resources and the externalization of health and environmental costs (and risks) to low-income regions of the world. By demanding resource extraction, labor exploitation, and the unrestrained release of pollution and toxic waste, this system depends on ecological sacrifice zones and disposable populations. Transforming this neo-colonial apparatus requires a deep shift in priorities and a profound remaking of practices. Ecocritical assessment, considering not only the environmental or material dimensions of the "eco" but its social, political, ethical, and aesthetic dimensions, is mandatory.

Notes

1 This move is inspired by media infrastructure researchers who utilize the methodological trick to change the query of "what is an infrastructure?" to "when is it an infrastructure?" (Plantin and Punathambekar 2019, 168).
2 The queries cited in this chapter were performed using ChatGPT-3. The purpose is less about ChatGPT's abilities and more about revealing socially produced conventional thinking about media, technology, and the environment that a trained artificial intelligence (AI) is churning out. Playing with ChatGPT demonstrates the nature and limitations of algorithmic knowledge, and how the assumptions we put into our "searches" are hugely important. AI chatbot natural language processing tools embody not only algorithmic bias but also the cultural and institutional prejudices that form their knowledge base. They are inherently machines of ideology. As Ruha Benjamin (2019) notes, algorithmic codes "operate within powerful systems of meaning that render some things visible, others invisible and create a vast array of distortions and dangers" (7).
3 This follows an approach devised by Andreas Hepp (2019) in his formulation of mediatization:

> At this point it is helpful to remember again the argument that mediatization is a 'sensitizing concept', that is, it sets out to sensitize us to current social transformations. As such, the term cannot stand on its own as a self-contained theory but another point of view might be more helpful: Mediatization is a sensitizing concept around which various researchers have gathered, researchers who are interested in an empirically based investigation of the significance of the role media plays in the transformation of culture and society … From this point of view, the term mediatization refers to an open, ongoing discourse of theorizing social and cultural transformation in relation to media and communications.
>
> (9)

Further Reading

Cubitt, S. 2016. *Finite Media: Environmental Implications of Digital Technologies*. Durham, NC: Duke University Press.
Maxwell, R., Raundalen, J., and Vestberg, N. L. eds. 2015. *Media and the Ecological Crisis*. London; New York: Routledge.
Peters, J. D. (2015). *The Marvelous Clouds: Toward a Philosophy of Elemental Media*. Chicago, IL: University of Chicago Press.
Rust, S., Monani, S., and Cubitt, S. eds. 2016. *Ecomedia: Key Issues*. London; New York: Routledge.
Starosielski, Nicole and Janet Walker, eds. 2016. *Sustainable Media: Critical Approaches to Media and Environment*. New York; London: Routledge.

References

Abram, David. 1996. *The Spell of the Sensuous: Perception and Language in a More-than-Human World*. New York: Pantheon Books.
Anderson, C.W. 2016. "News Ecosystems." In *The SAGE Handbook of Digital Journalism*, edited by Tamara Witschge, C.W. Anderson, David Domingo, and Alfred Hermida, 410–23. London: SAGE Publications Ltd. https://doi.org/10.4135/9781473957909.
Benjamin, Ruha. 2019. *Race after Technology: Abolitionist Tools for the New Jim Code*. Medford, MA: Polity.
Bollmer, Grant. 2019. *Materialist Media Theory: An Introduction*. New York: Bloomsbury Publishing, Inc.
Bozak, Nadia. 2011. *The Cinematic Footprint: Lights, Camera, Natural Resources*. Piscataway, NJ: Rutgers University Press.
Bratton, Benjamin H. 2015. *The Stack: On Software and Sovereignty*. Cambridge, MA: MIT Press.
Büscher, Bram. 2021. *The Truth about Nature: Environmentalism in the Era of Post-Truth Politics and Platform Capitalism*. Oakland: University of California Press.
Castree, Noel, and Bruce Braun, eds. 2001. *Social Nature: Theory, Practice, and Politics*. Malden, MA: Blackwell Publishers.
Chang, Alenda, Adrian Ivakhiv, and Janet Walker. 2019. "States of Media+environment: Editors' Introduction." *Media+Environment* 1 (1). https://doi.org/10.1525/001c.10795.
ChatGPT. 2022. Personal Communication, December 16.
Citton, Yves. 2017. *The Ecology of Attention*. Cambridge: Polity.
Cubitt, Sean. 2016. *Finite Media: Environmental Implications of Digital Technologies*. Durham, NC: Duke University Press.
Cucchietti, Fernando, Joana Moll, Marta Esteban, Patricio Reyes, and Carlos García Calatrava. 2022. "Carbolytics: An Analysis of the Carbon Costs of Online Tracking." *Carbolytics*. February 16, 2022.
Davis, Heather M. 2022. *Plastic Matter*. Durham, NC: Duke University Press.
Deleuze, Gilles, and Félix Guattari. 1987. *A Thousand Plateaus: Capitalism and Schizophrenia*. Minneapolis: University of Minnesota Press.
Demos, T. J. 2016. *Decolonizing Nature: Contemporary Art and the Politics of Ecology*. Berlin: Sternberg Press.
Emejulu, Akwugo, and Callum McGregor. 2019. "Towards a Radical Digital Citizenship in Digital Education." *Critical Studies in Education* 60 (1): 131–47. https://doi.org/10.1080/17508487.2016.1234494.
"Environmental Media Lab." n.d. https://environmentalmedialab.com.
Escobar, Arturo. 1995. *Encountering Development: The Making and Unmaking of the Third World*. Princeton, NJ: Princeton University Press.
Fuchs, Christian. 2020. "Everyday Life and Everyday Communication in Coronavirus Capitalism." *TripleC: Communication, Capitalism & Critique. Open Access Journal for a Global Sustainable Information Society* 18 (1): 375–98. https://doi.org/10.31269/triplec.v18i1.1167.
Fuller, Matthew A. 2005. *Media Ecologies: Materialist Energies in Art and Technoculture*. Cambridge: MIT Press.
Gabrys, Jennifer. 2016a. *Program Earth: Environmental Sensing Technology and the Making of a Computational Planet*. Minneapolis: University of Minnesota Press.
———. 2016b. "Re-Thingifying the Internet of Things." In *Sustainable Media: Critical Approaches to Media and Environment*, edited by Janet Walker and Nicole Starosielski, 180–95. London: Routledge.

Goldstein, Jenny, and Eric Nost, eds. 2022. *The Nature of Data: Infrastructures, Environments, Politics*. Lincoln: University of Nebraska Press.
Guattari, Félix. 2008. *Three Ecologies*. London: Continuum.
Haraway, Donna Jeanne. 2008. *When Species Meet*. Minneapolis: University of Minnesota Press.
Hepp, Andreas. 2019. *Deep Mediatization*. London; New York: Routledge. https://doi.org/10.4324/9781351064903.
Hörl, Erich, and James Burton, eds. 2017. *General Ecology: The New Ecological Paradigm*. London: Bloomsbury Academic.
Horn, Eva. 2007. "Editor's Introduction: 'There Are No Media.'" *Grey Room* 29 (October): 6–13. https://doi.org/10.1162/grey.2007.1.29.6.
Hu, Tung-Hui. 2016. *A Prehistory of the Cloud*. Cambridge: MIT Press.
Iheka, Cajetan Nwabueze. 2021. *African Ecomedia: Network Forms, Planetary Politics*. Durham, NC: Duke University Press.
Innis, Harold Adams. 1999. *The Bias of Communication*. Toronto: University of Toronto Press.
Ivakhiv, Adrian. 2013. *Ecologies of the Moving Image: Cinema, Affect, Nature*. Waterloo: Wilfrid Laurier University Press.
———. 2014. "Beatnik Brothers? Between Graham Harman and the Deleuzo-Whiteheadian Axis." *Parrhesia* 19: 65–78.
———. 2017. "Nature." In *The Oxford Handbook of the Study of Religion*, edited by Michael Stausberg and Steven Engler, 414–29. Oxford University Press. https://doi.org/10.1093/oxfordhb/9780198729570.013.29.
———. 2018. *Shadowing the Anthropocene: Eco-Realism for Turbulent Times*. Goleta, CA: Punctum Books. https://doi.org/10.21983/P3.0211.1.00.
———. 2021. "In Defense of Ecological Metaphor." *Immanence* (blog). February 19, 2021. https://blog.uvm.edu/aivakhiv/2021/02/19/in-defense-of-ecological-metaphor/.
Jue, Melody. 2020. *Wild Blue Media: Thinking through Seawater*. Durham, NC: Duke University Press.
Kaplan, Stuart Jay. 1990. "Visual Metaphors in the Representation of Communication Technology." *Crtical Studies in Mass Communication* 7: 37–47.
Kittler, Friedrich A. 1993. *Draculas Vermächtnis: Technische Schriften*. 1. Aufl. Reclam-Bibliothek 1476. Leipzig: Reclam.
Kuntsman, Adi, and Esperanza Miyake. 2022. *Paradoxes of Digital Disengagement*. London: University of Westminster Press. https://doi.org/10.16997/book61.
Latour, Bruno. 2005. *Reassembling the Social: An Introduction to Actor-Network-Theory*. Oxford: Oxford University Press.
———. 2010. *On the Modern Cult of the Factish Gods*. Durham, NC; London: Duke University Press.
Law, John. 2004. *After Method: Mess in Social Science Research*. London; New York: Routledge.
Manning, Erin, Anna Munster, and Bodil Marie Stavning Thomsen, eds. 2019. *Immediation I*. Place of Publication Not Identified: Open Humanities Press.
Maxwell, Richard, and Toby Miller. 2012. *Greening the Media*. New York: Oxford University Press.
McQuail, Denis. 2012. *McQuail's Mass Communication Theory*. Los Angeles, CA: SAGE.
Mignolo, Walter D. 2007. "Delinking: The Rhetoric of Modernity, the Logic of Coloniality and the Grammar of De-Coloniality." *Cultural Studies* 21 (2–3): 449–514. https://doi.org/10.1080/09502380601162647.
Milstein, Tema. 2016. "The Performer Metaphor: 'Mother Nature Never Gives Us the Same Show Twice.'" *Environmental Communication* 10 (2): 227–48. https://doi.org/10.1080/17524032.2015.1018295.
Mitchell, W. J. T. 2003. "Foreword." In *Animal Rites: American Culture, the Discourse of Species, and Posthumanist Theory*, edited by C. Wolfe, ix–xiv. Chicago, IL: University of Chicago Press.
Morton, Timothy. 2013. *Hyperobjects: Philosophy and Ecology after the End of the World*. Minneapolis: University of Minnesota Press.
Mumford, Lewis. 1970. *The Pentagon of Power*. New York: Harcourt Brace Jovanovich.
Nadler, Anthony. 2018. "Nature's Economy and News Ecology." *Journalism Studies* 20 (6): 823–39. https://doi.org/10.1080/1461670X.2018.1427000.
O'Gorman, Marcel. 2020. *Making Media Theory: Thinking Critically with Technology*. New York: Bloomsbury Academic.
Parikka, Jussi. 2015. *A Geology of Media*. Minneapolis: University of Minnesota Press.
Parks, Lisa. 2016. "Earth Observation and Signal Territories." In *Ecomedia: Key Issues*, edited by Stephen Rust, Salma Monani, and Sean Cubitt, 141–61. London; New York: Routledge.

Patel, Raj, and Jason W. Moore. 2018. *History of the World in Seven Cheap Things: A Guide to Capitalism, Nature, and the Future of the Planet.* Oakland: University of California Press.

Peters, John Durham. 2015. *The Marvelous Clouds: Toward a Philosophy of Elemental Media.* Chicago, IL: University of Chicago Press.

Plantin, Jean-Christophe, and Aswin Punathambekar. 2019. "Digital Media Infrastructures: Pipes, Platforms, and Politics." *Media, Culture & Society* 41 (2): 163–74. https://doi.org/10.1177/0163443718818376.

Plumwood, Val. 1993. *Feminism and the Mastery of Nature.* London; New York: Routledge.

Quijano, Aníbal. 2007. "Coloniality and Modernity/Rationality." *Cultural Studies* 21 (2–3): 168–78. https://doi.org/10.1080/09502380601164353.

Richter, Felix. 2022. "Are You Not Entertained?" Statista. December 12, 2022. https://www-statista-com.jcu.idm.oclc.org/chart/22392/global-revenue-of-selected-entertainment-industry-sectors/.

Rust, Stephen, Salma Monani, and Sean Cubitt. 2016. "Introduction: Ecologies of Media." *Ecomedia: Key Issues*, 1–14.

Schneider-Mayerson, Matthew, Alexa Weik von Mossner, and W P Małecki. 2020. "Empirical Ecocriticism: Environmental Texts and Empirical Methods." *ISLE: Interdisciplinary Studies in Literature and Environment* 27 (2): 327–36. https://doi.org/10.1093/isle/isaa022.

Serres, Michel. 1982. *The Parasite.* Translated by Lawrence R. Schehr. Baltimore, MD: Johns Hopkins University Press.

Shriver-Rice, Meryl, and Hunter Vaughan. 2020. "What Is Environmental Media Studies?" *Journal of Environmental Media* 1 (1): 3–13. https://doi.org/10.1386/jem_00001_2.

Starosielski, Nicole. 2019. "The Elements of Media Studies." *Media+Environment* 1 (1). https://doi.org/10.1525/001c.10780.

Starosielsk, Nicole, and Janet Walker. 2016. "Introduction: Sustainable Media." In *Sustainable Media: Critical Approaches to Media and Environment*, edited by Janet Walker and Nicole Starosielski, 1–19. London: Routledge.

Sultana, Farhana. 2022. "Critical Climate Justice." *The Geographical Journal* 188 (1): 118–24. https://doi.org/10.1111/geoj.12417.

Towns, Armond R. 2022. *On Black Media Philosophy.* Oakland: University of California Press.

Wahl-Jorgensen, Karin. 2015. "The Chicago School and Ecology: A Reappraisal for the Digital Era." *American Behavioral Scientist* 60 (1): 8–23. https://doi.org/10.1177/0002764215601709.

Warren, Karen J. 1993. "The Power and Promise of Ecological Feminism." *Environmental Philosophy: From Animal Rights to Radical Ecology*, 320–42.

Wickberg, Adam, and Johan Gärdebo. 2022. "Editors' Introduction: What Is Environing Media?" In *Environing Media*, edited by Adam Wickberg and Johan Gärdebo, 1–12. London: Routledge. https://doi.org/10.4324/9781003282891-6.

Williams, Raymond. 1980. "Ideas of Nature." In *Problems in Materialism and Culture: Selected Essays*, 67–85. London: Verso.

Ziser, Michael. 2016. "Ecomedia." In *Keywords for Environmental Studies*, edited by Joni Adamson, William A. Gleason, and David N. Pellow, 75–76. New York; London: NYU Press.

2
THREE ECOLOGIES
Ecomediality as Ontology

Adrian Ivakhiv

The chapter first examines contemporary notions of environment and ecology, which underpin not only the fields of ecomedia (or environmental media) studies but also environmental studies and ecocriticism more generally. It then introduces the tri-ecological framework, develops it in depth, and applies it to notions of mediation, mediatization, and ecomediality.

Environment vs. Ecology

Concepts of ecology underpin the great swath of environmental thinking of the last three-quarters century. Even as the words "environment," "environmental," and "environmentalism" have become deeply ingrained in contemporary usage, a rigorous examination entails acknowledging that there can be no *singular* notion of an environment—"*the* environment," "*our* environment"—unless it is counterposed against another singularity, which in most common usage is humanity. (The same can be said for cognate terms such as the French *environnement*, the German *Umwelt*, and the Spanish *medio ambiente*.) "The environment" is in this sense everything other than the human world, or at least everything that in any way surrounds that world. Together, the dyad "environment–humanity" exemplifies the longstanding practice of separating humans from nature, even if done relationally—a conceptual dualism that much of contemporary eco-theory abjures. In a very real sense, it could be said that there *is* no "the environment," a passive backdrop to an active agent within that environment, just as there is no active "humanity" which acts as a singular agent against this backdrop. Both are abstractions of aggregate forces. There are only *many* environments, an infinity of them in fact, each of which is an environment for something: you, me, that mole, this ant colony, "our civilization," that planet.

"Ecology" has often been proposed as a more holistic and relational starting point for theorizing relations between humans and others-to-the-human. In its first general uptake, ecology was conceived of as a science, the biological study of the interrelations between organisms and their environments. Humans were mostly peripheral in the ecological sciences until they became integrated into a second line of inquiry—*human* ecology, along with its descendants such as urban ecology and social ecology. But the impact of ecological thinking since the 1960s has incontrovertibly shaped another notion of ecology, variously labeled political ecology, ecologism, or a more specific variation such as deep ecology, (Bookchinite) social ecology, and feminist ecology (or ecofeminism).

The word "ecology" nevertheless carries connotations that sometimes get in the way of its intended meanings. A standard criticism of the use of the term in media studies is that it "naturalizes" whatever it is applied to, suggesting "spontaneous, self-ordering principles" in place of the social, political, and economic decisions that shape the media industries (e.g., Nadler 2019). Some version of this argument has plagued the field of "media ecology" since it emerged as an interdisciplinary interloper into media studies scholarship in the early 1970s (Cali 2017). Debates over the aptness of the metaphor have intensified as an ecologically oriented media scholarship has grown (Maxwell, Raundalen, and Vestberg 2014).

The word "ecology" is found today in a wide variety of scholarly contexts, some of them venturing far from the word's biological origins. As Erich Hörl and James Burton (2017) write in the introduction to a volume on "the new ecological paradigm," "There are thousands of ecologies today: ecologies of sensation, perception, cognition, desire, attention, power, values, information, participation, media, the mind, relations, practices, behavior, belonging, the social, the political" (1). Some of the term's *popular* uses remain conditioned by the competitivism of classical Darwinian accounts of life as "survival of the fittest," while others are more influenced by the holism of Gaia theory or the do-goodism of environmental virtuosity, where "ecology" acts as a signifier of "harmony" with scarcely a hint of competition or struggle. Many, as Hörl points out, are "denaturalized," their connection to "dogmas of authenticity" having been severed (1–2).

Contemporary ecological science, in any case, is complex and not easy to pigeonhole. Ecosystems, when they can even be identified as such, work in nonlinear ways. They do not always, and maybe not ever, attain the once-and-for-all stability of a "climax community." They are in this sense non-teleological: while they may reflect emergent, systemic features, they aren't directed toward a specific end goal. It is therefore unwarranted to assume that an economic system treated as ecological would be one where competition led "naturally" to the maximum flourishing of the whole. Ecosystems are made up of individuals doing what they do, and while that may sometimes look competitive, it can also be cooperative, symbiotic, or mutualistic. Most such activity is best considered statistical and emergent: what happens is a result of things settling into emergent patterns that find relative zones of stability punctuated by change and characterized by inherent dynamism. Reading social-Darwinist or neoliberal economic values into ecology is of course possible, but so is reading Kropotkinite anarchism, chaos theory, and almost anything else.

If there is an "essence" to ecology, or even just a "center of gravity" within the "family resemblances" among the "language games" the word features in (Wittgenstein 2001), it has something to do with relational networks or ensembles that, from an analytical perspective, are worth considering as systemically interactive and dynamic unities. *Things interact to create modellable wholes.* Scientifically speaking, the "modellable" part is crucial: if we cannot model something, then it cannot be treated as a system. But what is equally important is the interaction: ecology is the study of relational systems that are dynamic, changing, and processual. They can be studied *as* unities consisting of mutually adapting elements, even as they are recognized to be never fully closed systems. These characteristics will undergird the tri-ecological model proposed below.

Multiple Ecologies

With such a proliferation of meanings, it would appear useful to bring some order to concepts of ecology. It may be surprising, then, that no systematization has garnered much support and that it has fallen to French psychoanalyst and political activist Félix Guattari to present one of the more provocative formulations.[1] In his 1989 book *The Three Ecologies* (*Les Trois Écologies*), Guattari (2000) drew on novel articulations of psychology and biology, including the cybernetic anthropology of Gregory Bateson, with its notion of an "ecology of mind," the autopoietic cognitive systems theory of Humberto Maturana and Francesco Varela, the complexity theory of Ilya Prigogine and Isabelle Stengers, and Guattari's own post-Lacanian psychoanalytic work with patients to provide a provocative take on ecological affairs. In the book's opening sentences, Guattari declares what is at stake in this effort:

> The Earth is undergoing a period of intense techno-scientific transformations. If no remedy is found, the ecological disequilibrium this has generated will ultimately threaten the continuation of life on the planet's surface. Alongside these upheavals, human modes of life, both individual and collective, are progressively deteriorating.
>
> (2000, 27)

The book details these deteriorations at the individual and collective level and puts forward a proposal for an "ethico-aesthetic" revolution on three ecological registers: "the environment, social relations, and human subjectivity" (28).

For all the "transversal" complexity that characterizes Guattari's articulation of these three registers (cf. Berressem 2020; Heroux 2008), they represent a fairly conventional set of nested circles: at the center is the psyche or the "mental" sphere of human subjectivity, the self or *eigenwelt*; around it is the socius, the socio-ecological *mitwelt* of human relations; and around that is "nature" itself, or "environmental ecology," the *umwelt* that shades into the surrounding planetary ecology. There is an intuitive obviousness to this arrangement, especially to modern westerners for whom selfhood is clearly central, and with allegiance to humanity appearing natural in a way that allegiance to "nature," even to the category of "earthling," is more distant. This concentric cosmology is not exclusively a western view; Confucian "anthropocosmism" is among many variations of a cosmology which centers the human community (in its entirety) within a broader set of cosmic or universal referents (cf. Weiming 2012). Its popularity notwithstanding, a series of more recent intellectual developments—including the posthuman, ontological, and decolonial "turns" (Holbraad and Pedersen 2017; Ivakhiv 2020; Jackson 2018; Smith 2021)—all require that we place such "anthropocosmic" concentricity in abeyance, if only to recognize that not all humans have perceived humanity as one species-entity, with other kinship relations considered secondary or more distant. Many societies have been ordered according to kinship relations that cross-cut the modern categories of "humanity," "animals," "life," "nature," "environment," and so on.[2]

The last three decades have seen the rise of a range of "materialist" and "affective" engagements with the more-than-human world, and with relations between humans and that broader world: new materialism, actor-network theory, assemblage theory, agential realism, speculative realism, posthumanism, integral theory, and others (e.g., Alaimo and Hekman 2008; Bryant, Srnicek, and Harman 2011; Coole and Frost 2010; Mickey, Kelly, and Robbert 2017). Alongside the ontological and decolonial turns, these have collectively drawn attention to the dynamic mixtures of human and nonhuman forces, agencies, processes, and entanglements that constitute the world we know. No single metaphysical framework has emerged as dominant among this heterogeneous array, and my own attempt to "order the landscape" should therefore be considered as one among many.

The scheme that follows develops Guattari's initial conceptualization of social, mental, and material ecologies through a more rigorously processual turn by engaging with the process philosophy of A. N. Whitehead, and through a more deeply semiotic turn by engaging with the triadic, semiotic phenomenology of C. S. Peirce. (For the sake of space, the Peircian semiotic dimension will remain implicit in what follows.) Whitehead's growing influence in a range of "new materialist" and post-Deleuzian writings is fairly well known (e.g., Gaskill and Nocek 2014). Peirce's "categories," meanwhile, have been foundational to the growth of a range of semiotic approaches to the life sciences (biosemiotics, ecosemiotics, phytosemiotics) and to less well-known efforts at crossing semiotics with metaphysics and ethics (semio-ethics, et al.). My previous work has brought these two bodies of scholarship into dialogue with the goal of presenting an ontology that avoids both anthropocentrism and Eurocentrism (except insofar as its two most inspirational thinkers, Whitehead and Peirce, were both white, male, Euro-American philosophers; see Ivakhiv 2013, 2018). The remainder of this study will present the basics of this perspective in terms of three ecologies, which are resonant with Guattari's but rooted in a different ontological conception. I will introduce this ontology by building from a familiar foundation—that of scientific ecology—outward to a less familiar set of reference points.[3]

The Ecological Triad: Material, Social, and Medial-Perceptual

If the science of ecology studies the relationships between things, especially between living organisms and their environments, it does this because these are the things that *can* be studied from a scientific perspective. Organisms and their material constituents—carbon, nitrogen, water, solar energy, and so on—are objects of a scientific "gaze" or stance, a way of looking at and approaching the world that takes the world to be made up of observable, measurable phenomena. Scientific ecology has come up with a multitude of concepts, terms, and models for understanding ecological relations and processes. These can be our first ecology, *material* ecology, because it consists of material and energetic relations found in the observable world, a world we can study from its outside, as it were, bracketing out our own subjective experience and focusing on what is observed, measured, and rendered tangible.

Once we acknowledge *our* role in this study, a role that is enabled by the fact that we humans are beings that *can* study things—because we observe and interact with the world around us—then we also have to acknowledge that what is central to *us* is not those "things" but the fact that we experience anything at all. *We are subjects.* Experience is central to our subjective life; without it, there would be no "we" or "us" to study or discuss anything. And if experience is central to the life of humans, there is little reason to assume that it is not also central to the life of other living beings. There are good arguments that experience or something like it—at least a kind of responsiveness (of the sort that Whitehead called "prehension")—is also central to things we might not consider alive. If this is the case, that experience is central, then *what is experience?* For Whitehead, experience refers to events of relationship between subjectivity, or an experienc*er*, and objectivity, or the experienc*ed*. Every act of experience, every relational event that makes up the universe, consists of some relationship between subjectivity and objectivity. Every smallest bit of "universe" is a relational process.

If our first ecology, then, is an ecology of objective things—an *ecology of objects* (which may also be an ecology of processes), our second is an *ecology of subjects*. The latter concerns the subjective dimension, or subjective "pole," of a world that includes, and that in some respects is made up of, experience. It is the study (*-ology*) of the systemic relationships characterizing the subjectivities that make up our world: it includes the "I" who looks at you, the "you" who looks back, and the mutual acknowledgment of "youness" in our relationship. We can call this a *social* ecology because it is about the sociality by which agency is acknowledged and distributed throughout a system. For humans, it of course consists of other humans, but there is no necessary reason to leave nonhumans out of it. Indeed, most humans have historically included many kinds of nonhumans within their social ecologies: animals, mountains, trees, and various entities understood to be responsible for one thing or another, which are sometimes labeled gods, spirits, angels, or other "forces" of one kind or another. If scientific ecology is an ecology of *its*—objects like organisms, carbon and nitrogen, food webs, or DNA programs—then social ecology is an ecology of *I*'s, *you*'s, *we*'s, and *they*'s, an ecology of agency, and the negotiation of recognition. Who will get to qualify as a subject, with whatever rights that confers, and who will be cast into the category of objects? With what sorts of negotiations and agreements will we temper our actions with respect to each other and to other others? We can consider social ecology an ecology of mutual recognition.

What, then, is the third ecology? In a Whiteheadian process-relational view, the basic relational act, which Whitehead called "prehension," consists of an act of relationship between subjectivity and objectivity. A subject *responds to* or somehow *takes account of* an object or set of objects. *How* this is done makes all the difference. The third ecology is an ecology of the *hows* that constitute the world, the ways that subjects respond to objects and, in doing that, reshape both those objects and themselves. Subjectivity arises in respect to objects and *responds* to those objects. This *how* of relationality is a matter of perception (what is perceived and how it is perceived), which makes it a "perceptual ecology." And it is a matter of mind (for subjects that have the capacity for the sense-making or interpretive behavior we call thinking, cognition, mentation, and so on), which makes it a "mental ecology" (Guattari's term for it). Neither of these terms is quite sufficient: "mind" conjures up the Cartesian dichotomy of body-versus-mind, while "perception" is typically considered the way in which an organism takes in sensory data from its outside.

A more neutral term here is "medial," which places the focus on the *mediation* occurring: the precise ways in which a subjective arising responds to the data in its mental and perceptual fields, the things it encounters and acts upon. The third ecology is an *ecology of mediation*. The term "mediation" can also be confusing, since "media" tends to evoke either an infrastructural meaning (telephones, television, the internet, and so on) or an informational one (the data transmitted by those infrastructures). But it has the virtue of making plain that things—such as our sensory organs, or the bodies and technical media that make sociality possible—make a difference in our subjective perception, and that they also affect the objective materiality of the world. They are what draw the two together; without them, there is nothing.

In a genuinely process-relational account, *mediation is everything* because it is the processual, relational *eventing* by which the world occurs. This view comes close to that expressed in media philosopher John Durham Peters' (2015) view of media as the infrastructures that make up the world and echoes Sean Cubitt's (2016) phrase that "ecomedia" is "the study of the intermediation of everything" (166). In a certain sense, this mediation is what is ultimately real, while the ecologies of subjects and of objects are a study of the residues of mediations—their collected objectifications at either the subjective (social-ecological) or objective (material-ecological) end of the mediatory events that make up the universe. The "social" and the "material" are abstracted from these events as two ends of a continuum, with the first being the end of acknowledged "selves" and "others," and the second being the end of "things" known to exist but not socially acknowledged. But it is the continuum of ongoing mediatory production, the processual becoming, that makes up the world. Whatever the world happens to be at this moment (socially and materially), for whomever (subjectively), it can and will always be different.

In this tri-ecological framework, then, there is effectively only a single ecology—a monistic ecology of processual, relational, and mediatory becoming. Process-relationality *is* mediation; it is interaction, intra-action (to use Karen Barad's [2007] term), and transformation involving the sensory, perceptual, and technical modalities available to bodies—eyes, ears, air and radio waves, electronic devices, and so on—that cross and migrate between cognitive-affective systems and their technical mediators. Medial ecology is in this sense the core of a theory that accounts for subject relations (social ecology) and object relations (material ecology), even as its focus is on processes of mediation and mediatization.

The tri-ecological approach is in this sense directly relevant to theories of "mediatization," such as Couldry and Hepp's (2017), according to which "mediation" describes "the process of communication in general," while "mediatization" refers to "higher-order processes of transformation and change across society that result from mediation going on at every level of interaction," processes that include "mechanization, electrification, digitalization," and "datafication" (66). The technological systems we call media are extensions and transformers of how we perceive and respond to the world, a world that already includes political actors, social understandings, economic incentives, contractual agreements, design principles, and much more. Those media are a subset of the broader category of media, which are the technical, perceptual, and bodily modalities by which all things interact with other things. "Media" is thus a word for "mediating apparatuses," which mediate via the shaping of perceptual and responsive capacities. Mediation is *how the world works*.

In this sense, the notion of "media ecology" is not simply the importing of a biological metaphor into the social or media world (as Nadler argued). It is also the other way around: media constitute ecosystems and environments built by their constituent members, but so does biology itself. Both conceptions—of media and of biology—are radically constructivist in that both are understood to be constituted by the actions and processes that make them up. And by extension, "ecomediation" and "ecomediatization" refer to extensions of media into potential, even utopian, forms beyond the current phase of datafication toward something new on the horizon. Ecomedia studies, by this definition, is the study of ecomediation and ecomediatization as they may exist today and in a real or potential future.

Conclusion: Ecomediality

To summarize the tri-ecological model, we can ask why it is important to recognize and distinguish each of these three ecologies. Without the first, the ecological study of *objective materiality*, we wouldn't have as clear an idea of what is happening in our "natural environments." The science of ecology has revolutionized our understanding of the world; it wouldn't have been able to do that if it hadn't abstracted itself from subjective perceptions. Science's "bracketing out" of subjectivity arguably aided us in better understanding our effects on the world—even as this same bracketing made it possible for us to have greater impacts on that world; that is the paradox Bruno Latour (1993) and others have written much about. Without the second, the ecological study of *subjective relationality*, we lose our capacity for ethical and political action. Of course, we already practice social ecology; we just do not call it that, and in part as a result of that we have tended to restrict it to the human. Social ecology is an *ecology*, a study of the world, which encompasses the ethical and political dynamics by which all things relate to each other. And without the third, the ecological study of mediation, or of *perceptual mediality*, we render ourselves incapable of understanding the most important innovations in human sociality today—the media by which we make sense of and alter the world. Language has been a powerful medium for doing exactly that. Other creatures do it differently: by echolocation, by magnetoreception, and so on. Today we have learned to use more technologically sophisticated media for making sense of and altering the world, and these have had an even more profound impact on that world.

Media do not just describe the world (more or less faithfully), nor do they merely "carry information" from one place to another. They *constitute* the world, making possible the objectivities and subjectivities by which that world is organized. That is what makes this framework a theory of ecomediality. By defining media as broadly and inclusively as possible, and by articulating what it is that media do—how they enable the subjectivation and objectivation by which the world becomes a world of "subjects" and "objects," those (ostensibly) deserving political treatment and those merely deserving of instrumental action—we get an account of *the world as relational process*, a world to which we respond aesthetically (perceptually), ethically (socially), and logically (both scientifically and politically).

Notes

1 For another, much more comprehensive effort that has arguably obtained even less recognition, see Esbjorn-Hargens and Zimmerman, *Integral Ecology* (2011).
2 An interesting application of a Guattarian tri-ecological framework that avoids this "anthropocosmism" is Matthew Calarco's analysis of biologist Joe Hutto's multi-year interaction with mule deer, in "The Three Ethologies" (Calarco 2018).
3 The approach described here is developed in greater depth in Ivakhiv (2013, 2018). For applications of a tri-ecological approach to cinema, see Holtmeier (2017), Pisters (2018), and Wijaya (2019).

Further Reading

Guattari, Félix. 2000. *The Three Ecologies*, trans. by Ian Pindar and Paul Sutton. New Brunswick, NJ: Athlone Press.
Ivakhiv, Adrian. 2013. *Ecologies of the Moving Image: Cinema, Affect, Nature*. Kitchener-Waterloo: Wilfrid Laurier University Press.
Ivakhiv, Adrian. 2018. *Shadowing the Anthropocene: Eco-Realism for Turbulent Times*. Santa Barbara, CA: Punctum Books.
Ivakhiv, Adrian. Forthcoming. *The New Lives of Images: Digital Ecologies and Anthropocene Imaginaries in More-than-Human Worlds*.

Works Cited

Alaimo, Stacy, and Susan Hekman, eds. 2008. *Material Feminisms*. Bloomington: Indiana University Press.
Barad, Karen. 2007. *Meeting the Universe Halfway: Quantum Physics and the Entanglement of Matter and Meaning*. Durham, NC: Duke University Press.
Berressem, Hanjo. 2020. *Félix Guattari's Schizoanalytic Ecology*. Edinburgh: University Press.
Bryant, Levi, Nick Srnicek, and Graham Harman, eds. 2011. *The Speculative Turn: Continental Materialism and Realism*. Melbourne: re-press.
Calarco, Matthew. 2018. "The Three Ethologies." In *Exploring Animal Encounters*, ed. by D. Ohrem and M. Calarco, 45–62. London: Palgrave Macmillan.
Cali, Dennis G. 2017. *Mapping Media Ecology: Introduction to the Field*. Bern: Peter Lang.
Coole, Diana, and Samantha Frost, eds. 2010. *New Materialisms: Ontology, Agency, and Politics*. Durham, NC: Duke University Press.
Couldry, Nick, and Andreas Hepp. 2017. *The Mediated Construction of Reality*. London: Polity.
Cubitt, Sean. 2016. "Ecologies of Fabrication." In *Sustainable Media: Critical Approaches to Media and Environment*, ed. by Janet Walker and Nicole Starosielski, 163–79. New York: Routledge.
Esbjorn-Hargens, Sean, and Michael E. Zimmerman. 2011. *Integral Ecology: Uniting Multiple Perspectives on the Natural World*. Boston, MA: Integral Books.
Gaskill, Nicholas, and A. J. Nocek, eds. 2014. *The Lure of Whitehead*. Minneapolis: University of Minnesota Press.
Guattari, Félix. 2000. *The Three Ecologies,* trans. by Ian Pindar and Paul Sutton. New Brunswick, NJ: Athlone Press.
Heroux, Erick. 2008. "Guattari's Triplex Discourses of Ecology." In *An [Un]Likely Alliance: Thinking Environment(s) with Deleuze/Guattari*, ed. by Bernd Herzogenrath, 176–95. Newcastle Upon Tyne: Cambridge Scholars Publishing.

Holbraad, Martin, and Morton Axel Pedersen. 2017. *The Ontological Turn: An Anthropological Exposition.* Cambridge: Cambridge University Press.

Holtmeier, Matt. 2017. "Communicating Cascadia: Reichardt's Three Ecologies as Bioregional Medium." *Screen* 58(4), 477–96.

Hörl, Erich, and James Burton, ed. 2017. *General Ecology: The New Ecological Paradigm.* London: Bloomsbury Academic.

Ivakhiv, Adrian. 2013. *Ecologies of the Moving Image: Cinema, Affect, Nature.* Kitchener-Waterloo: Wilfrid Laurier University Press.

Ivakhiv, Adrian. 2018. *Shadowing the Anthropocene: Eco-Realism for Turbulent Times.* Santa Barbara, CA: Punctum Books.

Ivakhiv, Adrian. 2020. "Is the Post- in Posthuman the Post- in Postmodern? Or What Can the Human Be?" *Critical Theory* 4(2), 43–59.

Jackson, Mark, ed. 2018. *Coloniality, Ontology, and the Question of the Posthuman.* New York: Routledge.

Latour, Bruno. 1993. *We Have Never Been Modern*, trans. C. Porter. Cambridge, MA: Harvard University Press.

Maxwell, Richard, Jon Raundalen, and Nina Lager Vestberg. 2014. *Media and the Ecological Crisis.* New York: Routledge.

Mickey, Sam, Sean Kelly, and Adam Robbert, eds. 2017. *The Variety of Integral Ecologies: Nature, Culture, and Knowledge in the Planetary Era.* Albany, NY: SUNY Press.

Nadler, Anthony. 2019. "Nature's Economy and News Ecology: Scrutinizing the News Ecosystem Metaphor." *Journalism Studies* 20(6), 823–39.

Peters, John Durham. 2015. *The Marvelous Clouds: Toward a Philosophy of Elemental Media.* Chicago, IL: University of Chicago Press.

Pisters, Patricia. 2018. "Deep Blue Geomediations: Following Lapis Lazuli in Three Ecological Assemblages." *SubStance* 47(2), 36–58.

Smith, Linda Tuhiwai. 2021. *Decolonizing Methodologies: Research and Indigenous Peoples*, 3rd ed. London: Zed Books.

Weiming, Tu. 2012. "A Spiritual Turn in Philosophy: Rethinking the Global Significance of Confucian Humanism." *Journal of Philosophical Research* 37(supplement), 389–401.

Wijaya, Elizabeth. 2019. "Three Ecologies of Cinema, Migration, and the Sea: Anchorage Prohibited and Luzon." In *Ecology and Chinese-Language Cinema: Reimagining a Field*, ed. by S. Lu and H. Gong, 67–82. London: Routledge.

Wittgenstein, Ludwig. 2001 (1953). *Philosophical Investigations*, trans. by G. E. Anscombe. London: Blackwell.

3
MEANING, MATTER, ECOMEDIA

Christy Tidwell

Ecomedia studies engages with both the content and the creation of media, and this approach, which attends to how ecomedia are *of* and *about* the environment, parallels new materialism's declaration that "[m]atter and meaning are not separate elements" (Barad 2007, 3). New materialism includes many thinkers, not all of whom would use the same language or define it in precisely the same way. (Related philosophies that have much in common include material ecocriticism, material feminism, speculative realism, process-relational ontology, and others associated with the ontological turn; see Ivakhiv, this volume.) At its heart, new materialism recognizes the agency, liveliness, and vitality of the nonhuman world; it emphasizes the inseparability of human and nonhuman; and it argues for an ethical response to these relationships. As Stacy Alaimo and Susan Hekman write, "Nature is agentic—it acts, and those actions have consequences for both the human and nonhuman world" (2008, 5). Those consequences are wide-reaching, they argue, because "attending to materiality erases the commonsensical boundaries between human and nature, body and environment, mind and matter. In short, taking matter seriously entails nothing less than a thorough rethinking of the fundamental categories of Western culture" (2008, 17).

Trans-corporeality and agential realism, two feminist new materialist concepts, are useful for rethinking these categories. Stacy Alaimo's concept of trans-corporeality "denies the human subject the sovereign central position" (2010, 16) and acknowledges the ways "in which the human is always intermeshed with the more-than-human world" (2010, 2). Karen Barad's concept of agential realism understands "matter as a dynamic and shifting entanglement of relations, rather than as a property of things" (2007, 35), and it is accompanied by *intra-action*, the idea that "*agencies are only distinct in relation to their mutual entanglements; they don't exist as individual elements*" (2007, 33, italics in original). Trans-corporeality and agential realism emphasize the inseparability of humans from the rest of the world and indicate that no acts or entities exist truly on their own.

This chapter explores trans-corporeality and agential realism as useful concepts for applying new materialist approaches to ecomedia studies while also addressing how these concepts intersect with or echo insights from Indigenous philosophies. Sebastian De Line writes, "Intra-action works similar to *our relations* in that it is a binding agent, gluing subjectivity to all matter" (2016). The concept of *our relations* that De Line describes here appears in many accounts of Native science or epistemology (see Gregory Cajete, Robin Wall Kimmerer, Enrique Salmón, and Shawn Wilson). It requires an understanding that everything in existence is animate and that, as Leroy Little Bear says, "Everything, those rocks, those trees, those animals all have spirit just like we do as humans" (qtd. in De Line 2016). As Indigenous studies scholars point out, new materialist thought is new to Western paradigms but not new in the world.

Representations: New Materialism on Film

One way that ecomedia engages with new materialist thought is in its content, representing the interconnectedness of human and nonhuman through stories of encounters between people and animals or through narratives that emphasize other beings' agency. These ideas tend to evoke two distinct affective responses: wonder and fear.

Becoming Animal (2018, dir. Emma Davie and Peter Mettler) and *My Octopus Teacher* (2020, dir. Pippa Ehrlich and James Reed) do the former for many viewers by emphasizing human/nonhuman relationships and recognizing the complexity and intelligence of the nonhuman. These films reflect Jeffrey Jerome Cohen's argument that "[m]aterial ecocriticism is a story-laden mode of reenchantment. It demands an ethics of relation, entanglement, and wonder" (2014, x).

Becoming Animal is described as "an urgent and immersive audiovisual quest, forging a path into the places where humans and other animals meet, where we pry open our senses to witness the so-called natural world—which in turn witnesses us" ("Becoming Animal – The Film" 2018). This language resonates with new materialism's emphasis on connection, openness to other beings, challenges to anthropocentrism, and co-created meaning. Philosopher David Abram illustrates these ideas in his discussion of perception as "an ongoing improvisation between my body and the bodies of other beings." He says, "I experience my own coherence only by entering into relation with others. In touching things, I feel touched *by* those things. In gazing out at the world, I can't help but feel seen by that world." This expresses key elements of both trans-corporeality and intra-action. As Barad writes, "Existence is not an individual affair. Individuals do not preexist their interactions; rather, individuals emerge through and as part of their entangled intra-relating" (2007, ix). Abram argues for and revels in this intra-relation in his engagement with other beings.

My Octopus Teacher, a story of a human–octopus friendship, illustrates the possibility of cross-species communication and of creating meaning in an environment that is not centered on the human. The underwater setting of *My Octopus Teacher* offers an opportunity to consider how, as Melody Jue writes, "[s]eawater also changes how we think about the porosity of embodiment" (2020, 19), another instance of trans-corporeality. In an informal reflection on the film, Alaimo describes the way *My Octopus Teacher* reveals "the exuberant, sustaining relations at the heart of expansive environmental visions. Who better to teach Donna Haraway's ethic of 'significant otherness in relation,' than a curious cephalopod?" ("Love, Wonder, and the Nonhuman" 2020). The film highlights the positive emotions associated with trans-corporeality, cross-species intimacy, and the co-creation of meaning.

In their emphasis on connection and openness, these films diverge from traditional nature documentaries like Jacques Cousteau's work or the BBC's *The Blue Planet*. Hunter Vaughan describes such documentaries as "quintessential popular-media extensions of the philosophical subject-object binary at the heart of Western positivist empiricism: that we can taxonomize and categorize the universe into bits of information, which by organizing we then can control" (2019, 64). In those films, the human speaker observes from a distance and educates the even more distant viewer about the nature that exists separate from them (or us). Nature documentaries like *Becoming Animal* and *My Octopus Teacher*, however, eschew this distance and acknowledge the trans-corporeality inherent in relations with other creatures. As Alaimo writes, "matter—nature, if you will—is always an agent of change and always already within and without the permeable membrane of the human" (2010, 154). Abram's sense of himself in *Becoming Animal* and the openness to physical and emotional connection with the octopus in *My Octopus Teacher* blur rather than reinforce those boundaries and embrace "the permeable membrane of the human."

Other ecomedia – most notably, ecohorror – represent new materialist ideas more negatively, revealing anxiety about what it means to connect with the nonhuman or to lose a sense of human uniqueness. For example, films like *The Thing* (1982, dir. John Carpenter), *The Fly* (1986, dir. David Cronenberg), *Gaia* (2021, dir. Jaco Bouwer), and *In the Earth* (2021, dir. Ben Wheatley) find horror in the blurring of boundaries between species and in the agency of the nonhuman. The tagline from *The Thing* – "Man is the warmest place to hide" – represents the penetration of the human body by the nonhuman as a source of horror. The human body is, the movie reveals, dangerously permeable, vulnerable to being changed at the deepest level (even present in the blood). The blurring of lines between human and nonhuman in *The Fly* as Seth Brundle (Jeff Goldblum) becomes Brundlefly, a human-fly hybrid, is viscerally horrific (disgusting and disturbing) as well as tragic, a loss of individuality that concludes in Brundlefly pleading for death. And both *Gaia* and *In the Earth* – narratives about fungi controlling humans – point to anxiety about how much or little control we humans have over ourselves by showing how easily other forms of life influence human actions and how little separates the human body from the nonhuman. Images of human bodies covered with fungal growth disgust rather than amaze, and spores disorient rather than enlighten.

Whether wonderstruck or fearful, these films display elements of new materialist thought. They dramatize Alaimo's trans-corporeality, identifying both the joyful possibilities of connection and the risks inherent in boundary-crossing. As Alaimo notes, trans-corporeality "acknowledges the often unpredictable and unwanted actions of human bodies, nonhuman creatures, ecological systems, chemical agents, and other actors" (2010, 2), tracing not only connections between humans and others but their effects, "how they *do* things—often unwelcome or unexpected things" (2010, 146). New materialist ideas within ecomedia must then be complex and attuned to possible transformations – even if these transformations are not always desired.

Process: How Ecomedia Is Made

It is not only the content of ecomedia that matters, though. Alenda Chang, Adrian Ivakhiv, and Janet Walker emphasize that "media are active participants in the social construction *and* material production of the world" (2019); new materialism similarly asks us to attend to both the social construction and material production of ecomedia.

In their work, Sean Cubitt, Kyle Devine, and Hunter Vaughan build upon new materialist insights to explore how ecomedia (digital technologies, music, and film, respectively) use natural resources and are themselves material. Cubitt argues against "a myth of immaterial media" (2017, 13), Devine notes that "common understandings of music tend to exclude a lot of the sweat and stuff that musical cultures rely on" (2019, 21), and Vaughan takes an ecomaterialist approach that

> explores the material environmental impact of film practices, from the extraction of minerals to the chemical waste of its process, the centrality of natural symbolism in its marketing and crossover merchandising, and the restructuring of urban communities based on production culture ebbs and flows.
>
> (2019, 13)

In each case, it's not just the message but the medium that matters.

Because trans-corporeality and intra-action do not occur only between individuals, these concepts can be usefully applied not just to media texts but also to processes and systems. As Barad writes,

> Perhaps intentionality might better be understood as attributable to a complex network of human and nonhuman agents, including historically specific sets of material conditions that exceed the traditional notion of the individual. Or perhaps it is less that there is assemblage of agents than there is an entangled state of agencies.
>
> (2007, 23)

This expansion of intentionality means that systems of production – film and music industries, for instance – can be explored through these new materialist concepts. Cubitt emphasizes "the material processes connecting human and nonhuman events" (2017, 3–4) and "the primal connectivity shared by human and nonhuman worlds" (2017, 4), while Devine writes about music as "not a thing but an activity" (2019, 19). They draw attention to events and worlds, networks and assemblages, and processes and activities that exceed individual action or experience.

This is not simply a theoretical point, of course. The material consequences of these activities, events, and mediations must be considered, too, as Devine's analysis of the materiality of music makes clear: "The mediatic point here is that every system of inscription is tied to a system of extraction. Every discourse network is a resource network" (2019, 24). This recognition means acknowledging "the slow violence of music" (Devine 2019, 27), such as when shellac resin was harvested from lac beetles to make records, a process that killed many beetles, damaged forests, and relied on child labor and abuse of laborers.

New materialist thought – when applied in this way – raises questions about the ethics of ecomedia itself. Ecomedia often has the explicit goal of addressing environmental problems, but it simultaneously comes with dramatic environmental costs: "In *Racing Extinction*, [Louis] Psihoyos acknowledges on camera that the worst thing a filmmaker can do for the environment is *to make a film about the environment*, evoking a catch-22 that cannot be avoided here" (Vaughan 2019, 24). *Mad Max: Fury Road* (2015, dir. George Miller) provides a vivid example of this tension. The film presents a strong environmental vision, addressing climate change, water politics, pollution, oil dependence, ecofeminism, and environmental health. But, in addition to the typical environmental costs of filmmaking described by Vaughan, *Fury Road* also caused damage to a protected area in its Namib desert filming location. Ecologist Jon Henschel

> found that parts of the desert until now untouched by vehicles had been driven over, leaving tracks – in one area a 'ploughing device' had been used. Even worse, to try and level the tracks as they left, the crew had dragged nets across the ground, ripping out small plants.
>
> (Steadman 2013)

This dramatically illustrates the need for a change in which "ecological communications become much more than alerting the human public to environmental issues" (Cubitt 2017, 180). Providing information is not enough, and neither is telling environmentalist stories; the media we use to communicate these ideas must also take the insights of new materialism into consideration. We are not separate from our environment, and so the material impacts of our media cannot be ignored.

These analyses of ecomedia demonstrate that theory that simply applies new materialist terminology does not go far enough: "it will leave in place the traditional enlightenment dichotomy between knowledge and values. It will do this performatively, by engaging non-human agents first and foremost through a practice of representation, as opposed to through a practice of ethical reciprocity" (Rosiek, Snyder, and Pratt 2020, 336). It's not always clear what ethical reciprocity with nonhuman agents would look like, but attending to the costs of creating ecomedia perhaps offers a place to begin.

Matter: Enacting New Materialism in Ecomedia

Finally, I turn to two examples of ecomedia that embody new materialism's entanglement of meaning and matter: (1) museum taxidermy and (2) Yup'ik artist Peter Williams' "Inherent Right," an exhibition using the skins of fish, seal, and sea otters to create "striking geometries or fluid curves" (Williams n.d.). In these examples, the material presence of animal skins are a significant part of the works' meaning, and all address conservation, animality, and liveliness in ways that create meaning *through* that materiality.

There are many types of taxidermy, but here I consider museum taxidermy rather than trophies, pet memorials, or taxidermy for entertainment alone. Museum taxidermy has historically been used to bring the natural world closer, to help make faraway creatures and ecosystems material – three-dimensional and tactile. It has not only contributed to scientific understanding and categorization of the natural world but also promoted environmentalist goals: "environmental conservation campaigns required awe-inspiring visuals to promote legislative changes and mobilize public opinion: How could city dwellers care for and support the conservation of nature they could never see?" (Aloi 2018, 113). Before technologies like video or virtual reality, the physical presence of the animal – even if dead – was uniquely awe-inspiring and intimate.

Museum taxidermy consists of not only the animal itself but also its display. When Carl Akeley embraced the diorama as a way to present museum taxidermy in the late nineteenth century, it helped make the animal even more real to viewers. As Bridgitte Barclay writes, "Akeley wanted to give museum visitors a sense of the animal's life, to animate the inanimate behind glass" (2015). Dioramas "sought to drop viewers … into the African savannah or the mountains of western North America" (Wecker 2016) and so needed to be "both realistic and artistic" (Barclay 2015), requiring plants (transplanted or recreated), painted backgrounds, and the animals themselves.

This desired credibility can reinforce anthropocentric goals of mastery over the nonhuman world, but taxidermy has also worked against mastery through its very materiality and animacy. Contemporary artists' uses of taxidermy (what Giovanni Aloi calls "speculative taxidermy") can become "a deliberate destabilizer of anthropocentrism rather than as a tool of affirmation of man's superiority over nature" (Aloi 2018, 16). For artists like Mark Dion, Damien Hirst, or Kate Clark, such destabilizing moves are intentional, but this destabilization can be unintentional, too. As Rachel Poliquin writes, taxidermy can provoke a sense of "visceral knowledge: a bodily knowing that occurs in contact with physical things, a knowing that blurs emotion with materiality and may even defy reason, logic, and explanatory language" (2012, 39). This bodily knowing threatens the taxonomic logic of anthropocentrism and highlights the ways in which taxidermy does not stand alone, separate from the human spectator. Instead, taxidermied animals are "sensitive substrates upon which human/animal relationships co-shape discourses, practices, and, ultimately, ecosystems" (Aloi 2018, 31).

Peter Williams' "Inherent Right" intentionally challenges anthropocentrism and connects with both new materialist and Indigenous ideas. His work with furs and skins consists of "hand sewing scraps into art tapestries and stretching them over a canvas stretcher bar" (Williams n.d.), creating pieces that are insistently material (the fur of seals and skin of fish are front and center) while abstract in design. Williams writes that "The surface aesthetics are simple, accessible, and do not initially communicate a narrative; until the viewer notices the unusual texture of the painting" ("Inherent Right" 2021). That closer look "leads to dialogue about the materials and the story of their becoming" (Williams n.d.), turning the viewer's attention back to the materiality of the animal itself and the process of creation.

Williams' work presents an alternative to non-Indigenous ideas about conservation that assume that "we must 'preserve' nature by minimizing human interaction with it." Instead, Williams emphasizes "reciprocal, intimate relationships with plants and animals" ("Inherent Right" 2021). This language of reciprocity and intimacy parallels that of trans-corporeality and intra-action, and his description of his process, which "perpetuates Alaska Native protocol of developing a personal relationship with 'the materials of place,'" highlights not only the importance of interconnectedness but the necessity of placing this in a specific context:

> I source by hunting and fishing; I alter by tanning; I construct by the time consuming yet cathartic labor of hand sewing, each stitch a prayer. The start-to-finish intimacy of my work underlines the ethos of Indigenous practice: Our environment and its inhabitants are not to be treated as disposable resources, but as critical relationships. Before a hunt I smudge and pray, asking the animal for its life; after the hunt I honor the animal by giving it its last drink of water per Yup'ik custom.
>
> ("Inherent Right" 2021)

These details both reflect the particularity of Alaska Native practices and also operate alongside trans-corporeality's acknowledgement of the way "the human is always intermeshed with the more-than-human world" (Alaimo 2010, 2) as well as agential realism's understanding of "matter as a dynamic and shifting entanglement of relations, rather than as a property of things" (Barad 2007, 35). As Zoe Todd writes about contemporary Indigenous materialist art, the materials of this art "are no mere actants. They are ... enlivened with spirit. With relationship. With sentience, will, and knowing" (2015, 248).

Williams' work, therefore, illustrates new materialist ideas while also demonstrating that new materialist concepts echo what has long been present in many Indigenous philosophies. This is important because, as Todd argues, it is "easy for those within the Euro-Western academy to advance and consume arguments that parallel discourses in Indigenous contexts without explicitly nodding to them, or by minimally nodding to Indigenous intellectual and political players" (2016, 8). Furthermore, Todd writes, "When we cite European thinkers who discuss the 'more-than-human' but do not discuss their Indigenous contemporaries who are writing on the exact same topics, we perpetuate the white supremacy of the academy" (2016, 18). Acknowledging the work of Indigenous theorists and artists alongside new materialist philosophy is, then, an attempt to challenge white supremacy as well as a way to make the conversation richer and more productive.

Conclusion

Combining new materialism and ecomedia offers an opportunity to think differently about our relationships to both the nonhuman world and the media with which we understand it. Karen Barad's agential realism "gestures toward a practice of inquiry that involves transformations not just of our ways of knowing but also of our ways of being, feeling, committing, and living in the world" (Rosiek, Snyder, and Pratt 2020, 335). These transformations extend beyond epistemology and theory and into ontology and ethics. They connect both ecomedia and new materialism to Vine Deloria's call to consider the "proper way to live in the universe" (1999, 47), a moral or ethical stance built upon particular rather than general knowledge, and to Max Liboiron's argument that "relations do not universalize" (2021, 32). In new materialist terms, this means "prioritizing the performative establishment of particular relational entanglements with non-human agents over seeking generalizable understanding of that agency" and "considering the consequences of our actions—including our research—for all the communities with which we are in relation and on which our being depends" (Rosiek, Snyder, and Pratt 2020, 339, 340).

Ecomedia studies can benefit from new materialist thought in multiple ways – from exploring representations of trans-corporeality (shaped by both wonder and fear) to thinking through the ways that systems in media production have agency and material impacts. But perhaps the most important element of combining the two is the turn to ethics. If we are entangled with each other, the nonhuman, and the networks that produce ecomedia, then we cannot remove ourselves from the effects of ecomedia. Those effects are material, and those effects matter.

Further Reading

Alaimo, Stacy. 2016. *Exposed: Environmental Politics & Pleasures in Posthuman Times*. Minneapolis: University of Minnesota Press.
Iheka, Cajetan, 2021. *African Ecomedia: Network Forms, Planetary Politics*. Durham, NC: Duke University Press.
Jue, Melody, and Rafico Ruiz (eds.). 2021. *Saturation: An Elemental Politics*. Durham, NC: Duke University Press.
Rust, Stephen, Salma Monani, and Seán Cubitt (eds.). 2022. *Ecocinema Theory and Practice 2*. New York: Routledge.
Starosielski, Nicole. 2021. *Media Hot & Cold*. Durham, NC: Duke University Press.

References

Alaimo, Stacy. 2010. *Bodily Natures: Science, Environment, and the Material Self*. Bloomington: Indiana University Press.
Alaimo, Stacy, and Susan Hekman. 2008. "Introduction: Emerging Models of Materiality in Feminist Theory." In *Material Feminisms*, edited by Stacy Alaimo and Susan Hekman, 1–19. Bloomington: Indiana University Press.
Aloi, Giovanni. 2018. *Speculative Taxidermy: Natural History, Animal Surfaces, and Art in the Anthropocene*. New York: Columbia University Press.
Barad, Karen. 2007. *Meeting the Universe Halfway: Quantum Physics and the Entanglement of Matter and Meaning*. Durham, NC: Duke University Press.
Barclay, Bridgitte. 2015. "Through the Plexiglass: A History of Museum Dioramas." *The Atlantic*, 14 Oct. 2015. https://www.theatlantic.com/science/archive/2015/10/taxidermy-animal-habitat-dioramas/410401/.
"Becoming Animal – The Film." 2018. *Becoming Animal*. https://www.becominganimalfilm.com/.
Chang, Alenda, Adrian Ivakhiv, and Janet Walker. 2019. "States of Media+Environment: Editors' Introduction." *Media+Environment* 1, no. 1. https://doi.org/10.1525/001c.10795.
Cohen, Jeffrey Jerome. 2014. "Foreword: Storied Matter." In *Material Ecocriticism*, edited by Serenella Iovino and Serpil Oppermann, ix–xii. Bloomington: Indiana University Press.
Cubitt, Sean. 2017. *Finite Media: Environmental Implications of Digital Technologies*. Durham, NC: Duke University Press.
Davie, Emma, and Peter Mettler, directors. 2018. *Becoming Animal*. Edinburgh: Maximage/SDI Productions Ltd.
De Line, Sebastian. 2016. "All My/Our Relations: Can Posthumanism Be Decolonized?" *Open! Platform for Art, Culture & the Public Domain*, 7 Jul. 2016. https://onlineopen.org/all-my-our-relations.
Deloria, Vine, Jr. 1999. *Spirit and Reason: The Vine Deloria, Jr., Reader*. Golden, CO: Fulcrum.
Devine, Kyle. 2019. *Decomposed: The Political Ecology of Music*. Cambridge: The MIT Press.
"Inherent Right." 2021. *All My Relations Arts*, 29 Mar. 2021. http://www.allmyrelationsarts.com/inherent-right/.

Jue, Melody. 2020. *Wild Blue Media: Thinking Through Seawater*. Durham, NC: Duke University Press.

Liboiron, Max. 2021. *Pollution Is Colonialism*. Durham, NC: Duke University Press.

"Love, Wonder, and the Nonhuman: Recommendations from ASLE Leadership." 2020. *ASLE*. https://www.asle.org/features/love-wonder-nonhuman/.

Poliquin, Rachel. 2012. *The Breathless Zoo: Taxidermy and the Cultures of Longing*. University Park, TX: The Pennsylvania State University Press.

Rosiek, Jerry Lee, Jimmy Snyder, and Scott L. Pratt. 2020. "The New Materialisms and Indigenous Theories of Non-Human Agency: Making the Case for Respectful Anti-Colonial Engagement." *Qualitative Inquiry* 26, no. 3–4: 331–46. https://doi.org/10.1177/1077800419830135.

Steadman, Ian. "Fragile Namibian Deserts 'Damaged' by Mad Max Film Crew." 2013. *Wired*, 5 Mar. 2013. https://www.wired.co.uk/article/mad-max-namibian-desert-damage.

Todd, Zoe. 2015. "Indigenizing the Anthropocene." In *Art in the Anthropocene: Encounters Among Aesthetics, Politics, Environments and Epistemologies*, edited by Heather Davis and Etienne Turpin, 241–54. London: Open Humanities Press.

Todd, Zoe. 2016. "An Indigenous Feminist's Take On the Ontological Turn: 'Ontology' Is Just Another Word for Colonialism." *Journal of Historical Sociology* 29, no. 1: 4–22.

Vaughan, Hunter. 2019. *Hollywood's Dirtiest Secret: The Hidden Environmental Cost of the Movies*. New York: Columbia University Press.

Wecker, Menachem. 2016. "The History and Future of the Once-Revolutionary Taxidermy Diorama." *Smithsonian Magazine*, 11 Oct. 2016. https://www.smithsonianmag.com/science-nature/ode-once-revolutionary-taxidermy-display-180960707/.

Williams, Peter. n.d. "Fish Skin & Fur Paintings." *Shaman Furs*. http://www.seaotterfur.com/fish-skin-fur-paintings.

4
BLUE MEDIA ECOLOGIES
Swimming through the Mediascape with Sir David Attenborough

Stephen Rust and Verena Wurth

The mini-series *Life in Colour* (2021) finds Sir David Attenborough, in his signature style, traveling across the globe in less than three hours of runtime. In episode two, Attenborough leads viewers into the subaquatic world of the Great Barrier Reef off the coast of Northern Australia to introduce the bluestriped blenny, a species of that fish uses biomimicry "for a rather [] sinister reason" (31:23), he suggests. By changing its color to match the blue and black stripes of a non-predatory cleaner wrasse, which feeds off the parasites of larger fish, the blenny deceives and devours its prey more easily. In his familiar anthropomorphizing rhetoric, Attenborough adds that blennies are savvier than to overexploit their prey because would be "bad for business" (35:59). Recognized internationally as "the human voice of nature" (Mathur 2020), the British naturalist has concrete ideas about what is good for the business of wildlife media and natural history filmmaking, yet ideas that are not always an apt reaction to the global ecocrisis.

From his role as a host and producer of the early wildlife series *Zoo Quest* (1954–1963), to such projects as *Life on Earth* (1979), *Planet Earth* (2006), *Blue Planet II* (2017), and *Our Planet* (2019), Attenborough has become one of the most recognizable figures in television history and a vocal advocate for protecting the natural world from the impacts of human industrialization. Ironically, however, over his seven-decade career, nature film and television has become a multi-billion-dollar global industry that produces a substantial carbon footprint (Aitchison, Aitchison, and Devas 2021).

This chapter examines some of Attenborough's aquatic adventures to develop the concept of blue media ecologies. This conceptualization constitutes an effort to bridge the discourses of environmental media and media ecology studies. While we recognize that media productions are highly collaborative, the ubiquity of Attenborough's media avatar as a host/narrator and his repeated focus on blue, aquatic ecologies serves as the binding element (the *tertium comparationis*) through which we build this connection between discourse communities. By thinking blue rather than just green (cf. Alaimo 2019), ecomedia studies can develop robust conceptual frameworks for understanding the intertwined material and cultural impacts of media production, circulation, and consumption on the planetary environment.

We argue that metaphors of media ecology are most effective when they further our understanding of both the way that media technologies operate *and* how such technologies impact the material world humanity exploits to produce them. Three aspects of blueness assist us in thinking across the gap between media ecology and ecomedia studies using Attenborough's aquatic oeuvre. First, we approach blue media ecologies through textual analysis of metaphorizations of media and ecology and provide a snapshot of how new technologies impact the shooting of underwater environments in Attenborough's recent projects. Second, we explore new theorizations of underwater representational strategies, such as those developed by Melody Jue and consider water and air as blue mediated spaces that have come to play an increasingly important role in the transmission of audiovisual media across the planet, as elemental media scholars and material ecocritics such as John Durham Peters, Nicole Starosielski, Lisa Han, Sidney Dobrin, Sean Cubitt, and Laura Marks have documented in recent years. In tracking Attenborough's voice and image through the space of the modern mediascape, we consider how the materiality of the global media infrastructure is rendered through the use of undersea cable systems and airborne cloud networks that mask the expansive scale of media's physical presence in the environment. Third, we consider blue symbolically as a color often associated with sadness and depression and wade into the debate over whether the environmental footprint of Attenborough's productions created more harm for the planet than good. In this section, we build on ideas proposed by Eileen Joy to examine the shift in the tone and content of Attenborough's recent projects, which acknowledge the realities of climate change.

Metaphors

In her 2002 essay "Unnatural Ecologies," Ursula Heise explores the development of media ecology metaphors and anticipates the emergence of ecomedia studies as a field of discourse situated between ecocriticism and media studies. Since Marshall McLuhan and Neil Postman first conversed about the topic in the mid-1960s, media scholars have used metaphors of the environment to explain how forms and systems of electronic media evolve and interact with each other. The metaphor of mediascape has become shorthand to explain the way media content circulates through digital, satellite, radio, and other networks and wavelengths to reach consumers. Ecological metaphors like rhizome and web have become ubiquitous in media theory to help students and scholars make sense of the physical and abstract (eco)systems of modern media communications and thereby shape our understanding of media more generally. Beginning with Raymond Williams' (1974) term "flow" in the 1970s and Stanley Cavell's (1982) conceptualization of "current" in the 1980s to the modern discourse of "streaming," many metaphors associated with water have been deployed to explain how televisual productions (Attenborough's primary medium) are distributed and circulated through media infrastructures to reach viewers. Conversely, it is not uncommon for Attenborough to use media metaphors like "array," "relay," "program," and "machinery" to help viewers understand natural phenomena (*Blue Planet, Life in Colour*, etc.), a point that underlines the multitude of levels at which media and ecology are conceptually intertwined.

Heise explains that ecological metaphors in theories of media "can serve to articulate both systemic and antisystemic perspectives [...] because ecology offers both a holistic dimension that foregrounds universal connectedness, and a local one that points to the specificities of particular ecosystems" (2002, 164–65). Heise was also among the first ecocritics to push back against the limitations of ecological metaphors as a means of explaining how media technologies evolve and operate. Since the publication of Maxwell and Miller's *Greening the Media* (2012), the burgeoning field of ecomedia studies has disrupted the rhetorical strategies of media ecology by examining the material impacts of film and media production on the ecology of planet earth. Blueness as both metaphor and material is a useful term for bringing these two aspects of media ecology and ecomedia into more direct conversation.

From an ecocritical perspective, Attenborough's *Life in Colour* is not just interesting textually when it makes visible the mimicry color change of the bluestriped blenny but also through its use of new camera technologies that allow viewers to see the aquatic animal realm in a new way through polarized light (Ep. 3, 33:00). With such new technologies, some of which were "developed especially for this series" (Ep. 1, 01:15), *Life in Colour* goes further than any previous documentary to replicate the visual experience of animals using camera lenses that enable viewers to "understand" the "way of seeing" of these animals, bio-mimicking their "perspective" (Ep. 2, 01:22). In this way, *Life in Colour* implies that the medium of the camera *is* the animal's eye and that the series enables moments of "seeing" not just *with* but *as* these creatures. Thinking further, such representational strategies do not merely suggest the camera's mimicking of the fish's eye but a conceptual, metaphorical overlap of medium and ecology; of camera and aquatic animal; in which the *tertium comparationis* is a particular way of seeing. Such an enmeshment of media technology and ecology presented by *Life in Colour* is remindful of the intertwining of media and ecology in academic discourse since the 1960s. As Heise notes, "the concept of 'media ecology' relies on a metaphorical transfer that [...] developed out of a translation of categories from biological ecology" (Heise 2002, 149). Thanks to Postman, Lance Strate, and others, ecological metaphors have become common parlance for describing how media environments operate, and media ecology has developed into a robust field of discourse that "tries to find out what roles media force us to play, how media structure *what we are seeing* or thinking, and why media make us feel and act as we do" (2012, 205, our italics). To transfer this to the example of the bluestriped blenny, blue media ecology can help understand how the media structures our way of seeing to mimic that of the aquatic animal – and identify with it.

Blue Ecomateriality: Attenborough across the Blue Mediascape

As ecocritics, one interest of ours, are the camera technologies that structure what we are seeing or thinking when viewing such striking underwater images. New ultra-high-definition and mobile screen technologies allow viewers to appreciate the blenny's mimicry, while new polarized light cameras used to mimic the perspective of creatures like fiddler crabs allow us new insight into how concrete local ecosystems work. However, as Melody Jue argues, not just the cameras or different media technologies are a factor in how a film is perceived but also the specific environments in which cameras are placed must be examined. Such considerations of oceanic mediality led Jue to develop the concept of milieu-specific analysis: "By offering entirely different conditions than on land – increased pressure, three-dimensional movement, light refraction and magnification, and the inability to tell the directions of sounds," she writes, "the ocean is a material and imaginative space for the conditions of perception that we have taken for granted" (2020, 2). Viewing *Life in Colour, Blue Planet, Blue Planet II*, or other aquatic adventures of Attenborough, it is valuable to maintain perspective on how visual representations may distort our understandings of the ocean as much as inform them – for in short: the medium itself is the message. While many bodies of water in Attenborough's aquatic works narratively serve as protagonists, filmically they often remain invisible containers, i.e., an unnoticed media in which the fish (and the technologies that capture them) are situated – an analysis that bears similarities with McLuhan's insistence that "media are environments [...] in which individuals live like fish do in water" (Scolari 2012, 206), not realizing the element in which they live.

Through such a comparison, McLuhan raises interesting concerns of media consumer's awareness, but the somewhat far-fetched metaphorical transfer also raises questions about the point when the transfer reaches its limits and fails to make sense. There are many aspects of media ecology that remain in the rhetorical realm of comparison; using the media ecology metaphor to study Attenborough typically means to consider his media avatar on his journey across media environments; spatially across flows and streams. Furthermore, the media ecology metaphor can be temporally extended to a discussion of the historical development, that is, the *evolution* of media from broadcast television (black-and-white and color) to cable and satellite television, from celluloid film to video tape, DVD, Blu-ray, and from all earlier media to the internet and online streaming. While using such metaphors has shortcomings with regards to inaccuracy about the nonhuman world and evokes Darwinian associations, thinking of the historical development of Attenborough's oeuvre in terms of evolution can help make clear its nonlinear trajectory of change and flows. For example, his viewers in the contemporary media environment, particularly in the Global North, might have first seen him in black and white in his first BBC broadcast series *Zoo Quest*, which can now be discovered on digital platforms as YouTube, and as clips in documentaries about Attenborough or in programs like *Zoo Quest in Colour* (2016), which features original outtakes for the series shot on early color film. More recently, viewers encounter Attenborough using streaming media services such as Netflix in works like *Our Planet* (2019) or *David Attenborough: A Life on Our Planet* (2020).

Following the Attenborough avatar through this evolving media (eco)system, one cannot fail to notice the qualitative trajectory of his oeuvre through the use of high-definition cameras and enhanced sound and image editing that create hyper-real effects. In this context of technological development, the metaphor of evolution not only has its benefits but also suggests coincidental change and thus masks the key role Attenborough has played as a driving force in the media industry, for example in the shift from black and white to color television during the 1960s, which Attenborough promoted as controller of BBC2 (Murphy n.d.).

This incorporation of new generations of cameras and screens that show the world in ever higher definition is very much in keeping with his personal and professional desire to represent nonhuman life in all its magnificence. This depiction of the wonders of the natural world has long been Attenborough's strategy of advocating for environmental protections but such enthusiasm for technological advancement, which has been part of Attenborough's adventures, since the colonialist capturing of animals for the London Zoo in *Zoo Quest*, is not far from a celebration of linear, capitalist, and expansionist progress ideologies that have been involved in environmental destruction since the industrial revolution. Such a development of 'ever more stunning images,' 'ever further around the globe,' is clearly observable through Attenborough's series. This trajectory of increasing spectacularism is palpable if one looks at the development from *Planet Earth* (2006) as the first high-definition nature series, to the narratively climactic sequel *Planet Earth II* (2016) in ultra-high-definition, for which the crew spent more than 2,000 days of filming in 40 different countries (Lawless 2017). Because of its 4K-quality, the sequel was even shown on digital TVs as a selling point at department stores like Costco and Walmart.

From our blue media ecological perspective, what interests us beyond the new camera and screen technologies is the development of blue media infrastructures for cable/satellite and internet connections through which the Attenborough productions circulate. As Nicole Starosielski reminds us, the ocean is an environmental medium that calls not only for milieu-specific cultural and perceptual analysis but also for a materiality analysis. In the book *The Undersea Network* (2015) and its multimedia companion project "Surfacing" (2015), Starosielski has helped to make visible the environmental impacts and political dimension of cable networks used to transport media data like Attenborough's avatars around the world. Such work calls attention to the paradox that Attenborough helps us understand and appreciate the oceans at the very moment in history when we are doing the most damage to them; damage that Attenborough is complicit in.

Feeling Blue

While Attenborough endeavors to advance media technology to help viewers appreciate the natural world, his educational efforts rely heavily on technocapitalist development, thus evoking "ecomodernist" (Asafu-Adjaye et al. 2015) approaches that promote technological solutions to the ecocrisis. Other forms of criticism of Attenborough's environmental activism, especially as he nears the end of his illustrious career, come from folks like *Guardian* writer George Monbiot, who has accused Attenborough of escapism for "[k]nowingly creating a false impression of the world" (2018), because of a fear of losing viewers for sounding alarmist. For most of his career, Attenborough has arguably whitewashed Earth's malaise by only obliquely referencing it (Yong 2019).

The reason for such obliqueness might be that Attenborough succumbs to criticisms that label a mere thematization of the ecocrisis as alarmist and exaggerating – or he and his films do not account for the imbalance of some of his viewer's knowledge about anthropogenic destruction. When he focuses on the beauty of nature, Attenborough seems to assume that everyone else knows as much about the ecocrisis as he does and do not need to be constantly reminded of the problem (Zemanek 2022). This logic makes his conservationist approach slightly more understandable, but it does not ameliorate his oversight. In *Climate Change: The Facts* (2019), Attenborough insists that he has been addressing the ecocrisis since the turn of this century (02:55), probably referring to *State of the Planet* (2000) and he took part in productions like *The Truth About Climate Change*, aka, *Are we Changing Planet Earth?* (2006). An ecocritical perspective enables a fuller picture of Attenborough's environmentalism, complicating criticisms of his on-screen persona by pointing toward his off-camera activism, for example his patronage of the Wildscreen Arkive, a conservationist multimedia encyclopedia of the world's (endangered) species, and his participation in the Global Apollo Program, which aims at cutting the cost of carbon-free energy (Lawless 2017).

Recent Attenborough programs have foregrounded saddening environmental content (Lawless 2017). A comparison between *Blue Planet* (2001) and *Blue Planet II* (2017) highlights this shift in Attenborough's oeuvre with regards to overt environmentalism. In *Blue Planet*'s episode three, we see how flying fish lay their eggs on palm leaves floating in the open ocean and hear Attenborough add that fish in these realms lay are attracted by any type of floating debris – "even manmade junk" like plastic crates or discarded netting "attracts them"; serving as a "sanctuary" for fish (20:27). Such excitement in Attenborough's voice about anthropogenic influence on aquatic life is difficult to find in *Blue Planet II*. Unlike its similarly successful predecessor, the widely viewed sequel brings up the notion of environmental destruction at least once in every episode and is said to have "triggered a massive effort to reduce plastic pollution" (Monbiot 2018). Yet, while the series "positively influenced" viewers' perceptions of plastic consumption as having a negative environmental impact, it "did not [directly] translate into a behavioral change" according to researchers at Imperial College London (Dunn, Mills, and Veríssimo 2020, 1).

With *Blue Planet II*, Attenborough's shift toward more explicit environmentalism reached wider audiences, and also his other recent work is much more "blue" in sentiment; more emotionally impacted by human environmental destruction. Whatever has caused him to express such blueness in recent programs like his "witness statement" *David Attenborough: A Life on Our Planet* (2020) – perhaps criticisms from the likes of Monbiot – scholars like Gouyon and Yong argue that his recent projects like *Our Planet* (2019) and *Seven Worlds, One Planet* (2019), which manifest waves of sadness through Attenborough's narration, "mark the start of a new era for wildlife television—one which doesn't shy away from political and environmental problems" (Gouyon 2019). As Ed Yong notes in *The Atlantic*, *Our Planet* discusses the issue of eco-emergency "repeatedly, in shot after shot. It does what no other natural-history documentary has done. It forces viewers to acknowledge their own complicity in the destruction of nature, in the moment. It feels sad, but also right" (2019).

Our notion of such a crisis-conscious blue media ecology is informed by Eileen A. Joy's essay "Blue" (2013), which Joy presents as an effort "to think about depression as a shared creative endeavor, as a transcorporeal blue (and blues) ecology that would bind humans, nonhumans, and stormy weather together" (213). Joy's perspective prompts us to consider the more depressing (yet honest) approach of recent Attenborough films, such as whether "depression, sadness, melancholy—feeling blue" always only takes place within the individuum, or if it is also *"in the world* somehow, a type of weather or atmosphere, with the becoming-mad of the human mind only one of its many *effects* (a form of attunement to the world's melancholy)?" (213–14). Joy's approach arguably goes very far in anthropomorphizing the planet, but Attenborough's films do prompt us to ask – as we witness birds flying away from the melting glaciers in *Our Planet* (Ep. 1, 44:08) or researcher Terry Hughes shedding tears over bleached coral reefs in *Breaking Boundaries* (2021, 50:40) – do birds, corals, and other life forms notice what is happening to the planet, could they possess some sense of knowledge that the oceans are acidifying and warming, and, to go further, might they have any agency to respond to and even counter such changes? In *Life in Colour*, for example, Attenborough suggests that some corals have developed neon colors as a "sunscreen … to fight back" against acidification (Ep. 3, 40:00). Or is the blueness we perceive in Attenborough's recent work more accurately figured a response to humanity's global coming to terms with industrialization's impact on the planet – an impact disproportionately created by the nations of the Global North and the corporations and politicians who have the greatest agency to change the present dynamic? Thinking with blue media ecologies allows us to pursue these questions and for future scholarship to apply them to other contexts, such as the portrayal of Indigenous blue-skinned sea-inhabiting civilizations in blockbuster movies like *Black Panther: Wankanda Forever* (2022) and *Avatar: The Way of Water* (2022).

Outlook

Coming to terms with humanity's impact on the global environment is still not fully executed in the late Attenborough work, even in *Our Planet* or in its MOD (its Making-of-Documentary) *Our Planet: Behind the Scenes* (2019), where the filmmakers are morbidly happy to have witnessed large-scale melting of the cryosphere in Greenland, the unsettling images captioned with their comments on how "fantastic" (54:07) the melting landscape looks – comments that make us as ecomedia scholars feel rather blue. The scene clashes with its following one, which shows the filmmaker's distress about walruses falling off a cliff because global warming destroyed their glacial habitat (cf. Yong 2019). With this scene, *Our Planet* provides an exceptional case in which the cameras, the filmmakers, and their emotions of blueness are at least temporarily part of the ecosystem we see on screen – in other words, the scene provides a vivid, self-referential, and self-reflexive Anthropocene example in which the feelings of *blueness*, *media*, and the *ecology* appear together. However, even in such instances of blueness, more complex ecomaterial reflections are missing: the shows' own environmental impact and that of its media technologies are not discussed, although they are part of the ecologies depicted – a task that blue media ecology could pursue as it aims to bridge media ecology and ecomedia studies.

Further Reading

Cubitt, Sean. 2016. *Finite Media: Environmental Implications of Digital Technologies*. Durham, NC: Duke University Press.

Dobrin, Sidney I. 2021. *Blue Ecocriticism and the Oceanic Imperative*. Routledge Environmental Humanities. Abingdon, Oxon New York: Routledge.
Jue, Melody. 2020. *Wild Blue Media: Thinking Through Seawater*. Elements. Durham, NC: Duke University Press.
Peters, John Durham. 2015. *The Marvelous Clouds: Toward a Philosophy of Elemental Media*. Chicago, IL: University of Chicago Press.
Starosielski, Nicole. 2015. *The Undersea Network*. SST, Sign, Storage, Transmission. Durham, NC: Duke University Press.

Works Cited

Aitchison, John, Rowan Aitchison, and Fredi Devas. 2021. "Assessing the Environmental Impacts of Wildlife Television Programmes." *People and Nature*. doi:10.1002/pan3.10251.
Alaimo, Stacy. 2019. "Introduction: Science Studies and the Blue Humanities." *Configurations* 27 (4): 429–32. doi:10.1353/con.2019.0028.
Asafu-Adjaye, John, et al. 2015. "An Ecomodernist Manifesto." Accessed December 07, 2021. www.ecomodernism.org.
Blue Planet. Fothergill, Alastair, dir. 2001. BBC One. September 12, 2001.
Breaking Boundaries: The Science of Our Planet. Clay, Jonathan, dir. 2021. Netflix. www.netflix.com/de/title/81336476.
Cavell, Stanley. 1982. "The Fact of Television." *Daedalus* 111 (4): 75–98. www.jstor.org/stable/20024818. Accessed August 31, 2021.
Cordey, Huw, Sophie Lanfear, Ilaira Mallalieu, Kieran O'Donovan, Hugh Pearson, Gisle Sverdrup. 2019. *Our Planet: Behind the Scenes*. Netflix. www.netflix.com/de/title/81082125.
Davies, Serena, dir. 2019. *Climate Change: The Facts*. BBC One. April 18, 2019.
Dunn, Matilda E., Morena Mills, and Diogo Veríssimo. 2020. "Evaluating the Impact of the Documentary Series Blue Planet II on Viewers' Plastic Consumption Behaviors." *Conservation Science and Practice* 2 (10). doi:10.1111/csp2.280.
Gouyon, Jean-Baptiste. 2019. "A New Generation of Wildlife Documentaries Are Confronting the Climate Emergency. BBC Nature Documentaries Are Finally Confronting Climate Change." *Quartz*, December 12. Accessed August 03, 2021. https://qz.com/1767046/bbc-nature-documentaries-are-finally-confronting-climate-change/.
Heise, Ursula K. 2002. "Unnatural Ecologies: The Metaphor of the Environment in Media Theory." *Configurations* 10 (1): 149–68. doi:10.1353/con.2003.0006.
Joy, Eileen A. 2013. "Blue." In *Prismatic Ecology: Ecotheory Beyond Green*, edited by Jeffrey J. Cohen, 213–32. Minneapolis: University of Minnesota Press.
Jue, Melody. 2020. *Wild Blue Media: Thinking Through Seawater*. Elements. Durham, NC: Duke University Press.
Lawless, Jill. 2017. "Epic 'Planet Earth II' Offers Creatures'-Eye View of Nature." *Associated Press*, February 16. Accessed July 30, 2021. https://apnews.com/article/ddb30a91ecbc4893a49f25010f2ca35d.
Life in Colour. Geiger, Adam, Bridget Appleby, Nick Green, and Sally Thomson, dirs. 2021. Netflix. www.netflix.com/de/title/81036559.
Mathur, Swati. 2020. "David Attenborough the 'Human Voice of Nature', Manmohan Singh Says While Conferring Indira Gandhi award on Veteran Broadcaster." *Times of India*, September 7. Accessed June 11, 2021. https://www.thehindu.com/news/national/attenborough-is-the-human-voice-of-nature-manmohan/article32546288.ece.
Maxwell, Richard, and Toby Miller. 2012. *Greening the Media*. New York: Oxford University Press.
Monbiot, George. 2018. "David Attenborough Has Betrayed the Living World He Loves." *The Guardian*, November 7. Accessed September 3, 2021. https://www.theguardian.com/commentisfree/2018/nov/07/david-attenborough-world-environment-bbc-films.
Murphy, Amanda. n.d. "History of the BBC: 50 Years of BBC TV Colour." *BBC*. Accessed September 3, 2021. www.bbc.com/historyofthebbc/research/bbc-tv-colour.
Our Planet. Chapman, Adam, Hugh Pearson, Huw Cordey, Sophie Lanfear, Mandi Stark, Jeff Wilson, dirs. 2019. Netflix. www.netflix.com/de/title/80049832.Scolari, Carlos A. 2012. "Media Ecology: Exploring the Metaphor to Expand the Theory." *Communication Theory* 22 (2): 204–25. doi:10.1111/j.1468-2885.2012.01404.x.

Starosielski, Nicole. 2015. *The Undersea Network*. SST, Sign, Storage, Transmission. Durham, NC and London: Duke University Press.
"Surfacing." Starosielski, Nicole, Erik Loyer, and Shane Brennan. 2015. Accessed November 16, 2021. www.surfacing.in/.
Williams, Raymond. 1974. *Television: Technology and Cultural Form*. 2nd ed. Publ. 1990, reprinted. Routledge Classics. London: Routledge.
Yong, Ed. 2019. "Netflix's 'Our Planet' Says What Other Nature Series Have Omitted." *The Atlantic*, April 1, 2019. Accessed August 03, 2021. www.theatlantic.com/science/archive/2019/04/wildlife-series-finally-addresses-elephant-room/586066/.
Zemanek, Evi. 2022. "Between Fragility and Resilience: Ambivalent Images of Nature in Popular Documentaries with David Attenborough." *The Anthropocene Review* 9 (2): 139–60. doi:10.1177/20530196221093477.

5
POLITICAL AND APOLITICAL ECOLOGIES OF DIGITAL MEDIA

Sy Taffel

Introduction

Digital technologies are typically framed as objects: whether described as devices, gadgets, screens, or phones, the image conjured is of discrete individualized entities. Thinking ecologically about these technologies reconceptualizes them as assemblages dependent upon energy, matter, social exchange, labor, and knowledge, where ongoing functionality depends upon the continuing flows of these varied resources. This chapter outlines an approach to digital media ecologies which combines foregrounding ecology as the study of flows of energy and matter through complex dynamic systems, with insights drawn from the field of political ecology, which argues that "politics are inevitably ecological and that ecology is inherently political" (Robbins, 2004: XVII). This perspective necessarily critiques appropriations of ecological language that fail to engage with contemporary ecological crises.

A political ecology of digital media examines how technocultural systems form vast planetary assemblages that extract, purify, and transport millions of tons of matter around the globe, burn vast quantities of fossil fuels, and generate enormous volumes of toxic waste to maintain and extend the domain of media. Furthermore, digital media exemplify the process of ecologically unequal exchange, which political ecologists employ to describe the asymmetric flows of extracted materials from the global periphery toward the global core on the one hand, while on the other hand, nations situated within the core extract surplus value by exporting goods and services located further up the supply chain to peripheral nations (Hornborg, 1998).

A political ecology of digital media follows relational flows across a broad range of spatial and temporal scales, ranging from the microtemporal speeds of multi-gigahertz computational processing to the geological durations that e-waste will impact ecosystems, from imperceptibly small single-digit-nanometer transistors to planetary networks of global supply chain capitalism. This chapter begins by outlining key concepts surrounding ecological thought and ecological crises, moving through critiques of metaphorical and depoliticized applications of ecology to technology, before summarizing a political ecology-based approach.

Environments and Ecologies

While the terms "environment" and "ecology" are often used interchangeably to demarcate nonhuman or natural entities, there is a subtle yet important difference between them. Etymologically, ecology combines the anglicized version of the Greek *oikos*, meaning household (the same term that gives us the *eco-* part of economy), with the suffix *-logy*, denoting the study of. Ecology is not concerned with individual entities (the focus of biology, the study of life) but with relationships within our planetary household. Ecology traces entanglements between humans and nonhumans, across the scales of the individual organism and their relationship to their surroundings, population ecology (groups of the same species), community ecology (groups of different species), and ecosystem ecology (which also includes non-living elements such as water and the nitrogen and phosphorus cycles).

Conversely, environment is derived from the French *environ*, meaning "to surround," depicting an external nature which surrounds human society. While humans clearly depend upon this surrounding, for clean air, water, food, et al., it is fundamentally exterior to "us." By explicitly placing nature outside of society, "environment" indicates a dualistic ontology, one that has dominated Western, Christian thought for centuries. This approach separates nonhuman nature from human culture, in addition to a series of related dualisms that include mind/matter, body/soul, free will/determinism, and civilized/savage societies. The last of these oppositions functioned as a justification for the brutal exploitation and oppression of indigenous and other predominantly nonwhite humans associated with colonization and imperialism. Correspondingly, the nature/culture dualism reduced diverse ecosystems to "natural resources" that were amenable to expropriation, exploitation, and in many cases devastation. Within a western context,[1] the chief philosophical rival to dualism was physicalism (also referred to as mechanism), a monistic ontology which contends that all existence can be explained by the mechanical laws governing sub/atomic particles, thereby depicting living systems as analogous to complicated clockwork machines. Indeed, the apparent distinction between the agential capacities of humans, who were thought to possess free will, and mechanistic accounts of the natural world resulted in the proposition of dualistic ontologies.

Ecological thought fundamentally departs from both dualism and physicalism. It situates humans within ecosystems rather than placing nature outside "us," therefore rejecting the nature/culture dualism. It also rejects the micro-level reductionism found in physicalism. While classical/Newtonian mechanics contends that the behavior of physical systems can be deterministically understood through analyzing their constituent components, and that these behaviors are time reversible, ecology deals with living systems where behaviors are irreversible, which require flows of energy and matter to remain organizationally balanced at points far from thermodynamic equilibrium, and where causality can be an emergent property arising from interactions between assemblages. Ecology deals with complex systems. This does not mean systems that are complicated, as per vernacular applications of complexity, but rather that ecosystems are governed by non-linear dynamics and circular causality. Whereas linear systems involve proportional change, so small changes in inputs produce corresponding small changes in output, non-linear systems involve feedback loops, entailing outputs that can be wildly disproportionate to inputs. Feedback can be negative (also known as homeostatic), where the system is self-correcting, meaning that no change eventuates, or it can be positive, where minuscule changes are iteratively magnified so that they produce dramatic transformations. Often, complex systems exist within semi-stable states, where negative feedbacks suppress change within certain thresholds, but once tipping points are exceeded, positive feedbacks amplify change, impelling the system into a novel semi-stable state. Once tipping points are breached, these changes are often irreversible.

This description of ecology should be familiar from discussions of climate change and other contemporaneous ecological crises. The semi-stable climatic conditions that characterized the Holocene, the geological epoch which began approximately 11,650 years ago, enabled the flourishing of human societies and nonhuman life. During the twenty-first century, there is growing acceptance among scientists that the Holocene has ended. Since post-World War II "great acceleration," the planet has entered the Anthropocene, a new epoch where "human activities have become so pervasive and profound that they rival the great forces of nature" (Steffen et al., 2007: 614). The climate is being altered by the combustion of fossil fuels, biodiversity is plummeting approximately a thousand times faster than background levels, ecosystems are transformed as "unproductive land" is converted for industrial agriculture, the cyclical flows of key elements within the Earth system such as nitrogen and phosphorus have been altered, the oceans are warming and acidifying, and novel materials such as petroleum-derived plastics will suddenly appear in the geological strata. In each case, scientists have identified tipping points, beyond which the Earth system is likely to be destabilized and irreversibly exit the relatively benign conditions of the Holocene (Steffen et al., 2015). These analyses currently place climate change and land system change within the zone of increasing risk, while biodiversity and biogeochemical flows are already in high-risk areas, suggesting that they require remedial action as urgently as climate change. Indeed, one rationale for the Anthropocene is that it avoids reducing multiple entangled ecological crises to climate change.

However, the rhetoric of the Anthropocene has been heavily criticized within the social sciences and humanities for propagating an overly reductive discourse that homogenizes the impacts of diverse human activities. Humans are not equally responsible for greenhouse gas (GHG) emissions, material use, and the like; instead, ecological harms are largely produced by an economically affluent minority. Indigenous peoples and subsistence farmers cannot reasonably be compared, in their ecological impacts, to fossil fuel executives and merchant bankers. Homogenizing humanity not only repeats the universalizing doctrine of colonialism, but it also depoliticizes ecological crises, neglecting analyses of how certain groups of humans benefit from ecologically harmful actions. Consequently, the "Capitalocene" has been proposed as an alternative description of our present planetary situation, highlighting the role of the capitalist mode of production, with its requirement for endless compound economic growth in producing ecological crises that threaten to transgress planetary boundaries while widening economic inequalities (Moore, 2016).

Apolitical and Metaphorical Ecologies

While understanding ecological crises in terms of non-linear thresholds and tipping points is now an orthodox scientific perspective, the enduring legacy of the nature/culture dualism entails that human societies and technologies are typically assessed quite differently. Technologies are primarily understood through the lens of commodity fetishism, which positions them as discrete objects that are primarily evaluated through their monetary exchange value. Representations of technology are dominated by the global advertising industry, which spent US$749 billion in 2021 (Bruell, 2021), primarily serving humans located in geographically affluent regions thousands of daily reminders that an ecologically calamitous level of overconsumption is normal and desirable.

A dualistic approach based on the separation of nature and culture is exemplified by the media ecology associated with Marshall McLuhan and Neil Postman, which advocates:

> human beings live in two different kinds of environments. One is the natural environment and consists of things like air, trees, rivers, and caterpillars. The other is the media

environment, which consists of language, numbers, images, holograms, and all of the other symbols, techniques, and machinery that make us what we are.

(Postman, 2000: 11)

This metaphorical media ecology (Scolari, 2012) drew upon mid-twentieth century insights from cybernetics and ecology, proposing analogies between ecosystems and media systems, while maintaining a rigid distinction between them. This dualistic separation of nature and culture enabled Postman and McLuhan to solely focus on the technocultural media environment. Contemporary approaches to ecomedia instead foreground entanglements of technological and ecological systems, exploring how digital technologies and infrastructures are implicated in significant local, regional, and planetary ecological harms, a perspective which is effectively erased by treating media and ecology as distinct environments.

However, metaphorical and apolitical applications of ecological tropes to media still endure. Both popular and academic literatures frequently reference the apolitical metaphor of ecosystems, discussing the iOS, Android, mobile or app ecosystems, Facebook's ecosystem, or social media ecosystems. "Ecosystem" here denotes complex, negentropic systems which require flows of energy and matter to sustain themselves. While rainforests or savannahs require flows of sunlight, water, carbon, and nitrogen, digital ecologies require human attention, labor, code, and content (although material extraction and supply chains are obviously necessary to produce these systems, they rarely figure in these discussions). The use of ecosystem as a descriptor here is tied to that of the term "platform," indicating that value is not solely produced by Facebook, Apple, or Google, but that there exists a multisided market where a significant proportion of economic value results from harvesting users' data, the production of user-generated content, and/or the production of third-party apps, plug-ins, and other forms of executable code.

Similarly, the term "ecology'" is applied to cultural and creative production (Dovey et al., 2016), innovation (Dvir and Pasher, 2004), and information (Davenport and Prusak, 1997), examining how the production of digital media and other contemporary creative ventures involve dynamic networks that form cultural ecologies which function analogously to natural ecosystems. While these approaches yield economically useful insights for cultural production, they also fulfill a pernicious political role in validating and naturalizing the capitalist economic system in which contemporary cultural production occurs. Analyses of benevolent corporate superorganisms (Kelly, 2009) and capitalist cultural ecosystems which exclude discussions of contemporary ecological crises and the structural role of economic inequalities that are pivotal to capitalist economic development perpetuate the myths of progress and meritocracy that sustain the systems of exploitation, domination, and power responsible for pushing the planet toward the sixth mass extinction. Further, emphasizing dynamism and innovation reinforces widespread assumptions that capitalist innovation will generate technological solutions to these crises. Geo-engineering, carbon capture and storage, deep-sea mining, and other capital and technology intensive means of addressing the Capitalocene are transformed from dangerous and speculative strategies into common-sense solutions by naturalizing capitalism.

Political Ecologies

In contrast to apolitical and metaphorical digital ecologies, political ecology emphasizes the entanglement of power and ecosystems, highlighting that technocultural systems are not somehow divorced from natural ecologies. While commodity fetishism posits technologies as discrete objects devoid of social and environmental relations, political ecology instead addresses these seemingly stable objects as temporary crystallizations of flows of matter, energy, labor, and knowledge.

Analyzing technologies relationally means considering their life-cycle. This begins with the extraction of materials from the earth. The smartphone that may well currently be in your pocket contains around 70 of Earth's 84 nonradioactive elements. These materials are distributed across disparate and specific places. For example, most tantalum, which is used in capacitors, is extracted from the Democratic Republic of Congo. Tantalum is a conflict mineral that has financed long-standing civil warfare within the DRC (Taffel, 2019). Approximately two-thirds of the world's cobalt, which is used in batteries, is also located in the DRC, predominantly in the Katanga region which is removed from the civil war, but where tens of thousands of children as young as five-year-old labor in the extraction industry (Niarchos, 2021). Around two-thirds of lithium, which is primarily used in batteries, is sourced from the arid Atacama desert in South America where multinational mining companies have been in conflict with local indigenous peoples over access to scarce local water supplies and the ecological damage caused by extraction (Cubitt, 2016). Most of the lanthanides, a group of elements also referred to as rare earths whose unique properties are used in microelectronics for diverse purposes, including making lightweight permanent magnets, red phosphors for digital screens, and doping fiber-optic cables to amplify signals over long distances, are predominantly mined and refined in China, where production is associated with "cancer villages," where local residents and ecosystems are routinely poisoned by toxic and radioactive tailings (Klinger, 2017). These are just a handful of the tangible harms associated with extracting the raw materials necessary for digital technologies.

The extraction industries move immense quantities of matter from low-income nations toward high-income nations. This forms one half of a process that political ecologists describe as ecologically unequal exchange (Hornborg, 1998). The other, corresponding process involves high-income nations extracting significantly higher values from exporting products and services further up the supply chain to low-income nations. This structural inequality has been traced back to the early days of capitalism, where the colonies functioned as sources of cheap nature and labor that enriched European empires (Patel and Moore, 2017). High-income nations are net importers of over 10 billion tons of raw materials per annum, and all regions except high-income nations are net exporters of raw materials (Dorninger et al., 2021). While this is not a straightforward dualism, with China functioning as both a huge importer of materials from lower income nations and exporter of goods to higher income nations, since 1990, 81% of per capita growth in material footprint results from high-income nations (Hickel, 2020). Digital technologies exemplify this structural inequality; vast quantities of materials flow from low-income nations such as DRC toward higher income nations (the centers of technological consumption), while tech corporations based in high-income nations, especially the US, reap the financial rewards of selling technology and digital services to low-income nations.

After extraction, materials undergo numerous energetically and chemically intensive processes of separation and purification. The materials employed in high-performance computing, such as nine-nines silicon (99.999999999% pure) and electrolytic copper (>99.95% pure), are far removed from extracted ores; for example, the concentration of copper within chalcopyrite ore is typically less than 1% (Koppelaar and Koppelaar, 2016). The processes used for purification require precise control of temperatures that are often in excess of 1,000°C (Starosielski, 2016). Alongside energy-intensive extraction processes, this is a key reason why approximately 80% of the lifetime GHG emissions associated with smartphones arise from production (Apple, 2020). These extremely pure materials enable the production of digital technologies, whose microscopic and microtemporal scales are exemplified by the 5–7 nanometer transistors employed within microprocessors that perform billions of floating point operations per second. Manufacturing digital devices primarily occurs within enormous factories located in China and South-East Asia. Over the past decade, a series of scandals have revealed the inhuman conditions that migrant, mainly female workers are subject to at these facilities, and there have been regular revelations of workers being poisoned in factories where low wages and poor safety practices drive down the costs of production (Qiu, 2017).

After being used for an average of less than three years (Tröger et al., 2017), phones are replaced and become part of the >50 million tons of electronic waste (e-waste) produced annually. Rapid growth in digital technologies means that by 2030, that figure is expected to grow to 74 MT per annum (Forti et al., 2020). E-waste contains significant volumes of toxic material, and additional toxicants are released into the environment from processes such as plastic coatings being burnt to reclaim copper from inside wires, or strong acids dissolving silicon chips to recover gold pins. Artisanal e-waste processing produces numerous harms to workers, local communities, and ecosystems, including lead poisoning (Guo et al., 2014) and elevated cancer rates among local children (Davis and Garb, 2019). These harms are predominantly borne by impoverished workers, including children, located in the global periphery, which functions as both a source of raw materials for digital production, and a sink for toxic e-waste. Further, the ecological harms associated with materials such as plastics are operative over time-scales spanning centuries or millennia, demonstrating the temporal imbalance between digital capitalism and the planet (Farrelly et al., 2021). As with many ecological crises, responsibility correlates with wealth, with per capita e-waste generation rates in the US, UK, and Australia being over 40 times higher than that in Rwanda and Sierra Leone (Forti et al., 2020).

While examining the life-cycle of devices productively decenters the dominant way of conceptualizing them as commodities, it threatens to repeat their erroneous individualization by segregating them from the infrastructural relations required for their ongoing functionality. As an isolated device, a smartphone couldn't browse or search the web, post to, or peruse social media, download apps, stream media from Spotify or Netflix, show you how to get from A to B, or even make phone calls. Put simply, the smartphone relies upon a gargantuan planetary assemblage of infrastructure comprising hardware, software, and standards for the overwhelming majority of its functionality. This hardware includes the datacenters that host streaming content, social media platforms, videogames, cloud data and websites, the hundreds of millions of kilometers of undersea and underground fiber optic cables which carry over 99% of global internet traffic (Starosielski, 2015: 1), cable landing stations, internet exchange points, the cellular towers and antennas used for mobile internet, the routers and modems used for Wi-Fi networks, and the network of GPS satellites used for locative services. The software includes the Android and iOS operating systems, the Windows and Linux operating systems used on servers, the millions of applications downloadable from mobile app stores, databases, algorithms, user interfaces, file formats, programming languages and content management systems, websites, games, and so on. The multitude of standards and protocols, agreed rules, and regulations which enable diverse forms of IT hardware and software to interact (Galloway, 2004) include the Internet protocol, transmission communication protocol, hypertext transfer protocol, IEEE 802.11 family of Wi-Fi Standards, the 2/3/4/5G standards for broadband cellular networks, the Bluetooth short-range wireless technology standard, and so on.

While these lists are far from exhaustive, they indicate that digital technology involves assemblages, not discrete devices. All this hardware has similar issues throughout its life-cycle to individual devices. The software and standards require immense volumes of labor, communication, and knowledge. Our individualistic way of approaching digital media positions typically male, often white corporate CEOs, such as Mark Zuckerberg and Jeff Bezos, as innovative leaders who single handedly invented Facebook and Amazon. A relational way of situating these individuals instead places them within vast networks of labor, knowledge, energy, and matter. The centuries of common knowledge and culture that are leveraged by contemporary technologies are typically entirely unacknowledged by a system that fetishizes individualism and presentism. However, in reality, these systems exemplify Isaac Newton's famous statement that any apparent individual innovation is the result of "standing on the shoulders of giants." Approaching digital media this way reveals that addressing the ecological harms of this assemblage cannot be meaningfully accomplished by ethical consumption undertaken at an individual level – individuals do not purchase networks of satellites, data centers, or submarine fiber-optic cables. Rather, it requires systemic and structural changes requiring national and international regulation.

Conclusion

One possible objection to outlining the enormity of contemporary digital media ecologies is that they manifest as a terrifying level of complexity that propagates affects of apathy and hopelessness in the face of globalized digital capitalism and ecological catastrophe. However, it is useful to recall that complexity theory provides a conceptual framework for focusing upon differences that make a difference, rather than needing to know every detail of how systems work. Short-term noise in complex meteorological systems means weather forecasts for a months' time are inaccurate, but meaningful longer term predictions that should guide action to avert catastrophic climate change can still be made.

Thinking homologously about technology and ecology asks us to re-envision technocultural systems that are not predicated on inflicting significant and inequitably distributed harms to people and ecosystems. This means jettisoning the fantasy of infinite economic growth enabled by dematerialized digital technologies on a materially finite planet. It means addressing the substantive social and environmental harms that surround the life-cycle of digital technologies, including addressing the ecologically unequal forms of exchange that see low-income nations function as sources of materials and sinks for toxic waste, while high-income nations profit from selling or allowing access to technologies produced from those materials. It requires a fundamental re-evaluation of what should be produced and how those technologies should be owned, governed, and deployed. Ultimately, it urges a reorientation of technology, culture, and society toward a postcapitalist future, one where the digital ecology does not depend upon the exploitation and degradation of present and future human and nonhuman life.

Note

1 Indigenous and non-Western ontologies are markedly different here.

Further Reading

Cubitt, Sean (2016) *Finite media: Environmental implications of digital technologies.* Durham, NC: Duke University Press.
Hornborg, Alf (2015) The political ecology of the Technocene: Uncovering ecologically unequal exchange in the world-system. In *The Anthropocene and the global environmental crisis*, pp. 57–69. London and New York: Routledge.
Nost, Eric, and Jenny Elaine Goldstein (2022) A political ecology of data. *Environment and Planning E: Nature and Space* 5(1): 3–17.
Robbins, Paul (2020) *Political ecology: A critical introduction.* Third Edition. Oxford: John Wiley & Sons.
Taffel, Sy (2019) *Digital media ecologies: Entanglements of content, code and hardware.* New York and London: Bloomsbury.

References

Apple (2020) *iPhone 12 Product Environmental Report*. Available at: https://www.apple.com/environment/pdf/products/iphone/iPhone_12_PER_Oct2020.pdf.

Bruell A (2021) Global Ad spending expected to rebound faster than previously forecast. *The Wall Street Journal*, 14 June 2021.

Cubitt S (2016) *Finite media: Environmental implications of digital technologies*. Durham, NC: Duke University Press.

Davenport TH and Prusak L (1997) *Information ecology: Mastering the information and knowledge environment*. Oxford: Oxford University Press.

Davis JM and Garb Y (2019) A strong spatial association between e-waste burn sites and childhood lymphoma in the West Bank, Palestine. *International Journal of Cancer* 144(3): 470–75.

Dorninger C, Hornborg A, Abson DJ, et al. (2021) Global patterns of ecologically unequal exchange: Implications for sustainability in the 21st century. *Ecological Economics* 179: 106824.

Dovey J, Moreton S, Sparke S, et al. (2016) The practice of cultural ecology: Network connectivity in the creative economy. *Cultural Trends* 25(2): 87–103.

Dvir R and Pasher E (2004) Innovation engines for knowledge cities: An innovation ecology perspective. *Journal of Knowledge Management* 8(5): 16–27.

Farrelly T, Taffel S and Shaw I (2021) *Plastic legacies: Pollution, persistence, and politics*. Edmonton: Athabasca University Press.

Forti V, Balde CP, Kuehr R, et al. (2020) *The Global E-waste Monitor 2020: Quantities, flows and the circular economy potential*. Bonn and Rotterdam: United Nations University, International Telecommunication Union, and International Solid Waste Association.

Galloway AR (2004) *Protocol: How control exists after decentralization*. Cambridge: MIT press.

Guo P, Xu X, Huang B, et al. (2014) Blood lead levels and associated factors among children in Guiyu of China: A population-based study. *PLoS One* 9(8): e105470.

Hickel J (2020) *Less is more: How degrowth will save the world*. London: Random House.

Hornborg A (1998) Towards an ecological theory of unequal exchange: Articulating world system theory and ecological economics. *Ecological Economics* 25(1): 127–36.

Kelly K (2009) *Out of control: The new biology of machines, social systems, and the economic world*. New York: Hachette.

Klinger JM (2017) *Rare earth frontiers*. Ithaca, NY and London: Cornell University Press.

Koppelaar RHEM and Koppelaar H (2016) The Ore grade and depth influence on copper energy inputs. *BioPhysical Economics and Resource Quality* 1(2): 11.

Moore JW (2016) *Anthropocene or capitalocene?: Nature, history, and the crisis of capitalism*. Oakland, CA: Pm Press.

Niarchos N (2021) The dark side of Congo's Cobalt Rush. *The New Yorker*.

Patel R and Moore JW (2017) *A history of the world in seven cheap things: A guide to capitalism, nature, and the future of the planet*. New York: Verso.

Postman N (2000) The humanism of media ecology. *Proceedings of the Media Ecology Association* 1: 10–16.

Qiu JL (2017) *Goodbye iSlave: A manifesto for digital abolition*. Chicago: University of Illinois Press.

Scolari CA (2012) Media ecology: Exploring the metaphor to expand the theory. *Communication Theory* 22(2): 204–25.

Starosielski N (2015) *The undersea network*. Durham, NC: Duke University Press.

Starosielski N (2016) Thermocultures of geological media. *Cultural Politics* 12(3): 293–309.

Steffen W, Crutzen PJ and McNeill JR (2007) The Anthropocene: Are humans now overwhelming the great forces of nature. *AMBIO: A Journal of the Human Environment* 36(8): 614–21.

Steffen W, Richardson K, Rockström J, et al. (2015) Planetary boundaries: Guiding human development on a changing planet. *Science* 347: 6223.

Taffel S (2019) *Digital media ecologies: Entanglements of content, code and hardware*. New York and London: Bloomsbury.

Tröger N, Wieser H and Hübner R (2017) Smartphones are replaced more frequently than T-shirts. In *Patterns of consumer use and reasons for replacing durable goods*. Vienna: Chamber of Labour.

6
CENTERING AFRICA IN ECOMEDIA STUDIES
Interview with Cajetan Iheka

Miriam Tola, Kiu-wai Chu, and Stephen Rust

This conversation discusses how Cajetan Iheka's book *African Ecomedia: Network Forms, Planetary Politics* contributes to ecomedia studies by centering Africa as a key site for media production, consumption, and disposal. This volume, published by Duke University Press in 2021, combines the focus on the socioecological effects of global media processes in postcolonial African nations, with the attention to the transformative agency of African visual artifacts representing at once ecological violence and more sustainable modes of living. This work invites ecomedia studies to address the materiality of media in relation to Africa's place within planetary networks of extraction and waste while also considering the continent as a site of creative expressions of futurity. The book comprises five chapters addressing a rich media archive produced in African locations, from Ghana to Kenya, Senegal to South Africa, and spanning video art, photography, documentary, and fiction film. Ihneka's case studies include, among others, Wanuri Kahiu's science fiction short film *Pumzi*, set in a future of ecological devastation following the Water Wars in East Africa; Pieter Hugo's *Permanent Error*, a photograph series depicting the recycling of technological waste in Agbogbloshie, Ghana; the safari images of Cecil, the lion killed in 2015 by a white American shooting big game in Zimbabwe, and its connections to the Black Lives Matter protest in the United States. *African Ecomedia* is the winner of the 2022 Ecocritical Book Award of the Association for the Study of Literature and Environment (ASLE) and the 2022 African Studies Association Best Book Prize. This conversation took place online in July 2022 and was edited and condensed via email, with the participation of Miriam Tola, Kiu-wai-Chu, Stephen Rust, and Antonio López.

MIRIAM TOLA: Can you talk about your definition of ecomedia in *African Ecomedia*?
CAJETAN IHEKA: My focus in this book is on artworks and media practices that are set in Africa or produced by Africans. My thinking about ecomedia encompasses textual and visual materials, mass media and electronic media. I am also interested in resource media such as oil and uranium that are extracted in Africa and travel across the world, as well as their impact on elemental media such as air and water. The book is about the role of Africa in the process of producing, consuming and disposing media as well as the ecological significance of these media processes. I provide a broad definition of ecomedia that includes

This chapter has been made available under a CC-BY-NC-ND license.

KIU-WAI CHU: cultural artifacts as well as the infrastructural and material dimension of media. As I explain in the book, *African Ecomedia* offers a model for ecological media studies for the twenty-first century.

KIU-WAI CHU: Your book focuses mainly on visual media, particularly photography. What is the role of text and context in defining the significance of the visual in ecomedia studies? Can we detach an image from its specific textual descriptions when we study ecomedia?

CAJETAN IHEKA: In the book's introduction I address the question of the visual and why it is crucial in the way I am seeing ecomedia. I agree that what we see is constructed: in every media form, including the literary text we are getting a point of view, a perspective. But at the same time, it seems to me that in ecomedia, in media studies and the environmental humanities, the locations that I am interested in have been sidelined. African places have been out of sight. Addressing visuality becomes then a way for foregrounding a region that has not really gotten the centrality it deserves in scholarly conversations. Over the past decades there has been this proliferation of cultural and media production in Africa. Recently, African literary culture has gotten a lot of attention through the Booker Prize, the Nobel Prize and the French Goncourt being won by African writers. This is an acknowledgement of the vital literary ecosystem that is African literature right now but this renaissance is not just happening in literature; it is happening in visual culture too. Part of what I am doing is to deprivilege, to unsettle the logic that puts the printed text and the literary work above the visual. This is a way to pay respect to the amazing work that African artists and creatives produce, to acknowledge their role in our ecological imaginary. Further, the turn to the visual draws on a broader Black critical tradition where exposure has been central to the work of critique. Of course, there's a problem of commodification and objectification that comes with exposure, but overtime Black thinkers and Black people have used exposure as a way to draw attention to anti-Blackness, to racism and to the value of Black lives. In the book introduction I talk about the mother of Emmett Till and her decision to expose her son's body in order to force a reckoning with lynching and the racial climate. The visual turn draws from this tradition of really laying bare violence for the purpose of reckoning. A lot of the images that I discuss in the book are uncomfortable to watch, for example the images of workers connected to the oil economy in the Niger Delta (Chapter 3). The racial economy of Blackness contributes to this discomfort but we must confront these images. If we are consumers of what pollutes the Niger Delta inhabitants and other sites I discuss, the least we can do is to refuse to look away; to deal with the discomfort that comes from looking at those images. There are epistemological, ethical and political stakes in the visual turn, but I must also say that the visual is not studied in isolation here. In fact, that kind of isolationist critique is impossible. Visual materials are in collaboration with what you call "textual description" throughout my work, a move that foregrounds ecological relation not only as theme but also as method. Linking visual texts and other forms of texts and working across media, I uphold ecological relation as both matter and method.

MIRIAM TOLA: You mentioned the use of exposure in the Black critical tradition. Do you see ethical and political overlaps in Emmett Till mother's exposure of her son's body, and the photos of Pieter Hugo that expose electronic waste pickers in Ghana?

CAJETAN IHEKA: There is a clear distinction between Emett Till mother's decision and the work of a photographer like Hugo. I acknowledge and respect this difference. However, I also think that it is important for scholars in the humanities to pay attention to how artworks, including Hugo's images, can have a transformative ecological impact despite being entangled in processes of commodification. There are questions of commodification even when we're dealing with other representations, such as when someone writes fiction or nonfiction depicting minority communities. My point is: what else is possible in the visual economy of looking? I refuse to accept that what we're seeing here is *just* objectification and commodification. It seems to me that that's the overused answer; I am interested in what else these images can do. It is worth returning to the Black critical tradition of exposure again. In protests in the Niger Delta, for example, you see women exposing their upper bodies in protest against oil companies. These women's bodies risk objectification and even exoticization but there's something else that their exposed bodies can do. These are bodies in dissent and there is a spiritual dimension of resistance activated in their bareness that deserves serious consideration. I recognize the power dynamic between a photographer like Hugo and the people in his images in Chapter 2, but I still think that something redemptive can occur through those images. What interests me is the transformative agency of images.

STEPHEN RUST: One of the images you discuss is that of Cecil the Lion killed by a North-American big-game hunter in Zimbabwe in 2015. Depending on the viewer, this image could be read as "environmental" or simply as a trophy image. Could you address this point? On a more general level, how much emphasis do you place on the ecological intent of cultural producers as opposed to the viewer's interpretation of their texts?

CAJETAN IHEKA: The image of Cecil the Lion is a trophy image, one connected to white supremacy or racism. It was taken for specific reasons and purposes. But when it circulated, its meaning changed, it acquired other meanings, becoming for some an ecological image drawing attention to the depletion of wildlife. In thinking about Cecil the Lion's image in terms of ecological violence across bodies and across entangled spaces, I'm interested not just in the violence of Cecil the Lion's death but also of events happening in the diaspora very far from the Zimbabwean context of origin. I am concerned with the relation between the killing of Cecil in Africa and questions of anti-Black racism, in how his image allow us to raise uncomfortable but important questions about the entanglements between vulnerable Black people and decimated animal bodies. I'm interested in how this relation is of the present but also historical and allows us to make sense of this image as an ecological artifact. To address the second part of the question, I focus on the reader, the viewer and the meaning that emerges in the act of viewing. Meaning is negotiated through the relation between the intention of the producer, the text, and the context of viewing. It's this interplay that produces meaning.

KIU-WAI CHU: How are people in Zimbabwe and Africa reacting to the global circulation of Cecil the Lion's images? What does it say about local ecomedia?

CAJETAN IHEKA: People in Zimbabwe and Africa are aware of the global circulation of the images of Cecil the Lion. They point out that the death of one of them would not elicit the same kind of response across the world. They draw attention to an ecological imbalance, an ecological inequality that makes it possible for the life of Cecil as a charismatic animal to be more valued than human lives. There is an ecological hierarchy of beings in privileging the life of Cecil over the lives of African people. This is not new, it is an historical problem. It is the same problem for which local communities have been displaced to make room for animals and for white people who can enjoy wildlife. Thus, for local people the global response to Cecil's killing fits into a history of dispossession and centuries of oppression. To connect this point to discussions on ecomedia, it is important to recall that the logic of dispossession and marginalization also applies to media production. So, when the image of Cecil is produced for the colonial gaze, it is done in such a way that it removes the local people from the frame, to present the landscape as empty. People in Africa are ephemeral in media production and even in what we call ecomedia today. In writing *African Ecomedia*, I wanted to bring them back into the frame. The exciting futuristic images in Chapter 5 titled *Shanty Megastructures* are important for centering Africans: as media makers, as knowledge producers, and as subjects of media production.

KIU-WAI CHU: Part of bringing Africans into the frame is also paying attention to local media production. This seems related to what you call "imperfect media." Could you expand on this concept? How are "imperfect media" related to fourth cinema? They are both low budget, smaller in scale, and environmentally much more sustainable. However, their social impact might be limited. How would you address this problem?

CAJETAN IHEKA: There is currently a cultural boom in Africa. There are young people in places like Lagos, Nigeria, who are doing remixes of major production. Working with basic equipment, they take samples of film and create new content out of them. I'm hoping that scholars going forward will pick up and will dig further into this more marginal production. "Imperfect media" are cultural artefacts with low carbon expenditure and are products of creative ingenuity and improvisation often seen in contexts of scarcity. We can call this form of media poor media. And yes, fourth cinema falls within the scope of "imperfect media" but this is not restricted to cinema. As I discuss in the book's epilogue, the scope extends to making art from recycled objects and cuts across media forms. I adapt "imperfect media" from Julio Garcia Espinosa's notion of "imperfect cinema," which names unpolished revolutionary cinema in the era of anticolonial struggle. "Imperfect media" updates the term for our current moment of climate catastrophe. In my usage, imperfect media embraces the more sustainable modes of media production that are cognizant of the planetary crisis. These works demonstrate the infinite resourcefulness that are necessary in our moment of finite resources. It is certainly a challenge to make such productions more visible. But it seems to me that addressing this challenge would involve our own reassessment of what constitutes a good film or art. In the age of digital media, those images have the potential to circulate a lot. Young people are producing images and putting them on the Internet so that they can make their way to different audiences. Part of the problem is that they don't meet the conventional taste of what a good media is. When we begin to think in terms of sustainability, it opens room to appreciate transformative work that is not Hollywoodian in orientation. These productions are not peculiar to Africa; they appear in the Americas where Indigenous people are producing lifegiving media. What might be needed is to reassess our taste of what a proper media production is. It is our responsibility to reconfigure our taste, our pleasure principle in ways that allow us to appreciate the import of ecologically conscious media.

STEPHEN RUST: Film and media scholarship can preserve the memory of works that may otherwise disappear and be forgotten, particularly low budget productions. Even in Hollywood, films are barely preserved. It is well known that discs are wiped so that new films could be made. I wonder if we could ask you about the infrastructure of preservation and sustainability, the sustaining of media, how texts are sustained and stored so that they can be recirculated over time.

CAJETAN IHEKA: Storage and archiving are challenges for African media. Sometimes media scholars struggle to find a film from the 60s or 70s because of the problem of conservation. But digitality has created new pathways, with agencies and organizations funding depositories, archives of African transcripts. I haven't done much work on media conservation in the African context but the Internet, the digital sphere, with all its problems, is offering African media spaces of archiving. I agree that scholars by writing, discussing these media, are somehow encouraging their preservation. It is also interesting that cultural productions now function as archives for environments that are disappearing due to economic development in parts of Africa, due to mineral extraction. It is important to preserve these cultural forms but also to think of the way they are preserving something.

MIRIAM TOLA: Your book engages with scholarship of digital labor. Could you explain your contribution to these debates?

CAJETAN IHEKA: In considering this scholarship I realized that it tends to prioritize the digital sphere over the material. It is the glamourous work that happens on the Internet that gets most attention in discussions on digital labor. But the digital does not exist a vacuum, there is a material structure that makes possible working in the digital sphere. Part of my intervention is highlighting some of the material dimensions of digital labor. What happens when digital equipment becomes obsolete, how will it be replaced, how and where will it be disposed? To attend to the materiality of the digital, I focus on electronic waste pickers working in Agbogbloshie, Ghana (see Chapter 2). Is their work part of digital labor? Focusing on the recycling work of the metal pickers and the ecological pollution in this location, I argue that we cannot dissociate these dirty processes from the shiny part of digital labor. When we bring the material and immaterial together, we get a more realistic sense of digitality as it is in practice.

KIU-WAI CHU: This question is coming from my work with Chinese ecomedia. We often talk about China as a whole, but then there are important regional specificities that tend to be overlooked. The same is true with Africa. Do you see any significance in developing more regional approaches to African ecomedia, looking for instance to Nigerian ecomedia?

CAJETAN IHEKA: I think that there's room for that. The term African ecomedia is a useful categorical expression but the chapters in my book are grounded in specific localities. Of course, there is so much more that could be done. Based also on the work of young scholars that I am seeing, my sense is that in the future there will be more attention to the heterogeneity of African spaces in ecomedia studies, ecocriticism and the environmental humanities.

MIRIAM TOLA: Your book also focuses on race and the relations between Blackness and ecomedia. Do you see yourself in conversation with Armond Towns's book *On Black Media Philosophy*?

CAJETAN IHEKA: Part of what drives our projects is the concern with the ways in which Black people have been represented, misrepresented or marginalized from the media and how media philosophies and practices change when we put Black people at the center. In *African Ecomedia* (Chapter 2), I engage a question that the Kenyan farmer and activist Kisulu Musya asks in Julia Dahr's climate change film *Thank You for the Rain* (2017): "Why can't we be seen?" I think this is a shared concern but, in my case, African people and ecologies become central participants in media cultures, as producers, as subjects and as victims.

ANTONIO LÓPEZ: Where would you like to see the field of ecomedia go in the next future?

CAJETAN IHEKA: I would like to see more attention devoted to areas that so far haven't found much space in ecomedia and the environmental humanities. I hope that these fields will really expand and diversify in terms of geographies, topics and people being published. On a different note, I've been interested in ongoing discussions about the post-carbon world and I would like to ask: post-carbon for whom? What will happen in places such as the Niger Delta when we move into a post-carbon world? I hope we will pay attention to this question. Finally, I would like us to reach the point when media studies will address the materiality of *all* media and realize that *all* media practices have ecological consequences. When that happens, the descriptor eco- in ecomedia will become irrelevant. We are not there yet, but I think that this is the ultimate goal, and the hope that I have going forward.

Further Reading

Garcia Espinosa, Julio. 1979. "For an Imperfect Cinema." *Jump Cut* 20: 14–26.

Garritano, Carmela. 2020. "Waiting on the Past: African Uranium Futures in Arlit, Deuxième Paris." *Modern Fiction Studies* 66 (1): 122–40.

Iheka, Cajetan. 2022. *Teaching Postcolonial Environmental Literature and Media*. New York: Modern Language Association.

Moradewun, Adejunmobi. 2016. "African Media Studies and Marginality at the Center." *Black Camera* 7 (2): 125–39.

Nyamnjoh, Francis B. 2011. "De-Westernizing Media Theory to Make Room for African Experience." In *Popular Media, Democracy and Development in Africa*, edited by Herman Wasserman, 19–31. London: Routledge.

References

Iheka, Cajetan, 2021. *African Ecomedia: Network Forms, Planetary Politics*. Durham, NC: Duke University Press.

7
ECOMEDIA AND EMPIRE IN THE US–MEXICO BORDERLANDS, 1880–1912

Carlos Alonso Nugent

In 1881, the photographer Ben Wittick created *Acequia Madre, Albuquerque, New Mexico* (Figure 7.1). In blurry black and white, Wittick showed two children standing by an acequia—a type of irrigation ditch that Nuevomexicanas/os and Pueblos developed to survive in the Upper Rio Grande. But as he illuminated one environment, Wittick also incorporated several others—those that furnished the glass for his photographic plates, and those that became paper and ink for his final stereographic prints. And as he reflected on bonds among particular people and places, he also reshaped a wider variety of human-nonhuman relations, for along with other railroad photographers, he helped attract the settlers who would drink the Rio Grande dry.

Through these independent yet intertwined acts, Wittick epitomized the multiple meanings of the "eco-" in "ecomedia studies." For years, this prefix pointed to "media" that seemed avowedly "ecological," so just as ecocriticism emerged by analyzing nature writing, ecomedia studies first focused on wildlife films (Mitman 1999) and nature photographs (Dunaway 2005). However, as the field came together in articles, books, and collections, it endowed its eponymous prefix with additional meanings. Today, the "eco-" reflects a recognition that media are always material: whether their production is carbon-neutral or energy-intensive, and whether their consumption concludes in recycling centers or at scrapyards, they are always "environmental participants" (Maxwell and Miller 2012, 9). More abstractly, the "eco-" signals a sense that we might use media's materiality to rethink relations among humanity and nonhumanity—that we might read squid ink clouds as interspecies inscriptions (Jue 2020), or that we might measure radioactive particles for their meaning-making potential (Mukherjee 2020). As ecomedia studies plays with these possibilities, it thus "flip[s]" the "old idea that media are environments" to suggest that "environments are also media" (Peters 2016, 3). Considering the communicative capacities of complex video games, primordial elements, and so much more, the field helps us face planetary predicaments at once all-too-human and more-than-human.

With ecomedia studies taking new turns, the time is ripe to reassess older conversations. As readers of this *Handbook* will recall, Harold Innis helped create media studies in part through what we might call comparative imperial studies (1950, 1951). To understand how media technologies enabled and/or disabled imperial power, Innis ranged from ancient Egypt and Mesopotamia to twentieth-century Europe and North America. Out of this vast archive, Innis pulled a provocative hypothesis: if "durable" media like clay and stone were "biased" toward time (and well-suited

This chapter has been made available under a CC-BY-NC-ND license.

Figure 7.1 Ben Wittick, *Acequia Madre, Albuquerque New Mexico* (1881a,b)

to religious ideology), and if "light" media such as paper were "biased" toward space (and useful for bureaucratic management), then empires rose and fell by balancing or failing to balance these "biases." Although he was not known for his modesty, Innis acknowledged that proving his hypothesis would be all but impossible. Yet in the following decades, his ideas became conditions of possibility. Even when not cited explicitly, these ideas animated influential approaches to media and/against imperialism: they echoed through Angel Rama's account of the "lettered cities" that ruled the Spanish Empire (1984), they resounded with Benedict Anderson's argument about "print capitalism" and/as nationalism (1983), and they reverberated in scholarship on Indigenous and settler sign systems (from Mignolo 1995 to Garcia 2020). However, as Innis's ideas spread across the humanities, they became less fashionable within media studies: among the thousand or so paper and panel titles at the 2021 and 2022 Conferences of the Society for Cinema and Media Studies, the words "empire," "imperial," and "colonial" (along with their prefixes and suffixes) appeared just 51 times.

If this number turns out to be a low point instead of a last gasp, it will likely be in large part thanks to ecomedia studies. Whether engaging images like Wittick's *Acequia...* or infrastructures like actual acequias, the field has proven that even the most apparently all-too-human empires always have more-than-human dimensions. Most broadly, it has shown how empires rest on the "geology of media" (Parikka 2015). More specifically, it has explained how empires exploit resources from precious metals to (non-)renewable energy sources (Maxwell and Miller 2012; Cubitt 2017). Crucially, it has demonstrated that empires extend through infrastructures—and that, as empires embed these infrastructures into the earth, they make even the largest dams and longest fiber optic cables start to seem natural (Starosielski 2015; Hu 2016; Mukherjee 2020). Through these insights, ecomedia studies has put comparative imperial studies on a firmer footing. But though it no longer advances such sweeping arguments, the field still comes to compelling conclusions. In one of her chapters, Jennifer Fay reexamines films of the nuclear bombs that the US detonated at its Nevada Test Site; as she demonstrates, these "atomic screen tests" "transform[ed] explosions into aesthetic experiences ... [and thereby] naturalize[d] this regime that leaves a stratigraphic signature in the planet's geological record" (2018, 17). In a different direction, Nick Couldry and Ulises Mejias reinterpret search engines, social media platforms, and the "social quantification sector"; by "tracing continuities from colonialism's historical appropriation of vast territories ... to data's role in contemporary life," they theorize a "data colonialism" in which "human life is ... annexed to capital" (2019, xi).

While ecomedia studies has reinvigorated comparative imperial studies, it has also driven debates about anti-imperial activism. On the one hand, the field has focused on writers and artists who expose "the ecological footprint of media technologies": bringing "insightful reading" to bear on both established and emerging voices, Cajetan Iheka explains that though Africa's environments may have "finite resources," its people possess "infinite resourcefulness" (2021, 2–3). On the other hand, the field has turned to social movements that fight against power plants, waste dumps, and similar sites: proving "there is no one kind of environmentalism in India," Rahul Mukherjee describes the "innovative ways that Indian environmental activists deploy media to spotlight" problems (2020, 28). Through these projects, ecomedia studies has illuminated anti-imperial activism in all its environmental complexity. In so doing, the field has contributed to conversations beyond its borders. Much as ecomedia scholar Hester Blum investigates (in)commensurabilities among US explorers and Inuit leaders (2019), Hemispheric American studies scholar Edgar Garcia highlights human-nonhuman networks that take shape as settler texts remediate Anishinaabe pictographs, Mayan hieroglyphs, and other Native signs (2020). Similarly, whereas I employ ecomedia studies in my article on "Latinx Literature in the Anthropocene" (2020), Curtis Marez works much more obliquely with the field in his book on migrant farmworkers who use visual media "for projecting competing futures" (2016, 3).

To deepen discussions about ecomedia and empire, the rest of this chapter reinterprets the rise of the New Mexico Bureau of Immigration (NMBI). Between 1880 and 1912, the NMBI printed at least 500,000 copies of at least 124 grandly written and lavishly illustrated publications (Nieto-Phillips 2004, 119). Since these ecomedia were comedically self-referential—in 1884 (6), one counted "2,450,000 octavo pages of carefully prepared, classified matter setting forth the advantages of the Territory"—it is easy to establish that they were related to resource extraction (Maxwell and Miller 2012; Cubitt 2017). In turn, since these ecomedia circulated along railroad routes, in irrigation districts, and at events like the 1904 Louisiana Purchase Exposition, it is simple to show how "new and old medias [became] layered atop of each other" so that they shaped environments (Hu 2016, 2). But while the ecomedia went so far as to thematize their tight links to resources (at the top of Figure 7.2, smoke billows from the "Colossus of Roads") and infrastructures (throughout the image, the railroad is a cardiovascular system), they did so in the service of something even more extraordinary. If John Durham Peters is right that all media are "containers of possibility" (2016), the NMBI's ecomedia are unusual in their commitment to—and eventually, their creation of—impossibilities. In an era when Natives and Nuevomexicanas/os controlled much of New Mexico, these ecomedia set the stage for Anglo sovereignty. And in a region whose heat and aridity challenged even sustainable agriculture, the ecomedia played fueled the rise of extractive agribusiness. At once material, infrastructural, and imaginative, these ecomedia of empire helped make the US–Mexico borderlands.

Figure 7.2 NMBI, *Illustrated New Mexico* (1883, 23)

Naturalizing Empire

In 1880, the New Mexico Territory had an immigration problem: under the US racial logic, it was not home to enough whites to become a fully fledged state.[1] To solve this problem, leaders founded the NMBI. Whereas their later counterparts would obsess over policing Latina/o migrants, these nineteenth-century leaders experimented with strategies for attracting white settlers. Initially, they tried to lure settlers to specific places, so in their second year (1881), they published *Report on Bernalillo County*, *Report of Doña Ana County*, and more. Eventually, they started providing settlers with ways of sensing vast spaces, rebranding the Territory as a *Land of Sunshine* (1904) and *Land of Abundant Water* (1908). As scholars have shown, the NMBI advanced derogatory arguments about Natives (Gutiérrez 1989) and Nuevomexicanas/os (Nieto-Phillips 2004, 118–43).[2] But as its geographically oriented titles attest, the NMBI never simply focused on Indigeneity or race: instead, it refracted these human identities through nonhuman environments. For every explicitly imperialist idea (in 1904, 133, it generalized about "the Indian [and] the Spaniard"), the NMBI devised dozens of environmental images (on that page, it spoke of "scenic attractions" as "beautiful … as any in the world"). At some points, it rendered these images in lithographs or photographs. At other points, it routed them through charts or tables in an early version of "infowhelm," Heather Houser's term that "captures [the] ready availability of information" and that "evokes emotional inundation without specifying the content of the emotion" (2020, 1). At every point, it complicated Jussi Parikka's claim that "nature affords and bears the weight of media culture" (2015, viii): while turning to "nature" for the material makings of its "media," it used these very media to naturalize empire.

The NMBI began this process in the all-important arena of sovereignty. Throughout its 32-year tenure, it was often forced to admit that New Mexico had an unsettling history, so while some of its ecomedia opened optimistically with sixteenth-century colonization (and thus longstanding Europeanization), others dwelled on the seventeenth-century revolt (when Pueblos drove settlers south of the Rio Grande) and still others evoked eighteenth-century wars (when Apaches and Comanches turned settlements into their servants).[3] However, when the NMBI recognized harsh realities, it sought reassurance not only in the ideology of Manifest Destiny (Gutiérrez 1989; Nieto-Phillips 2004) but also in theories of environmental (mis)management. In *Farming by Irrigation in New Mexico* (1897, Figures 7.3 and 7.4), the NMBI argued that Native Pueblos and Spanish land grants had "no foundation in law or equity" (55), that their water infrastructures were "rough" and "crude" (19), and that their inhabitants were "embarrass[ing]" (55). Then, just as later "agribusiness futurisms" would keep "workers of color" in view so they could be "subordinate[d] to the machinery of production" (Marez 2016, 11), the NMBI acknowledged Native and Nuevomexicana/o presence to create illusions of absence—to assert falsely that these peoples were unable to build big irrigation projects, develop private properties, or sell crops in a cash economy. Positing racial inferiority as both cause and consequence of environmental inefficiency, the NMBI thus offered readers ways of rearticulating violent dispossession as benign modernization. When squatters stole lands, they

Figure 7.3 NMBI, *Farming by Irrigation in New Mexico* (1897)

were able to feel like "law" and "equity" were on their side. And when bureaucrats redesigned acequias, they could justify themselves by celebrating "examples of modern irrigation construction" (1912, 2).

From undermining Native and Nuevomexicana/o sovereignty, it was only a small step to ameliorating Anglo environmental anxiety. In *Farming...* (1897), the NMBI began by noting "misapprehension ... in regard to the water supply." However, it then insisted that "nothing [could] be further from the fact" (12) and that the Rio Grande was the "Nile of America" (11). To support these claims, the NMBI offered "ocular demonstration[s], so far as a printed page [made possible], of the fact that there [was] plenty of water" (10). With lithographs (Figure 7.3), it helped readers see what it would be like to have "rain when [they] want[ed] it and seldom when [they] don't want it." In turn, with fold-out maps (Figure 7.4), it let them chart courses to either existing irrigation infrastructures or big blank spaces. By describing and then dismissing fears about arid environments, the NMBI prefigured the later institutions that built the Indian government's "radiant infrastructures": momentarily, it aligned itself with skeptical readers (in India, such readers criticized "carcinogenic radiations"), but eventually, it entrenched a public of gullible followers (in India, as in New Mexico, these basked in the "radiance" of a bright future) (Mukherjee 2020, 6–7). But while the Indian institutions found that "mediation accentuate[d] both aspects of radiance," with "the material effects of impalpable radiations" obscuring "the mediated radiance of...glistening objects," the NMBI ended up in a much more straightforward situation. Concealing crises of settler colonialism, racial capitalism, and ecological degradation, the NMBI's ecomedia were "an

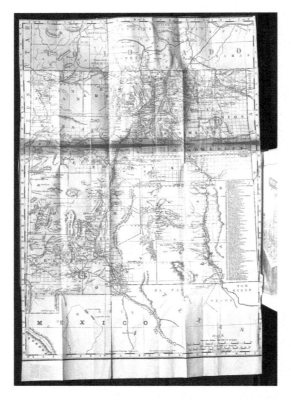

Figure 7.4 NMBI, *Farming by Irrigation in New Mexico* (1897)

'eye-opener' to people of the east, whose hazy ideas about 'the west'…receive[d] a strong and wholesome readjustment" (1904, ix). Like the photos and films that provided publics with "natural visions" (Mitman 1999; Dunaway 2005), the NMBI's ecomedia became all-too-human ways of conceiving and controlling more-than-human worlds.

Irrigation Media

Over the course of the twentieth century, US Americans came to rely on "petroleum media," Stephanie LeMenager's term for "the objects derived from petroleum that mediate our relationship … to other humans, to other life, and to things" (2013, 6). But in the late nineteenth century, they engaged with a wider range of ecomedia, and following LeMenager's lead, we might refer to the NMBI's as irrigation media. As we might expect, irrigation media often used the narrative templates of Manifest Destiny: a passage in *Farming...* (1897, 41) began in the past, when Natives and Nuevomexicanas/os believed that the "vast desert wastes" were "untillable for lack of water"; it then shifted into the present, with Anglos creating "constantly improving processes for the development and distribution of water"; and it concluded in the future, when "water will come—'white man' will get it, and those now vast desert wastes will teem with all the energies of American conquest." However, irrigation media also transcended templates, and if we accept Hester Blum's argument that "environment[s] and forms of communicative media are mutually constituted" (2019, 29), we will be able to see how and why. Embedded in an arid "environment," the NMBI came up with suitable "communicative" strategies, and from the old story of the frontier, it forged new bonds between scientific expertise, bureaucratic management, and utopian dreams (or dystopian nightmares?) for the borderlands. To some extent, it told readers what to believe, but for the most part, it taught them how to perceive—that is, how to use two techniques to reimagine and reshape the borderlands.

First, the NMBI showed readers how to transfigure physical forms—how to turn arroyos into aqueducts, deserts into cities, and, to quote the Pecos Irrigation and Improvement Company (1894, 1), drought-stricken plains into "land[s] of verdure and fruitfulness." After statehood, transfiguration was reduced to mere juxtaposition; thus, Burton Frasher's 1932 postcard *Yuccas in Bloom/Elephant Butte Dam* suggested that intimidating deserts could become magnificent dams in the blink of an eye (or the glance over a 4/6-inch page). In the territorial period, by contrast, transfiguration remained a complex series of esthetic and conceptual reorientations. Think back to *Farming...* (1897, 41). Despite its commitment to "conquest," the irrigation media hinged on the moment of (mis)perception when "mesas" and "plains" appeared as "productive farms" and "thriving towns." Amidst cliché claims about Manifest Destiny, it thus experimented with ways of comparing possible worlds, and while lurching between anxiety and arrogance, it taught readers to transfigure the desert. Through this pedagogical project, the NMBI contributed to what Jennifer Fay calls "the central conundrum of the Anthropocene … namely, that our collective efforts to make the planet … productive for human flourishing … are precisely the measures that have made this a less hospitable earth" (2018, 1–2). At the same time, the NMBI concealed this "conundrum" from view: as whites made New Mexico "less hospitable" to most Natives, most Nuevomexicanas/os, and almost all nonhumans, they continued experiencing the Territory as a "veritable Eden" (1881a,b, 3).

As the NMBI taught the amazing arts of transfiguration, it also modeled less prominent (but no less powerful) approaches to calculation. Like the twentieth- and twenty-first-century scientists who interest Houser (2020) and Jue (2020), the NMBI rendered nonhuman environments as human data: in *"Heart of the Well Country"* (1912, i), it credited New Mexico with "3,500,000

Figure 7.5   NMBI, *Heart of the Well Country* (1912)

acres of irrigable land" and "5,000,000 acres of DRY FARMING land." However, to an extent that would surprise its later counterparts, the NMBI not only converted qualitative knowledge into quantitative data but also replaced material entities with monetary values such as "$16.50 per ton" and "$500 per acre" (6). Through these twinned types of calculation, the NMBI forged a feedback loop (Figure 7.5). At the start of the loop, the NMBI used "actual experiment[s]" to support statements like "50,000 pounds of onions can be produced to the acre *as a rule*" (1883, 111), and by extension to stir readers to build irrigation media into the land. In the second stage of the loop, the resulting infrastructures freed water from its spatio-temporal limits, so where Natives and Nuevomexicanas/os had lived near natural rivers, Anglos expanded along man-made aqueducts, and where earlier inhabitants had endured interminable dry spells and unpredictable monsoons, the new generation secured water from storage dams. From this point forward, the loop was self-sustaining: as irrigation infrastructures imposed capitalism's predictable and profitable cycles, irrigation media could boast that "there [could not] be, by any possibility, a failure of crops through either drouth or drowning" (1897, 20), and as extractive industries turned "the infinite [into their] familiar" (Cubitt 2017, 14), boosters could claim to "control the rainfall" (Pecos 1894, 52). In short, media and materiality could be mirrors (Figure 7.5).

"Imperfect [Eco]media"

Between 1880 and 1912, the NMBI often engaged with environments that were more fictitious than factual. But over time, it helped produce the conditions it seemed merely portray. Most concretely, it attracted enough Anglos to make New Mexico the 47th state. More broadly, it inspired the Rio Grande Project (1905), the Middle Rio Grande Conservancy District (1925), and the later work of both the Bureau of Reclamation and the Corps of Engineers. In these twinned areas, the NMBI became both imaginative and infrastructural: while remaining an "eye-opener" that gave readers "strong and wholesome readjustment[s]," it became a basis for the power plants (Mukherjee 2020) and information networks (Starosielski 2015; Hu 2016) that pushed the borderlands to a breaking point.

But though the NMBI became intertwined with empire, it could not stop the circulation of "imperfect media"—Iheka's term for "low-carbon media practices and infrastructures of finitude that are critical for ameliorating ecological precarity" (2021, 10). In the century-and-a-half since Wittick turned photographic plates and chemical emulsions into *Acequia...*, Nuevomexicanas/os and Pueblos have used millions of imperfect ecomedia to maintain actual acequias. From democratically developed "reglas y reglamentos" (rules and regulations) to individually maintained "libros del tesorero" (treasurer's ledgers) to an amazing array of paintings, poems, and performances, these ecomedia have preserved resilient subsistence ecologies at the heart of an extractive capitalist economy.[4] Since there is not enough space in this chapter to give these ecomedia their due, I ask you to look again at *Acequia...*: in the mysterious, *Mona Lisa*-like eyes of the little girl, you may yet be able to see possibilities outside of and in opposition to empire.

Notes

1 This chapter is too short to engage the excellent scholarship on Indigeneity, race, and nationality in New Mexico's territorial period. Entry points into these conversations include Nieto-Phillips (2004); Gómez (2007); and Mora (2010).
2 In addition to the fine work of Gutiérrez and Nieto-Phillips, I would be remiss not to mention the early essay by Lang (1976). However, I use this essay as little as possible simply because it is so racist: to take

just one example, it laments that "the Hispano…used his innate political talents to oppose [the] new social and economic order" (194).
3 On these histories, return to Gómez (2007) and Mora (2010). Then see Blackhawk (2008).
4 For a revelatory reading of these media, see Rivera (1998).

Further Reading

Blum, Hester. 2019. *The News at the Ends of the Earth: The Print Culture of Polar Exploration*. Durham, NC: Duke University Press.
Couldry, Nick and Ulises Mejias. 2019. *The Costs of Connection: How Data is Colonizing Human Life and Appropriating It for Capitalism*. Palo Alto, CA: Stanford University Press, 2019.
Hu, Tung-Hui. 2016. *A Prehistory of the Cloud*. Cambridge: MIT Press.
Iheka, Cajetan. 2021. *African Ecomedia: Network Forms, Planetary Politics*. Durham, NC: Duke University Press.
Mukherjee, Rahul. 2020. *Radiant Infrastructures: Media, Environment, and Cultures of Uncertainty*. Durham, NC: Duke University Press.

References

Anderson, Benedict. 1983. *Imagined Communities: Reflections on the Origin and Spread of Nationalism*. London: Verso.
Blackhawk, Ned. 2008. *Violence over the Land: Indians and Empires in the Early American West*. Cambridge: Harvard University Press.
Cubitt, Sean. 2017. *Finite Media: Environmental Implications of Digital Technologies*. Durham, NC: Duke University Press.
Dunaway, Finis. 2005. *Natural Visions: The Power of Images in American Environmental Reform*. Chicago, IL: University of Chicago Press.
Fay, Jennifer. 2018. *Inhospitable World: Cinema in the Time of the Anthropocene*. Oxford: Oxford University Press.
Garcia, Edgar. 2020. *Signs of the Americas: A Poetics of Pictography, Hieroglyphs, and Khipu*. Chicago, IL: University of Chicago Press.
Gómez, Laura. 2007. *Manifest Destinies: The Making of the Mexican American Race*. New York: NYU Press.
Gutiérrez, Ramón. 1989. "Aztlán, Montezuma, and New Mexico: The Political Uses of American Indian Mythology." In Rudolfo Anaya and Francisco Lomeli, eds. *Aztlán: Essays on the Chicano Homeland*. Albuquerque, NM: Academia/El Norte: 172–90.
Houser, Heather. 2020. *Infowhelm: Environmental Art and Literature in an Age of Data*. New York: Columbia University Press.
Innis, Harold. 1950. *Empire and Communications*. Oxford: Clarendon Press.
———. 1951. *The Bias of Communication*. Toronto: University of Toronto Press.
Jue, Melody. 2020. *Wild Blue Media: Thinking Through Seawater*. Durham, NC: Duke University Press.
Lang, Herbert. 1976. "The New Mexico Bureau of Immigration, 1880–1912." *New Mexico Historical Review* 51.3: 193–214.
LeMenager, Stephanie. 2013. *Living Oil: Petroleum Culture in the American Century*. Oxford: Oxford University Press.
Marez, Curtis. 2016. *Farm Worker Futurism: Speculative Technologies of Resistance*. Minneapolis: University of Minnesota Press.
Maxwell, Richard, and Toby Miller. 2012. *Greening the Media*. Oxford: Oxford University Press.
Mignolo, Walter. 1995. *The Darker Side of the Renaissance: Literacy, Territoriality, and Colonization*. Ann Arbor: University of Michigan Press.
Mitman, Gregg. 1999. *Reel Nature: America's Romance with Wildlife on Film*. Cambridge: Harvard University Press.
Mora, Anthony. 2010. *Border Dilemmas: Racial and National Uncertainties in New Mexico, 1848–1912*. Durham, NC: Duke University Press.
New Mexico Bureau of Immigration. 1881a. *Report on Bernalillo County*. Albuquerque, NM: Daily Journal Book and Job Office.

———. 1881b. *Report of Doña Ana County.* Santa Fe: New Mexican Printing Company.
———. 1883. *Illustrated New Mexico.* Santa Fe: New Mexican Printing Company.
———. 1884. *Report of the Bureau of Immigration.* Santa Fe: New Mexican Printing Company.
———. 1897. *Farming by Irrigation in New Mexico.* Santa Fe: New Mexico Bureau of Immigration.
———. 1904. *The Land of Sunshine.* Santa Fe: New Mexican Printing Company.
———. 1908. *San Juan County: A Land of Abundant Water* (1908). Santa Fe: New Mexico Bureau of Immigration.
———. 1912. "*Heart of the Well Country.*" Albuquerque: New Mexico Bureau of Immigration.
Nieto-Phillips, John. 2004. *The Language of Blood: The Making of Spanish-American Identity in New Mexico, 1880s–1930s.* Albuquerque: University of New Mexico Press.
Nugent, Carlos Alonso. 2020. "Latinx Literature in the Anthropocene." *ISLE: Interdisciplinary Studies in Literature and Environment.* 27.3: 453–71.
Parikka, Jussi. 2015. *A Geology of Media.* Minneapolis: University of Minnesota Press.
Pecos Irrigation and Improvement Company. 1894. *The Pecos Valley of New Mexico.* Colorado Springs, CO: Gazette Printing Company.
Peters, John Durham. 2016. *The Marvelous Clouds: Toward a Philosophy of Elemental Media.* Chicago, IL: University of Chicago Press.
Rama, Angel. 1984. *La ciudad letrada.* Hanover, NH: Ediciones del Norte.
Rivera, José. 1998. *Acequia Culture: Water, Land, and Community in the Southwest.* Albuquerque: University of New Mexico Press.
Starosielski, Nicole. 2015. *The Undersea Network.* Durham, NC: Duke University Press.

8
SPATIAL DOCUMENTARY STUDIES, *EL MAR LA MAR,* AND ELEMENTAL MEDIA REMEDIATED

Janet Walker

The borderzone that is the domain of this chapter was constituted as such in the mid-nineteenth century and turned into a corridor that people pass along, at risk of their lives and vulnerable to attack. As Sandro Mezzadra and Brett Neilson write in *Border As Method*, the "tracing and institution of borders since late antiquity" has been surrounded by "fog and dirt, violence and magic" (2013, vii). And yet, as these thinkers also emphasize, there is the possibility, indeed the reality, that "subjects in transit" contest the border on a regular basis (25).

The U.S.–Mexico border was drawn across the Sonoran Desert, a North American ecoregion of approximately 100,000 square miles known not only for its extremely high temperatures and aridity but also for summer thunderstorms and frigid lows in its subalpine valleys and high mountains. In 1994, the U.S. Border Patrol established a strategic plan known as Prevention through Deterrence. The plan aimed to pinch off access points in populated areas such as El Paso, Texas and San Diego, California, in order to force would-be migrants from Mexico and Central and South America through rugged areas, or, as the report baldly states, through "more hostile terrain, less suited for crossing and more suited to enforcement" (U.S. Border Patrol 1994, 7). However, since being deterred is not an option for many migrants, Prevention through Deterrence and its successive contortions have twisted this desert into a space of brutality and loss.

Jason De León's consequential book, *Land of Open Graves: Living and Dying on the Migrant Trail,* exposes the strategic plan as one that "outsource[s]" violence to desert "actants," including temperature and terrain (2015, 60), and advocates the amelioration of attendant harms (see also the Undocumented Migration Project directed by De León 2009–present). For its part, the Tucson-based humanitarian organization No More Deaths/No Más Muertes reports that the Border Patrol has recorded the remains of nearly 8,000 people recovered from the United States borderlands between 1998 and 2019, dead from exposure, dehydration, falls, wounds, animal causes, and human assaults (2021).[1]

Obviously, the desert is not a perpetrator. The violence of this zone is anthropogenic and systemic. It stems from the economic, sociocultural, and geopolitical substrates of policy-as-perpetration, which are themselves reliant on the historical and continuing racial animus against immigrants of color that shapes and is fanned by U.S. immigration policy (Ewing 2021, Gramlich and Scheller 2021). And then there is the violence of various actors, including smugglers, vigilante groups, and members of the Border Patrol.

The fossil-fueled heating of the Earth's climate system also operates in and through patterns of race-based prejudice and injustice, in both its extractive operations and its situational specificity. As Carmen Gonzalez states, there is an integral relationship among "climate change, race, and migration," namely the "disproportionate burdens [that climate change imposes] on racialized communities all over the world" who will be—are being—"expelled from their homes in record numbers as the climate emergency intensifies" (2020, abstract and 1). The dry corridor—extending from Panama north through Costa Rica, Nicaragua, El Salvador, Honduras, Guatemala, and parts of Mexico—is expanding due to climate disruption. Lessening and increasingly unpredictable rainfall is contributing to a loss of crops, widespread malnutrition, competition for resources, and a further necessity to relocate that, for this reason too, cannot be deterred (Feng, Kruegger, and Oppenheimer 2010, Blitzer 2019, Gramlich and Scheller 2021, Kennedy 2022).

This chapter probes what has been termed the weaponization of the Sonoran Desert as a case of the weaponization of geography more broadly (Boyce, Chambers, and Launius 2019, Shivone n.d., Navarro 2020) and offers several analytical moves against weaponization from the perspective I think of as critical environmental media justice studies: first, spatial documentary studies "as method" with roots in human geography; second, a cartographically attuned "shot mapping" of the feature documentary *El Mar La Mar* (Bonnetta and Sniadecki, 2017) in light of borderzone thinking that is anti-racist, environmentally just, and condemnatory of state violence[2]; and third, the insistence that elemental media be understood in relation to the "set of extractions, from particular subject positions, from black and brown bodies, and from the ecologies of place" to which inhuman geography is heir (Yusoff 2018, 15). With this chapter, I seek to countermap a multidirectional cartography being razed upon the Sonoran Desert, and to support the necessity—and vitality—of strenuous crossings into geosocial futures.

Spatial Documentary Studies

Spatial documentary studies, as I intend it, is a cartographically attuned analytic for the study of site-specific or situated documentaries. In practice, it involves the identification and shot mapping of specific locations where the camera was set up and shots taken, for the purpose of revealing the co-constitution of film and place (Gray, Petermon, and Walker 2011, Walker 2013). To know the meaning of a situated documentary's entanglement in sociopolitics as well as culture, it is necessary to understand the "where" of its mediatic inhabitation as well as the historical when and the rhetorical what, how, and why the film was made (Bowles and Mukherjee 2017).

The genealogy of this spatial study is that of Lefebvrian human or cultural geography, extended by scholars who understand space as socially produced, with power dynamics entailed (Harvey 2001, Lefebvre [1974] 1991, Massey 2005, Soja 1989). As Irit Rogoff explains, human geography's cognizance of palpable features such as "land masses, climate zones, elevations, bodies of water, populated terrains, nation states, geological strata and natural resource deposits" is accompanied by a defetishizing sense of space (2000, 21). From this perspective, geography is "an epistemic category in turn grounded in issues of positionality," in "questions of who has the power and authority to name" and the "power and authority to subsume others to its hegemonic identity" (21). I am particularly taken with Rogoff's insight that "every topography and every text is doubly inhabited by irreconcilable positions" (110–11).

The "geohumanities" or "spatial humanities" bring together critical GIS geography, art, history, and the moving image (Bodenhamer, Corrigan, and Harris 2010, Dear et al. 2011). Here my focus is at the intersection of mapping, borderzones, and documentary where geographic knowledges are formative of the struggles at hand. In John Pickles's view, a map can serve as "archive for geo-referenced data, as picture of the spatial order of the world, as tool for investigating spatial relations" (2004, 9). Indeed, critical cartography scholars, including Pickles, understand the investigative role of maps as fully *instigative* as well. Maps exercised power, wrote J.B. Harley, often "[running] ahead of the settled frontier, preceding the axe and the plough" (2002, 144).

Turning to cinema, we have the benefit of Tom Conley's and Giuliana Bruno's field-shifting cartographically inclined work (see also Aitken and Zonn 1994, Lefebvre 2006, Rhodes and Gorfinkel 2011). In *Cartographic Cinema* (2007), Conley describes the map-to-film relationship as "strangely coextensive." "Films *are* maps," he asserts (1, 20; see also Castro 2009, 9). Giuliana Bruno, for her part, writes about the motion picture as a form of "site-seeing" that is "the very synthesis of seeing and going—a place where seeing *is* going" (2002, 245). It is my conviction that the work of these two scholars who dwell on cinema in general with ample reference to fiction film is all the more applicable to the spatial study of situated documentaries. A documentary film shot in one or more particular locations is a map of the territory in which it inheres; that is to say, a documentary film—like all maps—is co-constitutive of a complex territory it may purport only to observe. And it is also a navigational technology that foregrounds the transit through the landscape of makers, perhaps subjects, and certainly spectators. Usually shot in multiple locations, over a period of time, and then assembled (out of shooting order) in the editing process, a situated documentary inhabits its filming locations while simultaneously constituting a creative geography—creative, like all geographies, but as a representational text, perhaps doubly so.

The map that the Prevention through Deterrence document provides below the signature line depicts four "Avenues of Approach" as chunky arrows through which migrants (labeled "aliens" in the report) would presumably stream northward across the border (U.S. Border Patrol 1994, 17).[3] The legend notes the use of hatch marks for "Obstacles"—overlaying mountainous and other extreme desert areas. But as I will show, *El Mar La Mar*-as-map gives lie to this Anthropocenic cartography with its neat edges and blank white space inside the arrows, revealing instead the Sonoran Desert as a space "inhabited by irreconcilable positions," persons, and more-than-human beings, elements, and forces. The next section puts into practice this cartographically induced heuristics[4] of spatial documentary studies to surface an alternative mapping of the desert, in which directional diversity suggests possibilities for a more just borderscape.

A Cartographically Attuned Reading: *El Mar La Mar* and "Unwalling" the Borderzone

The opening shot was filmed by J.P. Sniadecki with an Aaton LTR54 Super 16-mm camera on his shoulder as he leaned out of his Volkswagen window to frame and unframe—to make both visible and invisible—the border wall of this stretch of the Sonoran desert region. Sniadecki's operation of the camera, as he described it to me, was guided by actively "changing focal length, focus, and framing angle, while also adding different micro-movements and also letting … my hands or my body move along with the landscape, the wall, and the vehicle as well" (Sniadecki 2021) (Figure 8.1). The place was the U.S.–Mexico border; the car was moving from west to east (actually, from northwest to southeast) along a service road parallel to the border wall in the area of Sasabe, Arizona (Figure 8.2). Originally one long take, the finished sequence unspools for nearly three minutes, comprising the entire opening section of the film: "Rio." We see hard-edged iron-colored vertical posts, with greenery visible through the spaces between. As the focal length and focus change, "we" move forward, swivel sideways, and pull back out. A flash of white is visible at one point. Might this be the clothing of a person, running along on the other side of the wall?

Spatial Documentary Studies

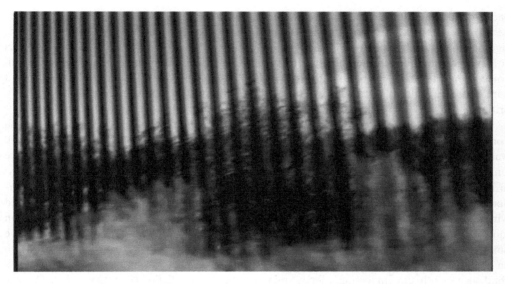

Figure 8.1 The border wall prior to its disappearance from *El Mar La Mar*. Image by Joshua Bonnetta and J.P. Sniadecki, included with permission

Figure 8.2 Shooting along the border wall, "changing focal length and ... focus"

As it happens, this is more or less the last we see in *El Mar La Mar* of this iconic, lethal border wall. Sniadecki has said that the film is not about the border per se but about the desert. Other images of human-built sectioning are also few and far between. For tribal nations who trace their belonging to the area back to time immemorial, international borderlines are a new development. With its compelling visuals—long takes of dry, drenched, and fiery desertlands—and its complex soundscape that includes the audio of more than seven speakers from different backgrounds, the film seems to pause attentively while people, nonhuman animals, and other desert features make their own impressions. One of Vinicius Navarro's main points in his significant article about the film is that it actively "produces" desert encounters of various types "often by creating unexpected juxtapositions between sound and image or by using the human voice as a means to imbue place with lived reality" (2020, 35). *El Mar La Mar*'s rendering of a borderless and multiply inhabited desert is astute, aspirational, performative—and cinematically brilliant.

The pattern, I submit, is one of "unwalling." Architect Teddy Cruz and political scientist Fonna Forman have developed the concept and set of practices of "unwalling citizenship" to "challenge walled-worlds everywhere" and the socially unjust perseveration on the wall that fortresses the United States (2020, 1; see also Rael 2017). The wall is material *and* semiotic, or more succinctly, in Brian Larkin's theorization of infrastructure, a "concrete semiotic" (2013, 329). Only a portion of the border has been physically fortified, and the various types of barriers—from barbed wire to high-tech surveillance systems (Rael 2017, 11)—vary in their permeability by people on foot. Humanitarian organizations and the U.S. Customs and Border Protection agency both have pointed to the wall's ample contradictions and porosity. The wall has *not* been shown to cut down on unauthorized entry. According to a Border Patrol spokesman, "a surveillance video filmed a child successfully circumventing a fence" minutes after its installation (Fan 2006, 716). There is no clear data on how many people are entering the U.S. by crossing the Southern border (Boyce 2019, 31). A significant percentage of people who are not authorized to be in the U.S. did not "sneak in" across the Southern border but arrived through other channels. These uncertainties call into question the "effectivity" of the wall in its Trumpian imagination. Exploring "unwalling" is not meant to downplay the harm that nativist physical or wishful walling has wreaked on would-be border crossers or asylum seekers, as a state of violence outsourced to the desert, and racism outsourced to the wall, but rather to approach it from a different perspective.

El Mar La Mar enacts its cinematographic and editorial schema of "unwalling" not only by avoiding images of the wall but also through the mosaicking of a multidirectional and multiscalar creative geography. With the enormous benefit of information shared with me by J.P. Sniadecki—spatial documentary studies depends on the generosity of filmmakers—I turn now to the work of orienting and wayfinding enabled by the film's mediatic, ambulatory, and—congruent with the third main section of this study—*inhuman* geographical logics.

Mediatic: Film as Map

The U.S.–Mexico national border is generally rendered as a distinct line, more horizontal than vertical and, in the westward logic of Manifest Destiny, put right through from the Gulf of Mexico to the Pacific Ocean. To take a media-rich example, the major interactive mapping project by USA Today Network prominently includes imagery of the more or less horizontal line overlaying the drawn landscape, with embedded videos shot from an east to west helicopter flight that readers/viewers access by clicking or dragging a helicopter icon to a spot along the borderline ("The Wall—Interactive Map Exploring U.S.–Mexico Border" 2021). In a certain way, trajectories from the south to the north also emphasize east-west linearity as a discrete boundary to be crossed. Miguel Fernández Labayen has discussed in the European context how, for migrants, "jumping the fence" can become ingrained and ritualized (2021). In other worlds, the "funneling" effect of Prevention through Deterrence, however paradoxically, serves to further emplot the horizontal border.

But if the map is in some sense the territory, it is also a form of mediatic statecraft that could be designed otherwise. As the wall disappears in the film, so does latitudinal movement along the border.[5] *El Mar La Mar*'s spatial logic attempts to "dissipate" or "destabilize," in Sniadecki's terms, the "physical material existence" and "symbolic power" of the typical border proximity and axis (personal communication with Snaidecki 2021). Sniadecki reported to Scott MacDonald that they "filmed in the hills or lost in a canyon, sometimes not sure which side we were on … to try to disrupt the perception of clear 'sides'" and the "dominant logic of the border" (MacDonald 2019, 492). Then too, during the filming periods, Bonnetta and Sniadecki hiked water and supplies with the Tucson Samaritans: on the Mexican side, from the port of entry in Nogales to the Juan Bosco Migrant Shelter; and on the U.S. side, along canyon trails frequented by economic refugees coming across (personal communication 2021).[6]

The second and longest section of the film, "Costas," establishes the film's primary visual esthetic of long, still takes, heart-stopping compositions marked by heat and shade and height and depths and all the ravages of this hardscrabble environ. And it scrambles horizontal linearity in favor of a creative geography that is diverse by virtue of scale, location, and direction. In other words, the film's shots have been taken from various spots (and at various times) throughout the Sonoran Desert (and beyond), composed on drastically different scales, with camera set-ups looking in different directions. A close-up of a Mexican banknote, object survivor of its owner, flutters on the ground in the Organ Pipe National Monument [1:19:00 min]. A close-up of a young woman's hand writing Neruda's poetic lines on a plastic water jug was shot near an altar for safe passage that border-crossers have created in the vicinity of Arivaca Lake [34:40 min] (Figure 8.3). A medium longshot of a woman lowering herself into a natural water source [38:27 min] was made in the Arivaca area "down toward the abandoned mining town of Ruby," as Sniadecki explained it.[7] The longshot of a flag marking an emergency spot for people in distress [55 min] was made north of Brown Canyon off of highway 286, North of Sasabe, "about 22 miles north, at the highway's middle region towards Three Points." In another stunning longshot, a train poised against the mountain curves toward the camera in Cochise County east of Benson [17:27 min].[8] Then, as

Figure 8.3 Image from *El Mar La Mar* by Joshua Bonnetta and J.P. Sniadecki

Figure 8.4 Grid infrastructure in the vicinity of the Arivaca Lake Reservoir. Image from *El Mar La Mar* by Joshua Bonnetta and J.P. Sniadecki

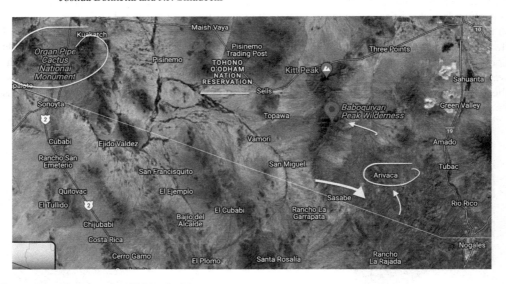

Figure 8.5 Shot-mapping *El Mar La Mar*

specific evidence of the film's insistent multidirectionality, compare a shot of communications grid infrastructure taken south of the Arivaca Lake Reservoir and oriented toward the northwest [53 min] (Figure 8.4) with a firescape, including Baboquivari Peak, taken from Brown Canyon looking west [9:30 min and 1:08:07 among other spots]. While distance and arrival remain pressing in this "fatal environment,"[9] viewpoints swivel as the natural and human-built environment meets the camera lens head-on (Figure 8.5).

Ambulatory: Navigating the Desert

This film's use of voiceover is extraordinarily compelling and acoustically accordant with this film-as-map. With one exception, the main speakers are not shown on camera. Instead, in their pairings with the visuals or with black screen as a kind of visual, the voices-over create an audible "map" that is also, like the film's visual edition, variable in its geometry and multidirectional. Some of the interviews were conducted in the immediate area (for example, at a dump that people call "the mall"), while others were conducted elsewhere. Some of the voices-over are used such that they emanate across images of the desert and, be it in addition or alternatively, over black screen (with white subtitles for Spanish language translation). A male speaker tells of his encounter with migrants who returned in search of the brother they had had to part from along the way in order to go for help. Although they had left provisions and a fire for his keep, the brother did not survive. Two other migrants who made it into the U.S. tell of the rigors of their journey accompanied by the audible weeping of one of the men. A young woman who contributed her interview from New York City tells of the volunteer work she had done as a college student with Tucson Samaritans and De León.

This young woman interviewee is a former archeology student who worked with De León (personal communication with Sniadecki 2021). What she describes is her experience when she and others, including De León, discovered the body of woman, dead from exposure. Carmita Maricela Zhagui Puyas, wife and mother of three who traveled from Ecuador and died, walking in the United States.[10] Rael (2017) refers to the whole border region as "Usonia," adapting Frank Lloyd Wright's original meaning of the term encompassing Mexico and the USA as the United States of North America. Depending on their location and sometimes not knowing where they are, crossers often must continue walking long after they pass the invisible line marking U.S. territory. Maricela Zhagui died of exposure at age 30 in the summer of 2012, in the Sasabe corridor, in the United States (De León 2015; see also Arizona OpenGIS Initiative for Deceased Migrants). Through her cartographic theory and practice, Tara Plath also provides a new and non-bordercentric understanding of the relationship among crossers, officials, humanitarian workers, and the ecology of the desert (2020).[11]

Another voice, speaking in Spanish, is that of a man who crossed some years ago and contributed his interview from Chicago (personal communication with Sniadecki). His voiceover, accompanied by English subtitles, is added over windblown grasses, a flower waving the breeze, shots of personal effects abandoned on the dry earth. He speaks of hearing his own footsteps "muted and hollow" and of staying with an older man who had fainted, of striving to follow "the traces of the others" lost in the wind. Then over black screen, we are given the story of how he eluded a patrol—and his philosophy of the desert: "walking again through a rocky area with shrubs" as if "arriving on the shore of the desert." The patrol finds a larger group of people and loads them into trucks. He sees them with dilated pupils, but they don't see him because he is just one person. He concludes:

> The desert at night is just like the day
> and your sky is like a roof of light
> At night you can see
> the reflection of the moon and stars on the sand
> It's an illuminated room
> You don't get lost because you can't see
> You get lost because you don't know where you are

Navarro writes that the film itself "evokes the disorientation voiced in migrants' testimonies" (2021, 35). I appreciate his point. Many crossers have perished due to the disorientation this speaker describes in stirring language. "You get lost because you don't know where you are." Yet, here I want to make two points that elude the paradigm of disorientation. First, listening to this speaker, we learn how his navigational process relied on qualities of the desert that withstand weaponization, and on his own abilities of sensing and proprioception: "the reflection of the moon and stars on the sand;" the dilation of his pupils. Then, too, it is possible to distinguish between, on the one hand, the disorientation of various "subjects in transit" and, on the other hand, the film's own multidirectionality as precisely, a distinct formal pattern that is thoroughgoing in the film and resistant to spatial practices of walling, funneling, and extraction.

Inhuman Geography: Remediating Elemental Media

In his "philosophy of elemental media," John Durham Peters quoting Jochen Hörisch affirms that "well into the nineteenth century when one spoke of *media*, one typically meant the natural elements such as water and earth, fire and air" (Peters 2015, 2). "In the life sciences ... gels and other substances for growing cultures" are media (3). Indeed, in many public-facing documents put out by government agencies in charge of land, air, and water, the term "media" is used for those elements. Peters proposes reversing the idea that "media are environments." "Environments are also media," he argues (3). Furthermore, since media are "vehicles that carry and communicate meaning" (3), environments-as-media also have a carrying capacity, existing as "repositories of readable data and processes that sustain and enable existence" (4). "[O]f course clouds have meaning," Peters concludes (4).

The Sonoran Desert and *El Mar La Mar* are readable repositories of existence sustaining data—media, if you will. In the desert, residents, crossers, trackers, and media makers; more than 500 species of animals and more than 2,000 species of plants; along with rivulets, sedimentary and volcanic rock, tectonic plates, 2-billion-year-old Precambrian outcroppings, and rays of sunlight; all of these over vastly varying timescales have found their way in place and taken up habitation there.[12] A massive fire at the base of Brown Canyon attracted Bonnetta and Sniadecki who spent a whole day and into the night filming, skirting the fire lines, edging closer and closer—and subsequently distributed the resulting images throughout the film. At another point, one of the unseen interlocutors speaks of learning to track, while a low rise silhouetted against a blue sky with pink clouds fixes our attention. He tells how the sand and wind inscribe—and disperse—footprints; how the body of a passing animal may have shed a twig that a person would likely carry a ways before dropping. The Sonoran Desert and *El Mar La Mar* in their respective idioms announce this environment as a more-than-human character and witness to the intense and multiscalar activity of its ecosystem.

As another dimension of this chapter's concentration on resistance in the borderzone, I want to advocate the remediation of elemental media studies from the perspective of Yusoff's "inhuman geography;" the latter being a field of study aware of the ways that nineteenth-century geology "mapped life and earth during a certain time with consequences for race" (Yusoff 2022). A central thread of *A Billion Black Anthropocenes or None* (Yusoff 2018) is the presentation of historical instances of the intertwinement of the "White Geology of the Anthropocene" with slavery and the plantation economy.[13] For Yusoff, these geological contingencies constitute a "racialized optic razed on the earth" (2018, 15 and 23). Here I am seeking to engage with the weaponization of the Sonoran Desert as another crucial entwinement of inhuman geography in the borderzone confluence of race, migration, climate, and mapping at the end of the twentieth and into the twenty-first century.

Spatial Documentary Studies

Figure 8.6 Baboquivari Peak. Image from *El Mar La Mar* by Joshua Bonnetta and J.P. Sniadecki

But then, pressing elemental media studies toward critical inhuman geography—remediating elemental discussions with their racialized historical antecedents and present-day geopolitics—we might comprehend the Sonoran Desert as a formidable environment that in and of itself challenges the borderlining, deterrence, and their racist consequences.[14]

In this connection, I will hazard a further reading of *El Mar La Mar*'s film-as-map and antiracist optic that defies narrowly elemental analytics. Through the dual lens of spatial documentary studies and inhuman geography, the film in its materiality also invokes oil extraction and Indigenous presence. First, and admittedly briefly, in its capacity as an archive of extraction, the film includes several images (a gate, a blimp) captured in the U.S.'s largest oil-producing state of Texas. These I regard as trace elements of a state among other states (including my own) where fossil fuel industry stakeholders are inflicting profound damages on human and more-than-human environments; and I urge the importance of recognizing the trace elements and petroeconomics as such.

Then, the inhuman geography of this film "about the desert" encompasses awareness of the decimation and dispossession of Native American peoples. Though not overtly or through the film's roster of speakers as far as I know, the film touches the unfathomably deep, atrocious, and ongoing history of the racist, extractive regime on which this settler state and its wealth are contingent. The Tohono O'odham Nation, or, that is, their predecessors and ancestors from thousands to hundreds of years ago, inhabited a huge area extending south into what is now Sonora, Mexico, north into what is now central Arizona, west to the Gulf of California, and east to the San Pedro River (official website of the Tohono O'odham Nation n.d.). They lived and continue to live with and protect the land and water, as "master dwellers of the desert" (Community Development Financial Institution: Tohono O'odham Nation n.d.) and through their traditional ecological knowledge. In 1854, the U.S.–Mexico border was solidified across this nation's tribal territory. In yet another destructive mapping, the borders of the Tohono O'odham reservation were drawn to exclude Baboquivari [15]

Baboquivari Peak is a mountain sacred to the Tohono O'odham peoples. With its distinctive outline, it is regarded as the navel of the world; here the earth opened up and the people emerged after the great flood. Indigenous mapping of Baboquivari Peak is relevant information that I do not purport nor presume to possess. But based on an effort to inform myself, my supposition is that Baboquivari Peak would loom large on Indigenous maps and not be confined to the modes of scale common to western topographic traditions (Binnema 2001, Hershey, McCormack, and Newell 2014, Rivard n.d.).

Sniadecki told me that they tried not to overuse images of Baboquivari but could not resist its pull (Figure 8.6). It is amply present in the film, seen in many lights and weathers and through the flames of a fire at its base. The film's visual celebration of this sacred mountain is another archive of a sort, one that is suggestive of desert geographies beyond borderlining.

Tormenta: Expanded Cartographies

The final section of the film—a stormy landscape shot west of Ambos Nogales (the communities of Nogales, Arizona and Nogales, Mexico) and east of the Tohono O'odham Nation Reservation—is aptly titled "Tormenta." The emotional power of these shots is amplified by the soundtrack, a reading of the poem "Primero Sueño" by seventeenth-century Mexican writer Sor Juana Inés de la Cruz. Indeed, the borderscape in the Sonoran Desert—at the present time—is a raging tempest.

Moving in sync with *El Mar La Mar*'s directional diversity, ambulatory paths, and remediatic qualities, I have sought to envision a countermap of the Sonoran Desert that is resistant, aspirational, and more fully humane. Then, moving in sync with inhuman geography and bringing this mode of thought together with elemental media studies, I have sought to understand this specific borderzone as part of the racist Anthropocene that Yusoff calls us to "rewor[k] and reconstitute[e] in terms of agency *for* the present, *for the end of this world* and the possibility of others" (2018, 105). This chapter embraces the potential of spatial documentary making and spatial documentary studies to help transform violent fixations of place, media, and environment into new forms of agency for the present and the future already upon us.

Acknowledgments

J.P. Sniadecki's insights, information, and generosity in talking with me about filming locations and the meanings of *El Mar La Mar* made this chapter possible. As did this extraordinary film by Joshua Bonnetta and J.P. Sniadecki. I would like to thank those who heard and offered thoughts about portions of this chapter-in-progress, including at SCMS 2021 and at the 2021 Steve Tisch School of Film and Television International Lecture Series at Tel Aviv University, with special thanks to Alisa Lebow, Patricia Zimmermann, Ohad Landesman, and Raya Morag, brilliant colleagues who invited, encouraged, and responded to this work in their official capacities, and in friendship. My thanks as well to the members of the 2022 Colby Summer Institute in Environmental Humanities workshop who engaged with this work-in-progress and shared their consequential projects: Waqia Abdul-Kareen, Eyad Houssami, Moritz Ingwerson, Jordan Kinder, Zeynep Oguz, Christiana Zenner, and Christopher Walker, the latter also an Institute convenor. Deep gratitude to Kathryn Yusoff as the leader of our workshop and for the profound inspiration of her work and her friendship. With special thanks to Elizabeth DeLoughrey for her radiant seminar leadership and for moving conversations along with Jill Didur. With appreciation for Stephen Borunda and Tara Plath, and the influence of their respective, activist commitments and desert grounding. And to Lisa Parks and Nicole Starosiekski with boundless gratitude. Finally, my warm thanks to the co-editors of this volume for their encouragement and astute suggestions at crucial moments.

Notes

1 While citing the Border Patrol's official figure of 7,805, the 2021 report by No More Deaths/No Más Muertes discusses the presence of and reasons for the Border Patrol agency's substantial undercounting. This topic is also documented in mainstream as well as human rights news sources, including a *New York Times* article by Varjacques and Ma (2019) where De León's estimate that "for every body found there are five to ten people who have simply disappeared" is reported.
2 In his important article on the film, Vinicius Navarro states that "The weaponization of nature by U.S. government agencies is a thread throughout *El Mar La Mar*" (2020, 36).
3 I wish to acknowledge that this chapter does not undertake the study of Mexican maps of Mexico's northern border.
4 Here I am adapting the term "geographically induced heuristics" used by von Lünen and Moschek (2011, 249).
5 In fact, Bonnetta and Sniadecki began their project by following the first leg of Alexis de Toqueville's and Gustav de Beaumont's 1831 journey to New Orleans, and then carried on by driving to west Texas, in sight of the border wall in El Paso/Juarez, and then in a westerly direction into New Mexico and Arizona (MacDonald 2019, 489). By the end of the filming, they had made several trips together.
6 I have not set foot in the Sonoran Desert, nor could I do so with the vulnerability and risk to life and limb that migrant crossers face. I offer this chapter in allyship, committed to reading and writing for environmental justice in the U.S.–Mexico borderzone.
7 Arivaca, Arizona was an important fieldwork site for De León who suggested it to Bonnetta and Sniadecki (personal conversation with Sniadecki 2021).
8 This image may be associated with "The Beast" ("La Bestia"), or the "Train of Death," that runs from Mexico's southern border into the capital, and then beyond to Mexico's northern border with the US, with hundreds of thousands of migrants in some years riding atop its roof.
9 This term is adapted from Richard Slotkin (1998, *The Fatal Environment*).
10 De León traveled to Ecuador to meet and get to know Zhagui's family members. He writes about them in *Land of Open Graves*, reconnecting a life lived to a woman who might otherwise have died with little notice, a statistic on roles of official and humanitarian organizations, a red dot on a map.
11 According to Plath (2020), migration is generally mapped by enforcement, official, and humanitarian organizations with a focus on searching in particular zones and plotting the coordinates where human remains have been located. The resulting patterns are usually seen as indicative of changing migration routes. But Plath's own cartographic research and activist and creative practice yields different findings. Remains of people who have perished on the way have been found, not only in crossing corridors but also in a much broader area—wherever they have been are sought. The pattern of deaths, Plath concludes, must be understood in relation to "patterns of authorized activity," as well as in relation to "spatial and ecological conditions of the desert" and "clandestine activities of migrants themselves" (11 of 29). Plath's "expanded reading of the map" (11 of 29) foregrounds *intersecting paths*, thereby providing a fuller border ecology. An undergraduate student in my documentary seminar, M.J. Macias, engaged with Plath's article, provided a brilliant reading of *El Mar La Mar*'s imagery, and added a personal interview of her own to the archive of testimonies by those who have crossed.
12 As Edward S. Casey writes so evocatively, "The lived body is coterminous with place because it is by bodily movement that I find my way in place and take up habitation there" (2000, 180).
13 One of Yusoff's particularly sharp examples of the intertwinement of the histories and realities of geology and slavery is the discussion of Geological Society of London's president Charles Lyell's mid-nineteenth century publications on geologic surveying in North America.
14 I would like to thank Jordan Kinder for his encouragement to understand the agential quality of the desert and his suggestion of specific language.
15 Currently the mountain is located in the Baboquivari Peak Wilderness, an area of Arizona administered by the U.S. Bureau of Land Management.

Further Reading

Borunda, Stephen. 2022. "A Body Downwind of the Atomic Attack at Trinity: Mediations of Atomic Coloniality in Nuevo México," *Media+Environment* 4, issue 1 (August): unpaginated. https://doi.org/10.1525/001c.36561.

Gonzalez, Carmen G. 2020. "Climate Change, Race, and Migration," *Journal of Law and Political Economy* 2020:109–46.

Plath, Tara. 2020. "From Threat to Promise: Mapping Disappearance and the Production of Deterrence in the Sonora-Arizona Borderlands," *antiAtlas Journal* #4:1–29.

Walker, Janet. 2018. "Media Mapping and Oil Extraction: A Louisiana Story," *NECSUS* 7, 2 (Autumn): unpaginated (https://necsus-ejms.org/media-mapping-and-oil-extraction-a-louisiana-story/).

Yusoff, Kathryn. 2018. *A Billion Black Anthropocenes or None*. Minneapolis: Minnesota University Press.

References

Aitken, Stuart C. and Leo Zonn, eds. 1994. *Place, Power, Situation, and Spectacle: A Geography of Film*. Lanham, MD and London: Rowman and Littlefield Publishers, Inc.

Arizona OpenGIS Initiative for Deceased Migrants (humaneborders.info/app/mapp.asp).

Binnema, Theodore. 2001. "How Does a Map Mean? Old Swan's Map of 1801 and the Blackfoot World," in *From Rupert's Land to Canada*, eds. Theodore Binnema, Gerhard J. Ens, and R.C. Macleod. Edmonton and Alberta: The University of Alberta Press.

Blitzer, Jonathan. 2019. "How Climate Change is Fuelling the U.S. Border Crisis," *The New Yorker* (April 19).

Bodenhamer, David J., John Corrigan, and Trevor M. Harris, eds. 2010. *The Spatial Humanities: GIS and the Future of Humanities Scholarship*. Bloomington: Indiana University Press.

Bonnetta, Joshua and J.P. Sniadecki. 2017. *El Mar La Mar*.

Bowles, Ryan and Rahul Mukherjee. 2011. "Documentary and Space: Introduction," and their co-edited Special Issue of *Media Fields Journal: Critical Explorations in Media and Space,* issue 3: unpaginated (http://mediafieldsjournal.squarespace.com/introduction-issue-3/).

Boyce, Geoffrey, Samuel N. Chambers, and Sarah Launius. 2019. "Body Inertia and the Weaponization of the Sonoran Desert in US Boundary Enforcement: A GIS Modeling of Migration Routes through Arizona's Altar Valley," *Journal on Migration and Human Society* 7, 1:23–35.

Bruno, Giuliana. 2002. *Atlas of Emotion: Journeys in Art, Architecture and Film*. New York: Verso.

Casey, Edward S. 1987. *Remembering: A Phenomenological Study*. Indianapolis: Indiana University Press.

Castro, Teresa. 2009. "Cinema's Mapping Impulse: Questioning Visual Culture," *The Cartographic Journal* 46, 1:9–15.

Conley, Tom. 2007. *Cartographic Cinema*. Minneapolis: University of Minnesota Press.

Cruz, Teddy and Fonna Forman. 2020. "Unwalling Citizenship," *e-flux Architecture* (November) (http://www.e-flux.com/architecture/at-the-border/358908/unwalling-citizenship/).

De León, Jason. 2015. *The Land of Open Graves: Living and Dying on the Migrant Trail*. Oakland: University of California Press.

Dear, Michael, Jim Ketchum, Sarah Luria, Doug Richardson, eds. 2011. *GeoHumanities: Art, History, Text at the Edge of Place*. London and New York: Routledge.

Ewing, Walter. 2021. "The Legacy of Racism with the U.S. Border Patrol," *Special Report by the American Immigration Council* (February 10) (https://www.americanimmigrationcouncil.org/research/legacy-racism-within-us-border-patrol).

Fan, Mary D. 2006. "When Deterrence and Death Mitigation Fall Short: Fantasy and Fetishes as Gap-Fillers in Border Regulation," *Law & Society Review* 42, no. 4:701–34.

Feng, Shuaizhang, Alan B. Kruegger, and Michael Oppenheimer. 2010. "Linkages among Climate Change, Crop Yields and Mexico–US Cross-border Migration," *PNAS* 107, 32:14257–14262.

Gonzalez, Carmen G. 2020. "Climate Change, Race, and Migration," *Journal of Law and Political Economy* 2020:109–46.

Gramlich, John and Alissa Scheller. 2021. "What's Happening at the U.S.–Mexico Border in 7 Charts," *Pew Research Center*, November 9 (https://www.pewresearch.org/fact-tank/2021/11/09/whats-happening-at-the-u-s-mexico-border-in-7-charts/).

Gray, David, Jade Petermon, and Janet Walker. 2011. "Mapping Documentary: Roundtable with Filmmaker Ido Haar and Film and Media Studies Scholar Janet Walker in Conversation with David Gray and Jade Petermon," *Media Fields Journal: Critical Explorations in Media and Space,* issue 3: unpaginated (http://mediafieldsjournal.squarespace.com/mapping-documentary/2011/8/21/mapping-documentary-roundtable-with-filmmaker-ido-haar-and-f.html).

Harley, J. B. 2002. *The New Nature of Maps: Essays in the History of Cartography*. Baltimore, MD: The Johns Hopkins University Press.
Harvey, David. 2001. *Spaces of Capital: Towards a Critical Geography*. New York and London: Routledge.
Hershey, Robert Alan, Jennifer McCormack, and Gillian E. Newell. 2014. "Mapping Intergenerational Memories (Part I): Proving the Contemporary Truth of the Indigenous Past," Arizona Legal Studies Discussion Paper No. 14–01.
Kennedy, Sarah. 2022. "The Deadly Connections between Climate Change and Migration," *Yale Climate Connections* (July) (https://yaleclimateconnections.org/2022/07/the-deadly-connections-between-climate-change-and-migration/).
Labayen, Miguel Fernández. 2021. "Dissenting Narratives and the European Border Regime: Mobile Phone Videos by Migrants at the Moroccan-Spanish Border," talk presented at the annual meeting of the Society for Cinema and Media Studies (March).
Larkin, Brian. 2013. "The Politics and Poetics of Infrastructure," *The Annual Review of Anthropology* 42:327–43.
Lefebvre, Henri. [1974] 1991. *The Production of Space*. Trans. Donald Nicholson-Smith. Malden, MA, Oxford and Victoria: Blackwell.
Lefebvre, Martin, ed. 2006. *Landscape and Film*. New York and London: AFI/Routledge.
MacDonald, Scott. 2019. *The Sublimity of Document: Cinema as Diorama (Avant-Doc 2)*. New York: Oxford University Press.
Macias, M.J. 2021. "Animating Red Dots: *El Mar La Mar*, Space, and Migration," Unpublished student paper for the course Film and Media Studies 189CD: Contemporary Documentary, University of California, Santa Barbara.
Massey, Doreen. 2005. *For Space*. London: Sage.
Mezzadra, Sandro and Brett Neilson. 2013. *Border As Method: Or, The Multiplication of Labor*. Durham, NC: Duke University Press.
Navarro, Vinicius. 2020. "On Uncertain Ground: Place and Migration in *El Mar La Mar*," *Film Quarterly* 73, 4:33–40.
No More Deaths/No Más Muertes and La Coalición de Derechos Humanos. 2021. "Left to Die: Border Patrol, Search and Rescue, & the Crisis of Disappearance," online (February 3) (https://nomoredeaths.org/new-report-left-to-die-border-patrol-search-rescue-and-the-crisis-of-disappearance/).
Peters, John Durham. 2015. *The Marvelous Clouds: Toward A Philosophy of Elemental Media*. Chicago, IL: University of Chicago Press.
Pickles, John. 2004. *A History of Spaces: Cartographic Reason, Mapping, and the Geo-Coded World*. New York: Routledge.
Plath, Tara. 2020. "From Threat to Promise: Mapping Disappearance and the Production of Deterrence in the Sonora-Arizona Borderlands," *antiAtlas Journal* #4:1–29.
Rael, Ronald. 2017. *Borderwall as Architecture: A Manifesto for the U.S.-Mexico Boundary*. Oakland: University of California Press.
Rhodes, John David and Elena Gorfinkel, eds. 2011. *Taking Place: Location and the Moving Image*. Minneapolis: Minnesota University Press.
Rivard, Étienne. n.d. "Colonial Cartography of Canadian Margins: Cultural Encounters and the Idea of *Métissage*," *cartographica* 43, 1:45–46 (doi:10.3138/carto.43.1.45).
Rogoff, Irit. 2000. *Terra Infirma: Geography's Visual Culture*. London and New York: Routledge.
Shivone, Gabe. n.d. "Death as 'Deterrence': The Desert as a Weapon," *Alliance for Global Justice* (https://afgj.org/death-as-deterrence-the-desert-as-a-weapon).
Slotkin, Richard. 1998. *The Fatal Environment: The Myth of the Frontier in the Age of Industrialization, 1800–1890*. Norman: University of Oklahoma Press.
Sniadecki, J.P. 2021. Conversation with Janet Walker via Zoom (February 28).
Soja, Edward W. 1989. *Postmodern Geographies: The Reassertion of Space in Critical Social Theory*. London: Verso.
"The Wall—Interactive Map Exploring U.S.-Mexico Border." 2021. USA Today Network (https://www.usatoday.com/border-wall/us-mexico-interactive-border-map/).
Tohono O'odham Nation. Official Website. n.d. (http://www.tonation-nsn.gov/history-culture/).
Tohono O'odham Nation, Community Development Financial Institution. n.d. (http://cdfiton.org/~ton/index.php/88-homepage).

Undocumented Migration Project. 2009–present. Director Jason De León. Hostile Terrain 94 is a participatory art project and exhibition series, mounted under the auspices of the Undocumented Migration Project (https://www.undocumentedmigrationproject.org/home).

U.S. Border Patrol. 1994. "Border Patrol Strategic Plan: 1994 and Beyond." *National Strategy* (July).

Varjacques, Leah and Jessica Ma. 2019. "To Stop Border Crossings, the U.S. Made the Journey Deadlier," *New York Times*, Opinion (May 29) (https://www.nytimes.com/interactive/2019/05/29/opinion/migrant-crisis.html).

von Lünen, Alexander and Wolfgang Moschek. 2011. Without Limits: Ancient History and GIS," in *GeoHumanities: Art, History, Text at the Edge of Place*. Michael Dear, Jim Ketchum, Sarah Luria, Doug Richardson, eds. New York and London: Routledge: 241–250.

Walker, Janet. 2013. "'Walking through Walls': Documentary Film and Other Technologies of Navigation, Aspiration, and Memory," in *Deeper than Oblivion: Trauma and Memory in Israeli Cinema*. Boaz Hagin and Raz Yosef, eds. London and New York: Continuum: 329–356.

Yusoff, Kathryn. 2018. *A Billion Black Anthropocenes or None*. Minneapolis: Minnesota University Press.

Yusoff, Kathryn. 2022. "Geoethics for an Anti-Racist Earth," lecture presented at the Colby Institute in Environmental Humanities (August 5).

9
ECOMEDIA LITERACY
Bringing Ecomedia Studies into the Classroom

Antonio López

For scholars and educators wanting to incorporate ecomedia into their instruction, this chapter introduces ecomedia literacy and offers a brief overview of analytical methods that can be used for teaching. Ecomedia literacy combines ecomedia studies scholarship explored in this book with the tools of critical digital and media literacy. At its core, literacy

> involves gaining the skills and knowledge to read and interpret texts of the world and to successfully navigate and negotiate its challenges, conflicts, and crises. Literacy is thus a necessary condition to equip people to participate in the local, national, and global economy, culture, and polity.
>
> (Kellner and Share 2019, 3)

Media literacy "has always been about demystifying the structures of media, information, and communications technologies and preparing students to identify how and why media are constructed, along with implications and effects related to social, economic, and political power" (López, Share, and Redmond 2022, 467). Ecomedia literacy expands this by prompting learners to make sense of how ecomedia infrastructures and our engagement with them connect with ecojustice for the present and future. Ecomedia literacy aims to foster a transformative shift in cultural behaviors, attitudes, and media practices by promoting eco-ethical norms and eco-citizenship. (López 2021).

Like legacy scholarly traditions associated with media studies, historically the field of media literacy has not addressed environmental concerns (López 2014). However, there are some examples of environmentally themed media education to draw from. Project Look Sharp authored several environmental media literacy curricula based on constructivist pedagogy (Sperry 2020), and Gabriele Hadl (2016) penned a Japanese textbook on ecomedia literacy. Critical media literacy scholars connect a variety of social concerns, such as ideology, class, patriarchy, racism, gender, violence, and war with ecojustice (Kellner and Share 2019). Jocelyn Miller et al. (2021) associate media and science literacy with evaluating climate claims. Jennifer Rauch's (2018) "slow media" approach joins media literacy and "unplugging" to cultivate environmental awareness. Greg Garrard's (2016) edited volume offers methods for teaching ecocriticism in the classroom. Tema Milstein et al. (2017) bridge environmental communication with pedagogy. As a contribution to the

This chapter has been made available under a CC-BY-NC-ND license.

field, I was involved with co-editing (along with Jeff Share and Theresa Redmond) a special joint issue of *The Journal of Media Literacy* and *Journal of Sustainability Education* on ecomedia literacy, which includes over 20 articles and feature case studies and teaching examples. My book *Ecomedia Literacy: Integrating Ecology into Media Education* (López 2021) bridges research with pedagogical approaches from ecoliteracy, education for sustainability, systems thinking, critical media literacy, science literacy, and visual studies.

The divergent paths and debates in media literacy are beyond the scope of this chapter; however, I want to highlight how ecomedia literacy's holistic approach does bridge different strands within the field. Standard media literacy principles and research methodologies are used to analyze/deconstruct media texts by drawing on ecocriticism in combination with content, semiotic, narrative, discourse, and multimodal analysis. Students research media and technology organizations to develop information literacy. Environmental impacts are calculated utilizing environmental, climate, and science literacy. News literacy is used to detect and critically engage media bias, propaganda, and disinformation. Artistic expression and aesthetics are explored through the literacy of media language. To holistically inventory media infrastructures, students require systems literacy. Engaging media affect and sensory experience can be achieved through mindfulness and medium literacy.

The suggestions in this chapter are prompts to inspire thinking across curricula and levels. This is not aimed at more advanced studies but more for "beginners" with entry points into basic media and journalism studies to include both theory and practice. In addition to giving an overview of curriculum development, I offer two analytical methods that can be used for specific research projects: the "ecomediasphere" and the "iceberg model" of systems thinking.

Ecomedia Studies and Curriculum Development

A curriculum overhaul is not necessary to get started. One can make minor changes or additions to build confidence and familiarity with the material (López, Share, and Redmond 2022). An essential move is to challenge the conventional definition of media to update it with the underlying premises of ecomedia discussed in this *Handbook* (media that are *about* and *of* the environment). Educators can then include a lesson that reflects the environmental impacts of various media being taught, whether it's Web 3.0 (blockchain, NFTs, cryptocurrencies), AI, film, video games, radio, news, TV, photography, or anything else covered in this volume. In addition to classic reading/textual analysis, there are various journalistic and production activities that can be utilized in ecomedia literacy, many of which are inspired by David Buckingham's (2019) extensive survey of media literacy education practices (for detailed examples see López 2021, 231–75).

Students can track their experience of space, place, and time with self-reflective practices, such as slow media approaches advocated by Jennifer Rauch (2018) by doing digital sabbaths, fasts, or detoxes that are meant to help reduce media usage and renegotiate media habits through mindfulness (for a nuanced discussion of digital "opting out," see Kuntsman and Miyake 2022). Students can engage how media impact a variety of emotional responses and physiological phenomena, such as alienation, biophilia (love of nature), biophobia (fear of nature), technophilia (love of technology), sense of place, sublime, technology addiction, disrupted natural biophysical rhythms, cognitive dispositions that drive responses to media (such as selective exposure or confirmation bias), and mental health. Sound, color, shape, form, and light are nervous system stimuli and should be explored as physiological phenomena. Sara Pink (2015) has developed sensory ethnography by exploring ways in which smell, taste, touch, and vision can be interconnected and interrelated within research. Phenomenological inquiry (Parks 2016, 148) and auto-ethnography are other methods. These approaches can broadly be defined as cultivating media mindfulness, which is the ability to be conscious of how our cognition and sensory experience interacts with media.

Building on Paolo Freire's (Freire and Macedo 1987) concept of reading the world as text and engaging in praxis, research projects and outcomes should be built around problem finding and problem solving that directly relate to students' lived experience. To achieve this, the method of backward design (see Wiggins and McTighe 2005) is recommended by practitioners of education for sustainability. It starts with what you want students to know and then works backward to scaffold skills and concepts. As a solution-based method, it's based on a predetermined rationale, such as how the curriculum unit prepares students to engage in eco-citizenship and technology design. It combines an essential question (a compelling question that focuses on teaching and drives inquiry and learning), outcomes (what students should understand, know, and be able to do), and assessment method (evidence used to demonstrate student learning) (Cloud Institute for Sustainable Education 2011, 60–61). For example, learners can be charged with the following query: How can the news media ecosystem be redesigned to afford collective climate action?

Ecomediasphere

Students can engage in holistic ecomedia analysis using a heuristic I developed called the "ecomediasphere," an analytical tool that facilitates the exploration of the symbolic, cultural, material, phenomenological, and ideological character of ecomedia objects (López 2021). An ecomedia object is a boundary object: something that has commonly agreed upon characteristics, but whose meaning and function changes according to context. For example, a smartphone will have different purposes according to designers, manufacturers, app developers, workers, cobalt miners, and users. An ecomedia object can scale from micro (text/gadget) to macro (ICTs, hyperobjects). The unit of analysis is one of four categories: (1) representational media text (advertisement, news article, film, TV commercial, website, food packaging, NFT, etc.); (2) platform (streaming service, social network, or media organization); (3) gadget (smart phone, tablet, computer, etc.); or (4) hyperobject (an amorphous disbursed phenomena that behaves like a system, such as the internet, cryptocurrency, disinformation, or media industry). Representational ecomedia objects that deal specifically with ecological issues have the dual condition of being "images of ecology" while also being part of an "ecology of images," i.e., an ecology of meaning systems (Ross 1994). Likewise, they are also "resource media" that are as essential and material to daily life as water and power (Bozak 2011).

Using the ecomediasphere as an orientation device, the ecomedia object is explored from four different zones: ecoculture, political ecology, ecomateriality, and lifeworld (see Figure 9.1). If we study climate disinformation as an ecomedia hyperobject, the *ecocultural* perspective examines the kinds of values driving the debate around the climate crisis. This means attending to how particular stories/memes/news items are shareable/spreadable through shared belief systems. *Political ecology* addresses how disinformation is driven by and thrives as a result of media oligarchy, carbon- and consumer-based capitalism, attention economy, far-right media ecosystems, and surveillance capitalism. This includes the impact of algorithms, clickbait, and actors producing climate disinformation. *Ecomateriality* focuses on medium properties, such as the affordances and constraints of a particular medium (like using a Facebook app on a smartphone) but also on the material infrastructure and energy consumption of surveillance capitalism at the heart of climate disinformation (López and Frenkel 2022). *Lifeworld* addresses the cognitive dispositions and sensory experience of individuals. One of the biggest obstacles to climate action is cognitive. As systems thinking theorists assert, people are invested and entrenched in worldviews, which are disrupted by the reality of the climate crisis (Meadows 1991).

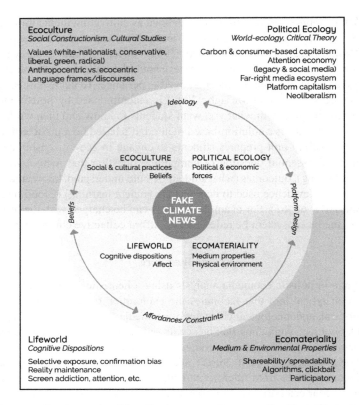

Figure 9.1 The ecomediasphere using fake climate news as the ecomedia object. Illustration by Priya Sage

The ecomediasphere guides students toward answering larger questions (like those developed using the backwards curriculum design method):

- Structure the class by dividing the semester into four zones as a general survey of ecomedia issues or choose one ecomedia object as the focus of the entire course and divide the schedule into four zones.
- Have students perform an analysis of an ecomedia object as a specific assignment (choosing from the categories of text, gadget, platform, or hyperobject).
- Assign students to investigate a personal gadget according to the four zones.
- Work in groups to study a category of ecomedia (streaming, print, phones, sound, video games, alternative media, art, film, entertainment, etc.) and do a multimedia presentation or build a website to go with it.
- Substitute the four zones with the elements: fire (energy), water, air, and earth, and examine the ecomedia object according to the lens of those elements.

In choosing ecomedia objects to study, one doesn't have to go for examples of environment per se (i.e., "mimetic or realistic depictions of nature") but can choose them for their *environmentality*, "for evidence of the way a text's language and form encodes a construction of and subsequent interaction with that text's environment" (James 2016, 66). Ecomedia objects should also be explored from the perspectives of those traditionally disenfranchised from the power structure.

Drawing insight from feminist standpoint theory, which situates knowledge and experience from the perspective of women and marginalized populations, students should study ecomedia objects from different vantages to explore power relations. For example, what if students examined their personal gadget from the perspectives of a Congolese child laborer extracting rare earth minerals, Chinese FoxConn assembler, "playbour" gamer, Amazon warehouse worker, or big box store sales associate? Roleplaying activities can be used to explore these different perspectives.

Iceberg Model of Systems Thinking

When probing an ecomedia object we are asking, how is the world in it? How is it in the world? And, where does it come from? (see Dumit 2014). One way of achieving this is the iceberg model of systems thinking, which treats ecological problems as design challenges rooted in knowledge systems (Goodman 2002). This approach posits that systemic problems are unsolvable if we only react to events without examining how they are caused by underlying patterns (trends over time), systemic structures (policies, laws, infrastructure, how parts connect), and knowledge systems (assumptions, beliefs, attitudes). For example, the proverbial tip of the iceberg is the visible and immediate event, such as ecological disasters like forest fires, hurricanes, or oil spills. Normally they are treated as momentary catastrophic occurrences in which the damage is repaired but business as usual continues without solving the underlying problem that caused the event to occur. Systems thinking attempts to transform the core pattern that caused these events by exploring beneath the surface of the tangible event, such as restructuring our system to reduce or eliminate fossil fuel emissions that trigger extreme weather. It is at the deepest level, knowledge systems, where solutions grow, leading to the design of new systems.

When applied to ecomedia literacy, the *event* is the expression of an ecomedia object. In the case of climate disinformation, the media object is a tangible *cultural artifact* (meme, clickbait, advertorial, publicity, video/film, social media post, news article, podcast, etc.). The first level underneath the visible surface features *patterns* and *trends* over time, such as how climate disinformation exists as part of a range of texts distributed throughout social media, search engines, and various media ecosystems over time. This requires recognizing framing patterns that connect discourses across different texts to build a particular story about the world, such as rightwing ideology, or market ideology and discourses about the ecological transition. A deeper inquiry delves into *system design*: the political, economic, and cultural structures that interact with and influence the production of climate disinformation. Understanding this requires developing an overview of legacy media, surveillance capitalism, the rightwing media ecosystem, and the financial and intellectual backend of the fossil fuel industry that exploits these different systems. It's essential to examine cultural norms and analyze hegemonic global capitalist institutions (including Big Tech) that inform how and why particular patterns of news, propaganda, and disinformation emerge over time. This requires exploring the economic status quo that enables a feedback loop between fake climate news, platform algorithms that amplify outrage and conspiracies, and digital media infrastructure that exacerbates the climate crisis. The wider social concerns of political polarization, post-truth epistemological crisis, structure and funding of rightwing media, and the market failure of journalism need to be addressed at this level. Here, we should ask, what long-term tech and media reform strategies are necessary to address this? A broader systemic analysis demonstrates that there must be a major shift in how media and tech structure their businesses and how governments regulate these industries.

At the deepest level of analysis is *knowledge systems*, in particular the anthropocentric worldview and ideology that drives the whole system of climate disinformation. Fake climate news circulates in a taken-for-granted fossil fuel cultural environment that shapes our beliefs about the world (Corbett 2021). The dominant worldview of media and tech accepts risks associated with the extraction economy. This status quo business environment normalizes sacrifice zones and the externalization of costs to the periphery of the global economy. In the United States, the most ardent defenders of fossil fuel culture are often steeped in a worldview of petromasculinity, evangelical Christianity, and white nationalism (López 2022).

The following four levels of inquiry can be used to perform an iceberg systems thinking analysis. Event: What is happening?

- *Systems thinking (react)*: Describe tangible elements (what we can see, hear, or touch) and what we notice.
- *Elements to identify*: Sensory experience; cognitive responses; form; aesthetics; and medium properties (affordances and constraints).
- *Ecomedia elements*: Experience of time, space, and place; materials (minerals, chemicals, etc.); and emotional experience.
- *Guiding questions*: What media languages are used? What are its medium and aesthetic properties? What is your sensory and emotional response? What can you do or not do with it? What are its material "ingredients"?
- *Ecological evaluation*: Does it invoke biophilia (love of nature) or biophobia (fear of nature)? Does it create alienation, disconnection, or connection with the world? What attention does it require? Are there any mental health impacts? Are there addictive characteristics?
- *Methods, theories*: Formalism, affect, phenomenology, aesthetics, media grammar, and media ecology.

Patterns of behavior: What are trends over time?

- *Systems thinking (anticipate trends over time)*: Map and diagram.
- *Elements to identify*: Discourses, frames, symbols, stereotypes, distribution outlets, locations, genre conventions, intertextuality, and cultural and social positionality.
- *Ecomedia elements*: Identify and map ecological discourses, eco-symbols, eco-metaphors, coding of environmental ideology (anthropocentric vs. ecocentric), and binaries (like Nature/nature, human/animal).
- *Guiding questions*: What is the story being told? How is it being told (narratives, symbols, discourses, metaphors)? What symbolic and cultural resources are required to understand it? How does it connect to one's own experience? How is one able to respond to it?
- *Ecological evaluation*: How is the environment/ecojustice represented or absent? What is its ecological meaning or significance? How does it promote particular ecocultural identities? What are its environmental impacts? What media ecosystem does it belong to? How is it coded for particular environmental ideologies? What communities does it impact?
- *Methods, theories*: Semiotic, narrative, critical discourse analysis, ecocriticism, ecolinguistics, environmental humanities, and environmental communication.

Systemic structures: How are parts related? What influences patterns?

- *Systems thinking (design)*: Identify policies, laws, infrastructure, and how parts connect.
- *Elements to identify*: Economic structure of organization/s producing object; infrastructures required for it to be distributed and exist; regulations and laws that govern its production and use; explore platform design.

- *Ecomedia elements*: Social, economic, and financial goals of organization and their environmental impacts; economic model and conditions it was produced under and its energy requirements; recognize if it's part of an open or closed system.
- *Guiding questions*: How was it made? Why was this made and produced? What is its purpose and function? What problem/s is it trying to solve? Who made this (individual, NGO, corporation, state, or other kind of organization)? What kind of organization (corporation, for-profit, nonprofit, public, audience supported)? Who is the intended audience/target market? What media ecosystem does it belong to? What infrastructure and resources does it require?
- *Ecological evaluation*: Is it ecologically beneficial or harmful? Is it fair, accurate, truthful, authentic, and credible? What is left out? Is it real and true to life? Does it benefit, harm, or disadvantage anyone? What kind of politics does it express? How does it perform ideological work? How is it disposed of or repurposed? Are there systemic reforms or policy changes that need to be made to regulate how it is made? Does it promote consumerism or greenwashing? What kind of energy infrastructure does it require? Does it promote or limit eco-citizenship? Are there neocolonial discourses that reproduce Orientalism or denigrate BIPOC? What kind of agency does it promote?
- *Methods, theories*: Political ecology, ecomaterialism, infrastructure studies, cultural studies, media studies, ecocinema studies, and postcolonial studies.

Knowledge systems: What values, assumptions, and beliefs shape the system?

- *Systems thinking (transform)*: Assumptions, beliefs, attitudes, and epistemology.
- *Elements to identify*: Underlying, taken-for-granted beliefs about how the system should function; stories being told about how we should live.
- *Ecomedia elements*: Identify environmental ideology and ethics; epistemological and ontological systems; ecological stories-we-live-by.
- *Guiding questions*: What is valued? How does the ecomedia object express ideology? What is marginalized, othered, or devalued? Are "common sense" assumptions being reinforced or challenged?
- *Ecological evaluation*: How would you evaluate it according to ecojustice? Whose perspective is missing? Is the story ecologically beneficial or harmful? Are there risks associated with its production or usage?
- *Method, theories*: Social constructionism, critical realism, ecojustice, ecofeminism, cosmovisions, traditional ecological knowledge, and eco-ethics.

In sum, the ecomedia literacy method analyzes texts to extrapolate much larger social concerns and systemic processes that are indexical of underlying structures, patterns, and knowledge systems. Harkening to Foucault's notion of discursive formations, the event (as expressed in an ecomedia object) is a node in the historical discourse of the particular moment it was produced.

Conclusion

Ecologically oriented education fosters a paradigm based on systems thinking and the ecocentric value of the interconnectedness of humans, the more-than-human world, technology, and economics. To achieve this, we can use backward curriculum design based on problem-solving and solution-generating outcomes. This enables students to engage in scenario and world-building activities to envision different futures; problematize human–nature binaries; transition away from abstract knowledge to experiential learning grounded in local ecosystems; contemplate models of political ecology based on ecological economics; and remediate ecology metaphors to encourage learners to perceive media as embedded within living systems. These approaches seek to rebalance the study of media and promote ecocentric knowledge systems for an ecojust world.

Further Reading

Buckingham, David. 2019. *The Media Education Manifesto*. Cambridge; Medford, MA: Polity.
Cloud Institute for Sustainable Education. 2011. "EfS Curriculum Design Workbook." No. Monograph.
ecomedialiteracy.org (website with lessons and resources for teaching ecomedia literacy).
Journal of Media Literacy and *Journal of Sustainability Education* special issue on ecomedia literacy (http://www.susted.com/wordpress/april-2020-eco-media-literacy/).
Iheka, Cajetan Nwabueze, ed. 2022. *Teaching Postcolonial Environmental Literature and Media*. New York: Modern Language Association of America.
López, Antonio. 2021. *Ecomedia Literacy: Integrating Ecology into Media Education*. New York: Routledge.

References

Bozak, Nadia. 2011. *The Cinematic Footprint: Lights, Camera, Natural Resources*. Piscataway, NJ: Rutgers University Press.
Buckingham, David. 2019. *The Media Education Manifesto*. Cambridge; Medford, MA: Polity.
Cloud Institute for Sustainable Education. 2011. "EfS Curriculum Design Workbook." No. Monograph.
Corbett, Julia B. 2021. *Communicating the Climate Crisis: New Directions for Facing What Lies Ahead*. Lanham, MD: Lexington Books.
Dumit, Joseph. 2014. "Writing the Implosion: Teaching the World One Thing at a Time." *Cultural Anthropology* 29 (2): 344–62. https://doi.org/10.14506/ca29.2.09.
Freire, Paulo, and Donaldo P. Macedo. 1987. *Literacy: Reading the Word & the World*. South Hadley, MA: Bergin & Garvey Publishers.
Garrard, Greg, ed. 2016. *Teaching Ecocriticism and Green Cultural Studies*. Cham: Palgrave Macmillan.
Goodman, Michael. 2002. "The Iceberg Model." Innovation Associates Organizational Learning. http://www.ascd.org/ASCD/pdf/journals /ed_lead/ el200910_kohm_iceberg.pdf.
Hadl, Gabriele. 2016. *Kankyou Media Riterashii (EcoMedia Literacy)*. Nishinomiya City: Kwansei Gakuin University Press.
James, Erin. 2016. "Teaching the Postcolonial/Ecocritical Dialogue." In *Teaching Ecocriticism and Green Cultural Studies*, edited by Greg Garrard, 60–74. Cham: Palgrave Macmillan.
Kellner, Douglas, and Jeff Share. 2019. *The Critical Media Literacy Guide: Engaging Media and Transforming Education*. Leiden; Boston, MA: Brill Sense.
Kuntsman, Adi, and Esperanza Miyake. 2022. *Paradoxes of Digital Disengagement*. London: University of Westminster Press. https://doi.org/10.16997/book61.
López, Antonio. 2014. *Greening Media Education: Bridging Media Literacy with Green Cultural Citizenship*. New York: Peter Lang.
———. 2021. *Ecomedia Literacy: Integrating Ecology into Media Education*. London; New York: Routledge.
———. 2022. "Gaslighting: Fake Climate News and Big Carbon's Network of Denial." In *Palgrave Handbook of Media Misinformation*, edited by Julian McDougall and Karen Fowler-Watt, 159–77. London; New York: Palgrave MacMillan. https://doi.org/10.1007/978-3-031-11976-7.
López, Antonio, and Olivia Frenkel. 2022. "Algorithms and Climate: An Ecomedia Literacy Perspective." *The Journal of Media Literacy*. https://ic4ml.org/journal-article/are-big-tech-algorithms-good-for-the-planet-an-ecomedia-literacy-perspective/
López, Antonio, Jeff Share, and Theresa Redmond. 2022. "Ecomedia Literacy: Ecojustice and Media Education in a Post-Pandemic World." In *The Routledge Handbook on Media Education Futures Post-Pandemic*, edited by Yonty Friesem, Usha Raman, Igor Kanižaj, and Grace Y. Choi, 463–70. New York: Routledge.
Meadows, Donella H. 1991. *The Global Citizen*. Washington, DC: Island Press.
Miller, Jocelyn, Linda Rost, Connor Bryant, Robyn Embry, Shazia Iqbal, Claire Lannoye-Hall, and Missie Olson. 2021. "Media Literacy in the Age of COVID and Climate Change." *The Science Teacher* 88 (6).

https://www.nsta.org/science-teacher/science-teacher-julyaugust-2021-0/media-literacy-age-covid-and-climate-change.

Milstein, Tema, Mairi Pileggi, and Eric Morgan. 2017. *Environmental Communication and Pedagogy*. New York: Routledge.

Parks, Lisa. 2016. "Earth Observation and Signal Territories." In *Ecomedia: Key Issues*, edited by Stephen Rust, Salma Monani, and Sean Cubitt, 141–61. London; New York: Routledge.

Pink, Sarah. 2015. *Doing Sensory Ethnography*. 2nd ed. London; Thousand Oaks, CA: Sage Publications.

Rauch, Jennifer. 2018. *Slow Media: Toward a Sustainable Future*. Oxford: Oxford University Press.

Ross, Andrew. 1994. *The Chicago Gangster Theory of Life: Nature's Debt to Society*. London: Verso.

Sperry, Sox. 2020. "Project Look Sharp's Decoding Media Constructions and Substantiality." *Journal of Sustainability Education* 23 (May). http://www.susted.com/wordpress/content/briefing-project-look-sharps-decoding-media-constructions-and-substantiality_2020_04/.

Wiggins, Grant P., and Jay McTighe. 2005. *Understanding by Design*. Alexandria, VA: Association for Supervision and Curriculum Development.

PART II

Ecomateriality

10
DISAGGREGATED FOOTPRINTS

An Infrastructural Literacy Approach to the Sustainable Internet

Nicole Starosielski, Hunter Vaughan, Anne Pasek, and Nicholas R. Silcox

As digital infrastructure has expanded over the past decade, researchers have drawn attention to the massive amount of energy it requires (Andrae and Edler, 2015; Varghese, 2020). Much of this discourse has focused on data centers, the energy-intensive warehouses of the internet. Perhaps predictably, less attention has been paid to measuring the network's least energy-intensive components or to comparative analysis of the network's many constituent parts. We still do not have a full picture, for example, of the relative carbon footprint of a network exchange, a terrestrial network, a last-mile connection, a satellite transmission, and a subsea cable link. This is in part an issue of data transparency and collection. However, it also reflects the fact that calculations of digital infrastructure's environmental impact have been largely driven by a desire to aggregate, to tie together various sections and sectors of internet infrastructure, and to assess harm at its broadest scale and scope.

Understanding where the biggest impacts can be made allows environmentalists to strategically advocate for technical and infrastructural change and could potentially play a crucial role in advancing the development and implementation of alternative energy futures. However, in this chapter, we advance a different—and as yet still marginal—approach to understanding digital infrastructure's impacts: a disaggregation of the internet's energy use, a focus on its localized and geographically specific parts, which can reveal the environmental specificity of critical digital infrastructure components. It is essential, we show, that both researchers and public stakeholders grasp the relative energy impact of data centers, subsea cables, and Internet of Things devices, among the multitude of other internet infrastructures.

Beyond understanding that data centers are energy-intensive, how can we assess them relative to one another and pose further questions regarding sector dynamics? How does our understanding of the environmental impact of digital infrastructure change when we consider different kinds of footprints—not only energy but also water or land footprints—in specific, local conditions? Knowing which part of the internet is more sustainable enables us to advocate more precisely for different models of internet organization—to design sustainability not only with a mindset of reduction or efficiency but also with a careful leveraging of pieces in relation to the whole. We describe this elsewhere as a turn to a *relational footprinting* rather than a complete accounting of the internet's carbon footprint (Pasek, Vaughan, and Starosielski, 2023). This isn't to say there is no value in a global approach, but rather there is much to be gained by supplementing such

This chapter has been made available under a CC-BY-NC-ND license.

approaches with attention to environmental variance and difference at the local level. Such specific critical understanding will not only advance a more holistic understanding of the network but also provide isolated and pragmatic targets for potential applied solutions and future best practices.

Crucial for this disaggregation of digital infrastructure, and the possibilities and advocacy for environmental change it opens, is an infrastructural literacy of ecomedia. Media scholars Lisa Parks (2009) and Shannon Mattern (2013) describe infrastructural literacy as the critical capacity to read, understand, and interact with the complex infrastructure systems in which we are enmeshed. In order to assess digital media's environmental dimensions, a basic literacy of the network—and its varied ecological effects—is necessary. For that reason, the first half of this chapter contains a breakdown of the parts of the internet's infrastructure and the environmental issues most pertinent to each. Evaluating the energy impact of a given set of digital media practices, whether executing a Google search, creating a TikTok video, or operating a server requires an infrastructural literacy in part because (1) different media practices activate different parts of our global digital infrastructure, and (2) individual platforms diverge in terms of policies of storage and organization. In the second section of this chapter, we discuss one relevant digital infrastructural trend—that of edge caching—and describe how this logistical technique dramatically reshapes the environmental effects of signal traffic. We discuss how applying a local ethos, such as edge caching, to the network could actually increase its environmental impact.

Data Centers: The Warehouses of the Internet

Data centers are the sites where computers (more specifically, racks and racks of servers) house the internet. What this means is that the content of websites, emails, and social media are all stored (at least within a cloud computing model) in a central location from which individuals can remotely access information. Within the landscape of data centers, there are a range of differentiations that affect environmental impact, most notably size and tenancy occupation, surrounding climate, and access to energy supply sources.

One distinction that shapes data centers' environmental impact is between the hyperscalers, the companies that have been able to build out massive data centers (e.g., Google, Facebook, and Amazon), and the much smaller data center players. Perhaps surprisingly, when it comes to the environment, bigger is often better. At scale, and in the development of massive new builds, it has been easier for companies such as Google to adopt increased efficiency measures and new technologies, and these companies have helped to drive sustainable development in the data center world. In contrast, a smaller data center or an older facility might fare much less well in an environmental assessment. Yet at the same time, the hyperscalers—in the acquisition and appropriation of additional land, energy, and water resources—still have a massive impact on the communities they inhabit.

Location also shapes data centers' overall environmental impact. Because of the need to maintain consistent temperatures, and because existing technologies are largely built for moderate climate (what Jen Rose Smith, 2020, calls "temperate normativity"), this means that data centers in cooler, often Northern climates typically use less electricity than comparable infrastructure built in tropical regions. Local energy grids also matter, since the mix of renewable versus carbon-intensive fossil fuel electrical generation varies dramatically from region to region (and even during times of day or the year). A data center powered primarily by wind, solar, or legacy nuclear and hydro will have a much smaller climate impact than one powered by coal, oil, or gas. This advantages and disadvantages certain areas of the world (and regions within a country) in terms of environmental performance.

Since its explosive growth in the 2010s, the data center industry has significantly advanced in its attempts to address sustainability compared to other sectors of network infrastructure development. The energy intensity of these infrastructures is a central economic and public relations concern for industry players, both in terms of operational cost and a growing trend of green finance that has incentivized this push. These efforts still have their limits, however: latency and national data sovereignty concerns, among others, mean that hyperscale data centers are not the best solution to every infrastructural problem.

Last Mile: The Driveways of the Internet

Alongside data centers, one of the most energy-intensive segments of internet infrastructure is last-mile infrastructure. By this, we mean the technologies and hardware that route traffic from internet exchange points (IXPs) to individual homes and businesses, as well as the routers, computers, screens, and periphery devices through which users interact. This equipment is generally less energy efficient than network traffic infrastructures, resulting in higher energy draw. While there has been improvement in overall energy efficiency per device with increasing regulatory standards over the past decade, the number of devices and consumption outpaces energy efficiency standards, a phenomenon known as Jevons Paradox. Despite variance in study data, there is broad agreement that last-mile infrastructures and end-user devices contribute a significant amount of the overall energy usage and carbon emissions of digital infrastructure networks. Some studies estimate that 47% of all ICT emissions can be attributed to last-mile infrastructures and end-user devices (Accenture Strategy, 2015). Others suggest that amount is greater than half (Malmodin et al., 2014). There is some evidence to suggest that this number might be lower, but still a significant portion of all ICT emissions (Ferreboeuf, 2019: 20). In addition to being energy-inefficient, last-mile infrastructure and end-user devices make up a significant portion of e-waste, expanding their environmental impact (Maxwell and Miller, 2012).

There have been efforts to make these devices and infrastructure more efficient, as well as the development of applications that monitor and report energy usage to consumers. There have also been some recent efforts to address consumer behaviors. Scholars have argued for the political and social possibility of an ethics of repair and accepting obsolescence in place of embracing the new (Mattern, 2018; Maxwell and Miller, 2012). Yet this focus on consumer behavior also risks redirecting the culpability of the environmental impact of digital infrastructure onto consumers themselves (Ericsson, 2020).

Internet Exchanges: The Transit Hubs of the Internet

A third key component of internet infrastructure is the internet exchange, the place where traffic is shifted between different kinds of networks. If data centers are warehouses and last-mile infrastructures are driveways, network exchanges are transit hubs, the train stations, and the airports for the data center metropolis. The energy use in these sites tends to be lower. While data centers are fairly mobile and can be established in preferable locations (taking into account environmental concerns ranging from the presence of renewable grids or cooler climates), network exchanges tend to be geographically situated as they are tied into and mediate between long-standing fixed lines. This sector of the network is often underexplored in terms of sustainability, partly because of its geographic situatedness, as well as lower energy consumption generally.

While IXPs are not energy-intensive, there have still been some efforts to increase their energy efficiency and sustainability. For example, some companies that manage IXPs have turned to renewable energy sources to power their facilities. This can be particularly advantageous for IXPs because they are so tightly tied to existing infrastructural geographies, and companies can adopt energy sources that are uniquely suited to the weather and climate conditions of the particular place in which they operate (Orghia, 2017). This can lower costs for companies, and for some, it can be a way of producing an energy surplus. Some companies have also invested in sustainable design of their buildings, further reducing their overall environmental impact (Equinix Initiatives, 2021).

The motivating factor for IXP location has rarely been ecological. Rather, IXP construction tends to follow a desire to keep the internet local and to provide higher quality internet access, especially in communities in which access is limited, as well as to increase the speed of data and information sharing within a local network (Internet Society, 2014). Given this reality, if local energy grids are primarily powered by fossil fuels, the decision to localize traffic through IXPs thus requires a trade-off between internet access, the cultural and business priority of maximum internet speeds, and emission of carbon. Thus, the more sustainable option in some cases might be to send data traffic to distant data centers that have more consistent access to renewable energy or more efficient standards overall. What are the implications of sending traffic to overseas data centers, even if this is more environment-friendly, instead of prioritizing local infrastructures? Thinking about IXPs and localization opens these critical questions about the geographical distribution of internet infrastructure.

Fiber-Optic Cables: The Highways of the Internet

Lastly, an oft overlooked aspect of the internet infrastructure is the long-haul fiber optic cable system through which network traffic is funneled underground and underwater. Satellites carry some transoceanic communication, but this is relatively small. In addition to being overlooked culturally, subsea cables are often overlooked in evaluations of the carbon and environmental impacts of the global internet infrastructure. This is, in part, because the emissions generated by subsea cables are so low that they are regarded as comparable to a rounding error in global calculations. Given the low-carbon footprint of subsea cables and the more general invisibility of the industry, there has been very little research dedicated specifically to cable infrastructure and its climate impacts. For example, in the subsea telecommunications industry, which constructs the transoceanic links that carry almost 100% of data traffic across the oceans, there has been almost no industry-wide carbon data exchange, collaboration around sustainability work, or discourse about the relative sustainability impacts of different cable landing stations or cables. In part because of its low-carbon footprint and its extensive focus on mitigating any potential marine environmental impacts, sustainability work has generally slipped through the cracks.

Since 2021, our team has been building the *Sustainable Subsea Networks* research project to document the energy use of this sector of the internet and develop mitigation strategies for its infrastructure. We have found many individual companies engaged in green practices, but on the whole, this has not been a sector-wide endeavor. To facilitate these green efforts, we have begun to generate basic environmental communication strategies (including the creation of a column on sustainability in the industry magazine and the generation of a sustainability map). Analyzing the internet's infrastructure in terms of its component parts, and understanding the specificity of different parts, reveals a multitude of places throughout the network where new strategies for making the system more sustainable, beyond degrowth and efficiency, are possible.

Case Study: Netflix and the Environmental Impact of Edge Caching

Given the pressing need to address climate change, much research on the energy use of the internet has been motivated by a desire to find the sites with the most significant impact, hone in on them, and develop solutions for reduction. Or, to aggregate and assemble the many different sites of energy use in order to demonstrate the magnitude of real or potential harm and to use this data to call for transformation. Such approaches bring with them several potential paths forward. Working at scale, aggregative approaches are particularly good at setting baselines for policy and regulation, for speaking to all parts of a network, and for connecting local actions into a greater whole. Yet they also carry the risk of eclipsing the specificity of different kinds of digital media practice and the infrastructures and places that support those practices. A big picture view does not as readily lend itself to solutions that involve reorganizing traffic, systems, and social practices, nor can strategies derived from their conclusions be easily implemented across the sector all at once.

Let us consider a specific case that illustrates the possibilities of disaggregation and the need for infrastructural literacy. Over the last decade, driven in part by the perceived need of consumers to receive streaming media content quickly, a new model of digital infrastructure organization developed: edge caching. In short, edge caching means that the content is stored in many edges in the global network, accessible in geographically proximate sites that are called cache servers, rather than distributed from a single central server. Edge caches are like smaller, regional airports, holding content that need not necessarily pass through and from major hub centers. A related development, "fog computing," relocates not simply content but computing capacity to the edges of the network. This reduces the time it takes to receive data and increases the speed at which one can consume data, which is important for a variety of time-sensitive activities from gaming and streaming video to stock trading. The motivations that have animated network development and new forms of network infrastructure prompt engineers to ask: how close can we get to the users? How quickly can we get them content? How can we predict what it is that they will want so that way we can keep it nearby?

One of the most well publicized versions of this movement to the edge has been Netflix's Open Connect, which involves Netflix partnering with Internet Service Providers (ISPs) in order to maximize efficiency and quality of streamed content. Working with over a thousand ISPs worldwide, Netflix utilizes a proprietary system of "embedded deployments" to localize data through what they call a "cooperative approach to content delivery." Ultimately, it means that the content provider and the internet provider work together in order to anticipate localized content needs and map, distribute, and maintain data accordingly. The Open Connect project is global with "14,000 Open Connect Appliances spread across 142 countries" which has made it possible for Netflix to store and access data locally from most places where streaming happens. This "cooperative model" of data storage and transfer has reduced costs for Netflix and increased efficiency while "increasing quality for consumers" (Netflix, 2021). However, it is not clear that this model has been effective in reducing the carbon footprint of Netflix. Netflix self-reports their use of "Amazon Web Services and the Open Connect content delivery network" accounted for 5% of the 1.1-million metric tons the company produced in 2020, or nearly 600,000 tons of carbon. Notably, this analysis excludes emissions from internet transmission or user-end electronic devices (Stewart 2021).

This is of particular importance given the exponential increase in online video streaming over the last decade (Kamiya, 2020), which has greatly outpaced environmental regulation of ICT and puts added strain on existing sustainability practices in the industry. Both academic (Marks, Makonin,

Rodriguez-Silva, and Przedpełski, 2021) and popular studies (Bedingfield, 2021; Kessler, 2017) have addressed the environmental impacts of digital streaming, primarily as an aggregate question of carbon footprinting: a certain amount of carbon per GB, or as the industry's share of overall global GHG emissions. Their conclusions are alarming, suggesting that edge caching and the user demand it supports and grows, pose substantial threats to the prospects of a greener internet.

Yet the question of digital streaming impacts might well be better understood—and made more available for intervention—by looking at its disparate elements and segmented design. One can evaluate the merits of edge caching versus centralization from various perspectives: Who controls the content? Under what regulations is that content controlled? Where can disruption occur? How fast are these systems? Are users subjected to increased forms of harm or surveillance in the movement to the edge? As yet, no one has calculated the relative environmental impact of different models of connection, whether edge caching, centralized delivery, or fog computing. We only have sketches of the network as a whole, and as it currently exists.

Here the analogy between internet infrastructure and the wider transportation system fails us. While we use the features of transportation systems to help make the dense layers of digital infrastructure intelligible—warehouses, transit hubs, highways—such transpositions also introduce potential misunderstandings. If we assumed that the length or duration of transmission is relative to environmental impact, we would easily adopt a localist perspective: like our food and commodity goods, local data would be lighter on the earth than a global import. However, while the transportation of goods via highway is a fuel- and power-intensive activity compared to leaving them stockpiled in a warehouse (provided this warehouse isn't climate-controlled), the opposite is true for digital signals. Long-haul transmission of information along digital highways is much more energy-efficient than local storage. Subsea routing is actually much less energy-intensive, relatively speaking, than storing data in perpetuity. In turn, the environmentalist ethos of situating things locally does not easily translate to digital networks. It is for these reasons that we need a clear disaggregation of the internet's energy use: a relational footprinting that locates usage in relation to national grids, energy policies, and the geography and displacements that govern movement across the internet (Pasek, Starosielski, and Vaughan, 2023). Greening the internet is both a decision about how much bandwidth one takes up and a matter of producing less or lower bandwidth content (Marks, Makonin, Rodriguez-Silva, and Przedpełski, 2022), but also a question of speed and network organization. Rather than only growing or shrinking the internet overall, we might also build different networks, taking advantage of geographic difference to move content along greener pathways, from greater distances. In turn, this might be an internet with content appearing slower, buffering for longer, and inaccessible at certain times and places. Recent critical creative projects such as Low-tech Magazine (https://solar.lowtechmagazine.com/about.html) and Solar Protocol (Brain, Nathanson, and Piantella, 2022) explore the role of sustainable design and solar-powered tech. Both projects center the idea of finite, limited energy resources as the political, esthetic, and technical motivations of design. They embrace intermittency, resiliency, and principles of degrowth as productive pathways through which to imagine low-carbon futures and reconsider our current understandings of the internet. These projects are less useful as specific blueprints—rather, they are useful examples that open up "new imaginaries of what web [and computing] systems designed within limits can be like" (Abbing, 2021).

Conclusion

In November 2021, Extinction Rebellion launched an anti-data center protest in Ireland. Standing outside of the Data Centres Ireland annual conference at the Royal Dublin Society, people gathered

Figure 10.1   Extinction Rebellion anti-data center protest

to protest the development and expansion of data centers in Ireland, a country that is at once a significant hub for internet traffic and particularly at risk for the impacts of climate change and rising sea levels. Protesters held signs that said simply "Ban New Data Centers" and, in echoing some of the sentiments of this paper, "System Change, not Climate Change" (see Figure 10.1). This is the kind of protest and public action that facts and figures about the environmental impact of the internet can help to motivate. The question remains: what is it that we want less of when we protest against emissions? Or rather, what does it mean to create "system change" with respect to internet infrastructure? Is it data centers that we need less of? Network exchanges? Subsea cables? No matter the answer, it is clear to us that infrastructural literacy is a precondition for creating more ecologically sound media.

Further Reading

Chang, Alenda, and Jeff Watson. 2022. "Steam Clouds and Game Streams: Unboxing the 'Future' of Gaming." In *The SAGE Handbook of the Digital Media Economy*, edited by Terry Flew, Jennifer Holt, and Julian Thomas, 240–59. London: Sage.

Freitag, Charlotte, Mike Berners-Lee, Kelly Widdicks, Bran Knowles, Gordon S. Blair, and Adrian Friday. 2021. "The Real Climate and Transformative Impact of ICT: A Critique of Estimates, Trends, and Regulations." *Patterns* 2 (9): 100340. https://doi.org/10.1016/j.patter.2021.100340.

Mattern, Shannon. 2018. "Scaffolding, Hard and Soft: Media Infrastructures as Critical and Generative Structures." In *The Routledge Companion to Media Studies and Digital Humanities*, edited by Jentery Sayers, 318–26. New York and London: Routledge.

Parks, Lisa. 2015. "Stuff You Can Kick: Toward a Theory of Media Infrastructures." In *Between Humanities and the Digital*, edited by Patrik Svensson and David Theo Goldberg, 355–73. Cambridge: MIT Press.

Pasek, Anne. 2019. "Managing Carbon and Data Flows: Fungible Forms of Mediation in the Cloud." *Culture Machine* 18 (April). http://culturemachine.net/vol-18-the-nature-of-data-centers/managing-carbon/.

References

Abbing, Roel Roscam. 2021. "'This Is a Solar-Powered Website, Which Means It Sometimes Goes Offline': A Design Inquiry into Degrowth and ICT." *Seventh Workshop on Computing within Limits*. https://computingwithinlimits.org/2021/papers/limits21-abbing.pdf.

Accenture Strategy. 2015. "#SMARTer2030: ICT Solutions for 21st Century Challenges." Brussels, Belgium. https://smarter2030.gesi.org/downloads/Full_report.pdf.

Andrae, Anders S. G., and Tomas Edler. 2015. "On Global Electricity Usage of Communication Technology: Trends to 2030." *Challenges* 6 (1): 117–57. https://doi.org/10.3390/challe6010117.

Bedingfield, Will. 2021. "We Finally Know How Bad for the Environment Your Netflix Habit Is." *WIRED*, March 15. https://www.wired.co.uk/article/netflix-carbon-footprint.

Brain, Tega, Alex Nathanson, and Benedetta Piantella. 2022. "Solar Protocol: Exploring Energy-Centered Design." In *Eighth Workshop on Computing within Limits 2022*, 7. https://computingwithinlimits.org/2022/papers/limits22-final-Brain.pdf.

Equinix Initiatives. 2021. "Map of Initiatives." *Equinix Sustainability*, September 20. https://sustainability.equinix.com/map-of-initiatives/.

Ericsson. 2020. "A Quick Guide to Your Digital Carbon Footprint: Deconstructing Information and Communication Technology's Carbon Emissions." Ericsson. https://www.ericsson.com/en/reports-and-papers/industrylab/reports/a-quick-guide-to-your-digital-carbon-footprint.

Ferreboeuf, Hugues. 2019. "Lean ICT: Towards Digital Sobriety. Paris, France: The Shift Project." https://theshiftproject.org/wp-content/uploads/2019/03/Lean-ICT-Report_The-Shift-Project_2019.pdf.

Internet Society. 2014. "The Internet Exchange Point Toolkit & Best Practices Guide." 25 February. https://www.internetsociety.org/resources/doc/2014/ixptoolkitguide/.

Kamiya, George. 2020. "The Carbon Footprint of Streaming Video: Fact-Checking the Headlines – Analysis." *International Energy Agency*, December 11. https://www.iea.org/commentaries/the-carbon-footprint-of-streaming-video-fact-checking-the-headlines.

Kessler, Matt. 2017. "The Environmental Cost of Internet Porn." *The Atlantic*, December 13. https://www.theatlantic.com/technology/archive/2017/12/the-environmental-cost-of-internet-porn/548210/.

Malmodin, Jens, Dag Lundén, Åsa Moberg, Greger Andersson, and Mikael Nilsson. 2014. "Life Cycle Assessment of ICT." *Journal of Industrial Ecology* 18 (6). https://doi.org/10.1111/jiec.12145.

Marks, Laura U., Stephen Makonin, Alejandro Rodriguez-Silva, and Radek Przedpelski. 2022. "Calculating the Carbon Footprint of Streaming Media: Beyond the Myth of Efficiency." In *Eighth Workshop on Computing within Limits 2022*, 7. https://computingwithinlimits.org/2022/papers/limits22-final-Makonin.pdf.

Mattern, Shannon. 2013. "Infrastructural Tourism." *Places*, July 1. https://doi.org/10.22269/130701.

Maxwell, Richard, and Toby Miller. 2012. *Greening the Media*. New York: Oxford University Press.

Netflix. 2021. "A Cooperative Approach to Content Delivery." *Netflix*. https://openconnect.netflix.com/Open-Connect-Briefing-Paper.pdf.

Orghia, Michael. 2017. "Sustainability in Armenia: ARMIX Adopts Solar Power." *Internet Society blog*, June 9. https://www.internetsociety.org/blog/2017/06/sustainability-in-armenia-armix-adopts-solar-power/.

Parks, Lisa. 2009. "Around the Antenna Tree: The Politics of Infrastructural Visibility." *Flow*, March 6. https://www.flowjournal.org/2009/03/around-the-antenna-tree-the-politics-of-infrastructural-visibilitylisa-parks-uc-santa-barbara/.

Pasek, Anne, Hunter Vaughan, and Nicole Starosielski. 2023. "The World Wide Web of Carbon: Toward a Relational Footprinting of Information and Communications Technology's Climate Impacts." *Big Data & Society* 10 (1): 205395172311589. https://doi.org/10.1177/20539517231158994.

Smith, Jen Rose. 2020. "'Exceeding Beringia': Upending Universal Human Events and Wayward Transits in Arctic Spaces." *Environment and Planning D: Society and Space* 39 (1): 158–75. https://doi.org/10.1177/0263775820950745.

Stewart, Emma. 2021. "Net Zero + Nature: Our Commitment to the Environment." *Netflix*, March 30. https://about.netflix.com/en/news/net-zero-nature-our-climate-commitment.

Varghese, Sanjana. 2020. "Is Streaming Music Growing Your Carbon Footprint?" *Al Jazeera English*, February 28. https://www.aljazeera.com/economy/2020/2/28/emissions-possible-streaming-music-swells-carbon-footprints.

11
COLLAPSE INFORMATICS AND THE ENVIRONMENTAL IMPACT OF INFORMATION AND COMMUNICATION TECHNOLOGIES

Laura U. Marks

This chapter gives an overview of the environmental impact of ICT, which comprise the interconnected webs of computing devices, networks, storage, and servers. Focusing on the important subcategory of ICT engineering research in sustainability, I argue that ICT's growth is unsustainable, even given the vaunted efficiency of the technologies, especially as it expands to developing countries. Reviewing some proposed best practices for making ICT use sustainable, I suggest that the movements of slow computing and collapse informatics offer a model for learning to live with decreased expectations.

ICT research occurs at the nexus of computer science, information systems, human-computer interaction, and economics. The majority of engineers working on ICT do not reflect a concern for the environment in their research but rather are driven to innovate solutions to make ICT more efficient. But as we shall see, efficiency usually translates to increased growth and a higher environmental footprint. I will focus on just one of the barriers to environmentally sustainable ICT: the rebound effect, whereby increased efficiency leads to greater demand.

Over the two years that I have immersed in the ICT engineering literature, I have come to empathize greatly with these hard-working engineers, much of whose research benefits telecoms and other corporations that extract profit from ICT services. Of those ICT engineers who do seek environmentally responsible solutions, some appear to end up, intentionally or willy-nilly, contributing to corporate greenwashing. Often this is because their analyses are limited in space and time: they study shorter term effects, or they exclude variables that are too hard to quantify. This greenish research creates a false sense of security that ICT's direct environmental effects, including resource extraction, carbon footprint, water use, and other pollution, can be mitigated and in any case are outweighed by ICT's good indirect environmental effects. I have the highest regard for those ICT engineers who, in the careful and precise language and methodologies of their discipline, do the more difficult work of studying the larger picture despite its many unknowns. They encourage us to convert the relativistic terms of efficiency and sustainability to the absolute terms of sufficiency and self-sustainability, as we will see later.

"We'll need a lot more energy"

When I first read "What Will the World Be Like in 20 Years?" in the *New York Times* of November 29 2021, I was so irritated by its glib contradictions that I flung the article across the room (luckily, I was reading the paper newspaper). Demographic studies indicate to the article's author, Andrew Ross Sorkin, that the majority of the world's population will live in cities, requiring more infrastructure. "We'll also need a lot more energy," he writes. Citing a 2017 US Energy Information Administration (EIA) report, Sorkin argues that the additional energy will come from renewable sources.

In fact, the EIA's long-term projection of world energy consumption is pretty gloomy. Its October 2021 update projects a 28% increase in world energy use by 2050 as populations and incomes rise. Almost every kind of energy consumption will rise: renewable, nuclear, natural gas, and petroleum. Crude oil and natural gas production will increase worldwide. The EIA projects coal consumption to slowly flatten worldwide, but this is not happening: China, India, and South Korea led the 2022 expansion of new coal plants, and Germany reopened coal plants after the Russian invasion of Ukraine (Global Energy Monitor 2023). The EIA's study shows that renewables will support *only* the increase; fossil fuels will maintain at a steady state. These predictions demolish any hope that global greenhouse gas (GHG) emissions will decrease to levels that make it possible to avoid catastrophic global heating.

Decarbonization Fallacies

ICT currently is estimated to use about 7% of the world's electricity and generate almost 4% of global GHG emissions (Belkhir & Elmeligi 2018, Bordage 2019). It is predicted to grab an ever-larger proportion of global electricity as numbers of data centers, network technologies, and devices continue to increase. As with the global trend, even if new electricity generation for data centers, networks, and devices comes from renewable sources, this is *in addition to*, not replacing, the existing fossil-fuel–powered electricity sources.

Mega-ICT corporations could claim, as Apple and Google do, that their data centers are sustainable because they are powered by renewable energy. In fact, data center operators purchase renewable energy credits, which allow them to claim that they are using renewable energy while continuing to use energy from fossil fuels (Chernicoff 2016). Moreover, that renewable energy could have been used to power the local grid. Take the Irish example. In Ireland, the infrastructural site of Google, Facebook, Amazon, and soon TikTok, data centers are projected to account for 25% of national electricity demand by 2030. In 2021, the state-owned electricity company EirGrid warned that the country would be short of 1,850 megawatts of energy in 2024–2025. Ireland's environment minister stated that EirGrid would fall back on diesel generators, among other things, to make up the shortfall (O'Doherty & Hyland 2021). Thus, the renewable energy demands of big media corporations force other folks to rely on fossil fuels.

Dreams of Dematerialization

Most people, especially in wealthy parts of the world, rarely consider that ICT has an environmental impact. That is partly because most of the infrastructure is invisible to us, as my diagram shows (Figure 11.1). Data centers are usually invisible; most parts of networks are underground and undersea; device manufacture takes place in factories in China; copper and rare metals are mined

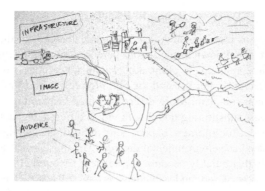

Figure 11.1 The infrastructure beyond the image

in Chile, Peru, China, the Democratic Republic of Congo, and elsewhere; dangerous disposal and the little recycling that occurs takes place most often in China, Brazil, and India.

ICT is generally thought to result in *dematerialization* or *virtualization*, the replacement of physical goods such as newspapers and DVDs with electronic media. Both terms are problematic. To call electronic media virtual grates on a Deleuzian like me, since electronic media are thoroughly actual. (Virtual describes, for example, a future world powered by renewable energy; or a future in which our planet becomes uninhabitable.) Nor are the products delivered by ICT immaterial. They use electricity, they are delivered on media composed of minerals, and they embody the labor of miners, assemblers, installers, and hardware and software engineers.

Moreover, ICT instates behaviors and expectations that have material effects. Streaming YouTube to a laptop or a large TV, instead of listening to the radio or your own CDs, or streaming audio music. "Reading" a video-heavy newspaper online instead of a paper newspaper. "Jumping on a Zoom" instead of talking on the phone. Streaming video for 35 hours a week instead of watching TV or going to the movies. Using AI-driven dictation software instead of typing. At first, these substitutions of one platform for another appear to result in a savings of energy and other resources. However, as behavior changes, they often end up consuming more energy. These are all examples of the rebound effects of ICT that result in increased demand on networks, data centers, and devices.

Infrastructure Anticipates Demand

ICT infrastructure is overbuilt to respond to anticipated demand. Preist et al. (2016) point out that in the dominant ideology of the "cornucopian paradigm," the internet is a limitless resource. Consumers expect internet services that are instantaneous, of huge variety, of high quality, and always available. Each one of these expectations has implications for data storage, network capacity, and energy consumption, setting up a feedback loop of increased capacity and increased demand. For example, the expectation for high-resolution audio, images, and video increases the demand on networks, servers, and storage. It also creates a demand for high-resolution devices. The resulting files are so large that users store more of the content they create on the cloud. Similarly, the expectation of instantaneous access to online content means that the infrastructure "must be sufficient to cater comfortably with peak demand, resulting in the need for more servers and network capacity than would otherwise be necessary" (2016, 1327).

Rebound Effects

As efficiency of technologies increases and costs decrease, demand for these technologies rises. This is the rebound effect, also known as the Jevons paradox: more efficient technologies encourage greater use of a resource, reducing or eliminating savings. Direct environmental effects of ICT include resource extraction and water use and the pollution resulting from fossil-fuel sources for electricity, i.e. ICT's carbon footprint. More difficult to measure are the indirect effects of ICT. Things like smart buildings, substituting travel with videoconferencing, and substituting tangible goods with electronic media (online newspapers, streaming music, streaming movies, distance learning) are thought to decrease environmental damage. But these initially energy-saving activities lead to new behaviors that quickly become normalized: rebound effects (Gossart 2015). In a market dynamic of obsolescence, rebound is cyclical, as new software drives renewal of hardware, which leads to more intensive use, which leads to new software (Belkhir & Hilty 2021). Inexpensive electricity—cheaper in the United States than in Nigeria or the UK—further drives demand (Ejembi & Bhatti 2015).

Many engineers argue that there are too many variables and unknowns to determine ICT's indirect environmental effects (Horner et al. 2016). Industry boosters and lobbyists prefer reports like that of Accenture and the Global e-Sustainability Initiative (GeSI) in 2015, which suggested that while the ICT sector causes only 2% of global GHG emissions through direct effects, ICT applications could prevent up to 20% of annual GHG emissions in 2030 through positive indirect effects (GeSI and Accenture 2015). But in a study based on an extensive literature review, the majority of researchers found that rebound effects are too high to prevent a sufficient absolute reduction in energy demand (Lange et al. 2020).

Surveys of ICT's indirect effects suggest that the more carefully you model, the more likely you will be to find that they are deleterious. The approach GeSI used is ICT-enabled modeling, a rough calculation based on estimating how ICT may decrease baseline emissions, for example in telecommuting. Bieser and Hilty, surveying 54 environmental impact assessments, note that ICT-enabled modeling almost always demonstrates favorable indirect effects of ICT. A more inclusive model is life cycle analysis, which models "all exchange of energy and matter between the product system and its environment" (Bieser & Hilty 2018, 12). At maximum, life cycle analysis takes into account the environmental effects of resource extraction, production, use, and disposal of a given product system (Global Energy Monitor 2023).

For researchers, a disheartening example of the digital rebound effect is that, because of online journals and databases, the numbers of academic journal articles have multiplied dizzyingly, diluting the quality of research and making it near impossible to assimilate new knowledge (Gossart 2015, 443). In my recent research, the overconsumption of streaming video is a carbon-intensive rebound effect of inexpensive high-bandwidth transmission (Marks 2021, Marks & Przedpełski 2022).

Rebound in Global Perspective

A question for ethical ICT design is, "If this service were to be used by all the world's population, what would the overall environmental impact of the infrastructure be?" (Preist et al. 2016, 1332). In well-infrastructured parts of the world, the global pandemic cemented unsustainable media practices. People streamed more hours of video per day; shared more videos on social media; played more online games, in increasingly high resolution; kept the videoconference platform open all day for working from home and attending webinars; and bought more stuff online.

Such users could protest that since they are no longer traveling by air and they drive less, their carbon footprint is smaller than it was before the pandemic. But the rebound effect teaches us that soon enough people will be traveling more *and* maintaining the high-bandwidth activities. On top of that, wealthy regions' high-bandwidth habits create a model for the expansion of ICT in less wealthy countries.

We have to blame the wealthy countries for establishing unsustainable and frankly ridiculous standards of consumption. Wealthy countries energy consumption is now quietly flatlining only because light and heavy industry moved to countries where labor is cheaper and energy is more likely to be unrenewable. I hesitate to use the term "developing" for countries whose GDPs are currently lower than wealthy countries, because (1) the current model of economic development is the cause of catastrophic global warming and (2) low-income countries offer many models of sustainable development, which wealthier countries ought to follow, as I suggest below.

Nevertheless, in developing countries' ICT infrastructure will expand even faster and consumers will be encouraged to expect the high bandwidth, high turnover of devices, etc. that are touted as the norm in wealthy countries. As a country's income grows, installing new ICT infrastructure leads to an increase in electricity consumption (Saidi et al. 2017, 801). In 2020, the network corporation Cisco (2020) projected a 42% increase in IP traffic in the Middle East and Africa (Belkhir & Elmeligi 2018, Ihayere et al. 2021). Cisco's projections tend to become factual because the ICT industry strategizes based on their predictions through planned obsolescence, market saturation, and corporate demands for government investment in new technologies.

Development cannot be sustainable if all countries seek to achieve the bloated infrastructure of wealthy countries. Rather than increase ICT capacity worldwide to be equivalent to that in wealthy countries—what Radek Przedpełski and I call bandwidth imperialism—it is more appropriate for the ICT capacity of low-income countries to serve as a model for the rest of the world (Marks & Przedpełski 2021).

ICT's environmental impact in developing countries is difficult to project, given disagreements about the relative impacts of direct, indirect, and rebound effects, alongside the ways ICT drives economic development. For example, one study finds that ICT initially increases CO_2 emissions in developing countries but later on can moderate them, for example in the use of smart electric grids (Danish et al. 2018, Park et al. 2018). It focuses on what Goldman Sachs identified in 2015 as the N11 or next 11 countries that could potentially become some of the world's largest economies: Bangladesh, Egypt, Indonesia, Iran, Mexico, Nigeria, Pakistan, the Philippines, Turkey, South Korea, and Vietnam. The authors recommend that government policy in these countries should focus on energy-efficient infrastructure and clean energy. But given that, as of 2019, all the N11 countries rely largely or overwhelmingly on fossil fuels for electricity generation[1]—indeed, that's one of the reasons why they're in this category—it is beyond unlikely that they will hasten to move quickly to renewable energy.

Prospects

Given this global context, prospects for mitigating the increasing carbon footprint of ICT are fairly dismal, but I will enumerate some of them, from individual to institutional to governmental levels.[2]

Like recycling, actions at the personal level can seem puny and ineffectual, but they add up. And like recycling, they're subject to larger forces of economy and regulation. So doing things like streaming less and in lower resolution, compressing videos before you upload them, minimizing subscriptions, avoiding cloud storage, and keeping your device for as long as possible have a cumulative effect. Oh, and don't buy cryptocurrency. You might ask, if our local grid is powered by renewable energy, can we stream without compunction? The answer is no. First of all, it's difficult to determine whether the servers and networks that support your streaming get their electricity from renewable sources. Second, even if they did, in all likelihood your devices were produced with energy from fossil fuels. Third, excessive use of ICT pushes global demand for consumption and resulting expansion of infrastructure.

At the medium scale, it is in the interest of media corporations and service providers to conserve energy and reduce digital waste. Streaming platforms can default to low resolution and not offer high resolution without users' consent (The Shift Project 2019, Obringer et al. 2021). YouTube can use audio-only detection, which would turn off the video when it is detected to be playing in the background (Preist et al. 2016). Google can delete less popular videos from all but a few central servers (Cubitt 2017). Service providers can sell longer subscription plans at discounted rates to encourage customers to keep their phone for longer (Belkhir & Elmeligi 2018). They should also charge per unit of data, rather than at a flat rate (Reinsdorf et al. 2018). ICT corporations should include rebound effects in self-assessments.

Ultimately, mitigating the carbon footprint of ICT can only be resolved by governmental and international regulation. For example, governments can impose a real carbon tax on streaming platforms, telecoms, and network managers, who would pass these costs on to consumers. They can regulate cryptocurrency, AI, and other highly electricity-intensive applications (Montevecchi et al. 2020).

Self-Sustainability and Computing within Limits

The ICT industry itself is influential and can model energy-saving practices that can become the basis of government regulation. The fields of sustainable computing and sustainable ICT engineering have burgeoned in the last several years, with dedicated journals and conferences. Engineers can come up with remarkably divergent analyses under the rubric of sustainability. Sometimes terms such as "sustainability" and "circular economy" are just greenwashing. As Lorenz M. Hilty and Bernard Aebischer, leaders in the field of sustainable IT, point out, sustainability is a relative term, as it refers to sustainable use in terms of a given context (Hilty & Aebischer 2015). Preferable are *sustainable development* and *self-sustaining systems*. "Networking technology should follow the principles of Appropriate Technology […]: be designed to be a) simple, b) locally reproducible, c) composed of local materials / resources, d) easily repairable, e) affordable, and f) easily recyclable" (Raghavan & Ma 2011). One group, Computing within Limits,

> is concerned with the material impacts of computation itself, but, more broadly and more importantly, it engages a deeper, transformative shift in computing research and practice to one that would use computing to contribute to the overall process of transitioning to a future in which the well-being of humans and other species is the primary objective.
>
> (87)

Embracing Collapse Informatics

When resources collapse, as in the declining periods of past civilizations, making do with less becomes a necessary art. Lambert et al. (2015) explore post-peak oil scenarios in which low-power networking is no longer optional but instead becomes a necessity due to an energy-intermittent future. This would also apply to other energy-constrained situations, such as disaster recovery or off-grid installations in developing countries. (e.g., Tomlinson et al. 2013, Lambert et al. 2015). The authors introduce the concept of "graceful decline."

Collapse informatics (a term introduced by Tomlinson et al. 2013) models what I believe is the only truly sustainable model of ICT. It necessitates making do with less electricity and therefore lower bandwidth and intermittent access. It amplifies the value of tinkering and DIY practices that people have always used in the absence of access to new technologies. It shifts the direction of emulation away from over-infrastructured regions and toward lightly infrastructured regions where people have devised ways to make do.

Models for collapse informatics thrive in informal media economies (Lobato & Thomas 2015). Tinkering, hacking, and making may begin as a response to deprivation, but once the tinkerer develops expertise, they can be elegant, effortless, and empowering (Larkin 2013, Marks 2017). Collapse informatics posits that everyone but the over-infrastructured elite will have to embrace oppositional technophilia, Ron Eglash's term for minority groups' practices of hacking received technologies (Eglash 2009).

Young people in highly infrastructured parts of the world have grown up taking high-speed access for granted. My colleague Yani Kong surveyed students and instructors at our university about their attitudes toward the use of streaming media in online teaching (Kong 2022). They argued that the best ways to decrease the carbon footprint of online teaching are to turn off video in videoconferences and decrease the resolution of streaming movies. Most of the instructors were open to, or actively preferred, decreasing the resolution of videos, especially lecture and demonstration videos. In contrast, the majority of students insisted on a high-resolution learning experience. "4K or bust, baby!", one student wrote. However, young people are also innovators of elegant media objects that require very little bandwidth: GIFs and memes (Figure 11.2). Both are tiny, intensive files—infinitesimal movies in the case of GIFs—that are perceived briefly but create a lingering affective and cognitive impact. Kong and Predpełski devised some memes to communicate their findings instantaneously, such as these.

A design question for the collapse-informatics scenario is, "Can a restricted version of the service be imagined, and what would its value and infrastructural burden be?" (Preist et al. 2016, 1332). The annual Small File Media Festival that I founded in 2020, which imagines a restricted version of the streaming-video service, models a paradigm for collapse-informatics art and entertainment. We invite media works of no larger than 1.44 megabytes per minute, a constraint that

Figure 11.2 Coughing cat meme

stimulates makers to radical experiments in content, style, and compression esthetics. Hundreds of media artists from all over the world have risen to our challenge, competing for prizes such as Lowest Bitrate, Best Cat Video, Best Postapocalyptic, and Best Haptic Renunciation. As the title of that last prize suggests, small-file movies are intensive, pulling viewers toward the screen and stimulating their imaginations, rather than push out in high resolution toward a viewer who remains passive. Small-file movies are often very short, giving viewers more time to relish their enjoyment.

An ICT Contribution to the Commons

Ultimately, as the more critical ICT engineers emphasize, rebound effects indicate destructive contradictions in a growth-based economic system (Gossart 2015, 445). As Hilty points out, the rebound effect is a self-fulfilling prophecy. For example, 5G is predicted to be seven times more efficient in 2030. But capacity is planned for *eight* times current capacity, in order for the companies to be financially successful, leading to a net increase in electricity consumption (Belkhir & Hilty 2021).

Between the lines of self-sufficiency in ICT engineers' proposals shimmers an ICT contribution to the Commons. If the capitalist compulsions for proprietary product competition, obsolescence, and immediate consumer gratification are subtracted, then indeed ICT can be sustainable. However, such a prospect to halt ICT's contribution to global warming is as unlikely as it is crucial, given that the vast majority of internet traffic is powered by and serves shareholder corporations.

Notes

1 Most of the N11 countries get over 90% of their electricity-generating energy from fossil fuels. The others are Nigeria: 77% fossil fuels, 23% hydro; Turkey: 63% fossil fuels, 25% hydro; South Korea: 70% fossil fuels, 27% nuclear; and Vietnam: 60% fossil fuels, 39% hydro. Sources: globalpetrolprices.com/energy_mix.php; ourworldindata.org; iea.org.
2 See the complete recommendations at https://www.sfu.ca/sca/projects---activities/streaming-carbon-footprint.

Further Reading

Hilty, Lorenz M., and Bernard Aebischer, eds. 2015. *ICT Innovations for Sustainability*. Dordrecht: Springer.
Marks, Laura U., and Radek Przedpełski. 2022. "The Carbon Footprint of Streaming Media: Problems, Calculations, Solutions." In *Film and Television Production in the Era of Climate Change: Environmental Practice, Policy, and Scholarship*, eds. Pietari Kaapa and Hunter Vaughan. Basingstoke: Palgrave Macmillan.
Nardi, Bonnie, et al. 2018. "Computing Within Limits." *Communications of the ACM [Association for Computing Machinery]* 61:10 (October), 86–93.
Patrignani, Norberto, and Diane Whitehouse. 2018. *Slow Tech and ICT: A Responsible, Sustainable and Ethical Approach*. Cham: Springer International Publishing.
Preist, Chris, Daniel Schien, and Eli Blevis. 2016. "Understanding and Mitigating the Effects of Device and Cloud Service Design Decisions on the Environmental Footprint of Digital Infrastructure." In *Proceedings of the 2016 CHI Conference on Human Factors in Computing Systems*. Santa Clara: ACM [Association for Computing Machinery], 1324–1337.

References

Belkhir, Lofti, and Ahmed Elmeligi. 2018. "Assessing ICT Global Emissions Footprint: Trends to 2040 and Recommendations." *Journal of Cleaner Production* 177, 448–63. https://www.sciencedirect.com/science/article/pii/S095965261733233X

Belkhir, Lotfi, and Lorenz M. Hilty. 2021, August 12. Remarks on the Panel "Engineering Heroes." The Small File Media Festival. https://vimeo.com/595550014

Bieser, Jan C.T., and Lorenz M. Hilty. 2018. "Assessing Indirect Environmental Effects of Information and Communication Technology (ICT): A Systematic Literature Review." *Sustainability* 10:8, 2662. https://doi.org/10.3390/su10082662

Bordage, Frédéric. 2019. "The Environmental Footprint of the Digital World." Report for GreenIT.fr. https://www.greenit.fr/wp-content/uploads/2019/11/GREENIT_EENM_etude_EN_accessible.pdf

Chernicoff, David. 2016. "How Data Centers Pay for Renewable Energy." Data Center Dynamics. https://www.datacenterdynamics.com/en/analysis/how-data-centers-pay-for-renewable-energy/

Cisco. 2020. "Cisco Annual Internet Report (2018–2023)." Technical report. https://www.cisco.com/c/en/us/solutions/collateral/executive-perspectives/annual-internet-report/white-paper-c11-741490.html

Cubitt, S. 2017. *Finite Media: Environmental Implications of Digital Technologies*. Durham, NC: Duke University Press.

Danish, Noheed Khan, Muhammad Awais Baloch, Shah Saud, and Tehreem Fatima. 2018. "The Effect of ICT on CO_2 Emissions in Emerging Economies: Does the Level of Income Matter?" *Environmental Science and Pollution Research* 25, 22850–60. https://doi.org/10.1007/s11356-018-2379-2

Eglash, Ron. 2009. "Oppositional Technophilia." *Social Epistemology: A Journal of Knowledge, Culture and Policy*, 23:1, 79–86. https://doi.org/10.1080/02691720902741407

Ejembi, Oche, and Saleem K. Bhatti. 2015. "Client-Side Energy Costs of Video Streaming." *IEEE International Conference on Data Science and Data Intensive Systems*, 252–59.

GeSI (Global e-Sustainability Initiative) and Accenture. 2015. "#SMARTer2030: ICT Solutions for 21st Century Challenges." https://smarter2030.gesi.org/downloads/Full_report.pdf

Global Energy Monitor. "Global Coal Plant Tracker." Consulted January 20, 2023. https://globalenergymonitor.org/projects/global-coal-plant-tracker/

Gossart, Cédric. 2015. "Rebound Effects and ICT: A Review of the Literature." In *ICT Innovations for Sustainability*, eds. Lorenz M. Hilty and Bernard Aebischer. Dordrecht: Springer, 20435–48.

Hilty, Lorenz M., and Bernard Aebischer. 2015. "ICT for Sustainability: An Emerging Research Field." In *ICT Innovations for Sustainability*, eds. Lorenz M. Hilty and Bernard Aebischer. Dordrecht: Springer, 3–36. https://doi.org/10.1007/978-3-319-09228-7_1

Horner, Nathaniel C., Arman Shehabi, and Iñes L. Azevedo. 2016. "Known Unknowns: Indirect Energy Effects of Information and Communication Technology." *Environmental Research Letters* 11:10. https://iopscience.iop.org/article/10.1088/1748-9326/11/10/103001

Ihayere, O., P. Alege, G. Obindah, J. Ejemeyovwi, and P. Daramola. 2021. "Information Communication Technology Access and Use Towards Energy Consumption in Selected Sub Saharan Africa." *International Journal of Energy Economics and Policy* 11:1, 471–82. https://iopscience.iop.org/article/10.1088/1755-1315/665/1/012039

Kong, Yani. 2022. "Examining the Carbon Footprint of Streaming Media in Online Teaching and Learning". Summary at https://www.sfu.ca/sustainability/commitments-initiatives/living-lab.html

Lambert, Sofie, Margot Deruyck, Ward Van Heddeghem, Bart Lannoo, Wout Joseph, Didier Colle, Mario Pickavet, and Piet Demeester. 2015. "Post-Peak ICT: Graceful Degradation for Communication Networks in an Energy Constrained Future." *IEEE Communications Magazine* 53 (11): 166–74. https://doi.org/10.1109/MCOM.2015.7321987.

Lange, Steffen, Johanna Pohl, and Tilman Santarius. 2020. "Digitalization and Energy Consumption. Does ICT Reduce Energy Demand?" *Ecological Economics* 176. https://doi.org/10.1016/j.ecolecon.2020.106760

Larkin, Brian. 2013. "The Politics and Poetics of Infrastructure." *Annual Review of Anthropology* 42, 327–43. https://doi.org/10.1146/annurev-anthro-092412-155522

Lobato, Ramon, and Julian Thomas. 2015. *The Informal Media Economy*. Malden: Polity.

Marks, Laura U. 2017. "Poor Images, Ad Hoc Archives, Artists' Rights: The Scrappy Beauties of Handmade Digital Culture." *International Journal of Communication* 11, 3899–916.

Marks, Laura U. 2021, August 3. "A Survey of ICT Engineering Research Confirms Streaming Media's Carbon Footprint." *Media + Environment*. https://mediaenviron.org/post/1116-a-survey-of-ict-engineering-research-confirms-streaming-media-s-carbon-footprint-by-laura-u-marks

Marks, Laura U. and Radek Przedpełski. 2021. "Bandwidth Imperialism and Small-File Media." In *Post-45, Special Issue on "New Filmic Geographies,"* ed. Suzanne Enzerink. https://post45.org/2021/04/bandwidth-imperialism-and-small-file-media/

Marks, Laura U. and Radek Przedpełski. 2022. "The Carbon Footprint of Streaming Media: Problems, Calculations, Solutions." In *Film and Television Production in the Era of Climate Change: Environmental Practice, Policy and Scholarship*, eds. Pietari Kaapa and Hunter Vaughan, 207–234. Cham: Palgrave Macmillan.

Montevecchi, Francesca, et al. 2020. *Energy-Efficient Cloud Computing Technologies and Policies for an Eco-Friendly Cloud Market*. Vienna: Borderstep Institute and European Commission Directorate-General for Communications Networks, Content and Technology.

Obringer, Renée, Benjamin Rachunok, Debora Maia-Silva, Maryam Arbabzadeh, Roshanak Nateghi, and Kaveh Madani. 2021. "The Overlooked Environmental Footprint of Increasing Internet Use." *Resources, Conservation & Recycling* 167. https://www.sciencedirect.com/science/article/pii/S0921344920307072?via%3Dihub

O'Doherty, Caroline and Paul Hyland. 2021, September 29. "Fossil Fuel Burning Plants to be Used in Emergency, Says Ryan as EirGrid Warns of Major Electricity Outages." *Independent.ie*. https://www.independent.ie/irish-news/fossil-fuel-burning-plants-to-be-used-in-emergency-says-ryan-as-eirgrid-warns-of-major-electricity-outages-40899079.html

Park, Yongmoon, Fanchen Meng, and Muhammad Awais Baloch. 2018. "The Effect of ICT, Financial Development, Growth, and Trade Openness on CO_2 Emissions: An Empirical Analysis." *Environmental Science and Pollution Research* 25, 30708–19. https://doi.org/10.1007/s11356-018-3108-6

Preist, C., Daniel Schien, and Eli Blevis. 2016. "Understanding and Mitigating the Effects of Deviceand Cloud Service Design Decisions on the Environmental Footprint of Digital Infrastructure." In *Proceedings of the 2016 CHI Conference on Human Factors in Computing Systems*. Santa Clara: ACM [Association for Computing Machinery], 1324–1337.

Raghavan, Barath and Justin Ma. 2011, August 19. "Networking in the Long Emergency". *GreenNet'11*. https://doi.org/10.1145/2018536.2018545

Reinsdorf, Marshall, Gabriel Quirós, and STA Group. 2018. "Measuring the Digital Economy". Washington, DC: International Monetary Fund. https://www.imf.org/en/Publications/Policy-Papers/Issues/2018/04/03/022818-measuring-the-digital-economy

Saidi, K., Hassen Toumi, and Saida Zaidi. 2017. "Impact of Information Communication Technology and Economic Growth on the Electricity Consumption: Empirical Evidence from 67 Countries." *Journal of the Knowledge Economy* 8, 789–803. https://doi.org/10.1007/s13132-015-0276-1

The Shift Project. 2019. "Climate Crisis: The Unsustainable Use of Online Video. The Practical Case Study of Online Video." https://theshiftproject.org/en/article/unsustainable-use-online-video/

Tomlinson, Bill, Eli Blevis, Bonnie Nardi, Donald J. Patterson, M. Six Silberman, and Yue Pan. 2013. "Collapse Informatics and Practice: Theory, Method, and Design." *ACM Transactions on Computer-Human Interaction* 20 (4): 1–26. https://doi.org/10.1145/2493431.

12
ELECTRONIC ENVIRONMENTALISM
Monitoring and Making Ecological Crises

Jennifer Gabrys

Electronics and all that they plug into are energy intensive. An increasing amount of energy powers everything from Google searches to text messages and smart appliances, which in turn require a vast range of resources to build and run data centers, digital devices, and communication networks. The quantity of electricity consumed to power digital devices and networks is now estimated to be 46% worldwide.[1] When the original version of this text was written in 2014, estimates were between 1.5 and 2%, with projected growth of 3% of energy use worldwide by 2020. Current ICT energy consumption is exceeding original projections. Fossil fuels, including coal and oil, are dominant energy sources that power electronics and their networks (IEA 2021). Greenpeace notes that data centers are the "factories" of modern-day economies. A 2011 report documents how coal supplied 50–80% of the electricity used to power data centers (Cook and van Horn 2011, 4–5). Fossil fuels also power the manufacture of electronics, principally in countries such as China, Taiwan, and India (Smith et al. 2006).

The materialities and media ecologies of fossil fuels, data, and digital devices do not significantly register when used. Yet digital technologies and infrastructures are highly energy-intensive. Eric Williams (2004, 6173) has explained that over their lifecycle, electronics are "probably the most energy-intensive of home devices aside from furnaces and boilers." The energy to manufacture, power, and connect electronics is consumed in far more significant quantities than these seemingly immaterial devices imply. Indeed, if one were to account for all the energy used to manufacture, power, connect, cool, maintain, and eventually recycle and dispose of electronics, estimates of electronics-related energy use would increase even further. While some estimates of energy use focus on the manufacture and use of digital devices, other ecomedia research engages with the extended environmental impacts of data centers and digital infrastructures (Hogan 2015; Velkova 2016). Moreover, as computing becomes more pervasive and additional forms of "smartness" are embedded in environments, questions emerge about the types, quantities, and distributions of energy resources required to power these digital worlds.

In this chapter, updated and extended from a version first written in 2014, I consider how electronics generate media ecologies through the distribution and use of energy. First, I discuss the amount and type of energy that electronics consume as a form of electronic waste. The pollution from digital energy consumption differs from the stacks of abandoned digital devices associated with electronic waste. However, such energy use demonstrates the inescapable materiality of

This chapter has been made available under a CC-BY-NC-ND license.

electronics and their networks. Second, I consider how electronics have become central in managing energy use to achieve sustainability. The smart meter—or energy monitor—is the emblematic technology for achieving energy efficiency. Many digital devices, apps, smart grids, and monitoring technologies have been developed to manage energy consumption to respond to climate change. These technologies are part of a broader trend to move toward sustainability and efficiency through the increasing use of digital technologies.

In this two-part analysis, I attend to how digital technologies enable energy efficiency while creating further environmental and material problems. Information technologies are often promoted as devices that help achieve efficiencies, from energy supply and distribution to transport and logistics. Digital technologies seem more green and immaterial, contributing to more efficient processes. With the proliferation of personal mobile and computing devices, there continue to be projections of considerable increases in smart technologies, digital infrastructures, the Internet of Things, and mobile digital devices, with estimated increases ranging between 12% and 27% (Hasan 2022). These projections include energy meters and smart grids, which are meant to make systems more efficient and environmentally sound. Yet the fallout from electronic energy materializes in the resources used to power these devices and the embedded energy, or power and resources used to manufacture them. Electronic energy use shows up in carbon footprints, coal dust, greenhouse gas emissions, and extensive land use taken up with data centers and power plants. These developments raise real dilemmas about what "green technology" means: can technology be green if it is hazardous in its manufacture, prone to obsolescence, and difficult to dispose of? Moreover, can technology be green if it is powered mainly by coal and contributes to increasing carbon emissions or requires rare earth or conflict minerals such as lithium or coltan that contribute to environmental injustice worldwide?

I develop the concept of *electronic environmentalism* to analyze how digital technologies organize ways of acting on environmental problems to arrive at potential solutions. On the one hand, electronic environmentalism describes digital technologies used to monitor and manage energy use. Such activities can replace potentially more carbon-intensive activities with energy-saving virtual parallels, for instance, meeting online rather than flying. On the other hand, the term signals how these practices require extensive digital infrastructures—including manufacturing to disposal sites, data centers, and server farms—that often enable these practices while obscuring the resources needed to support them. Digital technologies have become central to meeting environmental objectives, yet these same devices generate environmental problems. Electronic environmentalism is a term that captures and analyzes how digital technologies both monitor and exacerbate ecological crises. The media ecologies discussed here are ecologies in crisis.

Tracking the Material Processes of Digital Pollution

While energy use contributes to the material resource use and waste of electronics, the residues from digital devices include everything from discarded electronics at end-of-life to resource-intensive manufacturing processes, information overload, and software obsolescence. I have previously written about these other forms of electronic waste in the study *Digital Rubbish*, where I developed a processual and material approach to electronics by focusing on how they generate waste (Gabrys 2011). Electronic waste is one of the fastest growing waste streams worldwide. The volumes of e-waste generated have risen from estimates ranging from 20- to 25-million tons per year to 35–40-million tons per year in 2009 to 50-million tons per year in 2022.[2] Volumes of e-waste are also estimated to double by 2050 to 100-million tons per year.[3] Electronic waste is hazardous, difficult to recycle at end-of-life, and often processed in harmful ways, raising significant environmental justice issues. Lead, mercury, and brominated flame retardants are just a few of the harmful chemical-material components that make up electronics (Kuehr and Williams 2007). Electronics also require and generate hazardous waste products during manufacture, and the working conditions of electronics manufacturing and recycling are typically harmful to human health. However, there continues to be a widespread sense that digital media are relatively resource-free technologies and may even promote green alternatives by using fewer resources than analog equivalents or through ongoing monitoring of consumption activities.

The case of energy as a form of electronic waste raises related yet distinct issues concerning the materiality of electronics. Carbon footprints are often used to estimate how much waste electronics generate from energy use. For example, a Google search can create carbon emissions between 0.2 and 7 grams of CO_2, while an average spam email generates "emissions equivalent to 0.3 grams of carbon dioxide (CO_2) per message" (Clark 2011). By comparison, driving 1 mile in an average gas vehicle generates 404 grams of CO_2.[4] Multiply by 62 trillion spam emails sent in 2008, and this cumulative amount of emissions from spam is equivalent to "driving around the Earth 1.6 million times" (McAfee 2009). Whereas each search, page use, or email sent might have a comparatively small resource or greenhouse gas footprint, the amounts of data sent, received, stored, and otherwise processed contribute to overall energy use and emissions of considerable quantities.

These carbon footprints make evident the resource requirements of seemingly fleeting and immaterial activities such as internet searching and social media browsing. They can also demonstrate the increasing demand for energy needed to power and connect digital technologies. However, energy use inevitably has an impact beyond measuring how much CO_2 is entering the atmosphere and accelerating the effects of climate change. Indeed, with ongoing coal use, there are issues of coal-mining extraction as a highly damaging land use, and coal mining also as an occupation that generates significant health risks and environmental justice issues. Alternatively, with nuclear energy, a whole attendant set of issues emerge related to where power plants are sited, how they are subsidized, where the waste goes, and what happens if power plants fail. Moreover, with oil and gas production through fracking, the details of groundwater contamination, air pollution, or land-use conflicts also become significant energy-related problems. Even with these briefly noted energy dilemmas, it becomes evident that the energy used to power electronic technologies has political, social, and environmental effects that go beyond the increase of carbon emissions to encompass much more complex ecologies.

However, the pollution from electronic energy that circulates in the form of greenhouse gases and excess CO_2 is often not evident in an overt material form. Instead, it is present as indeterminate matter. Dirt and pollution do not register through first-hand encounters but through political, scientific, bodily, and environmental arrangements. The material infrastructures of energy and electronic networks—in the form of data centers, devices, and coal—might be made evident. But the emissions that are the primary form of pollution from energy are often detected only in their effects and material transformations within systems, bodies, and ecologies. Making emissions—particularly CO_2—sensible involves an assortment of infrastructures and practices, from scientific models to policy to ecological field studies (Edwards 2010). This is not a matter out of place, as much as pollution that becomes evident through mattering processes (Barad 2003; Stengers 2008).

The pollution from energy emerges through different modes of mattering. By undertaking a processual approach to materiality, it may then be possible to expand beyond treating materiality only as that which is tangible, visible, or physical, to suggest instead that materiality relates to sedimentations, arrangements, and power relationships that continue to hold our existing energy practices together. In this sense, a "material" intervention in the space of electronic energy might not necessarily even consist of an object as such. Instead, it might consist of different arrangements of energy practices that rematerialize or recast the taken-for-granted sedimentations that make up our everyday energy ecologies (Gabrys 2014). Immateriality, moreover, might be a critical part of the performance of materiality, where electronics operate as though they are resource-free; or where energy appears to be endless and in constant supply. Electronic energy consumption articulates distinct forms of mattering. Such an approach suggests that energy practices could be unsettled and rematerialized.

Digital Energy: Monitoring and Making Ecological Crises

Imagine a near future of electronic waste, where alongside the more prehistoric artifacts of desktop computers, piles of energy monitors and smart-grid technologies accumulate, which amass as the debris of the drive toward efficiency and, apparently, sustainability. Electronics such as smart meters have emerged to monitor and track energy processes to lessen environmental burdens, yet at the same time require resources and energy for their manufacture and use, and are eventual contributors to electronic debris at end-of-life. These digital technologies are the anticipated debris from using electronics to manage and monitor climate change. They contribute to ecological crises in the form of fossil fuel extraction and land use degradation, hazardous pollution, impairment of environmental and human health, and climate change. Identifying and managing one crisis gives rise to—and even occludes—others.

I now turn to examine one of the objects and ecologies of digital energy—the smart meter—to consider how electronics are entangled with the management and use of energy. Energy monitors and their associated infrastructures are not typically regarded as digital media. Still, these technologies can be approached as media forms, practices, and ecologies, which further function within and through processes of materialization and dematerialization characteristic of many other digital technologies. Such an approach draws attention to how digital functionalities are not exclusively located within an identifiable computational object. Furthermore, the sites and distributions of computation may even shift through electronic appliances as banal as energy monitors. What media ecologies emerge with smart meters, and how might a materialized digital media analysis shed light on their environmental effects?

Energy monitors might be considered one of many technologies now made up of electronic components and constitute electronic waste at end-of-life. A seemingly less "expressive" technology than social media and other digital media for which revolutionary claims are frequently made, energy monitors are one of many emerging electronics developed to increase sustainability through awareness and efficiency mechanisms. Energy monitors promise to be technologies that will remake our material practices to generate greater sustainability and efficiency. Moreover, energy monitors, smart meters, and energy use interventions become specific strategies to visualize and materialize energy use.

One smart meter, plugged into the electrical mains in any house, monitors domestic energy use from this central point. It gathers data on electricity (and gas) use and potentially talks to appliances through a local network in some scenarios. It collects and sends several hundred packets of data per day via cellular and other networks while potentially hopping across neighboring energy meters to find the most efficient pathway to the nearest mobile phone tower. From there, it talks to a data management company, likely a subsidiary of a multinational outsourcing corporation, that holds the data in a cloud architecture to process and make it available to energy companies, governments, and other "relevant parties" still to be determined. Software may be used at various stages across this cycle to manage energy use in the home and across the grid, to make predictions and optimize configurations while seeking to lower costs. The smart monitor requires a smart grid and the ability to program and reprogram meters remotely since additional meters will likely be rolled out in multiple phases of testing and updating.

In the computational project of implementing smart meters, electronics monitor, manage, use, and reroute energy. These devices create new materializations of computation and energy. Within these materializations and matterings of energy, smart meters, animated appliances, and smart grids are part of the apparatuses for measuring, balancing, displaying, and making relevant data on energy consumption to mitigate and reduce the levels of energy consumed. While they consume energy, electronics could point toward more efficient energy use, where smart grids may modulate demand and smart meters aid in energy reduction. Efficiency through digital means is also proposed to replace energy-intensive activities such as transport, where online meetings replace air travel. Electronics, in this sense, are technologies for rematerializing a whole number of inefficient energy uses. At the same time, electronics and computing companies are increasingly making pledges to run their operations and production through efficient (and at times renewable) energy sources (Raghavan and Ma 2011; UK POST 2008).

Setting out to study just how much energy the internet requires for its construction, operation, and maintenance, Barath Raghavan and Justin Ma (2011) arrived at a rough estimate of between 170 and 307 gigawatts (GW) yearly. Calculating energy and "emergy," or energy embodied in devices and infrastructure, the authors suggest that the overall share of energy consumption across internet-based technologies is comparatively small. In this sense, they suggest that computational technologies may even offer energy-saving strategies by substituting networked processes for resource-intensive industries such as transport or manufacturing. In this estimation and proposal, electronics may consume energy, but they also provide the basis for achieving greater levels of energy efficiency.

Despite these many initiatives, multiple critiques of efficiency as an energy-saving strategy exist. While there is insufficient space to discuss these arguments, discussions around the "rebound effect" in energy literature have pointed out that energy efficiency does not automatically lead to an overall reduction in energy consumption. Instead, efficiency may even have a "backfire" effect by contributing to increased production and consumption due to lower prices or greater availability of resources (Herring 2006). Efficiency, these analyses note, is not the same as conservation or using less energy overall, nor does it address the need to switch to non-fossil-fuel sources of energy. Within proposals for electronics to contribute to energy efficiency, it is notable how electronics are operationalized to make energy reductions and so become part of the materialities of energy and part of the understanding of what it means to materialize energy in order to reduce energy use. Electronics for energy efficiency is part of this process of mattering, where attention to the pollution from energy use leads to strategies to intervene within energy ecologies. The problems with an efficiency-only approach become further evident since it does not attend to the energy source, such as coal, shale oil, solar power, and waste heat. The process of making energy use more efficient, where energy sources may be sourced from highly polluting fossil fuels, is problematic if the overall objective of using less energy is to address climate change.

Here, a digital version of materiality encourages electronic environmentalism as a sort of sustainable behavior. However, what articulations of materiality are at play here? Electronics, on one level, are descriptive technologies that are ideal for capturing, monitoring, and managing current conditions. Energy use can be monitored, usage statistics described and captured, and communicated for supply and demand management. This descriptive monitoring capacity of electronics is important to consider in the context of environmental and material approaches to digital media. Energy monitoring performs through an informational approach to evidencing material resources as they are used. Nevertheless, electronics that monitor could also make energy sources more distant. By materializing energy use, what do electronics make matter or cause to be relevant? And how do these electronic versions of environmentalism sustain distinct approaches to material practices and politics while impeding others?

Electronic environmentalism could even sustain energy practices as they are. Electronics that enable the monitoring of environmental distress may also be contributing to those same problems. Displaying and materializing the "facts" of electricity consumption might not inform or change the material politics of energy use. This is why working with a processual approach to materiality could generate different considerations of how materialities form. This is also why asking after what expressions and forms of materiality are made operational is essential. Through these electronic environmentalist interactions, distinct materialities that promote distinct practices and actions—or inactions—become evident.

From Media Ecologies to Ecological Media

The energy required to power the vast server farms, networks, digital devices, and processes is a relatively remote but operative aspect of digital technologies as an industry. Increasing power demands can generate waste in the form of carbon emissions and land used for data server centers and through power failures and website disruptions. How would an internet of sporadic but regular blackouts change relationships to digital technologies? Would a more deliberate encounter with the energy of digital devices and practices generate alternative materialities for these technologies? Because electronics appear to be engines of the perpetually new, they are readily adopted to address environmental issues since they are technologies that enable change. What emerges here is not just the novelty and obsolescence of digital media but also new uses of media, the revolutions they promise to achieve, and the economies and ecologies they promise to generate. At the same time, as instruments developed to monitor and so lessen environmental burdens, energy monitors contribute to the material effects and transformations of environments. The electronic environmentalism that materializes at this intersection is characterized by a complex set of practices that monitor environmental impacts in the form of energy use. However, through monitoring, they potentially lead to information disconnected from effective or alternative actions to remake energy ecologies.

In other words, energy monitors in their manufacture, use, and eventual disposal could contribute to environmental issues while attempting to mitigate them. Energy monitors do not ostensibly register as digital media. However, this computational arrangement should be considered both for how it reworks the materialities of digital media and for the extended ecologies and processes it sets in motion. Electronics are doubly bound up with the mattering of energy, both in how energy sources, use, and infrastructures are relatively remote; and in how smart meters remake energy encounters into a project of electronic environmentalism that tracks and visualizes energy consumption.

As this chapter has argued, the management-based logics of energy meters potentially do little to change energy practices toward lessening overall greenhouse gas emissions, even if they achieve efficiencies. These descriptive approaches to energy monitoring give rise to a reconsideration of what practices, relations, and material politics we might articulate through digital modes of engagement. How do practices of electronic environmentalism, potentially even through their failure to remedy ecological crises, give rise to different ways of engaging with and addressing the problem of energy consumption and the materiality of electronics?

The computational functionalities of energy monitors and any number of digital media are not contained within a single computational object. From desktop PCs to ubiquitous sensors, computation takes place through an extended milieu. It may even inform how we conceptualize the problem of energy use—as a problem that must be computable to be addressed. This approach suggests ways of expanding, transforming, and reworking the ecologies of media not simply as a content-use relationship located within identifiable media carriers or genres but rather as media ecologies and relationships articulated through a concatenation of computational technologies and practices.

As digital technologies, energy monitors enable functionalities for tracking energy use to promote sustainable everyday practices and abate ecological crises. And yet, these technologies contribute at the same time to reworking and transforming the very environments and problems they would monitor. In this sense, the pollution and waste from our ongoing material practices generate residual materialities that spur new modes of monitoring and technological interventions, where these very computational modalities continually remake digital media in both their material arrangements and processes. In this way, digital ecologies are always in the making, giving rise to different material processes and relations. These modes of mattering could open up from electronic environmentalism to alternative engagements if we were to attend to how digital media organize and give relevance to our material practices, politics, and ecologies.

Acknowledgments

This handbook entry is an abbreviated and updated version of an earlier chapter, published as Jennifer Gabrys, "Powering the Digital: From Energy Ecologies to Electronic Environmentalism." In: Richard Maxwell, Jon Raundalen, and Nina Lager Vestberg, eds. *Media and the Ecological Crisis*, pp. 3–18. New York and London: Routledge, 2014. Research for this project was originally made possible through the ESRC-funded project, "Sustainability Invention and Energy Demand Reduction: Co-Designing Communities and Practice" (RES-628-25-0043).

Notes

1 The original version of this chapter published in 2014 referenced estimates based on ICT energy use in 2010, which was 1.5–2% of worldwide electricity consumption and was projected to grow to 3% by 2020. The latest estimates suggest that ICT energy consumption was between 4 and 6% in 2020. See Raghavan and Ma (2011); UK Parliamentary Office of Science and Technology (2008); and UK Parliamentary Office of Science and Technology (2022).
2 Varying estimates of e-waste quantities can be found at Robinson (2009); United Nations Environment Programme (2009); and Statista, "Global E-Waste - Statistics and Facts".
3 Digital Watch observatory. "E-waste." https://dig.watch/topics/e-waste.
4 US Environmental Protection Agency (2022).

Further Reading

Gabrys, Jennifer. 2011. *Digital Rubbish: A Natural History of Electronics*. Ann Arbor: University of Michigan Press.
Hogan, Mél, and Asta Vonderau, eds. 2019. "The Nature of Data Centers." Special Issue. *Culture Machine* 18. https://culturemachine.net/vol-18-the-nature-of-data-centers.
Lennon, Myles. 2017. "Decolonizing Energy: Black Lives Matter and Technoscientific Expertise amid Solar Transitions." *Energy Research & Social Science* 30: 18–27.
Mukherjee, Rahul. 2020. *Radiant Infrastructures: Media, Environment, and Cultures of Uncertainty*. Durham, NC: Duke University Press.

Starosielski, Nicole and Janet Walker, eds. 2016. *Sustainable Media: Critical Approaches to Media and Environment.* New York and London: Routledge.

References

Barad, Karen. 2003. "Posthumanist Performativity: Toward an Understanding of How Matter Comes to Matter." *Signs: Journal of Women in Culture and Society* 28, no. 3: 801–31.

Clark, Duncan. 2011. "Google Discloses Carbon Footprint for the First Time." *The Guardian* (September 8). www.theguardian.com/environment/2011/sep/08/google-carbon-footprint.

Cook, Gary and Jodie van Horn. 2011. *How Dirty Is Your Data: A Look at the Energy Choices That Power Cloud Computing.* Amsterdam: Greenpeace International.

Edwards, Paul N. 2010. *A Vast Machine: Computer Models, Climate Data, and the Politics of Global Warming.* Cambridge: MIT Press.Gabrys, Jennifer. 2009. "Sink: The Dirt of Systems," *Environment and Planning D: Society and Space* 27, no. 4: 666–81.

Gabrys, Jennifer. 2011. *Digital Rubbish: A Natural History of Electronics.* Ann Arbor: University of Michigan Press.

Gabrys, Jennifer. 2014. "A Cosmopolitics of Energy: Diverging Materialities and Hesitating Practices." *Environment and Planning A: Economy and Space* 46, no. 9 (September): 2095–109. https://doi.org/10.1068/a468.

Hasan, Mohammad. 2022. "State of IoT 2022: Number of Connected IoT Devices Growing 18% to 14.4 Billion Globally." IoT Analytics (May 18). https://iot-analytics.com/number-connected-iot-devices.

Herring, Horace. 2006. "Energy Efficiency: A Critical Review." *Energy* 31: 10–20.

Hogan, Mél. 2015. "Data Flows and Water Woes: The Utah Data Center." *Big Data & Society* 2, no. 2: 2053951715592429.

International Energy Agency (IEA). 2021. *Key World Energy Statistics.* Paris, France. https://www.iea.org/reports/key-world-energy-statistics-2021.

Kuehr, Ruediger, and Eric Williams, eds. 2007. *Computers and the Environment: Understanding and Managing their Impacts.* Vol. 14. Berlin; Heidelberg: Springer Science & Business Media.

McAfee. 2009. "The Carbon Footprint of Spam Email Report." Santa Clara, CA: McAfee. http://www.mcafee.com/us/resources/reports/rp-carbonfootprint2009.pdf [https://web.archive.org/web/20110515043705/http://www.mcafee.com/us/resources/reports/rp-carbonfootprint2009.pdf].

Raghavan, Barath and Justin Ma. 2011. "The Energy and Emergy of the Internet." *Proceedings of the 10th ACM Workshop on Hot Topics in Networks* (November): 1–6.

Robinson, Brett H. 2009. "E-Waste: An Assessment of Global Production and Environmental Impacts." *Science of the Total Environment* 408, no. 2, December: 183–91.

Smith, Ted, David Allan Sonnenfeld, and David N. Pellow, eds. 2006. *Challenging the Chip: Labor Rights and Environmental Justice in the Global Electronics Industry.* Philadelphia: Temple University Press.

Statista. "Global E-Waste - Statistics and Facts." https://www.statista.com/topics/3409/electronic-waste-worldwide/#topicOverview.

Stengers, Isabelle. 2008. "A Constructivist Reading of Process and Reality." *Theory, Culture & Society* 25, no. 4: 91–110.

Velkova, Julia. 2016. "Data That Warms: Waste Heat, Infrastructural Convergence and the Computation Traffic Commodity." *Big Data & Society* 3, no. 2: 2053951716684144.

Williams, Eric. 2004. "Energy Intensity of Computer Manufacturing: Hybrid Assessment Combining Process and Economic Input-Output Methods." *Environmental Science & Technology* 38, no. 22: 6166–74.

UK Parliamentary Office of Science and Technology. 2008. "ICT and CO_2 Emissions," no. 319 (December). https://www.parliament.uk/documents/post/postpn319.pdf.

UK Parliamentary Office of Science and Technology. 2022. "Energy Consumption of ICT," no. 677 (September). https://post.parliament.uk/research-briefings/post-pn-0677.

United Nations Environment Programme (UNEP). 2009. "Recycling: From E-Waste to Resources." United Nations Environment Programme and United Nations University, 2009, DTI/1192/PA. www.unep.org/PDF/PressReleases/ E-Waste_publication_screen_FINALVERSION-sml.pdf.

US Environmental Protection Agency (EPA). 2022. "Greenhouse Gas Emissions from a Typical Passenger Vehicle" (June 30). https://www.epa.gov/greenvehicles/greenhouse-gas-emissions-typical-passenger-vehicle.

13
RADIANT ENERGY AND MEDIA INFRASTRUCTURES OF THE SOUTH

Rahul Mukherjee

As Melody Jue (2020, 4) and Cajetan Iheka (2021) have noted, ecomedia studies is interested in the connections and possibilities as well as the contradictions and problematics of/across "media representations, media infrastructures, and media materiality." The environmental and health impact of radiation from radiant infrastructures, which help power media devices (electricity from nuclear reactors) and support cellular communication (cell antenna signals), is a key part of ecomedia studies. This includes analyzing the complex (in)visibilities of radiant infrastructures and their varied/extended materiality from steel and concrete structures to electromagnetic waves and ionizing radiation. Whether it is the domes of a nuclear reactor or cell antennas atop a billboard or water tank, radiant infrastructures themselves have mediatic dimensions in the way they address audiences and citizens. Barandiarán et al. (2022, 8) explain that media devices and infrastructures have had a constitutive role in environmental and energy matters: "Part and parcel of large-, medium-, and small-scale infrastructures, media sculpt and enable energy modernity." Radiant infrastructures like nuclear reactors, cell antennas, and solar panels are energy and media infrastructures. These infrastructures are imbricated in questions about energy transition and intersecting energy cultures which are also crucial questions for ecomedia and environmental justice.

Radiant infrastructures can also be considered through a historical understanding of the different materialities and technologies involved in lighting indoor and outdoor environments: bonfires, candle lanterns, gas lamps, and electric lights (Marvin 1987). Media technologies of "modernity" like X-rays and cinema, when theorized as radiant infrastructures, constitute the twentieth-century drive for hypervisibility, for lighting up the depths of the interior body, and for making the wider world transparent (Lippit 2005). Concomitant with discussions of hypervisibility and transparency is another form of radiant infrastructures, surveillance infrastructures, which are used to illuminate citizens and make them visible. As Simone Browne (2015) has demonstrated in her examination of lantern laws in eighteenth-century colonial New York City, surveillance infrastructures can illuminate in disturbingly racialized ways.

Studies of radiant infrastructures can help scholars gain a logistical understanding of various energy forms, whether it is atomic energy (nuclear reactors) or solar energy (solar panels). Solar panels and agricultural technologies that harness/harvest sunlight for energy or food production are radiant infrastructures reconfiguring radiant lives. Cell towers and nuclear reactors, like railways and hydroelectric dams, have often been credited as bringing (or associated with the symbolic glow of) development and progress. What differentiates radiant infrastructures like cell antennas and atomic power plants from railways and dams is that they emit radiant energies in the form of electromagnetic signals and radioactive rays (Mukherjee 2020).

It is important to go beyond theorizing radiant infrastructures as specific objects to consider the wider environment that radiation emissions permeate, along with the uncertain environmental (and health) effects of such infrastructures. Studying radiant infrastructures involves transcending visible light to account for other waves in the electromagnetic spectrum emitted (or modulated/filtered/mediated) by nuclear reactors, cellular antennas, X-rays, and solar infrastructures (sun), such as infrared, ultraviolet, and invisible light (Starosielski 2021). The uncertain effects of spectral exchanges between infrastructural emissions and human (and animal) bodies (that mediate radiation) are crucial to theorizing radiant infrastructures.

In what follows, I will begin with how a historical study of heat and light in relation to radiant infrastructures provides an account of the blending of media and energy narratives and materiality. Then I shall explore emissions and exposures as specific properties of radiant infrastructures that provide a way to engage with the differentiated visibilities of such infrastructures, addressing aspects of labor needed to run and maintain such infrastructures. Finally, I will examine both geopolitical and on-the-ground socio-material relations that emerge with the siting of radiant infrastructures in particular locations and regions. I hope that this conversation between political economy of infrastructural power and studies of ecological systems can contribute toward ecomedia studies.

Heat and Light: Media and Energy Infrastructures

In our contemporary times, there has been a movement away from fossil fuels toward directly harnessing solar radiation as a renewable form of energy. Much before the large-scale sale, distribution, and deployment of solar photovoltaic systems and solar-powered appliances, there have been other radiant infrastructures and technologies in the era of industrialized modernity that have drawn on or have been compared to solar rays in the form of metaphors, analogies, and materializations. Whether it is the capture of solar rays through the camera in early photography or the comparison of the light and heat emanating from nuclear tests to the "radiance of a thousand suns," there is a turn to the sun, a "heliotropism" to discussions of radiance and radiation (DeLoughrey 2009). This literal "turn" toward the sun is in the infrastructure of the solar panel which follows the path of the sun from morning till evening. Atomic reactors are also associated with the sun because nuclear power plants are considered to replicate the fusion process that occurs inside the core of the sun.

The mutually imbricated histories of radiation and modernity across media and energy technologies are also elucidated by what Paul Virilio (1989) calls the "wars of light." From lanterns and searchlights to satellites and drones, wars started being fought on optical representations and visual (or "light") media. The tests of atomic weapons spilling radiation were accompanied by the capture of their spectacular violence through films as hundreds of Hollywood photographers and filmmakers were brought in to shoot these nuclear test films in Bikini Atoll and other Pacific Islands. As Elizabeth DeLoughrey notes:

> This connection between nuclear radiation and photography is close and historic; participants in the tests were required to wear film badges that would fog when 'safe' radiation levels were exceeded, replicating the behavior of the nineteenth-century photographic plates that led to the discovery of radioactivity itself.
>
> (2009, 476)

These overlapping histories and practices of media (searchlight, photography, and camera) and energy technologies (militarized and civilian nuclear infrastructures) suggest how radiant technologies have been associated with both illumination (at times, dizzying blinding light) and spectral shadows.

Some other historical accounts also suggest this blending of energy and media, both in terms of elements and infrastructures: the media object "radio" and the element "radium" do not merely share etymological roots but also intersect scientific and social histories associated with luminescence. The discovery of X-rays, radio waves, and later microwaves—which constitute the electromagnetic spectrum—had much to do with the early twentieth century's preoccupation with the science and technology of energy, which birthed the discovery of radioactivity (Mukherjee 2020). While it might be easy to move from radio to mobile phones and then to cell antennas (as mobile phones and cell antennas can be said to exchange radio waves), and from radium and uranium to nuclear reactors (thereby establishing similarities between atomic reactor radiations and cell tower radiations), this would be hasty conjecture. As much as radiations are all-pervasive, it is important to differentiate between "ionizing" nuclear radiations and the "non-ionizing" electromagnetic magnetic fields that cell antenna signals are constituted of.

Infrastructural (In)Visibilities: Emissions and Exposures

The "infra" in infrastructures suggests that infrastructures work in the background providing the "foundation" or "substructure" for everyday operations, and therefore, infrastructures like sewage systems and oil pipelines tend to (generally) remain hidden or inconspicuous unless one smells stench or sees oil leaking out. While exaggerated display of the monumentality of infrastructures (like media showcase of the giant domes of a nuclear reactor) is one kind of infrastructural visibility; another kind of infrastructural visibility would further public understanding of what makes infrastructures work on a day-to-day basis (Bowker and Star 1999). It is crucial to study these differentiated (in)visibilities of infrastructures, but with radiant infrastructures like cell towers and nuclear reactors, one needs to carefully attend to their comparative invisibility and imperceptibility. Additionally, an expansion of scale happens as the radioactive emissions from a nuclear fallout travel widely downwind. The spatial impact of the Chernobyl nuclear disaster did not remain contained in Ukraine and Belarus but extended to Cumbria and Wales, where plumes of radioactive emissions from the reactor landed.

The environmental and health debates around radiant infrastructures like nuclear reactors and cell towers have often involved contests over ways of measuring radiant emissions, ascertaining whether emissions are within threshold levels, and most importantly, whether the bodily exposure to such radioactive toxins is within or beyond acceptable limits. During the cell antenna radiation controversy in various cities of India that I studied from 2010 to 2017, there were debates about the kind of radiation detectors being used to measure cell antenna signals (Mukherjee 2020). After the nuclear fallout in Fukushima, to ensure food and environmental safety for their children, it became important for Japanese parents to measure radioactive contamination with Geiger counters to determine appropriate threshold levels (Kimura 2016). EMF detectors and Geiger counters become ways of mediating radiation. These detectors provide phenomenological translations, thereby making radiation palpable to human senses.

Gabrielle Hecht (2012) has argued that it is not just radiation or nuclear waste that is imperceptible, but that the plight of nuclear workers, especially subcontract employees, has been eschewed in mainstream media stories. While theorizing the (in)visibilities of radiant infrastructures, it is important to examine how laborers are exposed to radiation while working every day in the atomic power plant and how they apprehend (and calibrate) their bodily exposure to radiation doses. Parks and Starosielski (2015) have called for foregrounding people's phenomenological encounters with infrastructures in terms of occupational hazard and public health.

The questions of emissions and exposures related to radiant infrastructures are difficult as the threshold levels or exposure standards set are often contested (Mukherjee 2020). The governance of radiant infrastructures involves exercising tight control over not only radiation emission levels but also information about those emission levels. If a seasonal worker falls ill, authorities at an atomic reactor plant do not want to release the worker's dosage levels, fearing disrepute or public slander.

Socio-Material Relations

Infrastructures are not just things but relations between things (Larkin 2013). Certain parts of an infrastructure are not visible because of the scale of operations of an infrastructure, and therefore, the relations between different parts of an infrastructure may not be visible or immediately apparent. The spectacular displays of the (exterior) nuclear dome should not only lead to questions about the internal workings of the coolant channel inside the reactor chambers but also questions about the (working conditions in the) mines from where the uranium is extracted for the reactor. In many cases, the uranium mining is done in regions and countries different from where the nuclear reactors are located. The nuclear reactors in France run because of the uranium mined in Niger (a former colony of France), and the uneven terms of this uranium trade between France and Niger gesture to the continuation of the colonial legacies of extraction in postcolonial times.

In his observational documentary film *Arlit, Deuxième Paris*, Idrissou Mora-Kpai presents what it has meant for the denizens of a small town in Northern Niger called Arlit to live amidst the uranium mining operations carried out by the French nuclear corporation Areva (partially owned by the French state). The subtitle of the film, "second Paris" (*Deuxième Paris*), indicates promises left unfulfilled for the city of Arlit, which began as a uranium mining boom town with anticipations and aspirations of jobs and electricity, on its way to become the "second Paris" (Iheka 2021). These promises of development remain unrealized as conveyed by the expressive testimonies of Arlit residents. Several parts of Arlit remain without electricity, and the initial boom that the town witnessed soon subsided because of the global fall in uranium prices, and the profits that the state of Niger earned from uranium exports were not shared with the population in Arlit. Paradoxically, the uranium from Arlit's mines lights bulbs in France, but many streets in this Nigerien town remain without electricity. Thus, the uneven socio-technical relations around radiant infrastructures lead to unequal distributions of radiance.

The film also expresses, in the words of Carmela Garritano (2020, 125), "the different modalities of waiting experienced in Arlit." Some are waiting for global uranium trade policies to change so that Arlit becomes a boom town again and they can have their prosperous jobs back. Some others are migrants from various regions of West Africa on their northward move toward Algeria from where they want to make their way to Europe. As these people wait in Arlit, radioactive contamination from uranium mining slowly decays inside their bodies, mutating and unleashing horrific effects on the living tissues. These various socio-material relations between radioactive uranium and miners' bodies, between Arlit denizens and the Nigerien state, between Niger and France, and between Areva and Arlit are all part of understanding the (radiant/nuclear infrastructures of) uranium mines and nuclear reactors.

The first time I began researching about Areva was when I heard that this French nuclear corporation was building the largest nuclear reactor in Sakhri-Nate, a small fishworkers' village in the state of Maharashtra along the Arabian Sea. At that time; I had no idea that Areva operated mines in Arlit. The importance of making some of these connections about the way the French parastatal organizations run uranium mines and build nuclear reactors in different parts of the Global South is crucial toward understanding the various socio-material relations at different scales of lived lives and political economies engendered by radiant infrastructures.

The promise of another radiant infrastructure, the solar energy infrastructure, is to put an end (finally) to the extractive long chains of ruthless profit-making and environmental degradation that the political economy of nuclear energy infrastructures (as well as those of the fossil fuels industries) have engendered. Solar energy also promises a new moral economy with far more inclusive socio-material relations than those existing in the coal mining or nuclear reactor sector (Cross 2021). This promise of solar energy is what Imre Szeman and Darin Barney (2021) call "solarity," and which I believe to be another crucial aspect of theorizing the radiance of solar energy infrastructures. That said, the emerging empirical studies of places in India and East Africa where concerted efforts to provide off-grid electricity through solar power have been made suggest that the promise of solar energy runs into both logistical troubles and moral ambivalences (Cross 2021). Is solar energy going to unleash solar capitalism and business as usual or will it lead to community-based alternatives? Beyond just the "good" or "bad" moral economies of "solarity," what I want to examine are the on-ground socio-material relations that are emerging with the introduction of off-grid solar energy infrastructures in the Global South.

The relationship of particular communities in India to solar energy is also shaped by their years of living in un-electrified places. Some community members of an off-grid de-electrified village in the state of Bihar would rent out solar lights without the solar panel and, after their solar light got discharged, would bring it back to the person from whom they had rented it to have the light charged again (through the solar panel), so that they could rent it once more. Some found this aspect of charging and discharging of solar lights to be cumbersome and, yet, since they could not afford the lumpsum money required to buy the solar panel themselves, they continued renting. One such family that design anthropologist Abhigyan Singh interacted with during his fieldwork noted that they found solar lights to be convenient and safe, since a child in their family burned their hand from a flame while studying under a *dhibri* lamp running on kerosene oil.

The selling, renting, and exchanging of solar devices and solar panels in India is marked by prevailing relations of caste, kinship, and friendship (Cross 2019; Singh et al. 2017), though not always in expected ways. A Yadav woman (from a non-Dalit caste), part of a family of landowners and peasants, preferred to rent out solar lights she had to members of the Dalit caste who worked in her husband's agricultural fields rather than to her own Yadav caste members. The Yadav woman, who owned solar panels and devices, felt she would be able to get money back from her Dalit workers more easily than her own caste members. Trustworthiness here, therefore, had its own logic. Furthermore, the Yadav woman did not always expect monetary repayments for loaning out solar lights. At times, for the solar lights, she expected her Dalit workers to help out for longer hours in the fields or help out with their skills in masonry, carpentry, and agricultural tool-making. The patron-client (and earlier co-dependent) relationship made it easier for this particular Yadav woman to negotiate with their Dalit workers (Singh et al. 2017). Given the earlier history of extractive and exploitative relationships across caste hierarchies, some of these Dalit-Bahujan households hesitated to borrow solar lights worrying that they might get caught in a debt trap sooner or later. Some Dalit-Bahujan households were suspicious about the Yadav household not asking monetary repayment for solar lights and insisted that they would rather just pay with money instead of through other services. The distribution of solar lights, or in other words, the distribution of solar radiance in India, thus shapes and is shaped by dynamic caste relations that constitute the uneven Indian social fabric.

From these ground-level anecdotes of living with radiant (solar) technologies, I now move to how certain imaginaries of some other radiant infrastructures (like 5G wireless technologies) are created through boosterist rhetoric even as their realization and implementation fall short of expectations.

Infrastructural Imaginaries

The network of 5G has been touted as revolutionary. Industry insiders have argued that 5G will not only have an impact on consumer mobile phone (or broadband wi-fi) usage but also bring about an industrial revolution: an "industry 4.0" with factories consisting of modular assembly lines and their constituent machines autonomously moving and configuring themselves based on their communications with one another powered by 5G (Goldman 2021). These radiant futures of wireless factories and smart cities, what Shannon Mattern (2019) has called "networked dream worlds," promise the absolute realization of the Internet of Things with automated vehicles and sensors continuously connected with one another. These promises remain shadowed by the on-ground logistical challenges of deployment of cell sites and the need to ensure (physical) fiber-izing of the cell towers to sustain high connection speeds. Therefore, the imaging and imagining of 5G that happens through government press conferences and corporate ads need to be tempered with "infrastructural imaginaries" that interrogate who lays claims on particular visions about 5G wireless technologies, what kind of values are embodied in such visions, and what specific relations between different stakeholders such emerging infrastructures engender (Mattern 2019, Parks 2015).

Even as the infrastructural imaginaries associated with 5G wireless infrastructures were marked with much fanfare and boosterism rhetoric, they run into the everyday problems and intricacies of financial investments, technological incompatibilities, and regulatory hurdles. While 5G wireless technologies promise tremendous improvements in data speeds and almost zero latency times, except for China, the rollout of this new technology has been slow in most countries. The delayed testing and deployment are because of many reasons involving micro- and macro-scale interactions between local, national, and global players. For instance, there were geopolitical disputes over trade and security, with the United States, citing security concerns, coercing the United Kingdom and Australia to not enter into deals regarding 5G network expansion with Chinese company Huawei (Woyke 2018). There have been domestic debates within countries regarding spectrum auctions between regulators and telecom operators (Singh 2020). There have been altercations between cell tower companies and local communities over siting and deployment of towers (citing concerns over potentially deleterious effects of 5G non-ionizing electromagnetic radiations in microwave and millimeter wave range). Telecom operators have run into compatibility concerns as they deploy telecom equipment from different global vendors such as Nokia, Ericsson, and Samsung (Singh 2020; Woyke 2018).

Coda

Radiant infrastructures associated with energy regimes (whether solar or nuclear) have been touted by nation-states (like India) as providing not only "green" electricity but also increasing "savings, spending, business creation, time spent working or studying" (Aklin et al. 2017). Contrary to the connection between radiant infrastructures and "enlightenment," there might be a generative epistemics of "endarkenment" to them, which questions the seamless association of light and illumination with socio-economic values like growth and development that such infrastructures are supposed to bring (Badami 2021).

With radiant infrastructures, whether it is radio towers and nuclear reactors, or 5G cell sites and solar panels, the analytical shift is from object/artifact to the environment as emissions from radiant infrastructures permeate the environment, and thereby extend into the milieu. Therefore, beyond an object-based analysis of radiant infrastructures, one requires a processual analysis, attendant to radiant energies (radio waves, radioactive spillage). Here is where ecomedia studies and infrastructure studies are connected in a deeper and wider understanding of ecological systems.

Acknowledgment

This chapter draws on some of my earlier work for my book *Radiant Infrastructures: Media, Environment, and Cultures of Uncertainty* (DUP, 2020). Conversations at the "Intersecting Energy Cultures" themed roundtable organized by Bethany Wiggin and Rebecca Macklin on Nov 17, 2022 at University of Pennsylvania helped in writing this essay. Thanks to Alenda Chang, Miriam Tola, and Nandita Badami for conversations and suggestions.

Further Reading

Badami, Nandita. 2021. "Let There Be Light (or in Defense of Darkness)," *The South Atlantic Quarterly*, 120 (1): 51–61.
Lippit, Akira. 2005. *Atomic Light (Shadow Optics)*. Minneapolis: University of Minnesota Press.
Mattern, Shannon. 2019. "Networked Dream Worlds: Is 5g Solving Real, Pressing Problems or Merely Creating New Ones?" *Real Life Magazine*, July 8. https://reallifemag.com/networked-dream-worlds/.
Mukherjee, Rahul. 2020. *Radiant Infrastructures: Media, Environment, and Cultures of Uncertainty*. Durham, NC: Duke University Press.
Starosielski, Nicole. 2021. "Beyond Sun: Embedded Solarities and Agricultural Practice," *The South Atlantic Quarterly*, 120 (1): 13–24.

References

Aklin, Michaël, Patrick Bayer, S. Harish, and Johannes Urpelainen. 2017. "Does Basic Energy Access Generate Socioeconomic Benefits? A Field Experiment with Off-Grid Solar Power in India." *Science Advances*, 3 (May): e1602153. doi.org/10.1126/sciadv.1602153
Badami, Nandita. 2021. "Let There Be Light (or in Defense of Darkness)," *The South Atlantic Quarterly*, 120 (1): 51–61.
Barandiarán, Javiera, Mona Damluji, Stephan Miescher, David Pellow, and Janet Walker. 2022. "Energy Justice in Global Perspective: An Introduction." *Media+Environment*, 4 (1). https://doi.org/10.1525/001c.37073
Bowker, Geoffrey, and Susan Leigh Star. 1999. *Sorting Things Out: Classification and Its Consequences*. Cambridge: MIT Press.
Browne, Simone. 2015. *Dark Matters: On the Surveillance of Blackness*. Durham, NC: Duke University Press.
Cross, Jaime. 2019. "Selling with Prejudice: Social Enterprise and Caste at the Bottom of the Pyramid in India," *Ethnos*, 84 (3): 458–79.
Cross, Jaime. 2021. "Viral Solarity: Solar Humanitarianism and Infectious Disease," *The South Atlantic Quarterly*, 120 (1): 123–36.
DeLoughrey, Elizabeth. 2009. "Radiation Ecologies and the Wars of Light," *Modern Fiction Studies*, 55 (3): 468–98.
Garritano, Carmela. 2020. "Waiting on the Past: African Uranium Futures in *Arlit, Deuxième Paris*," *Modern Fiction Studies*, 66 (1): 122–40.

Goldman, David. 2021. "China Is First Out of the Gate for Industry 4.0," *Asia Times*, June 26 2021. Available: https://asiatimes.com/2021/06/china-is-first-out-of-the-gate-to-industry-4-0/

Hecht, Gabrielle. 2012. "Nuclear Nomads: A Look at the Subcontracted Heroes," *Bulletin of Atomic Scientists*, Jan 9. https://thebulletin.org/2012/01/nuclear-nomads-a-look-at-the- subcontracted-heroes/

Iheka, Cajetan. 2021. *African Ecomedia: Network Forms, Planetary Politics*. Durham, NC: Duke University Press.

Jue, Melody. 2020. *Wild Blue Media: Thinking through Seawater*. Durham, NC: Duke University Press.

Kimura, Aya Hirata. 2016. *Radiation Brain Moms and Citizen Scientists: The Gender Politics of Food Contamination after Fukushima*. Durham, NC: Duke University Press.

Larkin, Brian. 2013. "The Politics and Poetics of Infrastructures." *Annual Review of Anthropology* 42: 327–43.

Lippit, Akira. 2005. *Atomic Light (Shadow Optics)*. Minneapolis: University of Minnesota Press.

Mattern, Shannon. 2019. "Networked Dream Worlds: Is 5g Solving Real, Pressing Problems or Merely Creating New Ones?" *Real Life Magazine*, July 8. https://reallifemag.com/networked-dream-worlds/

Marvin, Carolyn. 1987. "Dazzling the Multitude: Imagining the Electric Light as a Communications Medium." In Joseph Corn (ed.), *Imagining Tomorrow: History, Technology, and the American Future*. Cambridge: MIT Press, pp. 202–17.

Mukherjee, Rahul. 2020. *Radiant Infrastructures: Media, Environment, and Cultures of Uncertainty*. Durham, NC: Duke University Press.

Parks, Lisa. 2015. "'Stuff You Can Kick': Toward a Theory of Media Infrastructures." In D. T. Goldberg and P. Svensson (eds.), *Between Humanities and the Digital*. Cambridge: MIT Press, pp. 355–73.

Parks, Lisa, and Nicole Starosielski, eds. 2015. *Signal Traffic: Critical Studies of Media Infrastructures*. Champaign: University of Illinois Press.

Singh, Abhigyan, et al. 2017. "Towards an Ethnography of Electrification in Rural India: Social Relations and Values in Household Energy Exchanges," *Energy Research and Social Science*, 30: 103–15.

Singh, Pratik Vikram. 2020. "As 5G Spectrum Auctions Loom, Jio, Airtel Get Cold Feet," *The Ken*, Nov 18, 2021. Available: https://the-ken.com/story/as-5g-spectrum-auctions-loom-jio-airtel-get-cold-feet/

Starosielski, Nicole. 2021. "Beyond Sun: Embedded Solarities and Agricultural Practice," *The South Atlantic Quarterly*, 120 (1): 13–24.

Szeman, Imre and Imre Barney. 2021. "Introduction: From Solar to Solarity." *The South Atlantic Quarterly*, 120 (1): 1–11.

Virilio, Paul. 1989. *War and Cinema: The Logistics of Perception*. New York: Verso.

Woyke, Elizabeth. 2018. "China Is Racing Ahead in 5G. Here's What That Means," *MIT Technology Review*. Dec 18, 2018. https://www.technologyreview.com/2018/12/18/66300/china-is-racing-ahead-in-5g-heres-what-it-means/

14
MICRO/CLIMATES OF PLAY
On the Thermal Contexts of Games

Alenda Y. Chang

Video games are one of the paradigmatic media of the twenty-first century, despite Eric Zimmerman dubbing this the "ludic century" a tad prematurely in 2013 (Zimmerman 2015, 19). In a time so clearly marked by both rapid technological change and escalating environmental problems, I and others have already made the case that games merit interpretation as ecomedia (Abraham and Jayemanne 2017; Chang 2019; Woolbright and Oliveira 2015). In this chapter, however, I aim to flip the orientation from an ecocritical attention to game content—that is, the stories, images, and processes constitutive of gameplay—to a more elemental attention to the environmental contexts of digital gaming, which extend from the mining of rare earth minerals to game devices' disposal as electronic waste. Specifically, I want to draw the reader's attention to two ambient scales that pertain to play as it happens: first, the microclimates of play, or the site-specific, small-scale atmospheres in which play occurs, and second, the broader climates of play, where climate is what we typically understand scientifically to be the long-term general weather conditions for a region. We can think about this combination of approaches as a way to connect game studies, a kind of media analysis, to wider discussions about the cultures, infrastructures, and environments of play. Key to this will be the recognition that, as Finn Brunton once wrote in "Heat Exchanges," "the work of computation is the work of managing heat" (Brunton 2015, 159), and that the same goes for the work of bodies in motion.

On the one hand, the waste heat of powerful gaming computers and other gaming devices (along with other media black boxes) creates genuine microclimates of indoor weather, whether in the stereotypical "man cave,"[1] home office, living room, or internet café. As intensifying heat waves have demonstrated in recent years, many countries and individuals are woefully unprepared for the new realities of intemperate climate, from a lack of air conditioning to houses built to trap rather than release heat. Waste heat from electronic devices may soon be less a nuisance or even something entirely unremarked than a critical factor in when, whether, and how such devices are used, or left to gather dust. At the other end of the spectrum, we might examine climates of play around popular sporting events, or large-scale computing enterprises like the "hyperscale" datacenters described in Starosielski et al.'s (2023) chapter in this volume. Both rely, whether implicitly or explicitly, on an energetics of thermodynamic exchange between outside temperature and conditions within a facility, not to mention the warmth of robots and human bodies tasked with performing in these situations. As we will see, the case of winter sports is particularly instructive, although

This chapter has been made available under a CC-BY-NC-ND license.

all outdoor and increasingly indoor events are being impacted by rising ambient temperatures. That said, my intent is not just to point to the Sisyphean task of perpetuating mass commercial sporting events, or the pursuit of athletic records, in the face of sobering new climate records. Instead, it is to express worry that play, which by its nature depends on some level of experimental uncertainty, will face radical destabilization by mounting environmental uncertainty.

By now, media of many kinds, including computational media, have been productively read through such lenses as radiation (Mukherjee 2020), heat (Brunton 2015), climate control (Furuhata 2022), and thermopower (Starosielski 2021). In many ways, these make literal Canadian media theorist Marshall McLuhan's abstract notions of "hot" and "cold" media. But few scholars to date have directed targeted attention to game devices and infrastructures and their thermal excesses. Given that game hardware generally demands even more energy and produces more waste heat than conventional electronic devices, games become an important crucible for testing, or tempering, our expectations for leisure and ludic occupation in the decades ahead. Cryptocurrency mining and machine learning may be even more intensive in their processor use, but games are far more pervasive and as such demand our *energetic* critical attention.

As I hope to show, games, whether played on plastic and metal or grassy or snowy fields, handily demonstrate the lengths to which we will go to sustain an illusion—of fairness, fun, and climate normalcy. I argue that the tendency to apply technological solutions to overheated commercial, domestic, or in-case space, for instance through fans, air conditioning, or liquid cooling, mimics in microcosm the growing interest in geoengineering fixes to climate change, from orbital mirrors to genetically amplified carbon capture. When we look not just at outdoor games and their macroclimates, but equally at those we play on devices indoors, subject to our attempts to establish and control domestic microclimates, the inseparability of climate and gameplay manifests alongside a potential thermal approach to games. Here I am sensitive to Cara New Daggett's warning, in *The Birth of Energy* (2019), that with the science of thermodynamics the nebulous concept of energy gained a serious organizing principle, one that marshaled energy primarily in terms of productivity and susceptibility to conditions of industrial manufacture. Rather than use thermodynamics as an unproblematic, objective scientific truth, then, think of it as a way to defamiliarize what it is that we do when we play games, and to reconnect to the material conditions of play.[2]

The PlayStation in the Attic

At the beginning of *Digital Games After Climate Change* (Abraham 2022), a significant and troubling study of the global game industry's carbon footprint, Benjamin Abraham relates a personal, and telling, experience of overheated play. As an Australian teenager with a bedroom at the top of his childhood home, Abraham confronted a difficult choice on hot summer days: play his favorite games and thereby make his room unbearably hot, even at night, or forego them in order to be able to sleep. Increasingly, he argues, we will all face similar choices in our own spaces:

> Based on what we know about planetary bio-physical limits, as well as the political and economic constraints we face, it seems currently likely that we may all, much sooner than we would like, be faced with some stark choices as an industry, not to mention as scholars, researchers, designers, and as players. Choices that we face will become confrontingly intimate and personal, like the choice between running the air conditioning or turning on the PlayStation in summer months.
>
> (Abraham 2022, 12–13)

As Abraham's anecdote crystallizes, most of us encounter weather, not climate. Many a woeful environmental scientist and activist has noted that humans seem incapable of grasping larger scale variations in time and space, and predictably, that we thus have a tendency to prioritize our immediate safety and comfort over future conditions—what behavioral economists refer to as discounting. So it is with games, which are often played in family rooms, offices, or on the go, and typically require little cognizance of ambient temperature unless a particularly powerful computer or multiple devices are at work in an enclosed space, or one is playing on an unusually warm day. In the case of Abraham's dilemma, many readers will protest that all he needed, surely, was a window-mounted air conditioning unit, or, in more cutting-edge terms, a ductless mini split system, which have become hugely popular in the wake of historic heat waves in places typically unaccustomed to such temperatures and lacking in cooling infrastructure. Yet air conditioners have always been a climatic shell game, ironically contributing to the very problem they are meant to address by producing local cooling in exchange for ambient heating while using (likely fossil-fueled) electricity.

It turns out, then, that playing games is never just about devices and their tolerances but also about human bodies and their capacities. This has been well captured by Brendan Keogh in *A Play of Bodies* (Keogh 2018), a phenomenological attempt to capture the sensorium involved in digital gaming, but an aspect not addressed in his account of normative play is those moments, more common now, when play occurs at less-than-optimal levels. Heat is something that affects both machines and people and can cause problems and even failure for both kinds of systems. Perhaps you're exergaming on a warm day, in a room with little air flow, and drops of sweat roll in an uncomfortable line down your back. Or maybe your top-of-the-line gaming computer requires fans that whir so loudly that you can't properly appreciate a game's soundtrack. These quotidian microclimates of play, or device-influenced indoor weather, are reminders that heat work constantly happens around us, and through us.

Engines of Play

To begin bringing the emphasis on heat back to Daggett and her discussion of thermodynamics, we might productively resituate computers less as sleek, digital devices than as industrial-age engines. In a related demonstration in 2019, Zane Griffin Talley Cooper and his collaborators exhibited a cryptocurrency mining rig at the Annenberg Forum at the University of Pennsylvania, part of a larger project called "Alchemical Infrastructures: Making Blockchain in Iceland." The computer put on display at Cooper's institution was what is called an Application-Specific Integrated Circuit (ASIC), specifically a Bitmain Antminer S7 that was set to "mine" a popular cryptocurrency in Iceland known as Auroracoin. According to a report made at the time, "The machine is so loud when turned on that it must be submerged in mineral oil to stay cool and be suitable for a public space." The rig cost roughly $2 a day to run in terms of electricity use but made only $3.16 in Auroracoin in just over a month (Berger 2019). Of course, Cooper et al.'s goal was not to make money but to show that "the 'work' in PoW systems is principally heat-work" (Cooper 2021), referencing so-called proof-of-work (POW) blockchain systems.

So, in addition to highlighting the embodiment and ambient contexts of individual device use, heat quickly directs us to the limitations of computation. Although specialized tech subcultures have already routinized overclocking (running a computer's processor at higher speeds than specified by the manufacturer) and heat management through fans, sinks, and liquid cooling, for many the writing is on the wall. As Andrew Lison writes in "Toward a Theory of 100% Utilization," it behooves new media scholars to culturally situate the "historical hegemony and incipient exhaustion" (Lison 2020, 513) of Moore's Law, that dreamy prediction of the 1960s that computer processing power would increase exponentially as microchips grew more and more dense with transistors. In recent years, a growing chorus of skeptics has predicted the end of Moore's Law, given fundamental physical limits to transistor size reduction and heat as an inevitable byproduct. Lison notes that "Frequently offered solutions to the current impasse include switching from silicon to another base material that gives off heat at a much lower rate" (Lison 2020, 504). However, this obvious industry optimism does not accord with M. Mitchell Waldrop's observation that "'the maximum clock rate'—tied to the amount of instruction cycles a processor can carry out in one second—of modern CPUs 'hasn't budged since 2004,'" due to heat concerns (Lison 2020, 512).

Game hardware at work is therefore engine-like, but there is also a second, lesser-known way in which games and engines converge. Many game designers use game engines, that is, software suites specialized for game development, to create, organize, or publish their material. As described by Benjamin Nicoll and Brendan Keogh in *The Unity Game Engine and the Circuits of Cultural Software*,

> Game engines enable programmers, designers, and artists to build, collaborate on, and run real-time interactive digital content, including (but not limited to) videogames. In videogame development, game engines function as software hubs wherein a vast range of media forms and skills converge into singular videogame builds.
>
> (Nicoll and Keogh 2019, 3)

One question to then ask is, can a thermodynamically inflected media theory also account for the kinds of work that game engines do? Although game engines are software, and Daggett talks primarily about the hardware of steam engines and their role in developing the science of energy known as thermodynamics, there is some symmetry in her description of heat-work and the work of game engines, which in less obvious but still tangible ways also convert spatially coded matter to temporal experiences:

> As with fire, which had always seemed magical to humans, engines convert matter that is usually described in terms of spatial extension—cords of wood, seams of coal, and reservoirs of oil—into motion that is best described in time—acceleration, intensity, and work.
>
> (Daggett 2019, 25)

If, as Henry Lowood explains, game engines came into being in 1993, to describe a kind of separation between game assets (more discrete objects like art, textures, and so on) and game physics, the term engine performs a special work, the purr of an unseen motor driving the feel, if not the look, of one's game experience. Even the names of the most popular commercial (not proprietary) game engines—Unity, Unreal—gesture to similar magical tendencies, where we could replace Daggett's terms (acceleration, intensity, and work) with animation, iteration, and *collaborative* work.

In other words, multiple strains of heat work are operating in gameplay. As Lison puts it, "technological innovation is determined not only by the availability of its material inputs but also by their capabilities and arrangement" (494). Certainly, gaming—whether in its development or its consumption—produces heat. We need only stand behind a souped-up gaming computer, or in the "hot" aisles (where warm air is funneled) of the nearest gaming café or data center, to see why. But unlike traditional thermodynamic energy, which Daggett says lies in "its emphasis on heat-work, on the transformations made possible by burning fuel" (Daggett 2019, 20), the heat-work being done by game engines is less the conversion of fossil fuel to electricity than putting hardware to work. Heat in both cases can be both product and waste, something Daggett notes is confusingly enshrined in the laws of thermodynamics: the first law, which imagines a balanced view of nature in the conservation of energy, and the second, which qualifies the first, by saying that energy can be more or less useful (to humans) and can dissipate into more dispersed and unproductive forms (entropy). The quixotic aspiration for a lossless engine continues to reemerge in technoutopian fantasies of things like underwater data centers, like Microsoft's Project Natick, and cryptocurrency mining operations that channel waste heat into greenhouses. These literal pipedreams, wherein processor-intensive computing operations are portrayed not as environmentally damaging but rather ingeniously productive, have already been extended to a variety of commodities, among them "cryptomatoes," cannabis,[3] strawberries, and chickens. Digital frontierists believe that "with a little know-how and some PVC pipe and duct tape, bitcoin mining can generate profit while helping to cut power bills" (Kuhn 2021), while some cities have even contracted with bitcoin companies for their heating needs.[4]

If games could teach us anything, it might be enough to produce players suspicious of *win/win* rhetoric, where no one or nothing ever loses (Kim 2019). Thermodynamics conveniently explodes these closed-loop fictions, and everything from sweaty palms to warm rooms and exhaust vents belies them, as well. I give Lison the last word here, as he bids Moore's Law a less-than-fond adieu and gestures optimistically at the infrastructural literacy called for elsewhere in this volume:

Without the constantly increasing sophistication of our computing systems, the physical operations subtending them may gradually cease to be a source of mystery, rendering the computer closer to a hand tool than the arbiter of arcane instructions it is today.

(Lison 2020, 518)

Climate as Game Infrastructure

Finally, at much more macro levels than specific bodies, devices, and rooms, climate is again at work in the shifting realities for playful experiences of all kinds, from cloud gaming (games streamed from remote computers) to conventional sports. In other work, I have discussed in detail the problems posed by sea-level rise and rising ambient temperatures for all manner of sporting events (Chang 2023), particularly for golf, which favors scenic coastlines, and traditional "winter" activities like hockey and skiing. Whether outdoors or indoors, in stadiums or on open courses, mainstream sporting events happen to conveniently demonstrate the multiply layered sensitivities of games and playful activity to climate disruption, arguably even more so than digital games.

Like liquid cooling and high-powered fans for personal computers, the sunshades, genetically engineered turf, air conditioners, and technological gadgetry of the twenty-first century sport facility are indicative of our continuing technical orientation toward "solving" anthropogenic climate change. Take Qatar's Khalifa International Stadium, first opened in 1976 but since retrofitted and upgraded multiple times, most recently from 2014 to 2017 in time for the 2022 FIFA World Cup. In 2022, the FIFA championship was for the first time moved from its usual slot in the months of May through July to November and December, due to the intense summer heat in Qatar. Meanwhile, the stadium's newest retrofit added a 44,000 square-meter white canopy, or "membrane," to occlude an estimated 70% of the previous opening. This roof structure was designed to ward off sun, which in addition to the stadium's air cooling and purification system is expected to keep fans at comfortable temperatures (BESIX, n.d.; Midmac Contracting, n.d.). Much has been made of ubiquitous computing and the supposed "smart cities" of our future, but it is worth noting that these sorts of mesoscale atmospheric manipulations will be as much part of that "smartness" as public transportation and widely integrated information and communication technologies. Khalifa International Stadium is in fact part of the "Aspire Zone" in Doha, with Doha just one of the growing number of self-identified "sports cities" since it hosted the 2006 Asian Games (Smith 2010).

Granted, esports tournaments, which take place not only in a distributed way online but also in the same large venues used for sports, are equally if differently vulnerable to our new climate extremes. For instance, on July 19 2022, as the United Kingdom and most of Europe sweltered in the grip of an unprecedented, record-setting heat wave, the esports platform Hyperluxe postponed a scheduled *Apex Legends* tournament for European players, announcing on Twitter that "Due to the unbearable temperature in the UK we will be postponing todays [*sic*] event until everyone can compete comfortably. The health and safety of our participants is our top priority" (this accompanied by the hashtags #heatwave and #UKHeatwave). A spokesperson for the company explained that their anticipated European competitors were unlikely to have air conditioning, and that their UK-based staff were also affected, one of whom "likened their PC setup to having an unwanted space heater in a room that was already unbearably hot and humid" (Davison 2022).

Having contemplated all of this, for me what matters less is our ability to continue playing and watching as we have been accustomed to play and watch, with reliable snow cover or ice, or mild temperatures not likely to induce heatstroke in players or spectators. Those changes are coming for wide swaths of people, from neighborhood Little Leagues to the Olympic Games. Instead, what ought to concern us more is the unequal impact of those changes, which will be based on geography, socioeconomic status, and variable access to infrastructural largesse. Soon, perhaps, we may come to regard gaming computers or virtual reality setups or really any resource- and energy-intensive media rig as obsolete within our altered climates, like the characters in Paolo Bacigalupi's postapocalyptic *The Windup Girl* see an old, fossil-fuel–powered car—namely, as an almost unthinkable, definitely obscene expenditure of energy (in Bacigalupi's world, in terms of joules). Overclocking one's computer or playing soccer under 16 banks of stadium lights might in time come to resemble driving a sports utility vehicle or coal rolling an electric car with your diesel truck.

There will always be a value in playing, even as the world warms, whether it serves as a collective balm or an individual coping mechanism. But the indeterminacy so critical to games—How will the game play out? Who will win?—pales in comparison to the environmental upheaval ahead.

Notes

1 We might consider that the heating, ventilation, and air conditioning (HVAC) industry, like the game industry, often appeals to male consumers and their desires. Although the ideology of the "man cave," or the repurposed domestic sanctuary for men and their sports watching and playing of video games, may not originate with HVAC sales targets, hardly an HVAC company fails to extol the virtues of the man cave and to point out that these spaces, often relegated to peripheral or little used areas of the home like the basement, garage, or unfinished sheds, therefore require bespoke climate design. Whether for climatic comfort or for genre-based thrills, men are enticed not only on the basis of some kind of shared identity, and the ideal of a temperature- and light-controlled but also gender-controlled space for the full and free exertion of gameplay, cinematic viewing, and general noisiness.
2 *Playing Nature* (Chang 2019) devotes an entire chapter to the concept of entropy but skirts past debates in physics to focus on whether or not games or game systems could meaningfully present waste, labor, and other neglected aspects of games and game industries.
3 Enachescu sets out to investigate "whether a closed-loop gas-to-cryptocurrency design with integrated heat reuse can become a model for sustainable data centers in Canada" (Enachescu 2019, 1).
4 The city of North Vancouver (via Lonsdale Energy Corporation) recently agreed to add cryptomining (via bitcoin company MintGreen) to its list of heat sources. According to MintGreen's CEO, "Each digital boiler is said to recover more than 96 per cent of the electricity used for Bitcoin mining in the form of heat

energy" (Grochowski 2021). If the formal contract goes through, the city would then provide a publicly funded space for hundreds of MintGreen's crypto servers.

Further Reading

Abraham, Benjamin J. 2022. *Digital Games After Climate Change*. Cham: Palgrave Macmillan.
Chang, Alenda Y. 2019. *Playing Nature: Ecology in Video Games*. Minneapolis: University of Minnesota Press.
Daggett, Cara New. 2019. *The Birth of Energy: Fossil Fuels, Thermodynamics, and the Politics of Work*. Durham, NC: Duke University Press.
Furuhata, Yuriko. 2022. *Climatic Media: Transpacific Experiments in Atmospheric Control*. Durham, NC: Duke University Press.
Pasek, Anne, C.K. Lin, Zane Griffin Talley Cooper, and J. Kinder. 2023. *Digital Energetics*. Minneapolis: University of Minnesota Press.

References

Abraham, Benjamin J. 2022. *Digital Games After Climate Change*. Cham: Palgrave Macmillan.
Abraham, Benjamin, and Darshana Jayemanne. 2017. "Where Are All the Climate Change Games? Locating Digital Games' Response to Climate Change." *Transformations* 30: 74–94. http://hdl.handle.net/10453/121664.
Berger, Michele. 2019. "Exploring Cryptocurrency and Blockchain in Iceland." *Penn Today*, September 30, 2019. https://www.asc.upenn.edu/news-events/news/exploring-cryptocurrency-and-blockchain-iceland.
BESIX. n.d. "Khalifa Stadium Renovation." Accessed April 25, 2022. https://www.besix.com/en/projects/khalifa-stadium-renovation.
Brunton, Finn. 2015. "Heat Exchanges." In *MoneyLab Reader: An Intervention in Digital Economy*, edited by Geert Lovink, Nathaniel Tkacz, and Patricia de Vries, 159–72. Amsterdam: Institute of Network Cultures.
Chang, Alenda Y. 2019. *Playing Nature: Ecology in Video Games*. Minneapolis: University of Minnesota Press.
Chang, Alenda. 2023. "Perishing Twice: On Play in a Warming World." In *After Ice: Cold Humanities for a Warming Planet*, edited by Rafico Ruiz, Paula Schönach, and Rob Shields. Vancouver: University of British Columbia Press.
Cooper, Zane Griffin Talley. 2021. "The Deep Time of Bitcoin: Excavating the 'Work' in Proof-of-Work Cryptocurrency Systems." Paper presented at AoIR 2021: The 22nd Annual Conference of the Association of Internet Researchers. Virtual Event: AoIR. Retrieved from http://spir.aoir.org.
Daggett, Cara New. 2019. *The Birth of Energy: Fossil Fuels, Thermodynamics, and the Politics of Work*. Durham, NC: Duke University Press.
Davison, Ethan. 2022. "EU Apex Tournament Postponed Due to Extreme Heat." *Dot Esports*, July 19, 2022. https://dotesports.com/apex-legends/news/eu-apex-tournament-postponed-due-to-extreme-heat.
Enachescu, Monika Silvia. 2019. "Closed Loop Cryptocurrency Mining in Alberta." Master's thesis, University of Calgary.
Furuhata, Yuriko. 2022. *Climatic Media: Transpacific Experiments in Atmospheric Control*. Durham, NC: Duke University Press.
Grochowski, Sarah. 2021. "Bitcoin Mining Could Be Heating Homes in North Vancouver Next Year." *Vancouver Sun*, October 18, 2021. https://vancouversun.com/news/local-news/bitcoin-could-be-heating-homes-in-north-vancouver-next-year.
Keogh, Brendan. 2018. *A Play of Bodies: How We Perceive Videogames*. Cambridge: MIT Press.
Kim, Janette. 2019. "Win Win Board Games." CCA Architecture Division/Urban Works Agency. https://www.urbanworks.cca.edu/win-win-board-games.
Kuhn, Daniel. 2021. "Mining Bitcoin for Heat, Strawberries and Chickens." *CoinDesk*, March 1, 2021. https://www.coindesk.com/markets/2021/03/01/mining-bitcoin-for-heat-strawberries-and-chickens/.
Lison, Andrew. 2020. "Toward a Theory of 100% Utilization." *Configurations* 28, no. 4 (Fall): 491–519. https://doi.org/10.1353/con.2020.0024.
Midmac Contracting Co. W.L.L. n.d. "Khalifa Stadium and Museum – Total Renovation." Accessed April 25, 2022. https://www.midmac.net/project/khalifa-stadium-and-museum-total-renovation/.

Mukherjee, Rahul. 2020. *Radiant Infrastructures: Media, Environment, and Cultures of Uncertainty*. Durham, NC: Duke University Press.

Nicoll, Benjamin, and Brendan Keogh. 2019. *The Unity Game Engine and the Circuits of Cultural Software*. Cham: Palgrave Macmillan.

Smith, Andrew. 2010. "The Development of "Sports-City" Zones and Their Potential Value as Tourism Resources for Urban Areas." *European Planning Studies* 18, no. 3: 385–410. https://doi.org/10.1080/09654310903497702.

Starosielski, Nicole. 2021. *Media Hot and Cold*. Durham, NC: Duke University Press.

Starosielski, Nicole, Hunter Vaughan, Anne Pasek, and Nick Silcox. 2023. "Disaggregating the Network Footprint: Why Infrastructural Literacy is Essential to Mitigating the Internet's Environmental Impact." In *Routledge Handbook of Ecomedia Studies*, edited by Antonio López, Adrian Ivakhiv, Stephen Rust, Miriam Tola, Alenda Y. Chang, and Kiu-wai Chu. London: Routledge.

Woolbright, Lauren, and Thaiane Oliveira. 2015. "Where the Wild Games Are: Ecologies in Latin American Video Games." In *Ecomedia*, edited by Stephen Rust, Salma Monani, and Sean Cubitt, 196–212. New York: Routledge.

Zimmerman, Eric. 2015. "Manifesto for a Ludic Century." In *The Gameful World: Approaches, Issues, Applications*, edited by Steffen P. Walz and Sebastian Deterding, 19–22. Cambridge: MIT Press.

15
RELATIONAL ECOLOGIES OF THE GRAMOPHONE DISC

Elodie A. Roy

Phonographic Surfaces: The Land and the Grooves

Between the wars, home-recordists on both sides of the Atlantic borrowed from the lexis of topography when they discussed the 'land' and the 'grooves' of gramophone discs.[1] The former referred to 'the uncut space between grooves' while the latter described 'the channel-like spiral track[s] cut into a record by the stylus' (Anon. 1940, 120). For early, experimentally minded home-recordists, the surface of the disc operated as a valuable epistemic gateway: the depth, consistency and material spacing of the grooves provided tangible information about their sonic properties. Many visual artists of the period were similarly drawn to phonographic landscapes. In the 1920s, László Moholy-Nagy, then teaching at the Bauhaus in Weimar, produced close-up photographic studies of the gramophone disc, surveying its accidents, crater-like marks and countless scars. Across the twentieth century, a large number of visual artists were to sound out – and sometimes fetishize – the sedimented strata of gramophone discs.[2] More than a disposable icon of Jazz Age modernity, what they perceived in the grooved disc was a metaphorical route into the archaic substrate of modernity itself. The exhibition *Broken Music*, which took place at Berlin's daadgalerie in 1988 as part of the INVENTIONEN Festival for New Music, testified to the great appeal of phonographic surfaces for twentieth-century – and especially postwar – artists as they tore apart and reconfigured, through paintings, sculptures, performances and installations, what Cuban-born poet Octavio Armand once described as the 'peculiar reality' of the record (Armand 1994, 46). In the early twenty-first century, multimedia artists as well as designers have shifted their focus from the iconicity and inscriptibility of phonographic surfaces to an exploration of how the early materials of phonography (such as wax and shellac) connect to wider media-cultural practices and histories. This shift of emphasis may be compared to the broader tendency of ecomedia studies themselves, as they move from an early thematic preoccupation with issues of environmentalist representation to a consideration of how media objects themselves affect, alter and often contaminate the planet (Cubitt 2014, 163). Ecomedia studies, which often have a presentist agenda (typically discussing 'urgent' issues related to the global environmental crisis in the Anthropocene), have not engaged with 'historical' media objects and infrastructures in a systematic way. Yet an ecologically informed approach to obsolete media formats may allow us to counteract traditional media histories. In the case of sonic media, an emphasis on the so-called raw materials of phonography contributes to unveiling the complex and occasionally violent political processes of social, material and racial extractions which underpinned the emergent transnational record industry at the turn of the twentieth century (Gribenski, Pantalony, Tkaczyk 2021) – while prompting us to listen for their lasting, and unresolved, reverberations in the contemporary era.

In what follows, the disc is not deciphered as a discrete repository of symbolic traces. Rather than theorizing the gramophone record as a medium for writing and storing information (as in Marshall McLuhan's [1964] and Friedrich Kittler's [1999] earlier conceptualizations of phonography as a writing technology), I consider the cultural significance of phonographic materials themselves. If the gramophone record constitutes 'an archive of cultural engineering by its very material fabrication' (Ernst 2011, 243), it may conversely index the larger 'engineering' of industrial expansionism. The example of the enduring shellac trade, which began with the East India Companies in the early seventeenth century, certainly evidences a connection between colonial routes and ideology and the early record industry. The first part of this chapter discusses the implications of what I term 'ecomaterial thinking' for the study of media artefacts as well as providing a small theoretical toolkit for ecomaterial scholars. The second part outlines an ecomaterial study of the shellac disc, conceptually extending findings from some of my previous research (Roy 2021a,b).

Open Horizons: Ecomaterial Thinking and Its Implications

In the past ten years, there has been a shift from examining the organized 'material culture of music' (Straw 1999–2000) and its finished cultural commodities to retracing the discrete and unstable materials of music and their global trajectories (Smith 2015; Devine 2019a,b; Gibson and Warren 2021; Roy 2021a). This is accompanied by a questioning of the transnational material infrastructures or 'supply chains' sustaining the production, circulation and consumption of music (Devine and Boudreault-Fournier 2021; Gribenski, Pantalony, Tkaczyk 2021). Musicologist Kyle Devine – who has investigated the socio-material history of audio formats from shellac records to digital files – has made a daring and invigorating plea for a 'musicology without music' as a means to 'expand [*musicology and music sociology*] by highlighting the ways that they are not only necessarily tied to but also constituted by a variety of distributed and ostensibly non-musical conditions' (2019b, 17). This alternative form of musicology – or eco-musicology – equally concerns itself with 'seemingly meaningless textures' as it does with 'evidently meaningful texts' (2019b, 16). As we '[*unfold*] the constitutive material layers' of sonic textures, we may 'encounter political formations of labor, gender, colonialism, extractivism, ecology, and war' (2019b, 19). At the same time, the act of unfolding layers contributes to deconstructing monolithic abstractions such as 'labor, gender, colonialism, extractivism, ecology, and war' by drawing attention to their heterogeneous and multi-sited foundations. Emphasizing the myriad surfaces – as well as the broader production history – of media objects (rather than their commercial and critical trajectory as cultural goods) produces a decentred, multicentric – and perhaps even eccentric – narrative of media cultures. The reexamination of the deep material preconditions of (Western) musical and media cultures begins with a description of how, where and by whom past and contemporary media objects are assembled, processed and disseminated. What may initially appear to be a narrow premise requires in fact a more inclusive and refracted methodological approach to media, involving a great heterogeneity of sources.[3] Studies carried out by music and media scholars including Jennifer Gabrys (2011), Jacob Smith (2015), Shannon Mattern (2017) and Kyle Devine (2019a,b) – with their distinct points of departure, orientations and horizons – alert us to the vitality and potentialities of the ecomaterial impulse. As the growing body of ecological approaches to media suggests, there is not one way of doing ecomaterial studies.

A valuable source of inspiration for ecomedia scholars may be found in the field of art history, and especially in the branch of art history which doesn't artificially separate the 'natural' properties of materials from the cultural elaboration of aesthetic and epistemic forms (in a perspective where materials and meanings appear to be undissociated). For art historians Natalie Adamson and Steven Harris, '[t]he reward for an attentive questioning of how an artwork is made is a more nuanced and particular understanding of how specific material properties and processes contribute to a complex kind of knowledge' (Adamson and Harris 2017, 18; see also Anderson, Dunlop, Smith 2015). The same comment could be made about media objects: different – and complementary – media narratives and theories effectively emerge from examining production rather than consumption practices. Another important insight provided by art history is its insistence on the instability, plasticity and transformability of materials. While materials have discrete individual properties, they never fully exist in and of themselves. Rather, they influence one another, becoming 'vibrant' (to reuse Jane Bennett's [2010] term) and concretely (re)activated through moments of connection, collision and encounter. Highlighting the processual and generative relationality of materials – how they mutually and incessantly transform one another – further provides an important means of avoiding reification and commodity fetishism, for what continually comes into being cannot be easily fetishized. In the realm of painting, the 'medium' is defined as 'the binding material or vehicle that holds together pigment particles in paint' (Gettens and Stout 1966 [1942], 35). I am using aspects of the art historical definition of medium, for it helpfully highlights what could be termed the 'adhesive' dimension of ecological mediation, drawing attention to media cultures as concretely and dynamically bound together on a physical as well as symbolic level. Taking our cue from material art history, we may strive to temporarily forget what media objects were initially made *for* to concentrate on what they are made *of* – as this closely relates to what they might do and mean.

There are affinities between the embodied, experimental methodology developed in art schools and the undisciplined school of media archaeology which, in recent years, has reinvigorated the field of media studies. Theorists including Wolfgang Ernst, Siegfried Zielinski and Jussi Parikka have sought to turn media artefacts inside out, cracking open the 'black boxes' of media culture and examining what lay deep beneath the flat 'discursive surface (literally, the monitors and interfaces) of mass media' (Ernst 2011, 239). The practice of uncovering the material and symbolic foundations (as well as the decaying remainders) of media environments seems to echo Nietzsche's injunction to philosophize with a hammer – if only to resist the rampant reification or commodification of thought and its reduction to stagnant automatisms and clichés. Importantly, a focus on the long duration of materials implicitly decouples the study of cultural objects from the readymade narratives of consumers' culture (with their totemic insistence on finished objects and ephemeral character). In its most radical form, the media-archaeological method seeks to remove any cultural filter or intermediary which may '[hinder] knowledge and insight' (Ernst 2011, 249) so as to tentatively see, speak and listen from 'the perspective of the media themselves' (ibid., 240) – adopting their cold and dispassionately mathematical or diagrammatic 'language'. Contrary to the most radical – or ascetic – form of media archaeology, the ecomaterial approach does not seek to artificially suspend (or conceal) affect, embodied acts of narration or moments of 'hermeneutic empathy' (ibid., 249). Yet it similarly strives to off-centre (or estrange) our perception of cultural artefacts so as to create an effect of distanciation comparable, perhaps, to the one achieved by Francis Ponge and Georges Perec in their literary defamiliarizations of everyday objects. Such a defamiliarization may help us coin an alternative critical response to media rather than strictly replicating the logic of capitalism. Negotiating a differential zone of 'free play' seems especially crucial for the theorization of (new) technologies which are still frequently described with the readymade terminological apparatus and laudatory narratives provided by the industry. A discrete re-politicization of media studies, albeit from a different angle, may thus emerge from the reconsideration of materials – one which is rooted not in the classic Marxian systemic perspective but which begins in the apparently non-hierarchical tangle of ordinary, frequently overlooked substances.[4] These include, in this chapter, shellac – but could also encompass the minerals and metals central to the manufacture of screens, computer boards and smartphones (Berthoud et al. 2012), the mica mined for gramophone and radio production (Bronfman 2021) or yet again resources such as ivory, steel, rubber and carbon black used to build musical instruments and audio technologies (Gribenski, Pantalony, Tkaczyk 2021).

Ecomateriality in Action: The Poetics and Politics of Shellac

Shellac – a bioadhesive polymer of insect origin – was a key resource in the development of Berliner's gramophone record in the second half of the 1890s. I have retraced elsewhere, and in more detail, its material history (Roy 2021a,b) but for the sake of clarity will reiterate some of the key information. Shellac was, and continues to be, cultivated in the forest regions of India (principally in the region of Bihar, with smaller production areas in the United Provinces, Bengal and the Central Provinces; Adarkar 1945, 3) and has been known for thousands of years, being notably praised in ancient Sanskrit treatises for its medicinal properties. It is the only known plastic of insect origin, a by-product of the tiny parasitic *Laccifer lacca*[5] infesting such species of host trees as the kusum, the palas and the ber. In order to be used in record production, shellac was substantially processed by seasonal workers, including unskilled women and children, to obtain the heat-soluble shellac flakes – or crystals – which would be shipped away from the port of Calcutta and transformed in gramophone plants across the world (and particularly in Europe and North America). The labour practices in the shellac industry have been well documented and appear to have remained relatively unchanged across decades (though a notable development was the establishment of modern factories producing machine-made shellac; Adarkar 1945).

Despite its centrality in record production up to the late 1940s, there never existed a 'standard recipe' for records. As suggested by chemical research carried out in 2007 across the extensive disc collection of the French Bibliothèque Nationale, the composition of discs varied depending on available materials, eras of production and manufacturers (Nguyen, Sené, Bouvet, le Bourg 2011). Shellac was not the main component – proportionally speaking – of the deceptively called 'shellac discs',[6] as these also contained a range of natural and man-made materials such as copal, carbon black, asbestos, cement, clay, silk, cotton, flour, kaolin, magnesia, mica, slate dust or rosin. Shellac – rather than any of the inexpensive and more aleatory 'fillers' listed above – occupies such a central position in the present study because of its strategic adhesive status (in the sense described earlier in this chapter). In other words, it physically and chemically held the record together. Emile Berliner had initially experimented with a variety of inadequate materials including vulcanized rubber before resorting to shellac. Because of its toughness, the shellac-based disc was particularly apt to receive and retain sound engravings, without deforming or altering of them, thus ensuring a relative level of audio fidelity. The material was easily moulded at a moderate temperature of 130°F (Bell 1936, 37) and could be remoulded and recycled so that little waste occurred in the record-production process – this notably explains its multiple cultural uses over centuries as well as the particular transformations which would affect it in the two world wars (when it became used in the weapon industry). Before becoming a key phonographic material, shellac had been successfully used in the manufacture of myriad 'plastic' trinkets (including toys, jewellery items, brushes and photographic cases) across the second half of the nineteenth century, at a time when industrial processes of casting and thermosetting were developed (Heath et al. 2000, 23). These same processes allowed to mass-producing gramophone discs in a cost-effective manner. By 1935, half of the shellac that England exported was to manufacture records (Parry 1935, 170). The disc represented the most familiar and culturally ubiquitous shape taken by the material in the twentieth century. It is no surprise that the word 'shellac' should have become synonymous, in the contemporary cultural imagination, with the thriving phonographic era of the interwar period (see Millis and Taylor 2007; Petrusich 2014).

Though 78-rpm records have become a cult mediatic format, relatively little is known about shellac's colonial origins – even though discussing them would allow us to draw sobering parallels between past and contemporary extractive media cultures. Indeed, the history of the material predates by thousands of years the rise of the record industry at the turn of the twentieth century and understanding its embedment in a longer cultural duration casts a light on the lingering colonial vestiges which underpinned the early transnational record industry. It must be noted that shellac was not a novel material for late nineteenth-century European industrialists, as it had been traded by the East India Companies (notably the Dutch and the British EICs) from the early seventeenth century onwards. The British remained in control of the territories where shellac was cultivated for over three centuries, exploiting them until the violent Partition of India in 1947. During the Second World War, shellac stocks and factories (as in the previous war) were directly controlled by the War Office Authorities (both in the UK and the US) and were promptly put to non-musical and often deadly uses – such as the making of detonating and ignition compositions or the sealing and waterproofing of hand grenades (Parry 1935, 172–73). The events of the Second World War, and the geopolitical reorganization and redistribution of power of the post-war years, contributed to curtailing the media-cultural life of shellac in the West, if only because the material was now much less readily accessible. Research for chemical substitutes accelerated, and by 1950, the notoriously toxic polyvinyl chloride (PVC) had become the main substance in record composition (finer PVC-based pressings enabled the development of long play microgroove records). As such, shellac appears as a site of physical as well as conceptual crystallization which gives us a situated and concrete (yet inevitably partial) understanding – notably through archival recovery – of issues related to labour, race, gender, power relations, globalism and conflict spanning at least four centuries.

In the past ten years, a number of artists and designers have revived or recycled discarded cultural materials such as shellac, wax and copal.[7] Art and design practices are especially relevant here as they remind us of the continued actuality of so-called obsolete materials in the contemporary era. Importantly, the knowledge produced by artists and designers – as well as by all of those who continue to work with shellac in an industrial context – complement theory-driven research in that it gives us concrete information not only about production techniques – but also about the variable 'feel' of the substance. Although artists and designers ask different questions from the ones ecomaterial theorists may outline, their insights and findings are no less valuable than the ones obtained through theoretical routes and should be incorporated into our research. This is because a study which flattens or 'dematerializes' the dynamic materials of media cultures – reducing them to theoretical abstractions – misses a core (and perhaps the most important) dimension of ecomaterial thinking, that is to say its unreserved commitment to the substances, volumes and textures of the living world. An engagement with materiality produces a differential type of knowledge, which is filtered and formed through bodily, affective and sensory encounters: experience, in its irreducible diversity, must remain an integral part of ecomaterial studies if they are to flourish.

Conclusion

This chapter has drawn attention to some of the political implications of closely reexamining the material resources and foundations of both past and contemporary media-musical cultures. A material-driven approach recognizes that natural resources and energies – as well as cultural and epistemic formations including infrastructures – may be transformed but that they never simply vanish: rather, they live on as surplus or residual traces (in the sense of the Foucauldian archive), latently informing the contemporary matrix. The ecocritical project always already brings us back to the present moment, without erasing its origins. It is concerned with 'the past as a form of delayed presence' (Ernst 2011, 250). An ecomaterial approach to historical media (including gramophone discs) therefore emphasizes their lasting – and perhaps haunting – relevance to the contemporary rather than their pastness or musealization. This is not to say that the contemporary media condition may be explained away, elucidated or deduced from the material past. Indeed, we may be 'too much inside the streams of contemporary happening to chart their flow and volume' (Kubler 1962, 30) and will arguably never grasp or fully understand the moving contours and implications of the technological present. This does not mean however that we should not try to move closer to its edges.

Notes

1 Incidentally, topography consolidated as a discipline in the 1870s at about the same time as the first sound-recording devices were developed.
2 For an exhaustive survey of artists interrogating shellac discs and gramophones, see Block and Glasmeier (2018) [1989] and Schoonmaker (2010).
3 An ecomaterial study may therefore draw together such heterogeneous elements as archival findings, interviews with makers, industrial reports, philosophical accounts and so on. No theoretical a priori is assumed: rather, theory is understood as an open-ended and cumulative process of *getting to know* in the larger sense of the term.
4 This doesn't mean that the Marxian and the ecomaterial perspectives cannot be reconciled.
5 The insect is also known as *Tachardia lacca*, after Guy Tachard, the French Jesuit missionary who described it in the seventeenth century.
6 It only constitutes 30–50% of the total composition of the disc.
7 These include Annika Unger, Anja Lapatsch, Sascha Brosamer, Graham Dunning, Dinah Bird and Darsha Hewitt – to name but a few. See Chapter 4 of my monograph *Shellac in Visual and Sonic Culture: Unsettled Matter* (Amsterdam UP).

Further Reading

Devine, Kyle. 2019. *Decomposed: The Political Ecology of Music*. Cambridge: MIT Press.
Devine, Kyle, and Alexandrine Boudreault-Fournier, eds. 2021. *Audible Infrastructures: Music, Sound, Media*. New York: Oxford University Press.
Gibson, Chris, and Andrew Warren. 2021. *The Guitar: Tracing the Grain Back to the Tree*. London and Chicago, IL: The University of Chicago Press.
Huhtamo, Erkki, and Jussi Parikka, eds. 2011. *Media Archaeology: Approaches, Applications, and Implications*. Berkeley: University of California Press.
Smith, Jacob. 2015. *Eco-Sonic Media*. Berkeley: University of California Press.

References

Adamson, Natalie, and Steven Harris, eds. 2017. *Material Imagination: Art in Europe, 1946-72*. Chichester: Wiley Blackwell.
Adarkar, B. P. 1945. *Report on Labour Conditions in the Shellac Industry*. Delhi: Indian Labour Investigation Committee.

Anderson, Christy, Anne Dunlop, and Pamela H. Smith, eds. 2015. *The Matter of Art: Materials, Practices, Cultural Logics, c. 1250-1750*. Manchester: Manchester University Press.
Anon. 1940. *How to Make Good Recordings*. New York: Audio Devices, Inc.
Armand, Octavio. 1994. *Refractions*. Translated by Carol Maier. New York: Lumen Books.
Bell, L. M. T. 1936. *The Making & Moulding of Plastics*. London: Hutchinson.
Bennett, Jane. 2010. *Vibrant Matter: A Political Ecology of Things*. Durham, NC: Duke University Press.
Berthoud, Françoise, et al. 2012. *Impacts écologiques des Technologies de l'Information et de la Communication: Les faces cachées de l'immatérialité*. Paris: EDP Sciences.
Block, Ursula, and Michael Glasmeier, eds. 2018 (1989). *Broken Music: Artists' Recordworks*. New York: Primary Information.
Bronfman, Alejandra. 2021. "Glittery: Unearthed Histories of Music, Mica, and Work." In *Audible Infrastructures: Music, Sound, Media*, edited by Kyle Devine and Alexandrine Boudreault-Fournier, 73–90. New York: Oxford University Press.
Cubitt, Sean. 2014. "Ecomedia Futures." *International Journal of Media and Cultural Politics* 10(2): 163–70.
Devine, Kyle. 2019a. *Decomposed: The Political Ecology of Music*. Cambridge: MIT Press.
Devine, Kyle. 2019b. "Musicology without Music". In *On Popular Music and Its Unruly Entanglements*, edited by Nick Braae and Kai Arne Hansen, 15–37. Cham: Palgrave Macmillan.
Devine, Kyle, and Alexandrine Boudreault-Fournier, eds. 2021. *Audible Infrastructures: Music, Sound, Media*. New York: Oxford University Press.
Ernst, Wolfgang. 2011. "Media Archaeography: Method and Machine versus History and Narrative of Media." In *Media Archaeology: Approaches, Applications, and Implications*, edited by Erkki Huhtamo and Jussi Parikka, 239–55. Berkeley: University of California Press.
Gabrys, Jennifer. 2011. *Digital Rubbish: A Natural History of Electronics*. Ann Arbor: University of Michigan Press.
Gettens, Rutherford J., and George L. Stout. 1966 (1942). *Painting Materials: A Short Encyclopaedia*. New York: Dover Publications.
Gibson, Chris, and Andrew Warren. 2021. *The Guitar: Tracing the Grain Back to the Tree*. London and Chicago, IL: The University of Chicago Press.
Gribenski, Fanny, David Pantalony and Viktoria Tkaczyk. 2021. Abstract of the workshop 'Sound Supplies: Raw Materials and the Political Economy of Instrument Building'. Paris: IRCAM (online), 21–22 May 2021.
Heath, Adrian et al. 2000. *300 Years of Industrial Design: Function – Form – Technique 1700-2000*. New York: Watson-Guptill Publications.
Kittler, Friedrich. 1999. *Gramophone, Film, Typewriter*. Stanford, CA: Stanford University Press.
Kubler, George. 1962. *The Shape of Time: Remarks on the History of Things*. New Haven, CT and London: Yale University Press.
Mattern, Shannon. 2017. *Code and Clay, Data and Dirt: Five Thousand Years of Urban Media*. Minneapolis: University of Minnesota Press.
McLuhan, Marshall. 1964. *Understanding Media: The Extensions of Man*. London: Routledge and Kegan Paul Limited.
Millis, Robert, and Jeffery Taylor. 2007. *Victrola Favorites*. Atlanta: Dust-to-Digital.
Nguyen, Thi-Phuong, Xavier Sené, Stéphane Bouvet, Emilie le Bourg. 2011. "Determining the Composition of 78-rpm Records: Challenge or Fantasy?." *ARSC Journal* 42 (1): 29–42.
Parry, Ernest J. 1935. *Shellac*. London: Sir Isaac Pitman & Sons, Ltd.
Petrusich, Amanda. 2014. *Do Not Sell at any Price: The Wild, Obsessive Hunt for the World's Rarest 78 rpm Records*. New York, London, Toronto, Sydney, New Delhi: Scribner.
Roy, Elodie A. 2021a. "Another Side of Shellac: Cultural and Natural Cycles of the Gramophone Disc." In *Audible Infrastructures: Music, Sound, Media*, edited by Kyle Devine and Alexandrine Boudreault-Fournier, 207–26. New York: Oxford University Press.
Roy, Elodie A. 2021b. "The Sheen of Shellac – From Reflective Material to Self-Reflective Medium." In *Materials, Practices, and Politics of Shine in Modern Art and Popular Culture*, edited by Antje Krause-Wahl, Petra Löffler, and Änne Söll, 105–19. London, New York, Dublin: Bloomsbury.
Schoonmaker, Trevor, ed. 2010. *The Record: Contemporary Art and Vinyl*. Durham, NC: Duke University Press.
Smith, Jacob. 2015. *Eco-Sonic Media*. Berkeley: University of California Press.
Straw, Will. 1999–2000. "Music as Commodity and Material Culture." *Repercussions* 7–8: 147–172.

16

CORE DUMP

The Global Aesthetics and Politics of E-Waste

Mehita Iqani

Introduction

E-waste comprises defunct or obsolete electronics. This chapter maps out some of the key theoretical and empirical issues that arise in scholarly research to do with e-waste by examining South African artist Francis Knoetze's multi-modal project *Core Dump* (https://francoisknoetze.com/core-dump-2018/).

In the four short films that comprise *Core Dump*, the artist doubles as an urban scavenger, harvesting various forms of e-waste such as old headphones, circuit boards, cables, and mobile phone cases and sculpting these into wearable forms. Donning these sculptures, which present as robotic, post-human, cyborg creatures, sometimes charmingly monstrous, often unsettlingly creepy, Knoetze's characters interact with urban settings in each city in suggestive ways, highlighting complex assemblages between capitalism and waste. The four cities in which *Core Dump* (Figure 16.1) is set – Kinshasa, Shenzhen, New York, and Dakar – each serve as a time-space marker in the journey of e-waste.

Kinshasa: Extraction of Resources

One key set of aspects of e-waste that researchers and theorists working in the realm of eco-media need to consider are: the roots in the extractive economy, the presence of mined metals and minerals, colonial histories, labour issues to do with the mining of those materials, and the related social and economic impacts on the countries that are blessed (and cursed) with mineral resource wealth.

Kinshasa is the capital city of the Democratic Republic of Congo, the African nation still embroiled in grave political uncertainty resulting from the damages of colonialism, not least the pervasive exploitative extraction of its natural resources (Nzongola-Ntalaja 2021). Dangerous and dehumanising work is done to mine the rare earth metals used in the manufacture of many electronics: copper, cobalt, and a range of substances known as "rare earth elements," without which, "global finance, the Internet, satellite surveillance, oil transport, jet engines, televisions, GPS, and emergency rooms could not function" (Klinger 2018, 45). Congo is one of the key sites for colonial and post-colonial extraction, by external governments and corporations (Butler 2015; Mullins and Rothe 2008). Mineral resource extraction in Congo is linked to its ongoing war and criminal

Figure 16.1 Core Dump "E-Revenant" (2018) by Francois Knoetze

economy (Jackson 2002) and features massive human rights and labour abuses, including child labour (Mària, Josep, and Taka 2012; Williams et al. 2021).

The history of racist colonial-capitalism is a central theme in *Core Dump Kinshasa*. The narrative revolves around a young man who through the manipulation of a devious white man driving a car is transformed into a mutant: half-person, half-pig. The film explores themes of military violence and the brutal oppression and exploitation of Africans by the special horrors of Belgian rule. The protagonist journeys through the city, interspersed with images of robots from pop culture. After a bar fight, he becomes disoriented in a quiet back street, where a car driven by a creepy rubber-masked figure chases him, and he morphs into a pig. He creeps in the shadows – ashamed, scared. When he asks for help, a mob chases him, various nightmare scenes unfold, assembled into montages with archival footage and blurring effects. The closing scene shows figures vomiting chipboards and wires and tropical plants in a night breeze.

As *Core Dump Kinshasa* implies, colonial history, exploitative labour, and violent extraction processes should be understood to be at the heart of the problem of e-waste, because of where these valuable components come from, and how they are mined. Although many people in Congo – including children – risk their lives and health to mine cobalt and copper, they remain trapped in destitution and earn only a tiny shred of the value of the materials they unearth, thus excluded from the economy of the high-tech, touch-screen items manufactured from their raw materials. The conditions in DRC for mining cobalt and other minerals used in electronic commodities are appalling to any humane observer (Niarchos 2021). Despite Congo's wealth of natural resources, the exploitative extraction of minerals has not resulted in the broad-based economic empowerment of its people, who remain cut off from prosperity and happiness, much as they were during the brutalities of the colonial era. Further, contamination from cobalt mining has been shown to have an association with birth defects (Van Brusselen et al. 2020) – as the imagery of the mutant pig-person in film hauntingly symbolises.

Shenzhen: Tech (Over) Production

The second key set of aspects of e-waste that researchers and theorists working in the realm of eco-media need to consider are: the global geopolitics of technology production, including how it is linked to resource extraction; the rise of China as an economic superpower on the basis of "export industrialisation" (Lüthje and Butollo 2017, 216) and the role of labour exploitation within that rise; and the social and human cost of wealth creation through industrial manufacture. From the raw materials unearthed in Congo and elsewhere, electronic and technology items are produced, mostly in China. The city of Shenzhen is a hub for tech manufacture and innovation, named by some as "China's Silicone Valley" (Wang 2021). Part 2 of *Core Dump* follows the journey of raw materials to production.

Core Dump Shenzhen features a mysterious, blonde-wigged woman who represents an ancient river spirit, who was caught in an African river and brought against her will to China. Integrating archival images of maps and rivers, a voice tells us of underwater cables alongside images of a twisting body of water and applauding politicians. The supervisor looks into the water and sees something strange, a tangle of organic-looking cables. Images reference China-Africa relations, then arrive in Shenzhen: a fish is beheaded in a market, an old man sings in a square, and a group dances. A factory boss negotiates with the river spirit for power, and as a result becomes the richest woman in Shenzhen. She rules her factory with an iron fist as she teaches her son her ruthless ways. Scenes show machine production line workers, cables, and stock exchanges. The voice over tells us of worker fatigue, boredom, and suicide. But the tech components manufactured there attack the boss' son, burying into his flesh, until his body is integrated with circuit boards and chips. This cyborg monster wanders the empty halls of his factory then jumps off the roof.

Core Dump Shenzhen illuminates the technology production step in the journey of e-waste. With the mineral riches extracted, technology companies create devices bought by consumers around the world. Shenzhen is the production epicentre of the contemporary technology economy (Hossain 2022; Stevens 2019; Wang 2021). There are geopolitical and national implications to China's growing power as a manufacturer of technology. One is the relationship that China has with African states, especially those rich in mineral resources (Ebner 2015; Gulley, Nassar, and Xun 2018; Hodzi 2018). Another is domestic labour rights on Chinese soil. Research has shown that the tech industry in China continues to operate on the flexible employment of low-skilled and poorly paid migrant workers. Suicides – as represented by the fatal jump of the circuit board cyborg in *Core Dump* – have taken place at the factory that makes Apple and other famous brand products (Chan 2013; Waters 2017). With the rise of China as an economic superpower, extractive relations with African states are highlighted, as are socio-economic labour issues domestically.

New York: Media (Over) Consumption

The third key set of aspects to e-waste that researchers and theorists working in the realm of eco-media need to consider are: the central role that consumption plays in the generation of e-waste; the extent to which individual consumers can or should take ethical or activist positions in relation to their personal technology shopping choices; the responsibility that lies with the tech companies;

and the question of whether consumption can offer any solutions at all to the environmental problems it creates.

The brand new smartphones and other tech devices produced in Shenzhen are shipped around the world to be sold. Western shoppers, in particular, have the means and interest to replace their media devices often. And so, *Core Dump* moves to New York City.

The film opens with news clips on robotics. A military robot dog played by two actors seemingly fused at the upper body marches around New York City, their legs moving uncannily just like the robots from the news video. It is tragically cut in half in the subway by closing doors. A split screen follows the journey of the split robot, each half lost in a different part of the city, wires dangling. Each finds another half a thing to connect with, their adventures interspersed with images of tech billionaires, other robots, climate change-induced extreme weather events, facilities for the wealthy, stocks being traded by algorithms, abandoning Earth to colonise Mars, uploading minds to machines, escaped slaves, voodoo, the American War of Independence, marines returning home with racist stories and horror, zombies. At an e-waste site, a familiar pair of legs stick out of a big box of broken electronics. It is loaded onto a container ship which is shown crossing the seas.

Core Dump New York sums up key themes that animate late capitalism: the interlinking of the military-industrial complex with consumer commodities (Foster and McChesney 2014; Zuboff 2015), and the taken-for-granted centrality of tech items to everyday life and consumption in the global north (Economides and Cochoy 2017), the relation between racism and colonialism in capitalist structures of power (Wilson 1996), and the relation of waste to consumer culture (Iqani 2020). New York City is one of the most consumerist places on earth, where market exchange organises almost every aspect of life. The film demonstrates how media commodities and markets, and built-in obsolescence, is one of the main drivers for the proliferation of e-waste. As Eleftheria Lekakis writes, the smartphone is the commodity that perhaps best captures many of the deep ethical concerns that animate consumer society and its seemingly endless march towards the replacement of one item by a supposedly better but actually very similar version of itself (Lekakis 2022). Smartphones are highly polluting; the ethical choice for any consumer would be to never buy another smartphone ever again (Lekakis 2022; Maxwell and Miller 2020). But tech companies actively encourage consumers to get ever new models and even allegedly plan for their items to fail or degrade earlier than necessary, to force people into buying newer models (Lekakis 2022). The result of planned obsolescence is injury to the people who mine the minerals, as well as the workers who recycle the e-waste: environmental racism (Taylor 2014).

Dakar: Disposal, Dumping, Toxicity

The fourth and final set of concerns spotlighted by *Core Dump* are: the global inequities that excuse the trade in e-waste and its dumping on poorer nations; labour issues to do with recycling, including the dangerous and toxic work that takes place in the e-waste dumps in those locations and the risk to the health and happiness of the human beings who must do this work; and the social, economic, and environmental consequences for the cities where e-waste dumps are located.

The fourth part of *Core Dump* moves to the west coast of Africa (as the final scenes of the first film illustrate), where a huge amount of e-waste is taken for "recycling" – a term that might be best read as a euphemism for "dumping."

The film features a protagonist who picks apart and fixes electronics on the streets of Dakar. After being wounded by an accident, he "fixes himself the only way he knows how" with screwdrivers and soldering irons, using the various wasted tech parts he has gathered in his shop to fill in his gaping wounds, and 3D printing himself a new face/mask. Part inventor, part hack, part survivor, now he has two faces, the mask above lustrous, the skin below injured. Clips from news reports which speak of high-value metals in obsolete tech are juxtaposed with images of African statesmen and binary code. Scenes show an e-waste dump, where humans and animals scavenge for something of value.

E-waste is "end-of-life electronic equipment" (Perkins et al. 2014). The dump signals the everlasting nature of certain man-made materials and "new lives" of obsolete tech items.

> Waste pickers who salvage through the remains of dead electronics do not necessarily have the luxury of entertaining the wish fulfillment these devices promised; instead, in salvaging and recycling these machines, they reveal how these promised wishes fall apart.
> (Gabrys 2011, 137)

Core Dump Dakar brings the e-waste narrative back full circle, to Africa where the story began with extraction. The toxic, dangerous, and difficult work of picking through the e-waste to find materials of value for recycling compromises the human rights of those who are forced by circumstance to do it. In a detailed and fair discussion of Pieter Hugo's problematic photographs of waste workers at Agbogbloshie in Ghana, Cajetan Iheka argues that these subsistence workers, often barely out of childhood, are "toxified laborers" (Iheka 2021, 66) who are alienated and exploited by capital on multiple levels (not least by white artists who sell photographs in galleries for huge prices). Iheka (2021, 66) points out that these e-waste–pickers should be seen as digital labourers, as much a part of the digital economy as the coders, designers, manufacturers, and markets of tech gadgets. The "circular economy" of recycling (Lacy and Rutqvist 2015; Tonelli and Cristoni 2019) is revealed to benefit the rich and injure the poor.

E-Waste in Global Perspective: Aesthetic and Political Issues

This chapter has shown where e-waste comes from, where it goes, its affective links to global consumption patterns, and its afterlife as waste. According to the Global E-Waste Monitor,

> In 2019, the world generated a striking 53.6 Mt [*metric tons*] of e-waste, an average of 7.3 kg per capita. The global generation of e-waste grew by 9.2 Mt since 2014 and is projected to grow to 74.7 Mt by 2030 – almost doubling in only 16 years.
> (Forti et al. 2020, 13)

In high-income countries, small technology gadgets like smartphones are replaced every 18, or even 12 months, by consumers (Gaia Foundation 2013). Billions are spent annually on marketing the commodities, for example Apple alone devoted $1.8 billion to advertising in 2015 (Basulto 2018). E-waste is doubtless a problem that will remain central to critical eco-media studies for the foreseeable future.

There are more tech items in existence on the planet than ever before – and it is worth noting that along with precious metals, plastic is a key ingredient in their production, and plastic does not biodegrade, so it is safe to assume that some piece of every electronics item ever produced still exists in some form or another on the planet. There is no "away" (De Laney 2018). E-waste underlines this uncomfortable fact in stark relief. As the world goes increasingly online, more and more people depend on various devices to connect for work, politics, and pleasure. But these devices are not built to last – instead, various forms of planned obsolescence as well as the rent-to-buy contract economy for mobile phones and tablets (including aggressive marketing) mean that they often either have to be replaced within a couple of years or consumers are enticed to choose to replace them with promises of upgrades and glossier, trendier devices. From the analogue media age with its cassette and CD players, through to the converged mobile media economy, no member of global north society considers themselves complete without a smartphone and/or tablet. Meanwhile, members of global south society are working hard (often it seems in vain) to catch up to the same kind of connectivity. The result is greater than ever proliferation of old and useless devices, and the irresponsible disposal of these items – e-waste – has led to toxic waste dumps (mostly in global south cities) and new forms of precarious reclaimer work as people are pushed by economic circumstances to "mine" e-waste dumps for materials of value, precious and rare metals. *Core Dump*, as well as offering an exploration of the political issues linked to e-waste, also stands as an example of the kind of valuable and progressive creative work that can be made, tangible and materially, with e-waste itself.

This chapter has summarised the links between the voracious demands of consumer societies, both those well-established and entitled-feeling in the global north and those in the global south who are excluded, marginalised, and keen to catch up with the lifestyles that they see represented in global media discourses. E-waste must be understood as not only a material challenge for policy, trade, and even consumer activism but also a metaphorical device that captures all that is broken, wasteful, and anti-human in consumer capitalism. The material existence of e-waste raises several questions and concerns for critical researchers in the field of eco-media. These include the geopolitics of mineral extraction and the international trade in waste; the toxic risk posed both by mineral extraction and its recycling; labour issues during extraction work (both the mining and the removal of valuable items from discarded tech items); consumer cultures and over-consumption and the role of technology items in accessing the lifestyles that are denied by most people around the world; and the exploitative strategies used by tech production companies in order to buoy market demand for their wares. In summary, there is perhaps no item more connected to the multiple power structures and struggles that characterise late capitalism than e-waste. If critical research can succeed in exploring and explicating these multiple links, across space and time, we may be able to apply that knowledge to helping to change this deeply damaging way of life.

Further Reading

Gabrys, Jennifer. 2011. *Digital Rubbish: A Natural History of Electronics*. University of Michigan Press.
Iheka, Cajetan. 2021. *African Ecomedia: Network Forms, Planetary Politics*. Durham, NC: Duke University Press.
Iqani, Mehita. 2020. *Garbage in Popular Culture: Consumption and the Aesthetics of Waste*. Albany: SUNY Press.
Knoetze, Francois. Core Dump. Available at: https://francoisknoetze.com/core-dump-2018/.
Lekakis, Eleftheria J. 2022. *Consumer Activism*. London: Routledge.

References

Basulto, Jacqueline. 2018. 'Why Apple Spends $1.8 Billion On Advertising'. *Medium.Com*, 13 July 2018. https://medium.com/seedx-digital-marketing-guru/why-apple-spends-1-8-billion-on-advertising-38d3940270bf.
Butler, Paula. 2015. *Colonial Extractions: Race and Canadian Mining in Contemporary Africa*. Toronto: University of Toronto Press.
Chan, Jenny. 2013. 'A Suicide Survivor: The Life of a Chinese Worker: The Life of a Chinese Worker'. *New Technology, Work and Employment* 28 (2): 84–99. https://doi.org/10.1111/ntwe.12007.
De Laney, Velvette. 2018. 'Landfill Waste Is a Design Choice: Or, There Is No "Away"'. *Design Management Review* 29 (1): 12–17. https://doi.org/10.1111/drev.12103.

Ebner, Julia. 2015. 'The Sino–European Race for Africa's Minerals: When Two Quarrel a Third Rejoices'. *Resources Policy* 43 (March): 112–20. https://doi.org/10.1016/j.resourpol.2014.11.009.

Economides, Steve, and Franck Cochoy. 2017. *Digitalizing Consumption: How Devices Shape Consumer Culture*. Routledge Interpretive Marketing Research. London; New York: Routledge, Taylor & Francis Group.

Forti, V., C.P. Baldé, R. Kuehr, and G. Bel. 2020. *The Global E-Waste Monitor 2020: Quantities, Flows and the Circular Economy Potential*. Bonn/Geneva/Rotterdam: United Nations University (UNU)/United Nations Institute for Training and Research (UNITAR) – co-hosted SCYCLE Programme, International Telecommunication Union (ITU) & International Solid Waste Association (ISWA).

Foster, John Bellamy, and Robert W. McChesney. 2014. 'Surveillance Capitalism: Monopoly-Finance Capital, the Military-Industrial Complex, and the Digital Age'. *Monthly Review* 66 (3): 1. https://doi.org/10.14452/MR-066-03-2014-07_1.

Gabrys, Jennifer. 2011. *Digital Rubbish: A Natural History of Electronics*. Ann Arbor: University of Michigan Press.

Gaia Foundation. 2013. *Short Circuit: The Lifecycle of Our Electronic Gadgets and the True Cost to Earth*. Brighton: Gaia Foundation.

Gulley, Andrew L., Nedal T. Nassar, and Sean Xun. 2018. 'China, the United States, and Competition for Resources That Enable Emerging Technologies'. *Proceedings of the National Academy of Sciences* 115 (16): 4111–15. https://doi.org/10.1073/pnas.1717152115.

Hodzi, Obert. 2018. 'China and Africa: Economic Growth and a Non-Transformative Political Elite'. *Journal of Contemporary African Studies* 36 (2): 191–206. https://doi.org/10.1080/02589001.2017.1406191.

Hossain, Mokter. 2022. 'The Shenzhen Ecosystem: What It Means for the Western World'. *Technology in Society* 68 (February): 101919. https://doi.org/10.1016/j.techsoc.2022.101919.

Iheka, Cajetan. 2021. *African Ecomedia: Network Forms, Planetary Politics*. Durham, NC: Duke University Press.

Iqani, Mehita. 2020. *Garbage in Popular Culture: Consumption and the Aesthetics of Waste*. Albany: SUNY Press.

Jackson, Stephen. 2002. 'Making a Killing: Criminality & Coping in the Kivu War Economy'. *Review of African Political Economy* 29 (93–94): 517–36. https://doi.org/10.1080/03056240208704636.

Klinger, Julie Michelle. 2018. *Rare Earth Frontiers: From Terrestrial Subsoils to Lunar Landscapes*. Ithaca, NY: Cornell University Press.

Lacy, Peter, and Jakob Rutqvist. 2015. *Waste to Wealth: The Circular Economy Advantage*. London; New York: Palgrave Macmillan.

Lekakis, Eleftheria J. 2022. *Consumer Activism*. London: Routledge.

Lüthje, Boy, and Florian Butollo. 2017. 'Why the Foxconn Model Does Not Die: Production Networks and Labour Relations in the IT Industry in South China'. *Globalizations* 14 (2): 216–31. https://doi.org/10.1080/14747731.2016.1203132.

Mària, S.J., F. Josep, and Miho Taka. 2012. 'The Human Rights of Artisanal Miners in the Democratic Republic of the Congo: The Responsibility of Mining Companies'. *African Journal of Economic and Management Studies* 3 (1): 137–50. https://doi.org/10.1108/20400701211197320.

Maxwell, Richard, and Toby Miller. 2020. *How Green Is Your Smartphone?* Digital Futures. Cambridge; Medford, MA: Polity.

Mullins, Christopher W., and Dawn L. Rothe. 2008. 'Gold, Diamonds and Blood: International State-Corporate Crime in the Democratic Republic of the Congo'. *Contemporary Justice Review* 11 (2): 81–99. https://doi.org/10.1080/10282580802057678.

Niarchos, Nicolas. 2021. 'The Dark Side of Congo's Cobalt Rush'. *The New Yorker*, 24 May 2021. https://www.newyorker.com/magazine/2021/05/31/the-dark-side-of-congos-cobalt-rush.

Nzongola-Ntalaja, Georges. 2021. *The Congo from Leopold to Kabila: A People's History*. https://doi.org/10.5040/9781350223004?locatt=label:secondary_bloomsburyCollections.

Perkins, Devin N., Marie-Noel Brune Drisse, Tapiwa Nxele, and Peter D. Sly. 2014. 'E-Waste: A Global Hazard'. *Annals of Global Health* 80 (4): 286. https://doi.org/10.1016/j.aogh.2014.10.001.

Stevens, Hallam. 2019. 'The Quotidian Labour of High Tech: Innovation and Ordinary Work in Shenzhen'. *Science, Technology and Society* 24 (2): 218–36. https://doi.org/10.1177/0971721819841997.

Taylor, Dorceta E. 2014. *Toxic Communities: Environmental Racism, Industrial Pollution, and Residential Mobility*. New York: NYU Press.

Tonelli, Marcello, and Nicolò Fabrizio Cristoni. 2019. *Strategic Management and the Circular Economy*. Routledge Research in Strategic Management. New York: Routledge, Taylor & Francis Group.

Van Brusselen, Daan, Tony Kayembe-Kitenge, Sébastien Mbuyi-Musanzayi, Toni Lubala Kasole, Leon Kabamba Ngombe, Paul Musa Obadia, Daniel Kyanika wa Mukoma, et al. 2020. 'Metal Mining and Birth Defects: A Case-Control Study in Lubumbashi, Democratic Republic of the Congo'. *The Lancet Planetary Health* 4 (4): e158–67. https://doi.org/10.1016/S2542-5196(20)30059-0.

Wang, Grace Yuehan. 2021. 'Talent Migration in Knowledge Economy: The Case of China's Silicon Valley, Shenzhen'. *Journal of International Migration and Integration*, July. https://doi.org/10.1007/s12134-021-00875-5.

Waters, Sarah. 2017. 'Workplace Suicide and States of Denial: The France Telecom and Foxconn Cases Compared'. *TripleC: Communication, Capitalism & Critique. Open Access Journal for a Global Sustainable Information Society* 15 (1): 191–213. https://doi.org/10.31269/triplec.v15i1.801.

Williams, John T, Achim Mambu Vangu, Habib Balu Mabiala, Honore Bambi Mangungulu, and Elizabeth K. Tissingh. 2021. 'Toxicity in the Supply Chain: Cobalt, Orthopaedics, and the Democratic Republic of the Congo'. *The Lancet Planetary Health* 5 (6): e327–28. https://doi.org/10.1016/S2542-5196(21)00057-7.

Wilson, Carter A. 1996. *Racism: From Slavery to Advanced Capitalism*. Sage Series on Race and Ethnic Relations, v. 17. Thousand Oaks, CA: Sage Publications.

Zuboff, Shoshana. 2015. 'Big Other: Surveillance Capitalism and the Prospects of an Information Civilization'. *Journal of Information Technology* 30 (1): 75–89. https://doi.org/10.1057/jit.2015.5.

PART III
Political Ecology

17
CARBON CAPITALISM, COMMUNICATION, AND ARTIFICIAL INTELLIGENCE

Placing the Climate Emergency Center Stage

Benedetta Brevini and Daisy Doctor

Communication plays a vital role in organizing or mystifying public understandings of the climate crisis and promoting or impeding action for change. Greta Thunberg's rise to celebrity status and Donald Trump's manipulation of Twitter and supportive media channels led by Fox News exemplify this pivotal role. However, communication and computation systems also generate a number of environmental harms, staring with mineral extractions, water, energy, and natural resources necessary for hardware and machine production; and then generating additional resource depletion for distribution, transportation, post-consumption of material technology, to end with major e-waste disposal needs. Added to this is the major environmental cost of data extraction, computing, and analysis. According to the International Energy Agency (IEA, 2022), data center electricity use in Ireland has more than tripled since 2015, accounting for 14% of total electricity consumption in 2021, while in Denmark, data center energy use is projected to triple by 2025 to account for around 7% of the country's electricity use.

This chapter draws on the tradition of critical political economy of communication and in particular on the theoretical elaboration developed in the books *Carbon Capitalism and Communication: Confronting Climate Crisis* (Brevini and Murdock, 2017) and in *Is AI good for the Planet* (Brevini, 2021), where communication systems (including its latest developments, Artificial Intelligence (AI) *in primis*) are approached as assemblages of material devices and infrastructures, capable of depleting scarce resources in their manufacturing, usage, and disposal. In fact, it is important to connect how the accelerating impact of human interventions on the Earth's ecosystems identified by climate research coincides with the rapid expansion of communication and computational systems. This has in turn drastically accelerated our consumption of raw materials and energy, compounding our global environmental challenges.

Pandemic, Climate Crisis, and Energy Consumption

The pandemic has hastened our dependence on technology along with the massive acceleration and the adoption of AI, big data, cloud computing, and video technologies. We eat, socialize, work, study, exercise online, and plug into the cloud. New research from Milkround (2021) in the United Kingdom reveals that video conferencing has surpassed email as the most widely used form of business communication during the lockdown. So, we are reliant on communication systems as

This chapter has been made available under a CC-BY-NC-ND license.

never before, while the planet is facing the biggest crisis ever faced. We now know that unless emissions fall by 7.6% each year between 2020 and 2030, the world will miss the opportunity to get on track toward the 1.5°C goal. We also know that we are currently on a trajectory for a temperature rise of over 3°C (United Nations Environment Programme, 2019). Yet, for almost two years, we have been constantly bombarded by media reports that the pandemic has been incredibly good for the climate crisis by reducing climate emissions through taming transport, flights, and movement (Gössling and Humpe, 2020, 2). On the contrary, even despite the lockdowns of 2020, greenhouse gas emissions have remained stubbornly high. Daily global carbon dioxide emissions fell by as much as 17% in early April 2020. But, as the world's economy started to recover, emissions rebounded. The UN showed that 2020 only saw a 4–7% decline in carbon dioxide relative to 2019 (UN News, 2020). While transportation and industrial activity declined from January 2020, electricity consumption remained constant, which partly explains the minimal drop in emissions (IEA, 2020). How, you may ask? According to the World Energy Outlook 2019, globally 64% of the global electricity energy mix comes from fossil fuels (coal 38%, gas 23%, oil 3% [IEA, 2019]). Since fossil fuels are the largest source of greenhouse gas emissions, without fundamental shifts to renewable resources in global energy production, we shall not be able to prevent incalculable loss of life.

The book *Carbon Capitalism and Communication* has focused specifically on developing a type of communication scholarship that focuses on the materiality of communication systems: communication systems run on machines and infrastructures that deplete scarce resources in their production, consumption, and disposal, thus increasing the amounts of energy in their use, and exacerbating problems of the climate crisis (Brevini and Murdock, 2017). Researchers Lotfi Belkhir and Ahmed Elmeligi estimate that the tech industry's carbon footprint could increase to 14% by 2040, "accounting for more than half of the current relative contribution of the whole transportation sector" (Belkhir and Elmeligi, 2018, 448). Data centers will make up 45% of this footprint (up from 33% in 2010) and network infrastructure 24% (ibid., 457).

Understanding Artificial Intelligence and Its Environmental Toll

In dominant media debates, AI has been defined as the ability of machines to mimic and perform human cognitive functions. These include reasoning, learning, problem-solving, decision-making, and even the attempt to match elements of human behavior such as creativity. Human–Machine Communication (HMC), an emerging area of communication research, defined AI as the study of the "creation of meaning among humans and machines" (Guzman and Lewis, 2019, 71). Others instead focused on refinement and theory related to people's interactions with technologies such as agents and robots (Spence, 2019).

Most AI applications are already so embedded in our everyday life that we no longer notice. For example, the AI-enabled camera that helps control traffic, the facial recognition scan at airports, the latest smartphone applications recommending music videos on YouTube, and the smart homes powered by Amazon's Alexa. AI technologies are now employed in every sector of social, political, and economic relevance. They are used to translate languages, guide agricultural businesses, assess climate threats, advise corporations on HR and investments, fly drones, diagnose diseases, and protect borders. The AI industry is dominated by a handful of companies mainly, from the U.S. and China (Brevini, 2021; Kaplan and Haenlein, 2020). In both the leading countries, AI applications are controlled by "Digital Lords" (Brevini, 2020a), the tech giants who have come to dominate technology developments, both in the West (Google, Microsoft, Apple, Facebook/Meta, Amazon) and in China (Baidu, Tencent, Alibaba). In the last decade, these companies have become more aggressive in their competition for AI dominance by acquiring start-ups as well as heavily investing in compute capacity, leading to the concentrated AI industrial landscape we see today (Dyer-Witheford et al., 2019). Besides the U.S. and China, many countries in the northern hemisphere have invested heavily in funding for AI technologies and intellectual property. France, Israel, the United Kingdom, South Korea, and Japan have all joined the race for AI (Cognilytica, 2020).

In *Is AI Good for the Planet*, Brevini argues that the definition adopted by the latest *White Paper on Artificial Intelligence* issued by the European Commission serves as a good starting point to regain an understanding of the materiality of AI, highlighting the connection between AI, data, and algorithms: "AI is a collection of technologies that combine data, algorithms and computing power. Advances in computing and the increasing availability of data are therefore key drivers of the current upsurge of AI" (Brevini, 2021, 40). Embracing the tradition of critical political economy of communication, in which communication systems are approached as assemblages of material devices and infrastructures (Brevini and Murdock, 2017), AI then can be better understood as technologies, machines, and infrastructures that demand amounts of energy to compute, analyze, and categorize. As a consequence, these communication technologies use scarce resources in their production, consumption, and disposal, exacerbating problems of waste and pollution.

The Potentials of AI: Fixing the World, Fixing the Environment

AI – so we are told – is helping to solve some of the world's biggest challenges, from treating chronic diseases and reducing fatality rates in traffic accidents, to fighting climate change and anticipating cybersecurity threats (Brevini, 2020a,b, 2). AI is sold as the solution to the world's most pressing problems, so it's not surprising that it also promises to tackle the most urgent emergency: the climate crisis that the earth is facing. A report entitled *Harnessing Artificial Intelligence for the Earth*, published in January 2018 by the World Economic Forum, reiterated that the solution to the world's most pressing environmental challenges is to employ technological innovations – none more so than AI (World Economic Forum, 2018): "We have a unique opportunity to harness this Fourth Industrial Revolution, and the societal shifts it triggers, to help address environmental issues and redesign how we manage our shared global environment" (ibid., 3); "The intelligence and productivity gains that AI will deliver can unlock new solutions to society's most pressing environmental challenges: climate change, biodiversity, ocean health, water management, air pollution, and resilience, among others" (ibid., 19).

Technology has served for generations as the most efficient tool to address the inequalities of capitalism (Brevini, 2021), thus rescuing societies from unavoidable declines. Morozov (2013) describes how "Techno solutionism" entails an absolute faith in technology, carrying the power to change how we understand social phenomena. Embedded in this neoliberal, techno-determinist discourse is a belief digital technology can disrupt inequalities and power asymmetries. The concept of Ecomodernism (Asafu-Adjaye et al., 2015) echoes this sentiment. In contrast to those who place unequal capitalist power relations at the center of the climate emergency (Brevini and Murdock, 2017; Foster, 2002), the *Ecomodernist Manifesto* (Asafu-Adjaye et al., 2015) cites technology as our answer to the ecological crisis, shirking the need to confront the inherent environmental destructiveness of capitalism. Halting the many societal gains we have achieved through technological innovation, they argue, rules out the best tools we have for combating climate change, protecting nature, and helping humanity.

Authored by a group of sustainability figures from the Breakthrough Institute, including Nordhaus, Shellenberger, and Brand, 2015's *An Ecomodernist Manifesto* argues "meaningful climate mitigation is fundamentally a technological challenge" (Asafu-Adjaye et al., 2015). For ecomodernists, limitless economic growth is not disputed but encouraged. High-tech crops, tools for carbon capture and storage, and smart conservation, all have the potential to reduce human demands on the environment but also spark the economic growth needed to lift people out of extreme poverty. Ecomodernist ideas have been advanced in the last few years through the work of Harvard University cognitive linguist Steven Pinker who in his popular book, *Enlightenment Now* (Pinker, 2018), advocates for ecomodernism and the need for technologies such as nuclear energy. Ecomodernism is also being adopted in leftist circles (Isenhour, 2016), among scholars who claim "the idea that the answer to Climate Change is consuming less energy – that a shift to renewables will necessarily mean a downsizing in life – feels wrong" (Bastani, 2017). For Bastani, a proponent of fully automated green communism, "rather than consuming less energy, developments in wind and solar (and within just a few decades) should mean distributed energy of such abundance that we won't know what to do with it" (ibid., para. 33).

Despite its discussions around limiting greenhouse gas emissions, the International Kyoto Protocol also did little to dissuade an ecomodernist agenda, instead encouraging environmental advocates in the United States (see: Al Gore's presidential campaign) to push for technological improvement in energy efficiency as a way of averting environmental disaster (Foster, 2001, 2002). This view, which we similarly find in cybertarian Silicon Valley circles, turns into a powerful apology of the status quo and is embraced by the same corporate giants that traditionally opposed action on Climate Change.

Inequality and Exploitation: Understanding the Environmental Costs of AI as Communication Technologies

A study by the College of Information and Computer Sciences at University of Massachusetts Amherst (Strubell, Ganesh, McCallum, 2019) quantifies the energy consumed by running AI programs. In the case examined by the study, a common AI training model in linguistics can emit more than 284 tons of carbon dioxide equivalent. This is comparable to five times the lifetime emissions of the average American car. It is also comparable to roughly 100 return flights from London to NYC. Meanwhile, the converged communication systems upon which AI relies generate a plethora of environmental problems of their own, most notably energy consumption and emissions, material toxicity, and electronic waste (Brevini and Murdock, 2017). For example, while internet users increased globally by 60% from 3 billion to 4.9 billion in 2021, internet traffic increased by 440% with major consequences on the electricity supply. Data center energy usage increased by 60%, while for crypto mining, energy use went from 4 terawatt hours (TWh) to 100/140 TWh in five years between 2015 and 2021, an increase of over 300%/ (IEA, 2022).

AI relies on data to work. At present, cloud computing eats up energy at a rate somewhere between the national consumption of Japan and that of India (Greenpeace International, 2011; Murdock and Brevini, 2019). Today, data centers' energy usage averages 200 TWh each year (International Energy Agency, 2017; Jones, 2018), more than the national energy consumption of some countries, including Iran. Moreover, the information and communications technology (ICT) sector that includes mobile phones networks, digital devices, and television amounts to 2% of global emissions (Jones, 2018). Greenhouse gas emissions from the information and communication industry could grow from roughly 1 to 1.6% in 2007 to exceed 14% worldwide by 2040, accounting for more than half of the current relative contribution of the whole transportation sector. Moreover, data centers require large, continuous supplies of water for their cooling systems, raising serious policy issues in places like the U. S. and Australia where years of drought have ravaged communities (Mosco, 2017). As *Google's Deepmind* website explains,

> One of the primary sources of energy use in the data centre environment is cooling... Our data centres - which contain servers powering Google Search, Gmail, YouTube, etc. - also generate a lot of heat that must be removed to keep the servers running. This cooling is typically accomplished via large industrial equipment such as pumps, chillers and cooling towers.
>
> (Evans and Gao, 2016, para. 5)

According to *Deepmind*, the solution to this problem is, of course, Machine Learning, which is also extremely energy-consuming and generative of carbon emissions. When communication machines are discarded, they become electronic waste or e-waste, saddling local municipalities with the challenge of safe disposal. This task is so burdensome that it is frequently offshored, and many countries with developing economies have become digital dumping grounds for more privileged nations (Brevini and Murdock, 2017).

Finally, while promising to solve the climate emergency, AI companies are marketing their offers and services to coal, oil, and gas companies, thus compromising efforts to reduce the emissions and divest from fossil fuels. A report on the future of AI in the oil and gas market published by Zion Market Research (2019) found that the sector of AI in oil and gas is expected to reach around USD 4.01 billion globally by 2025 from 1.75 billion in 2018. AI companies around the world are pushing their capabilities to the oil and gas sectors to increase their efficiencies, optimize their operations, and increase productivity. In other words, they are selling their services to increase the pace and productivity of excavation and drilling. ExxonMobil, for example, signed a partnership with Microsoft to deploy AI programs, while oil and gas exploration in the fragile ecosystem of Brazil have seen the deployment of AI technology by state oil giant Petrobras. Similarly, European oil major, Royal Dutch Shell, signed a partnership with AI company C3.

Placing the Climate Emergency at the Center of Communication Scholarship

New developments of AI escalate demands on energy, water, and resources in their production, transportation, and use; reinforce a culture of hyper consumerism; and add to the accumulating amounts of waste and pollution already generated by accelerating rates of digital obsolescence and disposal (see Brevini, 2021; Gabrys, 2011). Instead of embracing new developments in communication technologies and AI as a new utopia that will fix the world and capitalism problems, we should start quantifying and considering the environmental costs and damages of the current acceleration of algorithm-powered data communication. We need to ask who should own and control the essential infrastructures that power data communication and AI and make sure to place the climate emergency at the center of the debate.

How can we shape the future of AI to be one of collective well-being and minimized climate impact? Certainly, an intervention at global and international public fora would be crucial. One interesting piece of policy in this regard is the European Commission report, "Strategic Foresight Report 2022" (European Commission 2022) on "Twinning the green and digital transition in the new geopolitical context" (ibid). It stresses the crucial role of the "twin transition" of green and digital at the top of the EU's political agenda. What is crucial is that for the first time, the European commission is explicit about the fact that digital technologies will also bring additional environmental burdens with them. In particular, it explains that,

> Unless digital technologies are made more energy-efficient, their widespread use will increase energy consumption ... Studies show that ICT power consumption will continue to grow, driven by increasing use and production of consumer devices, demand from networks, data centres, and crypto assets.
>
> (European Commission, 2022)

It further acknowledges that "further tensions will emerge in relation to electronic waste and environmental footprints of digital technologies." However, despite growing attention to the environmental costs of ICT systems, AI gets principally heralded as the key technology to solve contemporary challenges, including the environmental crisis, which is one of the goals of sustainable development. In fact, it seems that global discussions on the climate emergency – for example in the context of UN COP – are yet to connect the environment with technology policy.

We know many corporations now audit the production conditions of sub-contractors' factories, but there is still an urgent need to demand accountability for those who own data centers. One crucial intervention could be to government-mandated Green Certification for server farms and centers to achieve zero emissions. Given AI's increasing computing capabilities, the disclosure of its carbon footprint could be a first step in the right direction. This could take the form of a "Tech Carbon Footprint Label," which would provide information about the raw materials used, the carbon costs involved, and what recycling options are available, resulting in stronger public awareness about the implications of adopting a piece of smart technology. Making transparent the energy used to produce, transport, assemble, and deliver the technology we use daily would enable policy makers to make more informed decisions, and for the public to make more informed choices. Added to this could be policy intervention which requires manufacturers to lengthen the lifespan of smart devices and provide spare parts to replace faulty components.

Global policy making should encourage educational programs to enhance green tech literacy and raise awareness of the costs of hyper-consumerism, as well as the importance of responsible energy consumption. Green tech literacy programs should also entail interventions to ban production of products that are too data-demanding and deplete too much energy, such as the request by the EU commissioner to lower the default quality of video streams services by Netflix, YouTube, and Amazon to preserve bandwidth during the coronavirus lockdowns. As the global pandemic crisis has shown, governments around the world can act fast when urgent action is needed in the public good.

Further Reading

Brevini, Benedetta. 2022. *Is AI Good for the Planet?* Cambridge; Medford, MA: Polity Press.
Brevini, Benedetta. 2023. *Communication, Technology and the Environment*. Cambridge; Medford, MA: Polity Press.
Brevini, Benedetta and Graham Murdock. 2017. *Carbon Capitalism and Communication: Confronting Climate Crisis*. Cham: Palgrave.
Dyer-Witheford, Nick, Atle Mikkola Kjøsen, and James Steinhoff. 2019. *Inhuman Power: Artificial Intelligence and the Future of Capitalism*. Pluto Press. https://doi.org/10.2307/j.ctvj4sxc6.
Gabrys, Jennifer. 2011. *Digital Rubbish: A Natural History of Electronics*. Ann Arbor, MI: Univ. of Michigan Press.
Maxwell, Richard, and Toby Miller. 2020. *How Green Is Your Smartphone?* Cambridge; Medford, MA: Polity Press.

References

Asafu-Adjaye, John, et al. 2015. "An Economist Manifesto." *Breakthrough Institute*. http://www.ecomodernism.org.
Bastani, Aaron. 2017. "Fully Automated Green Communism." *Novara Media*. November 19. https://novaramedia.com/2017/11/19/fully-automated-green-communism/.
Belkhir, Lotfi, and Ahmed Elmeligi. 2018. "Assessing ICT Global Emissions Footprint: Trends to 2040 & Recommendations." *Journal of Cleaner Production* 177: 448–63.
Brevini, Benedetta. 2020a. "Black Boxes, Not Green: Mythologizing Artificial Intelligence and Omitting the Environment." *Big Data & Society* 7 (2). https://doi.org/10.1177/2053951720935141
Brevini, Benedetta. 2020b. *Conclusion in "Amazon: Understanding a Global Communications Giant"*. New York: Routledge.
———. 2021. *Is AI Good for the Planet?* Cambridge: Politi.
Brevini, Benedetta, and Graham Murdock. 2017. *Carbon Capitalism and Communication*. Sydney: Palgrave Macmillan.
Cognilytica Research. 2020. "Data Preparation & Labeling for AI 2020." https://www.aidatatoday.com/product/data-preparation-labeling-for-ai-2020/.
European Commission. 2022. "Strategic Foresight Report Twinning the Green and Digital Transitions in the New Geopolitical Context." *Communication from the Commission to the European Parliament and the Council*. Brussels: European Commission
Evans, Richard, and Jim Gao. 2016. "AI Reduces Google Data Centre Cooling Bill by 40%." *Deepmind*. July 20. https://www.deepmind.com/blog/deepmind-ai-reduces-google-data-centre-cooling-bill-by-40.
Foster, John Bellamy. 2001. "Ecology against capitalism." *Monthly Review* 53(5).
Foster, John Bellamy. 2002. "Capitalism and Ecology: The Nature of the Contradiction." *Monthly Review* 54 (4).
Gabrys, Jennifer. 2013. "Plastic and the Work of the Biodegradable." In *Accumulation: The Material Politics of Plastic*. London: Routledge, 208–227.
Gössling, Stefan, and Andreas Humpe. 2020. "The Global Scale, Distribution and Growth of Aviation: Implications for Climate Change." *Global Environmental Change* 65: 1–12.
Greenpeace International. 2011. "How Dirty Is Your Data? A Look at the Energy Choices That Power Cloud Computing." *Greenpeace*. May 24. https://www.greenpeace.org/international/publication/7196/how-dirty-is-your-data/.
Guzman, Andrea L., and Seth C. Lewis. 2019. "Artificial Intelligence and Communication: A Human–Machine Communication Research Agenda." *New Media & Society* 22 (1): 70–86.IEA. 2017. "Digitalisation and Energy." *IEA*. November. https://www.iea.org/reports/digitalisation-and-energy.
———. 2019. "World Energy Outlook 2019." *IEA*. November. https://www.iea.org/reports/world-energy-outlook-2019.
———. 2020. "Global Energy Review 2020." *IEA*. April. https://www.iea.org/reports/global-energy-review-2020.
———. 2022. "Data Centres and Data Transmission Networks." *IEA*. September. https://www.iea.org/reports/data-centres-and-data-transmission-networks.
Isenhour, Cindy. 2016. "Unearthing Human Progress? Ecomodernism and Contrasting Definitions of Technological Progress in the Anthropocene." *Economic Anthropology* 3 (2): 315–28.
Jones, Nicola. 2018. "How to Stop Data Centres from Gobbling Up the World's Electricity." *Nature*. September 13. https://www.nature.com/articles/d41586-018-06610-y.
Kaplan, Andreas, and Michael Haenlein. 2020. "Rulers of the World, Unite! The Challenges and Opportunities of Artificial Intelligence." *Business Horizons* 63 (1): 37–50. https://doi.org/10.1016/j.bushor.2019.09.003.
Milkround. 2021. "Gen Z Lead the Way Through Lockdown with Tech Skills That Boost Productivity." *Milkround*. January 24. Accessed February 8, 2022. https://www.milkround.com/advice/gen-z-lead-the-way-through-lockdown-with-tech-skills-that-boost-productivity.
Morozov, Evgeny. 2013. *To Save Everything, Click Here: The Folly of Technological Solutionism*. New York: PublicAffairs.
Mosco, Vincent. 2017. "The next Internet." In *Carbon Capitalism and Communication: Confronting Climate Crisis*, edited by Benedetta Brevini and Graham Murdock, 95–107. Sydney: Palgrave Macmillan.
Murdock, Graham, and Benedetta Brevini. 2019. "Communications and the Capitalocene: Disputed Ecologies, Contested Economies, Competing Futures." *The Political Economy of Communication* 7 (1): 51–82.

Pinker, Steven. 2018. *Enlightenment Now: The Case for Reason, Science, Humanism, and Progress.* New York: Viking.
Spence, Patric R. 2019. "Searching for Questions, Original Thoughts, or Advancing Theory: Human-Machine Communication." *Computers in Human Behavior* 90 (January): 285–87. https://doi.org/10.1016/j.chb.2018.09.014.
Strubell, Emma, Ananya Ganesh, and Andrew McCallum. 2019. "Energy and Policy Considerations for Deep Learning in NLP." *Proceedings of the 57th Annual Meeting of the Association for Computational Linguistics.* Florence, Italy, 3645–50.
United Nations. 2020. "Carbon Dioxide Levels Hit New Record; COVID Impact 'a Tiny Blip', WMO Says." *UN News.* November 23. https://news.un.org/en/story/2020/11/1078322.
United Nations Environment Programme. 2019. *Emissions Gap Report 2019.* Nairobi: UNEP.
World Economic Forum; PwC; Stanford Woods Institute for the Environment. 2018. "Harnessing Artificial Intelligence for the Earth." January. https://www3.weforum.org/docs/Harnessing_Artificial_Intelligence_for_the_Earth_report_2018.pdf.
Zion Market Research. 2019. "Global AI in Oil and Gas Market Will Reach to USD 4.01 Billion By 2025: Zion Market Research." July 18. https://www.globenewswire.com/news-release/2019/07/18/1884499/0/en/Global-AI-In-Oil-and-Gas-Market-Will-Reach-to-USD-4-01-Billion-By-2025-Zion-Market-Research.html.

18
ENVIRONMENTAL MEDIA MANAGEMENT
Overcoming the Responsibility Deficit

Pietari Kääpä and Hunter Vaughan

Introduction

As awareness of the environmental impacts of the screen media sector increases, new practices, frameworks, guidelines, and policy frameworks are developed by industry stakeholders. However, these frameworks are fraught with challenges ranging from questions over their economic viability to their role in the management infrastructures of the film industry. If media management concerns "the ability to supervise and motivate employees, and to operate facilities and resources in a cost-effective (profitable) manner" (Sherman 1995, 21; see also Albarran et al. 2018), *environmental media management* translates such concerns into the rhetoric of sustainable development. The challenges for transforming practice and policy are multi-fold. Key amongst them is what we refer to as the "responsibility deficit" in media management, that is, a lack of coordination between organizations, regulators, producers, and creatives, leading to gaps in accountability over the design and implementation of environmentally sound policies.

In response to these gaps, we have seen the development of local, national, regional, and international self-regulation mechanisms and tools (including ones by leading organizations like the Producers Guild of America [PGA] Green and the UK's Bafta albert), which have generated a slew of industry and public-facing public relations (PR) content to spotlight the industry's green turn. While some of these organizations are imposing careful and impactful measures like mandatory carbon reporting, infrastructural problems continue to plague the effective implementation of these approaches. Challenges arise from competing measurement tools (especially as these incentives have now become commercialized), lack of unilateral standards (heavily problematic for co-productions or runaway shoots for example), different environmental regulatory regimes, and diverse creative and managerial practices. This chapter provides critical analysis of these media governance infrastructures and suggests that contemporary scholarship on media materiality and ecomedia needs to incorporate such perspectives far more prominently into their DNA to address the complex realities of an industry balancing between external pressure and internal cultural, processual, economic, and managerial challenges that impose considerable limits on their implementation.

The intersection of environmental values and practical implementation offers a crucial point of investigation for the potential role of science communication in the enforcement and assessment of media corporate accountability amidst growing calls for climate-based solutions in screen culture production, messaging, and infrastructure. For us, sound climate change and environmental communication is an essential part of environmental media management and is instrumental in developing and enforcing corporate policies, as well as articulating and enacting green mission statements and communicating corporate responsibility to the public. By analysing corporate branding and green marketing techniques as well as green mission cultivation across studios and within production teams, we offer a critique of not only the gaps in the structures of management but also of the communications that in many ways make management possible.

Accordingly, this chapter investigates the structural obstacles and ideological motivations that have and will continue to hinder substantive transformation of the industry to meet the urgent needs of climate adaptation. However, the aim of this critique is constructively aimed at the potential for screen culture, as a whole and as distinct parts and places, to play an influential and effective part in mitigating anthropogenic environmental destabilization. While much remains to be done in assessing the environmental impacts of major industry practice and holding the guiltiest parties accountable, we hope here *also* to lay out a future of environmental media studies in celebration of potentially alternative approaches for green media policy and practice.

Environmental Media Production Management

Environmental sustainability strategies to mitigate the negative environmental impacts of film production exemplify the global film industry's attempts to address the anthropogenic climate crisis. As environmental crises escalated towards the end of the twentieth century, much of the industry's early response was to emphasize creative content, from the proto-neoliberal 1990 "Earth Day" US network television special to doomsday narratives such as *The Day After Tomorrow* (dir. Roland Emmerich 2004) (see a wide range of "ecocinema" scholarship including Brereton 2005, Ingram 2004, Rust, Monani and Cubitt, 2012, 2023) to glitzy paratextual public relations drives and awards ceremonies by the Environmental Media Association. Despite this understandable focus on content, the global film and television sector has also developed practical solutions like carbon calculators and seals of approval for green productions. Among these, the albert carbon calculator and sustainability certificate – developed in collaboration between the BBC and BAFTA – has emerged as a key industry standard in the UK and is now being adapted on an international level.

Yet, many problems continue to persist with this "material turn." While Hollywood occasionally produces environmentally sensitive content and has pivoted slowly towards curtailing its footprint, the tone and scope of such strategies raise pressing questions. Many scholars (see Maxwell and Miller, 2012, Rust, Monani and Cubitt, 2023) argue that these practices largely consist of corporate rebranding efforts, amounting to little more than greenwashing instead of full-scale rerouting of the value chains and workflows of the industry. This is a problem only exacerbated by the transition to digital, as can be seen in the excessive analogue costs, digital infrastructure ramifications, and energy dependency of Hollywood's first self-marketed "fully digital" film, *Avatar* (dir. James Cameron 2009, see Vaughan 2019). For smaller industrial contexts, policy development and enforcement dynamics act as key drivers as they tend to be reliant on subsidies from national film institutes. Yet, often these incentives mix in an increasingly collaborative international film industry reliant on tax incentives and off-location shoots. Here, imposing constraints on a creative industry spread widely across a range of parts and players, often collaborating between nations with radically different labour and environmental regulatory policies, often arrives at the environmental dead end offered by the underlying logic of capitalist globalization: financial motivations trump environmental decisions.

Further concerns arise from the ways environmental production choices can be considered as impositions on the creative process or as legal concerns over the right to freedom of speech, especially if they are included as part of financial arrangements or policy recommendations. Such concerns especially apply to small to medium industries reliant on public funding, where film production is coordinated by gatekeepers such as national film funds or institutes. Accordingly, the environmental impacts of the media industry can be classed into two categories: context and content. We separate analysis of these two areas below to explore how the responsibility deficit applies to them.

The Responsibility Deficit in Media Production

The "responsibility deficit" as we define it involves the absence of a clear line of decision-making regarding governance over and application of green production measures in the film industry. It can involve the absence of regulators (for example, to do with ministries in charge of environment and/or culture), or the lack of a clear governing sectoral body to oversee green policy development and implementation. It often involves the lack of a transparent trail of governance that, consequently, leads to the evasion of responsibility, facilitating an approach where responsibility becomes someone else's problem. The responsibility deficit, in short, suggests a structural gap in the governance structures of the film industry.

In analysing the implications of this gap, the primary and most overriding concern is funding and its implications for regulation: even if we do not attempt to correlate explicitly commercial operations like Hollywood with small cinemas, the basic clash (especially in terms of developing mandatory solutions) lies in the discrepant motives to implement green policies into practice. Here, the prioritization of financial interests over other goals such as environmental values and social inclusion poses as a key question. For commercial operators, the implications of green practice will predominantly be reputational as there is relatively minor commercial pressure to consider them: producers in film industries where green incentives remain underdeveloped and where finance is mostly private stand to profit far more from environmentally negligent filmmaking practices than they do in minor tax breaks or energy reduction through green practice. As the initial implementation of green practices requires monetary investment and changes to working protocols, they can be perceived as costly and too long-term in orientation. Yet, for productions reliant on public finance in regulatory dynamics more attentive to environmental sustainability, as small film cultures often are, motivation towards green practice is more explicitly connected to long-term strategy (that is, governance and regulation) that has already been or will be immediately developed. We have seen examples of such practices in, for example, Belgium with The Flanders Film Fund requesting an emissions report in advance of awarding of the 10% of final finances for a film production or, similarly in the UK, with the BBC and its mandate for all original or commissioned content to use the albert certification for green production.

Second, labour regulations make any attempt to impose environmental measures challenging since they are not currently considered vital to health and safety (which also carry great liability factors), or urgent (as, for example, COVID-19 mitigation efforts). Such a lack of mandate underpinning their adoption fundamentally undercuts their efficiency. While industry literature, especially from consultants and policymakers, is full of positive stories about improved performance and enhanced motivation, these are generally meant as encouragement leading to improved activity and do not necessarily indicate a fundamental cultural change. It is notable that many of the success stories still revolve around a handful of large-scale productions (*Amazing Spider-Man 2*, 2014, continues to be an industry touchstone), while small productions are often discussed in terms of minor improvements in recycling performance or cutting back on crew travel arrangements, indicating that there have been few giant leaps made in the industry. We have suggested elsewhere a cultural transformation is required, one which would fundamentally upend the economic/ecological logic of the industry, but such measures do not take place in a pressured industry like film and TV without due moderation and governance decisions. If there are no clear laws or regulations for work practice, it is unlikely they will be implemented, as financial forces and venture capital underlying the film and TV industry have yet to begin leveraging environmental sustainability as an important priority for long-term financial benefit.

Third, the increasing reliance on international collaboration – whether this be through co-production arrangements, the use of outsourced digital production and post-production, and runaway or mobile production shoots in countries and cities far from the finance, talent, and creative base – poses significant managerial and strategic concerns. While industrial coordination by organizations like Cine-Regio – which brings together the various film institutes of European countries – has enabled the European film and television sector to build momentum on addressing their footprint, from a regulatory perspective, the international principles of film production clash with any established green regulation. This problem stems from the diversity of industry practices worldwide. The mechanisms established in the major commercial industries would not necessarily apply in a more regulated context and vice versa, as they are premised on entirely different economic and industrial systems. Imposing any type of globalized standard would be similarly complicated by their localized relevance as by their administrative applicability.

Conversely, though, the transnational nature of contemporary production also offers key strategies for leveraging financial and aesthetic appeal to mitigate screen media production's contribution to greenhouse gas emissions, fossil fuel use, and ecosystem disruption. Examples of this can be seen in Vancouver and Sardinia, two sites that – due to a combination of idyllic natural settings and tax incentives – have become heavily sought-after locales for mobile production from Hollywood, Europe, and elsewhere. While runaway and mobile production cultures have historically set the scene for unprecedented ecosystem disruption and environmental negligence (see the reef and biodiversity destruction wrought by beacons of globalized Hollywood *The Beach* and *Titanic*, two blockbuster hits ironically starring self-branded eco-celebrity Leo DiCaprio), the demand for these settings has also been converted into dynamics for environmental policy and enforcement. Vancouver, for example, has proven that stern municipal regulations and shooting fee reduction incentives successfully allow for leveraging the use and further development of alternative and renewable energy; in Sardinia, inter-sectoral collaboration with other institutions of cultural heritage has converted incoming production money into native biodiversity protection and local cultural heritage preservation.

Finally, perhaps the ultimate concern facing an environmental assessment of media practice is to do with Scope 3 emissions, which are generated by life cycle supply chain manufacturing and provision for the material infrastructures, from camera technologies to data centre operations, that make screen culture possible. Dismissed as externalities by most industries, Scope 3 emissions are generally considered to be outside of the direct control of the film industry. Concerns like the energy sourcing to power productions, the lifecycle of food or production materials, the "petrol" used for travel, the accommodation used, and the wider digital infrastructural apparatus of streaming culture are considered beyond the purview of producers or studio executives. They can find suppliers (and best provider catalogues and recommendations do exist), but these can be very complex to securely ascertain and integrate into the wider production structure. Furthermore, the regulations that pertain to these sectors do not coincide with the policy imperatives and overseers of the film industry. Organizations like The Responsibility Media Forum have argued that existing frameworks for environmental regulation in all these down- and upstream sectors already cover much of the emissions of the media sector. Such an evasion tactic is easy to pull off considering the scope of the operations of the film industry, which, unlike publishing, for example, does not have visibly tangible products or emissions on the scale of paper. The argument goes that not only was the dream factory's original product a quantum of light, and its current product beamed from satellites and streamed through subsea cables under the auspice of the immaterial, but also the reach of its footprint is incalculable due to its reliance on travel and its connection to other carbon-intensive industries such as catering, hotels, and textiles. Yet, all of these activities leave traces that can be quantified and hence mitigated by sustainability measures if there is a sufficient willingness to do so.

The Responsibility Deficit in Media Content

While it may be possible to instil mandatory guidelines and best practices equivalent to regulatory oversight with more easily quantifiable criteria such as production equipment, waste disposal, and energy sourcing, the ethical and legal concerns are much more complicated when they apply to content. While many major organizations and institutions evaluated here, from traditional broadcasters like the BBC to twenty-first–century streaming behemoths like Netflix, have suggested that content, not context, can create the largest environmental impact, critical questions must be asked about how to instigate awareness generation and how some of the concerns discussed in Section "The Responsibility Deficit in Media Production" might apply here, especially when complicated by the distinction between explicitly commercial and publicly financed media. While BAFTA, for example, often suggests that the impact of a media company on audience brainprint (that is, on the audience's levels of knowledge and awareness of environmental concerns) is much more substantial than the impact of its operational footprint, they cannot set standards or insist that creatives implement such measures. Their arguments rely on the idea that by influencing popular opinion, mediamakers will influence societal transformations. Accordingly, incentives such as Planet Placement (2020) propose best practices for environmental content which BAFTA summarizes as follows:

> We are working to help creatives make content that supports the transition to a sustainable future. Programme makers have two complementary content opportunities:
>
> 1 to look for exciting new ways to place the planet into the picture
> 2 to ensure content's editorial ambition isn't unduly normalizing unsustainable behaviour.
>
> (BAFTA 2022)

While Planet Placement now extends BAFTA albert to cover content, it only includes a few recommendations; thus, it is difficult to conceptualize how mandatory, not voluntary, suggestion would shape practice. Largely in response to social media campaigns like #MeToo and #OscarsSoWhite, the US Academy of Motion Picture Arts and Sciences has recently instituted criteria of social diversity and representation for films to be considered in the Best Film category; could the same be done for environmental messaging? Can we establish a similar quantitative framework for content as is now in place for production? Perhaps even more pressingly, should we do this?

Ultimately, these questions revolve around whether the emphasis on footprinting the media industry is a sensible approach, or would these energies be better used for conceptualizing the impact of content and, especially, in developing appropriate audience measurements. Focusing on the creation of environmental content and targeting behavioural transformation make a lot of sense considering the "key performance indicators" (KPIs) by which the industry is measured to generate content in an economically profitable way, not to "save the world." This is reflected in the Responsible Media Forum's emphasis on how the sector considers environmental matters an operational aspect of their performance as useful for reputation management and increasing corporate profiles, but not in providing improvements on economic or legal performance. Environmental issues can, in some instances, impact the economic operations of a company, for instance, when a broadcaster develops a reputation for environmental material (such as with The BBC's collaboration with David Attenborough) or a film breaks out at the box office (as with David Guggenheim and Al Gore's 2006 *An Inconvenient Truth*). These successes are rare (even with streaming companies like Netflix investing in documentaries with environmental themes such as *Seaspiracy* 2019 and *My Octopus Teacher* 2020) and do not provide an economically sustainable strategy adaptable across the industry, especially regarding the discrepancies in international modes of financing and production.

Yet, establishing any form of policy to promote environmental content is a very difficult task complicated by a range of factors. Freedom of expression is considered a fundamental cultural value (at least in many Western societies), and challenges to any sort of content management come in various forms, such as the arm's length principle in Nordic countries, which prohibits cultural institutions from any explicit encouragement or influence over content, including environmental programming. Simultaneously, leaving content to develop according to the guiding hand of the free market does not seem like a solid strategy either, especially in terms of the ethical dimensions of environmental arguments. While there are gains to be had from environmental content (especially in terms of reputation and awards, including capitalizing on celebrity self-promotion), prioritizing environmental content may require both audience studies to gage the actual influence of content on social values and behaviours, as well as box office data to suggest that such content can be economically profitable in the long run. As private companies can, arguably, conduct content management more efficiently than publicly funded companies, it is questionable whether they will choose to do so in beneficial ways (i.e., not simply capitalizing on pseudo-environmentalist rhetoric in blockbusters and children's animation). At the same time, perhaps a more practical approach to generating environmental content in publicly funded production is to place elements into narratives or backgrounds of sets, such as the use of recycling bins in *EastEnders* (see BAFTA 2022). Such minimal interventionism may be palatable to creatives and the developers of green policies, but whether they have sufficient influence on general audiences can only be ascertained through sustained research on reception.

Conclusion

While there is now general academic and industrial understanding that the environmental and political economy dynamics of each production and distribution context matter, there continue to be fundamental challenges that complicate the implementation of systemic or majorly impactful measures to mitigate the environmental costs and consequences of film and television production. Concerns range from the explicitly material, as in the types of resources available to productions; to the politics of administrative regimes and their perspectives on sustainability; to the development of physical and digital infrastructure; and finally, and arguably most importantly, of cultural value systems that ultimately guide these choices.

If legislating for content faces considerable hurdles and cannot ever be a truly comprehensive or quantifiable measure, a focus on footprint may, in contrast, provide an efficient means to install a solid level of control on the industry's environmental impact. Policy for measuring and reporting screen media's footprint requires the industry to focus on its own actions by providing quantifiable data on its emissions and explaining these measures in qualifiable ways to its staff and stakeholders. While imposed top-down control is never the most efficient management tool, especially on a topic as personal and value-oriented as climate change, it does indicate a viable way to introduce environmental sustainability to production practice. Supporting this is the fact that the industry continues to be at a relatively early stage of adopting such measures. Establishing guidelines and policies, published through industry events and festivals – i.e., through soft power strategies – may be sufficient to encourage the industry to accept sustainability as an everyday part of production. Simultaneously, correlating these strategies for the sector as a whole, as Bafta and Cine-Regio are now doing, could provide a pragmatic way to avoid the responsibility deficit and, instead, leverage environmental accountability through corporate networks and multi-stakeholder pressure.

Even if, say, the EU was to accept responsibility for establishing common European green media production standards, perhaps alongside its digital single-market strategy, there would need to be national variations in practice. Currently, fragmentation is one of the key obstacles facing the industry. The EU has a range of codes and directives that govern the infrastructure of the media. The EU Green New Deal covers both resource management and recycling, which directly impacts the media. There are plans in place to establish centralized European coordination of green media policies and practices, but their applicability and content are yet to be determined. The confluence of centralized policies and the individual needs of national media industries remains a likely sticking point. Currently, environmental best practices remain scattered and isolated (often the internal imposition of municipalities or islands highly sought-after for mobile production) and for the most part an afterthought on the priority list of productions. Sectoral differences act as one of the obstacles to developing functional policy for the media as a whole, and a better understanding of the distinctive strategies required to meet each part of the industry appropriately would move the debate forward considerably. Thus, there would need to be a correlation between the regulatory and operational environments of each sector.

Another increasingly crucial factor that will have repercussions across the screen media discussed here is the role of digital technologies in both production and dissemination of content. The emissions involved in housing, circulating, and streaming content, as well as the mining impacts, manufacturing footprint, and operational and waste implications of digital media devices (designed for planned obsolescence), are only now beginning to be understood by climate scientists. Similarly, the significance of renewable energy infrastructures will transform with, for example, the introduction of large-scale server farms in Finland and Sweden and elsewhere by Google and Facebook to make use of the cool climate. While launching domestic data centre operators such as GreenQloud and Green Mountain in Iceland and Norway will influence the total media footprint of these countries, the ways they will influence the overall footprint of screen media production are questionable. Not only are there questions over the "sustainability" of the methods used (the air cools their servers, but the servers also warm the air), but the reliance on infrastructural solutions can also lead to fallacies endemic to the responsibility deficit.

If digital or wider infrastructural solutions are the answer to cutting back on screen media's environmental impacts, then responsibility over what equates to Scope 3 emissions can once more evade the remit of media production companies and creatives. Understanding environmental sustainability as a network of different agents – regulators, companies, producers, crew, consumers, consultancies, institutes, and a whole range of other stakeholders – would ensure environmental concerns gain an even more prominent role in media management. Significantly, we are now witnessing such attempts take place with many of the regional and international efforts chronicled in this chapter. It is in such ventures that the futures of green film and TV lie, not in attempts to evade these difficult questions by, for example, greenwashing them through policy and guideline documents which often frame them as easy opportunities. If these rhetorical tools are used to paper over the responsibility deficit gap, then further critical attention on the fallacies of such communication strategies will be required.

Further Reading

Kääpä, P. (2018). *Environmental Management of the Media: Industry, Policy Practice*, New York: Routledge.
Kääpä, P. and H. Vaughan (2021). 'From content to context (and back again): new industrial strategies for environmental sustainability in the media', in Hjort, Mette Ted Nannicelli (ed.) *Motion Pictures and Public Value*, Chichester: Wiley-Blackwell.
Kääpä P. and H. Vaughan (ed.) (2022). *Film and Television in the Age of the Climate Emergency*, Basingstoke: Palgrave MacMillan.
Rust, Stephen, Salma Monani and Sean Cubitt (eds.) (2023). *Ecocinema: Theory and Practice 2*, London: Routledge.
Vaughan, H. (2019). *Hollywood's Dirtiest Secret: The Hidden Environmental Costs of the Movies*, New York: Columbia University Press.

References

Albarran, Alan, B. Mierzejewska and J. Jung (eds.) (2018). *Handbook of Media Management and Economics*, London: Routledge.
BAFTA (2022). https://wearealbert.org/editorial/why/ (Accessed 8 January 2022).
Brereton, Pat (2005). *Hollywood Utopia*, Bristol: Intellect.
Ingram, David (2004). *Green Screen: Environmentalism and Hollywood Cinema*, Exeter: University of Exeter Press.
Maxwell, R. and T. Miller (2012). *Greening the Media*, Oxford: Oxford University Press.
Rust, Stephen, Salma Monani and Sean Cubitt (eds.) (2012). *Ecocinema: Theory and Practice*, London: Routledge.
Sherman, B. (1995). *Telecommunications Management, Broadcasting/Cable and the New Technologies*, New York: McGraw-Hill Humanities.
Vaughan, H. (2019). *Hollywood's Dirtiest Secret: The Hidden Environmental Costs of the Movies*, New York: Columbia University Press.

19
PROPERTY RIGHTS CONTROL IN THE DATA-DRIVEN ECONOMY
The Media Ecology of Blockchain Registries

Jannice Käll

Introduction

The year 2021 saw the boom of NFTs (non-fungible tokens), as well as creative and less creative ways of using and understanding them. As NFTs became popularized by celebrities as the next big thing in art and sold for up to almost 92 million dollars (see, e.g., Dexerto 2021), artists flocked around the thought of creating scarcity in cultural expressions, long (conceived of as being) lost in the era of digital media. By utilizing blockchain technologies, the idea is to create a distributed registry for digital cultural expressions of different kinds. Recently, interesting ways to rematerialize the environment into the digital economy have been pursued by artists and organizations with varying results. For example, the World Wildlife Fund UK (WWF) started selling NFTs in the form of digital art comprising 13 endangered species, which they called "non-fungible-animals" (NFAs). Further aligned with the ecological realities of such species, they announced an ambition to mint NFTs/NFAs in a number limited to the number of animals left in each specific species on Earth (Gizmodo 2022). This specific project was however cancelled after just two days on the market, following critique from the "crypto community" (Farand 2022).

In the legal discipline, the discussion has circled around how to make sense of what made the NFT phenomenon "new" from a legal perspective, considering its similarities to digital rights management (DRM). Another aspect discussed is what laws may apply when copyrights are put on the blockchain registry (European Commission 2022), hence making NFT constructs even less clear than DRM. As debunked by Guadamuz, NFTs cannot necessarily be viewed as establishing unique property rights, but rather serve as contractual agreements over metadata placed on-chain (Guadamuz 2021). Copyright, DRMs, and NFTs, however, all share the aim of producing *scarcity* in intangible goods in the sense that they are supposed to function as a means to control creative expressions. However, this production of scarcity as a means to better sustain a cultural ecology, often claimed to be put at hardship through digitalization, rarely addresses the larger societal aspects of "giving back rights" to artists and, even less so, the other ecological costs such manufactured scarcity involves.

This chapter suggests connecting the ecology of blockchains, smart contracts, NFTs, and copyrights to a longer trajectory of the function of control vested in property rights by placing more focus on the registry as a means of creating proprietary control than on the possibility to control cultural expressions via NFTs. In doing this, we can draw upon similarities to the filing of property rights of land. This extended historizing of property pulls together materialities and materialisms that are generally kept apart in legal theory and philosophy as cultural or "intangible" expressions being different from land or other "physical" expressions. To draw such materialities together is beneficial from a media ecological perspective as it enables us to see how property rights also can be understood as an ecology of control (c.f. Bhandar 2018; Käll 2022) over connected media.

The need to pursue such ecological understanding of how different matter, or media, connect (or disconnect) to each other, is an urgent task considering the diagnosis, such as how ecomedia scholars call to limit capitalist exploitation of everything from the environment to knowledge (Cubitt 2016). Cultural ecologies, together with environmental ecologies, need to consider the vast amounts of resources needed for new, and supposedly radical, data-intense phenomena. In pursuing such a route, we can also begin to make visible a fuller picture of the effects of ownership and exploitation in digitalized societies. The notion of thinking environmentally in relation to intellectual property rights (IPRs) in digital settings was deployed famously already by James Boyle (1997: 109). What Boyle suggests for the information economy is cultivating an information environment or an information commons. This is a first step to understand how IPRs have functioned as a wider means of control than imagined, as more and more aspects have been turned into information/intangibles that may be captured by IPRs. However, this type of commons focuses only on the cultural aspects of technological media. Therefore, it can be criticized for continuing the general move by capital to make invisible the layers that go into the production of media. For example, the extraction of minerals and energy demanded for information to be transmitted is not inside the picture of such idea of the commons.

Property as a Registry of Control

The idea of property rights as the means for some to control different elements of society is an old concept in the Western legal discipline. Over the years, property rights have been created and used to rationalize patriarchal and racist forms of control (Harris 1993; Davies and Naffine 2001; Bhandar 2018). Current conceptions of property rights still tend to work with certain ideas about what is the normal property object, or even the ideal property object, in relation to Westernized (capitalist) societies. In property law today, property rights tend to be modeled around fixed or movable properties. Both of these types of property have in common a physical representation, which makes it possible to identify what they are in terms of a property object. In this manner, such forms of property objects are understood to be qualitatively different than property objects in knowledge or culture, which are regarded as intangible and not immediately representable.

The potential to identify something as property is not in itself part of the nature of the property object but forms part of legal techniques that renders them into commodities. Bhandar (2018) points out, for example, the construction of land as private property was made into a legal standard connected to expressions of colonial power. This includes how the widely theorized concept of *terra nullius* functioned for states to claim land as a resource, when they had no such land under their possession before. It also involves several linked concepts related to colonialism, such as depicting the people living on the land the colonial powers entered as "savages." This "savagery" is then utilized to rationalize why the relationship to the land by the colonialized people needs to be replaced with an alternative idea of land-use and exploitation by the colonial power (2018: 23–28; 49). One of the legal inventions to change the notion of control over land during early colonial times was the construction of a registry for property rights in land (Bhandar 2018; Keenan 2019). The use of registration of property was first enforced within laws for ships, as ships could not be kept in possession in the way that one did with lands and also other (smaller) movable goods. Hence, for people to transact upon them, a registry was established (Bhandar 2018). This model was later adapted as a form of experiment in the colonies, via the so-called Torrens system (Bhandar 2018: 84–113; Keenan 2019). In other places, registration of land also became standard practice as industrial capitalism emerged and later came to be rationalized as an important means for successful capitalism (e.g., notably De Soto 2004). It is therefore not surprising that the possibilities of creating an even more tamper-proof registry of land through blockchain were suggested earlier than the emergence of NFTs (de Filippi and Wright 2019: 109).

Moving down a bit in the conventional property hierarchy, one can identify similar ideas in relation to the validation of moving chattel. For the non-lawyer, chattel is considered a traditional form of commodity object, since it is easy to identify as a separate object (it "is" the object that it represents) and to trade one can pass it along with some ease compared to land property that, before land registries, had to be occupied. This of course does not necessarily mean that the commodification of chattel was always uncontroversial or detached from the colonialism pursued via land rights, both historically and today. The harrowing examples of the slave trade point us toward the role of the registry and the specifications of goods needed, such as insurance claims, as in the well-known case of the slave-ship *Zong* (Hartman 2008: 136–53).

With industrialization and mass production, chattel, or *tangible* goods, became more standardized; however, some tangible goods, such as livestock, were not necessarily as easy to standardize as, let's say a pencil, yet are today under increased requirements to hold a certain standard for purposes such as food safety. As Wang (2020) described in her much-cited book on blockchain chicken farms in China, the question of food safety has become increasingly important. In a case described by Wang, a small farmer in the Chinese countryside decides to put the chicken he tends to on the blockchain to prove that they have been kept in the way that has been described. The consumer can then unlock this data about the chicken to make sure that it has not been tampered with. Consequently, the move from the accountancy in the form of simple trades, or trades accompanied by lists and specifications of goods, makes it into a blockchain registry.

In intellectual property law, processes of dematerialization can be likened to the enclosure of land pursued via colonialism and capitalism, and their respective "findings" of *terra nullius* (c.f. Boyle 2003). The processes which render something into a commodity are, however, many and multifaceted, but for the purpose of NFTs (to the extent of being built up as registries of metadata), there is reason to look further into the role that the registry plays for commodification. The connection between the commodity object and the property right, in turn, is constructed via IPR laws and what they define as the object covered under property control. It is this distinction between the object and the IPR that becomes further difficult to uphold, for example, when cultural expressions are turned into information objects via digitalization. This process unfolds via legal concepts that grant property rights, such as copyright to the "creator" of "works of art," and one of the ways the right holder can effectuate such rights is via the dissemination of "copies" of such "works." To continue the production of scarcity that IPRs afford, the above-mentioned construct of DRMs was put in place in copyright (Schollin 2008), and the unfolding construct of NFT, and the registration of metadata on the blockchain, can be said to do the same. In comparing these phenomena to land rights as described by Keenan (2019), it becomes clear that the registry here fulfills a role to expand proprietary control over intellectual expressions, such as works of art.

A Lack of Ecology

IPRs and other forms of property rights rely on different abstractions as a means to rationalize and make invisible forms of control vested in certain humans over other bodies (human and nonhuman).

As shown by Keenan (2019), legal techniques such as property registries have the capacity to create a time machine where the relationality between some humans and the spaces they inhabit are recast as past, while the future of the land is inscribed by the ones who benefit from the registry. Keenan (2019) and Bhandar (2012) both point out that the registry was vital to creating a colonialist, racist form of ownership, both in the colonies and in mainland UK. Current forms of property rights do not stop this development, which can be seen not the least in the critique of access to knowledge forwarded in relation to IPRs (Boyle 1996, 1997, 2003; Kapczynski 2010; Bhandar 2012).

Today, this understanding of land as a capital asset is obvious, not the least in the way in which property in land has become a capital asset used for the liquidation of capital. The connection to the "knowledge-driven" economy is obvious in many ways, as it is perceived of as more difficult to evaluate the value of intellectual assets (Andreasson 2010). Production as well as speculation in innovative industries can therefore depend on ownership of land. Despite this, the dominant idea in legal theory and practice is still that intellectual property can be distinguished from physical property, including both movable chattel and property rights in land. This legal technique of keeping different types of properties apart arguably facilitates the disconnection between resources needed to create "intangible" expressions as art from the physical resources involved. To not recognize the material means needed for the effectuation of IPRs has been discussed widely, both in relation to biotechnologies related to the human body (Bhandar 2012), as well as in relation to natural resources such as the extraction of crops and plants (Kapczynski 2010).

Critical research on cultural rights has been particularly vital in showing how IPRs are formed around capitalist ideas of culture, as well as nature. Hence, the institution of IPRs has come to recast perceptions of knowledge, rendering Indigenous knowledge particularly at risk. This in turn implies that a spatiotemporal ordering takes place as space is re-arranged via what is understood as modern knowledge, or a modern relationship to one's surroundings. Here we can again remind ourselves about how the concept of "the savage" and its relationship to land as being unmodern. In the same manner, Indigenous knowledge, including Indigenous cultures, has been understood as inferior to Western science. As Shiva (1993) proposes, this is in spite of the uniform way that Western knowledge can affect agriculture and turn it into monocultures, via a monoculture of the mind. Without ignoring the actual advances in medicine and technology pursued over the past centuries, it is still feasible to point out how such advances have, at least to some degree, occurred through the capture and dissolution of alternative cultural ways of engaging with both human and nonhuman life, as well as our environments. Building upon Keenan's (2019) insight into the spatiotemporal ordering assigned via the registry of land rights, it would consequently not be far off to state that the technique of IPRs allows a re-ordering of both culture and space into a capitalist relation of cultural and environmental spacetime.

In relation to intellectual property in digitally mediated spheres, the placelessness of intellectual property control has been felt, both as a form of resistance and as a form of enclosure, as described by Boyle (2003) and Lessig (1999). Cyberspace has been deemed a free space where jurisdictions cannot reach. From a critical perspective, there is much to say about this idea about digital space as being something culturally disconnected from physical spaces, as has been pointed out by several researchers for over two decades (Nakamura 2002; boyd 2012; Srnicek 2017; Noble 2018; Benjamin 2019). Such "placelessness" is however also mirrored in the way that digital elements and their property rights are being disconnected from the resources needed for these spaces to be actualized. This can be illustrated particularly well with how the data-driven economy utilizes information derived from both humans and nonhumans as a resource just waiting to be *mined*; however, it can also be illustrated by the general disengagement with the natural resources needed to effectuate blockchain technologies in general and NFTs in particular.

The possibility of using blockchain as a registry to create more sustainable or resilient ecologies, which possibly could resist the placelessness of data-driven capitalism, comes through in many emerging projects, as mentioned in the introduction. The most famous of the latter type of project is likely the terra0 project, which involves visualizing an existing forest that can "own itself" through the use of blockchain technology (https://terra0.org). In their 2016 white paper for this project, Seidler, Krolling, and Hampshire describe terra0 as a "self-owned" forest, with the aim of setting up a self-utilizing piece of land to create a scenario where the forest would be able to sell licenses that would log other trees through "automated processes, smart contracts and Blockchain technology" to accumulate its own capital. In their understanding, this would mean that the forest would be able to realize its real exchange value, and "eventually buy (thus own) itself." The augmented forest would then be able to function as an owner, and with capital be able to buy more ground and expand its territory (Seidler, Kolling, and Hampshire 2016: 1). In a similar manner, the project and installation Nature Cognita, endorsed by the Amsterdam-based Sovereign Nature Initiative, is a research project that embeds technology with plants to produce renewable energy (https://cognita.dev). What seems to be lacking in these projects, however, is the critique of what happens when one creates the possibility to put more and more objects into a registry and facilitate proprietary control, whether it is full ownership, licensing, or something different altogether (c.f. Guadamuz 2021).

A Media-Ecological Registry of Property Rights

As has been stressed throughout, the rationalization of IPRs in law involves the idea that one can distinguish between intellectual and physical expressions. Hence, the ecologies involved in IPR discourse are those considered as an expression of (the) mind, including culture and scientific discoveries. However, this understanding runs partially contrary to tools used in management theory and practice, where what matters for the value proposition, or innovation object, includes more elements than control through IPRs. The idea of the intellectual object in such thought also includes understanding the need to have access to physical resources, such as factories and workers, whether they are employed directly by the organization or not (Petrusson 2004: 76, 136; c.f. Chesbrough 2003). For example, platforms are built up around a logic of proprietary control over a constellation of different assets. IPR is no longer the legal technique to control intellectual expressions, or "information." Instead, contracts form an important part of legal techniques to establish control over the different elements, whether these contracts are end-user license agreements, platform guidelines, or developer agreements. Furthermore, technological design as such becomes a means of control in these types of platforms (c.f. Lessig 1999). Thus, ironically business practices where information is commoditized have ways to visualize and enable the different materialities that build up proprietary control over information, or intangible, assets.

In further utilizing insights made in ecomedia studies, such layered visualization can also be elaborated to show what is at stake in terms of proprietary control in the digitalized society. First, one can here draw inspiration from software studies as set out by Fuller et al. who advocate "an understanding of the materiality of software being operative at many scales" (Fuller 2008, 4). This extended view of software, and other digital matter, such as data and metadata, can be aligned with the collapse of a limit between organic/non-organic or living/non-living forms of commodity that have existed in relation to de facto property rights for a long time in history (Hartman 2008; Bennet 2020). Such a conceptual apparatus is useful when we think through the ecomedia perspective of property rights, as it affords a way of connecting not only the intellectual expressions with the physical media that they are embedded in but also the commodification of organic life that is in the firing line when technologies such as blockchain and NFTs are being deployed.

This chapter has explored some examples where other than human elements, or bodies, are being placed onto the blockchain, rendering them part of a digitalized ecology, in order to serve different political or economic purposes. Whether the aim is to make a forest "self-owning" or to create an opportunity for increased revenues for creators of art or other traditional cultural expressions, the blockchain introduces the opportunity to think through the multiple ecologies that such registries brush up against. Meanwhile, the production of scarcity in knowledge expressions offers a strengthened form of control, such as with artists. How it is done is of vital importance so as not to disrupt the ecologies upon which both human and other than human life-forms rest upon. This is particularly visible when NFTs run on energy-intensive blockchains where the digital ownership granted through this system undercuts the resources needed for artistry to take place. On a local European level, this is also felt directly under the banner of the unfolding energy crisis, leading to high costs of residing in physical properties when the energy market and states offset the costs for electricity on private persons. An increased cost in art creation due to "scarcity" in energy may hence render the perceived positive scarcity produced via NFTs to art expression, insufficient or impossible. This form of local ecological crisis, furthermore, then exists besides the political and ethical hesitations one might have to expand property registry ecologies advancing the possible apocalypse of human life on Earth.

Consequently, all these aspects further imply that even if one puts an entire ecology on the blockchain, one still needs to account for the spatiotemporal consequences that such a time machine might create. As demonstrated throughout the history of property registries, objects might be locked in the hands of a "rightful" owner, but they also enclose both culture and nature in ways that may prevent alternative futures to come into being. For this reason, the future of ecological perspectives of property rights in data needs to be mindful of what it puts on registry, since the ecological future they promised may already have been determined and destroyed, in a tamper-proof manner.

Further Reading

Benjamin, Ruha (2019). *Race After Technology*. Medford: Polity Press.
Bhandar, Brenna (2018). *Colonial Lives of Property: Law, Land, and Racial Regimes of Property*. Durham, NC/London: Duke University Press.
Boyle, James (1996). *Shamans, Software, & Spleens, Law and the Construction of the Information Society*. Cambridge, MA: Harvard University Press.
Harris, I. Cheryl (1993, June). Whiteness as property. *Harvard Law Review*: 1707–1791.
Keenan, Sarah (2019). From historical chains to derivative futures: title registries as time machines. *Social and Cultural Geography* 20 (3), pp. 283–303. ISSN 1464-9365.

References

Andreasson, Jens (2010). *Intellektuella resurser som kreditsäkerhet: En förmögenhetsrättslig undersökning*. Doctoral Diss. Gothenburg: The Gothenburg Law Department Working Paper Series No. 6.
Benjamin, Ruha (2019). *Race after Technology*. Medford: Polity Press.
Bennet, Joshua (2020) *Being Property Once Myself, Blackness and the End of Man*. Cambridge, MA: Harvard University Press.
Bhandar, Brenna (2012). Disassembling legal form: Ownership and the racial body. In Stone, M., Wall rua, Illan, and Douzinas, Costas, eds., *New Critical Legal Thinking*, 112–27. New York: Routledge.
Bhandar, Brenna (2018). *Colonial Lives of Property: Law, Land, and Racial Regimes of Property*. Durham, NC/London: Duke University Press.
boyd, danah (2012). White flight in networked publics? How race and class shaped American teen engagement with MySpace and Facebook. In Chow-White, Petet A. and Nakamura, Lisa, eds., *Race after the Internet*, 203–22. New York: Routledge.

Boyle, James (1996). *Shamans, Software, & Spleens, Law and the Construction of the Information Society*. Cambridge, MA: Harvard University Press.

Boyle, James (1997). A politics of intellectual property: Environmentalism for the net?, *47 Duke Law Journal* 87–116. https://scholarship.law.duke.edu/dlj/vol47/iss1/2

Boyle, James (2003). The second enclosure movement and the construction of the public domain, *66 Law and Contemporary Problems* 33–74 (Winter 2003). https://scholarship.law.duke.edu/lcp/vol66/iss1/2

Chesbrough, Henry (2003). *Open Innovation: The New Imperative for Creating and Profiting from Technology*. Boston, MA: Harvard Business School Press.

Cubitt, Sean (2016). *Finite Media: Environmental Implications of Digital Media*. Durham, NC/London: Duke University Press.

Davies, Margaret and Naffine, Ngaire (2001). *Property as Persons. Legal Debates about Property and Personality*. Aldershot/Burlington: Dartmouth Publishing Company and Ashgate Publishing Limited and Ashgate Publishing Company.

de Filippi, Primavera, and Wright, Aaron (2019). *Blockchain and the Law, The Rule of Code*. Cambridge, MA: Harvard University Press.

De Soto, Hernando (2004). *Kapitalets mysterium: varför kapitalismen segrar i västerlandet och misslyckas på andra håll*. Stockholm: Atlantis.

Dexerto (2021). https://www.dexerto.com/tech/top-10-most-expensive-nfts-ever-sold-1670505/

European Commission, News Article: Making sense of NFT's and what they mean from an IP standpoint in India, 22 March 2022. https://intellectual-property-helpdesk.ec.europa.eu/news-events/news/making-sense-nfts-and-what-they-mean-ip-standpoint-india-2022-03-25_en, accessed 19 December 2022.

Farand, Chloé (2022). WWF-UK ends sale of NFTs after backlash, angering the crypto community. *Climate Change News*. 9 February. https://www.climatechangenews.com/2022/02/09/wwf-uk-ends-sale-nfts-backlash-angering-crypto-community/

Fuller, Matt (2008). "Introduction." In Fuller, Matt, ed. *Software Studies: A Lexicon*, 1–13. Cambridge: MIT Press.

Gizmodo (2022). You can now buy 'non-fungible animals,' and I hate it The World Wildlife Foundation announced this week it would mint nfts linked to endangered species in the wild. *Gizmodo*, 3 February 2022: https://gizmodo.com/wwf-non-fungible-animal-nft-endangered-spieces-1848474978

Guadamuz, Andrés (2021). The treachery of images: Non-fungible tokens and copyright. *Journal of Intellectual Property Law & Practice* 16(12), 1367–85.

Harris, I. Cheryl (1993, June). Whiteness as property. *Harvard Law Review*: 1707–91.

Hartman, Saidiya (2008), *Lose Your Mother: A Journey Along the Atlantic Slave Route*. New York: Farrar, Straus and Giroux.

Käll, Jannice (2022). *Posthuman Property and Law: Commodification and Control through Information, Smart Spaces and Artificial Intelligence*. New York: Routledge.

Kapczynski, Amy (2010). Access to knowledge: A conceptual genealogy. In Kirkorian, G., and Kapczynski, A., eds. *Access to Knowledge in the Age of Intellectual Property*, 17–56. New York: Zone Books.

Keenan, Sarah (2019). From historical chains to derivative futures: Title registries as time machines. *Social and Cultural Geography* 20(3), 283–303.

Lessig, Lawrence (1999). *Code and Other Laws of Cyberspace*. New York: Basic Books.

Nakamura, Lisa (2002). *Cybertypes. Race, Ethnicity, and Identity on the Internet*. New York: Routledge.

Noble, Safiya Umoja (2018). *Algorithms of Oppression: How Search Engines Reinforce Racism*. New York: New York University Press.

Petrusson, Ulf (2004). *Intellectual Property and Entrepreneurship, Creating Value in an Intellectual Value Chain*. Gothenburg: Center for Intellectual Property Studies.

Schollin, Kristoffer (2008). *Digital Rights Management, the New Copyright*. Stockholm: Jure.

Seidler, Paul, Kolling, Paul, and Hampshire, Max (2016). "terra0: Can an augmented forest own and utilise itself?" May Berlin University of the Arts, Germany. https://terra0.org/assets/pdf/terra0_white_paper_2016.pdf 3, accessed March 2022.

Shiva, Vandana (1993). *Monocultures of the Mind*. London/New York/Penang: Zed Books Ltd and Third World Network.

Srnicek, Nick (2017). *Platform Capitalism*. Cambridge/Malden, MA: Polity Press.

Wang, Xiaowei (2020) *Blockchain Chicken Farm, and Other Stories of Tech in China's Countryside*. New York: Farrar, Straus and Giroux.

20
COMMON POOL RESOURCES, COMMUNICATION, AND THE GLOBAL MEDIA COMMONS

Patrick D. Murphy and E. Septime Sessou

Introduction

This chapter considers how today's highly interlaced and mobile media landscape discursively constructs the "problem of the commons" by examining how the positions of the social actors involved in common pool resource (CPR) disputes are represented and in whose interest. This is an important area of analysis for communication scholars because within CPR conflicts reside underlying assumptions about what is a resource and who or what has "the rights" to that resource. This includes fears of one or more parties misusing or overusing it to the detriment of the others. Chances for overuse/misuse are much higher when some actors are or become more powerful than others, leading to ecological mismanagement. Within the public sphere, contemporary CPR conflicts are communicated to citizens in a number of ways. Broadly speaking, globally networked media systems act as a "media commons" by presenting a range of environmental discourses that represent regimes of truth. While these discourses establish the parameters of debate, exposing disjunctures and antagonisms between distinct political, cultural, and ecological interests, they are nevertheless profoundly shaped by a dominant discourse of perpetual growth which promotes the private control over resources (Murphy 2017). At a more granular level, how clashes over CPRs evolve can be impacted by the "communication commons," which are sites of emergent value systems and alternative ideas about the care of the commons. These two spheres are often entangled and, when examined closely, can reveal who or what is granted agency as well as ontological assumptions about the human relationship with the earth.

Drawing from the scholarship on "the commons" (Buck 2017; Hardin 1968; Ostrom 1990, 2010) and the media and communication commons (Birkinbine and Kidd 2020; Kidd 2020; Murphy 2017), this chapter explicates how CPR conflicts can be shaped by dominant interests as well as more citizen-based forms of adaptive governance. After a brief introduction to the concept of "the commons," the chapter defines both "the global media commons" and "the communication commons" and how these communication spheres function to constrict or expand the sociocultural boundaries of environmental thought and action. Two condensed case examples of CPR conflicts are then provided, focusing on how the actors in these disputes have been represented by media and communication networks. The conclusion argues that, since the discursive construction of the commons is enmeshed in the interests of the powerful, the gaps between the media commons and communication commons can reveal how conflicts over CPRs present or leave out voices from the margins that may offer a different set of ecological values.

The Commons

CPRs are generally understood as natural resources, such as forests, fisheries, and freshwater basins, in which multiple interests have access and/or expressed a desire to consume. A CPR can be "owned and managed as government property, private property, community property, or owned by no one," but this does not mean that all who wish to access it acknowledge that "ownership" (Ostrom 2010, 650). These interests operate with different and often even opposing ideas about who or what has "rights" to the CPR and how it should best be utilized, thus conflict often results. Contemporary examples of CPR conflicts have involved the Amazon, the Salish Sea, and the Whanganui River in New Zealand. With the rising global populations and expanding levels of consumption, larger conceptualizations of the commons such as the global atmosphere and planet Earth itself are increasingly seen as CPR conflict zones (Buck 2017).

Garret Hardin's 1968 essay "The Tragedy of the Commons" is taken by many scholars as an entry point into questions about the underlying tensions that shape the use of CPRs. In his essay, Hardin famously used the metaphor of a medieval commons—a pasture open to all villagers—to illustrate the struggle to maintain ecological balance. The metaphor powerfully illustrated the concern over "carrying capacity," painting a picture of how a growing population with expanding needs could exhaust an ecosystem (Murphy and Castro-Sotomayor 2021).

This line of thinking, which Dryzek (2013) dubbed "the Limits discourse," was deeply enmeshed in the question of "maximum good." Hardin considered the maximum good for all an unresolvable situation because people cannot agree on *what is good*. "To one person it is wilderness, to another it is ski lodges for thousands" (Hardin 1968, 1244). With this impasse in mind, he and other Limits scholars called for greater social control of the commons through expert-led oversight, enclosures, and privatization (Ophuls 1977; Pirages and Ehrlich 1974). Fearful of an ever-increasing world population, Hardin (1974) later argued for an even more extreme and xenophobic path, calling for a "lifeboat ethics" to guide which groups would be granted and which ones denied access to ecological safe zones.

Other Limits scholarship conceptualized the "problem of the commons" in less draconian terms. For instance, the work of the Bloomington School of Institutional Analysis and Development approached it from a framework of "adaptive governance" (Murphy and Castro-Sotomayor 2021). Led by the pioneering scholarship of Elinor Ostrom, the Bloomington School moved the focus to multidimensional interrelationships, presenting a vision of CPR stewardship anchored in community rulemaking, monitoring, and trust to overcome dilemmas that might otherwise lead to ecological collapse. In doing so, where the earlier Limits scholarship pushed for management models that involved social control dictated from above, the Bloomington School advocated "nested" CPR monitoring processes exercised through group-oriented, participatory, and interconnected dynamics. Within this polycentric decision-making model, communication surfaces as an essential characteristic.

Finally, an important distinction that the Bloomington School makes is how "subtractability of use" should be understood in relation to public problems and "public good" (Ostrom 2010). For instance, whereas CPRs are defined in relation to their subtractability, something that would fall under "public good," such as "democracy" or "public health," is not exhaustible. Therefore, as public goods have no finite limits, they are not exposed to the dangers of too many users (e.g., the "supply" cannot run out)—a distinction that has implications for how we can apply the notion of the commons to the study of media, communication, and the environment.

The Commons in Media and Communication Scholarship

Many of the underlying issues that the commons literature wrestles with are in fact communication centered. First, how environmental stewardship and the "problem of the commons" are understood in contemporary societies is deeply tied to how "resources," "nature," and "the environment" are articulated through media and communication landscapes. Second, the capacity of agents to respond to contemporary problems of the commons is profoundly shaped by access to and use of media and communication tools to voice their concerns and challenge taken-for-granted assumptions. These dynamics thus fall broadly under the realm of "public good" in that they define the contours for how conflicts over CPRs are represented, defined, and responded to, and who or what has standing. This also points to questions concerning the capacity of media and communication to engender or derail adaptive governance. To get a purchase on this landscape thus requires considering some of the ideological and discursive terrain and generative practices that shape and define the environmental action in the public sphere.

The Global Media Commons

The global media commons, as developed by Murphy (2017), is a space of mixed regimes of truth where competing discourses co-author the terms of agreement and dispute over the (global) commons. Drawing from Dryzek's (2013) charting of "Earth discourses," Murphy argues that while apparently "open" to different discourses, the global media commons primarily traffics in Prometheanism, a discourse grounded in abundance and perpetual growth. Significantly, this discourse has historically enjoyed a place of prominence under colonialism, western expansion, and industrialization and has been expanded by neoliberal globalization. Indeed, for much of the planet today, the Promethean discourse is hegemonic and advances core ideas such as private control over resources, anthropocentrism, and nature as object that run counter to establishing more progressive and sustainable frameworks for the care and treatment of the commons.

This hegemonic status has unfolded in relation to the growth and global expansion of networked commercial media systems and mobile technologies controlled by tech firms that advance an environmental imagination anchored in consumption and material excess (Murphy 2017). This has complicated the presumption that the commons is finite because as the discursive field of everyday life for which billions of Earthlings are now enmeshed, Prometheanism normalizes market-based logic. So, even when these global mediascapes present environmentally progressive commentary (e.g., Netflix's *Don't Look Up*, Animal Planet's *Whale Wars*) or cautionary post-apocalyptic themes (AMC's *The Walking Dead*, History Channel's *Life After People*, Netflix's *Kingdom*), they seem like fugacious deviations from discursive arrangements that are otherwise fully committed to promoting growth. This is also often the case of environmentally engaged journalism, which can work to reframe the climate crisis and related ecological concerns (e.g., *The Guardian's* decision to use "climate crisis" over "climate change" language in reporting), but which is presented within a sea of narratives that otherwise suggest that shared crises (e.g., droughts, rising seas, species extinction) are best approached through economic remedies.

The Promethean discourse thus remains dominant, allowing the invisible hand of the market to allay concerns over ecological limits with promises of a better future through innovation and more efficient technologies (e.g., electric vehicles, sustainable fashion, recycled consumables). Within the global media commons, environmental stewardship is therefore typically presented as simply a matter of adopting "better" consumption practices and sustainable services, not radical change.

The Communication Commons

In contrast to the global media commons' construction of Earth discourses is the "communication commons." According to Birkinbine and Kidd (2020), the notion of the communication commons is positioned as an "alternative to capitalist productive and social relations" (152) within the field of communication. Scholarship centered on the communication commons situates citizens as actors with the capacity to generate forms of collective management. The common thread is an understanding of the commons as "sites of emergent value systems in which a new subjectivity, characterized by mutual aid, care, trust, and conviviality, may be reproduced over time through 'commoning' activities" (152). This conceptualization of citizen-actors within the communication commons dovetails with the more heterogenous vision of environmental stewardship advanced by the Bloomington School, which emphasizes the distinct roles that different actors and networks of concern play in shaping the question of value (e.g., "public good") and organizing action (e.g., "adaptive governance").

Within this framework, when infringements threaten CPR management, (e.g., when capitalist extractivist ventures clash with local people's relationship with their ecosystems), citizen-actors can respond through multidimensional, horizontal modes of communication that mobilize communities that share their values and respect their rights. Relatedly, within these generative exchanges, values and action can also manifest in the form of resistance to confront powerful interests in an upward fashion (e.g., protests, media events, reclamation of land). Whether manifesting horizontally, vertically, or in combination, these forms of communicative action and resistance are often grounded in legacy knowledge, notions of communal life, territoriality, and protocols of reciprocity with nature (Castro-Sotomayor 2020; Kidd 2020) that run counter to Promethean logic.

Finally, given these dynamics, it is important to recognize that the center of the communication commons resides issues of voice. Couldry (2010) urges scholars to think of voice as both a process and a value. In both respects, voice is a form of reflexive agency. For instance, within participatory or consultative processes, the presence or absence of voice is highly significant when evaluating access and influence within contentious CPR decision-making (Senecah 2004). And as a value, narratives of place and land can reveal, for example, how many indigenous communities in the Americas articulate an environmental ethic based on nonexploitation, reciprocity, and coexistence tied to their cultural identities (Brady 2011; Castro-Sotomayor 2020). The place of voice in the communications commons is therefore an indication of standing, providing a sense of what interests are emphasized and which are marginalized or simply erased.

Two Short CPR Case Examples

As outlined in these overviews, the notion of the global media commons emphasizes the discursive power of media systems and their products, focusing on how hegemonic culture shapes the environmental imagination, while the defining characteristic of the communication commons is struggle and how communing activities can be engendered through different modes of cooperative communication. By looking at specific CPR cases through these lenses, communication scholars can get a better sense of how media's treatment of CPR conflicts are sites of discursive struggle which may simply reify hegemonic logic (e.g., Prometheanism) or demonstrate how dominant storylines can be subverted and/or agency transferred to more ecologically conscious actors motivated by other social and cultural concerns.

Grand Ethiopian Renaissance Dam

One example of a major CPR conflict is the Grand Ethiopian Renaissance Dam (GERD) project on the Nile River. While conflicts about the Nile River have persisted since the 1950s, in the current context, Ethiopia's building of the large infrastructure on the Blue Nile branch of the historic river received a vehement reaction from both Egypt and Sudan, which fear that their supply of water will be held back to fill the reservoir (Abdullah et al. 2020; Kushkush 2015). Filling the dam's reservoirs is estimated to reduce the Nile's flow in Egypt by 25% (Wirtschafter 2017), a scenario that puts Egyptians in a very vulnerable position, as their country's agricultural industry depends exclusively on the Nile (Walsh and Sengupta 2020), thus heightening worries about food security (Abdullah et al. 2020). The Nile River is also central to Egyptian cultural identity and political influence as it is associated with the nation's Pharaonic and Kush eras. In 1929, Egypt and Great Britain signed the "Nile Waters Agreement," a treaty granting monopoly in the management and use of the waters to Egypt, including veto power over construction projects on the main river and its tributaries anywhere upstream (Lazarus 2018). As a result, Egyptian leaders feel that they have longstanding rights to the river.

For Ethiopia, the GERD is imagined as a path to the future (Fortin 2014). Once the theater of poverty and hunger (Kushkush 2015), the country has worked hard to achieve a positive economic growth rate. This effort has produced a +30% per year need in electricity production, and the GERD project was designed to meet this growing need (Abdullah et al. 2020). The $4.8 billion dam is a symbol of national pride, as it is almost entirely funded by Ethiopians who bought government-issued bonds for this project (Walsh and Sengupta 2020). While Sudan shares many of the same fears as Egypt, and after opposing the project initially, it has worked with Ethiopia on how they can benefit from the irrigation facilities and electricity generated from the dam. All three countries continue to forge a deal on the management of their common resource, and negotiations have produced agreements on over 90% of the issues (El-Fekki and Malsin 2021). Nevertheless, Egypt and Ethiopia are still not agreeing on the rate at which the dam should be filled. As result, Egypt is putting international pressure on Ethiopia by appealing to extra-national entities like the United Nations Security Council, the Arab League, and other African, Middle Eastern, and European states to urgently intervene (El-Fekki and Malsin 2021). The Trump administration tried to arbitrate the conflict, taking the side of Egypt and initiating punitive actions against the Ethiopian government (Bearak and Raghavan 2020).

As this negotiation around the GERD has evolved, the conflict moved from a regional dispute to a global issue, thanks in large part to the amplifying role of international media, especially from US-based news organizations. These organizations have mainly focused on the conflict between Egypt and Ethiopia, with lesser attention on Sudan. On February 9, 2020, *The New York Times* published "For thousands of years, Egypt controlled the Nile. A new dam threatens that," (Walsh and Sengupta 2020), an article that provocatively stated, "without the Nile, there is no Egypt." Later, that year *The Washington Post* published a story titled "Africa's largest dam fills Ethiopia with hope and Egypt with dread" (Bearak and Raghavan 2020). A few days later, the authors updated the piece with a new headline reading, "Africa's largest dam powers dreams of prosperity in Ethiopia — and fears of hunger in Egypt." As these titles suggest (Marks and Alamin 2021), the US press has largely framed the conflict as a water war defined oppositionally by dreams of prosperity (modernization) and fears of scarcity (limits), while also evoking the river's symbolic currency. These discursive elements indicate an underlying Prometheanism (Ethiopia's river-as-resource transformed for human good, Egypt's "ownership" of the river, Sudan's interest in electricity), along with the symbolic dimensions of the project as related to cultural identity.

Given this discursive rendering, what bears attention is what parts of the GERD conflict have been neglected within the media commons, a question enmeshed in the perceived risks and benefits of this highly complex commons. As a CPR, 97% of the water flowing into the Nile originates outside Egypt's territory (Lazarus 2018). The Nile basin is shared by 11 African countries—Burundi, Democratic Republic of Congo, Egypt, Eritrea, Ethiopia, Kenya, Rwanda, South Sudan, Republic of Sudan, Tanzania, and Uganda. This region is home to nearly 300 million people, a number expected to double by 2030, thus increasing demands on the use of the river's waters for agriculture and economic activities (Abdullah et al. 2020). Moreover, within these nations people relate to the river in many ways (commercial, household, religious, transportation, food), especially for riparian communities which are considerable in number. There is also the question of how the GERD will impact the Nile's ecosystems and the non-human life dependent upon it. Yet few if any of the interests of these countries have been explored by the Western media. Moreover, voices of the people representing these interests have largely been muted, leaving issues related to access, infringements, biocentric, and spiritual concerns to be articulated by others, if at all.

The Dakota Oil Access Pipeline and the Standing Rock Sioux

Another recent CPR dispute that has drawn international attention is the construction of the Dakota Access Pipeline (DAPL) and its incursion over land sacred to the Standing Rock Sioux Tribe. Like the GERD project, the controversial construction of the DAPL moved from a regional dispute to an event involving a host of national and international actors. The central conflict, however, was between the Standing Rock Sioux and the Texas-based project developer Energy Transfer Partners (ETP) and US Army Corps of Engineers. The Standing Rock Sioux asserted its status as a sovereign nation and its rights according to past treaties which guaranteed the "the undisturbed use and occupation" of lands (Smithsonian National Museum of the American Indian 2018). The tribe objected that the planned route of the pipeline crossed sacred grounds and threatened the reservation's water. Conversely, ETP asserted that the DAPL was the "safest and most environmentally sensitive way to transport crude oil…to American consumers" (Dakota Access Pipeline Facts 2016–2017) and that its path ran through privately owned land that "does not encroach or cross any land owned by the Standing Rock Sioux Tribe" (Dakota Access Pipeline Facts 2021–2022). Within the increasingly antagonistic push-pull over the DAPL stood the US Army Corps of Engineers, which had to determine whether or not to grant a permit to ETP, a decision that was ostensibly guided by the preparation of a consultative environmental impact statement. The Corps eventually let ETP lay pipe in the contested land, despite using a fast-track approval process rife with political pressures and powerful insider interests (Kormann 2017).

Both mainstream and alternative media chronicled the clash, an interest sparked by the growing number of protestors and visual elements of the protests. Led by Standing Rock Sioux, the protest grew from American Indian grassroots activists and tribal governments in collaboration with Indigenous people from elsewhere in the Americas and allies of from around the world (Johnson 2017; Steinman 2019). The broad-based social movement drew its energy from on-site encampments in the contested land as well as a host of online sites of engagement and exchange. As Kidd (2020, 233) notes, the encamped protest spaces were expansive and "supported by every single Native American tribe, hundreds of other Indigenous nations from across the Americas and northern Europe, U.S. Military veterans, and a very wide coalition of environmental and social justice movements."

The key interventions were performed by Indigenous actors, who called themselves "Water Protectors," and their supporters using a host of strategies and tactics to mobilize resistance (Johnson

2017; Steinman 2019). These involved both direct action and media activism tied to Indigenous sovereignty and cultural preservation. Specific social media campaigns included #StandingRock, #NoDAPL, #ReZpectOurWater, and many others that employed media platforms such as Twitter, Instagram, Facebook, and YouTube videos, designed to communicate key issues, gain broader support, and circulate petitions. Although much of the leadership resided with Native elders (many of them women), many of the more media-centered tactics and pan-tribal collaborations were initiated by Indigenous youth (Steinman 2019). These efforts amplified the movement's core principles and messaging and were crucial to the multidimensional nature of the protest.

While both on-the-ground and virtual-site locations provided opportunities to self-organize community and co-produce strategies of resistance, the "communing practices" (Kidd 2020) that unfolded also revealed a number of dynamics that complicated more simplistic notions of horizontal communication, including underlying tensions between resistance tactics (e.g., direct action as opposed to more ceremonial forms of confrontation), gender roles expectations, generational fissures, and competing discursive formations (e.g., climate change discourses versus Indigenous environmental knowledge and governance) (Kidd 2020). Nevertheless, the combination of land-based and virtual encampments was crucial in fostering regenerative communing activities that strengthen kinship while also functioning as sites of knowledge recovery, further rooting the Water Protectors connection with the land, past and present. These dynamics served to reify key principles of the movement, like "Water is sacred" and the notion of humans being caretakers of the more than human world. Kidd (2020) observes that this ethic of land stewardship not only pushed against a history of settler colonialism and anthropocentric notions of nature-as-object but also emphasized "caring and solidarity, not conflict" (242).

The movement's interlaced presence in virtual mediascapes forced mainstream media to contend with the dispute in terms that broke with Prometheanism. For example, #NoDAPL drew the attention of a broad range of news and entertainment media, from the *New York Times*, BBC News, Aljazeera, and NPR to *Vogue, The Rolling Stone*, and *Food and Wine* Magazine, as well as more progressive media like Democracy Now!, *Yes Magazine*, *Vice*, The Maori News, and the conservation news site *Mongabay.com*. Folk singer Neil Young and heavymetal artist Dee Snider, both of whom spent time in the encampments, wrote anti-pipeline songs celebrating the resistance that went viral. In *The New Yorker*, noted environmental activist Bill McKibben (2016) drew from the Indigenous frames to place the conflict into a broader historical context, writing "The fight for environmental sanity—against pipelines and coal ports and other fossil-fuel infrastructure—has increasingly been led by Native Americans, many of whom are in that Dakota camp today. They speak with real authority—no one else has lived on this continent for the longterm. They see the nation's history more clearly than anyone else, and its possible future as well."

CPRs and the Media and Communication Commons

Media and communication representations are a function of the discursive construction of events, problems, and positions by social actors (Carvalho 2008). When interpreting these representations in relation to how CPRs are constructed, we need to recall that while dominant discourses are typically driven by powerful interests, they are still fundamentally unstable and contingent sites of struggle (Laclau and Mouffe 1985).

One key distinction between the GERD and the DAPL/Standing Rock cases is that the latter is an example of a CPR conflict profoundly shaped by a citizen-based form of adaptive governance. The #NoDAPL was deeply moored in an American Indian-centered experience. Drawing from a host of communication tools and tactics, the movement worked against a history of settler colonialism and ethnic erasure while resisting contemporary practices of extractivism by rearticulating Indigenous knowledge, leadership, and a land ethics of care and spiritual connection (Steinman 2019). While place-based and grounded in Indigenous sovereignty, the movement's decentralized speaking-for-the-land form of struggle was participatory and consultative, permitting alliances, community rulemaking, and other types of sociopolitical collaborations open to non-indigenous actors (Johnson 2017), many of which unfolded online through collectively governed communications. In short, a communication commons was elaborated that allowed for coalition building and an understanding of public good to be articulated that was, to put it in Ostrom-like terms, grounded in "local rules-in-use" practices and processes of "adaptive governance." In contrast, the GERD case has been constructed almost entirely within the global media commons as a water war shaped and framed by constructs central to Prometheanism (growth, progress, prosperity, modernity), and even the river's link to Egyptian cultural identify is evoked as a form of ownership. While the public construction of this conflict may change as more actors insert their voices, for now this case represents the interests of powerful state actors.

Both cases revolve around the value of a CPR and how that valuation is evoked in terms of "rights," yet the "problem of the commons" looks very different because of the way that media and communication networks have presented the actors involved and *who has standing*. If judged from those mediated renderings, the GERD conflict remains uniquely the domain of elite actors attempting to position their interests over their rivals, while the dispute over the DAPL is a complex and nested struggle involving a much more diverse range of voices capable of challenging taken for granted assumptions about the care and treatment of the commons. Scholarship that engages contemporary CPR conflicts through both lenses—the global media commons and the communication commons—can help map how such conflicts unfold discursively, revealing not only issues of power and standing but also underlying assumptions about what has ecological value and why.

Further Reading

Birkinbine, Benjamin J., and Dorothy Kidd. 2020. Re-Thinking the Communication Commons. *Popular Communication*, *18*, no. 3: 152–54.
Buck, Susan. J. 2017. *The Global Commons*. London: Routledge. https://doi.org/10.4324/9781315086415
Murphy, Patrick D. 2017. *The Media Commons: Globalization and Environmental Discourses*. Champaign: University of Illinois Press.
Murphy, Patrick D., and José Castro-Sotomayor. 2021. From Limits to Ecocentric Rights and Responsibility, *Communication Theory*, *31*, no. 4: 978–1001. https://doi.org/10.1093/ct/qtaa026
Ostrom, Elinor. 2010. Beyond Markets and States. *American Economic Review*, *100*: 641–72.

References

Abdullah, Adam. M. A., Celia Dyduck, and Taha Y. Ahmed. 2020. Transboundary Water Conflicts as Postcolonial Legacy. *Vestnik RUDN. International Relations*, *20*, no. 1: 184–96. https://doi.org/10.22363/2313-0660-2020-20-1-184-196
Bearak, Max and Sudarsan Raghavan. 2020. Africa's Largest Dam fills Ethiopia with Hope and Egypt with Dread. *Washington Post*. https://www.washingtonpost.com/world/interactive/2020/grand-ethiopian-renaissance-dam-egypt-nile/
Birkinbine, Benjamin J. and Dorothy Kidd. 2020. Re-Thinking the Communication Commons. *Popular Communication*, *18*, no. 3: 152–54.
Brady, Miranda. 2011. Mediating Indigenous Voice in the Museum. *Environmental Communication*, *5*, no. 2: 202–20. https://doi.org/10.1080/17524032.2011.562649
Buck, Susan. J. 2017. *The Global Commons*. London: Routledge. https://doi.org/10.4324/9781315086415
Carvalho, Annabel. 2008. Media(ted) Discourse and Society. *Journalism Studies*, *9*, no. 2, 161–77.

Castro-Sotomayor, José. 2020. Territorialidad as Environmental communication. *Annals of the International Communication Association*, 44, no. 1: 50–66. https://doi.org/10.1080/23808985.2019

Couldry, Nick. 2020. *Media, Voice, Space and Power.* New York: Routledge.

Dakota Access Pipeline Facts, 2016–2017. The Dakota Access Pipeline Is the Best Way to Move Bakken Crude Oil to Market. https://daplpipelinefacts.com/

Dakota Access Pipeline Facts, 2021–2022. Addressing Misconceptions about the Dakota Acess Pipeline. https://daplpipelinefacts.com/The-Facts.html

Dryzek, John. 2013. *The Politics of the Earth*. Oxford: Oxford University Press.

El-Fekki, Amira and Jared Malsin. 2021. Egypt, Ethiopia Tensions Escalate as Nile Dam Talks Falter. *The Wall Street Journal*. April 7, 2021. https://www.wsj.com/articles/egypt-ethiopia-tensions-escalate-as-nile-dam-talks-falter-11617808239?mod=Searchresults_pos1&page=1

Fortin, Jacey. 2014. Dam Rising in Ethiopia Stirs Hope and Tension. *The New York Times*. https://www.nytimes.com/2014/10/12/world/dam-rising-in-ethiopia-stirs-hope-and-tension.html?searchResultPosition=15

Hardin, Garret. 1968. The Tragedy of the Commons. *Science, 162*, no. 3859: 1243–48.

Hardin, Garret. 1974. Lifeboat Ethics. *Psychology Today, 38–43*: 124–26.

Johnson, Hayley. 2017. #NoDAPL: Social Media, Empowerment, and Civic Participation at Standing Rock. *Library Trends, 66*, no. 2: 155–75.

Kidd, Dorothy. 2020. Standing Rock and the Indigenous Commons. *Popular Communication, 18*, no. 3: 233–47.

Kormann, Carolyn. 2017. For the Protesters at Standing Rock, It's Back to Pipeline Purgatory. *The New Yorker*, Feb. 3, 2017. https://www.newyorker.com/tech/annals-of-technology/for-the-protesters-at-standing-rock-its-back-to-pipeline-purgatory

Kushkush, Isma'il. 2015. Ethiopia, Long Mired in Poverty, Rides an Economic Boom. *The New York Times*, 3–7. https://www.nytimes.com/2015/03/04/world/africa/ethiopia-an-african-lion-aspires-to-middle-income-by-2025.html?searchResultPosition=12

Laclau, Ernesto and Chantell Mouffe. 1985. *Hegemony and Socialist Strategy*. London: Verso.

Lazarus, Sarah. 2018. Is Ethiopia Taking Control of the River Nile? *The Philadelphia Tribune*. 2018, Oct. 22, https://www.phillytrib.com/news/is-ethiopia-taking-control-of-the-river-nile/article_edd62093-60b2–5ad1-a2af-eeff0f01e644.html

Marks, Simon and Mohammad Alamin. 2021. Giant Dam Is Messing Up Water in Africa Even Before It Is Filled. *Bloomberg*, July 9, 2021.

McKibben, Bill. 2016. A Pipeline Fight and America's Dark Past, *The New Yorker*, September 6, 2016. https://www.newyorker.com/news/daily-comment/a-pipeline-fight-and-americas-dark-past

Murphy, Patrick D. 2017. *The Media Commons: Globalization and Environmental Discourses*. Champaign: University of Illinois Press.

Murphy, Patrick D., and José Castro-Sotomayor, 2021. From Limits to Ecocentric Rights and Responsibility. *Communication Theory, 31*, no. 4: 978–1001. https://doi.org/10.1093/ct/qtaa026

Ophuls, William. 1977. *Ecology and the Politics of Scarcity*. San Francisco, CA: Freeman.

Ostrom, Elinor. 1990. *Governing the Commons*. New York: Cambridge Univ. Press.

Ostrom, Elinor. 2010. Beyond Markets and States. *American Economic Review, 100*, 641–72.

Pirages, Dennis, C. and Paul Ehrlich. 1974. *Ark II: Social Response to Environmental Imperatives*. San Francisco, CA: Freeman.

Senecah, Susan. L. 2004. The Trinity of Voice. In *Communication and Public Participation in Enviornmental Decision Making*, edited by Stephen Depoe, John Delicath and Marie-France S. Elsenbeer, 13–33. Albany, NY: SUNY Press.

Smithsonian National Museum of the American Indian. 2018. "Treaties Still Matter: The Dakota Access Pipeline," *Native Knowledge. 360*. https://americanindian.si.edu/nk360/plains-treaties/dapl

Steinman, Erich. 2019. Why Was Standing Rock and the #NoDAPL Campaign so Historic? *Ethnic and Racial Studies, 42*, no. 7: 1070–90.

Walsh, Declan and Somini Sengupta. 2020. For Thousands of Years, Egypt Controlled the Nile. *New York Times*, 26. https://www.nytimes.com/interactive/2020/02/09/world/africa/nile-river-dam.html?searchResultPosition=6

Wirtschafter, Jacob. 2017, October 3. Here's Why Egypt's Nile River Is in Danger, *USA Today*. https://www.usatoday.com/story/news/world/2017/09/29/egypt-nile-river-danger/679222001/

21
#NOLNG253! MEDIA USE IN MODERN ENVIRONMENTAL JUSTICE MOVEMENTS

Ellen E. Moore and Anna Bean

Introduction

What are the benefits and challenges of using social media for modern, Indigenous-led environmental justice movements? This chapter addresses this question through the lens of a specific case study in an interview with an Indigenous leader of an ongoing environmental justice movement on the shores of the Salish Sea in Washington State. Creating a dialogue through a series of questions and responses, the voice of Anna Bean, Puyallup Tribal Council member and leader of the Puyallup Water Warrior movement #NOLNG253, provides a critical perspective on the role of the media in environmental justice movements. This interview, conducted by media scholar Ellen Moore, summarizes existing problems in legacy media's coverage of environmental justice issues, including the "gatekeeping" function and the framing of environmental justice issues as unworthy of widespread concern or decisive action. The focus then shifts to an exploration of how Indigenous environmental justice leaders have utilized social media, highlighting key examples from two movements: #NOLNG253 and #NODAPL. The two questions that shape this interview are: (1) How have local news outlets framed the concerns of the *Puyallup Water Warriors* regarding the installation of a liquified natural gas (LNG) plant in the Port of Tacoma located on the Tribe's ancestral lands?; and (2) What are some of the benefits of using social media for this specific movement? The #NOLNG253 case study is thus situated broadly in relation to other environmental justice activism, including #NODAPL at Standing Rock to address a key question for ecomedia studies: if social media can bypass more traditional forms of media in cases like these, does it provide the chance for a "digital democracy" for all?

Background: LNG and Fossil Fuel Projects in the Twenty-First Century

Located on the "Tacoma Tideflats" on the shores of Puget Sound and the Salish Sea in Washington State, the recently constructed Puget Sound Energy LNG plant (located in the 253 area code for Tacoma) is an 8-million–gallon fossil fuel refinery and storage facility recently completed on the ancestral land of the Puyallup Tribe of Indians. In concert with the fact that it was proposed and built during a time of heightened awareness of the climate crisis, this has made it a highly

This chapter has been made available under a CC-BY-NC-ND license.

controversial project amongst local communities, environmental organizations, and Indigenous groups. In 2018,

> the Puyallup Tribe and leaders from 14 other Northwest Tribes called on Gov[ernor] Jay Inslee to stop the construction of Puget Sound Energy's liquefied natural gas plant ... until an environmental review is complete and all permit requirements are satisfied.
>
> (Ruud, 2018)

In 2019, the Puyallup Tribe, along with Earthjustice, filed a series of legal challenges to oppose the project:

> 'The Tribe continues to be frustrated that the Puget Sound Clean Air Agency is not considering the appropriate science and putting dangerous impacts on an already disproportionately impacted community,' said David Z. Bean, chairman of the Puyallup Tribal Council. 'Even more shocking to us is that this facility would operate in a densely populated urban area, and yet no authority has taken a serious look at the consequences of a catastrophic incident at this facility. That's not just unfair to the people who live here–it's dangerous'
>
> (Puyallup Tribe of Indians 2019)[1]

Environmental groups have stood with the Tribe, including Stand Earth, Advocates for a Cleaner Tacoma, and Washington Environmental Council (Cockrell 2021) as well as Earthjustice, Greenpeace, and now Washington State Attorney General Bob Ferguson. In December 2019, on the same day that the Puyallup Tribe "made history by becoming the first tribe in the nation to declare a climate emergency," PSE received the final permit needed for the LNG facility (Native Daily Network 2019).

Essential for understanding the perspectives in this interview and research is a consideration of the broader context for the LNG plant, as the glut of fracked gas from Canada's Alberta "oil patch" and the US Bakken shale has been moving westward in recent years for transport to overseas Pacific Rim markets. At a time of heightened awareness of the climate crisis, PSE's website notes that the LNG facility would ship fossil fuels across the Pacific Ocean to markets in Japan, China, Singapore, and Indonesia. The fossil fuel surplus enabled by fracking thus has exerted significant pressure on local communities and Tribes living on the western shores of North America to accept large-scale fossil fuel projects.

Interview with Anna Bean

Anna Bean has served on the Puyallup Tribal Council as a council member since 2018 and is one of the founding members and leaders of the *Puyallup Water Warriors*. Her perspectives on the LNG plant and the #NOLNG253 movement complement my interviews and research with the Standing Rock Sioux Tribe on the #NODAPL movement (Moore 2019). Taken together, consideration of these two nearly simultaneous movements highlights key patterns in the role that legacy and new media play in covering environmental justice movements. We had this conversation in December 2021 over Zoom in our respective offices in Tacoma.

LNG on the Salish Sea – "The More You Read, The More Concerned You Got"

Ellen: What is your perspective on why Puget Sound Energy's LNG plant – why do you think it is harmful from the perspective of environmental justice for the Puyallup Tribe and the surrounding community? Is this about the health of the water, the air, the Tribe – or all of the above?

Anna: Most LNG sites are nowhere near any area such as where the Port (of Tacoma) is – within, I believe, one mile of houses, a little over a mile from schools, daycares, areas like that, less than 500 feet from the Puyallup Tribe's marina. It's located in an area that, in my research, I have not seen (other) LNG sites to exist so close to life, businesses, waterways. I'm not happy about it at all. It's within feet of current Tribe land, but it is within my current ancestral lands ... That they have chosen to place this here without proper consultation with the Puyallup Tribe of Indians is disgusting.

I'm learning about fracked gas in general, and how it has to be heated or cooled: that's of great concern to me in an already highly developed industrial port that we have down there. In the original environmental impact statement that was done early on, (Puget Sound Energy) had folks to consider or speak to, and they listed the Puyallup Tribe…at least we were considered in the EIS, but we weren't considered in actual, proper consultation. Learning more about fracked gas and this plant, and knowing through maps ... how they were going to have 16 or 18" pipes ... that were to go through Fife, a school or daycare, and as far back as [*an apartment building*] in Tacoma.

So, the more you dug into it, the more you read, the more concerned you got.

Anna noted that both the Puyallup and the Muckleshoot Tribe were listed as potential stakeholders in the original impact statement from PSE (perhaps revealing the scope of potential impact in an emergency), but that both Tribes were removed as stakeholders later: "so then you start wondering why they were removed: because they [PSE] didn't feel they were getting their permits approved along the way." She further noted how PSE had been "riding the line" (with stakeholders and their estimate of greenhouse gas emissions) to get approval for the project. "Why? Because they were able to."

Anna's acknowledgment of the harm and disruption caused by the lack of formal communication between PSE and the Tribe directly echoes statements made by the Standing Rock Sioux Tribe in my interviews with them in 2018, where they acknowledged that they received little to no government-to-government consultation at any stage in the project. They recognized that being "unique by treaty" meant that consultation was required but was bypassed by the pipeline corporation and the government (Moore 2019, 172). While "there is an increasing trend to engage with indigenous communities for research and collaboration, including indigenous groups as active participants in resource management decision making" (Harmsworth and Robb 2016, 8), neither the Puyallup nor Standing Rock Sioux Tribe were consulted. It is the lack of formal, respectful communication and consultation in the development of these large fossil fuel projects on Indigenous ancestral lands that emerges as a harmful trend for both #NODAPL and #NOLNG253, for "legal affirmations of tribal sovereignty are positively associated with ... ecosystem health" (Ballantine 2017, 46).

The Climate Crisis in Washington State: "We Should Be the Front Runners on Renewable Energy"

Ellen: Does LNG make sense with where we are now with the climate crisis, with where we are now in terms of Indigenous rights?

Anna: It absolutely doesn't. It encompasses everything: human life, water, air, land, everything. We live in the state of Washington, considered the "Evergreen State." We should be the front runners on renewable energy. In this current day and age, we know that climate change is real. Anyone looking at Mount Rainier over the summer of 2021 and seeing barely any snow – it's scary.

We have to do better: it's an emergency for us to take all of these things seriously. We should be finding ways to be energy efficient, to go off of solar, and stop utilizing all these gases. I think it's absolutely crazy that we aren't holding very strict regulations in our state, to be more centered on climate change. It's beyond me. There's talk that PSE LNG is cleaner than the alternative, but it's by such a small amount that it's not even worth mentioning.

Anna's observation regarding the obvious incongruity of starting new fossil fuel infrastructure at a time of increased concerns about the global climate crisis was also highlighted in my research on #NODAPL, which underscored the claim made in the United Nations climate change reports that we cannot fight the climate crisis if we keep investing in and building permanent fossil fuel infrastructure. Exemplifying Anna's important point about the urgent need to switch our infrastructure, Phyllis Young, a revered elder I interviewed at Standing Rock, was awarded the "Oceti Sakowin SOLVE Fellowship" grant from the Massachusetts Institute of Technology to create a tribal utility company based on solar energy (Moore 2019, 171). Anna's call to "do better" speaks directly to the idea that the climate crisis is built on values and ideas related to entrenched colonial structures, and to address the climate crisis, we need to adopt a different set of values and norms (Cameron et al. 2021).

The Start of the Water Warriors Movement – "Showing Up Puyallup"

Ellen: Tell me about the Water Warriors movement that you lead – how did you come to create the movement, and has the focus solely been on LNG?

Anna: We answered a call in April of 2017 to come join folks who were at the time called "Red Line Tacoma."[2] They ... asked us to come stand with them, and at that time there was nothing built at the PSE LNG site. There was an individual there named Steve Storms and there was Native Daily Network. Steve Storms starts telling us about LNG ... and so when I go home, I have to look all this up ....

People started calling on us as Tribal members to come ... speak at Tacoma City Council (meetings), because there were a lot of people speaking for the Puyallup Tribe, as our neighbors, but Tribal members needed to come out and speak up on our own behalf. This is really serious because once you know what's going on, you can't unknow it and you can't just go to sleep at night: it's no longer out of sight.

We had a lunch meeting one day and it seemed like everybody we were around, they all had [group] names: we were just showing up Puyallup, [so] we sat around a table as folks who were getting called on, and just slowly started coming up with what our name would be. And so ... we were the Puyallup Water Warriors.[3] I have to be honest, you know, it used to make me really uncomfortable how much folks wanted us to be at the forefront. And I get, "Indigenous led" and all of those things, and this is our area, but it was almost like at some point, we felt like "token Indians." And so, if we believed we were just there to be a token Indian, we wouldn't even show up. We would decline offers.

Once we got involved in this work, people from other reservations and other movements ... started reaching out to us (on different issues). A lot of folks were really reaching out to us on how to get their own movements going and how to be heard. It's all been environmental: Puyallup Water Warriors are really focused on getting back to the basics of being heard and protecting the air, water, and land for future generations.

Legacy News Media Coverage: "Media Can Really Make Or Break A Movement"

Ellen: How have you experienced legacy news coverage (traditional news sites like our local paper, TV news, etc.) of Water Warrior's resistance to the plant? What have you noticed about the coverage – in the past and now?

Anna: The papers never just covered the Puyallup Water Warriors. We would be quoted amongst other groups: we called ourselves the "LNG253 Family." We also had folks from Seattle ... It wasn't often that the Water Warriors were featured outside of the entire "253" family, unless we were doing something for the Puyallup Tribe at an event.

Honestly, when it comes to newspapers, I don't think we got as much coverage as we should have. Native Daily Network [*was*] why anybody was really paying attention to what was going on down at the Tacoma Tideflats. I definitely know that it was Native Daily Network on the social media sites ... who were really giving full attention to what was going on at all.

Dakota [*Case*]4 had this long interview: his grandmother's a part of AIM, and she was interviewed, and th[*e media*] took one line, one snippet, out of what he had to say. Sometimes I think the way it ended up looking is just like we were uneducated on the movement we were a part of.

When you're talking about framing and what happens: the editing of what is said or done can totally change the portrayal. We did a Women's March here, and they had the news crews come in a helicopter as people started to come in. So, it looks like nobody's there, like there's 30 people [*when instead*] there were hundreds of people here. It didn't capture the momentum of that day ... **Any kind of media can ultimately make or break a movement by minimizing what is really going on.**

The thing is, ensuring that your message is clear: looking back, if I knew then what I know now ... I remember somebody said, "what is your message?" We should have just been ensuring that no matter what we did or said that we always started off with that, so no matter what was captured, that was always there – the heart of what we were trying to say. People's attention span is held for only so long. Now we know: [*the media are*] going to kind of chop up what you're going to say, so make sure every single one of your sentences hit; that, no matter what they take, your message is always there.

Ellen: Why do you think newspapers and TV news didn't give attention to the LNG plant the way you wanted or hoped?

Anna: There's a contradiction of information. Probably because of who pays for these papers. Depending how they wanted government officials to be viewed, and whose hands were in whose pockets, maybe. It may be 2021 right now, but [*the news media*] still function ... very old school. I think folks set out to do good work and be unbiased maybe, but ultimately somebody's got to pay somebody and those people decide.

There are several important critiques in Anna's statement. First, she notes the importance of legacy media coverage to "make or break" the start of a movement or resistance. Second, she underscores an essential point about media framing: the news media choose how to present an issue for their readers or viewers (often through selective editing), and that framing is often based on economic relationships. Third, her experience acknowledges that the media can minimize a story by not covering/ignoring it. Finally, leaders of environmental movements know that the burden is on them to have a clear message when dealing with the media. In fact, Anna's critique of legacy news media coheres seamlessly with well-known media framing scholars (Entman 1993; Schudson 2011) who study media, social movements, and power (Boykoff 2006).

In my interviews with the Standing Rock Sioux Tribe, these same themes emerged clearly. Just as their concerns had been ignored by the pipeline company and the government, so it was with the news media. This was so much a trend in my work on the #NODAPL movement that the Standing Rock Sioux Tribe members I interviewed openly discussed (with critical humor) exaggerated ways that they could act that would earn them local newspaper coverage. Even then, they said, newspaper coverage was mostly centered on conflict: even when they did get local news coverage, it often was a "negative" portrayal. It is difficult to overemphasize the necessity for environmental justice movements like #NOLNG253 and #NODAPL to receive coverage: "When it comes to environmental justice ... it is clear that these issues involve deep questions about value, especially in regards to who merits attention, consideration, and respect" (Moore 2019, 69).

The Role of New Media: "Social Media Became the Heart of the Movement"

Ellen: What role do you see that social media play in environmental justice movements like #NOLNG?

Anna: Social media became the heart of the movement ... It's how we communicated: you know, your videos would get shared at Native Daily Network. There's a movie that was created out of all of these recordings – Ancestral Waters.[5] And honestly, that was like a full accounting of everything that we've been going through ... in this movement.

You know, [*through*] likes and shares, you could get this out to just anyone, and we had folks who were reaching out to us because they had been at Standing Rock ... occasionally it would be somebody in who'd say "Hello, I seen your video, I really want to know what's going on down here." On social media we were just eating, sleeping, and drinking PSE LNG – "No way, Jose" Yeah, social media played a massive role: it wasn't just Facebook: it was any social media site that we could get into.

Ellen: How and why did you choose the hashtag #NOLNG253? Why is a hashtag important for a movement?

Anna: It was a chant and it just stuck. You just put in a hashtag (like #NOLNG253) and then shirts were made. It became something that was the heart of what we were saying ... It has a ring to it: you won't forget it. If you really want something to pick up, you have to be willing to be a part of whatever time frame you're in. And right now we're in the age of ... here we are, right now, in this interview: we are on a social site, we're utilizing our phones. If you want to reach more folks, you have to have something that works for every single person: you put that hashtag out there and people will pick up way quicker on that. All of these things can be so easily linked ... It's also cataloguing.

When I asked the Standing Rock Sioux Tribe for their perspectives on social media, I heard a similar theme: social media permits a message to get "out there" to people, bypassing traditional news media and getting rid of the "filter" placed by corporate gatekeepers. Elder Phyllis Young liked the phrase "digital democracy" because social media could increase awareness and participation directly from sender to (millions of) receivers. Thus, when Anna discusses the power of a hashtag to propel a movement forward, it coheres with this idea of social media as a form of power that goes to a movement's central core, or "heart." Just as #NOLNG253 and #NODAPL became a key identifier of the movement, it's clear that social media provide a cornerstone in the fight against fossil fuels that has the potential to be transformational. This is not just because it can "go around" old media gatekeepers but because it can enable the firsthand experiences of members of a movement to communicate directly to audiences around the globe. Anderson (2014) identifies this type of social media use as "mass self-communication," which she believes provides the opportunity for social movements to resist and challenge the status quo while also allowing significantly more voices to be heard (21).

Tensions in Using One Extractivist Industry to Fight Another? "It's A Double-Edged Sword"

Ellen: Do you perceive any kind of irony, or tension, in using the tools of social media (which are polluting themselves) to fight against another polluting industry like the fossil fuel industry?

Anna: That's such a loaded question – it really is. In environmental [movements] there's a lot of – I don't know – hypocrisy. And it's unintentional, because you've grown accustomed to the lifestyle and the times that you're in. And, if you want to get information out there, well, people are all on social media so you're going to get a hold of a lot of people. That means you're holding this phone [with its] environmental and health impacts that they may have. It's a double-edged sword when you've evolved with the changes [*in society and technology*] but you're also fighting to restore things to their original.

This is, as Anna observes, a "loaded question," and it may be unfair as well. First, it runs the risk of unproductively shifting the focus away from the change we need to see from larger, impactful structures – here I include both the fossil fuel industry and the corporate news media industry – in the fight for environmental justice. A point made in my research on Standing Rock was that a fundamental shift in those industries will produce large-scale, positive environmental changes: if the news media would start paying more attention to environmental movements, and if the fossil fuel industry would use its infrastructure and economic power to support renewable energy, we can start to fight climate injustice. In addition, the question also seems to presume a shared burden of responsibility for environmental degradation, but it should not be up to leaders of environmental justice movements to justify why they feel they need to use social media; instead, we need systemic, industry-wide change on the polluting, extractivist ways in which technology is produced and social media information is stored.

Conclusion

In their work on ecosystem threats in the Salish Sea, which is considered an "international treasure," Gaydos and Donatuto (2015, 3) highlight the need for inclusion

> Tribes have been significantly absent from ecological and health risk assessments and risk management as most assessments and management strategies fail to mention the impacts that resource-based development activities can have on tribal communities, tribal homelands ... or treaty-guaranteed hunting, fishing, and gathering rights ... Current risk assessment methods fail to account for the fundamental worldviews and relationships that connect Native peoples with the physical, ecological and spiritual worlds, which form the foundation of health and wellbeing.

The work of the *Puyallup Water Warriors* in Washington State, as well as the *Water Protectors* at Standing Rock, provides insight into the ways that resistance takes place, including the different perspectives that can be offered as an alternative to polluting fossil fuels. As we enter a time of heightened awareness of climate change, it is clear a fundamental shift in values is needed. Writing on the *Indigenous Knowledge Keepers*, Cameron et al. (2021, 42) argue

> for a new approach to engaging with Indigenous knowledge in climate research, which acknowledges it not only as a source of environmental observations, but a wealth of values, philosophies, and worldviews which can inform and guide action and research more broadly.

The media industry can do more to be the keystone of change in this regard by removing its coverage "blindspot" – on both environmental issues as well as historically marginalized groups – to effect change rapidly when it's needed the most.

Notes

1 The Tribe provides more information, including background and context for LNG and fossil fuels, at http://puyallup-tribe.com/lng/.
2 The group is now called "Redefine Tacoma."
3 The *Water Warriors* have been featured in the documentary *Ancestral Waters* (Native Daily Network, 2019) as one of the key groups in the fight against the plant.
4 Dakota Case is a member of the Puyallup Tribe and one of the founders of the Water Warriors. He has been featured in *Ancestral Waters* and also by Greenpeace and other organizations for his environmental work.
5 *Ancestral Waters* can be viewed through Native Daily Network at https://nativedailynetwork.org/ancestral-waters/.

Further Reading

Alia, V. (2004). *Media ethics and social change*. New York: Routledge.
Bullard, R. (2000). *Dumping in Dixie: Race, class, and environmental quality* (3rd ed.). Boulder, CO: Westview Press.
Grossman, Z. (2017). *Unlikely alliances: Native nations and white communities join to defend rural lands*. Seattle: University of Washington Press.
LaDuke, W. (2017b). *The Winona LaDuke chronicles: Stories from the front lines in the battle for environmental justice*. Nova Scotia: Fernwood Publishing.
Wasko, J. (2014). The study of the political economy of the media in the twenty-first century. *International Journal of Media & Cultural Politics*, 10(3), 251–79.

References

Anderson, A. (2014). *Media, environment and the network society*. New York: Palgrave Macmillan.
Ballantine. (2017). The river mouth speaks: Water quality as storyteller in decolonization of the Port of Tacoma. *Water History*, 9(1), 45–66. https://doi.org/10.1007/s12685-016-0179-5
Boykoff, J. (2006). Framing dissent: Mass-media coverage of the global justice movement. *New Political Science*, 28(2), 201–28. https://doi.org/10.1080/07393140600679967
Cameron, Courchene, D., Ijaz, S., & Mauro, I. (2021). 'A change of heart': Indigenous perspectives from the Onjisay Aki Summit on climate change. *Climatic Change*, 164(3–4), 43. https://doi.org/10.1007/s10584-021-03000-8
Cockrell, D. (2021, November 23). Divisive Tacoma LNG project wins approval from key state board, upsetting Puyallup Tribe. *The News Tribune*.
Entman, R. M. (1993). Framing: Toward clarification of a fractured paradigm. *Journal of Communication*, 43(4), 51–58. https://doi.org/10.1111/j.1460-2466.1993.tb01304.x

Gaydos, Thixton, S., & Donatuto, J. (2015). Evaluating threats in multinational marine ecosystems: A coast salish first nations and tribal perspective. *PLoS One*, 10(12), e0144861. https://doi.org/10.1371/journal.pone.0144861

Harmsworth, Awatere, S., & Robb, M. (2016). Indigenous Māori values and perspectives to inform freshwater management in Aotearoa-New Zealand. *Ecology and Society*, 21(4), 9. https://doi.org/10.5751/ES-08804-210409

Moore, E. (2019). *Journalism, politics, and the Dakota Access Pipeline: Standing Rock and the framing of injustice*. London: Routledge.

Native Daily Network (2019, December 10). An 'act of war' – Puyallup Tribe and Water Warriors respond to permit approval. *Native Daily Network*. Accessed from https://nativedailynetwork.org/2019/12/10/final-lng-permit-approved-in-violation-of-treaty/

Puyallup Tribe of Indians (2019, December 2019). Puyallup Tribe, environmental groups hit Tacoma LNG with legal challenges. Accessed from http://news.puyalluptribe-nsn.gov/puyallup-tribe-environmental-groups-hit-tacoma-lng-with-legal-challenges/

Ruud, C. (2018, February 03). Northwest tribes ask Gov. Inslee to halt construction of Tacoma LNG plant. *Tacoma News Tribune*.

Schudson, M. (2011). *The sociology of news* (2nd ed.). New York: W.W. Norton & Company.

22
CONTESTING DIGITAL COLONIAL POWER

Indigenous Australian Sovereignty and Self-Determination in Digital Worlds

Corrinne Sullivan and Jessica McLean

Introduction

Digital worlds are manifestations of power relations and can potentially challenge existing hegemonic regimes, such as those that produce settler colonialism and racial hierarchies. Ruha Benjamin's thinking about racial hierarchies in digital worlds offers a powerful critique of already existing problematic representations within digital worlds, while inviting us to consider constructive ways of remaking these worlds and negotiating better ones. Rather than stopping at critique, Benjamin challenges us to offer constructive alternatives:

> an emancipatory approach to technology entails an appreciation for the aesthetic dimensions of resisting the New Jim Code and a commitment to coupling our critique with creative alternatives that bring to life liberating and joyful ways of living in and organizing our world.
>
> (Benjamin 2019: 197)

Benjamin's central concern is that racial biases are built into the formation of digital worlds, effectively reproducing Jim Crow racist and separatist regimes, in coding systems that are hidden but have powerful effects.

We respond with enthusiasm to Benjamin's exhortation by structuring this chapter about possibilities for decolonizing digital worlds in settler-colonial Australia in two parts. The first begins by sharing insights from Aboriginal and Torres Strait Islander peoples about inappropriate digital worlds, outlining how problematic digital worlds referring to, or about, Aboriginal and Torres Strait Islander peoples continue to exist, despite widespread critique of them. The second part shares how Aboriginal and Torres Strait Islander peoples are creating alternative digital worlds that are grounded in sovereignty and self-determination. It is important to note that Benjamin is referring to different histories and power relationships in her analysis, but we see value in drawing on her challenge to social processes that (re)produce racial inequities in the digital as similar injustices are produced through colonial digital practices. Here forth we will use the collective terms "Indigenous" and "Indigenous Australians" to refer to Aboriginal and Torres Strait Islander peoples. Where possible we will name the Nation of Indigenous individuals and communities.

In commencing this chapter, it is essential that we introduce ourselves by detailing our positionality, including our accountabilities and responsibilities, in relation to Indigenous Australians and the work that we produce. Corrinne Sullivan is a Wiradjuri scholar living and working on Dharug Country. Jess McLean is a white Australian geographer living on Gadigal Country, working on Darug Country, and who grew up on Wiradjuri Country. These positions affect how this chapter has developed. We write together in solidarity for a just present and future that not only acknowledges Indigenous people's self-determination but also the absolute and undeniable sovereign owners of the lands and waterways, of what is now known as Australia. It is from this position that we discuss the digital worlds that Aboriginal and Torres Strait Islanders build and inhabit in Australia.

The proposition of decolonizing digital spaces offers challenges and contradictions arising from the structural realities of the Internet and its political and economic dimensions. For instance, Fredericks et al. (2021) describe in their analysis of social media usage how Indigenous peoples have leveraged opportunities to assert presence and resist settler-colonial practices in the digital. They describe how Indigenous peoples disrupt "colonial algorithms" that result in problematic understandings of Indigenous peoples and identities. Algorithms, for Fredericks et al., are "a set of rules, processes and instructions that are followed for a desired outcome" (2021, 2). Social media includes colonial algorithms as it rearticulates, and at times amplifies, the marginalization and misrepresentation of Indigenous peoples that has been a part of broader society since invasion.

In their book *Indigenous Digital Life*, Carlson and Frazer (2021) offer analysis of what Indigenous Australian social media users experience in settler-colonial nations. The research underpinning that book covered several substantial projects over a 15-year time period, during which the Internet morphed from a separate realm that was connected to circumscribed settings to a technology enmeshed with everyday life. Carlson and Frazer (2021, 11) draw on interviews with Indigenous Australians to get a sense of how and why they use social media and carefully represent these points of view as a powerful intervention aimed at decentering colonial practices, "[p]rivileging the voices and practices of Indigenous people acts as a kind of 'corrective' to the dominant approach to research, which tends to objectify, essentialize and, in turn, infantilize Indigenous peoples." Indigenous Australian people's agency is key here in challenging wrong conceptualizations of digital lives.

Decolonizing digital spaces is a challenging proposition as it assumes that they are indeed colonized, and that a decolonial strategy is feasible and possible (Barker 2015; McLean 2020). Further, false allies can emerge if decolonizing efforts fail to address structural inequities and ultimately maintain the status quo of settler privilege (Powys White 2018). The concept "decolonizing the digital" is used in this chapter as a way to talk about centering Indigenous knowledges in the digital and challenging those that continue to misrepresent and misconstrue the same. Drawing on Barker (2015), we want to capture how Indigenous resistance to colonial digital practices disrupts these and also reasserts Indigenous presence while "altering the spatialities of both" (Barker 2015, 46).

Part 1: Dismantling Problematic Digital Worlds That Perpetuate Colonial Power

Despite sustained critiques of settler-colonial practices in digital worlds, it is clear that inappropriate representations of Indigenous knowledges persist, sometimes with a high profile. Critiques of these practices have proliferated in recent times and it is telling that the authors and managers of such settler-colonial digital spaces seem impervious to this commentary.

In a wonderful paper about digital racism, Fredericks and Bradfield (2021, n.p.) argue that "social media can be likened to liminal monstrous worlds as they create environments that remain within existing social structures, yet provide freedoms that would otherwise not be acceptable, accessible, or doable in the physical world." They put forward that social media provides freedoms for individuals and organizations to assert settler-colonial power, express racist views, and undermine Indigenous knowledges. We extend Fredericks and Bradfield's critique in this chapter to acknowledge that similar liminal monstrous worlds are created in digital settings, as well as on social media, in the form of settler-colonial–controlled websites.

Within Australia, Indigenous Australians have been creating digital worlds that are vibrant and contribute to self-determination efforts while also calling out digital presences that appropriate knowledges without permission or collaboration. A website that has persistently misappropriated and misrepresented Indigenous knowledges is *Creative Spirits*, a digital space that has offered information about Indigenous peoples since 2006. The site was created by white Australian Jens Korff, a web developer who "holds a postgraduate degree in IT" and operates Creative Spirits as a "passion."

Despite the longevity of the website, and innumerable critiques from Indigenous peoples, it continues to perpetuate false claims while providing a settler-colonial–controlled presence. In an exchange with Indigenous Studies scholar Sandy O'Sullivan, who is Wiradjuri and an Australian Research Council Future Fellow in the Department of Indigenous Studies at Macquarie University, when Korff asked O'Sullivan to educate him about what cultural appropriation is happening on his website, O'Sullivan responded: "I'm not doing your labour for you, at least learn about what is appropriate. It's your business that makes money off Aboriginal people, not mine. You do the work" (O'Sullivan, 2022, n.p.). Earlier, Prof O'Sullivan had written a critique of the appropriation on the site:

> What I wrote: 'Please don't cite Creative Spirits as an authoritative source. If you don't know why, read the About Us, it should explain it all or PM me. It appropriates information, takes material published elsewhere and uses it out of context, and is generally problematic.'
> (O'Sullivan, 2022, n.p.)

A related article critiquing settler-colonial practices and decolonizing education by Tabitha Lean (Gunditjmara) and Pip Henderson (White) described Creative Spirits as "a site that contains much misinformation and racist myths" (2020, n.p.).

When writing this chapter, the authors experimented with common search terms to ascertain how search engines rank various pages within the *Creative Spirits* architecture. A Google search of the term "Aboriginal people self-determination" listed a *Creative Spirits* page as seventh, while "stolen generation Australia" offered a *Creative Spirits* story in twelfth position. We find it alarming that these relatively high positions are held by a website that has been widely discredited and shares representations of Indigenous Australians without their control or input. (Of course, these algorithmic page rankings are contingent on where you are located in the world and your own search results may not be the same as ours.).

In a Twitter thread recommending resources for Australian school teachers to use during National Aborigines and Islanders Day Observance Committee Week, known now as NAIDOC Week, Elizabeth Flynn (Aboriginal, Chinese Malaysian, and Muslim academic) shared a series of links to help educators use the right material. The thread included links to NAIDOC-produced material, public broadcaster sites, and several collated sites such as one by @IndigenousX, an

Indigenous-owned and -operated organization that specializes in digital media and training. The thread included a clear and unequivocal recommendation to avoid *Creative Spirits*:

> Never, ever use the website Creative Spirits unless you're after an example of cultural (mis) appropriation and racist content. That site is run & filled by a non-Indigenous man, is not scholarly, and is filled with inaccuracies. It's 🗑 [*emoji of rubbish bin*].
>
> (@IndigenousX E Flynn June 28, 2019)

Flynn's exhortation to avoid Creative Spirits has been shared regularly by other @IndigenousX hosts. It is quite likely that the host of the site would have encountered these arguments, yet he persists in maintaining these pages. The cultural (mis)appropriations and inaccuracies are key to this critique and belie any claim to authenticity on the site. Another exhaustive list of educator resources, by Amy Thunig, a Gomeroi education academic, similarly notes:

> DO NOT USE THE SITE 'CREATIVE SPIRITS'. Whilst it appears professionally created, it is riddled with misinformation, and racist myths. The site is produced and populated by a non-indigenous man. It is, in my opinion, the worst site online when it comes to spreading misinformation about First Nations, and unfortunately it is often the first site when you google anything to do with mob. DO NOT USE IT.
>
> (Thunig, 2018, n.p.)

Thunig's critique of Creative Spirits includes reference to the data discrimination that underpins the ongoing popularity of the site. The power of colonial algorithms, in the sense that Fredericks (2021) offers, to drive the spread of misinformation is important for understanding how digital worlds continue to claim authority despite ongoing and pointed critiques.

Search engines do not prioritize high-quality or ethical websites above others as they are driven by popularity and can be gamed by search engine optimization (SEO) processes. As Noble (2018) points out in her analysis of the oppressive forces of algorithms, search engines do not work as a level playing field. Rather, data discrimination means some identities and information dominates others; this skewing is a result of private interests perpetuating the privileging of certain sites, and the small number of popular search engines.

The ethics of SEO by corporations and individuals have been examined by critical data scholars who engage with the complex realities of "gaming the system." For instance, Ziewitz (2019) draws on extensive ethnographic work within SEO consultancies and recounts the efforts of those who are "being ethical" even when the possibilities for doing so are marginal. It is one thing to create a website without the input and authority of peoples that it deigns to represent, and another to forward the material as easily discoverable and a part of making a living off of that representation. Being ethical does not seem to come into play in that strategy.

Creative Spirits appears to fall into a longer tradition of New Age proponents appropriating and misrepresenting Indigenous Australian people's knowledges in Australia for their own benefit. For example, Robert Lawler's (1991) book *Voices of the First Day: Awakening in the Aboriginal Dreamtime* offers a White man's perspective on Aboriginal peoples, using a spiritualist stance that is reductive and error-ridden. In a lengthy critique of Lawler's book, Rolls (2000) recounts how Lawler depicts Tasmanian Aboriginal peoples as "pure" due to the perceived simplicity of their tools for use in daily life and surmises that they are therefore closer to sacredness than others. The tendency for spiritualist misrepresentations of Indigenous Australians by settler-colonial people and institutions is not particularly new and suggests that addressing such practices is also well overdue.

Part 2: Making New Digital Worlds That Assert Sovereignty and Self-Determination of Indigenous Australians

There are two main ways that Indigenous Australians are remaking digital worlds to assert sovereignty and self-determination: first, by claiming territory in digital spaces by strategic use of already existing digital technologies; and second, by making spaces that are controlled and managed by Indigenous peoples as a form of self-determining digital citizenship.

A clear demonstration of how Indigenous Australians are pursuing self-determination via the digital is in owning and controlling digital spaces. An example of this is Mukurtu CMS (content management system), a digital storage and management space that is based on self-determining principles. From the Mukurtu CMS website:

> Mukurtu (MOOK-oo-too) is a grassroots project aiming to empower communities to manage, share, and exchange their digital heritage in culturally relevant and ethically-minded ways. We are committed to maintaining an open, community-driven approach to Mukurtu's continued development. Our first priority is to help build a platform that fosters relationships of respect and trust.
>
> (Mukurtu CMS, n.p.)

Mukurtu (https://mukurtu.org/) exists in part thanks to globally situated technologies: it uses GitHub programming, which is owned by Microsoft, and is supported by the US-based Washington State University. There is an Australian branch of the Mukurtu CMS in NSW which is led by UTS Jumbunna (University of Technology Sydney) and the State Library of NSW. Mukurtu CMS builds on earlier forms of self-determining digital spaces that are created "both out of and in spite of ongoing structural inequalities" (Christen 2005, 334). Self-determining digital citizenship draws on complex networks of affiliation in the case of Mukurtu.

Self-determining digital citizenship relates to radical digital citizenship as a strategy and concept. Radical digital citizenship has been conceptualized by Emejulu (2014) as a way to actively build better digital and social spaces that prioritize social justice. Emejulu argues that critiquing digital technologies and constructing technologies that enable freedom are two key elements that underpin radical digital citizenship. This iteration of digital citizenship is "a process by which individuals and groups critically analyze the social, political and economic consequences of technologies in everyday life and collectively deliberate and take action to build alternative and emancipatory technologies and technological practices" (Emejulu 2014, n.p.).

Radical digital citizenship is mostly framed as a technical process by Emejulu and McGregor (2019) who argue that the designing and programming processes of digital technologies provide a way to talk about how the digital can reconstruct older contestations of social justice. A radical digital citizenship is achievable, Emejulu and McGregor argue, and is preferable if we are invested in building new human-technology relations. In a straightforward sense, radical digital citizenship may be demonstrated by learning code to create digital presences and/or hacking existing sociotechnical systems to improve them. Similarly, McLean (2021) has argued that Emejulu's proposition for emancipatory technologies could be extended by drawing on more strategic and pragmatic use of digital technologies rather than just technical interventions. In the context of decolonization of the digital, Indigenous peoples may not be interested or invested in technical interventions and may prefer to intervene in other ways.

The making of new digital worlds reformulates and recreates old and emerging social/cultural/political spaces; it even challenges and asserts what sovereignty and self-determination mean in the digitally mediated era. Indigenous Australian peoples have long had similar ways of translating and sharing knowledge, histories, language, and cultural expressions primarily through oral traditions and storytelling practices that have been handed down through the generations (Janke 2005). The emergence of digital media has prompted Indigenous Australians to embrace new media to establish, propagate, and organize individual and collective online spaces to continue and expand these oral traditions and storytelling practices.

The exploration of Indigenous Australians' use and creation of digital technologies assists to discern a range of structures and networks within digitally mediated presences and futures. The rise in the use and operationalization of digital spaces by Indigenous Australians has been rapid (Carlson 2013). What is compelling about this everyday escalation of activity is the manner in which Indigenous Australians embody, represent, and embolden their identities through their social/cultural/political positions and affiliations. An example of this is IndigenousX, an Indigenous-owned and Australian-based media organization begun in 2012 that has a website as well as a prominent Twitter presence (IndigenousX 2022). Its founder and CEO, Luke Pearson (Gamilaraay), built the platform in a manner that underpins "his commitment to Indigenous self-determination, truth-telling, and education" (IndigenousX 2022, n.p.). The @IndigenousX Twitter handle (mentioned earlier in this chapter as critiquing *Creative Spirits*) is a rotating account that is hosted by a different Indigenous person each week, though some have done this several times over the course of the last decade (Pearson 2022). This platforming and amplification of multiple Indigenous people, their voices, content, knowledges, and opinions over a sustained period of time locates IndigenousX's position on self-determination and the importance of Indigenous sovereignty. These practices could also be read as forms of network sovereignty, as Duarte (2017) outlines, that work to refute settler-colonial stereotypes in important ways.

IndigenousX's intent, therefore, is a space that is delineated as a continuous and uninterrupted space for Indigenous peoples to express, share, and discuss matters that are of importance to them. The creation and maintenance of digital spaces that are Indigenous-owned and determined such as IndigenousX are paramount. They are the spaces that hold Indigenous histories, contemporaneities, knowledges, and thought production. Indigenous governance of the ownership, transmission, and transformation within digital spaces is vital to ensuring that Indigenous people have control of not only of the information produced, but also the manner in which it is reproduced and circulated.

Conclusion

Alongside Indigenous peoples' efforts to center Indigenous knowledges and to assert self-determination, academic scholarship has generated and shared narratives of effective decolonization and Indigenization. For instance, ecomedia scholarship such as Lowan-Trudeau's (2021) evaluation of how journalists use digital maps was shaped by a critical lens drawing on the interrelated concepts of decolonization and Indigenization, while Eichberger (2019) considers the use of physical and digital maps in the Sacred Stone Camp base of the protest against the Dakota Access Pipeline construction as instrumental. Ecomedia scholarship should continue to address the imperative to think through and enact ways to center Indigenous knowledges rather than risk reproducing colonial power, either deliberately or unintentionally. Also, future research could examine the implications of shifting framings of what decentering settler-colonial presence in the digital involves and how it works, building on Couture and Toupin's (2018) analysis of the multiple framings of digital and technological sovereignty.

By sharing some examples of the different ways that self-determination is foregrounded in Australia, we have shown how alternative digital worlds that centre sovereignty and self-determination are already in existence. Building and supporting more, while challenging those that speak from positions of authority that they are not entitled to, are viable ways forward. Digital spaces offer freedoms and particular constraints that make it difficult to dismantle or remove digital presences that misrepresent and/or do not have the authority to share knowledges. Further, sovereignty and self-determination are undermined when persistent claimers of territory refuse to remove themselves. The persistence of non-Indigenous site owners and content developers who continue to profiteer from sharing information and knowledge that they knowingly and deceptively suggest is of their own making should no longer, if ever, be tolerated. It is a flagrant and abusive wielding of their own White power and privilege that holds no shame or remorse. To be continuously called out by Indigenous peoples across multiple platforms is damning, and to ignore it and persist in the (ab)use of content that is not your own is reprehensible. If you see it, call it out, loudly. If you have been called out multiple times by those who have the authority to do so, it is likely time to leave!

Further Reading

Benjamin, R. (2019). *Race after technology: Abolitionist tools for the new jim code*. Polity, Cambridge.

Carlson, B. and Frazer R. (2021) *Indigenous digital life: The practice and politics of being Indigenous on social media*. Palgrave Macmillan, London.

Emejulu, A. & McGregor, C. (2019) Towards a radical digital citizenship in digital education, *Critical Studies in Education*, 60:1, 131–47, https://doi.org/10.1080/17508487.2016.1234494

Fredericks, B. et al. (2021). Disrupting the colonial algorithm: Indigenous Australia and social media. *Media International Australia*. https://doi.org/10.1177/1329878X211038286.

Powys White, K. (2018). White Allies, Let's be honest about decolonization. *Yes*! Available: https://www.yesmagazine.org/issue/decolonize/2018/04/03/white-allies-lets-be-honest-about-decolonization/. Accessed 30 Sept 2022.

References

Barker, A. J. (2015). 'A direct act of resurgence, a direct act of sovereignty': Reflections on idle no more, indigenous activism, and Canadian settler colonialism. *Globalizations* 12:1, 43–65. https://doi.org/10.1080/14747731.2014.971531

Benjamin, R. (2019). *Race after technology: Abolitionist tools for the new Jim code*. Polity, Cambridge.

Carlson, B. (2013). The 'new frontier': Emergent indigenous identities and social media. In M. Harris, M. Nakata & B. Carlson (Eds.). *The politics of identity: Emerging indigeneity*. University of Technology Sydney Press, Sydney, pp. 147–68.

Carlson, B. and Frazer R. (2021) *Indigenous digital life: The practice and politics of being Indigenous on social media*. Palgrave Macmillan, London.

Christen, K. (2005). Gone digital: Aboriginal remix and the cultural commons. *International Journal of Cultural Property* 12:3, 315–45.

Couture, S. & Toupin, S. (2018) .What does the concept of 'sovereignty' mean in digital, network and technological sovereignty? (January 22, 2018). *GigaNet: Global Internet Governance Academic Network*, Annual Symposium 2017. http://dx.doi.org/10.2139/ssrn.3107272

Duarte, M. E. (2017). *Network sovereignty: Building the internet across Indian country*. University of Washington Press, Seattle.

Eichberger, R. (2019). Maps, silence, and standing rock: Seeking a visuality for the age of environmental crisis. *Communication Design Quarterly* 7:1, 9–21.

Emejulu, A. (2014). Towards a radical digital citizenship (for *E-learning, Politics and Society*). https://digital.education.ed.ac.uk/showcase/towards-radical-digital-citizenship (Accessed 8 April 2022).

Emejulu, A. & McGregor, C. (2019). Towards a radical digital citizenship in digital education. *Critical Studies in Education* 60:1, 131–47, https://doi.org/10.1080/17508487.2016.1234494

Flynn, E. (2019). Twitter. June 28. Available at: https://twitter.com/indigenousx/status/1144473447600234496?lang=en (Accessed 2 December 2021).

Fredericks, B. & Bradfield, A. (2021). 'Waiting with bated breath': Navigating the monstrous world of online racism. *M/C Journal* 24:5. https://doi.org/10.5204/mcj.2825

Fredericks, B. et al. (2021). Disrupting the colonial algorithm: Indigenous Australia and social media. *Media International Australia*. https://doi.org/10.1177/1329878X211038286

IndigenousX (2022). About us. *IndigenousX.* https://indigenousx.com.au/about-us/ (Accessed 15 January 2022).

Janke, T. (2005). Managing indigenous knowledge and indigenous cultural and intellectual property. *Australian Academic & Research Libraries* 36:2, 95–107.

Lean, T. & Henderson, P. (2020). For parents, teachers and children, some resources for decolonizing education. *Croakey Healthy Media*. https://www.croakey.org/for-parents-teachers-and-children-some-resources-for-decolonising-education/

Lowan-Trudeau, G. (2021). Mapping (as) resistance: Decolonizing↔indigenizing journalistic cartography. *Media+Environment* 3:1. https://doi.org/10.1525/001c.19057

McLean, J. (2020). *Changing digital geographies: People, technologies and environment.* Palgrave Macmillan, London.

McLean, J. (2021). 'Gives a physical sense almost': Using immersive media to build decolonial moments in higher education for radical citizenship. *Digital Culture and Education* 13:1, 1–19. https://www.digitalcultureandeducation.com/volume-13-papers/mclean-2021 (Accessed 10 October 2022).

Noble, S. U. (2018). *Algorithms of oppression.* New York University Press, New York.

O'Sullivan, S. (2022). Twitter. January 2022. Available at https://twitter.com/sandyosullivan/status/1482990289027756039 (Accessed 29 September 2022).

Pearson, L. (2022). Reporting on Indigenous issues is still woeful but we will keep making noise and keep showing up. *The Guardian.* https://www.theguardian.com/commentisfree/2022/mar/15/reporting-on-indigenous-issues-is-still-woeful-but-we-will-keep-making-noise-and-keep-showing-up

Powys White, K. (2018). White Allies, let's be honest about decolonization. Yes! Available: https://www.yesmagazine.org/issue/decolonize/2018/04/03/white-allies-lets-be-honest-about-decolonization/ (Accessed 30 September 2022).

Rolls, M. (2000). Robert Lawlor tells a 'white' lie. *Journal of Australian Studies* 24:66, 211–18. https://doi.org/10.1080/14443050009587627

Thunig, A. (2018). Educator resource: 'But I am NOT ABORIGINAL I don't know how to do this stuff!'. *Amy Thunig: Baby Academic.* https://thebabyacademic.com/2018/09/07/but-i-am-not-aboriginal-i-dont-know-how-to-do-this-stuff/ (Accessed 2 December 2021).

Ziewitz, M. (2019). Rethinking gaming: The ethical work of optimization in web search engines. *Social Studies of Science* 49:5, 707–31. https://doi.org/10.1177/0306312719865607

23
WHO MAKES OUR SMARTPHONES? FOUR MOMENTS IN THEIR LIFECYCLE

Richard Maxwell and Toby Miller

Introduction

This chapter examines the hazards and despair faced by workers who labor across continents to produce and recycle smartphones. Drawing on research conducted over the past decade, we argue that institutional and individual consumer demand for new smartphones sets in motion a chain of events that pressurizes working conditions—in the mines where key minerals are extracted, through the production of components, and on to factories for final assembly until their end of life, when these devices become another part of the electronic waste (e-waste) stream of discarded electronics.

We examine four moments in their life cycle—mining, manufacture, subcontracting, and e-waste—to show that the best way for consumer-citizens to lessen the pressure on electronics workers is to keep their smartphones for as long as possible without buying new ones, urge the institutions where they work, study, or volunteer to do the same, and push governments to implement effective regulation of working conditions. Along the way, we touch upon ecosystem threats associated with the smartphone's life cycle.

Mining Hazards and Conflict Minerals

There are many good reasons to share stories about the hardships faced by workers who extract minerals and labor in the factories that supply the world with smartphones. The most obvious is that a compelling account of hidden labor can open our eyes to the human origins of our devices. It is a healthy reminder that someone, somewhere, makes the things we need and want. Of course, that doesn't just apply to electronics. We rarely think about the origins of our soap, clothes, or cars; they seemingly appear in retail outlets fully formed, without any outward sign of their histories. In this case, billions of electronic gadgets arrive with a toxic pedigree that most of us never hear about (Merk, 2021). For these objects are profoundly material, in ways that are largely invisible to users (a word it is worth pondering further, in all its implications).

Seventy stable (non-radioactive) elements from the periodic table are present in smartphones. Copper, gold, platinum, silver, and tungsten are the main metals in basic microelectronic components, wires, and solders. Aluminum and cobalt are used in casings and batteries. Numerous rare-earth metals enhance smartphone functions in speakers and microphones, from signature vibrations to brilliant colors (Crowston, 2018, 9; Jardim, 2017, 4). While critical metals like neodymium and indium are found in small quantities, they provide important functions to digital devices: neodymium is used for the magnets in speakers and indium tin oxide is electrically conductive and transparent, making it a key material in screens (Thiébaud et al., 2018, n.p.).

Mining these metals is hazardous for workers in Asia, Africa, South America, and locations where ores are exported for processing. They are exposed to respiratory hazards and radioactive elements, often in countries where the industry is unregulated or laws are poorly enforced. Miners frequently work on unstable terrain or in vulnerable underground sites where they confront combustible dust, fires, and mine collapses. Breathing ore dust can lead to lung diseases, including bronchitis, silicosis, and cancer. Gold-mining byproducts include such poisonous neurotoxins as lead, cyanide, and mercury (Grossman, 2016, 67–68; Ronsse, 2019).

Some metals used in smartphones—gold (for circuitry), tin (for soldering), tungsten (for capacitors aiding vibration), cobalt (for batteries), and tantalum (capacitors for audio)—are known as "conflict minerals." They are mostly found in the Democratic Republic of Congo (DRC), where they help fund the country's ongoing civil war, in which millions of lives have been lost. Armed groups profit from mines, which they control through violence, child labor, sexual abuse, and rape. The materials are then bought primarily by international mining and commodity traders, sectors dominated by Chinese and Indian firms (Pattisson, 2021; Penke, 2021; Scheele et al., 2016).

Anyone wishing to hear the testimony of those suffering from this brutal industry can view numerous documentaries and reports. They provide chilling testimony (Conflict Minerals, 2012; Conflicted, 2019; Congo, 2011; Special Report, 2017). As a consequence of such media coverage, these crimes are highlighted much more than the region's complex social and economic realities (Musamba and Vogel, 2021) or the wider political economy of the labor process and its toxicity, both of which are kept far distant from smartphone owners' attention (Laudati and Mertens, 2019). Major US electronics manufacturers continue to profit from the trade, despite having pledged to abide by the Dodd-Frank Wall Street Reform and Consumer Protection Act, which prohibits obtaining these minerals from the DRC. Due diligence and support for "conflict-free sourcing opportunities" are good things, but companies down the line such as Samsung or Apple still can't be confident they are buying conflict-free minerals, because it is notoriously difficult to ascertain the origins of these metals: once processed, ore is mixed with the overall global supply, then sold on the international market, often using financial instruments to further "clean" their record (Callaway, 2017; MacGarrigle, 2021; van den Brink et al., 2019).

Manufacturing and Assembly

Most component manufacture and smartphone assembly take place in East Asia; over half of smartphone exports originate from China (Jardim, 2017, 5). This arrangement depends on global supply chains that feed the assembly lines. When stable, they allow electronics businesses to plan with relative confidence. US trade tariffs imposed on Chinese imports in 2019 unsettled such confidence, causing major consumer electronics brands to draw up plans to reconfigure existing supply chains, with attendant changes to the international division of labor.

Taiwan is especially important in the global supply chain. Its centrality is based on the deep dependency that the biggest tech brands have developed on contract manufacturers, who assemble the bulk of the world's smartphones and other devices that institutional and individual customers have come to love. Hon Hai (better known as Foxconn), Largan, Wistron, Pegatron, Quanta, and TSMC are the main players. TSMC's specialized microprocessors form the heart of iPhone and

Huawei products. Workers at Largan grind the lenses used in high-end phone cameras; Pegatron and Quanta employees make cheaper devices; Foxconn runs mega factories in China, with the capacity and logistical know-how to hire "armies of workers" on-demand to create new iPhones and associated gadgets rapidly ("Taiwan's computing titans," 2019).

These Taiwanese companies have anchored much of their production in the factory zone of Shenzhen in southern China, which has led to their own dependency on a highly developed cluster of industries and expertise in the region. Recent trade conflicts have seriously disrupted this arrangement, pressing major brands to relocate factories and suppliers, which would be costly and take years to establish the "efficiency" of current norms. Pegatron looked to establish a factory in Indonesia, while Foxconn and Wistron built factories in India to assemble iPhones. Samsung now makes most of its smartphones in Vietnam ("Taiwan's computing titans," 2019; "The technology industry is rife with bottlenecks," 2019).

High-end or leading-edge chips are key components in digital devices. A leading-edge chip could start its life at a silicon dioxide mine in the US, be turned into pure ingots of silicon in Japan, sliced into wafers, then go to a factory in Taiwan or South Korea to be printed with advanced Dutch photolithography equipment. This supply chain is vulnerable to geopolitical threats because of its high level of concentration: only five companies produce leading-edge chips, down from 29 in 2001 ("The semiconductor industry," 2018).

When these firms relocate, workplace hazards accompany them (Swedwatch, 2021). Making silicon wafers, semiconductors, batteries, and other basic components of smartphones involves exposure to toxic chemicals. "Solvents—such as benzene, glycol ethers, methylene chloride, trichloroethylene (TCE), trichloroethane, acetone, toluene—acids, heavy metals, and perfluorinated compounds are among the many hazardous chemicals used" (Grossman, 2016, 70; also see Kim, Kim, and Paek, 2014). They have been linked to brain and kidney disorders, brain cancers, leukemia, and lymphoma among workers. Other chemicals used to manufacture smartphones are associated with reproductive disorders, infertility, miscarriages, and birth defects. Many such diseases do not manifest for years, and the industry only reports harms that occur at work, so the statistics underreport long-term health risks facing employees and their families (Grossman, 2016, 71; Sung-Won, 2019). Research on factories throughout East Asia finds that workers receive little or no training in the safe handling of "chemicals that include phenol, chloroform, TCE, mercury, glues, solvents, flux and solder, degreaser, hexane, n-hexane, methanol, trimethyl fluoride, benzene, nickel, lithium, methylene chloride, and isopropyl alcohol" (Grossman, 2016, 71–72).

The semiconductor, the heart of all electronic equipment, is produced by hundreds of companies around the world for a market dominated by Intel, Samsung Electronics, Toshiba Electronics, Texas Instruments, Qualcomm, and ADM. Workers in semiconductor facilities can be exposed to skin irritants, acids that harm mucous and pulmonary tissue, and chemicals that may cause cancer, reproductive complications, and debilitating illnesses. Long after culpable firms have departed, the durable half-life of toxic waste emitted into the soil from semiconductor plants leaves groundwater and land unusable or highly dangerous for populations who live atop them. Entire communities, like Endicott, New York—the original home of IBM—have seen their aquifer and soil cursed with such carcinogenic compounds as TCE (a solvent) that remain active for decades (Grossman, 2006, 109–11; Silicon Valley Toxics Coalition, n.d.). The Biden White House has sought to make local mineral extraction an industrial priority in order to lessen its dependence on international supply chains (FACT SHEET, 2022). That may lead to a repatriation of occupational health risks.

The Inhumane Business Model of Subcontracting

The business model that brands like Apple pioneered has solidified the behavior of subcontractors like Foxconn, ensuring constant pressure on workers to speed up under inflexible, hazardous, and unhealthy conditions (Harris, 2014). Contractual rules ensure a percentage mark-up of price at each stage, from factory floor to retail store. The contract manufacturer's selling price combines assembly costs (including labor) and materials costs (determined by the brand company) plus a small profit (usually no more than 3% of the factory-selling price). After that, Apple and other corporations have assured a mark-up of 30% to pay for "development, shipping, distribution, marketing." They may enjoy a further 30% as profit. In the end, the total price for a smartphone or other gadget can be five times or more than the subcontractor's price. In 2014, factory labor costs amounted to about 0.5% of the final retail price; the total amount paid for workers to make a $500 device was about $2 (Harris, 2014). That was not $2 for each employee; it was the collective share for all the labor incarnate in the device. That amount today is no more than $6, a pittance given the retail prices for new iPhones (Mickle, 2022).

As a consequence of this model, companies like Foxconn have little incentive to raise wages or improve working conditions. Although profit margins are small, they can finagle increased revenue from suppliers without increasing their selling price by holding down wages, cutting safety corners, and speeding up the pace of work. The result has been years of unsafe and illegal subcontractor operations, including cases of exposure to poisonous chemicals that damage the peripheral nervous system and cause chronic weakness, fatigue, and hypersensitivity to heat and cold (Maxwell and Miller, 2012, 95, 157). Searing conditions at one Chinese Foxconn factory making iPhones led to mass suicides in 2010–2011, which Foxconn's leadership initially refused to investigate (Chan et al., 2016). Apple would later order its subcontractors to halt unsafe and illegal practices, though company representatives kept their distance, never meeting with affected workers or offering support, financial or otherwise, to rehabilitate or compensate them for physical and emotional privation (Chan et al., 2020; Gong, 2019; Pun et al., 2019).

Some social scientists have characterized this inhumane system as a new form of slavery (Qiu, 2016). The system removes young people from family, friends, freedom of association (they are prohibited from talking to one another on the assembly line), and forms of cultural enjoyment and release, which might help them adjust to sequestration in high-tech, high-speed, and high-security compounds. Working days can be as long as twelve hours, with overtime (often unpaid) to follow. Stress levels are high, and repetitive motion and other ergonomic problems are common (Lu, 2019). Again, you can view testimony from those on the front line of this abuse (Chan et al., 2020; "Made in China," 2017; Qiu, 2010). Because many workers are on short-term contracts, it is "difficult for them to become informed about their working conditions, difficult for them to organize [and] difficult to trace workplace exposures and ... any resulting health problems" (Grossman, 2016, 72).

Our Global E-Waste Problem

Moving on from mines and factories, smartphones have an existence after users have abandoned them as e-waste. They fall into the category of small information and communication technology (ICT) equipment that includes Global Positioning Systems, pocket calculators, routers, personal computers, printers, and telephones (Baldé et al., 2018, 11) and overlaps with monitors, televisions, laptops, notebooks, and tablets. Discarding these devices creates large quantities of waste—ICTs overall account for just over 10% of total e-waste globally. An estimated 53.6 million metric tonnes (MT) was generated in 2019. That represented a 21% jump in the five years since 2014. In 2021, the worldwide mountain of e-waste totaled an estimated 57.4 million MT—greater than the weight of the Great Wall of China, Earth's heaviest artificial object. E-waste is predicted to amount to 74 MT by 2030. Global e-waste generation is therefore growing annually by 3–4%, a problem attributed to higher consumption rates of electronics (annual increases of 3%), shorter product lifecycles, and limited repair options (WEEE Forum, 2021). (It should be said that measuring this level is notoriously difficult—only 20% of the recorded volume comes from fully documented e-waste that has been designated for recycling; the remaining 80% is a statistical projection drawn from sales, trade volume and weight, and the average lifespan of equipment.) One-third of the world's population lives where there is no e-waste legislation, and only 41 countries produce official e-waste statistics. The fate of undocumented waste is uncertain, though it's probably dumped in landfills or recycled in low-tech, high-hazard conditions (Baldé et al., 2018, 30–35).

Most digital waste produced in the US is sent to Asia for recycling or dumping (Baldé et al., 2018, 44). Precise data on the flow is as murky as the overall picture. US recyclers claim that most documented e-waste is locally recycled (Public Broadcasting Service, 2016). But evidence of "export denial in the recycling industry" shows that 40% of tracked e-waste is dispatched overseas, nearly all of it illegally (Basel Action Network, 2016). The export of waste containing toxic materials is regulated by the Basel Convention on the Control of Transboundary Movements of Hazardous Wastes and Their Disposal, which was adopted in 1989 and ratified three years later. The Convention imposes strict rules on transporting and handling e-waste, and even stricter ones limiting or prohibiting its export to the Global South. It is illegal for any signatory to receive e-waste from the US—the only wealthy country that has refused to sign (Basel Convention, 1989).

Until 2017, China was the final resting home for 70% of the world's e-waste, much of it ending up in landfills, sub-standard treatment sites, and low-tech salvage yards. While new restrictions in China have shifted e-waste flows to smaller Asian countries (Larmer, 2018), a portion still ends up there after arriving in Hong Kong as an entrepôt, while much of the remainder finds its way to Pakistan, Thailand, Taiwan, Cambodia, the United Arab Emirates, Togo, and Kenya (Lepawsky, 2015). The European Union leads the world in e-waste collection and recycling but is far from innocent of illegal exports to the Global South. Much of the Union's electronic waste goes to Asia and West Africa, specifically Benin, Côte d'Ivoire, Ghana, Liberia, and Nigeria. Ghana and Nigeria are the main regional ports of entry for e-waste from around the world. Over three-quarters of e-waste entering Nigeria originates in Europe, most of it smuggled inside motor vehicles shipped as "roll on/roll off" cargo to Lagos (Gault, 2018; Odeyingbo et al., 2017, 36; Shaw 2019).

There is a dreadful human cost to these illegal shipments, visible in such documentaries as *Electronic Waste in Ghana* (2008) and *ToxiCity* (2016). As we have seen, smartphones contain a range of toxic components that can cause human and ecological damage. Plastics are a particularly pernicious problem in e-waste treatment, because flame retardants, toxic elements, and heavy metals used in their production can release hazardous chemicals into the environment and food chain if not properly recycled (Beurteaux, 2018; Wëger et al., 2010). Health risks include brain damage, headaches, vertigo, nausea, birth defects, diseases of the bones, stomach, lungs, and other vital organs, and disrupted child development (United Nations University/StEP Initiative, 2016). There is also ecological damage from low-tech, high-hazard recycling of e-waste, as demonstrated by the recent history of Guiyu, a village in south-eastern China that was a preferred dumping ground for decades ("Chinese City," 2015; "In Guiyu," 2016).

There are very few government incentives to manage e-waste transparently and legally, despite suggestions that the recovery of high-value components through the formal economy could be worth as much as $63 billion, with some estimates of potential value for high-tech, low-hazard recycling amounting to "more than the 2016 Gross Domestic Product of most countries in the world" (Baldé et al., 2018, 7, 54).

The multiple issues associated with e-waste present us with compelling reasons to hold on to our phones for as long as possible. The waste stream is already filled with enough discarded digital devices to overwhelm e-waste management systems. If we must replace our smartphones, let's wait until they are truly beyond repair, and insist that our employers do the same. Then we should do our damnedest to make sure they get to a reputable and tested recycler or back to the original manufacturers, who have successfully blocked people's ability to exercise the right to repair by mimicking the sealed-set model of radios adopted by commerce almost a century ago. That "damnedest" should also include citizen action, via calls for democratic regulation to protect the Earth and worker solidarity. Governments must be forced to take decisive action on all these fronts.

Conclusion

This brief chapter has shown that smartphones are products of an exploitative and toxic system that beats up on workers in mines, factories, and e-waste disposal sites. We have tried to connect the dots between the premia consumers pay for smartphones and a political economy designed to guarantee corporate profits by ensuring that working conditions remain inhumane (La Monica, 2018). It doesn't have to be this way. We hope we have provided reasons for holding on to smartphones for as long as possible, if for no other reason than to help release some of the pressure on workers laboring across the supply chain. Through that simple action, we can eliminate some of the estrangement between worker and consumer and think more routinely about the political-economic ties that bind us in order to deepen our ethical commitments to electronics workers, based on mutuality, justice, and equality, and ensure that such exploitation is banished from supply chains.

Further Reading

Baldé, C. P., Forti, V., Gray, V., Kuehr, R., and Stegmann, P. (2018) *The Global E-Waste Monitor* 2017. Bonn/Geneva/Vienna: United Nations University, International Telecommunication Union, and International Solid Waste Association. https://ewastemonitor.info/
Chan, J., Selden, M., and Ngai, P. (2020) *Dying for an iPhone: Apple, Foxconn, and The Lives of China's Workers*. Chicago, IL: Haymarket Books
Iheka, C. N. (2021) *African Ecomedia: Network Forms, Planetary Politics*. Durham, NC: Duke University Press.
Maxwell, R. (ed.) (2016) *The Routledge Companion to Labor and Media*. New York: Routledge.
Maxwell, R. and Miller, T. (2020) *How Green is Your Smartphone?* Cambridge: Polity.

References

"Chinese City Moves Electronics Recycling Activities to Industrial Park" (2015, December 18) *Recycling Today*. http://www.recyclingtoday.com/article/ban-guiyu-industrial-park-visit/.
"Conflict Minerals, Rebels and Child Soldiers in Congo" (2012, May 22) *Vice*. https://www.youtube.com/watch?v=kYqrflGpTRE.
"Conflicted: The Fight Over Congo's Minerals" (2019, March 3) Al Jazeera. https://www.aljazeera.com/programmes/faultlines/2015/11/conflicted-fight-congo-minerals-151118084541495.html.
"Congo: Blood, Gold and Mobile Phones" (2011, September 6) *Guardian*. https://www.youtube.com/watch?v=gGuG0Ios8ZA.

"Electronic Waste in Ghana" (2008, August 4) *Greenpeace International*. https://www.youtube.com/watch?v=pr1zQrXM_7s.

"In Guiyu, the E-Waste Nightmare is Far From Over" (2016, November 4). *Toxic Leaks*. https://toxicleaks.com/wiki/In_Guiyu,_the_e-waste_nightmare_is_far_from_over.

"Made in China: Mobile Phone Factory Behind the Scenes" (2017, November 28). *BBC News*. https://www.youtube.com/watch?v=hwMZtdTcM7A.

"Special Report: Inside the Congo Cobalt Mines That Exploit Children" (2017, February 27). *Sky News*. https://www.youtube.com/watch?v=JcJ8me22NVs.

"Taiwan's computing titans are caught up in the US-China tech war" (2019, June 8). *The Economist*. https://www.economist.com/business/2019/06/08/taiwans-computing-titans-are-caught-up-in-the-us-china-tech-war

"The semiconductor industry and the power of globalization" (2018, December 1). *The Economist*. https://www.economist.com/briefing/2018/12/01/the-semiconductor-industry-and-the-power-of-globalisation

"The technology industry is rife with bottlenecks" (2019, June 8). *The Economist*. https://www.economist.com/business/2019/06/08/the-technology-industry-is-rife-with-bottlenecks

"ToxiCity: Life at Agbobloshie, the World's Largest E-Waste Dump in Ghana" (2016, June 1) RT. https://www.youtube.com/watch?v=mleQVO1Vd1I.

Baldé, C. P., Forti V., Gray, V., Kuehr, R., and Stegmann, P. (2018) *The Global E-Waste Monitor* 2017. Bonn/Geneva/Vienna: United Nations University, International Telecommunication Union, and International Solid Waste Association.

Basel Action Network (2016) "Scam Recycling: E-Dumping on Asia by US Recyclers," https://www.re-source-recycling.com/images/BANReportTwo.pdf.

Basel Convention (1989) "Convention on the Control of Transboundary Movements of Hazardous Wastes and Their Disposal," http://www.basel.int/TheConvention/Overview/TextoftheConvention/tabid/1275/Default.aspx.

Beurteaux, D. (2018, April 9) "Is Plastic Waste Poisoning Our Seafood?," *Pacific Standard*. https://psmag.com/environment/isplastic-poisoning-our-oci.

Callaway, A. (2017) "Demand the Supply," *The Enough Project*. https://enoughproject.org/wp-content/uploads/2017/11/Dem andTheSupply_EnoughProject_2017Rankings_final.pdf.

Catholic Agency for Overseas Development (2004) *Clean Up Your Computer: Working Conditions in the Electronics Sector*. https://www.peacelink.it/cybercultura/docs/176.pdf.

Chan, J. and Ho, C. (2008) *The Dark Side of Cyberspace: Inside the Sweatshops of China's Computer Hardware Production*. Berlin: World Economy, Ecology and Development.

Chan, J., Pun, N., and Selden, M. (2016) "Chinese Labor Protest and Trade Unions," in Maxwell, R. (ed.). *The Routledge Companion to Labor and Media*. New York: Routledge, pp. 290–302.

Chan, J., Selden, M., and Ngai, P. (2020) *Dying for an iPhone: Apple, Foxconn, and The Lives of China's Workers*. Chicago, IL: Haymarket Books.

Crowston, B. (2018) "Smartphones: Behind the Screen," *Resonance* 8: 9–10.

FACT SHEET. (2022, February 22) "Securing a Made in America Supply Chain for Critical Minerals," https://www.whitehouse.gov/briefing-room/statements-releases/2022/02/22/fact-sheet-securing-a-made-in-america-supply-chain-for-critical-minerals.

Gallagher, M. (2019) "Childhood and the Geology of Media," *Discourse: Studies in the Cultural Politics of Education*. https://doi.org/10.1080/01596306.2019.1620481.

Gault, M. (2018, April 23) "Europe Is Smuggling its E-Waste to Nigeria Inside Used Cars," *Motherboard*. https://motherboard.vice.com/en_us/article/59jew8/e-waste-smuggling-nigeria.

Gong, Y. (2019) *Manufacturing Towns in China*. Singapore: Palgrave Macmillan.

Grossman, E. (2016) "The Body Burden: Toxics, Stresses and Biophysical Health," in Maxwell, R. (ed.). *The Routledge Companion to Labor and Media*. New York: Routledge, pp. 65–77.

Harris, A. (2014) *Dragging Out the Best Deal: How Billion Dollar Margins Are Played Out on the Backs of Electronics Workers*. GoodElectronics. https://goodelectronics.org/dragging-out-thebest-deal/.

Iheka, C. N. (2021) *African Ecomedia: Network Forms, Planetary Politics*. Durham, NC: Duke University Press.

Jardim, E. (2017) *From Smartphones to Senseless: The Global Impact of 10 Years of Smartphones*. Greenpeace. https://www.greenpeace.org/usa/wp-content/uploads/2017/03/FINAL-10YearsSmartphones-Report-Design-230217-Digital.pdf.

Kim, M.-H., Kim, H., and Paek, D. (2014) "The Health Impacts of Semiconductor Production: An Epidemiologic Review," *International Journal of Occupational and Environmental Health*, 20, no. 2: 95–114.

La Monica, P. R. (2018, August 2) "Apple Reaches $1,000,000,000,000 Value," CNN Business. https://money.cnn.com/2018/08/02/investing/apple-one-trillion-market-value/index.html.

Larmer, B. (2018, July 5) "E-Waste Offers an Economic Opportunity as Well as Toxicity," *The New York Times*. https://www.nytimes.com/2018/07/05/magazine/e-waste-offers-an-economic-opportunity-as-well-as-toxicity.html.

Laudati, A. and Mertens, C. (2019) "Resources and Rape: Congo's (Toxic) Discursive Complex," *African Studies Review*, 62, no. 4: 57–82.

Lepawsky, J. (2015) "The Changing Geography of Global Trade in Electronic Discards: Time to Rethink the E-Waste Problem," *The Geographical Journal*, 181, no. 2: 147–59.

Lu, D. (2019) "Everyday Modernity in China: From Danwei to the 'World Factory'," *Fudan Journal of the Humanities and Social Sciences*, 12, no. 1: 79–91.

MacGarrigle, K. (2021) "The Bloodiest Trade: Conflict Minerals in the DRC," *Penn Political Review*, April 10. https://pennpoliticalreview.org/2021/04/the-bloodiest-trade-conflict-minerals-in-the-drc/

Maxwell, R. and Miller, T. (2012) *Greening the Media*. New York: Oxford University Press.

Merk, J. (2021) *Human Rights Risks in the ICT Supply Chain*. Edinburgh: Make ICT Fair. https://www.ed.ac.uk/files/atoms/files/human_rights_risks_in_the_ict_supply_chain_0.pdf

Mickle, T. (2022, September 6) "How China Has Added to Its Influence Over the iPhone," *The New York Times*. https://www.nytimes.com/2022/09/06/technology/china-apple-iphone.html.

Musamba, J. and C. Vogel (2021) "The Problem with 'Conflict Minerals'," *Dissent*, October 21. https://www.dissentmagazine.org/online_articles/the-problem-with-conflict-minerals.

Odeyingbo, O., Nnorom, I., and Deubzer, O. (2017) *Person in the Port Project: Assessing Import of Used Electrical and Electronic Equipment into Nigeria*. Bonn: United Nations University. http://collections.unu.edu/eserv/UNU:6349/PiP_Report.pdf.

Pattisson, P. (2021) "'Like Slave and Master': DRC Miners Toil for 30p an Hour to Fuel Electric Cars," *The Guardian*, November. https://www.theguardian.com/global-development/2021/nov/08/cobalt-drc-miners-toil-for-30p-an-hour-to-fuel-electric-cars.

Penke, M. (2021) "How China's Mines Rule the Market of Critical Raw Materials," *Deutsche Welle*, April 13. https://www.dw.com/en/how-chinas-mines-rule-the-market-of-critical-raw-materials/a-57148375.

Public Broadcasting Service (2016, May 10) "Where Does America's E-Waste End Up? GPS Tracker Tells All," *News Hour*. https://www.pbs.org/newshour/science/america-e-waste-gps-tracker-tellsall-earthfix.

Pun, N., Tse, T., and Ng, T. (2019) "Challenging Digital Capitalism: SACOM's Campaigns against Apple and Foxconn as Monopoly Capital," *Information, Communication and Society*, 22, no. 9: 1253–68.

Qiu, J. L. (2010, December 16) *Deconstructing Foxconn*. China Labor Watch. http://www.chinalaborwatch.org/newscast/74.

Qiu, J. L. (2016) *Goodbye iSlave: A Manifesto for Digital Abolition*. Champaign: University of Illinois Press.

Ronsse, S. (2019) *Toward a Fairer ICT Supply Chain—Research and Fact-Finding Mission in the Context of the Project 'Make ICT Fair' in Oruro, Bolivia*. Edinburgh: Make ICT Fair. https://www.ed.ac.uk/sustainability/what-we-do/supply-chains/initiatives/make-ict-fair-project/towards-a-fairer-ict-supply-chain

Scheele, F. with de Haan, E. and Kiezebrink, V. (2016) *Cobalt Blues: Environmental Pollution and Human Rights Violations in Katanga's Copper and Cobalt Mines*. Good Electronics. https://www.somo.nl/cobalt-blues/.

Shaw, N. (2019, January 5) "For Ghana E-Waste Recyclers, a Safer Option Amid Toxic Fumes," *Associated Press*. https://phys.org/news/2019-01-ghana-e-waste-recyclers-safer-option.html.

Silicon Valley Toxics Coalition (n.d.) *Electronic Industry Overview*. San Jose: Silicon Valley Toxics Coalition.

Sung-Won, Y. (2019, January 18) "Samsung Asked to Pay for Leukemia Victims," *The Korea Times*. http://m.koreatimes.co.kr/phone/news/view.jsp?req_newsidx=183426.

Swedwatch (2021) *Electronics Brands Must Protect Workers from Hazardous Chemicals in the Philippines*. Edinburgh: Make ICT Fair. https://swedwatch.org/publication/report/electronics-brands-must-protect-workers-from-hazardous-chemicals-in-the-philippines-sub/.

Thiébaud, E., Hilty, L. M., Schluep, M., B.ni, H. W., and Faulstich, M. (2018) "Where Do Our Resources Go? Indium, Neodymium, and Gold Flows Connected to the Use of Electronic Equipment in Switzerland," *Sustainability*, 10, no. 8: 2658.

United Nations University/StEP Initiative (2016) "Guiding Principles to Develop E-waste Management Systems and Legislation," *Solving the E-Waste Problem (StEP) White Paper*. http://collections.unu.edu/eserv/UNU:6119/step_systems_and_legislation_final.pdf.

van den Brink, S., Kleijn, R., Tukker, A., and Huisman, J. (2019) "Approaches to Responsible Sourcing in Mineral Supply Chains," *Resources, Conservation and Recycling*, 145: 389–98.

WEEE Forum (2021) "International E-Waste Day: 57.4 mm Tonnes Expected in 2021," https://weee-forum.org/ws_news/international-e-waste-day-2021/.

Wäger, P., Schluep, M., and Müller, E. (2010) *RoHS Substances in Mixed Plastics from Waste Electrical and Electronic Equipment, Swiss Federal Laboratories for Materials Science and Technology*. http://www.weee-forum.org/sites/default/files/documents/2010_rohs_substances_in_weee_plastics.pdf.

PART IV

Ecocultures

24
MEDIA AND ECOCULTURAL IDENTITY

Tema Milstein, Gabi Mocatta, and José Castro-Sotomayor

All identities are sociocultural as well as ecological. These ecocultural identifications – whether conscious or not or whether destructively anthropocentric or restoratively ecocentric – shape individual, group, and institutional environmental meanings, relations, and practices.[1] The task of understanding ecocultural identities is deeply important to the urgent project of transforming dominant destructive environmental identifications to have capacity to transition to more regenerative futures (Milstein & Castro-Sotomayor, 2020).

This chapter illuminates media's role in reflecting, shaping, and shifting ecocultural identities and challenges dominant mediated environmental narratives that fuel destructive planetary positionalities. We explore tensions between media functioning to reproduce status quo anthropocentric identities (which hierarchically center humanity and privilege a mastery gaze upon the world's life systems) and, conversely, to nourish and mediate mass paradigm shifts to ecocentric identities (which center the ecological web of life and position humans as part of the web). To illustrate these dynamics, we present four international case studies that explore a range of ecocultural contexts, including visitor online reviews of a United States marine mammal sanctuary dependent upon a coal-burning power plant, a blockbuster South African documentary about an octopus' relations with a human, Indigenous uses of community-based media for transition discourses in Latin American borderlands, and mediatized environmental conflict in Chile leading to widespread protest and emancipatory catastrophism around environmental injustice and inequality.

In investigating a range of media in interaction with different publics and places, we illustrate the reproductive and transformative potential in the mediation of ecocultural identities and the diversity and dynamism of such identities in stasis and shift. We also query whether we have reached a moment in time in which much-needed overarching identity shifts from anthropocentrism to ecocentrism will be driven less by media and more by immediacy – embodied experiences, including lived experience of extreme droughts, bushfires, floods, and temperatures. Will the ecocultural identity revolution not be televised – particularly if the majority of media is reproducing anthropocentric views? We close with a case-informed discussion about ways different forms of media can play meaningful roles in increasing ecocentric identification.

This chapter has been made available under a CC-BY-NC-ND license.

Current Research

To provide context for the case studies that follow, in this review of current research, we first explain why the framework of ecocultural identity is a crucial lens for studying ways media serve as a central force in reflecting and shaping environmental relations. We then dig into how environmental issues and conflict engage mediatized ecocultural identities in the new public sphere (Castells, 2008) of largely online media. We close this section with an exploration of ways heightened media digitization and technologies can further distance media users from immediate ecological relations and identifications.

Ecocultural Identity

The transdisciplinary study of ecocultural identity provides an important lens for understanding personal and collective identities as always both sociocultural and ecological (Milstein & Castro-Sotomayor, 2020). Ecocultural identity is crucial to consider in the realm of environmental communication and meaning-making (Milstein et al., 2019; Milstein, 2020) and, more specifically, in the realm of media, as "narrations and navigations of identity intersect with politics, society, and processes of reinvention, reconstruction, and renewal" that are represented, reproduced, and challenged throughout the media sphere (Milstein & Castro-Sotomayor, 2020, p. xviii). Situating human forms of identification as always ecocultural overrides the tendency in media studies (and in most realms of study and in the media) to separate environment from, or treat ecosystems as subsidiary to, sociocultural, economic, political, and historical dimensions. As such, the ecocultural identity framework offers an ecologically expanded and potentially recuperative lens for research and media practice.

The framework allows for the study and engagement of *all* ecocultural identities from the most anthropocentric to the most ecocentric. In other words, "ecocultural" is not a normative frame but instead an expanded scope for understanding ecological and more-than-human elements of identities as they relate to and are shaped by (and shape) sociocultural elements. We argue all people – from media makers to consumers to hybrids of the two – start and engage from ecocultural standpoints, whether latent or conscious. These ecocultural positionalities and identifications inform embodied, emotional, mental, political-economic, and sometimes spiritual sensibilities with/in/as "nature," and these standpoints (from the most environmentally distanced to the most infused) are foundational to how media are produced, accepted, interrogated, or transformed.

Ecocultural identity also expands notions of intersectionality in both environmental communication and media studies to include not only sociocultural categories but also generally overlooked more-than-human groupings and processes, leading to potential for intraspecies, interspecies, processual, and elementally shared questions, concerns, and actions (Castro-Sotomayor, 2020b; Freeman, 2020; Parks, 2020; Thomas, 2020). In both immediate and mediated realms of influence, this relational potential can open ways to more effectively address increasing feelings of disconnection, disempowerment, and polarization and provide pathways to alternative public spheres and platforms that support points of unification.

Indeed, the relationship between media and identity is always iterative. "As sites of contested representations, media outlets and technologies (re)produce, challenge, and amplify ecocultural perceptions, practices, and identifications" (Milstein & Castro-Sotomayor, 2020, p. 223). Media are reflective and formative of ecocultural identity and both dominant and counter-hegemonic ecocultural identities are engaged in struggle for media voice and amplification. Further, a focus on media helps illuminate ways "people identify within contexts of ecological distress and social, political, and environmental complexity" (p. 224).

Environmental Conflict and Mediatized Identities in the "New Public Sphere"

It's been fewer than three decades since our network society (van Dijk, 1999; Castells, 2011) has fundamentally changed the ways we construct both power and identity. Beyond the Habermasian public sphere, the whole spectrum of traditional media and social media platforms now forms a vastly broadened *new public sphere* (Castells, 2008), in which media gatekeeping has given way to a multiplicity of competing voices. This can be regarded as a shift from "mass mediation" to "mass self-mediation" (to borrow from Castells). In this new public sphere, identities are crafted and power is held. This has changed the long-established balance of media power, siting such power increasingly with the media prosumer (Toffler, 1990), who is engaged in both media *production* and *consumption*, or produsage (Bruns, 2006) – that is, user-led production of media content.

Not only does the contemporary media sphere represent a site of produsage, but also, given the now extraordinary breadth of what constitutes "media," such diverse media are also sites for the formation of a multiplicity of mediatized identities – and the polarization of such identities (Büscher, 2021). While media have long been actors in mediatized conflicts, disseminating ideas and images about them (Cottle, 2006), media of the new public sphere provide increasingly diverse sites for the strategic enactment of mediatized environmental conflict (Hutchins & Lester, 2015) and identity formation relative to such conflicts. Historically, better resourced institutions have greater potential to buy communication influence, more agenda-setting potential, and, ultimately, more "communication power" (Castells, 2007), which leads to vested interests reproducing the status quo – in the case of ecocultural identity, reproducing anthropocentric identity. In the networked public sphere, however, resource-poor organizations – and even individuals – also can make significant interventions.

Counter-movements that point out, protest, or highlight alternatives to environmental harm are often led by skilled media makers, and these less powerful actors can sometimes triumph over the powerful in a deeply mediatized world (Hepp, 2019). Media *produsers* (Bruns, 2009) can make headway by using "social appropriation to transform collective relations toward a political project of structural change" based on "emancipatory ideological assumptions" (Parra, 2015, p. 3686). In the present chapter's case studies, we provide a snapshot of assorted media locations within this broad and active mediascape – from user-produced online reviews to strategic communication for resistance – and examine the varied productions of mediatized ecocultural identities.

Mediacy and Immediacy

Today's media largely involve layers of digital technology. Reflections on technology's role in shaping humanity's condition are not new (e.g., Ferkiss, 1993), but studies have shown that the rapidly increased mediation of human experience through electronic screens has deepened negative impacts on interpersonal and social relationships (Eriksen, 2001; Turkle, 2015). It is not until recently that intersections between the accelerated degradation and destruction of Earth's ecosystems and the recent unprecedented technological development have come under critical scrutiny. From the toxic e-waste produced by extraction of resources for digital devices (Kuntsman & Rattle, 2019) to attempts through sophisticated technological innovations to not only mediate but also emulate and replace the "natural world" by augmenting or simulating it (Breves & Greussing, 2022; Levi & Kocher, 1999; Milstein, 2009; Stinson, 2017), mediated communication profoundly shapes human-environmental and interspecies relations.

While media and their technologies most often inform both individual and group senses of self by hindering identifications with the more-than-human world, in some cases media can foster ecological immediacy by expanding audience's senses through counter ecocultural imaginaries (Nielsen,

2020), stimulating pro-environmental behaviors (Holbert et al. 2003), and providing interactive ways to garner public support and further conservation goals (Ducarme et al., 2013; Büscher, 2016; Crawford et al., 2017; Fletcher, 2017; Thomson & Rog 2019).

Immediate, or direct, contact with the more-than-human world, however, is still arguably more impactful in developing and highlighting entanglements and interdependencies intrinsic to ecological relations (Greenwood & Gatersleben, 2016). Beyond media's overarching reproduction of dominant anthropocentric discourses, technology and mediation can inhibit or frustrate "the spontaneous reciprocity between our sensing bodies and the sensuous Earth around us," as Abram argues, by "short circuiting this instinctive reciprocity" (Abram with Milstein & Castro-Sotomayor, 2020, p. 10). Amid unprecedented climate-induced extreme weather events, embodied experiences may increasingly be overriding mediated abstractions – curtailing the ecological numbness that both springs from and accelerates some of the most destructive dynamics at work in the global ecological emergency. Immediate, visceral experiences with environmental and climate catastrophes can override dominant anthropocentric media framing and lead to reassessed values, realigned politics, and fundamentally transformed ecocultural identities, as new rationalities and sensibilities emerge from disruptions of people's daily lives, senses of normalcy, and expectations of safety and security (Raynes & Mix, 2020). Everyone's spaces have become the backyard of the environmental crisis and, while the burden of climate disruption unjustly and disproportionately still falls on marginalized communities and regions, visceral and corporeal immediate experiences may force even the most privileged to question what it means to identify as human. Media could delay this reevaluation by prioritizing dominant society's anthropocentric inertia or can accelerate this reevaluation by bringing forward alternative and ancient and enduring ecocentric ways of framing ourselves and our environmental futures.

Case Studies: Mediated Ecocultural Identities

To bring these frameworks for understanding ecocultural identity, media, and immediacy to life, we present four micro case studies. From the commercial to the grassroots, these international cases highlight ways a wide range of media serve as sites for the production of diverse forms of ecocultural identity. In particular, through these comparative cases, we exhibit ways media makers and users alternately produce blindness to ecological and more-than-human immediacy, seek out immediacy, share a lived sense of immediacy, or attempt to reclaim immediacy.

Blind to Immediacy: Can't See the Coal-Burning Power Plant for the Manatees

Our first case study emanates from Carr and Milstein's (2021) research on ways people use commercial social media, specifically online review sites such as Google Maps, Yelp, and Tripadvisor, to make sense of human ecological relations. The case is an incongruous wildlife tourism site in North America, the coal-burning Tampa Electric Company's Manatee Viewing Center, where people view threatened Florida manatees, who are present because they must depend upon a fossil-fueled power plant's hot water effluent channel to survive winters. The effluent channel is officially protected as a federal and state marine mammal sanctuary – a sanctuary required directly because of power plant-driven and supported unsustainable human development that destroyed essential warm-spring manatee winter habitat.

Visitors to the site may have a chance of seeing manatees but can't avoid seeing (and smelling) an immense fossil-fuel power plant towering immediately in front of their eyes. So, it is particularly striking for such an ironic and discordant site that the vast majority of visitor online reviews (92.5% of 8,100 reviews) never mention the power plant. Further, of the 7.5% of reviewers who note the plant, nearly all mention it favorably (e.g., the power plant is the savior of the manatees), and none mention the anthropogenic causes for manatee survival dependency on the power plant. While visitors experience visceral immediacy in this site, the collective mediatized ecological blindness they construct as media produsers draws attention to the prevalence and power of dominant anthropocentric ecocultural identity, even among those drawn to wildlife reserves as tourism destinations.

While a fossil-fuel-industry–run wildlife sanctuary and viewing center may not be a site where anthropocentric identities will likely transform to ecocentric, the willful ecological blindness at the heart of visitor online reviews exemplifies a broader tendency. Indeed, in this case, we see produser propensity to hegemonically reproduce anthropocentric spaces of *ecological invisibility,* obscuring humanity's ecological embeddedness and impact. Such anthropocentric identity production work is perhaps especially pronounced when confronted with jarring places and events in which the reigning binary between human and "nature" spectacularly collapses and one's embodied self seems to remain unthreatened (Carr & Milstein, 2018, 2021).

Beyond industry framing, however, willful collective ecological blindness reproduced by visitor reviews may serve a profound ontological need to protect anthropocentric identities and the associated catastrophic status quo. Carr and Milstein (2021) posit the act of ecocentrically identifying one's own implication in and reliance upon ecologically destructive (in this case, fossil fuel) sites would demand a fundamental reevaluation of the very bases of anthropocentric identity, including lifeway choices in housing, consumption, transportation, career, and politics. Consciously or not, it's far easier to reproduce the status quo than it is to face such an ontological crisis. This first case exhibits how everyday people – who voluntarily and publicly take on media produser roles – overwhelmingly tend to reproduce anthropocentric identities, reinforcing inattentiveness to their connections with and damage to shared irreplaceable ecosystems (Carr & Milstein, 2018). Such mediatized hegemonic work is fundamental to making anthropogenic ecological destruction unremarkable and, therefore, unfixable.

Seeking Immediacy through Mediatized Empathy: My Octopus Teacher

The 2020 documentary *My Octopus Teacher* tells an intricate story of one human and one wild octopus. Producer and narrator Craig Foster documents his year-long odyssey of daily meeting with an octopus in the cold-water kelp forests of South Africa's False Bay. These meetings provide sanctuary from Foster's own overwork-induced near-mental breakdown. Foster also seeks the intimate environmental knowing he observed in trackers among the San bushmen of the Kalahari Desert, with whom he made a documentary years earlier. He seeks connection and immediacy as an antidote to his own mental distress, which is a product of the neoliberal project and, more broadly, of modernity.

Foster chronicles the octopus's life and the gradual formation of an inter-species bond. In the process, the filmmaker also documents his own developing empathy for the whole marine environment, and indeed with "nature" at large, including humanity. He narrates:

> I hadn't been a person that was overly sentimental towards animals before. I realised I was changing. My relationship with humans was changing. What she taught me was to feel that you are part of this place, not a visitor – and that's a huge difference.

Such nature-immersion as illustrated in *My Octopus Teacher* centers the importance of immediacy in shaping the media-maker's ecocentric ecocultural identity. In the film, strategic, empathetic anthropomorphism (Arnold et al., 2021), brought onto the screen and into our living rooms, also affords the perception of oceanic immediacy for the documentary's viewers. This Oscar-winning and much-viewed film likewise has had widespread influence on viewers' own ecocultural identities. On Google Reviews of the film (as with reviews above, another mediatized sphere for production of ecocultural identity), reviewers are effusive about how the film touched them. Many describe being brought to tears, describing the documentary as "profoundly moving" and "spellbinding and inspirational." Indicating ecocentric manifestations in their own ecocultural positionalities, viewers write the film "connects to that part you recognize in yourself that you thought you had lost," shows that "our salvation … may lie in making deep and nurturing connections with the astonishing natural world around us," and reminds us that "we are ultimately, all connected."

In this case, we can see how mediatized transformations of ecocultural identity are iterative processes that may have the potential to reach beyond the screen and how media products can profoundly evoke empathy, change attitudes – even touch people's hearts. *My Octopus Teacher* is exemplar of ecomedia that has moved from the margin to the mainstream, becoming an environmental communication "blockbuster" and, thereby, an influential force for shaping viewers' potentially biocentric (all life-centered) and ecocentric ecocultural selves.

Living Immediacy: Indigenous Community Media and the More-Than-Human World

As we have seen with the first two cases, media can be used to reinforce the anthropocentric (and ecologically blind) status quo or to raise or amplify awareness of habitats and other species with whom people interact and dwell, fostering more ecocentric (and biocentric) forms of ecocultural identity. Across Indigenous media narratives, shifting gaze to the more-than-human world is common (e.g., Rodríguez, 2011, see ch. 3; Magallanes-Blanco, 2015; Pereira & Chagas, 2019). The symbolic and material realities outside and beyond the screen are decanted through Indigenous cosmologies to foreground a world that exceeds and contains humanity's existence. Thus, the production of Indigenous media content is central to amplifying embodied ecocentric knowledges and elevating "submerged perspectives that challenge obliteration" (Gómez-Barris, 2017, p. 12). The principles of interculturality, territoriality, and communitarianism frame Indigenous media (Krohling et al., 2019), which further challenge the distinction between human and nonhuman (Gómez, 2017), foreground relationality with territory (Martínez, 2019; Castro-Sotomayor, 2020a), and embrace human and nonhuman actors (Gudynas, 2011).

These three principles guide the narratives found in the four radio stations of the Awá, binational Indigenous peoples living at the border between Ecuador and Colombia: Radio Ampara Su from Ecuador, and Radio Camawari, Radio La Voz de los Awá, and Radio Ñampi Telembi from Colombia.[2] Understanding Indigenous media demands recognizing the cosmopolitics (De la Cadena, 2015) implicated in the production of media content. For instance, Radio Ampara Su – which in the Awá's native language, Awapit, means "four worlds," in reference to Awá's cosmology of creation – seeks "to promote social inclusion and cohesion, peaceful coexistence and a culture of peace, eradicating all forms of discrimination" (Nastacuaz, 2019).

In Awá media production, regenerative ecocultural identities emanate from embodied forms of sense-making and earthly co-existence. Gabriel Dorado, a radio producer of Radio La Voz de los Awá, states the programs capture "the practice of ancestral medicine, and the return to our own nutrition and care for our territory through our community guardians" (Cultural Survival, 2021).

The radio station also amplifies how multinational mining companies threaten the more-than-human territory's health and emotions:

> In the Pital gorge there is a very tall waterfall. A long time ago, it bellowed very hard. It was like a whistle. It bellowed hard, so the elders named it La Quebrada del Pital (the whistle gorge). But not anymore. Now he [*the waterfall*] no longer bellows like before. Now he's a bit quiet.
> (Colectivo de Comunicaciones Camawari y Corporación Chacana, 2016)

Extractivist activities make "the mountain mad" (ibid.) as they impact the Awá sense of immediacy and conviability with their territory's animate world. Relations to the territory are central to the shifting and recovery of Awá restorative ecocultural identities, which know "Nature as the locus of thought and consciousness" (Castro-Sotomayor, 2020b, p. 67). Awá media production, therefore, becomes central to their Indigeneity, supporting long-term endurance and survival and fostering alternative forms of activism that transcend geographical borders.

Reclaiming Immediacy through Emancipatory Catastrophism: Transforming Identity in Chile

As the gravity and far-reaching effects of the global environmental crisis have become clear – with "sacrificial zones" permanently impaired by resource extraction – people have increasingly mobilized, using their power as media prosumers and produsers and their bodies in the streets, to express their outrage. Beck (2015) has written of "emancipatory catastrophism" as the hidden liberatory possibilities that derive from the "bads" of modernization. Such "bads" (like the climate crisis) can result in "anthropological shocks" (p. 79), which can provide opportunities to transform ways of seeing the world and change politics. In particular, re-politicization through mediatized environmental protest can ultimately lead to "social catharsis" and improved environmental and social justice. As part of such re-politicization, activists – running the gamut from the media-ready spectacle of Extinction Rebellion to the righteously outraged students of School Strike 4 Climate – are reclaiming the visceral immediacy of protest against environmental injustice. Environmental concern has also become a point of confluence for outrage about social injustice, given the fundamental links between inequality and environmental degradation.

In this section, we turn to our final micro case study, that of an 11-year environmental conflict in Chile, in which a social movement and a transnational hydroelectric megaproject developer engaged in extended mediatized conflict. This case study focuses on traditional and social media, as well as protest and advertising material to trace mediatized discourse as the conflict evolved (Mocatta, 2020). Within this conflict, ecocultural identity formation was shaped from outrage over environmental harm and, sustained through symbolic use of media, transformed into outrage about social inequality. The now-defunct HidroAysén sought to build five dams on two of Chilean Patagonia's last wild rivers, and a 2,300 km power line to bring the power of glacier meltwater to Chile's dry north. The project was resisted by "Patagonia sin Represas" (Patagonia without Dams), a loose coalition of more than 30 organizations, which organized sustained mediatized protests ranging from alternative and radical media (Rodríguez et al., 2014) to traditional media to social networks. Although HidroAysén met its demise in 2018, Patagonia sin Represas' skillful conflation in its strategic message of outrage over environmental harm together with outrage over social injustice arguably fed into the large-scale mobilizations protesting inequality in Chile during 2020, leading to calls for a new, more democratic, constitution.

Mediatized environmental conflict can spill over into broader social conflicts, especially if social movements appropriately harness mediatized "communication power" (Castells, 2007). In such conflicts, we see the capacity of modernity's "bads" to galvanize people for the environment, for emancipation, and for greater social fairness. We might describe this kind of conflict as *emancipatory ecocultural identity transformation* – that is, an opportunity for identities to centrally incorporate ecocentric social and environmental justice in the face of collective threat.

Will the Ecocultural Identity Revolution Be Televised?

The four international micro case studies illustrated above demonstrate the centrality of a wide range of media to both crystallizing and shifting ecocultural identities in these times. The cases exhibit ways mediated identities reflect and produce a spectrum of identifications, ranging from the willful ignoring of one's ecological embeddedness, to active recovering of interspecies kinship, to centering enduring convivial more-than-human relations, and to politicizing identities of environmental and social fairness and justice.

In addition to illustrating the ecocultural identity reproductive and transformative functions of media, especially the impact of produsage (Bruns, 2009) in the networked public sphere (Castells, 2008), we also draw attention to elements of immediacy at play in these mediated sites. From visitors who turn a mediated blind eye to their immediate experiences with place to a documentary maker who turns his camera *toward* place to bring immediacy back to himself and global audiences, and from Indigenous media makers who put immediacy first by grounding in territoriality to awakened activists who find their power in aligning with place through mediated channels, we see ways media can reflect and be a platform for distanced, shifting, integrated, or emplaced ecocultural identities. We also see ways the more-than-human world exerts agency and senses of immediacy and interconnection, if one's ecocultural identity is open to listening – from an octopus extending a tentacled arm to waterfalls no longer bellowing.

The urgency of these times – the present "decisive decade," in which we must change the ways we dominantly ecoculturally identify and behave as a species to avert escalating anthropogenic environmental disaster (McGrath, 2021) – reintroduces immediacy to many who have retreated to largely technologically mediated spheres. Certainly the mediasphere can be a space to broadcast more-than-human reality more widely and within which to raise senses of immediacy with places we live or those places and species more distant or all-encompassing. However, we also see in the first case, media can be a space in which blindness to more-than-human interconnection can be hegemonically reinforced so anthropogenic destruction and industry's and people's unsustainable actions remain unimplicated and anthropocentric identities unphased.

It's useful to dig deeper into the layers of mediation at play in these cases. In the first case, the manatee viewing site is mediated by a fossil fuel power company's framing and visitors further reproduce everyday hegemonic willful ecological blindness at the heart of anthropocentric identities in their online reviews. In contrast, in the second two cases, immediacy takes precedence and is broadcast through film documentary and radio, producing shifts toward, or representations of, enduring, ecocentric identities. In the final case, in part by linking social and environmental injustice, activists engage media to foster a fertile space for transformative ecocultural identity – and structural political change – to emerge.

When it comes to ecocultural identity, the lens of *identity crisis* may be especially useful to observe and understand these times. Carr and Milstein (2021) argue that, for the majority of Western/ized and/or industrial/ized people, recognizing one's own implication in and reliance upon destructive and extractive infrastructure, such as coal-burning power plants or one's own distressing overwork as a product of the neoliberal project, brings on ontological crisis. Such recognition, on the one hand, can shake the foundations of dominant anthropocentric identities that most Western/ized and/or industrial/ized people have been raised to adhere to and rarely question. On the other hand, reproducing mediatized anthropocentrism – for instance, via constructing ecological blindness – helps willfully keep dominant anthropocentric identity intact, however tenuously.

While the ecocultural identity revolution may not be televised through media in which anthropocentric narratives dominate, we do see potential for disruption. For instance, purposeful posting of ecocentric visitor reviews on Google Maps and Tripadvisor of sites of anthropogenic disruption could produse a counter-discourse, provoke ecocultural questioning, and help manifest very different ways of identifying and being. In the latter three micro cases presented here, productions of ecocentric identity come to the fore.

Such instances of mass mediating ecocultural identity toward inter-species, ecocentric, and transformative exhibit powerful potential beyond their locational spheres. We saw this, for example, in global mass media coverage of Australia's 2019–2020 catastrophic "climate fires" resulting in transnational (and deeply galvanizing) ecocentric concern and care. While, on the ground, the embodied and visceral loss immediacy of the climate fires sparked ecocultural identity shifts that can be credited – along with new young voters who overwhelmingly voted green – for ushering in a more climate-friendly government in Australia's federal election that followed. As we presume and produce diverse media in these times and encounter palpable anthropogenic disruption – ranging from global pandemics (Tollefson, 2020) to deadly extremes of the climate emergency – ecocultural identities will likely shift quickly and, in some cases, collectively. This chapter has begun the task of illustrating media hurdles and pathways for such shifts toward healing, restoring, and empathetic ways of knowing and being.

Notes

1 For the purposes of this chapter, we use anthropocentric and ecocentric as overarching terms for two ends of a spectrum of ecocultural identities. This shorthand, however, can risk oversimplifying the wide range of enduring, evolving, and emerging ecocultural identities, including dualistic vs. mutualistic (see Debelo et al., 2017; Alhinai & Milstein, 2019), egocentric vs. relational, and technocentric vs. biocentric, as well as the intersectionality (Parks, 2020; Thomas, 2020) and dynamism and diversity of ecocultural identities (Banham, 2020; Bendixsen et al., 2020; Bloomfield, 2020; Carlin, 2020; Carr & Milstein, 2020; Dahake, 2020; Freeman, 2020; Hallgren et al., 2020; Karikari et al., 2020; Méndez Cota, 2020; Milstein, 2020; Quick & Spartz, 2020; Raynes & Mix, 2020; Seraphin, 2020; Stibbe, 2020; Tarin et al. 2020; Tuitjer, 2020).
2 Radio Ampara Su is run by Federación Centros Awá del Ecuador; Ecuadorian Federation of Awá Centers; Radio Camawari belongs to the Cabildo Mayor Awá de Ricaurte (Main Council Awá of Ricaurte); Radio La Voz de los Awá is run by Unidad Indígena del Pueblo Awá; Indigenous Unit of Awá People; and Radio Ñampi Telembi is run by Asociación de Cabildos Indígenas del Pueblo Awá del Putumayo; Association of Indigenous Councils of the Awá People of the Putumayo.

Further Reading

Carr, J. & Milstein, T. (2021). "See nothing but beauty": The shared work of making anthropogenic destruction invisible to the human eye. *Geoforum.* 122 (June), 183–92. https://doi.org/10.1016/j.geoforum.2021.04.013
Castro-Sotomayor, J. (2020). Ecocultural identities in intercultural encounters. In Tema Milstein and José Castro-Sotomayor (Eds.), *Routledge Handbook of Ecocultural Identity*, pp. 66–85. London: Routledge.
Milstein, T. (2020). Ecocultural identity boundary patrol and transgression. In Tema Milstein and José Castro-Sotomayor (Eds.), *Routledge Handbook of Ecocultural Identity*, pp. 26–52. London & New York: Routledge. https://doi.org/10.4324/9781351068840-2

Milstein, T., & Castro-Sotomayor, J. (Eds.) (2020). *Routledge Handbook of Ecocultural Identity.* London: Routledge. https://doi.org/10.4324/9781351068840

Mocatta, G. (2020). When water is energy: Tracing mediatized discourse in Chile's mega-hydro debate. In Schmitt, C., Thomas, C. and Castor, T. (Eds.), *Water, Rhetoric, and Social Justice: A Critical Confluence.* Lanham, MD: Lexington books.

References

Abram, D. with Milstein, T., & Castro-Sotomayor, J. (2020). Interbreathing ecocultural identity in the Humilocene. In Tema Milstein and José Castro-Sotomayor (Eds.), *Routledge Handbook of Ecocultural Identity*, pp. 5–25. London: Routledge. https://doi.org/10.4324/9781351068840

Alhinai, M., & Milstein, T. (2019). From kin to commodity: Ecocultural relations in transition in Oman. *Local Environment*, 24 (12), 1078–96. https://doi.org/10.1080/13549839.2019.1672635

Arnold, C., Atchison, J., & McKnight, A. (2021). Reciprocal relationships with trees: Rekindling Indigenous wellbeing and identity through the Yuin ontology of oneness. *Australian Geographer*, 52 (2), 131–47.

Banham, R. (2020). Empathetic ecocultural positionality and hte forest other in Tasmanian forestry conflicts. In Tema Milstein and José Castro-Sotomayor (Eds.), *Routledge Handbook of Ecocultural Identity*, pp. 5–25. London: Routledge.

Beck, U. (2015). Emancipatory catastrophism: What does it mean to climate change and risk society?. *Current Sociology*, 63(1), pp. 75-88.

Bendixsen, C. G., Durbin, T. J., & Hanschu, J. (2020). 'Progressive ranching' and wrangling the wind as ecocultural identity maintenance in the Anthropocene. In Tema Milstein and José Castro-Sotomayor (Eds.), *Routledge Handbook of Ecocultural Identity*, pp. 5–25. London: Routledge.

Bloomfield, E. F. (2020). The rewording of evangelical Christian ecocultural identity in the Creation Care movement. In Tema Milstein and José Castro-Sotomayor (Eds.), *Routledge Handbook of Ecocultural Identity*, pp. 5–25. London: Routledge.

Breves. P. & Greussing, E. (2022). Virtual and Augmented reality in environmental communication. In Takahashi, B., Metag, J. and Thaker, J. (Eds.) *The Handbook of International Trends in Environmental Communication*, pp. 449–65. New York: Routledge.

Bruns, Axel (2006) Towards Produsage: Futures for User-Led Content Production. In Charles Ess, Sudweeks, F, and Hrachovec, H (Eds.) *Proceeding of the 5th International Conference on Cultural Attitudes towards Technology and Communication.* School of Information Technology, Australia, pp. 275–284.

Bruns, Axel (2009) From Prosumer to Produser: Understanding User-Led Content Creation. In Transforming Audiences 2009, 2009-09-03 – 2009-09-04.

Büscher, B. (2016). Nature 2.0: Exploring and theorizing the links between new media and nature conservation. *New Media & Society*, 18 (5), 726–43.

Büscher, B. (2021). *The Truth about Nature: Environmentalism in the Era of Post-Truth Politics and Platform Capitalism.* Oakland: University of California Press.

Carlin, C. (2020). Navigating ecocultural Indigenous identity affinity and appropriation. In Tema Milstein and José Castro-Sotomayor (Eds.), *Routledge Handbook of Ecocultural Identity*, pp. 5–25. London: Routledge.

Carr, J., & Milstein, T. (2018). Keep burning coal or the manatee gets it: Rendering the carbon economy invisible through endangered species protection. *Antipode: A Radical Journal of Geography*, 50 (1), 82–100. https://doi.org/10.1111/anti.12355

Carr, J., & Milstein, T. (2020). Political identity as ecocultural survival strategy. In Tema Milstein and José Castro-Sotomayor (Eds.), *Routledge Handbook of Ecocultural Identity*, pp. 5–25. London: Routledge.

Carr, J., & Milstein, T. (2021). "See nothing but beauty": The shared work of making anthropogenic destruction invisible to the human eye. *Geoforum* 122 (June), 183–92. https://doi.org/10.1016/j.geoforum.2021.04.013

Castells, M. (2007). Communication, power and counter-power in the network society. *International Journal of Communication*, 1 (1), 29.

Castells, M. (2008). The new public sphere: Global civil society, communication networks, and global governance. *The Annals of the American Academy of Political and Social Science*, 616 (1), 78–93.

Castells, M. (2011). *The Rise of the Network Society* (Vol. 12). Chichester: John Wiley & Sons.

Castro-Sotomayor, J. (2020a). Territorialidad as environmental communication. Special issue "Decolonizing Communication Studies: A view from the Global South". *Annals of the International Communication Association*, 1 (44), 50–66. https://doi.org/10.1080/23808985.2019.1647443

Castro-Sotomayor, J. (2020b). Ecocultural identities in intercultural encounters. In Tema Milstein and José Castro-Sotomayor (Eds.), *Routledge Handbook of Ecocultural Identity*, pp. 66–85. London: Routledge.
Colectivo de Comunicaciones Camawari y Corporación Chacana (2016). La Voz del Mundo Awá. Radio Programs.
Cottle, S. (2006). *Mediatized Conflict: Understanding Media and Conflicts in the Contemporary World*. McGraw-Hill Education.
Crawford, M. R., Holder, M. D., & O'Connor, B. P. (2017). Using mobile technology to engage children with nature. *Environment and Behavior*, 49 (9), 959–84. https://doi.org/10.1177/0013916516673870
Cultural Survival (2021). Weaving Community Communication of the Great Awá Family in Ecuador and Colombia. Retrieved from. https://www.culturalsurvival.org/news/weaving-community-communication-great-awa-family-ecuador-and-colombia
Dahake, S. (2020). The making of fluid ecocultural identities in urban India. In Tema Milstein and José Castro-Sotomayor (Eds.), *Routledge Handbook of Ecocultural Identity*, pp. 5–25. London: Routledge.
Debelo, A. R., Legesse, A., Milstein, T., & Oda, O. (2017). "Tree is life:" The rising of dualism and declining of mutualism among the Gedeo of southern Ethiopia. *Frontiers in Communication: Science and Environmental Communication*, 2 (7). https://doi.org/10.3389/fcomm.2017.00007
De la Cadena, M. (2015). *Earth beings: Ecologies of Practices across Andean Worlds*. Durham, NC: Duke University Press.
Ducarme, F., Luque, G. M., & Courchamp, F. (2013). What are "charismatic species" for conservation biologists? *BioSciences Master Reviews*, 1 (July), 1–8.
Eriksen, T. H. (2001). *Tyranny of the Moment: Fast and Slow Time in the Information Age*. London: Pluto Press.
Ferkiss, V. C. (1993). *Nature, Technology, and Society: Cultural Roots of the Current Environmental Crisis*. New York: New York University Press.
Fletcher, R. (2017). Gaming conservation: Nature 2.0 confronts nature-deficit disorder. *Geoforum*, 79, 153–62. https://doi.org/10.1016/j.geoforum.2016.02.009
Freeman, C. P. (2020). Perceiving ecocultural identities as human animal earthlings. In T. Milstein and J. Castro-Sotomayor (Eds.), *Routledge Handbook of Ecocultural Identity*, pp. 26–52. London & New York: Routledge. https://doi.org/10.4324/9781351068840-2
Gómez, J. (2017). Aproximaciones semióticas a la interculturalidad. In Jorge Gómez (Ed.), *Repensar la Interculturalidad*, pp. 109–157. Guayaquil: Artes Ediciones.
Gómez-Barris, M. (2017). *The Extractive Zone: Social Ecologies and Decolonial Perspectives*. Durham: Duke University Press.
Greenwood, A., & Gatersleben, B. (2016). Let's go outside! Environmental restoration amongst adolescents and the impact of friends and phones. *Journal of Environmental Psychology*, 48, 131–139. https://doi.org/10.1016/j.jenvp.2016.09.007
Gudynas, E. (2011). Buen Vivir: Today's Tomorrow. *Development*, 4 (54), 441–447.
Hallgren, L., Ljunggren Bergeå, H., & Nordström Källström, H. (2020). Conservation hero and climate villain binary identities of Swedish farmers. In Tema Milstein and José Castro-Sotomayor (Eds.), *Routledge Handbook of Ecocultural Identity*, pp. 5–25. London: Routledge.
Hepp, A., (2019). *Deep Mediatization*. London & New York: Routledge.
Holbert, R. L., Kwak, N., & Shah, D. V. (2003) Environmental concern, patterns of television viewing, and pro-environmental behaviors: Integrating models of media consumption and effects. *Journal of Broadcasting & Electronic Media*, 47, 177–96.
Hutchins, B., & Lester, L., (2015). Theorizing the enactment of mediatized environmental conflict. *International Communication Gazette*, 77 (4), 337–58. https://doi.org/10.1177/1748048514568765
Karikari, E., Castro-Sotomayor, J., & Asante, G. (2020). Illegal mining, identity, and the politics of ecocultural voice in Ghana. In Tema Milstein and José Castro-Sotomayor (Eds.), *Routledge Handbook of Ecocultural Identity*, pp. 5–25. London: Routledge.
Krohling, C., Chaparro, M., & Torrico, E. (2019). Comunicación comunitaria, políticas y ciudadanía. *Chasqui*, 140, 33–42.
Kuntsman, A., & Rattle, I. (2019). Towards a paradigmatic shift in sustainability studies: A systematic review of peer reviewed literature and future agenda setting to consider environmental (un)sustainability of digital communication. *Environmental Communication*, 13 (5), 567–81, https://doi.org/10.1080/17524032.2019.1596144

Levi, D., & Kocher, S. (1999). Virtual nature: The future effects of information technology on our relationship to nature. *Environment and Behavior*, 31 (2), 203–26.

Magallanes-Blanco, C. (2015). Talking About our mother: Indigenous videos on nature and the environment. *Communication, Culture & Critique*, I (2), 199–216. https://doi.org/10.1111/cccr.12084

Martínez, G. (2019). La radio comunitaria indígena: alternativa para la descolonización, la interculturalidad y la construcción del bien común a través del sonido emanado del territorio. *Chasqui*, 140, 31–46.

McGrath, M. (2021, April 22). Biden: This will be "decisive decade" for tackling climate change. *BBC News*. https://www.bbc.com/news/science-environment-56837927

Méndez Cota, G. (2020). A queer ecological reading of ecocultural identity in contemporary Mexico. In Tema Milstein and José Castro-Sotomayor (Eds.), *Routledge Handbook of Ecocultural Identity*, pp. 5–25. London: Routledge.

Milstein, T. (2009). 'Somethin' tells me it's all happening at the zoo:' Discourse, power, and conservationism. *Environmental Communication: A Journal of Nature and Culture*, 3 (1), 25–48. https://doi.org/10.1080/17524030802674174

Milstein, T. (2020). Ecocultural identity boundary patrol and transgression. In Tema Milstein and José Castro-Sotomayor (Eds.), *Routledge Handbook of Ecocultural Identity*, pp. 26–52. London & New York: Routledge. https://doi.org/10.4324/9781351068840-2

Milstein, T., & Castro-Sotomayor, J. (Eds.) (2020). *Routledge Handbook of Ecocultural Identity*. London: Routledge. https://doi.org/10.4324/9781351068840

Milstein, T., Thomas, M., & Hoffmann, J. (2019). Dams and flows: Immersing in Western meaning systems in search of ecocultural reflexivity. *Environmental Communication*, 13 (1), 104–17.

Mocatta, G. (2020). When water is energy: Tracing mediatized discourse in Chile's mega-hydro debate. In Schmitt, C., Thomas, C. and Castor, T. (Eds.), *Water, Rhetoric, and Social Justice: A Critical Confluence*, pp. 43–62. Lanham, MD: Lexington books.

Nastacuaz, O. (2019). Radio Ampara Su: La Voz del Pueblo Awá. Retrieved from https://www.culturalsurvival.org/news/radio-ampara-su-la-voz-del-pueblo-awa-de-ecuador

Nielsen, H. (2020). Identifying with Antarctica in the ecocultural imaginary. In Tema Milstein and José Castro-Sotomayor (Eds.), *Routledge Handbook of Ecocultural Identity*, pp. 225–39. London: Routledge. https://doi.org/10.4324/9781351068840

Parks, M. (2020). Critical ecocultural intersectionality. In T. Milstein and J. Castro-Sotomayor (Eds.), *Routledge Handbook of Ecocultural Identity*, pp. 26–52. London & New York: Routledge. https://doi.org/10.4324/9781351068840-2

Parra, D. (2015). Latin American struggles| alternative media in Latin American grassroots integration: Building networks and new agendas. *International Journal of Communication*, 9, 21, 3680–3701.

Pereira, L., & Chagas, C. (2019). Comunicação cidadã na Amazônia brasileira: em defesa das atingidas e dos atingidos pela Vale S.A. *Chasqui Revista Latinoamericana de Comunicación*, 140, 174–194.

Quick, J., & Spartz, J. T. (2020). Competing models of ecocultural belonging in highland Ecuador. In Tema Milstein and José Castro-Sotomayor (Eds.), *Routledge Handbook of Ecocultural Identity*, pp. 5–25. London: Routledge.

Raynes, D. & Mix, T. (2020). Induced seismicity, quotidian disruption, and challenges to extractivist ecocultural identity. In Tema Milstein and José Castro-Sotomayor (Eds.), *Routledge Handbook of Ecocultural Identity*, pp. 293–310. London: Routledge. https://doi.org/10.4324/9781351068840

Rodríguez, C. (2011). *Citizens' Media Against Armed Conflict Disrupting Violence in Colombia*. Minneapolis: University of Minnesota Press.

Rodríguez, C., Ferron, B. and Shamas, K. (2014) Four challenges in the field of alternative, radical and citizens' media research. *Media, Culture & Society*, 36 (2), 150–66.

Seraphin, B. (2020). Wildtending, settler colonialism, and ecocultural identities in environmental futures. In Tema Milstein and José Castro-Sotomayor (Eds.), *Routledge Handbook of Ecocultural Identity*, pp. 5–25. London: Routledge.

Stibbe, A. (2020). Toward a grammar of ecocultural identity. In Tema Milstein and José Castro-Sotomayor (Eds.), *Routledge Handbook of Ecocultural Identity*, pp. 5–25. London: Routledge

Stinson, J. (2017). Re-creating Wilderness 2.0: Or getting back to work in a virtual nature. *Geoforum*, 79, 174–87. https://doi.org/10.1016/j.geoforum.2016.09.002

Tarin, C. A., Upton, S. D., & Sowards, S. K. (2020). Borderland ecocultural identities. In Tema Milstein and José Castro-Sotomayor (Eds.), *Routledge Handbook of Ecocultural Identity*, pp. 5–25. London: Routledge.

Thomas, M. O. (2020). Intersectional ecocultural identities in family stories. In Tema Milstein and José Castro-Sotomayor (Eds.), *Routledge Handbook of Ecocultural Identity*, pp. 26–52. London & New York: Routledge. https://doi.org/10.4324/9781351068840-2

Toffler, A. (1990). *Powershift: Knowledge, Wealth, and Violence at the Edge of the 21st Century*. New York: Bantam.

Tollefson, J. (2020). Why deforestation and extinctions make pandemics more likely. *Nature*, 584 (7820), 175–76. https://doi.org/10.1038/d41586-020-02341-1

Tuitjer, L. (2020). Scapegoating identities in the Anthropocene. In Tema Milstein and José Castro-Sotomayor (Eds.), *Routledge Handbook of Ecocultural Identity*, pp. 5–25. London: Routledge.

Turkle, S. (2015). *Reclaiming Conversation: The Power of Talk in a Digital Age*. New York: Penguin Press, 2015.

van Dijk, J. (1999). *The Network Society*. London: Sage.

25
ECO-TERRITORIAL MEDIA PRACTICES
Defending Bodies, Territories, and Life Itself in Latin America

Diana Coryat

Introduction: Eco-Territorial Media Cultures and Their Relevance to the Ecomedia Field

While the field of ecomedia studies continues to expand, the scholars, journals, conferences, and related field-building activities have largely taken root in the Global North. Yet, the emergent eco-territorial media cultures and practices in Latin America that could contribute to this field of study exist mostly outside of its purview. This chapter attends to this gap by analyzing these multifaceted and dynamic processes. The media cultures and practices in defense of bodies, territories, and life itself are a constitutive part of a broad range of efforts, mostly led by indigenous and Afro-descendent communities and social movements, to resist the growing onslaught of extractive projects that represent grave threats to their ancestral lands. Increasingly, these socio-environmental struggles are conceptualized as the defense of life and territory. It would be difficult to overstate the dramatic rise in scale and scope of extractive activities in Latin America and the terrible consequences. According to Eduardo Gudynas (2021, 1), one of the leading scholars that study this issue, "the incidence of extractivisms has multiplied, as reflected in a huge volume of studies, reports and analyses, both scholarly and from within civil society, that it has generated."

Relatedly, the Argentinian sociologist Maristella Svampa (2019) has called the present conjuncture, with its heterogenous mixings of indigenous, communitarian, ecologist, and anti-patriarchal ethos and movements, the "eco-territorial turn." While this environmentalization of social struggles varies across contexts, there is a commonly held language and set of values they share, including a rejection of hegemonic notions and practices of extractive capitalism and development, and attention to the intertwined relations of humans and other-than-human beings. Rather, they uphold the rights of Nature and look toward postdevelopment and post-extractive horizons, which include the need to cultivate more sustainable, equitable forms of living. Hence, a deeper engagement with these media practices can enrich ecomedia studies by foregrounding the materiality of all life, including Nature as a subject of rights, that is expressed in eco-territorial audiovisual work that focuses on situated lived experiences, images, songs, sounds of the forest, and more. This type of "ecological communication" (Cubitt, 2017, 80) rises above "the abstraction of indigenous knowledge," "environments," and "workers" that Sean Cubitt critiques as being part of the "very root of Western alienation from populations and lands" (Cubitt, 2017, 152–53). At the same time, the work of ecomedia scholars could contribute to anti-extractive media collectives through their deep reflection on the materiality of media and its imbrication with extractive practices.

While understudied, I propose that the contributions of the audiovisual dimension of the eco-territorial turn, that is, collectives that create media to help defend territories, bodies, and life itself from extractive projects, are essential to bringing much-needed attention to socio-environmental conflicts. This chapter conceptualizes and analyzes the characteristics of eco-territorial media cultures and practices and discusses some of the key media-makers, their projects, and the vital role they are playing in the region. While the practices and networks are transnational, the essay focuses on Ecuador as a vibrant site of audiovisual defense, highlighting instances of collaboration that occur at the intersection of social movements and media activism. I conclude the chapter by reflecting on their contributions to the field of ecomedia and indicate directions for further research. My work in this area is mainly based on media practice and ethnography from a committed practitioner-scholar stance.

Historical and Conceptual Notes

Since at least the 1980s, Latin American media-makers, anthropologists, filmmakers, journalists, and others have worked with indigenous and other social movements to produce media and films on an array of critical issues. Media made by (and not just about) indigenous peoples (*video indigena*) emerged in the 1980s and 1990s (Salazar, 2022). Since then, indigenous media production has continued to expand and diversify with the increasing accessibility of digital production tools; the professionalization of indigenous filmmakers; a growing demand for diverse audiovisual content; a growing interest by film boards and film financing initiatives; and the proliferation of festivals and streaming platforms that help make the work visible. With respect to audiovisual defense of territory, indigenous communities that have long trajectories of defending their territories have been some of the first to establish their own media projects, including the Mapuche (Argentina and Chile), the Nasa (Norte de Cauca, Colombia), the Kichwa Sarayaku (Amazonía, Ecuador), and the Zapatistas (Mexico). In the second decade of the twenty-first century, many projects sprung up in response to the extractive industries that have presented immediate threats to the lives, livelihoods, and territories of countless communities. Griselda Sanchez, a community media activist from Oaxaca, Mexico who has worked with communities facing territorial dispossession for over two decades, analyzes the shift in communicational strategy:

> For a long time, among the demands [of the indigenous movement] were the defense of collective, agrarian, and political rights, autonomy, territory, self-determination, the democratization of media, etc. But in the last several years, communication has occupied a very specific place on the agenda. Now it is no longer about democratizing the existing media or fighting for access to our own media, but rather how to organize against the advance of neoliberalism and its extractivist model. Community media is positioned as a political-communicational practice. (29) ... the common denominator is the premise that what is at stake is the reproduction of indigenous *pueblos*, and above all, life itself.
> (Sanchez, 2018, 29).

Relatedly, the notion of territory became a working political concept in the early 1990s at the time of large mobilizations by indigenous, Afro-descendent, and peasant communities in Bolivia, Ecuador, Colombia, and Brazil (Escobar, 2016). Social movement-led dialogues with scholars and activists constituted some of the most advanced theoretical-political debates of the time about nature and territorial rights. These dialogues and related advocacy led to several important international documents, most notably the UN Declaration of the Rights of Indigenous Peoples (2007), "recognizing other ways of living, appropriation of space and inhabiting the world."

Contemporary movements and ancestral communities consider their territories as sites for the reproduction of life that embody memory, historic struggle, and cultural continuity, among other material and symbolic elements. As such, territorial conflicts are not just material, but rather represent ontological struggles about nature/culture. Here, I am referring to the vast differences between modernist notions of nature and land as a resource for human beings, and indigenous conceptualizations of human and nonhuman inter-being and relationality. On the one hand is the dominant worldview that adheres to a notion of development linked to capitalist modernity and the push to exploit land for profit. On the other hand are ancestral and contemporary worldviews and practices that articulate territory to the reproduction of life. Vilma Almendra (2017), an indigenous (Nasa Misak) scholar and activist from Norte del Cauca, Colombia, succinctly expresses what is at stake. She argues that with the loss of territory comes "…the destruction of spontaneity, of human power to start something new using their own resources, something that cannot be explained as reactions to a context and a few events" (Almendra, 2017, 33). Almendra draws a sharp distinction between the Nasa concept of territory, which includes land, bodies (human and nonhuman), and imaginaries, and the capitalist logics that drive the need to accumulate and occupy ever-increasing amounts of land.

Emergent Eco-Territorial Media Cultures

In the twenty-first century, there is an increasing number of media collectives that explicitly situate their work within communities and social movements that are defending their territories against extractive projects led by governments and corporations. I argue that, taken together, they constitute emergent media cultures that contribute to the eco-territorial turn. They include a diverse array of individuals, groups, practices, and discourses that are activating communicational processes and strategies that make visible socio-environmental conflicts. They make media in a multiplicity of spaces: ancestral territories, communally held land, highly biodiverse areas that are legally protected, as well as urban settlements. Through the production and circulation of this work, they make these struggles known to other anti-extractive social actors, policymakers, the general public, in the media, in urban areas, and across national borders. Within communities, media creation is often part of a larger response to territorial defense, and the need to organize against, resist, intercept, and evict mining, oil drilling, hydroelectric plants, monocultural agriculture, and other extractive activities that are causing grave harm to human and other-than-human bodies, territories, and life itself.

A key characteristic of many collectives and their networked alliances is their intercultural composition across race, class, ethnicity, and geography. They are Afro-descendant, indigenous, and mestizo; they are from popular sectors and the middle class; they are urban, rural, and also live in Amazonian rainforests. Many are students, oftentimes representing the first members of their families to attend university. Many are neither professionally trained nor identify primarily as media-makers. They have acquired digital production tools and have worked together to learn to produce media. Members of collectives are ecologists, geologists, anthropologists, filmmakers, artists, feminists, and LGBTQI activists. Given the rise and effervescence of diverse feminisms in the region, eco-territorial media cultures often feature strong leadership by women who articulate the defense of their bodies as the first territory to defend (Cabnal, 2019; Gago, 2019).

The works created by eco-territorial collectives are not defined by one medium, genre, methodology, or focus. In addition to working in radio and video, many of them incorporate online radio, zines, multimedia blogs, and social media platforms. They produce short- and long-form documentaries, fiction, music videos, and journalistic narratives. Individuals within the collectives are often activists, and as such often incorporate repertoires that are emblematic of the twenty-first–century movements. They are horizontally organized and use a combination of direct democratic practices (assemblies, consensus-building, street protest) and mediated practices. Even those that are professionally trained filmmakers are not interested in reproducing the hierarchies implicit in the film industry. They also utilize artistic expression and performative practices to mobilize postdevelopment imaginaries.

The independent, multilingual, and web-based streaming platform Bombozila (dubbed by the Brazilian founders as the "Netflix of social struggles") provides a window onto the breadth and depth of recently produced work. It features films and web series from 16 countries and autonomous territories in Latin America and the Caribbean created by small producers and community film collectives that, according to the platform, "respond to the political urgency of our struggling and enduring territories." The members of Bombozila, also a collective, form part of several networks across Latin America. Like many media collectives, they also create their own media, produce itinerant audiovisual trainings and residencies, and organize festivals and screenings.

The Convergence of Social Movements and Media Activism in Ecuador

Ecuador is a rich site of convergence for media practitioners that are part of the eco-territorial turn. It has a long history of vibrant social movements related to Afro, indigenous, peasant, student, worker, ecological, feminist, LGBTQI, and communication rights. Given the relatively small size of Ecuador, movement actors have often shared the streets during protests, providing multiple opportunities for them to build relationships across struggles. For example, when Amazonian women have walked to Quito to speak out against extractive practices, and when indigenous groups have marched on the capital during national strikes, local activists have ensured that they obtained food, shelter, clothing, and medical care. Quito is an important intellectual center in the region with two internationally renowned graduate schools that attract students, scholars, activists, and public intellectuals from across Latin America, particularly from nearby Andean nations (Bolivia, Colombia, Peru, Venezuela). Ecuador's 2008 Constitution attracted global attention, as it was the first nation in the world to consider Nature a subject of rights. While such rights have not been respected by the government, the fact that they are inscribed in the constitution marks an important legal "leg" to stand on. In 2013, the rights of Nature once again entered the international spotlight with the emergence of Yasunidos. This new collective took to the streets immediately following then President Rafael Correa's announcement to abandon a popular initiative to "leave the oil in the soil" in the Yasuní, one of the most biodiverse places on the planet, located in the Ecuadorian Amazon. While not a media collective themselves, they were able to catalyze a wide range of mainstream and alternative media, as well as the occupation of public places, to gather support for a referendum on the issue, the results of which are still being disputed in 2022 (Coryat, 2015). Ecuadorian social movement actors and intellectuals like Esperanza Martínez of Acción Ecológica and Alberto Acosta have made significant contributions to the field of political ecology (Porto-Gonzalves, Carlos Walter, and Enrique Leff, 2015).

Working with social movements, several collectives in Ecuador use audiovisual means to defend bodies, territories, and life itself. Each project has evolved over time, with regards to its own professionalization, construction of networks, and films produced. These groups have also collaborated among each other over the years while filming street protests, at audiovisual residencies and film festivals, and when they travel to each other's territories to assist in each other's productions. Collectively, a long-term commitment to audiovisual defense of territory is evident in their work. The following projects provide a glimpse into the varied ways in which media collectives are defending territory. They include filmmakers embedded in their own territories, hybrid urban-rural projects, and collectives that have national and international reach and a role in bringing this field together.

Eriberto Gualinga is an indigenous filmmaker that works with and on behalf of his community, the Kichwa Sarayaku, also known as Pueblo del Mediodia (People of the Midday). This legendary community, known for its fierce resistance to oil drilling, is located deep in the Ecuadorian Amazon, reachable only by aircraft or canoe. I would argue that his *oeuvre* makes visible ontological struggles in distinct ways, depending on whether they are documentaries made for general audiences, or short, more experimental films. I briefly discuss some of them here. One of Gualinga's first documentaries, *Children of the Jaguar* (2012) chronicles the case that the Sarayaku people filed in 2003 with the Inter-American Commission on Human Rights against the Ecuadorian government, which illegally permitted a multinational oil company to prospect for oil. The Sarayaku won this case and have continued to resist subsequent efforts to enter their territory.[1] Another work, *Kawsak Sacha* (2018) chronicles how his community built a "canoe of life" and transported it to Paris during COP 20 to bring attention to their struggles to remain autonomous and free from extractivism. He also directed *Helena from Sarayaku* (2021), which follows 17-year-old Helena Gualinga as she works to protect her community from extractive development. These documentaries all discuss their core philosophy, Kawsak Sacha (Living Forest), which is a relational ontology.[2] While the work is powerfully told by Gualinga and his community, the structure and style of the films is similar to that of conventional documentaries. In addition to these mid- and full-length documentaries, Gualinga has produced several short films. Aesthetically distinct from the longer format documentaries, these short works visually express a relational ontology. For example, in *Los dueños de la selva preocupada/Guardians of the forest are worried* (2012), the images and words of guardians of the forest are made visible and audible in the Kichwa language through the performance of young actors, as they witness a logger seeking to cut down an ancient tree and beg him to stop. Eriberto Gualinga's work is at once that of an auteur that, as he often says, speaks for his community. At the same time, it is highly collaborative, as he regularly works with indigenous and mestizo filmmakers from Ecuador and elsewhere.

Etsa Nantu/Cámera Shuar[3] is an Amazonian-based collaborative project that, since 2013, has made visible the Shuar's efforts to resist large-scale mining projects. It is an urban-Amazonian collaboration; one of the directors is a historic Shuar leader, Domingo Ankuash; the other is a mestiza Ecuadorian filmmaker, Verenice Benítez. Like Eriberto Gualinga's work, the collective utilizes various genres, styles, and aesthetics, with documentaries that are observational, investigative, and archival. The language and songs are mainly in Shuar and include Spanish subtitles. The collective has filmed the uninvited "visits" of Chinese mining company officials (*Visita Inesperada/Unexpected Visit*, 2014), the forced evictions they have endured (*Nankints, La otra historia/Nankints, the other story*, 2019) and have chronicled the assassination of land defenders (*Quién mató a José Tendetza/Who killed José Tendetza*, 2017). Etsa Nantu/Cámera Shuar also makes films about Shuar history, cultural practices, resistance, and stories (*Genealogía de un territorio en disputa/Genealogy of a disputed territory*, 2017). The ancestral story of the spirit Tsunki seeks to express visually the relations between the Shuar and Nature, and the intercultural dialogue between spirits and human beings (*Tsunki Aumatsamu, el mito de Tsunki/Tsunki Aumatsamu, the myth of Tsunki*,

2014). In 2022, as a result of a collective scripting process, Camera Shuar produced a short film based on one of their most important stories, Nunkui Aujmáttsamu (*La historia de Nunkui/the history of Nunkui*).[4]

El Churo Comunicación[5] located in Quito, Ecuador, began as a radio project led by working-class mestizo youth. More than a decade later, it has evolved into a leading independent multimedia organization that works in radio, video, and analysis of breaking news. Its work with Afro-descendant, indigenous, and feminist social movements, collectives, and communities has focused on audiovisual training, territorial defense, and LGBTQI rights. El Churo has also been one of the leading organizers for the allocation of community radio frequencies. A recent project of El Churo, Ojo Semilla Feminista: Laboratorio de Cine y Audiovisual Comunitario (Feminist Eye Seed: Community Film and Audiovisual Laboratory) began in 2017. It convenes women from across the country to participate in week-long residencies where participants learn to produce films on topics such as reproductive rights, gender violence, and bodily and territorial defense. Like the other collectives mentioned here, Ojo Semilla's productions work in various genres and styles, including documentary, fiction, experimental, music video, video poem, and animation. What they have in common is that they all draw from the lives, experiences, and imaginaries of the nascent filmmakers. Many have an expressive, poetic quality. For example, *El retumbar de las voces/The roar of our voices* (2020) is a music video sung in indigenous languages and scored with Afro-Ecuadorian and indigenous voices and rhythms. It celebrates women that maintain their ancestral legacies, defend their bodies and territories, and claim the right to make their own decisions. In one part of the music video, women exclaim:

> If I want to be a mother, or if I want to wait
> My body and my land will not be abused
> I am a woman who does not lower her gaze
> In defense of the land
> *El Retumbar de las Voces* (The roar of our voices)

The number of media collectives in Ecuador continues to rise, as well as the multiple collaborations among them and with others at local, regional, and transnational levels.[6] Over the past several years, there have been face-to-face gatherings in Argentina, Bolivia, Colombia, Ecuador, Guatemala, Mexico, and Peru to share communication strategies that call attention to the issues elaborated here. These nodal points have made for a mobile, cosmopolitan audiovisual field that works at the intersection of media, territorial defense, and social justice. Taken together, the growing number of media projects powerfully communicates to diverse publics the threats to modes of living and the destruction of biodiverse habitats, as well as possible solutions from indigenous and territorially grounded perspectives. The films provide oral and visual testimony to these cultures' contributions to various fields of knowledge, including biology, agroecology, astronomy, history, medicine, philosophy, and art and aesthetics, to name a few. While there is a lack of research and publications by and about this emerging media culture and individual projects, this is changing as more media collectives document and write about their practices (Maizal, 2018–2022; Sanchez, 2018; Red de Maestres de Cine Autonómico, 2020–2022).

Concluding Remarks

This chapter has discussed the eco-territorial turn and the emergent media cultures that share its sensibilities, values, and commitments. It offers a window onto their common characteristics, practices, and goals. It argues that audiovisual resistance to extractivism is an integral part of Latin America's field of political ecology, diverse feminisms, and other scholarly and movement tendencies of the twenty-first century. These eco-territorial audiovisual practices that are situated within local cultures should be of vital interest to ecomedia scholars. They explore relational ontologies, indigenous knowledge production, and shed light on processes that are often out of sight in urban centers, particularly in the Global North.

When analyzing the impact of these emergent media cultures, it is essential to keep in mind an expanded meaning of territory, which involves historic memory, culture, language, and protection of local ecologies and modes of living. Additionally, an analysis of their impact should consider the critical information they offer, the alternative and relational ontologies they capture, and the postdevelopment visualities they create. Griselda Sanchez's (2018) analysis of the contributions of Oaxacan community radio can be extended to include the larger field of audiovisual action.

> The rough geographies of the state and the lack of highways, newspapers, telephone lines, cell phones – not even to mention the Internet – means that communities are isolated. Many of the community radio stations in Oaxaca have been able to build linkages between communities that promote the culture that one lives, and to provide pertinent information about reality and everyday life.
>
> (2018, 71)

Media cultures that defend bodies, territories, and life itself are helping to generate a collective outcry, strengthen resistance, and help communities learn from each other. They help shift the narrative that has mainly been told by states, corporations, and the mainstream media. Research is needed about particular media collectives, as well as the larger impact that these emergent media cultures produce. Questions that could be posed of each one might include: where does their effectivity lie? Are they mostly positioned to make visible the struggles to those who are unaware or uninformed about these struggles, or do they mainly serve to connect like-minded movements, communities, and networks? Are their visual and aesthetic strategies better at revealing capitalist development, or do their visualities explore relational ontologies and postdevelopment imaginaries? How have audiovisual projects helped communities in specific legal battles? How can audiovisual collectives themselves be strengthened so that their efforts are more effective? These are just a few questions that ecomedia scholars might address in their work.

Notes

1 Children of the Jaguar (Amnesty International 2013) can be viewed in its entirety with English subtitles at https://www.youtube.com/watch?v=Ma1QSmtuiLQ&t=121s Eriberto Gualinga's YouTube channel has several of his films. See https://www.youtube.com/user/TrayaMuskuy.
2 The Kawsak Sacha cosmovision is outlined in a declaration published on the Sarayaku website in 2022. See https://kawsaksacha.org/en/.
3 See http://www.camara-shuar.org/.
4 https://www.nua-films.com/la-historia-de-nunkui?fbclid=IwAR0I1F8lel5eGehLYLVx-IkjSOZcXcJq-28sV7lyljh1GFBqIIgMBfFnjX0.
5 See El Churo's main website, the Ojo Semilla website and videos: https://elchuro.org/; http://ojosemilla.elchuro.org/; https://www.youtube.com/channel/UCUWek35pFjCMEsVFW3wZdvg/videos.
6 Other collaborative, grassroots film initiatives located in Ecuador that focus on territorial defense include two indigenous-led initiatives, Tawna (https://tawna.org/) and Lanceros Digitales (https://lanceros.confeniae.net/). See Tawna's film, Piatua Resiste at https://www.youtube.com/watch?v=j7mrjuNV4BE.

Further Reading

Borunda, Stephen N. 2019. "Mapuche Cosmovision and the Cinematic Voyage: An Interview with Filmmaker Francisco Huichaqueo Pérez (English Version)." *Media+Environment* 1, no. 1: 10788.
Coryat, Diana, Christian Leon and Noah Zweig. 2023. *Small Cinemas of the Andes: New Aesthetics, Practices and Platforms*. London; New York: Palgrave MacMillan: Palgrave MacMillan.
Gudynas, Eduardo. 2021. *Extractivisms: Politics, economy and ecology*. Halifax: Fernwood.
Kidd, Dorothy. 2020. "Mobilizing with Video in the Extractive Zone." In Chris Robé and Stephen Charbonneau (editors) *InsUrgent Media from the Front: A Media Activism Reader*. 151. Bloomington: Indiana University Press.
Waldmüeller, Johannes. 2021. "The Eco-Territorial Turn in Latin America: A Conversation with Maristella Svampa." Accessed at http://www.alternautas.net/blog/2021/3/31/the-eco-territorial-turn-in-latin-america-a-conversation-with-maristella-svampa

References

Almendra, Vilma. 2017. *Entre la emancipación y la captura: Memorias y caminos desde la lucha Nasa en Colombia*. Mexico: Barricadas Colección.
Amnesty International, dir. 2013. *Children of the Jaguar*. https://www.youtube.com/watch?v=Ma1QSmtuiLQ.
Cabnal, Lorena. 2019. "El Relato de las Violencias desde Mi Territorio Cuerpo-Tierra." In *En Tiempos de Muerte: Cuerpos, Rebeldías, Resistencias*, Volume 4, edited by Xochitl Leyva Solano and Rosalba Icaza, 113–123. Chiapas; Buenos Aires; La Haya: CLACSO, Cooperativa Editorial RETOS, International Institute of Social Studies (ISS) Erasmus University Rotterdam. https://www.congresoed.org/wp-content/uploads/2021/07/071119-En-tiempos-de-muerte.pdf#page=114
Coryat, Diana. 2015. "Extractive Politics, Media Power, and New Waves of Resistance against Oil Drilling in the Ecuadorian Amazon: The Case of Yasunidos." *International Journal of Communication* (Online): 9: 3741–61.
Cubitt, Sean. 2017. *Finite Media: Environmental Implications of Digital Technologies*. Durham, NC and London: Duke University Press.
Escobar, Arturo. 2016. "Thinking-Feeling with the Earth: Territorial Struggles and the Ontological Dimension of the Epistemologies of the South/Sentipensar con la Tierra: las luchas territoriales y la dimension ontologica de las Epistemologias del Sur." *Revista de Antropologia Iberoamericana* 11, no. 1: 11–32.
Gago, Veronica. 2019. *La potencia feminista: o el deseo de cambiarlo todo*. Madrid: Traficantes de sueños.
Maizal. 2018–2022. *La otra cosecha*. No. 1, 2, 3 y 4. Ecuador, Peru, Mexico: Maizal. www.maizalaudiovisual.wordpress.com
Porto-Gonzalves, Carlos Walter, and Enrique Leff. 2015. "Political Ecology in Latin America: The Social Re-Appropriation of Nature, the Reinvention of Territories and the Construction of an Environmental Rationality." *Desenvolvimento e Meio Ambiente* 35, no. 1: 65–88.
Red de Maestres de Cine Autonómico. 2020–2022. Autonomías, cine y re-existencias. Botero-Gómez, P; Leyva-Solano, X, köhler, A; López-Suárez, M.G; Morales-Guzmán, J., Costa, A.M.; Sánchez, A.; Trejo-Sánchez, J.A Villamaría, Caldas-Colombia, Chiapas-México; Buenos Aires-Argentina: Centro de estudios independientes, Color tierra; RETOS, CLACSO en colaboración con colectivos de cineastas en el Abya Yala.
Sanchez, Griselda. 2018. *Aire, no te vendas: La lucha por el territorio desde las Ondas*. México: IWGIA.
Salazar, Juan Francisco. 2022. "Social Movements and Video Indígena in Latin America: Key Challenges for 'Anthropologies Otherwise.'" In *Media, Anthropology and Public Engagement*, edited by Sarah Pink and Simone Abram, 122–44. New York; Oxford: Berghahn Books. https://doi.org/10.1515/9781782388470-008.
Svampa, Maristella. 2019. *Las fronteras del neoextractivismo en América Latina: Conflictos socioambientales, giro ecoterritorial y nuevas dependencias*. CALAS Collection. Germany: Bielefeld University Press.

26
MAPPING FOR ACCOUNTABILITY
Decolonizing Land Acknowledgment Initiatives

Salma Monani and Sarah Gilsoul

Introduction

In August 2022, a digital ArcGIS StoryMap collection titled *Indigenous Pennsylvania: Past, Present and Future* went live on the Land Acknowledgment Statement (LAS) page of Gettysburg College's website.[1] As a digital mapping endeavor, a primary goal of the collection, which includes a page with an interactive Google map layer, is to spotlight places of Indigenous presence in a settler nation state where such presence is often erased. As we will describe, this primary goal goes hand-in-hand with the larger objective to serve as an Open Educational Resource (OER) that is grounded in re-thinking the very process of visualizing maps and thus, their role in how we might imagine our relations to the environment. Specifically, as an ecomedia project, *Indigenous Pennsylvania* turns to growing scholarship in Indigenous cartographies to foreground spatial and temporal mediations that offer us a storied sense of Indigenous place-based relations. In this chapter, we trace how Indigenous cartographies situate *Indigenous Pennsylvania* as an example of *d-ecomedia*, a shorthand we offer for ecomedia projects that foreground decolonial methodologies.[2]

Before we turn to Indigenous cartographies, it is worth spotlighting the immediate imperative that shapes this endeavor—Gettysburg College's recent move to incorporate a LAS. The LAS is a first for our institution as well as for other colleges and universities here in the south central part of the U.S. state of Pennsylvania. Those of us working on this initiative recognize it as long overdue to acknowledge Indigenous peoples' connections to the lands we currently occupy—specifically that these are "the traditional homelands of the Susquehannock/Conestoga, Seneca and the Haudenosaunee Confederacy, Leni Lenape, Shawnee and other Indigenous Nations" and that "these connections continue today" (Land Acknowledgment Committee, 2021). At the same time, given that LASs often pay nothing more than lip service to Indigenous peoples' experiences of historical and contemporary (dis)enfranchisement, we are acutely aware of the pitfalls of mere performativity, especially in light of recent work that reveals how colleges and universities in the United States are complicit in land grabs instigated by the Morrill Act of 1862. The act appropriated stolen Indigenous lands designated as "public domain" lands for the nation's burgeoning land-grant universities (Lee and Ahtone, 2020; Lomawaima et al., 2021; Sobo, Lambert, and Lambert, 2020).

Despite these criticisms, there are many who champion LAS initiatives when done carefully. Sobo, Lambert and Lambert (2020) write that keeping an unflinching focus on Indigenous pasts, presents and futures in ways that are informative *and* empower Indigenous voices can engender "respect and restoration" of Indigenous relations to stolen lands. One approach to do this work is through digital mapping. As geographer Mark Palmer writes in the special issue of the *Journal of Native American and Indigenous Studies* focused on land-grant universities, in such initiatives, digital mapping can be a powerful means to engender restorative attention:

> Mapping for accountability creates a context for discussing past injustices and contributions of Native people to land-grant universities, as well as thinking about ways to achieve remedies and reciprocity.
>
> (2021, 109–10)

Gettysburg College, like many settler institutions, can do better to "map for accountability." It is not a land-grant institution, and while it proudly advertises its foundation by anti-slavery advocate Thaddeus Stevens, it has done little to acknowledge its occupation on stolen Indigenous lands or interrogate how it remains complicit in upholding norms of racial discrimination (Bias Awareness Resource Committee, 2021). The *Indigenous Pennsylvania* StoryMaps project is a small step toward the on-going process of building relations of "respect and restoration." We also offer it as a cartographic model of d-ecomedia to the field of ecomedia studies.

Before we turn to the particulars of how, it is important to note that *Indigenous Pennsylvania* is an undergraduate senior honors thesis conducted by Sarah and advised by her faculty mentor, Salma (the two co-authors of this chapter). Neither researcher identifies as Indigenous, however, we bring Salma's many years of working with Indigenous collaborators on ecomedia studies projects to inform the project. Specifically, as described in the introduction of *Indigenous Pennsylvania*, the project is guided by Indigenous intellectual and activist voices as is essential to decolonial methodologies (Gilsoul, 2022). We discuss potentials and challenges of attempting such decolonial work within the context of institutional LAS initiatives.

Why Mapping for Accountability Matters

In his recent *Media+Environment* article, Greg Lowen-Trudeau (2021) reminds us that maps, much like all mediated representations, can fit within educational scholar Elliot Eisner's (2002) theory of the three curricula—the explicit, the implicit and the null:

> In a cartographic context, the explicit curriculum comprises the geographical, political, and cultural features explicitly included in a given map. The null is what is not shown at all through intention or ignorance. The implicit curricula are the lessons that are implied through the explicit and the null.

Settler colonial cartographies usually make explicit the geopolitical spatial boundaries of ownership and modes of access (e.g., state lines, private vs. public property, and roads). Such features are often decoupled from their complex sociocultural and ecological histories and depict "space as universal, homogenized, and devoid of human experience" (Pearce and Louis, 2008). Such cartographies, borrowing media scholars Candis Callison (Tahtan) and Mary Lynn Young's phrasing, legitimize the authority of a "view from nowhere" (Callison and Young, 2019). As geographers Margaret Pearce and Renee Louis (2008) note, colonial mapping is often "inscriptive" or veneers of "objectivity" where the map is understood as a static, stand-alone final product. In contrast, Indigenous cartographies are generally "process-oriented," that is they place emphasis on the relations involved in mapping—"stories expressed in the meanings, connections, and interrelationships of those place names" (Pearce and Louis, 2008). For example, "the map extends from the community into the landscape through inscriptions on trees and rocks, drawings on the ground, or dance and ceremony ... [and] *emphasize[s] experienced space, or place*" (Pearce and Louis, 2008, 110).[3]

Even when settler colonial cartographies map places as community experiences, they usually do so in ways that expunge or de-contextualize Indigenous relations to the land. Such a de-contextualized example exists in close proximity to Gettysburg College, on the famed Gettysburg Military Park, a designated national park that maps the experiences of one of the most iconic moments in the history of the United States (the turning point of the American Civil War). One can visit the park and experience it through tours that narrate the battle via audio, waysides and other monuments on the landscape. Along Hancock Avenue, a crucial stretch in the park's narrative tour of the battle, there is a monument dedicated by the 42nd New York Infantry, known as the "Tammany Regiment" (Figure 26.1).

It features an imposing granite pedestal on which a metal-cast Native American stands in front of a teepee; he is buck-skin clad, feathered and clasping a bow. It is the only such explicit gesture to Native presence on the battlefield. Erected by the Society of Tammany (also known as the Columbian Order), a self-identified fraternal order of White settlers who modeled their "Americanness"

Figure 26.1 Two views of the Tammany Regiment monument on Hancock Avenue on the Gettysburg National Military Park—looking north, and looking south with the Pennsylvania monument in the background.

on requirements of "native birth," the statue mythologizes Lenape Chief Tamanend as the noble savage who peaceably welcomed William Penn to America (New York Public Library, 2021). Unlike other landmarks mapped along this section (like the Pennsylvania Monument) that are part of the park's official tour, visitors have to dig to learn this context. Most passing by might briefly wonder, "who is this impressive figure?"; some might think, "why is he wielding a bow when the war was fought with guns?" and yet, all will soon be drawn away from such "distracting" thoughts to engage instead the park's more explicitly narrated features of this battle—the strategies of Confederate and Union generals commanding their troops in a patriotic struggle to determine the future of the United States of America.

Mapped onto the land within such settler colonial contexts, the Tammany Regiment statue mirrors the critiques Sobo, Lambert and Lambert (2020) level at LAS: it is "little more than [a] feel-good public gesture signaling ideological conformity…" The mythologized appropriation of a welcoming noble savage nulls any sense of genocide suffered by Lenape peoples as settlers encroached on their lands. Standing as a cipher in a place commemorating stories of patriotism to the nation, its presence—barely visible on the region's maps—does little justice to the complicated story of Chief Tamanend and his peoples' relations to their homelands as well as their dispossession by the settler state.

Such settler colonial cartographies that null Indigenous presence are common across the state of Pennsylvania, which contains no state or federally recognized Indigenous lands. Instead, features on the land, like Tammany Monument, Conestoga township and Big Indian Rock in the Susquehanna River, signal settler appropriations that do little to acknowledge Native peoples' contemporary connections to these lands and/despite legacies of brutal dispossession. The examples referred to in the last sentence demand a re-framing to demonstrate how, as the Gettysburg College's Land Acknowledgment notes, "these connections continue today" and are not merely hauntings of pre-colonial occupation. As a decolonial act, such re-framing involves approaching the very process of mapping through strategies of interpretation and theories of cartography that are grounded in Indigenous, not Western, epistemologies. They require a process-oriented and relational framework, which we discuss below.

Socio-Ecological Conceptions of Space and Time in Indigenous Cartographies

Indigenous Pennsylvania: Past, Present and Future is conceptualized as a digital mapping project grounded in Indigenous cartographic scholarship. Lowen-Trudeau's *Media+Environment* article cited above provides a rich overview of the field, drawing our attention to how such cartographies are understood variously as "countermapping," or "mapping back" (when they superimpose Indigenous epistemologies on Western style maps) and "communocentric"—when they "diverge from Western cartographic practices in favor of more locally and culturally relevant representations" (Lowan-Trudeau, 2021). As he notes, often Indigenous cartographies combine both modes of representation—countermapping and communocentric.

This combination is central to Indigenous cartographers working with Geographic Information Systems (GIS) tools, which, as Pearce and Louis note, while developed within Western paradigms, are "flexible and capable to being adapted to suit traditional Indigenous cultural geographies" (Pearce and Louis, 2008, 113). In particular, the continued development of Environmental Systems Research Institute's (ESRI) StoryMaps as a "trans-media" tool where "maps … could be combined with multimedia content and woven into new, immersive experiences" (Carroll, 2019) is one that lends itself well to Indigenous conceptions of space as "storied" versus as a "view from nowhere."

Salma Monani and Sarah Gilsoul

We chose the StoryMaps tool for the *Indigenous Pennsylvania* project for this reason and also for its ease of use. In doing so, we looked to a number of existing projects as exemplars while prioritizing a website with a relatively low carbon footprint (Peel, 2021). *Mapping Indigenous L.A.* (2022), a collaborative project led by Mishuana Goeman (Tonawanda Seneca) at the University of California, Los Angeles inspires our own map because as Indigenous studies scholar Siobhan Senier writes, "Nobody can visit *Mapping Indigenous L.A.* without seeing immediately that Indigenous people, spaces, and traditions are not static objects or pinpoints but living, dynamic, and future-oriented entities" (Senier, 2018). Given that our LAS seeks to spotlight "connections that continue today," this sense of Indigenous presence as "living and dynamic" is a guiding process-oriented principle—both in acknowledging Indigenous presence as an on-going process of survivance and in framing our mapmaking as an on-going dialogue with Indigenous intellectual thought and practice.[4]

Much like *Mapping Indigenous L.A.*, and other Indigenous mapping projects, our StoryMaps Collection makes full use of text, images and audio and video multimedia to generate what Senier describes as "narrative mapping" (Indigenous Mapping Workshop, n.d.; Senier, 2018). Our StoryMaps Collection includes a main menu to navigate through several pages. One of the pages includes a map with a "bird's-eye view." We do this deliberately to, as geographer Palmer reminds us, note that Indigenous cartography doesn't reject the tools of Western mapping but rather incorporates it into a different frame of context (Palmer, 2021). Our map allows visitors to orient sites in "how the crow flies" geospatial relation to each, *and* it does more. Clicking on any of these locations pulls up the side-bar scroll, which presents a textual synopsis and links to another page, which is rich with multimedia that deliberately *re*-presents the location as entangled in storied relations occurring in place *and through time*.

In other words, temporal relations become as central to this mapping project as are spatial ones. *Mapping Indigenous L.A.* (and Senior's review of it) provide a strong justification for attending to time, reminding us of the importance of "countermapping" settler colonial representations of Indigenous people as primitive hauntings. *Indigenous Pennsylvania's* multimedia provides rich evidence of Indigenous presence existing on a continuum into the present. Whether it's a quote from a Tuscarora student on Gettysburg's campus incorporated into the text, audio from an interview with an Onondaga activist and organizer who calls our region home, or images and video of the three sister's garden (corn, beans and squash) planted on campus, the project unequivocally reminds us that Indigenous collaborators are alive and part of the process of what Goeman has described as (re)mapping—that is, "remembering important connections to land and community" through the act of storytelling (Goeman, 2013, 29).

Grounding the project in such Indigenous collaborations reaffirms our desire to showcase Indigenous conceptions of temporality. Specifically, we organize our narratives regarding each place not as chronologically linear, but, rather, as what Kyle Powys Whyte (Potawatomi) has described as "spiraling": a sense of "intergenerational time" that captures:

> the varied experiences of time that we have as participants within living narratives involving our ancestors and descendants. Experiences of spiraling time, then, may be lived through narratives of cyclicality, reversal … The spiraling narratives unfold through our interacting with, responding to and reflecting on the actual or potential actions and viewpoints of our ancestors and descendants. They unfold as continuous dialogues.
>
> (2018, 228)

Thus, for example, we could have represented the Conestoga massacre of 1763 that haunts the Fulton Theatre in downtown Lancaster (located as the bird flies approximately 60 miles east of

Gettysburg) as one isolated historical moment in the settler nation's founding. Instead, we spotlight the multimedia and graphic novel project, *The Ghost River: Rise and Fall of Conestoga* (2019). Spearheaded by Will Fenton for the Library Company of Philadelphia, authored by Lee Francis IV (Laguna Pueblo), the owner of Red Planet, the largest Indigenous comic book retailer in the United States, and showcasing the remarkable work of illustrator Weshoyot Alvitre (Tongva), *The Ghost River* is a collaboration with local Pennsylvanian Natives and an exploration of the on-going meanings of this massacre from Indigenous points of view. For example, in one snippet of our video interview with her, MaryAnn Robins (Onondaga), the president of the local Native group, the Circle Legacy Center and a consultant for *The Ghost River* project, reflects on the intergenerational continuum of trauma imposed by such events on Native peoples into the present. Linking such video snippets to audio clips from an interview with Fenton and to the website of the project itself, our StoryMap's narrative further contextualizes how such reflections become spaces for on-going healing. Much like *The Ghost River* project itself, which is available online as a free educational resource for school and college classrooms, *Indigenous Pennsylvania* seeks to generate an open space for inter- and intra-generational dialogues all too often silenced by the settler state, including by its formal educational systems.

While *Indigenous Pennsylvania* refuses chronological linear time as an ordering structure for its narrative mapping, it remains faithful to Indigenous epistemologies that center place-based learning as socio-ecologically entangled. The navigation menu and the interactive map emphasize locations, and the narratives of each page attend to place as a web of human and more-than-human relations. For example, As Robins points out in her video interview regarding *The Ghost River* project, including "river" in the title of that project was no coincidence—it reminds us of the vitality of the Susquehanna River to the lifeways of the Conestoga peoples (Robins, 2021). In our StoryMap Collection, ecological groundings interwoven with sociocultural lifeways remain a central theme. For example, the page describing the Painted Turtle Farm, a college-owned farm, illuminates the agroecology and culture of local Indigenous planting practices. Pointing out how the three sisters—corn, beans and squash—are understood as sentient, reciprocal beings, the page narrates stories of colonially enforced food dispossession and the continuing fight for Indigenous food sovereignty.

In addition, the project actively works to put individual sites into a relational context with other places to remind us how these particularized places exist in larger matrices of socio-ecological influence, Native and colonial. Thus, for example, while the Fulton Theatre page references the Big Indian Rock page (and vice versa) to situate the river as a regional connective tissue, all pages also narrate and use the digital hyperlink feature to cast a wider geospatial and temporal net. Such a move is a constant reminder of similar Native experiences across the nation state and situates our region within collective community networks of resistance and resurgence.

In all, *Indigenous Pennsylvania: Past, Present and Future* seeks to unbury "past injustices and contributions of Native peoples… as well as [to] think about ways to achieve remedies and reciprocity" (Palmer, 2021, 109–10). It draws on historical and contemporary Indigenous scholarship and local collaborations to deploy decolonizing methodologies that are process-oriented and relational in its framing. As we discuss below in our concluding remarks, there are specific challenges to this work within the context of institutional LAS initiatives.

Conclusions

When Gettysburg College committed to a LAS, the glaring absence of a coherent (co)curriculum that helps the campus (and local) community understand what it means to occupy Indigenous lands fueled our desire to make visible the rich and continuing relations that Indigenous peoples have with these lands.[5] The college's institutional license to ESRI's StoryMaps tool facilitated a way to generate a publicly accessible means to visualize this work. In conducting this representational work, we are very cognizant of the need to, as Theresa Stewart-Ambo (Tongva/Luiseño) writes, "move beyond the rhetoric" to "materialize … tribal-university relationships" (Stewart-Ambo, 2021, 166). The *Indigenous Pennsylvania: Present, Past, and Future* project is founded on generating ongoing, on-the-ground collaborations with local Native members that extend beyond the map to community engagements of respect and restoration. Yet, there is a rub. The map itself, as noted at the start of this chapter, is an undergraduate student's honors thesis. As a senior thesis project, it is time bound to a year. Because each chosen site is dense with researched and original content, there are currently only four locations featured. We know that there are many more within our region, and while we envision the project being picked up by other students once Sarah graduates, there is no surety of this. This is because at the institutional level there is as yet no formal administrative guarantee of support to the LAS other than the promise to ensure the "practice of reciting the statement at major campus events" (President's Office, 2021).

The formal language raises red flags for the LAS more broadly, and within it, the viability of a digital mapping project like *Indigenous Pennsylvania*. Both are dependent on more concerted institutional support to survive in ways that do more than, as we have noted, lip service to the cause. Much like community relations, digital projects require care and attention to thrive. At a logistical level, as Senior writes, "Like many digital projects of this size, maintenance over time becomes an issue" (Senier, 2018, 947). Parts of the current mapping toolbox going defunct are part and parcel of how digital technologies function today—links need to be constantly checked as the internet re-calibrates its available content; as ESRI constantly updates its StoryMap software, glitches can develop in the existing design. At the same time, this particular project is envisioned with what Senier notes is the advantage of such web-based digital publications—it is meant to be a space for "continually expanding authorship, recursiveness, and revision" (2018, 949) to best reflect the process of growing relations with Indigenous partners in ways that can, as Sobo, Lambert and Lambert (2020) note, "respect and restore." This process-oriented framework requires institutional commitment.

Knowing that institutional challenges exist, we pin our hopes for the project's continued part in productive relationalities that our LAS can grow, if done right. Specifically, while the mapping project is primarily shepherded by the two of us, our work is part of the broader mission of a dedicated group of faculty, students and staff who constitute the LAS committee. The committee is intently focused on capacity building. For example, because Sarah's project is research based we reached out to the Provost's Office, which extended co-sponsorship for an on-campus event that featured the *The Ghost River* project collaborators through a small Mellon grant. Twelve other departments and programs across campus signed on as well. The success of this event has fueled additional institutional possibilities. Since then the LAS committee has worked actively on a number of curricular and co-curricular initiatives, which we showcase on the timeline on college's LAS homepage (LAS Timeline, 2021–Present). We hope that these will pave the way for more substantial support that can, as Stewart-Ambo notes, extend "external, economic, curricular, and cocurricular relationships existing between American Indian nations and universities that recognize, reinforce, and respect tribal sovereignty and self-determination" (Stewart-Ambo, 2021, 166). As an Indigenous cartographic project, *Indigenous Pennsylvania* plays a small part in a larger, process-oriented framework of relations that not only involve real challenges but also exciting possibilities for d-ecomedia practice and theory.

Acknowledgments

We are grateful to many who have assisted with this project. Our community collaborators provided primary research expertise, while our librarian and IT specialist, R.C. Miessler helped with getting our StoryMaps Collection off the ground, colleagues at Gettysburg College's Land Acknowledgment Committee were the spark for this project. Along with the editors of this handbook, we are also grateful to Sarah Wald and Nicole Seymour for reading drafts of this chapter and to Kyle Powys Whyte, Joanna Hearne and Angelina Lawson for important feedback on the StoryMaps Collection itself.

Notes

1 On this page, the link resides under the sub-head Indigenous Resources: https://www.gettysburg.edu/offices/diversity-inclusion/land-acknowledgement-statement/#indigenous-resources.
2 Salma's current monograph project *Indigenous Ecocinema: Decolonizing Media Environments* (forthcoming) outlines the idea of d-ecocinema, which shines a spotlight on cinema's ecological and decolonial possibilities, an idea she has presented in many conference presentations. Here we extend the terminology to all media, hence the term d-ecomedia.
3 We have added the italicized emphasis on experienced space.
4 Survivance as forwarded by Gerald Vizenor (Anishinaabe) in his seminal *Manifest Manners: Narratives of Post Indian Survivance* (1994) indicates a sense of Native agency beyond simple survival and instead as a marker of positive endurance.
5 There is no Native Studies program on campus; and in terms of co-curriculum activity, we have the recently formed the Land Acknowledgment Committee and the student club, Students for Indigenous Awareness.

Further Reading

Basso, Keith H. 1996. *Wisdom Sits in Places: Landscape and Language Amongst the Western Apache*. Albuquerque: University of New Mexico Press.
Goeman, Mishuana. 2013. *Mark My Words: Native Women Mapping Our Nations*. Minneapolis: University of Minnesota Press. http://ebookcentral.proquest.com/lib/gettysburg/detail.action?docID=1362032.
Lee, Robert and Tristan Ahtone, 2020. "Land-Grab Universities." *High Country News*, March 30, 2020. https://www.hcn.org/issues/52.4/indigenous-affairs-education-land-grab-universities.
Rose-Redwood, Reuben, Natchee Blu Barnd, Annita Hetoevėhotohke'e Lucchesi, Sharon Dias, and Wil Patrick. 2020. "Decolonizing the Map: Recentering Indigenous Mappings." *Cartographica: The International Journal for Geographic Information and Geovisualization* 55 (3): 151–62. https://doi.org/10.3138/cart.53.3.intro.
Smith, Linda Tuhiwai, Eve Tuck, and K. Wayne Yang. 2019. *Indigenous and Decolonizing Studies in Education: Mapping the Long View. Indigenous and Decolonizing Studies in Education*. New York: Routledge Press.

References

Bias Awareness Resource Committee. 2021. "Report on Diversity & Inclusion." Gettysburg College. 2021. https://www.gettysburg.edu/offices/diversity-inclusion/bias-awareness-resource-committee/.
Callison, Candis, and Mary Lynn Young. 2019. *Reckoning: Journalism's Limits and Possibilities*. Journalism and Political Communication Unbound. New York: Oxford University Press. https://doi.org/10.1093/oso/9780190067076.001.0001.
Carroll, Allen. 2019. "A Quantum Leap for Story Maps." *ArcGIS Blog* (blog). April 10, 2019. https://www.esri.com/arcgis-blog/products/arcgis-storymaps/mapping/a-quantum-leap-for-story-maps/.
Eisner, Elliot. 2002. *Educational Imagination: On the Design and Evaluation of School Programs*. Upper Saddle River, NJ: Merrill Prentice Hall.

Gilsoul, Sarah. 2022. *Indigenous Pennsylvania: Past, Present and Future*. Gettysburg College. https://cupola.gettysburg.edu/student_scholarship/1002/.

Goeman, Mishuana. 2013. *Mark My Words: Native Women Mapping Our Nations*. Minneapolis: University of Minnesota Press. http://ebookcentral.proquest.com/lib/gettysburg/detail.action?docID=1362032.

"Indigenous Mapping: Our Story." n.d. *Indigenous Mapping Workshop*. https://www.indigenousmaps.com/ourstory/.

Land Acknowledgement Committee. 2021. "Land Acknowledgment Statement." Gettysburg College. 2021. https://www.gettysburg.edu/offices/diversity-inclusion/land-acknowledgement-statement/.

Land Acknowledgment Timeline of Activities and Events. 2022. Gettysburg College. https://www.gettysburg.edu/offices/diversity-inclusion/land-acknowledgement-statement/#timeline

Lee, Robert and Tristan Ahtone, 2020. "Land-Grab Universities." *High Country News*, March 30, 2020. https://www.hcn.org/issues/52.4/indigenous-affairs-education-land-grab-universities.

Lomawaima, K Tsianina, Kelly Mcdonough, Jean M O'Brien, and Robert Warrior. 2021. "Editors' Introduction: Reflections on the Land-Grab Universities Project." *NAIS: Journal of the Native American and Indigenous Studies Association* 8 (1): 89–91. https://doi.org/10.5749/natiindistudj.8.1.0089.

Lowan-Trudeau, Greg. 2021. "Mapping (as) Resistance: Decolonizing↔Indigenizing Journalistic Cartography." *Media+Environment* 3 (1): 19057. https://doi.org/10.1525/001c.19057.

Monani, Salma (forthcoming). *Indigenous Ecocinema: Decolonizing Media Environments*. Morgantown: University of West Virginia Press (Salvaging the Anthropocene Series).

Palmer, Mark. 2021. "'Drawing a Line from Their Institution': One Origin Story of Indigenous GIS Design." *Native American and Indigenous Studies* 8 (1): 106–11.

Pearce, Margaret, and Renee Louis. 2008. "Mapping Indigenous Depth of Place." *American Indian Culture and Research Journal* 32 (3): 107–26. https://doi.org/10.17953/aicr.32.3.n7g22w816486567j.

Peel, Joanna. 2021. "(43) Seven Best Practice Tips to Design Low-Carbon Websites | LinkedIn." July 7, 2021. https://www.linkedin.com/pulse/how-design-low-carbon-websites-joanna-peel/.

President's Office. 2021. "Diversity, Equity, and Inclusion Midyear Update." Gettysburg College. 2021. https://www.gettysburg.edu/offices/president/communications/news_detail.dot?id=d31fc323-f548-46a4-8888-efc517428875.

Robins, MaryAnne. 2021. In Person Communication. Recorded Interview from November 13, 2021.

Senier, Siobhan. 2018. "Where a Bird's-Eye View Shows More Concrete: Mapping Indigenous L.A. for Tribal Visibility and Reclamation." *American Quarterly* 70 (4): 941–48. http://dx.doi.org/10.1353/aq.2018.0076.

Sobo, Elisa J., Michael Lambert, and Valerie Lambert. 2021. "Land Acknowledgments Meant to Honor Indigenous People Too Often Do the Opposite – Erasing American Indians and Sanitizing History Instead." The Conversation, October 7, 2021. Accessed February 14, 2022. http://theconversation.com/land-acknowledgments-meant-to-honor-indigenous-people-too-often-do-the-opposite-erasing-american-indians-and-sanitizing-history-instead-163787.

"Society of Tammany, or Columbian Order Records." 2021. The New York Public Library Archives & Manuscripts. 2021. https://archives.nypl.org/mss/2946.

Stewart-Ambo, Theresa. 2021. "The Future Is in the Past: How Land-Grab Universities Can Shape the Future of Higher Education." *Native American and Indigenous Studies* 8 (1): 162–68.

Vizenor, Gerald Robert. 1994. *Manifest Manners: Postindian Warriors of Survivance*. Hanover: Wesleyan University Press.

Whyte, Kyle P. 2018. "Indigenous Science (Fiction) for the Anthropocene: Ancestral Dystopias and Fantasies of Climate Change Crises." *Environment and Planning E: Nature and Space* 1 (1–2): 224–42. https://doi.org/10.1177/2514848618777621.

27
BLACK MEDIA PHILOSOPHY AND VISUAL ECOLOGIES

A Conversation between Armond Towns and Jeremy Kamal

Armond Towns and Jeremy Kamal

On May 12, 2022, Carleton University's Armond Towns met with Southern California Institute of Architecture's Jeremy Kamal Hartley via Zoom to discuss the interconnections between their work on art, race, blackness, and media ecology. This transcribed and edited conversation outlines the unique approaches both Towns and Hartley take in their respective art and research projects, both of which they view as central to imagining a world beyond racism and planetary destruction. In their shared discussion lies an expansion of media ecology into questions concerning the colonial assumptions of nature, Black radical thought, and artistic design and resistance.

Mojo: Da Floods is an animated short film that introduces a world in which the rituals of Black culture shape geological phenomena (Figures 27.1–27.3). The film is a portal into a speculative ecology where vast machines operated by music producers hover over a floodplain landscape, using bass notes from amplified music to vibrate bodies of water. These vibrations form cymatic

Figure 27.1 *Mojo: Da Floods* (2019) is one of a series of animated vignettes that depict a world where the rituals of Black culture shape geological phenomena. Each vignette is a portal into speculative ecosystems, landscapes, atmospheres, and climates that synchronize with the movement of black bodies in space. In this animated vignette, a music producer/sound engineer utilizes a tactile interface in order to operate a gantry crane used to mix and master sound spatially.

This chapter has been made available under a CC-BY-NC-ND license.

patterns in the water used to visually mix and master sound. Spillage from the process irrigates surrounding soil and flora distributed by seed-dropping drones. Through the production of music, the ecological system is sustained and the landscape is transformed. The film is one of a series of animated vignettes that depict a world where ecosystems and landscapes are birthed by the movement of Black bodies in space.

ARMOND TOWNS: My name is Armond Towns. I'm an Associate Professor of Communication and Media Studies at Carleton University. My research interests lie generally in media and communication history and the history of Black studies. I've recently been examining the relationship between media ecology and questions of race. I guess maybe one of the ways I've done that is by writing about the way that Europe and North America have talked about concepts of nature, particularly building off their philosophical assumptions of a "state of nature," which they largely associate with us, as black people. So there's a conflation of Black people with the Western conception of nature.

But one of the things that I found out when we met the first time, Jeremy, is your work also points me to something else that I'm interested in, and that's the way that we as Black people not only dismiss that Western construct of nature, but we also have our own types of media-making processes. I really enjoyed that in the small piece of your work that I was able to see last time.

JEREMY KAMAL HARTLEY: My name is Jeremy Kamal. I am a teacher at the Southern California Institute of Architecture (SCI-Arc), as well as a visual artist who engages storytelling and worldbuilding as a way of exploring relationships between Blackness, technology, and ecology. My work explores themes of landscape and fiction as a way of envisioning speculative futures. Through fiction, I'm interested in expanding our understanding of how abstractions such as myths, values, rituals, addictions, and emotions are part of a continuum with the material landscapes around us.

I absolutely love the jump-off points of your work Armond. You're looking at the premise that we have been grouped into this idea of nature from a Westernized perspective. I'm really excited about having more conversations into what you've discovered from your exploration. My starting point into a related topic was through looking at very basic patterns in the relationships between three things: landscape culture, Black culture, and Western colonialism. The biggest differences being that one group's relationship to landscape was highly leisure based, and the other was highly labor based. Black bodies were technologies that manipulate nature for Western profit. So, I always saw us, from the perspective of a technology, but from your viewpoint we were regarded as nature itself as well, that's a fresh take I would love to dive into some more.

ARMOND TOWNS: Well, there's a lot of overlap with that question of nature and technology—the pulling of raw materials for our technologies from nature. I'm influenced by this scholar R. A. Judy, who has a new book called *Sentient Flesh* (2020). And in it, one of the things that he talks about is how Europeans fabricated the state of nature. Coming out of social contract theory, so Thomas Hobbes and John Locke and [Jean-Jacques] Rousseau. Judy argues that Rousseau's understanding of the state of nature was too radical for the United States, because Rousseau's argument was that in the state of nature, people were free, while in civilization, in society, people were in chains. So, for Rousseau, we needed to go back, as a human species, to that state of nature. Whereas John Locke argued that the state of nature was something that civilizations had to progress out of. So, I'm really fascinated by thinking about those relationships between race and nature. And how we break them, which is one of the things that I found really fascinating in your work, like how can we think about nature differently.

JEREMY KAMAL HARTLEY: This is incredible, and as you're talking about the relationship of technology and this idea of extraction, it reminds me of a series of talks from Benjamin Bratton, a contemporary theorist who wrote a book titled *The Stack* (2015). He frames it as an accidental megastructure that arose as a result of global computation. One of the things that's most interesting is that his idea of the Stack lumps technology and what we would interpret as "nature" into the same system. Global computation is very much a part of "nature." It feels very much like a call for the inclusion of a "new nature" or ideas about "nature." He refers to the Stack as both fluid and hard surfaced. It's very much about water, it's very much about minerals, as much as it is about swiping left or swiping right on our small devices. All of it is inextricably linked. I really appreciated that viewpoint, and I'm curious what happens when you start to dig into that perspective and how might you filter it through your lens?

ARMOND TOWNS: Could you say more, maybe, about the new nature? I found that really fascinating.

JEREMY KAMAL HARTLEY: I'm paraphrasing, but I think it's the idea that this megastructure that we are a part of, that is defined as the Stack, almost has a will of its own. And it's so vast and so difficult to conceive of, much like how climate change feels a bit beyond our ability to understand fully. For instance, you or myself may have really good intentions in regards to how we can contribute to climate change in a positive way. But at the same time, I have an iPhone constructed of minerals extracted from Africa, a process which may have included labor practices and carbon emission levels that I may not agree with. It's beyond my ability to actually grapple with holistically and it begins to take on an effect that's as ubiquitous as any other form of "natural" phenomena like climate. Like "nature," our computational systems are vast; the reality of it, the idea, and the concept of it. In the same way that "nature" and the sublime have historically

ARMOND TOWNS: recontextualized our position, the vastness of global computation is forcing us to do the same thing.

ARMOND TOWNS: Thinking about the vastness of it, right. One of the things I've been trying to think about is, how do we think about massive forms of extraction and their relation to the massive digitalization of society? And one of the things that I talked about at the end of my book (Towns 2022) is the interconnected relationship between the networked world that we live in and reparations. As opposed to just kind of a nationalist understanding of reparations, we should move to a more global understanding of reparations, especially thinking about the way that the climate crisis is disproportionately happening in the Global South. Not to mention, as we've been talking about, the extraction of resources from places like Africa that go into our digital devices.

So many people are impacted by the massive need of Western societies to over-extract resources, and that impact is happening in the Global North as well. So at some point, we can't avoid what's happening to the climate, right? We're trying to push it off, as if "yeah, you know, that's going to be later generations," but it's not going to be that much later. We're kind of in it right now. So how can we think about a different type of world now? Because the climate crisis is disproportionately happening in the Global South, it's often the view that, "oh that's not really here." But that's a fiction. You know, we got wildfires on the West Coast and we got flooding on the East Coast. So we're looking at transformations of our living environments. At some point, we have to start having these real fundamental conversations about what's the next step. Beyond just massive extraction.

JEREMY KAMAL HARTLEY: Love it, love it, love it. I never looked at it that way. Love the idea that there's fire on the West and water on the East and they're both kind of washing away or transforming territory.

ARMOND TOWNS: Right.

JEREMY KAMAL HARTLEY: That conversation, of getting more people from different areas and backgrounds to look at the topic of climate, is also a motivator for me. Landscape and environmental fields often don't know how to engage minority audiences, but that's the project, figuring out how to engage the communities we often don't have the language to engage with. It forces us to change the way we do things. My premise was, what would a landscape look like if the rapper 2 Chainz designed it?

And this simple question that I was scared to ask myself in school, because it didn't seem like a "viable" academic trajectory, turned into one of my most profound explorations. It caused me, to your point, to rethink everything about landscape and revealed to me how Eurocentric it was.

I would ask my peers, if you could design a landscape what would it look like? And I think several times, people described manicured lawns, with fountains made out of golden Caucasian baby deities spitting out water from their mouths. But these images are all bathed in mythologies that come from the European and Western point of view. And *Mojo: Da Floods* was me saying let's wipe that away and completely reinterpret what a fountain might look like (Figures 27.2 and 27.3). I used the phenomenon of cymatics, and the idea of using raw sound itself in order to create patterns on a surface of water. And the origin of that sound would come from trap music in our culture. That's a jump-off point, now how do we expand on that and build a landscape around that system? So I started to get into water reclamation technologies and infrastructures and creating a whole system that would traditionally be used for very engineer-driven purposes, to serve the purpose of music production and culture.

The type of radical thinking about these landscapes and our environments is what I'm interested in, for the specific reason that you brought up, expanding the conversation but doing it in a real radical way. So a lot of my work deliberately tries to be unapologetically black, I'm taking up all topics from gang culture to trap culture, from African American rootwork and folk medicine

Figure 27.2 Mojo: Da Floods (2019); bass notes from amplified music vibrate large bodies of water held in cisterns. The vibrations register cymatic patterns on the water surface used to help tune and EQ sound. Excess spill-over irrigates surrounding soil and flora distributed by seed-dropping drones.

Figure 27.3 Mojo: Da Floods (2019); the film reframes the historic narrative of the black body as a landscape technology for colonial profit. Distinctions between the body and the landscape are blurred as technological systems allow black creativity, expression, and spirituality to materialize on an ecological scale. Tundras, grasslands, and forests are now the sites of music studios, cookouts, and kickbacks. Hands that worked the land for labor now shape the land for leisure.

to Memorial weekend cookouts, I'm taking up everything. Because it's very important that we broaden the spectrum of who this applies to and who's actually a part of it, which is everyone.

ARMOND TOWNS: What's so fascinating about that to me is the relationship between sound and architecture. Sound is itself touch right? Like sound vibrates your eardrum. And thinking about that in relationship to trap music, it just seems like they are polar opposites in my mind, but you bring them together. What does the 2 Chainz architecture look like? Right? Like I have an idea in my mind of what it looks like. I want to see it, you know.

JEREMY KAMAL HARTLEY: I don't think it's an answerable question. That 2 Chainz question is a safeguard for me. Because 2 Chainz exists in a very different space, as a lot of us do, right? And that's that wild card that I need to keep myself in check, and not get into the habit of moving too far this way or that way. Whereas from a capitalist point of view, water is a commodity that you sell. From a green point of view, water is an entity that you preserve and you give rights to and shouldn't pollute or interact with it. That's what tends to happen, you take on a preservationist mentality, where it's like don't touch it anymore, we're not going to touch anything. While capitalists are like let's touch it, but let's not only touch it, let's sell it. And then I'm trying to find that in-between space, where it's like, let's touch it, yes, but let's not sell it, let's also preserve it and respect it, but let's not be afraid to interact with it. Let's not use water to sell, let's not use water to just protect, but let's use water to create. In the case of *Da Floods*, create music. And I think that's what the 2 Chainz question gives me, but it's never an answered question. It's just an ongoing mantra.

ARMOND TOWNS: I love it. In a lot of ways, it seems like the capitalist approach to water and the green approach to water are kind of the same thing, or two sides of the same coin. One is excessive overuse and the other is this mythic protection narrative. And that history of protection is itself oftentimes related to a colonialist understanding of conservation. The argument is that "the indigenous populations don't know how to protect these resources, so we have to move them out, so we can conserve this natural resource that only we know how to fully do." And that middle ground, it seems like you're talking about, is we have to do something different than the capitalist or the green movement. We're just living.

JEREMY KAMAL HARTLEY: Right, exactly.

ARMOND TOWNS: It's not resistance, it's just living. Can we just live in the world? I was saying the other day to my partner, it would just be nice for me to just go out and be fine. The imposition of difference onto black people is like a constant relationship that the society puts on you. I'm reminded here of the work of Frantz Fanon (2021), and one of the things he says in the fourth chapter of *Black Skin, White Masks*, is he's on a train and this small white child says, "look mom, a Negro." And it's in that moment that he is brought back into his blackness when he was just chilling. Just minding his own business. And that's a constant possibility. And it seems like what you're doing with trap music and water and architecture is refusing those categories right? You're saying we just are.

JEREMY KAMAL HARTLEY: You paraphrase it so well—it's like, just take water and put it through blackness and then this is what happens. That's it. And that's why in this series I deliberately don't show any type of comparisons between white culture and black culture. I just want you to be immersed into what we do when we are able to just be, and what happens when you scale that up to the context of a landscape.

Your position is my first time hearing that sentiment in terms of how we have been lumped into this idea of nature. And I guess in some way subconsciously I've felt that with regards to our history of being used like chattel or property. However, once again I regarded those things as technologies. You've expanded my understanding of what that actually entails by saying it's actually nature. And I'm curious as to how many other people in our community are aware of that perspective. Do you think it's important that we understand that perspective and what are the ramifications of that going forward? You know, is that something we disrupt? Is that something we go into with a new perspective on what nature is supposed to be? Is it something we stand apart from? What is your take on that kind of perspective?

ARMOND TOWNS: In my work what I tried to do is really point out that relationship between nature and technology right? Because you know, one of the things that I talk about is how Europe imagines Africa. In the book *The Invention of Africa*, V. Y. Mudimbe (1988) talks about how Africa is imagined as this kind of archaic state of nature. And then, the movement of Black people to the New World is itself a part of this kind of technological making of us from nature into the Negro, into a media technology. So that discussion of technology is already a part of who we are. So you've had this kind of intimate connection between us and nature but also us and these Western technological concepts for this modern capitalist project of enrichment for specific populations.

We could say that the practices after racial slavery have been designed to continue that kind of technological-labor relationship that we have with the state. Whether that's the Black Codes or Jim Crow, or mass incarceration, we can kind of see the racism of the state as a way of trying to prevent us from ever leaving behind that kind of technological relationship. But also Black people have always understood the relationship between ourselves and nature and utilized nature in ways that have basically transformed what this entire modern world is. I always say to my students that poor black people know [*Karl*] Marx, without ever reading him. Making something out of nothing is itself a kind of understanding of the problems of the capitalist project that a lot of us live under and that involves a remaking of nature. This is what really interested me in your new approaches to nature, this remaking of nature.

JEREMY KAMAL HARTLEY: Aw man, this is good. I just would love to see what happens when Bratton's work and yours meet. Because a lot of his discussion about technology was also deeply rooted in a reinterpretation of who we are as human beings. I think it's like this new thing that emerged, this new kind of huge technological dependence, reliance, relationship that crosses race, politics, minerals, and is so interwoven in our existence, in our fabric, and our perception of the world around us, that it has kind of displaced us from, or demystifies our human centric viewpoint—here's human, here's nature, and we are the governors of it.

Bratton's take on it is, if you looked at the history of the earth, at first, you'd see a bunch of hot rocks melded together. Slowly those rocks would cool down. You'll then see the formation of ice. Slowly you'll see the formation of water; that ice would thaw into water. And then you'll start to see little plants sprout, and eventually you'll start to see forests, and eventually from these forest grounds and various bodies of water, organisms will evolve. And then you'll see humans. Next, you'll see fiber optic cables crossing the sea floor, and then you'll start to see satellites populating the earth's orbit and so on. And we are an aspect within that continuum versus this hierarchical role that we try to assume. And the thing that I don't really hear about is how this perspective intersects Black culture. In a lot of ways, blackness is also asking that we reinterpret our humanity.

ARMOND TOWNS: You're asking, where does Blackness fit into that frame right? And the way that Europe has written Black people is that we are left behind and are the natural.

JEREMY KAMAL HARTLEY: Right right right.

ARMOND TOWNS: If you read some of the early slave documents in North America, the way that many white people framed slavery was like this way of bringing us out of the jungle. It's part of this civilizing mission of Europe to enslave Black people. So in their minds, regardless of the violence, they're the ones who are helping us, through the extraction of resources from Africa and Asia. If we want to be real, like a lot of this just really goes back to them kicking the Moors out of Europe. They were only able to do that because they got gunpowder from China. Let's just be real. So they got lucky because of Chinese trade routes. Europeans rewrite themselves as constantly evolving and developing figures, you know with the phonetic alphabet, but that comes from the Phoenicians. That also comes from Asia. Everything that is Europe comes from somewhere else. Europe's idea of technological development, its idea of hierarchy is really based off this older fabrication that Europe and North America are somehow just better than everybody else, but this is just fabrication.

JEREMY KAMAL HARTLEY: I'm still curious, though, with that trajectory, of course, we can agree we're not left behind in the jungle. Where are we, in that line, to you? There's a clear idea that that's not where we are, and sometimes I'm like, are we ahead of it? Or where do you feel like we are in that process of the evolution of the Earth, if you use that as the analogy?

ARMOND TOWNS: W. E. B. Du Bois (1990, 7) has this kind of constantly quoted line, "How does it feel to be a problem?" And everybody talks about that, and they only talk about that question, which is this question that the white society is asking us as black people. This means it is white people's problem, not ours. But after that question, Du Bois also says, "I answer seldom a word" (7). Which to me suggests that, for Du Bois, he doesn't care what white society is worried about. But the framing of a lot of his work has been this kind of obsession with what the white society thinks about us. And I think Nahum Chandler's (2014) work also kind of speaks to this, but what I think Du Bois is speaking to in his answer is this relationship between blackness and a completely alternative understanding of what it means to be human. For Du Bois, the Negro is this alternative form of intelligence. Of course, Du Bois is using the Negro in his context, which doesn't mean the same thing for us today. But that alternative understanding of intelligence and alternative understanding of consciousness, I think, for Du Bois doesn't suggest that we as Black people are better than white people. He's not trying to create another hierarchy. He's trying to say that there are other forms of humanity, we don't have to continually mirror Europe's form of humanity. If we do, we're just going to extract everything to its end, until there's nothing left. I don't think that we have that option. And I think it's not just Black people who have this approach. I think there's a long history of multiple forms of humanity that are not European, and we as Black people are merely one important example.

JEREMY KAMAL HARTLEY: Yes, yes.

ARMOND TOWNS: It's just like at what point are we going to have to accept another form of humanity for us all to survive?

JEREMY KAMAL HARTLEY: I think that's the mic drop. It starts to bring in the idea of a climate disaster being kind of that moment of reckoning. And that resurfacing of considering the relationship between nature and Black people in a whole different way. Climate disaster is asking us to consider Blackness. You know what I mean? It's prompting us to consider Blackness and in a way, and to your point, also other alternative forms of humanity, because this ain't working at the moment. Yeah, I love it, I love it.

ARMOND TOWNS: We don't have a choice.

JEREMY KAMAL HARTLEY: Right, yeah.

ARMOND TOWNS: It's going to make the choice for us. So either we can make the choice now, or we can just wait until we have the choice made for us.

JEREMY KAMAL HARTLEY: Right, right.

ARMOND TOWNS: This conversation has been great.

JEREMY KAMAL HARTLEY: Absolutely!

References and Further Reading

Bratton, Benjamin H. 2015. *The Stack: On Software and Sovereignty*. Software Studies. Cambridge: MIT Press.

Chandler, Nahum Dimitri. 2014. *X–The Problem of the Negro as a Problem for Thought*. First edition. American Philosophy. New York: Fordham University Press.

Du Bois, W. E. B. 1990. *The Souls of Black Folk*. New York: Vintage Books/The Library of America.

Fanon, Frantz. 2021. *Black Skin, White Masks*. London: Penguin Classics.

Judy, R. A. 2020. *Sentient Flesh: Thinking in Disorder, Poiēsis in Black*. Black Outdoors: Innovations in the Poetics of Study. Durham, NC: Duke University Press.

Kamal Hartley, Jeremy. 2019. *Mojo: Da Floods*. Video, 2:15. https://jeremykamal.com/Mojo-Da-Floods.

Mudimbe, V. Y. 1988. *The Invention of Africa: Gnosis, Philosophy, and the Order of Knowledge*. African Systems of Thought. Bloomington: Indiana University Press.

Towns, Armond R. 2022. *On Black Media Philosophy*. Environmental Communication, Power, and Culture 2. Oakland: University of California Press.

28
ON THE ECOLOGICAL FUTURABILITIES OF EXPERIMENTAL FILM LABS

Noélie Martin and Jacopo Rasmi

This chapter considers the experience of the "experimental film lab network" from the contemporary perspective of ecological thought. Even though we, as authors, don't belong directly to such a network, we both have spent time within this cinematographic universe, not just as researchers but as friends, audience, and collaborators working mostly in France. Thus, the chapter articulates a conceptual and general approach to this phenomenon that is coupled with an ecocritical point of view "from the field" based on two case studies observed through direct participation. First, we will provide a sketch of ecomedia theory as it can be applied to cinema and give some general insights into the history of independent film labs, whose recent expansion follows the temporal trajectory of society's environmental concerns. Then, we will discuss the ecological implications of their work by introducing two specific experiences. Framed by references to ecomedia studies, such a double focus wishes to underline the actual and the potential ecology of these kinds of media environments thriving on the margins of the official world of visual communication.

What Does Cinema Look Like When Observed Through Ecomedia Glasses?

Since the early 2000s, the traditions of ecological theory and media theory have started to merge and mingle. This encounter gave birth to the field of "ecomedia" (Cubitt, 2005), despite some key thinkers – for example, the French author Félix Guattari (1989/2000) – had interrogated this intersection much earlier. To sketch out an approximate cartography of such a hybrid reflection, we identify three approaches to ecomedia inquiry: (1) mediation *as* an environment; (2) mediation *in* an environment; and (3) mediation *of* the environment. The first approach conceives human techniques of communication more broadly than simple instruments in the hands of a willing subject. For instance, according to the media archaeologist Jussi Parikka (2011) who draws on a deep philosophical tradition including McLuhan and Simondon, media are processes that set and modify the environmental conditions – time and space, and therefore agency – in which subjects operate. The second approach focuses on all the connections between a situation of mediation – for instance, an e-mail correspondence or a movie production – and the multiple environments within which it unfolds: material as well as social. This perspective attempts to account for the various relations of dependence and reciprocity but also exploitation between a media situation and the environments surrounding it: the labour conditions, the energy uses, the material production of tools, etc. The third approach, perhaps the most common, studies how the perceptions of our environments are shaped by media representations and considers how the semantic and aesthetic inventions of a media operation lead us to perceive and understand the environments we inhabit.

Cinema can be analyzed through each layer of this theoretical diagram. As we analyze the relationship between the cinematographic universe and ecological issues via these conceptual schemes, we widen the thematic horizon of "environmental films" (beyond well-known works such as the non-fiction inquiry *An Inconvenient Truth* and the cli-fi blockbuster *The Day After Tomorrow*) and land in a more complex territory that we will define as "cinematographic ecologies". Experimental film labs will be considered within this wider and not so literal understanding.

Another three-fold model could be proposed to describe our multilayered approach of "cinematographic ecologies"[1] based on the different phases of the film's existence: (1) *before* the film; (2) *within* the film; (3) and *after* the film. Considering the ecology that precedes a film means paying attention to all the environmental implications of its creative process: the relations among the crew, the waste produced during the shooting, and the impact on the living beings that inhabit the spaces where the production takes place. This is an *ecology of creation and production*, which is the main focus of our study of the film labs network. The second ecology mentioned concerns the films themselves, considered as formal and semantic objects, allowing us to experience our environments in particular ways. This could be named an *ecological esthetics*. Last but not least, we should acknowledge an ecology that describes how publics get access to films: these situations of attention also need to be observed from the perspective of their environmental conditions. It is an *ecology of distribution and of reception*.

How much water and energy were "wasted" in California in order to shoot one of the most famous sequence of *Singing in the Rain* (Vaughan, 2016)? What experiences of the animism that infuses living environment are provoked in watching *Princess Mononoke* by Hayao Myazaki (Cubitt, 2005)? To what extent can Michelangelo Frammartino's *Alberi*, a looped, high-definition video installation representing a plant ritual, bring its spectators into a new enactment of a cross-species event (Rasmi, 2021)? Each example embodies one of the lines through which the inquiry of cinematographic ecologies unfolds. We could find similarities within the wider field of reflections on cinema and environmental problems that was inaugurated in the Anglo-Saxon context at the end of the 1990s (e.g. Hochman, 1998; Mitman, 1999). This chapter asks: How might the relatively little-known movement of the independent film lab be valorized within ecomedia studies? We will address such question via two case studies, after a brief historical presentation.

How Did the Independent Film Lab Movement Emerge and Proliferate?

Independent film labs are shared spaces focusing on analogue film that foster creations, meetings, debates, and projections. They take different forms according to their history, the city, and the country where they are located, the equipment they possess and their artistic commitments. Sometimes they are run by salaried members or, more often, by volunteers. In these spaces, filmmakers experiment with a real freedom of action: as stated by *L'Abominable* film lab in Paris, these "workshops" are devoted "to open new territories of cinema". Previously an invisible stage in the cinematographic production, the work in the laboratory becomes here an occasion for exploring new possibilities of creation (Thouvenel & Constant, 2014).[2]

The emergence of the independent film lab movement is linked to the cinematographic forms that are often called "experimental cinema", "pure" cinema (Henri Chomette, Germaine Dulac), "metric cinema" (Kurt Kren, Peter Kubelka), and "abstract cinema". These terms designate above all an unconventional experience of cinema that reflects on cinematic form. But they are also connected to new economic and material infrastructures. In this context, Jonas Mekas founded the *Film-Makers' Cooperative* in New York in 1962, which specialized in the distribution of experimental films. He then encouraged other independent filmmakers to set up their own infrastructures. The *London Filmmakers Co-op*, inaugurated in 1966 by a group of British structural filmmakers, became the main source of distribution of experimental films in Europe during the 1960s and 1970s. Such cooperatives were created with the idea of reducing film production costs and developing the practice of 16 mm, a professional television format. Their independence was made possible by donations of technical equipment from commercial laboratories and the filmmakers' DIY spirit.

Film screenings have always been decisive opportunities for meetings between filmmakers, critics, and curators. In the French context, two important event programmers were *Le Collectif Jeune Cinéma*, a distributor of experimental cinema established in 1971, and *Light Cone*, a distributor and technical support provider, founded in 1982. These events inspired the establishment of additional film labs. The pioneer *Atelier MTK*, founded in 1992 in Grenoble, welcomed film projects from French-speaking Europe and encouraged filmmakers to set up their own structures. *Mire* was formed in Nantes in 1993, followed two years later by *L'Abominable* in Paris. In the same period, a first network of French-speaking laboratories – connecting organizations in Nantes, Le Havre, Strasbourg, Geneva, Marseille, and elsewhere – were set up and accompanied by the self-published magazine *L'Ébouillanté* (1995–1999).[3]

Today, laboratories like *L'Abominable* can cover the whole production chain of analogue films. In parallel to their daily activity, the labs also conduct technical research through workshops focusing on various aspects of filming, including shooting, processing, and making emulsions. Over the past decade these projects have intersected environmental concerns. Today, film labs are developing a number of initiatives around non-polluting and plant-based chemical techniques: we provide an account of this rich range of ecological gestures by describing two case studies that we have closely observed.

Brewing Images in the Ruins of Industry

While the cinema industries have chosen a radical but not yet fully achieved transition to the "new world" of digital technologies, the "old world" of the analogue ecosystem has collapsed. Within a handful of years, an entire world of technical equipment, skills, and spaces has been quickly dismantled by the brutal force of the digital turn and its economic efficacy. Thus, during the last decade, the survival of analogue cinema has become mostly a matter of institutional conservation and marginal resistance that seeks to take advantage of this epochal transformation for deindustrializing (as much as possible) cinematographic creation. Settling in the ruins created by the technical shift of the film industry, the international network of experimental film labs has managed to invent new forms of media life by turning the technical heritage from the past into the basis of a future of surprising filmic shapes and publics. In this sense, we could conceive the film labs as hubs of a "collapsonaut" experience of media (Citton & Rasmi, 2020) that learns to travel and create through a technical universe supposedly killed off by the self-destructive logic of capitalist system.

As socio-technical environments devoted to the cinematographic experience, experimental film labs enact several tactical gestures in line with the environmental movement's attempts to address the looming disaster: a slow and post-growth attitude, a range of relatively low-tech and convivial tools (Illich, 1973), a social organization based on mutual aid and a certain degree of spontaneous wildness, and a non-commercial economy relying on donating and up-cycling. As showed in the volume *Kinetika* (2011), the fact that most of these labs occupy old industrial buildings that were abandoned following deindustrialization in the twentieth century couldn't be a more explicit symbol of their "collapsonaut" status. Another clear example of this status is the seminars held in the rural venue of Les Aubanneaux (France) in the summer of 2020 and 2021 with the goal of producing a plant-based and non-polluting developer for celluloid film. These seminars are the focus of the following case study.

Processing Films in the Company of Nettles and Ashes

Coordinated by the MTK lab team, the experimental seminars at Les Aubanneaux gathered filmmakers from different European labs and people with different skills including young researchers in chemistry and cinema, local experts in plants and harvesting, and graphic artists. Everyone joined the adventure on the basis of the personal interest and brought along specific abilities. The objective shared by the participants was attempting to produce a black-and-white developer corresponding as much as possible to the following specifications: (1) being made with local, non-industrial, and inexpensive ingredients; (2) using gestures and recipes that wouldn't demand complicated training, a lot of energy, or high-tech infrastructures; (3) having an efficacy relatively comparable to standard products; and (4) having a minimal impact on the surrounding environment in terms of extraction of natural materials, pollution, and waste.

A trial-and-error process was adopted. The starting reference for the collective work was the widely known recipe of Caffenol, a developer based on supermarket goods: instant coffee, vitamin C, and soda bicarbonate. In its protocol, the first two ingredients operate as combined revealing agents while the last prevents the PH from becoming too acidic and stopping the process of developing. Even if the recipe fulfilled some of the criteria fixed by the group, for instance the easiness of the process, it failed to meet other requirements such as avoiding reliance on industrial and commercial products. The investigation quickly took the shape of media archaeology research (Catanese & Parikka, 2018) meant to explore the blind spots of the technical development of cinema under capitalist conditions, namely mass production, standardization, and speed. The group made several attempts to substitute the basic ingredients of Caffenol with common materials from everyday life.[4] Often these attempts drew inspiration from older studies, yet, problematically, they did not manage to get rid of some key industrial ingredients such as vitamin C. Claiming neither an ambition for purity nor complete "survivalist" autonomy, the seminars tried to achieve a more radical result by avoiding the purchase and use of this kind of product.

After a first phase that consisted of testing several ingredients, mostly plant-based ones that contained acids meant to trigger the developer (green tea, lemons, thyme), the collective decided to focus on nettles. The choice was based on several factors: not only a certain degree of efficacity, but also wide and immediate accessibility as these plants grow abundantly around the location of the workshop. Despite their broad availability in anthropized spaces (because this plant, a sort of "companion species", loves the chemical composition of soil "polluted" by animal and human life) and a rich tradition of various uses (food, medicine and cosmetics), most people are concerned about this plant's capacity to sting and therefore try to eliminate it from their gardens. Another ingredient was necessary to make the developer work: ashes. Easily available in a rural context where firewood is still widespread, this ingredient replaces the soda bicarbonate and keeps the reaction moving by ensuring an alkaline milieu. The collateral effects of this kind of chemistry – such as the coloured veils on the film – could be considered interesting surprises from the aesthetic point of view of someone who looks more for artistic experimentation than for clean realist reproduction.

The two seminars also provided the opportunity for crafting two collective films titled *Crête* (2020) and *L'amitié, ce n'est pas toujours du ski de fond* (2021) that – besides being a fun, experimental space for the participants – also became a "pedagogical" instrument to be screened in workshops and talks about this experience. Since the initiative remains a work in progress, sharing its results and recipes does not just mean showing outcomes but also discussing open problems together. This collective intelligence has also been put to work through an online wiki page compiled by the people who took part in the seminar.[5] It was important to make everything public in order to look for support (within and beyond the film community) to improve these practice and research.

Crafting Homemade Emulsions

The research of a plant-based developer described above is not unique. The Maddox seminars at *L'Abominable* that brought together approximately twenty artists between 2014 and 2016 are another interesting example to consider (Martin, 2016). The workshop's name is a homage to Richard Leach Maddox (1816–1902), a pioneer of photography, who in 1876 invented the gelatin-silver bromide process and the collodio-bromide process, without patenting it and allowing the following generations to take advantage of it. The Maddox seminars focused on the main component of film, the photochemical emulsion, with the goal of developing a handmade panchromatic emulsion, reproducing a pioneering colour technique (autochrome) and the coating of the emulsion onto the film strip. Two new DIY machines were created during these gatherings: the *Larry box* and the *MiniMadBox*. The key principles of the Maddox seminars, understood as places of research and experimentation rather than "artistic creation",[6] were the reappropriation of skills and the reinvention of pioneering film techniques.

This initiative could be considered as part of a global individual and collective ecological impulse (MacKenzie & Marchessault, 2019). Some of its members have adopted a self-sufficient, sustainable living and the crafting of self-made emulsion is consistent with their lifestyle. In 2003, Robert Schaller created the *Handmade Film Institute* not only to promote the knowledge necessary for making film but also to propose retreats offering a particular experience of the environment, either in the form of an expedition ("the Wilderness Expedition") or in the form of a camp ("Film Camp") on Orcas Island in the State of Washington.[7] Some compare the craft practice of emulsion with the wider crafting of a sustainable habitat, as in the case of Alex MacKenzie who, while living primarily in Vancouver (Canada), built a cob house with his partner on a Pacific island. For MacKenzie, making his own house is an extension of what he does with film.[8] Others combine their art with activist practices and vegan choices. It is worth noting that for some participants of the Maddox seminar, the research of alternatives to the animal gelatin present in industrial emulsion was motivated by an antispecist ethic. Robert Schaller has made many films with an emulsion made of Arabic gum, which is naturally sensitive to light. Alex MacKenzie made a film with agar-agar and used as a gel in food production.[9] Esther Urlus and Josephine Ahnelt, founder and member of WormFilmwerkpaatz, have replaced animal gelatin with polyvinyl alcohol.[10]

What Moves in Their Movies?

Without any doubt, a lot of films in the experimental lab movement represent interesting aesthetic attempts at the visual representation and the perception of our common (and threatened…) earthly life: from the classic *The Garden of Earthly Delights* (1981) by Stan Brakhage to the recent *La Trilogie Carnassière* (2018) by Carole Thibaud or *Atomic Garden* by Ana Vaz (2018). Therefore, we could have easily chosen to present this cinematic universe from the perspective of what we have called the "mediation *of* environments". Instead, we prefer to consider the peculiar conditions of existence and the collective work of a media ecosystem that resist the logic of the cultural industries, not only by the means of the filmic forms that it develops.

By paying attention to such experiences, we can understand how their ecology is likewise rooted in the relation that these filmmakers have to the film material as a living phenomenon (Knowles, 2020). Situated somewhere between mineral and plant life, the revealed image seems to have its own agency with attributes that could be called "animistic" if we believe, with Perig Pitrou (Castro, Pitrou & Rebecchi, 2020, 26), that "animism" means "to consider alive what isn't supposed to be so". Working *with* (instead of *on*) these "vibrant matters" (Bennett, 2010) establishes a distance from the illusion and neutral construction of industrial cinema based mainly on naturalist reproduction. It is interesting to highlight that this practice leads to a pre-modern conception of both matter and nature, closer to an organicist vision of the world that allows a rehabilitation of plural ways of doing, seeing, and feeling. The independent film labs produce new ecologies insofar as they create and maintain networks of relations between beings, human, and non-human, living and non-living in what Donna Haraway (2016) would call "sympoiesis".

Observed in light of our analyses focusing on the ecologies of production, the practices of the analogue cinema network represent an interesting ecomedia model in as much as they: (1) care about their own environmental impact as well as about the living companionship of the materials and the tools taking part in these particular activities; (2) practice a relation to knowledge and to techniques that is open, creative, and collective – opposed to attitudes of competition and control, of progress and obsolescence belonging to the market and part of the modern scientific world; and (3) rummage through the ruined outskirts of our times (the blind spots of past ages or abandoned items in the present) in order to invent media worlds that are more "futurable" and desirable. Here, a "horizon of possibility" for cinematographic invention appears: the "futurability" (Berardi, 2019) of analogue film beyond the "impotence" of the standardized and unsustainable productivism of the mass-mediatic industry.[11]

Notes

1 This expression borrows from "media ecologies" suggested by Matthew Fuller (2007).
2 Genevieve Yue (2015) has published a synthetic introduction to this "kitchen sink cinema" on *Film Comment* (2015): https://www.filmcomment.com/blog/artist-run-film-laboratories/.
3 The fanzine is archived online at https://www.filmlabs.org/dissemination/fanzines/.
4 The seminars worked on topics and practices that were discussed and shared within the event "Photographic Garden" run by Filmwerkplaatz (Rotterdam) in 2021. This programme of the lectures and workshops – including proposals like "Regenerating outdated film materials" (A. Cousins) or "Tinting toning with plants and other materials from nature" (J. Mayes) – focused on "low toxic", "alternative chemistry that will yield a different, new film aesthetic". For more insight on the event and its contents see https://worm.org/2021/06/01/filmwerkplaats-project-photographic-garden/. Among the "counter-practices" presented in those interventions, one finds the inspiring examples of Esther Urlus (working on a urine-based developer: https://estherurlus.hotglue.me/urine) or Ricardo Leite (processing film with different plants: https://vimeo.com/138099218).
5 The wiki pages are available at https://www.filmlabs.org/wiki/fr/emulsion/start.
6 An accurate overview of the Maddox experience is available at https://www.filmlabs.org/wiki/en/start.
7 See https://hmfi.handmadefilm.org/.
8 See its personal website: https://www.alexmackenzie.ca/.
9 The movie « Agar-Agar » is online: https://vimeo.com/213913982.
10 Their research around a vegan silver-bromide emulsion is available on the internet (https://www.youtube.com/watch?v=r1g7d2ypm-w&t=25s) as a text on this experience (https://www.filmidee.it/2021/03/vegan-analogue-film/).
11 This text was written with the generous collaboration of Marc Higgin (scholar – Université Grenoble Alpes); Joyce Lainé (filmmaker – MTK lab); and Mariya Nikiforova (scholar – Light Cone).

Further Reading

Bozak, Nadia. 2012. *The Cinematic Footprint. Lights, Camera, Natural Resources*. New York: Routledge University Press.
Della Noce, Elio, and Murari, Lucas, 2022. *Expanded Nature. Ecologies du cinéma expérimental*. Paris: Light Cone.
Knowles, Kim. 2020. *Experimental Film and Photochemical Practices*. New York: Palgrave Macmillan.
MacKenzie, Scott & Janine Marchessault (eds). 2019. *Process Cinema. Handmade Film in the Digital Age*. Montreal: McGill-Queen's University Press.
Thouvenel, Eric & Constant, Carole. 2014. *Fabrique du cinéma expérimental*. Paris: Paris Experimental.

References

Bennett, Jane. 2010. *Vibrant Matter. A Political Ecology of Things*. Durham, NC: Duke University Press. Berardi, « Bifo » Franco. 2019. *Futurability. The Age of Impotence and the Horizon of Possibility*. London: Verso Books.
Castro, Teresa, Pitrou, Perig & Rebecchi, Marie (eds). 2020. *Puissance du végétal et cinéma animiste. La vitalité révélée par la technique*. Dijon: Les Presses du réel.
Catanese, Rossella & Jussi, Parikka. 2018. "Handmade Films and artist-run Labs: The chemical Sites of Film's Counterculture". *Necsus*. Url: https://necsus-ejms.org/handmade-films-and-artist-run-labs-the-chemical-sites-of-films-counterculture/
Citton, Yves & Jacopo Rasmi. 2020. *Générations Collapsonautes. Naviguer par temps d'effondrement*. Paris: Seuil.
Cubitt, Sean. 2005. *Eco Media*. Amsterdam/New York: Rodopi.
Fuller, Matthew. 2007. *Media ecologies. Materialist Energy in Art and Technoculture*. Cambribdge: MIT Press.
Guattari, Félix. 1989/2000. *The Three Ecologies*, translated by Ian Pindan and Paul Sutton. London: Athalon Press.
Haraway, Dona. 2016. *Staying with the Trouble: Making Kin in the Chtthulucene*. Durham, NC: Duke University Press.
Hochman, Jhan. 1998. *Green Cultural Studies: Nature in Film, Novel, and Theory*. Caldwell: University of Idaho Press.
Illich, Ivan. 1973. *Tools for Conviviality*. London: Calder and Boyars.
Knowles, Kim. 2020. *Experimental Film and Photochemical Practices*. New York: Palgrave Macmillan
MacKenzie, Scott & Janine Marchessault (eds). 2019. *Process Cinema. Handmade Film in the Digital Age*. Montreal: McGill-Queen's University Press.
Martin, Noélie. 2016. *Ethnographie d'une pratique filmique actuelle : la fabrication des emulsions artisanales*. Graduate thesis under the direction of Patricia Falguières, EHESS (published on-line on *La Furia Umana*, #33, #35 et #36).
Mitman, Gregg. 1999. *Reel Nature: America's Romance with Wildlife on Film*. Cambridge, MA: Harvard University Press.
Parikka, Jussi. 2011. "Ecologies and Imaginary Media: Transversal Expansions, Contractions, and Foldings", *Fiberculture Journal*, n. 17, 34–50.
Rasmi, Jacopo. 2021. *Le hors-champ est dedans! Michelangelo Frammartino, écologie, cinéma*. Villeneuve d'Asq: Presses Universitaires du Septentrion.
Thouvenel, Eric & Constant, Carole. 2014. *Fabrique du cinéma expérimental*. Paris: Paris Experimental.
Vaughan, Hunter. 2016. "500,000 Kilowatts of Stardust: An Eco-Materialist Reframing of Singin' in the Rain", in *Sustainable Media. Critical Approaches to Media and Environment*, edited by Nicole Staroelski and Janet Walker, 23–37. London/New York: Routledge.
Yue, Genevieve. 2015. "Kitchen Sink Cinema: Artist-Run Film Laboratories." Film Comment. March 30, 2015. https://www.filmcomment.com/blog/artist-run-film-laboratories/.

29
POPULAR MUSIC
Folk and Folk Rock as Green Cultural Production

John Parham

This essay draws upon folk music and its now proliferating subgenres to address a key question in ecomedia studies – to what extent can ecological awareness be nurtured by green popular culture? Popular music exists as a configuration of "organic" folk culture, oppositional subculture, and mass market "pop." The consensus is that this particular "circuit of culture" (du Gay et al. 1997) is not especially conducive to meaningful environmental representation. Few pop or rock artists engage with environmental issues and when they do it's invariably tokenistic (Parham 2016, 151). Likewise, rock music's narcissism, individualism, and consumerist values are, David Ingram argues, "largely antithetical to radical environmentalism" (2010, 120).

But circuits, like ecosystems, mutate. They evolve in response to changing conditions, emergent risks, and new opportunities. The ecological and climate crisis has accelerated globally since 1945, shortly before modern pop and rock emerged. Mutating established categories is one way for new perspectives to be generated, perspectives perhaps better fitted to an altered world. I'll argue here that popular music is evolving hybrid forms that address diverse and complex ecological issues, from how we treat the physical environment or other animals to questions of plastic use, pollution, and climate change. My focus will be on one artist in particular, Ani DiFranco.[1]

Parameters: "Green" Popular Music

There are different ways to think about green popular music. One approach could be the ecomateriality examined elsewhere in this book. A *Rolling Stone* article on "The 15 Most Eco-Friendly Rockers" highlights, for example, how musicians ranging from Bonnie Raitt to Radiohead have promoted environmental issues and green lifestyle in practical terms – such as touring ecovillages – and in material terms, through adopting sustainable low-impact touring practices, by recycling, and using biodegradable materials and biofuels (Coscarelli 2010).

Environmental advocacy might also come (in the sense of *political ecology*) through the music itself. Previously studied examples include the Beach Boys (Carter 2013) and U2 (Parham 2016, 165–69), while Ingram identifies a sustained environmentalist tradition in folk artists such as Malvina Reynolds, Pete Seeger, Tracy Chapman, and Neil Young. Such analyses are mindful, nonetheless, of potential contradictions between environmental advocacy and the priorities of the music industry or rock culture itself. The Beach Boys' commitment to environmental protection was seemingly checked by "the risk averse logic of the Commercial music industry" (Carter 2013, 44). U2's advocacy of "more sustainable ways of life" appears to be contradicted by the industrial infrastructure that underpins their studio recording and world tours (Pedelty 2012, 18).

Green popular music also encompasses artists focused on environments, animals, or humans' increasingly hazardous impact on the Earth. Timothy Morton's "dark ecology" conceptualises a sense of our now troubled and ominous relationship with other species. This is articulated, Morton suggests, in "uncanny" songs like The Cure's "A Forest" that convey the "environment as creepy" (Morton 2010, 54). The avant-garde or "freak" folk of Joanna Newsom likewise posits nature as impenetrable and dangerous. Newsom deranges our sense of place and other animals via indecipherable lyrics, a jarring, childlike voice, and harp arrangements which mess with our expectations of how both folk and classical music should sound (see Ingram 2010, 117).

The ecocultural approach I take in this essay can examine where music originates from, how genres adapt to and circulate environmental themes, and the success (or otherwise) with which "green music" reaches a mass audience. For all their faults, U2's blend of "indigenous" Irish music, American folk, and global rock might well have been effective in translating an environmentalist sense of place and an urgent realisation of ecological crisis into popular awareness (Parham 2016, 165–66). DiFranco is another example, one who makes a direct case for how folk's evolution into folk rock can function as green popular music.

Folk into Rock

On a spectrum between Anglophone folk music and electrified rock music, traditional folk, alongside country music, is usually seen as the popular form closest to "nature." Its roots lie in the land, in songs articulating an earlier, everyday agrarian life. Both the US folk revival of the 1960s and its British equivalent contrasted a rural ideal to the alienations of modern industrial, urban life (Gruning 2006, 2). Commentators have complicated that portrayal, but it still recurs frequently and, in the assessment of some critics, remains a valid one. David Ingram argues that a "folkish anti-modernism" and "radical" nostalgia critiques the present, while folk is also oriented towards the future for instance by exemplifying modes of "local, sustainable cultural production" (2015, 221, 229). Rightly or wrongly, however, folk can also be seen as a genre constrained, in terms of being truly *popular*, by archaism, parochialism, and somewhat stale genre conventions. Describing the English Folk Revival of the twentieth century, Georgina Boyes concludes that "the Folk, by definition, re-created, rather than innovated" and suggests that folk music would not develop unless the "fundamental" principles of "tradition" and "authenticity" were rejected (2010, 240–41).

Yet folk music is evolving. Dick Weissman (2020) highlights how in North America the genre has co-mingled with blues, Celtic, hip hop, punk, pop, and world music (Chapters 12, 16), while Rowan Bayliss Hawitt (2020) detects movement beyond the "surface markers" of folk towards "globalised forms such as popular music" (336). Such adaptations can help address environmental challenges. In respective studies of Canadian and Scottish folk music, Ellen Waterman (2016) and Rowan Bayliss Hawitt (2020) both argue that a melding of local sensitivity and global ecological concern has engendered new environmental ethics of "responsibility and redress" (Waterman) and "solidarity and care" (Hawitt). However, can these new forms of folk music achieve the audience reach of the mainstream music industry? And why does this matter?

Both the science underlying ecological crisis and the required adjustments in policy and politics are complex. They seem to require challenging texts able to encapsulate and represent that complexity. However, as Richard Kerridge has pointed out, the speed at which the crisis is escalating means we probably don't have time to wait for "avant-garde" aesthetics and ideas to reach a larger audience (2014, 368–69). He concludes that while awakening urgency about climate change will need the dramatic jolt offered by experimental forms of culture, a more moderate disturbance of popular genres might also coax viewers, readers, or listeners relatively quickly towards environmental awareness. Kerridge cites science fiction, horror, and recent television nature documentaries as examples (372). Folk music is evolving in a similar way.

In *Electric Eden*, Rob Young concurs that folk music embodies important environmental values – organic local culture, a critique of modernity – while also arguing that in the 1960s it avoided stagnation through electrification and the emergence of folk rock (2011, 5–10). Since then folk has intersected more and more with music industry staples such as electronic rock and mainstream pop. Just as country music now encompasses "alt-country," rapper Little Nas X's genre-busting "Old Town Road," and commercial superstardom (Taylor Swift), folk, too, has splintered into almost innumerable variants. These are both subcultural – "chamber folk," "psych folk," and "weird folk" – and mainstream: "folk rock," "indie folk," "pop folk," and arena fillers such as Mumford and Sons and Fleet Foxes.

The most logical space for environmentalist folk music to move into is rock. Like folk, rock is guitar music. Lyrics are important, as is live performance. Rock has inherited core values from folk: authenticity, community, critique of mass culture, and political protest (see Bennett 2001, 30; Keightley 2001, 120). Rock also emerged from "pop music," inheriting its melodies and production values, its thematic emphasis on love, romance, and sex, and its commercial instincts and audiences (see Frith 1983, 32–38). While this potentially creates a tension between social dissent and commercial appeal, it is a tension that can be harnessed by environmentally minded artists. Folk rock has the capacity to stretch green discourse beyond prevailing modes – earnestness, fury, and sermonising – that lack traction amongst a mass audience. Correspondingly, folk rock could move rock beyond its narcissistic limitations – perhaps even its "waning vitality" as a genre (Pedelty 2011, 19) – thereby enabling rock music to rediscover the ground beneath its feet. Ani DiFranco arguably shows us how.

Ani DiFranco

Originally from Buffalo, New York, and now settled in New Orleans, DiFranco was introduced by her music teacher to Buffalo's folk scene at the age of nine and began learning guitar. DiFranco left home at 15 and toured extensively, selling tapes at shows and building a fan base via open mic events and festivals. Her connections with the folk scene run deep. DiFranco has worked with both contemporary artists (e.g. Bon Iver's Justin Vernon) and folk icons (Utah Phillips, Pete Seeger). The Woody Guthrie Center in Oklahoma curates her fortnightly radio show. DiFranco's music likewise identifies her as a folk artist: the centrality of lyrics, a conversational stage style (Garrett 2008, 379), and an emphasis on live performance over recording. Music is "something you *did*, not something you *bought*," she has said (Rodgers 2000). Nevertheless, DiFranco has currently recorded 22 studio albums, on her own label, Righteous Babe Records, established so that she would never be beholden to corporate money. The label maintains the community ethos of folk – employing friends, being based in a renovated Buffalo church, and striving to "work with local designers and manufacturers." As such, Righteous Babe corresponds with the ecocritical values espoused by critics like David Ingram and Mark Pedelty, who advocate folk as local, sustainable music. The label nurtures the music itself. More than twenty other artists are signed to Righteous Babe, ranging from Anaïs Mitchell's post-apocalyptic folk opera *Hadestown* to Peter Mulvey's wintry soundscapes.

In other respects, DiFranco conforms less readily to the folk archetype. Interviews often query her categorisation as a folk singer. DiFranco's largely self-produced albums recreate the "authenticity" of live performance central to folk, keeping the music close to her audience (Barlow 2019). Yet intermittent regrets about not doing her songs justice ("sometimes I do look back at my records and I think 'sorry, songs'"! [CBS Mornings 2021]) locate DiFranco somewhere between folk and the pop music tradition of the singer-songwriter. More visible still is a distinct subcultural attitude that DiFranco has helped introduce into folk culture. Tom Gruning's *Millennium Folk* offers entertaining accounts of her pierced and tattooed, gender and sexually fluid fans descending on folk festivals (2006, 125, 151). DiFranco herself describes her music as "one degree of separation between Pete Seeger and Prince" (another collaborator) and underlines a version of folk closer to the countercultural:

> folk music is not an acoustic guitar – that's not where the heart of it is. I use the word "folk" in reference to punk music and rap music. It's an attitude, it's an awareness of one's heritage, and it's a community. It's subcorporate music that gives voice to different communities and their struggle against authority.
>
> (Rodgers 2000)

DiFranco also transcends the place specificity of folk. She is a national, even international, artist who unwaveringly confronts a world stewing in neoliberal capitalism. Her songs attack big business, consumerism, patriarchy, sexism, racism, war, and gun crime. They incorporate references to climate change, global warming, the ozone layer, chemical and river pollution, plastic waste, and nuclear disaster. Correspondingly, while her eclectic music can accurately be called "folk rock" or "indie folk," these are just the foundations on which DiFranco overlays just about every other popular genre imaginable: jazz, soul, and funk; electronic, ambient, and environmental sound; hip hop, punk, and rock.

How does this translate into green popular music? Keir Keightley has distinguished between two rock music traditions. The first, "Romanticism," is organic. It cherishes a "pre-industrial" past and "locates authenticity principally in the direct communication between artist and audience." The second, "Modernism," values music that breaks from the past and shocks. Here, authenticity means being "true to […] experimentation, innovation, development, change" as a means of expressing estrangement from and a challenge to society (2001, 136). Romanticism encompasses folk, blues, and country styles. It emphasises roots, place, sincerity, liveness, "natural" as opposed to technological instruments, and a belief in a "core […] rock sound." Conversely, Modernism – closer to "art music" or pop – privileges radical or experimental sound, technology, and artifice (137). DiFranco swings between the two. And just as her musical fluidity has been seen to push the boundaries of feminist expression (Love 2013, 159), so, too, it meets the challenges of dark ecology by colliding the traditional signifiers of folk with the dissonant sounds of "modernist" rock.

Reprieve (from 2006) is a beautiful album haunted by natural disaster and human malignancy (or stupidity). Recorded before and after Hurricane Katrina, *Reprieve* also recalls the atomic bomb; its cover image shows a Nagasaki eucalyptus tree truncated by the bomb. Several tracks address ecological malaise by mixing seemingly incompatible sounds. On "Subconscious," electronic sound unsettles a largely conventional folk song to underscore its theme: personal anxiety compounded by a world of plastic water bottles, air conditioning, and cell phone radiation. In "Millennium Theater," pollution, melting ice caps, and a commodification of natural resources and of people are conveyed by a folk song that struggles to be heard beneath *Twilight Zone* electronica. There is no reprieve; the track ends in white noise. We live in "hell," says DiFranco on "Decree," the "darkest darkness." Mollified by media, consumer goods, and celebrity culture, nobody notices pollution, health hazards, or (it's implied) the death of nature. So DiFranco inflicts even greater injury to the folk sound. "Decree" is prefaced by noise: frightened animals and malign technologies. Discordant electronica tramples the guitar. The lyrics end prematurely, the folk voice annulled by 45 seconds of empty technological and percussive sound not unlike the outer limits of Radiohead. Gesturing towards the avant-garde, this experimental track sounds like the victory of "Modernist" rock over "Romantic" folk. The songs are a palimpsest: modernity writes itself over the values of folk.

The liberal use of studio-engineered, abstract sound – reverberation, eeriness, echo, and silence – often bleeding from one track to the next and implies an ontology of blurred lines, unsettled states, distortion, and disorientation brought about by the neoliberalism DiFranco is denouncing. Yet these sounds are also paired with environmental or animal sounds: wind through trees, birds singing and twittering, and honking and squawking geese (or ducks). Synthesised studio effects intrude, for example, in "Unrequited," where DiFranco is baffled at the urge to kill a "beautiful" animal just to hang it on the wall. The track ends, however, with a surprise – the fleeting sound of a horse whinnying. Written before Katrina struck, "Millennium Theater" mentions New Orleans biding its time. These environmental sounds imply not only a technologically altered posthuman world hurtling towards disaster but also the other type of posthumanism, the one where nature returns.

Earlier DiFranco songs had sometimes adopted an animal's perspective. On the title track of *Evolve* (2003), for example, folk guitar becomes a pounding funk bass as a moth frantically circles a lightbulb. It thinks it's "trying to evolve," just like we do while increasingly disorientated by a mediatised, technological world. On *Reprieve*, "In the Margins" opens with an acoustic guitar but played in a way critics and DiFranco herself have identified as "chunky," "ripping," and "powerful and percussive," a style apparently achieved by wrapping duct tape around artificial fingernails (Garrett 2008, 381, 388; Love 2013, 161). The guitar is overly forceful. Coupled with heavy bass, reverberation, and synthesised instruments it suggests again modern(ist) disorientation. The focus this time is on fractured personal relationships, disillusioned love, and the "cheap" insignificance of the human "saga." Until, that is, DiFranco takes on an animal's perspective. A "rare bird" flickers by; a stray dog looks on. Noticing these, DiFranco realises that love (the "pop" theme at the core of many of her songs) is a fool's game. These animal perspectives shift from the margins of the city to the centre of the song to see the world as it should be. Truth to Earth equates to truth to self. This understanding is met by a return to folk, the song concluding with unadorned vocals and scratched acoustic chords. By using animal, environmental, and technological sounds, DiFranco allows for ecological perspectives that would not be possible in a folk music conventionally grounded in *human* concepts of place, community, authenticity, and social solidarity. Yet Ani is nothing if not agile. Elsewhere she utilises the human perspective of the singer-songwriter tradition, extending the range of her green popular music.

Simon Frith has argued that, as folk music became increasingly intertwined with rock and pop, authenticity to the "folk" was replaced with personal authenticity: "truth to self rather than truth to a movement or an audience" (1983, 32). Something gets lost, it's implied. Yet shaped by feminism, DiFranco's songs have "always reflected an acute connection between my personal life and the life of my society" ("About Ani" 2022). Desire and aspiration, personal trauma and anxiety, sit alongside cultural, political and environmental hazards, creating a link between what she has called "macro" and "micro" melancholy ("Serpentine" 2003). Broken hearts happen (in part) because capitalism fosters transactional relationships, paranoid female identity, and the wrong kinds of masculinity. Moreover, DiFranco's music puts environmental desecration into dialogue with recent thinking around mental health and climate anxiety (see, for example, Clayton 2020; Thompson 2021).

"Simultaneously," from 2021's *Revolutionary Love*, is framed around a series of conjunctions. It conjoins a "fragile" self with a "dumb" social world. It suggests a cultural bipolarism – we feel (simultaneously) "fractured" and "free." The agents of our fractured selves are both political ("oppression") and personal ("disrespect") but so too are the solutions. The album was influenced by Valarie Kaur's book *See No Stranger: A Memoir and Manifesto of Revolutionary Love* (2020). Kaur argues for a politics of dissent and protest based on understanding, compassion, and dialogue with others. "Simultaneously" has no reference to climate change, plastic, or pollution. Yet in a context, in which the environmental crisis is increasingly personal, even in the global North – with forest fires in California and Australia, flash flooding in Britain and Germany – DiFranco appears to acknowledge this as green popular music. The video for "Simultaneously" was filmed on oil company land. DiFranco landed up in court charged with trespass. In articles and interviews, she has repeatedly articulated "revolutionary love" in ecological terms, expressed in the view that "we can't kick each other off the planet" (see Barlow 2019; Baltin 2020).

Conclusion: The Past Didn't Go Anywhere

"Simultaneously" can't really be called a folk song; it's about as close to pop as any DiFranco track I've heard. Critics and reviewers have, however, frequently noted DiFranco returning to her folk roots. *Revolutionary Love* is a good example. On her website, DiFranco writes:

> This thing was made more like it was 1968, with people performing on instruments made of wood and metal, laying down a few takes and moving on. It really brought out the prowess of the musicians involved and the immediacy of offering up a song to another human.

It was on a much earlier album, *The Past Didn't Go Anywhere* (1996), that DiFranco set Utah Phillips' stories to music: "I would find the BPM [*beats per minute*] of the story and try to negotiate a rhythm track to it" (Rodgers 2000). The purpose, DiFranco said at the time, was to unite the energy of youth and the wisdom of age. If younger musicians would only listen to Phillips, she insisted, they'd be inspired. And then they could "take the same old tools—an acoustic guitar—and be working in an old crusty medium like folk music, and do something totally new" (Rodgers 2000).

Now, folk artists are creating something new. Green ideas often lie at the heart of this, whether it's Edgelarks, Sam Lee, or Karine Polwart reworking traditional folk or artists like Cloud Cult, DiFranco, or the British indie band Sea Power explicitly colliding genres. Yet a question remains: how do we know whether these innovative forms of popular music really are helping nurture environmental awareness, changes in lifestyle, and even social action? A very rudimentary analysis indicates that some fans, at least, share or are inspired by musicians' environmental principles. On Twitter, if you pair "Ani DiFranco" with "climate," "environment," or "pollution," you will find people quoting DiFranco, citing her lyrics, or simply reflecting on the state of the planet after listening to her music:

> Untouchable Face by Ani DiFranco is taking on new, considerable meaning in the political and biological climate
> (One Shtick Ari (@arisbarmitzvah), March 5, 2020).

> Listening to Ani DiFranco this morning pretending it is the 90s and we still have time to avert climate catastrophe
> (Hiel, Adrian (@AdrianHiel), February 29, 2020).

Corroborating claims about green music's effect will ultimately require large scale, longitudinal analysis of fan literature, and/or social media. Addressing a lack of research into the audience reception of environmental texts is, I believe, still the key future task facing ecomedia studies (Parham 2016, 3). If we can answer those questions, the hope will be that these texts *do* speak to people, and in large enough numbers. They certainly deserve to.

In one of the few books on popular ecomusicology, Mark Pedelty writes that, "To be considered truly musical, organized sound also needs to contain selective and purposeful violations of culturally defined patterns, violations that both surprise and please an audience" (2011, 18–19). Avant-garde music is unlikely to please any audience at the scale environmental values must reach, nor will audiences be "surprised" (i.e., stimulated) by any forced repatriation back to "traditional" music. Splintering, mashing, and recombining genres are essential if we are to articulate and confront increasingly urgent challenges. But we should also retain core ecological values embedded into our cultural circuits by more traditional folk music. For there's pleasure to be had here: the pleasure of music charged by a visionary mix of folk, rock and pop, punk and hip hop, and free jazz and electronica, and that brings along with it the sound of horses, birds, and trees.

Note

1 With thanks to my friend and colleague David Arnold who introduced me to Ani DiFranco and shared his thoughts on environmental themes in her work.

Further Reading

Ingram, David. 2010. *The Jukebox in the Garden: Ecocriticism and American Popular Music*. Amsterdam: Rodopi.
Love, Nancy A. 2013. "Ani DiFranco: Making Feminist Waves." In *Political Rock*, edited by Mark Pedelty and Kristine Weglarz, 159–76. Burlington, VT: Ashgate.
Parham, John. 2016. *Green Media and Popular Culture: An Introduction*. London: Palgrave Macmillan.
Pedelty, Mark. 2011. *Ecomusicology: Rock, Folk and the Environment*. Philadelphia, PA: Temple University Press.
Young, Rob. 2011. *Electric Eden: Unearthing Britain's Visionary Music*. London: Faber and Faber.

References

"About Ani." 2022. Accessed January 15, 2022. http://anidifranco.com/about.
Baltin, Steve. 2020. "Q&A: Ani DiFranco on the Importance of Voting, Feminism, Billie Eilish, Beyonce and More." *Forbes*, October 20, 2020. https://www.forbes.com/sites/stevebaltin/2020/10/20/qa-ani-difranco-on-the-importance-of-voting-feminism-billie-eilish-beyonce-and-more/?sh=30ae170f4868.
Barlow, Eva. 2019. "Ani DiFranco: 'I'm sorry if I'm not what you need me to be'" *The Guardian*, May 17, 2019. https://www.theguardian.com/music/2019/may/17/ani-difranco-im-sorry-if-im-not-what-you-need-me-to-be.
Bennett, Andy. 2001. *Cultures of Popular Music*. Buckingham: Open University Press.
Boyes, Georgina. 2010. *The Imagined Village: Culture, Ideology and the English Folk Revival*. Leeds: No Masters Co-Operative Limited.
Carter, Dale. 2013. "Surf Aces Resurfaced: The Beach Boys and the Greening of the American Counterculture, 1963–1973." *Ecozon@: European Journal of Literature, Culture and Environment* 4 (1): 44–60.
CBS Mornings. 2021. "Singer Ani DiFranco on Career, New Album "Revolutionary Love." *YouTube* video 5: 56. February 20, 2021. https://www.youtube.com/watch?v=MmMpcakNxsk.
Clayton, Susan. 2020. "Climate Anxiety: Psychological Responses to Climate Change." *Journal of Anxiety Disorders* 74: 1–7.
Coscarelli, Joe. 2010. "The 15 Most Eco-Friendly Rockers." *Rolling Stone*, December 16, 2010. https://www.rollingstone.com/culture/culture-lists/the-15-most-eco-friendly-rockers-10751/thom-yorke-3-74268/.

du Gay, Paul (et al.). 1997. *Doing Cultural Studies: The Story of the Sony Walkman*. London: Sage/The Open University.
Frith, Simon. 1983. *Sound Effects: Youth, Leisure, and the Politics of Rock*. London: Constable.
Garrett, Charles Hiroshi. 2008. "The Musical Tactics of Ani DiFranco." *American Music* 26 (3): 378–97.
Gruning, Thomas R. 2006. *Millennium Folk: American Folk Music Since the Sixties*. Athens: University of Georgia Press.
Hawitt, Rowan Bayliss. 2020. ""It's a part of me and I'm a part of it": Ecological Thinking in Contemporary Scottish Folk Music." *Ethnomusicology Forum* 29 (3): 333–55.
Hiel, Adrian (@AdrianHiel). 2020. "Listening to Ani DiFranco this morning pretending it is the 90s and we still have time to avert climate catastrophe." Twitter, 8:03 AM, Feb. 29, 2020. https://twitter.com/AdrianHiel/status/1233649030552522753
Ingram, David. 2010. *The Jukebox in the Garden: Ecocriticism and American Popular Music*. Amsterdam: Rodopi.
———. 2015. "Ecocriticism and Traditional English Folk Music." In *Current Directions in Ecomusicology: Music, Nature, Environment*, edited by Aaron S. Allen and Kevin Dawe, 221–32. London: Routledge.
Keightley, Keir. 2001. "Reconsidering Rock." In *The Cambridge Companion to Pop and Rock*, edited by Simon Frith, John Street, and Will Straw, 109–42. Cambridge: Cambridge University Press.
Kerridge, Richard. 2014. "Ecocritical Approaches to Literary Form and Genre: Urgency, Depth, Provisionality, Temporality." In *The Oxford Handbook of Ecocriticism*, edited by Greg Garrard, 361–76. Oxford: Oxford University Press.
Love, Nancy A. 2013. "Ani DiFranco: Making Feminist Waves." In *Political Rock*, edited by Mark Pedelty and Kristine Weglarz, 159–76. Burlington, VT: Ashgate.
Morton, Timothy. 2010. *The Ecological Thought*. Cambridge, MA: Harvard University Press.
One Shtick Ari (@arisbarmitzvah). 2020. "Untouchable Face by Ani DiFranco is taking on new, considerable meaning in the political and biological climate." Twitter, 3:27 AM, Mar 5, 2020. https://twitter.com/arisbarmitzvah/status/1235391460364750851
Pedelty, Mark. 2012. *Ecomusicology: Rock, Folk and the Environment*. Philadelphia, PA: Temple University Press.
Rodgers, Jeffrey Pepper. 2000. "Profile: Ani DiFranco and Utah Phillips." In *Rock Troubadours: Conversations on the Art and Craft of Songwriting*, edited by Jeffrey Pepper Rodgers, 157–80. New York: String Letter Publishing. https://web.archive.org/web/20140130090622/http://jeffreypepperrodgers.com/difranco.htm.
Thompson, Tosin. 2021. "Young People"s Climate Anxiety Revealed in Landmark Survey." *nature.com*, September 22, 2021. https://www.nature.com/articles/d41586-021-02582-8.
Waterman, Ellen. 2016. "Witnessing Music from the New Wilderness." *Contemporary Music Review* 35 (3): 336–61.
Weissman, Dick. 2020. *A New History of American & Canadian Folk Music*. New York: Bloomsbury Academic.
Young, Rob. 2011. *Electric Eden: Unearthing Britain"s Visionary Music*. London: Faber and Faber.

Discography

DiFranco, Ani. 2003. *Evolve*. Righteous Babe.
———. 2003. "Serpentine." On *Evolve*.
———. 2006. *Reprieve*. Righteous Babe.
———. 2021. *Revolutionary Love*. Righteous Babe.
DiFranco, Ani, and Utah Phillips. 1996. *The Past Didn't Go Anywhere*. Righteous Babe.
Lil Nas X. 2019. "Old Town Road." Columbia.
Sea Power. 2005. *Open Season*. Rough Trade.
———. 2008. *Do You Like Rock Music?* Rough Trade.
The Cure. 1980. "A Forest." Fiction.

30
WOMEN IN THE GLOBAL PANDEMIC MEDIA IMAGINATION
Mimetic Desire, Scapegoating, Buddhist Hermeneutic, and Beyond

Chia-ju Chang

In the current white-patriarchal-capitalist world order, minorities, women, and nonhumans are caught in what René Girard calls "the mimetic triangle."[1] This theory postulates that a subject's desire for an object is mediated through the desire of a model. Mimetic desire or triangle leads to rivalrous competition with the model (the person modeling desire) and eventually prompts a subsequent cathartic solution: the scapegoating mechanism. Mimetic and scapegoating mechanisms are omnipresent in daily life and media and become intensified in our time of pandemic and ecological crisis, where they manifest in forms of racism, sexism, and eco/homo/xenophobia.

How does media, such as internet, social media, and particularly film, contribute to or ameliorate the mimetic triangle in which minority groups and women are victims or scapegoats for pan-epidemic and climate change Anthropocene? This essay zooms in on the gender dimension of mimetic triangle and scapegoatism, I consider the figure and trope of woman as Other in three pandemic films, *Hong Kong: A Winner* (Stephen Chow, Hong Kong, 2003), *Contagion* (Steven Soderbergh, USA, 2011), and *The Che Brother* (Anysay Keola, Laos, 2020). Two of the films are shorts, compared to the Hollywood feature film, *Contagion*, and help demonstrate how smaller productions, less beholden to box office bottom lines, can make more daring statements. These films demonstrate the plight of women—as a scapegoat or object of desire—in patriarchal, imperialist, and capitalist systems. They also provide ways of thinking about how bodies of women/Other are implicated in the construction of trans/nationalist, post/colonial, and capitalist/environmentalist discourses.

Since media technology has become an indispensable part of the mind-media-world ecology, tackling representation of mimetic violence will inevitably require critical toolkits such as Marxist/postcolonial/ecological feminist/Latourian critiques and Buddhist hermeneutics to dismantle the political unconscious of mimetic triangle and scapegoatism where women are the loci of blame or exploitation. This essay suggests that the Buddhist hermeneutic gestures at a deeper level of consciousness, called "emptiness" (Skt. *Śūnyatā*), which can dissolve the unconscious underpinnings of mimetic violence. Film and media at large have the potential of catalyzing alternate consciousness, hence, they can be retooled for making an ontological shift beyond representational resolution. This essay concludes with a call for a new field, which I tentatively call "contemplative ecomedia studies."

Scapegoating the "Other" in the Covid-19 Era

As I compose this chapter amidst the Covid-19 pandemic, the phenomena of mimetic rivalry and scapegoating have become prevalent across the globe. We see widespread, contagious herd mentality, such as panic buying and hoarding, and the rise of attacks against ethnic others. A case in point is the drastic increase of online hate speech and crime toward China, the Chinese, and Asian Americans. According to collected data from websites, teen chat rooms, and gaming platforms, a 900% increase in hate speech on Twitter was directed toward China and the Chinese ("Rising" 2020).

Just as Asian Americans have come under the spotlight of hate crime, what is often obscured in the grand narrative of mimetic violence in a world order that is still predominantly patriarchal is the gendered dimension which co-constitutes the social face of the Covid-19 pandemic. For example, women fighting over emergency commodities and the shooting of Asian women may easily be subsumed under the gender-neutral category of mimetic violence or hate crime. However, the predominance of women as scapegoats may be a synecdoche of gender inequality and sexism that the pandemic contributes to and aggravates. Research shows that women across the globe have been disproportionately impacted by the pandemic; they perform the primary unpaid household duties, including food shopping and caring for children and the elderly. In addition to an increase in inequality in the sector of both paid and unpaid labor, domestic violence against women has also increased. The United Nations Secretary-General António Guterres states, "Nearly one in five women worldwide has experienced violence in the past year" (UN 2020: n.p.) and exposure to Covid-19 is being used as a threat by the abusers.

Digital communication has become the pivotal mode for everyday dissemination of information to the point where it has become the primary site to perpetuate violence and hence is responsible for the rise of online bullying and hate speech. What redemptive role can digital media play in addressing or ameliorating the problem? Practical solutions such as moderation policies have been improvised. For example, media companies such as Tik Tok and WhatsApp filter toxic content that is poisoning the psychology of our younger generation. While platform moderation is employed to safeguard the digital environment, media policing to stamp out mimetic bigotry does not get at the root problem and it can easily provoke backlash since such moderation can feel like censorship.

While it is true that film media shares responsibility as a mimetic and scapegoating machine, as a creative and speculative medium, film can also contribute to our understanding of the political unconscious of gendered mimetic aesthetics in the negotiated space between national/indigenous and transnational/capitalism and even offer a non-mimetic, restorative vision for the future to come.

Women in Global Pandemic Films

Contagion: Hollywood Scapegoats and Latourian Mode of Redemption

During the early outbreak of Covid-19, Steven Soderbergh's *Contagion* became the most searched and watched film on Google and streaming services (Geal 2021, 242). The narrative unfolds with a white female professional, Beth Enhoff, going to Hong Kong for a business trip and bringing an infectious disease to the West. On her way back to Minnesota, Beth meets with a former lover during a Chicago layover. She dies two days later after returning home to Minneapolis, as does her son. This is the beginning of the pandemic.

Beth's tragedy evokes the figure of Oedipus in Sophocles's *Oedipus Rex*. In this modern version centering on woman's transgression, Beth is likened to the superspreader Oedipus (Wald 2008, 15–16), her ignorance of her "two crimes"—adultery and filicide— necessitates the punishment: her death, her son's death, and the pandemic outbreak. The metonymic link between two forms of transmissible diseases, the fictional MEV-1 and STD, together with details of her at the casino unwittingly spreading the disease to strangers all work to symbolize her independent and mobile status as promiscuity. Her outgoing nature and global travel is in sharp contrast with her domestic husband and protective father, endowed with his unique immune characteristics. Peckham points out that imagining an airborne viral infection with STD spread by a loose woman is "reminiscent of Second World War disease prevention films" (2016, 138). This cinematic sexism and misogyny can be viewed as a reaction against female autonomy, which discloses a gender unconscious in the Hollywood film industry. While cultural anxiety about uncertainties is projected on women in times of pandemic-precarity, male figures are often figured as the positive source of stability. In contrast with the powerful careerwoman Beth, Mitch Emhoff is portrayed as the everyday hero who is a protective father and Dr. Cheever (the CDC director) is an embodiment of the superhero who protects "the American way of life" (Bereton 2015, 94).

In an ecofeminist reading of disaster films, Cynthia Belmont argues that misogyny, fear, or the drive to conquer nature is often injected into the genre of disaster films. In *Contagion*, we see a link between evil nature (the menacing virus) and Beth, a woman who disrupts the current anthropocentric-patriarchal order. Moreover, the desire to scapegoat or tame Beth is juxtaposed against bulldozing the forest that sourced the disease, an abject Other that needs to be conquered. Here the trope of women as pandemic threat in the white-patriarchal-capitalist outbreak narrative not only links with ecophobia, it is also interlocked with xenophobia and racism, where the origin of disease is often located outside of one's own imagined community. As noted by Wald, in outbreak accounts, there is a tendency to establish the disease outbreaks as "'foreign' or 'alien' agents that posed a national threat" (2008, 2). In *Contagion*, Hong Kong is imagined as a hotspot of outbreak, rather than a locale of solution. The orientalist excess is deliberately employed in the depiction of the Chinese chef's unhygienic food preparation and the stereotypical representation of "Chinaman," short, fat, and filthy, in juxtaposition in the same frame with Beth, a tall blonde, white woman.

The redemption of the woman comes at the end of the film via a Latourian intervention, where a diffused-network perspective allows us to see the temporal and spatial distribution of cause, agency, and liability, in which issues of viral communicability, wildlife habitat loss, animal farming, urbanization, global consumerism, international corporations, the global transportation network (air travel industry), and even human physiology and behaviors of coughing and touching things are interlinked. In light of this Latourian sociology of associations, which "insists on the processual nature of the socio-material" (Müller 2015, 30), the cause of the pandemic is democratically distributed thus exonerating women, minorities, or nonhuman animals, as the primary cause of the pandemic.

The systemic network reconfigures the scapegoat (be it woman/Beth, the ethnic Other/the Chinese chef, or the nonhuman Other/the pig or bat) as being implicated in a larger global network of causal chain reactions that leads up to the pandemic. Here Beth symbolizes Western corporations in the transnational web of patriarchal-ecological-neoliberal system, which is responsible for the deforestation that kicks off the outbreak.

Though such a Latourian aesthetics deconstructs or demystifies the scapegoat mechanisms that the film previously set up, it also helps shield the deeper culprit, which has remained invisible in the narrative: AIMM (Alderson International Mining and Manufacturing), the transnational mining company that employs Beth, only appears for ten seconds on-screen, undermining its significance. In addition, the same Latourian sociological aesthetic strategy also fails to address the problem of secular modernity where demystification leaves us in a state of spiritual stasis and the illusory construct of mimetic rivalry (Chang 2022). The Latourian treatment as a solution to mimetic rivalry and scapegoatism differs from the other films, particularly with the re-sacralization approach found in *The Che Brother.*

"Hong Kong: A Winner": Cinematic Strategy of Anti-Western Hegemony

As a global, highly populated city, which survived several serious pandemic episodes, Hong Kong is "frequented in the media and in pandemic thrillers as an emerging disease hotspot" (Peckham 2016, 315), that is, as the ethnic Other. During the SARS epidemic, UK newspapers imagined Hong Kong as a zombie land, evoking post-apocalypse horror-film imagery, while reassuring their readers through the mechanism of othering: "it couldn't happen here' because the Chinese are so different to 'us'" (Washer 2004, 2570). In this context, one can interpret Stephen Chow's *Hong Kong: A Winner*—part of the *1:99 Short Film Series* produced by the Information Service Department of the Government of HK SAR during the SARS outbreak in 2003 to boost morale and civic pride of Hong Kongers—as a national allegory (Jameson 1986, 69) that also combats Western media's ongoing cultural Othering. This short film tells of a mother who is hospitalized in an isolated ward. She remains in touch with her family via telecommunication technology. From the conversation between the mother and daughter and images of father and son on the other end of the video conference, viewers are duped to believe that the whole family are distressed over the mother's illness, only to realize at the end that the daughter is playing Mah-jong against her brother and father and that the *recovering* mother is teaching the daughter how to play (and win!).

The film's contemporary Hong Kong family subverts the traditional patriarchal mimetic structure and scapegoat narrative where mothers are either vilified or sacrificed as a communal cathartic purge to sustain the patriarchal order. Such a scapegoat mechanism is reproduced in this short since the mother is the only member who is infected with the disease and segregated from the rest of the family. But the inversion of the plot at the end rejects this mother-scapegoating scenario and surprises its viewers with a happy ending. The ending also subverts mainstream perception of shelter-in-place, hospitalization, etc. as inhuman by reframing it as strengthening familial bonding.

Chow's employment of psychological manipulation (perceived either as sadist or masochistic) can be deceptively dismissed as a simply mean-spirited and childish trick, like most of his works. However, if we put Chow's signature blending of farce and pathos (Yu 2020) in the context of Hong Kong's turmoil where the city is internally facing the menacing threat of SARS and externally facing Western media's relentless stigmatization of the city, its people and their way of life, then Chow's plotline can be understood as a sophisticated psychological tactic, as it operates on both internal and external levels and demands a double reading to recognize the complexity.

First, if we situate the short in a transnational spectatorship, the film can then be conceptualized as a nativist, grassroot response to the empire's pathologizing gaze. For external or unsympathetic viewers, who may view Hong Kong as a totally alien and inferior cultural Other, as portrayed in the UK newspapers during SARS, Chow challenges the sadistic gaze (finding pleasure or showing no sympathy in seeing the suffering of the cultural Other) by way of challenging the Western mainstream projection of HK as the cultural Other in misery with an unexpected happy ending to undermine its hostile viewers' biases. Secondly, if we situate the short in a domestic context for internal or sympathetic viewers, who identify with or as Hong Kongers, the short provides the pathos of SARS with a "masochistic" tease (enduring the pain that the filmmaker torments them with a heartfelt tragic scenario with a reassuring twist at the end) that can be read as the trickster comedian director's quirky shtick, which comforts the local audience and offers hope.

Chow employs a postcolonial strategy of self-narration or subjectification that inverts Western stereotypes of Hong Kong as a primitive place of disease and filth via a twist that boosts domestic confidence and self-image. A similar strategy of self-narration that inverts the pandemic narrative coming from the West is seen in Samson Chiu's *Golden Chicken II* (2003), a film also made during SARS. This film portrays the consumption of food such as animal intestines positively. The scene of offering and eating pig lung soup subverts Western media's orientalist and much demonized portrayal of Chinese consumption of offal. It contrasts the representation of the Chinese chef and conceptualization of food in *Contagion*. Having said this, Chow's anti-hegemonic, postcolonial strategy of "self-other" inversion does not directly confront the onto-epistemological assumptions of mimeticism.

The Che Brother: Ecofeminist Redemption of Mother/Nature and Buddhist Hermeneutics

Written and directed by the Laotian filmmaker Anysay Keola, *The Che Brother* is part of the *MEKONG 2030* film anthology project, produced by Laos' Luang Prabang Film Festival (LPFF) in 2020. As a transregional project aimed at addressing the plight of the Mekong Delta, five filmmakers from the ASEAN countries were tasked to envision the Mekong River in 2030. The longest river in Southeast Asia and one of the largest freshwater ecosystems in the world, the Mekong River is facing an unprecedented transboundary crisis, not only as one of the most contaminated waterways in the world but also because of the construction of massive dams by the joint efforts of governments, transnational developers, and financiers. Laos is projected to build 100 dams across its lands by 2030, adding to 78 that are already operational. Future construction of dams will further endanger aquatic species as well as threaten the livelihood of local communities in the lower Mekong basins.

Set in Cambodia in 2030 when the world is suffering from both a pandemic and the effects of climate change, the film features the young urbanite and Che Guevara enthusiast Xe (or "river" in Laotian) returning to his dilapidated fishing village and finding himself in the midst of a feud between his elder brother and sister. Xe is informed that their brother has kidnapped their mother, who has a rare antibody, to sell her blood to a Western pharmaceutical company seeking to develop a potential cure for the ongoing pandemic. Xe succeeds in rescuing her but finds out that his sister is also engaging in the dirty business. After Xe confronts her, she points out his unwitting complicity as a college-educated man with an urban lifestyle which were paid for by their mother's blood. Horrified by this realization, he walks into the river; the film ends with Xe's mysterious smile after he hears the sound of a broken string.

This premise of mimetic desire takes on an ecofeminist critique of the ongoing Western capitalist appropriation and plundering of women's bodies, indigenous knowledge and resources, and the complicity of local governments. A case in point is the use of third-world women's bodies by transnational pharmaceutical industries as guineapigs for clinical tests on long-term effects of contraceptives, as they are "cheaper, faster and politically more convenient (…) than it is to run clinical tests on samples of women in the West" (Shiva and Mies 2014, 216). Here the passive body of the mother caught in a scathing sibling rivalry is figured as an object of desire, a raw "material" coveted by a Western pharmaceutical corporation. The mother in *The Che Brother* is in sharp contrast to the mother (Beth) in *Contagion* who, as an employee of AIMM, represents the Western plundering resources of non-Western regions.

While the mother/wife in *Hong Kong the Winner* is linked to the notion of "mother country" in a nationalist discourse, in the case of *The Che Brother*, the human mother represents Mother Nature, or more specifically, the Mekong River. The word Mekong or "Mae Nam" in Thai and Lao literally means "Mother of Rivers." The human mother as a trope for Nature is unequivocally dramatized in the blood-river analogy. All the needles, tubes, and machines that attach to her immobile body suggest the technologies that intercept the river's water for producing hydroelectric power for the consumption of neighboring countries. In one shot, the mother is placed at the center of a building under construction against the backdrop of a river. This image theatricalizes the Girardian idea of sacred scapegoat and human sacrifice (Figure 30.1). The human mother functions as *both* object of desire and scapegoat.

The rivalry over their mother's precious blood against the backdrop of the transnational exploitation of Mother River is demonstrated in the juxtaposition of the woman and the Mekong/mother, where extraction of third-world woman's blood and extraction of water are linguistically contextualized and visually linked. While narratorially the mother is constructed as the object of desire and sacrifice, the spectacular visual composition opens up different hermeneutic possibilities. Here we can alternatively interpret the image of the mother against the backdrop of the Mekong River as an evocation of a cultural memory in the context of a folk Buddhist practice where the river is the site of sacred shrines and where the local people make offering to river deities (Hongsuwan 2011). The reverential gesture repeated twice (one in a scene when Xe touches his mother's foot and then his forehead and the other where he touches the water and his forehead) (Figure 30.2) not only retrieves the folk memory in the process of Lao's industrialization but also reminds us of the Buddha's earth-touching gesture (*bhumisparsha*). It is said that the historical Buddha, Gautama Shakyamuni, called the earth goddess, Sthavara, to bear witness to his awakening under the Bodhi tree. Here, *The Che Brother* provides a more-than-political reading that allows us to think more deeply into cinematic imagination and hermeneutics of non-mimetic potential.

In *The Che Brother*, we see the director's resort to local, traditional culture such as Buddhism to redress the problem of mimetic triangle, resacralizing and reenchanting the land that is undergoing massive hydraulic transformation. Here a Zen perspective helps further a nondualistic hermeneutic. After he realizes that his identity as an urban, materialist Che unwittingly turns out to be complicit in the exploitation of his motherland, Xe joins the victim by literally physically immersing himself in the water. We can say that Xe's phenomenological encounter with the surroundings or

Figure 30.1 The tubed-up mother in a building under construction is juxtaposed against the backdrop of the Mekong River in *The Che Brother* (2020)

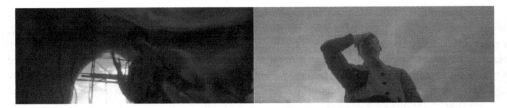

Figure 30.2 Two stills from *The Che Brother* (2020). These are perspective shots from the mother's and River's perspectives, showing Xe paying homage to both his mother and Mother Nature. The one on the left is Xe's semi-conscious, tube-ridden mother in bed looking up at her son who, after caressing her feet, touches his forehead. The one on the right is from the River's perspective, where Xe first touches the water and then his forehead.

elements initiates a nondualistic Zen-like awakening (or opening up) experience. His smile upon hearing the sound of a mandolin string breaking reminds us of the story of the Flower Sermon where Mahākāśyapa, the Buddha's principal disciple, smiled as a recognition of the meaning of the Buddha's holding up a flower (Dumoulin 2005, 54). Here we can interpret the smile as a realization that the Other (be it human or non-human) is none other than our own selves. If anything, the message from *The Che Brother* is a non-mimetic Buddhist gesture of transcendence where self-other are unified.

Conclusion

All three pandemic films provide a glimpse into the way film media addresses the issue of mimetic entanglement involving women, minorities, and nature either as scapegoats or objects of mimetic desire, across various genres, contexts, scales, aesthetics, and even length. I argue that, in dealing with the tenacious nature of unconscious mimeticism, Asian short films offer alternative perspectives compared to mainstream Hollywood productions. However, I am not content with settling down on the level of representational or hermeneutic amelioration, be it Latourian, ecofeminist, postcolonial, or even Buddhist. Instead, I suggest that these discursive strategies serve as intermediary transitions into a non-discursive, onto-epistemological call into a form of ecomedia praxis that brings forth a subjective, first-person, onto-existential, or phenomenological transformation for the audience so as to make a genuine impact.

The ending of *The Che Brother* gestures at aesthetic immersion as a mode of decolonizing "the trinity of the minor" (women/minorities/nature) as exemplified in Xe's striding into the river to immerse himself with Mother River, a feminized space or primal element. The gestural and representational model of calling for reintegration with the source from which we come—very Buddhist indeed—though making a step forward compared to the Latourian network-oriented approach and the postcolonial strategy still falls one step short of knocking down the semiotic façade of representation. Such a representational gesture has yet to take full advantage of the power film media or ecomedia offers.

Scholars such as George Watkins, Francisca Cho, and Murray Pomerance, to name a few, have already provided a theoretical platform to think about the power of film media to bridge the ontological subject-object dualistic divide and bring us back to the here and now (Watkins 1999; Cho 2008; Pomerance 2008). Future research directions concerning the power of ecomedia to destroy mimetic dualism (hence colonial exploitation and injustice) can glean some wisdom from this body of transdisciplinary scholarship. Situated in a broader environmental humanities framework, this work, which I tentatively call "contemplative eco-media studies," will intersect media and religious studies and contributes to the new sub-field of Contemplative Studies (Roth 2008). Contemplative eco-media studies will highlight the filmic or medial potential of non-Cartesian onto-epistemological transformation of spectatorship that emphasizes the first-person, first-hand, and subjective experience of the participants as a way to detoxify our unconscious mimeticism.

Acknowledgments

I thank Robert Geal and the editors, particularly Stephen Rust, for reading the early drafts and providing useful comments.

Note

1 For a detailed explanation of mimetic triangle, see Chang (2022).

Further Reading

Chang, C. (2019). "The Missing View in Global Post-Secular Cinema: Crouching Tiger Hidden Dragon as a Visual Kōan/Gong'an." *Paragraph Journal*, Special Issue: "Critical Theory, Religion and Film" 42(3), pp. 370–86.
Cho, F. (2017). *Seeing Like the Buddha: Enlightenment Through Film*. Albany, NY: State University of New York.
———. 2008. "Buddhism, Film and Religious Knowing: Challenging the Literary Approach to Film." In G. Watkins (ed.) *Teaching Religion and Film*. Oxford: Oxford University Press, pp. 117–27.
Pomerance, M. 2008. *The Horse Who Drank the Sky: Film Experience beyond Narrative and Theory*. New Brunswick, NJ: Rutgers University Press.
Watkins G. (1999). "Seeing and Being Seen: Distinctively Filmic and Religious Elements in Film." *Journal of Religion and Film* October, 3(2), Article 5.

References

Bereton, P. (2015) *Environmental Ethics and Film*. New York: Routledge.
Chang, C. (2022). "Scapegoating in Times of Pan-Epidemic: Mimesis, Identity Crisis, and the Buddhist *Phármakon*." In Co-edited by S. Slovic, S. Rangarajan, and V. Sarveswaran (eds.) *Handbook for Medical and Environmental Humanities*. London: Bloomsbury Academic, pp. 223–34.
Cho, F. (2008). "Buddhism, Film, and Religious Knowing: Challenging the Literary Approach to Film." In Gregory J. Watkins (ed.) *Teaching Religion and Film*. New York: Routledge, pp. 117–28.
Dumoulin, H. (2005). *Zen Buddhism: A History, India & China*. Bloomington, IN: World Wisdom.
Geal, R. (2021). *Ecological Film Theory and Psychoanalysis: Surviving the Environmental Apocalypse in Cinema*. New York: Routledge.
Guterres, A. (2020). "Secretary-General's video message on Women and COVID." April 9. https://www.un.org/sg/en/content/sg/statement/2020-04-09/secretary-generals-video-message-women-and-covid-scroll-down-for-french-version.
Hongsuwan, P. (2011). "Sacralization of the Mekong River through Folk Narratives." *Manusya: Journal of Humanities*, Vol. 14, Special Issue No. 19, pp. 33–45.
Jameson, F. (1986). "Third-World Literature in the Era of Multinational Capitalism." *Social Text* 15(Autumn), pp. 65–88.
Müller, M. (2015). "Assemblages and Actor-networks: Rethinking Socio-material Power, Politics and Space." *Geography Compass* 9(1), pp. 27–41.
Peckham, R. (2016). *Epidemics in Modern Asia*. Cambridge: Cambridge University Press.
"Rising Levels of Hate Speech & Online Toxicity During This Time of Crisis." 2020. L1ght. https://l1ght.com/Toxicity_during_coronavirus_Report-L1ght.pdf.

Roth, H. (2008). "Against Cognitive Imperialism: A Call for Non-ethnocentric to Cognitive Science and Religious Studies." *Religion East & West* 8, pp. 1–26.

Shiva, V. and Mies, M. (2014). *Ecofeminism*. London: Zed Books.

United Nations. (2020). *Policy Brief: The Impact of COVID-19 on Women.* https://www.un.org/sites/un2.un.org/files/policy_brief_on_covid_impact_on_women_9_april_2020.pdf.

Wald, P. (2008). *Contagious: Cultures, Carriers, and the Outbreak Narrative*. Durham, NC: Duke University Press.

Washer, P. (2004). "Representations of SARS in the British Newspapers." *Social Science & Medicine* 59, pp. 2561–71.

Yu, E. K. W. (2010). "Farce, Pathos, and Absurdity in Stephen Chow's Film Comedies: From Beijing with Love and CJ7 Reconsidered." *Concentric: Literary and Cultural Studies* 36(2), pp. 213–41.

PART V

Eco-Affects

31
ECOMENTIA, FROM TELEVISED CATASTROPHE TO PERFORMATIVE ASSEMBLY

Collapsonaut Attention in a House on Fire

Yves Citton

Introduction

"Our house is on fire, and we look the other way." So (in)famously spoke a French President at the Johannesburg Earth Summit in 2002 (without doing much about it when he returned to Paris) (Kokabi 2019). How does one communicate in a burning house? How does one think? We are (earth)bound to be haunted by such questions. They tie a daunting knot between *ecocultures* (what perceptions, representations, values, arguments should circulate among us?), *ecomedia* (how can we mobilize our extractivist smartphones in struggles against extractivism?), and *eco-affects* (how to keep insanity at bay?).

The question of knowing how properly to mediate our attention to our surroundings, and especially to its dangers, is anything but new, of course. The (relative) novelty of our situation comes from the fact that those of us comfortable enough to consume more than our sustainable share of resources play simultaneously the double role of firefighters and arsonists. Our mediality is doublebound: our devices are shooting flames and burning oil by the same breath as we are shouting fire.

In such a situation, *media ecology* can be understood both in the sense of minimizing the environmental impact of our collective use, production and waste of media devices, and in the sense of retooling (mass) media in order to speed up the ecological mutations of our social organizations (at a planetary scale). Both aspirations may seem out of reach: how can we, with our limited means, understand, let alone reign in, the hyper-complex and often terribly dirty (environmentally and socially) supply chains that provide us with our smartphone? Similarly, how can we, at our modest scale, deflect, let alone repurpose, the powerful media institutions and the hegemonic platforms whose interest and infrastructures shape our public debates?

No wonder many of us find it increasingly hard to resist the sirens of eco-anxiety, solastalgia (Albrecht et al. 2007), and collapsology (Servigne & Stevens 2020). Neither a civilizational disease nor a private insanity, the distress we experiment within our burning house deserves to be identified as a form of dementia—an "ecomentia," i.e., *a collective state of mind resulting from the attentional ecology of our mediated relations to our collapsing ecological milieus*. Some studies and theories can help us analyze, if not come to terms with, the medial determinants of this collective state of mind.

This chapter has been made available under a CC-BY-NC-ND license.

Mapping the Mediarchy

Before his untimely death in 1992, French philosopher Félix Guattari (1989) invited his readers simultaneously to consider three ecologies in tight co-evolution: the natural ecology of our bio-physical surround, the political ecology of our social organizations, and the mental ecology of our subjectivities. There is no "purely" psychological distress: our nervous systems react to imbalances in our social relations, which are conditioned by (and condition in return) the state of our bio-physical environment. In his foundational book *Understanding the Media*, Canadian theorist Marshall McLuhan (1964) had already pushed us to consider "media"—later broadly defined by German media archaeologist Friedrich Kittler (1986) as whatever transmits, records, and/or treats data—as extensions of our nervous system. Through the infrastructures of the printing press, the gramophone, the telephone, the radio, the television, the portable video, the personal computer, and the Internet, our sensibility has expanded so as to reach finer data ever faster and further in space and time.

A few years later, French philosopher Bernard Stiegler (1998) analyzed how the "primary retentions" (i.e., perceptions) selected by our attention in the sensory data that immediately surround us were ceaselessly interpreted and reconsidered in the light of the "secondary retentions" (memories) remembered in our nervous system, as well as of the "tertiary retentions" recorded for us on the external supports of various media. Simultaneously, German philosopher Niklas Luhmann (1996) portrayed mass media as a regulating system that provides our societies (more or less satisfactorily) with the amount and type of information they need to reproduce their social ordering. A couple of decades later, media and design theorist Benjamin Bratton (2015, 8) conceptualized the "accidental mega-structure" of the Internet as a vertical *Stack* of diffracted sovereignties composed of six strata: *Earth* (our biophysical environments and resources), *Cloud* (the interconnected network of servers powered by these resources), *City* (the logistical nods that allow human bodies to live, gather and communicate), *Address* (the new form of human and non-human identity relevant for the internet), *Interface* (our predesigned formats of interaction through digital devices), and *User* (as much a function and a target of the mega-structure as its punctual activator).

All in all, in half a century of cybernetic imagination, these (mostly white male) theorists have provided us with a powerful depiction of the ways in which our (supposedly personal) sensations and thoughts are never really "our own." We do not live in "democracies," as free willed individuals merely "informed" (or misinformed) by the media. We live in "mediarchies" (Citton 2017): our individual nervous systems appear as the "wetware" moment in a global circulation of information/electricity which is largely preformatted and predetermined by the software and hardware ever more tightly integrated within the global Stack. Ecomedia and ecomentia are one and the same: the evolutions of our personal psyches follow the magnetic fields powered by our medial environment. Our thoughts cannot be separated from their magnetization and modulation through the flows of discourses, sounds, and images that are carried by electricity through cables, satellites, waves, screens, and headphones. Our media are neither a superstructure (in the old Marxist sense), nor merely an infrastructure (in the ecomedia sense), but more properly an *intra*structure. They structure and substantiate our minds as they feed them. Hence our disarray: the house is burning, but the house is us!

The Disconnection of Affects and the Displacement of Saliences

Of course, such totalizing and universalizing discourses ought to be considered with the greatest suspicion. As we all know by now, the "Anthropocene" is a lure: not *all* humans are equally responsible for setting our common house on fire ("Eurocene," "Capitalocene," and "Plantationocene" are more accurate labels for our age). Similarly, "we" are not equally responsible for the structure and the contents of the mediarchy. It is important to identify *specific features* of our current digitalized mediarchy that need to be held more particularly responsible for our ecomentia (Zuboff 2019, Joler 2020, Chun 2021, Crawford 2021)—as a brilliant collection of essays has just done, whose title strikingly aligns our computing machines with our planet and our brains: *Your Computer Is on Fire!* (Mullaney *et al.* 2021).

It is increasingly clear that our current ecology of media is intrastructured first and foremost through the commodification of our attention. Most of the techno-institutional vectors that fuel our nervous systems with stimuli are organized along the competitive rules that originated in the 1830s, simultaneously in France, England, and the USA, when innovative press barons started to sell their daily newspaper half-price of their production costs, making up for the difference by selling ad space to advertisers (Wu 2016). What they were actually selling was their readers' attention, which became from then on a traded commodity. Two centuries later, the commodification of our attention has become the hegemonic economic base of "neuropower" (Neidich 2013) within our mediarchies.

Since economic survival in our current mediarchies is indexed upon the agent's capacity to attract (and monetize) attention, our communicational environment pushes emitters of messages toward the use of *saliences*, i.e., signals that cannot remain unnoticed by our nervous system. These saliences are partly "absolute," when they trigger a response from any able-bodied person (fire alarms, flashing lights, etc.), and partly "targeted," when online platforms analyze our personal data flows in order to predict which artist, brand, word, or notification will hit one of our personal soft spots. The overall result of this captological arms race is that discourses, images, and sounds flow among us, not mostly on the basis of their personal and collective relevance or empowering promises, but first and foremost on the basis of their potential to attract, capture, and sell our attention—with the frequent result of distracting and alienating us from more urgent or more emancipating concerns (Citton 2014).

This is why we look the other way while our house is on fire. But it is not written that we should continue to do so. On the contrary, the mere existence of a *Handbook of Ecomedia Studies* is only one among the many symptoms of a recalibration of our collective attentional focuses—an evolution of our ecomentia, an increasing awareness that our media are on fire. Our attention cannot be directly commanded by what philosophers identify as our "reason": they are much more tightly linked to our "affects" (our emotions, passions, desires, hopes, and fears). "Affects" should less be conceived as ego-centered "feelings," experienced "inside" our mind or heart, than as the inner manifestations of *an outer relation* which attaches us to some aspect of our (human or other-than-human) surroundings (Manning 2013). We become (subjectively) aware of a certain feeling when we "are affected" by a certain transformation in one of our (material) relations with our environment. And yet, this apparently passive affection by our surroundings generates in us an affect that can sometimes unleash a tremendously active and powerful reaction.

The increasingly insistent association between references to climate change and scenes of destruction (hurricanes, floods, megafires) is another symptom of the same recalibration of our attentional focuses fueled by our affective experiences. The extension of our sensory apparatus through the development of printed and electronic media that has happened over the past centuries has not managed to keep pace with the parallel extensions of our collective agencies and affectabilities, which have reached a planetary scale since at least the 1850s. We (relatively affluent members of the Western middle class) have lived on borrowed time, in a bubble disconnected from its actual environmental conditions, for more than 150 years. Most of us have not been (directly) "affected" by the remote consequences of our shopping sprees. Our media have failed to adjust our (personal) affectability to our (collective) agency. Our ecomentia has been schizophrenic: split by a technological power disconnected from its social and environmental response-ability (Haraway 2016).

The intensified commodification of our attention precipitated by digital media only exacerbates this schizophrenic ecomentia—and it is certainly at the root of a great deal of our feelings of powerlessness, solastalgia, and collapsologist anxieties. The bad news is that catastrophies are multiplying (and it is already too late to completely reverse their course). The mixed news is that they are hitting closer to the homes of the Westernized middle classes who are the main culprits of our environmental degradations. The good news is that stronger affects command stronger attention. We are witnessing (too late and too slowly) the beginning of painful realignment of medial images toward the actual implications of our individual and collective behaviors. Through shocking and highly salient mediatized scenes of destruction, our affects are starting to displace our attention—causing yet another form of schizophrenia, since part of us is led to rejoice in the broadcasting of our affliction.

The Great Disconnection between impacts and affects that has allowed the West to ravage our planetary living milieus over the past 150 years is starting to be mended by a simultaneously frightening and salutary Great Displacement of traumatizing saliences closer to "home," favoring an ecomedial reconnection between our behaviors and their visible consequences. Other people's houses—in the former colonies as well as in disenfranchised neighborhoods—have been burning for decades, and mainstream media have mostly looked the other way (see for instance Vergès 2017, Ferdinand 2021). Now that "our" house is burning, will we spontaneously look "our" way? That may be simultaneously too cynical and too hopeful.

Ecomedial Counter-Activism: From Sovereign Individuals to Undercommon Assemblies

Traumatic events rarely prompt reasonable reactions. In a burning house, some may prefer to weaponize their door rather than putting out the neighbor's fire. There is a long way from cursing a hurricane to deconstructing the Capitalocene. Fantasies of a megamachine rob us of any agency—leading to disturbingly rational conspiracy theories which trap us in reactionary forms of activism. Similarly, televised catastrophes won't put out our fire by the sole virtue of their screened scares. If we hope to coexist peacefully in our common hothouse, we need to collectively restructure our ecomentia (as well as our ecomedia, since they are but two sides of the same coin).

Such a restructuring calls for a number of caveats, which can be read as a set of conditions for ecomedial activism. The following five points do not pretend to be anything else than a very preliminary and unsatisfactory fridge list.

1 *Power is rarely surrendered.* The vectoralist class (Wark 2004) which currently benefits from the commodification (and distraction) of our attention is likely to hold on to its power and privileges. Displacements of saliencies and reconnections of affects will have to overcome mighty resistances. These struggles will require much tactical mediactivism (Lovink & Garcia 1997).
2 *Sovereign individualism may be a deeper (inner) enemy than the resistance of the vectoralist class.* Capitalist extractivism certainly needs to be opposed and defeated as an organizational form and as a business model, taught in MBA programs, and rewarded by financial revenues. But as Sylvia Wynter (2015) and other radical thinkers have taught us, extractivism is anthropologically rooted in a certain conception, and in a certain practice, of what it means to be

human. *Homo mediaticus* will not put out the fire of his current ecomentia if he doesn't shed the skin of *homo oeconomicus*. This calls for the greatest suspicion toward the ubiquitous ideology of sovereign individualism which permeates the current debates about platform sociality, visibility, privacy, and surveillance. In most of them, the assertion, discussion, exaltation, or accusation of individual performances monopolize most of our attention. Not only do "the semiotics of celebrity bodies" overheat our server farms (Bratton 2019, 41). The tyranny of the self-possessed subject—imagined in an original position of transparent self-sufficiency before he enters in "interactions" with "others" (supposed to be exterior to him)—remains firmly in place in our dominant view of communication, in spite of its imposture denounced by race theorists like Denise Ferreira da Silva (2007). Our house is burning, in great part, because every sovereign individual is encouraged to attract as much light as possible on his overheating self. How soon will we reach what M.C. Abbott, María Buey González, and Carl Olsson (2021) have termed "peak face"—the historical turning point after which our infatuation with our face and our self-possessive conception of identity will start its decrease? The praxis of being human without claiming the status of sovereign subject starts (and ends) with the "consent not to be a single being" (Moten 2017, quoting Édouard Glissant), i.e., with an acceptance to share one's incompleteness (Robinson 1980). This theme, so powerfully developed by Stefano Harney and Fred Moten in *All Incomplete* (2021), provides in a nutshell all the lessons one needs to know about ecomedia. Instead of an extractivist mediarchy of self-possessive individuals competing against each other to attract visibility/attention/revenue, the sharing of our incompleteness opens up modes of communication where a pre-individual solidarity and a mutual participation in each other always precede and underpin any form of interaction with each other. Guattari's three ecologies are thus recast in their ecomental entanglement: my individual affective and mental state is part and parcel of my social (and political) relations, whose materialities are themselves woven through and through into the fabric of our environments. After having been accustomed to surf on the reassuring illusion of one's subjective sovereignty, however, learning to relate with each other on the basis of incompleteness is a major challenge. It calls for a new ethics, a new politics, a new rhetoric, a new pedagogy, and a new epistemology—no less. "Ecomedia" could be the proper name for such a challenge—a radical mutation from our current ecomentia.

3 *Black study may serve as our ecomedial indiscipline in exploring the challenges of shared incompleteness*. In their book and discussions devoted to the *Undercommons* (2013), Harney and Moten offer and practice "black study" which, in their minimal definition, is "what you do with other people" on the basis of a sharing of our incompleteness (Harney & Moten 2013, 110). This provides an ecomedial environment devoid of any central authoritative point of reference, where ordinary people become extraordinary accomplices through their common activity of studying *with* and *for*: "studying with people rather than teaching them" and "studying with people in service of a project" chosen together (which could simply be "more study") (147–148). Of course, practices of study can also be more narrowly focused, as in the case of the counter-captology workshops whereby people share skills and sensing devices, in order to document obfuscated environmental damages (Gabrys 2019). Most importantly, if we are to recover from the collective pathologies of sovereign individualism and appropriative self-possession inherent to the very definition of *homo oeconomicus*, black study appears as a pagan, heretic, and scandalous form of black magic, explicitly experienced as "a kind of dispossession of what you might otherwise have been holding onto, […] where you allow yourself to be possessed by others as they do something" (Harney & Moten 2013, 109).

4 *Black Studies and media theory ought to ally forces in order to rethink what media are and what media do in times of (Western man's) collapse*. Armond R. Towns' important book *On*

Black Media Philosophy (2022) delineates several ways in which the "reactionary intercommunalism" implicit in (white) media theory illustrated by Marshall McLuhan's global village can be reformulated toward a "revolutionary intercommunalism" illustrated by Black Panther Party leader Huey P. Newton's 1970s reflections on media (83). The countless medial inventions imagined by fugitives in their escape from slavery, during the initial, "unorganized," phase of the Underground Railroad, transformed wood sticks, rivers, rocks, clothes, and constellations into Improvised Emancipatory Devices which "continue to plot out new worlds than what Western man could ever fully comprehend—they create radical, alternative conceptions of Black life […] where media and Black liberation collide outside of the limitations of white, Western epistemic imaginations" (66). The "Black futurities" (63) brought to life by such improvised media may inspire and flesh out our best common collapsonaut hopes.

5 *The practices of performative assembly are crucial, both to re-anchor our mediated communications in the social solidarities and in the living materialities of our surrounding and to provide them with powerful mediatic rebounds.* The more extended our nervous systems (through media networks now extending to a planetary scale), the more exposed we are to selected distant realities, and the more we need physically to assemble in the co-presence of the here and now. Practices of study, necessarily restricted to a small number of participants, gain to be complemented by practices of assembly, gathering larger crowds around a broader political purpose. Marches, demonstrations, and occupations: the various forms of what Judith Butler has named "performative assemblies" share five common features that allow them uniquely to bridge the gap between proximate community-building in the undercommons and broadcast mediactivism at a planetary scale (as illustrated by the Black Lives Matter movement). (a) They are a peculiar form of pre-expressive communication, since "forms of assembly already signify prior to, and apart from, any particular demands they make" (Butler 2015, 8). (b) Insofar as they are motivated by a resistance against precarity, they make possible minority coalitions by "bringing together women, queers, transgender people, the poor, the differently abled, and the stateless, but also religious and racial minorities" (58). (c) They operate as factories of coexistence and cohabitation since, "when we arrive, we do not know who else is arriving, which means that we accept a kind of unchosen dimension to our solidarity with others" (152). (d) In the best-case scenario, they may establish a quasi-symbiotic relation with the media which "constitute the scene in a time and place that includes and exceeds its local instantiation": "the media requires those bodies on the street to have an event, even as those bodies on the street require the media to exist in a global arena" (91–94). (e) Here again, some form of magic takes place, since the same virtue of presence in numbers that makes the bodies expressive, even if they remain silent, makes them qualitatively meaningful, even if they remain quantitatively insignificant: "they perform *as if they were a majority*, even though they are factually a minority" (Staal 2017, 8–10).

Conclusion: Collapsonaut Attention

We could certainly use a little magic to lighten up our ecomentia—and to jump start our eco-political struggles. But we clearly need more than mumbo jumbo to put out the fire burning our common house. Over the past decade, the perspective of a dramatic collapse of "Western man's empire" (Towns 2022) has been increasingly discussed in the French public sphere, including mainstream media, all the way to a former Prime Minister (Édouard Philippe), who confessed the anxiety kept him up at night. Collapsologists attempt to elaborate a scientific discourse to anticipate the institutional collapse of our thermo-industrial civilization (Servigne & Stevens 2020). Collapsonauts, by contrast, attempt to gather forces and wits to navigate, as ethically and effectively as possible, on the crumbling expectations raised by Western profligacy (Citton & Rasmi 2020). In analyzing our societies as mediarchies rather than democracies, they direct our attention toward the intrastructural fragilities of ecomedia.

Collapsonaut attention is desperately needed to correct the excesses and negligence of our dominant extractivist attention. Capitalism identifies resources, it extracts, exploits, and exhausts them, indifferent to questions of unsustainability or collateral damage. Collapsonaut attention is first and foremost household keeping—in line with the Greek etymology of the prefix *eco-* (from οικος: "home" and "household"). More concretely, collapsonaut attention urges us to shift our focus from the figures (GDP) to the background (the environment), from growth to maintenance, and from the networks to the common forms of cooperation that look after them. As Benjamin Peters reminds us, "networks do not resemble their designs as they take after the organizational collaborations and vices that tried to build them" (Peters 2016, Mullaney *et al.* 2021, 87).

Our house is threatened because our dominant extractivist attention fails to account for its (un) natural crumbling. Whether in mapping the intrastructures of our mediarchies, in practicing black studies, or in performing assemblies, collapsonaut attention helps us maintain our common house and care for each other—sticking with the trouble of cohabitation (Haraway 2016), while sharing the thrills of commonly imagined alternative futurities (Gumbs 2018).

Further Reading

Bratton, Benjamin. 2019. *The Terraforming*. Moscow: Strelka Institute.
Citton, Yves. 2017. *Mediarchy*. Cambridge: Polity.
Harney, Stefano & Fred Moten. 2021. *All Incomplete*. Wivenhoe: Minor Composition.
Mullaney, Thomas S. et al. 2021. *Your Computer Is on Fire!* Cambridge: MIT Press.
Towns, Armond R. 2022. *On Black Media Philosophy*. Oakland: University of California Press.

References

Abbott, M.C., María Buey González & Carl Olsson. 2021. "Peak Face." In *The Terraforming*. Moscow: Strelka Institute. https://peakface.strelka.institute. Accessed December 22, 2022.
Bratton, Benjamin. 2015. *The Stack. On Software and Sovereignty*. Cambridge: MIT Press.
Butler, Judith. 2015. *Notes toward a Performative Theory of Assembly*. Cambridge, MA: Harvard University Press.
Chun, Wendy Hui Kyong. 2021. *Discriminating Data: Correlation, Neighborhoods, and the New Politics of Recognition*. Cambridge: MIT Press.
Citton, Yves. 2014. *The Ecology of Attention*. Cambridge: Polity, 2017.
Citton, Yves & Jacopo Rasmi. 2020. *Générations collapsonautes*. Paris: Seuil.
Crawford, Kate. 2021. *Atlas of AI. Power, Politics, and the Planetary Costs of Artificial Intelligence*. New Haven, CT: Yale University Press.
Ferdinand, Malcolm. 2021. *Decolonial Ecology: Thinking from the Caribbean World*. Cambridge: Polity.
Ferreira da Silva, Denise. 2007. *Toward a Global Idea of Race*. Minneapolis: Minnesota University Press.
Gabrys, Jennifer. 2019. *How to Do Things with Sensors*. Minneapolis: University of Minnesota Press.
Glenn Albrecht, Gina-Maree Sartore, Linda Connor, Nick Higginbotham, Sonia Freeman, Brian Kelly, Helen Stain, Anne Tonna, and Georgia Pollard 2007. "Solastalgia: The Distress Caused by Environmental Change." *Australasian Psychiatry: bulletin of Royal Australian and New Zealand College of Psychiatrists* 15, Suppl. 1, S95–S98. doi:10.1080/10398560701701288.
Guattari, Félix. 1989. *The Three Ecologies*. London: Bloomsbury, 2014.
Gumbs, Alexis Pauline. 2018. *M Archive. After the End of the World*. Durham, NC: Duke University Press.
Haraway, Donna. 2016. *Staying with the Trouble. Making Kin in the Chthulucene*. Durham, NC: Duke University Press.
Harney, Stefano & Fred Moten. 2013. *The Undercommons. Black Study and Fugitive Planning*. Wivenhoe: Minor Composition.

Joler, Vladan. 2020. *New Extractivism. Assemblage of Concepts and Allegories*. www.extractivism.work
Kittler, Friedrich. 1986. *Gramophone Film Typewriter*. Stanford, CA: Stanford University Press, 1999.
Kokabi, Alexandre-Reza. 2019. "Jacques Chirac: l'histoire de sa phrase culte "Notre maison brûle et nous regardons ailleurs". Entretien avec Jean-Paul Déléage." *Reporterre*. September 26, 2019.
Lovink, Geert & David Garcia. 1997. *The ABC of Tactical Media*. https://www.nettime.org/Lists-Archives/nettime-l-9705/msg00096.html
Luhmann, Niklas. 1996. *The Reality of Mass Media*. Stanford, CA: Stanford University Press, 2000.
Manning, Erin. 2013. *Always More Than One*. Durham, NC: Duke University Press.
McLuhan, Marshall. 1964. *Understanding Media: The Extensions of Man*. New York: McGraw-Hill.
Moten, Fred. 2017. *Black and Blur*. Durham, NC: Duke University Press.
Neidich, Warren. 2013. *Glossary of Cognitive Activism*. Berlin: Archive Books.
Peters, Benjamin. 2016. *How Not to Network a Nation*. Cambridge: MIT Press.
Robinson, Cedric J. 1980. *The Terms of Order. Political Science and the Myth of Leadership*. Chapel Hill: University of North Carolina Press, 2016.
Servigne, Pablo & Raphael Stevens. 2020. *How Everything Can Collapse: A Manual for Our Times*. Cambridge: Polity.
Staal, Jonas. 2017. "Assemblism." *e-flux Journal*, no 80, March 2017. https://www.e-flux.com/journal/80/100465/assemblism/
Stiegler, Bernard. 1998. *Technics and Time*. Stanford, NC: Stanford University Press.
Vergès, Françoise. 2017. "Racial Capitalocene." In Gaye Theresa Johnson and Alex Lubin (eds), *Futures of Black Radicalism*, 72–82. New York: Verso.
Wark, McKenzie. 2004. *A Hacker Manifesto*. Cambridge, MA: Harvard University Press.
Wu, Tim. 2016. *The Attention Merchants*. New York: Alfred Knopf.
Wynter, Silvia. 2015. *Sylvia Wynter: On Being Human as Praxis* (Katherine McKittrick, ed.). Durham, NC: Duke University Press.
Zuboff, Shoshana. 2019. *The Age of Surveillance Capitalism*. New York: Public Affairs.

32
FEELING *WILD*
The Mediation of Embodied Experience

Alexa Weik von Mossner

Ecomedia play an ambiguous role in people's affective relationships with their environments. They demand and condition attention (Carroll & Seeley 2013; Citton 2016) and are often seen as an obstacle to healthy human-nature relationships because they "exhaust" our attentional resources in ways that affect our perception of our actual surroundings. At the same time, they also mediate such relationships (Cubitt 2005), immersing us in environments other than those we physically inhabit and treating us to embodied experiences that are both imaginary and real.

This chapter explores the psychological mechanisms behind this complex interplay of attention, cognition, embodiment, and emotion, focusing on the example of film. The first part of the chapter considers the ways in which film production and exhibition take into account the affective and embodied nature of human perception and cognition. The second part uses the example of Jean-Marc Vallée's biopic *Wild* (2014) to demonstrate how cinematic techniques enable viewers to viscerally experience a character's experience of a natural environment through processes of "embodied simulation" (Gallese & Guerra 2012). Vallée's film engages a form of cinematic language that lends itself particularly well to embodied experience: from its production mode, using natural light and a tiny crew, to its acting, mise-en-scène, sound design, music, pacing, and editing, it is geared toward engaging viewers in the embodied experience of one woman who immerses herself in nature and finds herself unprepared for the challenges of that encounter. Analyzing *Wild*'s material, narrative, and visual strategies through a cognitive ecocritical lens provides us with a better understanding of the affective reality of mediated embodied experience.

Film and the Nature of Human Perception, Emotion, and Cognition

Cinematic experience depends on *motion* in more than just one way. As Gilles Deleuze once put it, "cinema not only puts movement in the image, it also puts movement in the mind" (qtd. in Flaxman 2000, 366). The biology of the human brain, and the limitations of its processing capacity, is what enables us to see actual movement in motion pictures (Thompson-Jones 2013, 116), and it is also what allows us to understand and feel with characters. Neuroscientist Jeffrey Zacks notes that "movies evolved to take advantage of the brains we have" (2015, 4), including our innate capacity to *mimic* other people and simulate their actions, thoughts, and feelings, "whether we intend to or not, often without noticing" (5). Complex sets of information, communicated not only through dialogue, but also through an actor's body postures and facial expressions, cue viewers to mimic or simulate a character's embodied experience in their minds. In this context, Vittorio Gallese's influential work on the role of the mirror neuron system in processes of embodied simulation has far-reaching implications. As an embodiment theorist, Gallese proposes an approach to "the lived body" which focuses on the "tight interrelated connections" (2014) between the brain and the body while also paying attention to that body's situatedness in an environment.

Long before anyone had ever heard of Gallese's theory of embodied simulation, filmmakers and distributors figured out that viewers feel most immersed in a movie when their actual environment has very few affordances that they must pay attention to. That is why, at least in the context of Western exhibition traditions, everything about viewers' actual environments in a movie theater is geared toward keeping their eyes focused on the screen and the rest of their bodies motionless, making them the perfect sounding boards for the "liberated embodied simulation" (Gallese and Wojciehowski 2011) of the storyworld of the film. Other viewing situations – like watching a movie at home on a television set, computer screen or phone display – may be less conducive to full immersion, because they do not focus viewer attention to the same degree. But as long as some attention is paid to the film, we can expect a certain degree of immersion in its storyworld.

Important in my context here is that we simulate not only the motions and emotions of human protagonists. fMRI (functional magnetic resonance imaging) research suggests that we also map the movement of inanimate objects onto the motor systems of our brains, thus understanding them in relation to our own bodies (Keysers et al. 2004, 339). Only a fraction of these mapping processes is conscious, and yet most film viewers remember moments in which they held their breath, jumped back in fright, or teared up in response to a particular scene. Such affective responses are often related to the fate of central characters (who may or may not be human), and it is in part through them that viewers connect to a film's larger storyworld.

Patrick Colm Hogan has argued that narrative settings might "foster emotions either directly or indirectly. For example, a landscape might directly invite aesthetic delight, whatever its place in the story" (2018, 135). In this case, said landscape would cue emotions directly in the recipient. However, Hogan also points out that "the emotional consequence of a setting may be a function of its relation to the story. For example, a place that is neutral in itself may indirectly provoke fear through the dangers it poses to the hero" (135). In this case, our emotional response to the narrative environment takes a detour via our concern for a character – our sympathy and what film scholar Murray Smith has called "moral allegiance" (1995, 84), along with our resulting hope that the character will not be harmed. I have argued elsewhere (Weik von Mossner 2017, 28) that characters play an even more fundamental role in readers' and viewers' affective relationship to narrative environments: it is in part through the character's embodied existence in that environment that they understand it in the first place. A brief discussion of Jean-Marc Vallée's *Wild* will serve to illustrate this point.

Material, Narrative, and Visual Strategies in Jean-Marc Vallée's *Wild*

Wild opens with the sound of wind and a woman panting. Before we even see Cheryl Strayed, played by Reese Witherspoon, we can hear her gasping and huffing from what could (not by coincidence) be mistaken for sexual pleasure but is in fact caused by severe pain and exhaustion. Together with the wind, Cheryl's ragged breathing provides the soundtrack for a stunning shot of the Sierra Nevada as she takes off her uncomfortable hiking boots. A drone shot shows us that she is sitting high up on a mountain ridge, on the very edge of the abyss, before the film cuts to a closeup of her foot as she takes off her socks and reveals a bloody mass where her toes used to be.

Cheryl continues to pant as she tells herself – in a closeup of her face – that she would "rather be a hammer than a nail," and then – in a closeup of her foot – proceeds to rip off her loose toenail with a scream that echoes back to her from the surrounding mountains.

First-time viewers likely watch this opening scene with an unsettling combination of feelings – from the awe and admiration evoked by the beauty of the wide-angle landscape shot to the disgust and horror cued by the closeup on the bloody toenail and the empathic pain and, perhaps, admiration, caused by watching the character courageously rip it off her toe to alleviate her suffering. In terms of embodied simulation, it is important to note that the closeup of the bloody toe – and the fact that Cheryl can lift her toenail, something we know to be extremely painful – will cause a strong visceral reaction in most viewers, perhaps to the degree that they have to look away. Equally important, though, for the effect of the opening scene, is the closeup of Witherspoon's face since we inevitably read the actress's facial expression and are thus cued to empathize with her pain through processes of affective mimicry (Platinga 1999, 239). And it is the art of deception involved in acting that Witherspoon did not, in fact, feel any pain in her toe during the shooting of this scene (unlike the real Cheryl Strayed who lost no less than six toenails during her trip), but that she was nevertheless able to produce facial expressions that viewers read – both consciously and unconsciously – as a sign of great pain.

No less important than its visual dimension is the soundtrack of the opening scene. Building on the work of Vivian Sobchack, Laura Marks, and Jennifer Barker, Alison Walker bemoans critics' frequent focus on the visual (and narrative) dimensions of film and argues that, in Vallée's movie, a "combination of subtle and stylish sonic elements" helps "render the experience of the female character's embodiment" (2018, 120). The sounds of ragged breathing in the opening scene create what Walker calls "resonant empathy" with Cheryl's "physical exertions" (124). Empirical research supports the assumption that hearing Witherspoon's breathing as well as her sharp cry of pain at the moment when she (seemingly) rips off her toenail is an important component of the overall viscerality of the opening scene. Eye-tracking research has shown that "sound contributes to concentrating attention, particularly when subjective sound cues deeper character engagement" (Redmond et al. 2016, 19–20; see also Robinson et al. 2015; Smith 2015). "When sound is present in a scene," write psychologists Redmond et al., "it helps direct and focus where and for how long viewers look" (21), and processes of embodied simulation are guided by sound as well as sight (Kohler et al. 2002; Ward 2015). It is therefore both the edited sequence of images – including the strategic use of wide-angle shots and closeups – and the soundtrack of the opening scene that focus viewer attention on Cheryl's plight and, only moments later, on the material conditions that seem to have inflicted it on her. Viewers' affective relationship to the depicted mountain environment will inevitably be influenced by that knowledge, even though what really causes the pain in Chery's feet is the fact that she did not buy her boots in the correct size. But viewers will learn that only later.

What kind of woman they are dealing with is revealed in the very next shot of the film when one of Cheryl's boots accidentally tumbles down the mountain slope, and she reacts to the loss by throwing her other boot after the first one and screaming "Fuck you, bitch!" at the mountain, at herself, or at no one in particular. While she continues to scream, the film cuts to a quick succession of images – including a sex scene, a dictionary entry for the word "strayed" defining it as "to be lost," and the faces of a girl, a horse, and a fox – before it cuts to black and to the opening titles of the film. Only then does it flash back in time to the day, several weeks earlier, on which Cheryl Strayed embarks on her one-thousand-mile hiking trip along the Pacific Crest Trail for what she hopes will be a journey of self-discovery and healing.

At the time of its release in 2014, the reviews of *Wild* tended to highlight two aspects of the film. One was that Witherspoon had bought the rights to Strayed's bestselling memoir, *Wild: From*

Lost to Found on the Pacific Crest Trail (2009), for her recently founded production company, Pacific Standard, because she wanted to break out of the stereotypical (romantic) comedy roles that had made her a Hollywood star. The other important aspect highlighted in reviews of the film was the extreme physical challenges it posed to the crew and its female lead. As Witherspoon put it in an interview, "*Wild* is by far the hardest movie I've ever made in my life. I didn't hike a thousand miles, of course, but it was a different kind of physical rigor" (Buchanan 2014). Director Vallée had a reputation for his zeal for authenticity, and so the long shooting days meant a grueling routine for the actress in her role as Cheryl Strayed as well as for the small film crew that was shooting on location with natural light. While *Wild*'s main focus is on Cheryl's inner journey from the daughter of a beloved and terminally ill mother (Laura Dern) to promiscuous heroin addict to successful PCT hiker, it is the often brutal physical conditions of her hike that are shown to cause her healing, and it is one of the film's strengths that it invites viewers to imaginatively join Cheryl on a challenging trip they may not have the inclination or stamina to embark on themselves.

The metaphorical baggage Cheryl is taking along on that trip is both symbolized and made palpable for viewers by the much too heavy backpack she carries at the beginning of the film. The young woman is not an experienced hiker, and after she has crammed in everything she wants to take along, it is nearly impossible for her to even lift her pack from the floor of her motel room. Just how impossibly heavy her baggage has become is shown when Witherspoon – who is 5'6" and thus much shorter than the actual Cheryl Strayed – closes the straps across her chest and then struggles for over a minute to somehow get to her feet. Vallée insisted, in this scene and in others, on using a 75-pound backpack (rather than just a prop stuffed with paper) to make the scene more authentic (Buchanan 2014), and so, unlike in the opening scene, the physical strain we see on Witherspoon's face is real. Watching her, viewers automatically map her struggle onto their own bodies through processes of embodied simulation, understanding on a visceral level that Cheryl is not cut out for the task she has set for herself.

We see her swaying under the weight as she finally embarks on the trail, her heavy breathing begging the question of how on earth she is going to keep this up for over one thousand miles. What she has on her mind at this point is a sentence viewers heard earlier from her friend Aimee: "You can quit any time." But Cheryl does not want to quit, and so she stumbles on, sweating and swearing, through the merciless heat on a wilderness trail that – perversely – at this point runs parallel a six-lane interstate. After walking five miles, she is so exhausted that she is ready to camp for the night. Once again, the movie highlights that she is unskilled and underprepared for her wilderness trip. Not only does she have to consult the written instructions as she is trying to build her tent, but she also has brought the wrong kind of fuel for her camping cooker and thus is forced to eat a dinner of cold mush as she is reading Adrienne Rich and thinking of her dead mother.

Whether it is the heat and stark sunlight of the desert or the snow and cold of the mountains – throughout the film the natural environments along the Pacific Crest Trail come alive for viewers on the visual and aural level through panoramic shots of the landscape and accompanying sounds, cuing in them directly an emotional response. What it means to be exposed, physically, to the extreme *material conditions* of these environments, however, is related first and foremost through the embodied presence of the film's central protagonist. Whether she is sweating and panting in the heat or shivering in the cold, it is Witherspoon's body – the way it looks, moves, and expresses emotions – along with her dialogues and voiceover that allows viewers to simulate and imagine in a deeply visceral way what *it is like* to hike more than a thousand miles, alone, on the PCT.

As mentioned earlier, the hike itself is only one narrative dimension of the film, which keeps flashing back to the time when Cheryl's mother was still alive, to her illness, and to the time after her death, when Cheryl tries to cope with the loss by using heroin and engaging in promiscuous behavior, which in turn ends her marriage. *Wild* is as interested in the events that led Cheryl to embark on her brutal hike as it is in the hike itself, and it uses either her own physical states or her visual and aural impressions of her surroundings to interweave past and present. To name one example, as she is lying in her tent in the dark, the night sounds of the desert filling the air, it is her feeling hungry that triggers a flashback to a lunch she shared at a restaurant in Minneapolis with her friend Aimee. She is yanked out of that memory when something brushes against her body, returning her attention to her actual material environment and the potential dangers in it – like the rattlesnake she saw earlier that day (the culprit turns out to be a harmless caterpillar, though). Leaving her tent in panic, Cheryl uses a whistle she bought – "The Loudest Whistle in the World" – startling all the wildlife around her and triggering another flashback as her own ears are ringing from the piercing sound. This time, her mind returns to a moment in a car with her then-husband Paul, who is yelling at her. We cannot hear what is being said, but we see Cheryl covering her ears as the soundtrack changes from the continued ringing back to the sound of the cicadas in the desert night, and then to distant music as we see Cheryl in yet another flashback, naked and drugged up with some other guy, and then back to the earlier scene in the restaurant with her friend Aimee, whom she tells that she is "the girl who says yes instead of no." Here and elsewhere in the film, past and present, addiction and sobriety, wilderness and city, images and sound all interweave and melt into one another to help viewers understand how Cheryl got to this place and why she believes she needs to "put [her]self in the way of beauty" and hike a thousand miles to heal and survive.

It also bears mentioning that, despite her extreme aloneness for much of the trip, it is other people who save Cheryl from perishing in her chosen environment or at the very least alleviate some of her physical pain. As one of only two women hiking the trail at the time, some of the men she meets seem to pose a physical danger to her (though she never gets harmed by any of them) but others help her in crucial ways. It is the farmer Frank and his wife Annette who provide her with her first warm meal on the trail and help her get the right fuel; she learns from Ed, an older man she meets at Kennedy Meadows, that her heavy pack, nicknamed "Monster" by now, is filled with unnecessary things she can leave behind, and that she can order a free replacement for the hiking boots that have mangled her feet, delivered to her next stop. But despite all the human help she receives, it is first and foremost her strenuous physical encounter with nature that allows her to work through her painful past. At the end of the film, she has completed the mourning process for her mother – symbolized by a red fox that seems to be following her – and can forgive herself for the things she has done. As she crosses the Bridge of the Gods, the destination of her four-month trip, she stops to admire the glittering beauty of the Columbia River and seems, for the first time in the film, free of pain.

Conclusion

Ecomedia such as film can immerse us in environments other than those we physically inhabit and treat us to embodied experiences that are both imaginary and real. Taking a closer look at how Vallée's biopic *Wild* engages viewers in the physical struggle of its female protagonist in a demanding natural environment helps illustrate the psychological mechanisms behind this complex interplay of attention, cognition, embodiment, and emotion in viewers' engagement with characters and the cinematic environments that sustain and challenge them.

While viewers' embodied immersion in a cinematic environment such as the one presented in *Wild* remains to a large degree imaginary, it is also real in the sense that they use their own bodies as sounding boards for the imagination. When Witherspoon's Cheryl Strayed alternates between admiring the views along the PCT and suffering from its physical demands, her performance allows viewers to understand that environment not only visually (through the landscape shots) and aurally (through the soundtrack) but to relate to it also more indirectly through their empathetic alignment with the protagonist. The film thus illustrates well what is true for all movies – that we understand their larger storyworlds, including their cinematic environments, in part through characters' embodied interactions with them. And that it is our capacity to mentally simulate the actions, perceptions, and feelings of other people as well as the world around us that enables the sensations and emotions we feel at the movies.

Further Reading

Gallese, Vittorio, and Michele Guerra. 2012. "Embodying Movies: Embodied Simulation and Film Studies." *Cinema: Journal of Philosophy and the Moving Image* 3: 183–210.

Plantinga, Carl. 2009. *Moving Viewers: American Film and the Spectator Experience*. Berkeley: University of California Press.

Weik von Mossner, Alexa. 2017. *Affective Ecologies: Empathy, Emotion, and Environmental Narrative*. Columbus: Ohio State UP.

Weik von Mossner, Alexa, ed. 2014. *Moving Environments: Affect, Emotion, Ecology, and Film*. Waterloo: Wilfrid Laurier UP.

Zacks, Jeffrey M. 2015. *Flicker: Your Brain on Movies*. Oxford: Oxford UP.

References

Buchanan, Kyle (August 27, 2014). "How Getting *Wild* Saved a 'Lost' Reese Witherspoon." *Vulture*. https://www.vulture.com/2014/08/how-wild-saved-a-reese-witherspoon.html

Carroll, Noël, and William P. Seeley. 2013. "Cognitivism, Psychology, and Neuroscience: Movies as Attentional Engines." In *Psychocinematics: Exploring Cognition at the Movies*, edited by Arthur Shimamura, 53–75. New York: Oxford UP.

Citton, Yves. 2016. *The Ecology of Attention*. London: Polity.

Cubitt, Sean. 2005. *EcoMedia*. New York: Rodopi.

Flaxman, Gregory, 2000. "The Brain Is the Screen: An Interview with Gilles Deleuze." In *The Brain Is the Screen: Deleuze and the Philosophy of Cinema*, edited by Gregory Flaxman, 365–74. Minneapolis: Minnesota UP.

Gallese, Vittorio. 2014. "Bodily Selves in Relation: Embodied Simulation as Second-person Perspective on Intersubjectivity." *Philosophical Transactions of the Royal Society* 369 (1644). doi: 10.1098/rstb.2013.0177

Gallese, Vittorio, and Michele Guerra. 2012. "Embodying Movies: Embodied Simulation and Film Studies." *Cinema: Journal of Philosophy and the Moving Image* 3: 183–210.

Gallese, Vittorio, and Hannah Wojciehowski. 2011. "How Stories Make Us Feel: Toward an Embodied Narratology." *California Italian Studies* 2 (1).

Hogan, Patrick Colm. 2018. *Literature and Emotion*. New York and London: Routledge.

Keysers, Christian, Bruno Wicker, Valeria Gazzola, Jean-Luc Anton, Leonardo Fogassi, and Vittorio Gallese. 2004. "A Touching Sight: SII/PV Activation during the Observation and Experience of Touch." *Neuron* 42: 335–46.

Kohler, E., C. Keysers, M. A. Umiltá, L. Fogassi, Vittorio Gallese, and Giacomo Rizzolatti. 2002. "Hearing Sounds, Understanding Actions: Action Representation in Mirror Neurons." *Science* 297 (5582): 846–48.

Platinga, Carl. 1999. "The Scene of Empathy and the Human Face on Film." In *Passionate Views: Film, Cognition, and Emotion*, edited by Carl Plantinga and Greg M. Smith, 239–55. Baltimore, MD: Johns Hopkins UP.

Redmond, S., S. Pink, J. Stadler, J. Robinson, D. Verhagen, and A. Rassell. 2016. "Seeing, Sensing Sound: Eye Tracking Soundscapes in Saving Private Ryan and Monsters, Inc." In *Making Sense of Cinema:*

Empirical Studies into Film Spectators and Spectatorship, edited by CarrieLynn Reinhard and Christopher Olson, 139–64. New York: Bloomsbury.

Robinson, Jennifer, Jane Stadler, and Andrea Rassell. 2015. "Sound and Sight: An Exploratory Look at *Saving Private Ryan* through the Eye Tracking Lens." *Refractory* 25. Last modified February 6, 2015. http://refractory.unimelb.edu.au/2015/02/06/robinson-stadler-rassell/.

Smith, Murray. 1995. *Engaging Characters: Fiction, Emotion, and the Cinema*. Oxfordand New York: Oxford University Press.

Smith, Tim J. 2015. "Read, Watch, Listen: A Commentary on Eye Tracking and Moving Images." *Refractory* 25. https://refractoryjournal.net/smith/

Thompson-Jones, Katherine J. 2013. "Sensing Motion in Movies." In *Psychocinematics: Exploring Cognition at the Movies*, edited by Arthur Shimamura, 115–31. Oxford: Oxford UP.

Vallée, Jean-Marc, director. 2014. *Wild*. Los Angeles, CA: Fox Searchlight.

Walker, Alison. 2018. "Embodied Resonances: The Sonic Pathways in Jean-Marc Vallée's Film *Wild*." *The New Soundtrack* 8 (2): 119–34.

Ward, Mark S. 2015. "Art in Noise: An Embodied Simulation Account of Cinematic Sound Design." In *Embodied Cognition and Cinema*, edited by Maarten Coëgnarts and Peter Kravanja, 155–86. Leuven: Leuven University Press.

Weik von Mossner, Alexa. 2017. *Affective Ecologies: Empathy, Emotion, and Environmental Narrative*. Columbus: Ohio State UP.

Zacks, Jeffrey M. 2015. *Flicker: Your Brain on Movies*. Oxford: Oxford UP.

33

SOCIAL REALISM AND ENVIRONMENTAL CRISIS

Clio Barnard's *Dark River*

David Ingram

Established modes of aesthetic realism have come to appear problematic for the representation of the ecological crisis, because, as Timothy Clark writes, "crucial forms of environmental destruction cannot immediately be seen or localized, and resist representation at the kinds of scale at which most poetry, narrative or drama operate" (Clark 2015, 175). The editors of the *Climate Realism* collection (2021) similarly begin from the premise that "the immediate events of the present have become not only an index to larger dynamic systems but also deep historicity and futurity" (Badia et al. 2021, 8). Climate change has thus become a special case of what Clark calls a "global issue opaque to immediate or empirical representation" because its complex spatialities and temporalities mean that it is too large and difficult a concept to be represented adequately in realist modes of fiction (Clark 2015, 177). Clark observes that many narrative forms tend to simplify complex realities outside the text into stories with clear lines of cause and effect and clearly identified perpetrators (178). He is interested in new aesthetic forms which question these conventions in order to draw attention to "our normal entrapment in the delusory and potentially destructive projections of the personal scale" (191–92).

Yet is there a way of looking at narrative forms, whether in literature or in film, that does not see them as merely delusory or "evasive" (Clark 2015, 178)? Following ecological psychologist James J. Gibson, a more positive way of considering such forms, beyond the rhetoric of failure that Clark favours, is as "affordances" which not only constrain but also enable a range of cognitive and affective experiences (Gibson 1979, 129; Levine 2015, 6). Gibson defined the "affordance" of an environment or an object as "what it *offers* the animal, what it *provides* or *furnishes*, either for good or ill" (Gibson 1979, 129). What follows is an exploration of the affordances of social realist film, a tradition that has played a critically important role within British cinema since the work of documentarist John Grierson in the 1930s (Brown 2001, 248). If the large temporal and spatial scales required to represent ecological concepts are unavailable to the small-budget social realist film, what are the affordances of social realism as an aesthetic mode in a time of environmental crisis?

Scepticism about realism amongst critics in the environmental humanities tends to focus on realism both as a mode of art and as a position in the philosophy of knowledge. If realism is assumed to be a quest for the total reproduction or exact reflection of reality, then any act of representation will always be a failure. However, if realism is considered a partial and fallibilistic process, then excessive pessimism about realism, based on what cognitivist theorist Torben Grodal calls the "negative epistemological claim concerning the inherent uncertainty of our knowledge," is unfounded (Grodal 2009, 269). The philosophy of critical realism, which is the basis for Grodal's cognitivist theories of film, proposes a more modest and less totalising understanding of realism than rival postmodernist positions allow. As understood by critical realists, philosophical realism is an open and pragmatic process which can produce relatively trustworthy knowledge of the world (Soper 1995; Norris 1997). Aesthetic realism, on the other hand, produces representations of that world which are mediations, rather than simple reflections, of reality. Representations in film are thus informed, as Samantha Lay puts it, by "specific social perspectives. These perspectives in turn are products of distinct moments in time and are specific to the social realities of these times" (Lay 2002, 14). Understood in this way, realist art works can produce salient and moving representations of the environments in which they are created.

Yet the constraints imposed on aesthetic realism by limitations of scale remain. In the nineteenth-century novel, Dickens' invention of the network narrative was an effective way of representing a globalised world made up, as Levine puts it, of "the overlapping of multiple networks" which included the "social, economic, electronic, ecological, viral, bacterial, legal, familial, national and transnational" (Levine 2015, 115, 130–31). In *Bleak House* (1853), Dickens multiplied the usual number of characters in a novel and expanded its length in order to represent the enlarged scale of a complex, networked society (Levine 2015, 126). Yet these affordances specific to the novel are unavailable for films because a film is subject to temporal constraints. Hence the network narratives of films such as *Syriana* (2005) are "much simpler in plot because of their restricted length" and "all rely on a single principle of interconnection, like the oil industry, to undergird their plots" (Levine 2015, 127). They also tend to narrow the focus of their plot to events which happen to a single family (Levine 2015, 128). Although long-form television drama has the potential for complex characterisation and plotting, these affordances are also unavailable to a stand-alone movie of standard length. The network narrative is beyond the range of a small social realist film. A close analysis of such a film, *Dark River* (2017), written and directed by Clio Barnard, will show how the writer-director uses aesthetic strategies more typical of the social realist film to approach the challenge of representing rural English society in a time of economic and ecological crisis.

Social Realism, Metonymy, and Stylistic Hybridity in *Dark River*

Dark River was made for Film4 and funded by the BFI Film Fund, Screen Yorkshire, and the Wellcome Trust. Such mid- to low-budget films are necessarily constrained to be small in scale, often based in a single locality with a small number of characters and a single plot line. They are thus unsuited to the kind of network narrative that can explore the global temporalities and spatialities of environmental and climate crisis. Instead, the film explores the psychology of a broken family relationship, out of which emerges an ethical discourse on guilt, responsibility, and blame. Alice (Ruth Wilson) returns to the family farm after 15 years away to claim the tenancy that her late father (Sean Bean) promised her, while her elder brother Joe (Mark Stanley) has taken over the running of the farm. Alice is traumatised by the sexual abuse she suffered as a child at the hands of her father, which is represented in the film in flashback from Alice's point-of-view. Eventually Joe confronts his complicity in his father's abuse of his sister and the siblings are reconciled.

In social realism, this dramatic focus on individual characterisation and character interaction is placed within a particular environment which plays a determining role in the action (Bayman 2009, 56). *Dark River* thus includes the concrete details of everyday farm work in a specific rural environment in the North of England. As a Film4 film, these narrative concerns follow Channel 4's remit to represent the under-represented on television; funded by Screen Yorkshire, the film brings to the screen a relatively neglected region in the North of England (Lay 2002, 79). *Dark River* is thus the type of social realist film which Lay identifies as focussing on the "public and the social (the working class at work, struggles connected to the wider society or community)" rather than "the private and the personal (the focus on family life and problems with little reference to social, political and economic conditions)" (Lay 2002, 118).

Stories of generational conflict and dysfunctional families have always been central to this mode of British cinema. These family dramas, often centred on bad fathers and attendant themes of power, blame, reconciliation, and resilience, can be seen as commentaries on the workings of patriarchal power within wider networks than those of the immediate locality in which they are set. In this way, the subject matter of social realist films, as Hallam and Marchment write, aims to be of "'universal' human significance" (Hallam and Marshment 2000, 185). If the inverted commas here suggest uneasiness over the existence of human universals, social realist films at least move from the particular to the general in their representation of specific environments.

A limitation of such narrative focus on the local, and on the lived, personal experience of the protagonists, is that it is anthropocentric, although this bias may be justified in commercial, aesthetic, and ethical terms. As a commercial medium, cinema is constrained to concentrate mostly on human interest stories in which a potential audience may be interested and can empathise. Anthropocentrism may also be justifiable in ethical terms, in that what is often dismissed as anthropocentrism, as Tim Hayward argues, can include "legitimate human concerns" (Hayward 1997, 49). In the case of *Dark River*, these include the psychological effects of family trauma, sexual abuse, poverty, and economic competition. As with other "centrisms," whether "bio-" or "eco-," anthropocentrism may have a provisional validity in a particular discursive context.

In any case, *Dark River* moves at times beyond the anthropocentrism expected of social realist films to include the natural world and the nonhuman as explicit content. The film is a story about a conflict over land, its ownership, inheritance, and use, which makes reference to a wider ecology beyond the human by placing its central conflict between siblings within a social context of sustainable farming methods and the decline in biodiversity in the English countryside. The film thus creates a realist environment in which agency is multiple, both human and nonhuman, while nevertheless emphasising the powerful role played by "human decisions and omissions" as a determining force in the world (Bennett 2010, 25). In this way, the film demonstrates how social realism can infer ecological considerations beyond the human, the local, and the particular.

The opening shot of the film, a close-up of a sheep's face, is an example of this approach. Other cutaways and establishing shots feature animals, such as a hare in a field and a crow on a dry-stone wall. These shots, although brief, are held long enough to create the impression that the human drama is taking place within a wider environment that includes nonhuman participants. Martin Lefebvre writes that, in some films, the

> contemplation of the setting frees it briefly from its narrative function (but perhaps, in some cases, only for the length of a thought); for one instant, the natural, outdoor setting for the action is considered in its own right, as a landscape.
>
> (Lefebvre 2006, 29)

Dark River thereby hints at wider ecological networks within a multispecies environment, even if there is an inevitable limit to the extent and depth of its coverage of such concepts. Aesthetic realism is always selective, partial, and provisional, so that some conceptual content will inevitably be either simplified or omitted altogether from any act of representation. For example, the film does not explicitly link the issue of biodiversity loss to climate change, nor place the treatment of animals within an animal rights agenda. Compared to the global spatialities and temporalities required to represent an era of ecological and climate crisis, then, the focus of *Dark River* may appear narrow. Yet this does not have to be considered as a sin of omission, still less "delusory" or "evasive" (in Clark's words), but rather as a reasonable aesthetic decision made by the writer-director and producers, whether consciously or unconsciously, concerning what makes for a good film within the given budgetary constraints.

Metonymy is the main aesthetic means by which social realist filmmakers communicate concepts to the viewer, such as ideas about ecological crisis and climate change, without using either expository dialogue or voice-over commentary. In metonymy, the viewer derives a general concept from a shot of a particular object associated with that concept. For example, the inclusion in a film of a "ramshackle farmer's hut, perhaps in the nineteenth century" may signify "the transference of the idea of labour, of pastoralism, of the pre-industrial or agrarian existence" (Harper and Rayner 2010, 20). The aesthetic challenge for social realist filmmakers is to avoid disrupting plausibility and verisimilitude with overt didacticism; metonymy allows a film to construct wider conceptual meaning without obtrusive exposition. *Dark River* thus uses metonymy to connote concepts such as responsibility and care for the natural world, thereby placing its central family relationship within a realist sense of the wider environment of the Yorkshire Dales at a particular moment in English history.

The use of metonymy is augmented in the film by documentary-style scenes, most notably the sheep-shearing and auction sequences, in which nonhuman organisms are given a degree of agency in the action of the film. Indeed, the presence of animals advances both characterisation and plot and constructs the story world as an interaction of human and nonhuman participants. The rats that infest the farm are a sign of Joe's neglect of the farm; the old family dog is useless as a ratter and is now more a companion animal than a working dog. The climax of the plot, when Alice shoots the bailiff dead, is instigated when the new dog, which Alice brought in to deal with the rats, escapes and kills a sheep. The lives of animals are thus closely tied in with those of the human occupants of the land in a complex web of cause and effect. As Herman notes, the branch of narrative theory derived from A. J. Greimas talks of "participants" or "actants" in a fiction in a way that includes nonhuman agents such as animals and inorganic objects as well as human beings. Herman's notion of "participant roles and relations" is thus useful for an ecocritical approach to fiction that considers agency in an environment as multiple and nonhuman (Herman 2002, 115). Yet in *Dark River,* as in social realism in general, the main focus is on the human characters who make the crucially determining decisions about how to act in and on their environment. Decentring the concept of agency thus does not mean underestimating the importance of human actions in affecting a particular environment.

Consideration of nonhuman agency in *Dark River* comes across particularly in the dispute between sister and brother over farming methods, which reveals their differing attitudes to the land and its nonhuman inhabitants. Alice has worked as an itinerant sheep shearer, and this practical, economic relationship with the land lies behind her desire to improve the farm which Joe has neglected. The contrast in attitudes is reiterated several times in the film, as Joe prefers older, more environmentally benign farming methods to the more modern, industrial approach proposed by Alice. The siblings thus disagree over when to sell the sheep; Joe wants to "sell 'em fat," whereas Alice wants to sell the lambs quickly to make money. Joe prefers to dip the sheep, whereas Alice wants to spray them with chemicals using new technology. Joe is also concerned that cutting the grass for a cash crop will endanger the rare wildflowers and insects that thrive in the meadow and opposes Alice's plan to poison the rats in the barn because it might threaten the fledgling owls living in the eaves.

The scene in which Alice and Joe disagree on when to cut the grass in the meadow is a good example of a social realist drama moving outward to suggest a relatively complex, wider environment. When you cut for silage, Joe explains to Alice, "all you end up doing is killing everything that's under it." He tells her about the millions of insects, spiders, butterflies, bees, voles, and shrews "in one acre of hay." This scene, along with the scene when brother and sister watch the owls in the roof eaves, shows them relaxed and smiling, as their mutual love of the natural world brings out their familial care for each other. These simple gestures elicit emotional empathy in the viewer and suggest metonymically the therapeutic role that the natural world plays for both the characters in the film and for the viewer. Although the film also dwells on what reviewer Trevor Johnston called "the violence in the pastoral: the traps for vermin, the culling of a lame animal, the tussles required to shear and dip sheep" (Johnston 2018, 62), the presence of death and violence in the rural environment does not undermine the positive affect it also affords and the utopian potential for a more benign relationship with the land that this implies.

Yet the social realist treatment of the environment in the film also suggests that the reality of farming is based on difficult, messy choices, in which the farmers choose between two different ways of commodifying the land. Alice needs to make money to survive in a capitalist farming economy, while Joe shows more concern for wildlife and biodiversity than Alice but is also depressed, self-sabotaging, and ultimately willing to sell the land to developers. *Dark River* thus does not set up a simplistic, binary opposition between a villain who commodifies the land and a hero who values it from a non-capitalist perspective, as a more melodramatic fiction would do. Rather, the narrative raises the complex question of whether the conservationist methods preferred by Joe are less economically profitable than the more industrial methods favoured by Alice. Yet the narrative ultimately avoids this difficult question because of Joe's decision to sell the farm to developers, which means that Alice is denied the opportunity of demonstrating that her methods are better. Nevertheless, Joe's emotional, even sentimental desire to conserve the land becomes central to his ultimate reconciliation with his sister. After Joe takes the punishment for her crime, the coda shows Alice visiting him in prison. Alice gives her brother a seed from the shepherd's needle she has picked in the hay meadow, a gift that emerges from their mutual love of nature rather than its commodification. This scene typifies the way in which *Dark River* demonstrates a key affordance of social realism: the drama centres on the psychological complexities of human relationships while suggesting through metonymy how these relate to the wider social and environmental contexts within which they take place.

Another means by which a social realist film can suggest a large environmental scale, in addition to metonymy, is by augmenting realist verisimilitude with what Hallam and Marshment call "stylistic hybridity" (Hallam and Marshment 2000, 185). *Dark River* thus adds melodrama to realism as an aesthetically salient means not only of resolving its narrative but also of suggesting the protagonist's relationship to the wider natural environment. As the plot of *Dark River* moves in the direction of retribution and redemption, the mise-en-scène evokes elements of Gothic horror and action thriller. When Alice's new dog escapes and kills a sheep, she chases after it, accompanied by Joe and the bailiff who has arrived to evict her from the farm. Arriving at the nearby waterfall, the landscape triggers in Alice's childhood memories of her abusive father. In her rage, she fires her gun at an image of her father in her mind and accidentally kills the bailiff. Bayman observes that melodrama, which he describes as "the pathos of the expressive elevation of fundamentally ordinary feelings," is a fictional mode which is often drawn on in social realist films in order to reinforce the "vividness" of the drama, and therefore the viewer's experience of emotion and empathy in relation to the story (Bayman 2009, 48, 60).

From an ecocritical perspective, the melodramatic mode can also suggest a larger, cosmic scale to events than that possible within realism. The stormy weather that accompanies the dramatic climax of *Dark River* is, of course, commonplace in melodrama. Grodal writes that melodrama

> employs the type of weather, the type of time-space, which emphasizes the way in which human beings live at the mercy of nature (…) This means weather-types like darkness and fog, which block the act-supporting remote sensation, and strong thunder, wind, rain, which activate the contact-senses.
>
> (Grodal 1997, 257)

In this respect, the inclusion of the thunderstorm and the waterfall at the climax of *Dark River* connotes Alice's lack of control over her environment. When she fires the gun, her actions are ruled by her unconscious mind as the traumatic memories take over her motor actions. She is thus at the mercy of nature, both inner and outer. For Grodal, the use of such weather effects in melodrama encourages a viewing position that reflects the decentred place of human beings in the natural world: that "even if it is correct that we are conscious, intentional beings, it is also correct that we are a biomass in space, and that our sensibility is partly linked to this fact" (Grodal 1997, 263). Adding melodrama to social realism thus gives a wider, even cosmic scale to the fiction, demonstrating how stylistic hybridity expands the scale of social realist drama to include the relationship between the protagonist and the natural world she inhabits.

Amitav Ghosh has written influentially of the need for non-realist genres such as fantasy and science fiction if the novel is to represent the global spatialities and long temporalities of the Anthropocene era (Ghosh 2017, 24). Franny Armstrong's *The Age of Stupid* (2009) anticipated this theoretical move by drawing on the realist genre of expository documentary to present complex ideas about climate change while also including a science fictional frame-story to add the necessary long temporal scale to its argument about climate change. Yet *Dark River* is more a case of stylistic hybridity than of full-blown genre mixing, as the narration goes through various shifts in mode rather than larger shifts in genre. The film thus downplays the use of metaphor and symbol favoured by non-realist genres such as melodrama, science fiction, and fantasy, preferring instead to use metonymy to emphasise the materiality of the fictional environment it creates. In doing so, *Dark River* demonstrates how the affordances of social realism continue to be modest but salient means by which British cinema is addressing the contemporary realities of ecological crisis.

Further Reading

Bayman, Louis. "Melodrama as Realism in Italian Neorealism," in *Realism and the Audiovisual Media*, edited by Lúcia Nagib and Cecilia Mello. Basingstoke: Palgrave Macmillan, 2009.

Clark, Timothy. *Ecocriticism on the Edge: The Anthropocene as a Threshold Concept*. London: Bloomsbury, 2015.

Grodal, Torben. *Moving Pictures: A New Theory of Film Genres, Feelings, and Cognition*. Oxford: Clarendon Press, 1997.

Lay, Samantha. *British Social Realism: From Documentary to Brit Grit*. London and New York: Wallflower, 2002.

Soper, Kate. *What is Nature? Culture, Politics and the Non-Human*. Oxford: Blackwell, 1995.

References

Armstrong, Franny, director. *The Age of Stupid.* Spanner Films, 2009.

Badia, Lynn, Marija Cetinić and Jeff Diamanti. "Introduction," in *Climate Realism*: *The Aesthetics of Weather and Atmosphere in the Anthropocene*, edited by Lynn Badia, Marija Cetinić and Jeff Diamanti, 1–16. London and New York: Routledge, 2021.

Barnard, Clio, director. *Dark River.* Film4, Left Bank Pictures, Moonspun Films, 2017.

Bayman, Louis. "Melodrama as Realism in Italian Neorealism," in *Realism and the Audiovisual Media*, edited by Lúcia Nagib and Cecilia Mello, 47–62. Basingstoke: Palgrave Macmillan, 2009.

Bennett, Jane. *Vibrant Matter*: *A Political Ecology of Things.* Durham, NC and London: Duke University Press, 2010.

Brown, Geoff. "Paradise Found and Lost: The Course of British Realism," in *The British Cinema Book*, edited by Robert Murphy, 28–38. London: BFI Publishing, 2001.

Clark, Timothy. *Ecocriticism on the Edge: The Anthropocene as a Threshold Concept.* London: Bloomsbury, 2015.

Ghosh, Amitav. *The Great Derangement*: *Climate Change and the Unthinkable.* Chicago, IL and London: The University of Chicago Press, 2017.

Gibson, James J. *The Ecological Approach to Visual Perception.* Boston, MA and London: Houghton Mifflin Co., 1979.

Grodal, Torben. *Moving Pictures: A New Theory of Film Genres, Feelings, and Cognition.* Oxford: Clarendon Press, 1997.

———. *Embodied Visions*: *Evolution, Emotion, Culture, and Film.* Oxford: Oxford University Press, 2009.

Hallam, Julia and Margaret Marshment. *Realism and Popular Cinema.* Manchester and New York: Manchester University Press, 2000.

Harper, Graeme and Jonathan Rayner. "Introduction – Cinema and Landscape," in *Cinema and Landscape*, edited by Graeme Harper and Jonathan Rayner, 15–28. Bristol and Chicago, IL: Intellect, 2010.

Hayward, Timothy. "Anthropocentrism: A Misunderstood Problem," *Environmental Values.* 6, no. 1 (February 1997): 49–63.

Herman, David. *Story Logic*: *Problems and Possibilities of Narrative.* Lincoln, MI and London: University of Nebraska Press, 2002.

Johnston, Tom. "Land and Freedom." *Sight and Sound.* 28, no. 3 (March 2018): 10–11.

Lay, Samantha. *British Social Realism: From Documentary to Brit Grit.* London and New York: Wallflower, 2002.

Lefebvre, Martin. "Between Setting and Landscape in the Cinema," in *Landscape and Film*, edited by Martin Lefebvre, 19–60. London: Routledge, 2006.

Levine, Caroline. *Forms: Whole, Rhythm, Hierarchy, Network.* Princeton, NJ and Oxford: Princeton University Press, 2015.

Norris, Christopher. *Against Relativism: Philosophy of Science, Deconstruction and Critical Theory.* Oxford: Blackwell, 1997.

Soper, Kate. *What is Nature? Culture, Politics and the Non-Human.* Oxford: Blackwell, 1995.

34
ECOPOLITICAL SATIRE IN THE GLOBAL NORTH

Nicole Seymour and Anthony Lioi

In 2015, speaking about his satirical "cli-fi" (climate-change fiction) novel, *The Subprimes*, U.S. author Karl Taro Greenfeld told the *Los Angeles Times*, "I worry real life will eclipse this book very quickly" (Kellog). Similar musings have recently circulated around satire, irony, and comedy more broadly – capturing a growing sense that there is no place, or purpose, for such heightened or absurdist modes in an already absurd landscape defined, at least in the global North, by the ridiculous (former?) rule of Donald Trump and the bonkers theories of QAnon. Indeed, some have wondered if those modes might even be "responsible for enabling Trump's rise amid a pathologically entertaining political media landscape" (Hennefeld 2016). Meanwhile, the majority of ecomedia in the Anglosphere takes its tone from the tradition of nature writing, whose earnestness and sincerity have been widely noted. Ecocritics and ecomedia scholars have frequently followed suit, assuming that the "best," or most effective, eco-texts are those that inculcate earnest, sincere devotion to nature.

But as Nicole Seymour has shown, there exists a notable but underappreciated counter-tradition of environmentalist art that engages in modes including satire, irony, and comedy to, among other things, highlight the ironies and absurdities of climate policy – in which politicians, faced with overwhelming evidence of climate change, choose *not* to act, much as Trump did when he withdrew from the Paris climate accords. As she argues, "it is not that environmentalist artworks that engage with and employ irony, absurdity, and so forth are necessarily so rare. But they may go unrecognized *as environmentalist* due to environmentalism's prevailing reputation for seriousness, sentimentality, and the like" (32). Seymour thus participates in a small but growing intellectual tradition of seeing ecopolitical potential in non-serious modes – a tradition that we might trace back to Joseph Meeker's *The Comedy of Survival: Literary Ecology and a Play Ethic* (1974).

Our contribution to this handbook builds on this tradition, surveying works of eco-satire that have emerged during this recent era in which satire's very capacities have come under scrutiny: the Netflix comedy special *Sarah Cooper: Everything's Fine* (2020) and the Netflix film *Don't Look Up* (2021). While Samuel Johnson's classic definition of a satire is "a poem in which wickedness or folly is censured" (Greenberg 2019, 3), that definition has since widened. First, most contemporary definitions would have it that satire involves representing (*re-presenting*) certain realities in absurdist, exaggerated, or bizarre ways in order to "censure," or critique, said reality. Second, as Jonathan Greenberg has recently argued, it is important to move beyond the idea that satire is only

This chapter has been made available under a CC-BY-NC-ND license.

a form, such as a poem, to the broader claim that satire is a *mode and a practice*, permitting us to include any media that behave satirically (2019, 9–11). Though classical and neoclassical satire in the European tradition targets the folly of humanity across class – including the lower classes – it is characteristic of the eco-satire examined below to "punch up," to aim at the folly of powerful individuals and institutions such as politicians, corporations, nation-states, and other agents that can shape our response to environmental crises at the scale of the planet. As ecological crises become more severe, the lines between traditional forms of satire blur. The classical Latin tradition produced Horatian satire, in which foolish but loveable people muddle through, and Juvenalian satire, in which the meretricious human race destroys itself through vice. In the satire we examine, the urge to mock and preserve goes to war against the urge to punish and destroy, often in the same work.

Sarah Cooper: Everything's Fine and *Don't Look Up* are notable works insofar as they engage, to varying degrees, with multiple issues in addition to environmental ones – including racism and misogyny – thereby encouraging an intersectional approach to politics. They focus on affect, paying close attention to how environmental and other crises make us feel, while also evoking particular feelings themselves. Finally, they model specific, sometimes unexpected, techniques in addition to broader-strokes, common satirical techniques such as exaggeration. For example, *Sarah Cooper* employs lip synching. Throughout our discussions of these features, we remain attuned to Taro Greenfeld and others' concerns about the potential limits of satire as an ecopolitical mode of communication – but find that those concerns are, to a large extent, unfounded or at least beside the point.

"Everything's Fine with the Weather!": *Sarah Cooper* and Climate Anxiety

"I'm not denying climate change, but it could very well go back." So spoke Donald Trump during an aborted *60 Minutes* interview, in relation to the aforementioned Paris accords withdrawal – and so lip synched Sarah Cooper, in one of the many videos for which the comedian rocketed to attention in Spring 2020 ("How to Climate Change"). Cooper's juxtaposition of her Black/mixed-race female body with the words of our sexist, white supremacist former president (re)positioned those words as particularly absurd and bizarre. Further, through the dysphoric mismatch between voice and body, Cooper captured the kind of paranoia that has defined many citizens' relations to the president, while also depicting what many of those citizens have tried to avoid: letting Trump "get under your skin." By Fall of 2020, Cooper had landed a Netflix comedy special in which she plays the host, also named Sarah Cooper, of a *Good Morning America*-type program titled *Everything's Fine*. The special follows her through increasingly surreal and dark segments (figuratively but also literally so; the color palette dims as the special proceeds), tackling topical issues including the coronavirus pandemic, the QAnon conspiracy theory, racist microaggressions – "*you're* Sarah Cooper? Can I see some ID?" demands a baker named, obviously, Karen, when the host arrives for a cooking segment – the #MeToo movement, and, of course, climate change.

For our purposes, the most interesting segment of *Everything's Fine* is the weather report delivered by meteorologist Andrea Steele, played by Maya Rudolph. It includes a five-day forecast that ranges from 123 degrees to -12 degrees ("SPICY HOT & HUMID," and "WIND CHILL???" read the respective associated chyrons). Steele, like Cooper's character throughout the special, maintains a forced cheeriness that borders on hysteria – suggesting that the act of downplaying horror deepens the horror rather than lessening it. "It's gonna be a cold one, folks. Most likely not survivable, so wear a jacket!" chirps Steele. Only after Steele turns things back to an unnerved Cooper – "Everything's fine with the weather. … Back to you, Sarah!" – does the meteorologist actually start to break down: "Stay the fuck in your house. Reporting live from Hell on Earth, this is Andrea Motherfucking Steele!!!"

Cooper's own breakdown is more prolonged, only coming to a head at the end of the special. Fed up with pretending that "Everything's Fine," she finally storms out of the studio and goes to play golf, Trump's favorite sport – at which point she notices a giant asteroid heading straight toward Earth. As viewers will recall, Cooper's character preempted her own reporting on this major news development in order to take a phone call from the president – a clear reference to Trump's tendency to call into various new programs such as *Fox & Friends*. The special ends with Cooper taking shelter, uselessly, behind a tree.

In these depictions of both Cooper and Steele – at least, before their respective breakdowns – *Everything's Fine* comments upon the continued dominance of "infotainment" on both the left and right (*The Daily Show*, the aforementioned *Fox & Friends*, etc.), the media's misleading "both-sidesing" of issues such as climate change, and the general abdication of journalistic responsibility ("stick to the news," the showrunner lectures her, "[and] leave the politics out of it"). Of course, these head-in-the-sand reactions are not unique to journalists; countless thinkers, from psychologists to literary critics, have observed how grasping the enormity of climate change threatens our emotional and mental stability. Denial is thus adaptive in the short term – but maladaptive in the long term and on a mass scale.

At the same time, *Everything's Fine* suggests that anxiety over issues such as climate change, not to mention the (in)ability to speak out about such issues, is circumscribed by race and gender, among other factors. Indeed, we would connect the climate change segment with earlier segments in the special, such as when Cooper's showrunner tells her that "35% of our audience likes that you're Black ... and 80% ... feels extremely threatened by you" – an absurd point made even more absurd by the questionable math therein. "It's that *attitude*," the showrunner's second-in-command chimes in. "I don't think I have an attitude," Cooper replies mildly. "There it is! There it is!" the second in command insists. Reading such scenes alongside each other, we see how only certain (read: white) people are allowed to express anxiety, anger, fear, or other heightened emotions. Scholar Sarah Jaquette Ray has argued that "climate anxiety is an overwhelmingly white phenomenon," explaining that "people of color are disproportionately harmed by climate change, but whites disproportionately fret publicly about it" (2021). Extrapolating from Ray's work, we would argue that *Everything's Fine* indicates how marginalized people's emotions are discouraged, suppressed, and pathologized – consider the "Angry Black Woman" stereotype – thus potentially stifling political action, among other things.

It might at first sound contradictory to suggest that Cooper and Rudolph are supposed to stand in for *both* privileged, mainstream media pundits – who are typically, but not exclusively, white – *and* the average beleaguered Black woman. But such overlapping meanings, not to mention such play with race, are central to Cooper's work. After all, Cooper invited us to read the main figure onscreen in more than one way from the start, giving her a real name but placing her in a fictional scenario. Further, Cooper's character jokes at one point about the extent to which she can pass as white, given her name, in addition to her straightened hair and relatively light skin; in the special, she quips, "I feel like, when my parents named me Sarah, a white lady just moved into my body and kind of gentrified my whole personality!" – a joke that also gestures toward the weird nature of Cooper's lip synching of Trump. (In this sense, we could argue that the lip synching in question does not *rely on* juxtaposition per se but actually *creates it*; if Cooper is otherwise relatively racially ambiguous, she becomes "more Black" in contrast to Trump's troubling racial and other commentary.) Further, we might consider that part of the point of the Cooper/Steele depictions is to show that marginalized people are *allowed to be* part of the mainstream *as long as* they are willing to play along. (Interestingly, *Don't Look Up*, discussed in greater depth below, features two cheery newscasters, one white woman, played by Cate Blanchett, and one Black man, played by Tyler Perry.) Crucially, then, in both Steele's and the fictional Cooper's cases, they eventually reach their limit for doing so.

We should also remember here how Cooper's news segments are interspersed with other media forms including product commercials, movie trailers, home-shopping airtime, and historical documentary programs. At times, *Everything's Fine* thereby seems to indicate that it wants to mimic the experience of channel-surfing – as when we see a brief shot of a Black woman pointing a remote at a TV. But at other times this mix of media feels incoherent or confusing. For example, *Everything's Fine* includes a random documentary-style segment featuring a magician named Sarah Evak (also played by Cooper) who attempts to do close-up magic at a parking lot drive-in event during the pandemic. It's unclear whether this segment is meant to be part of the fictional Cooper's broadcast, or if it relates in any particular way at all to the latter's diegetic world.

We propose multiple ways of reading this formal and ontological chaos. The simplest, it seems, would be that *Everything's Fine* thereby mirrors the distraction and divided attention of the American populace: with our noses too deep in myriad consumerist media, we cannot muster any outrage about or opposition to environmental, racial, and other problems. Changing the channel, literally or figuratively, seems easier than changing the status quo. On a less mimetic level, we would suggest that this incoherence represents the (to some) crazy-making nature of the absurd political landscape – in which, to repeat the example from above, evidence of climate crisis does *not* lead to action on climate crisis. Ironically, then, we could say that the special's chaotic, nonsensical, and overwhelming format, in addition to paranoia-inducing techniques such as lip synching, serve a kind of making-sane function, insofar as they indicate that such feelings are shared by others and, therefore, at least somewhat valid.

Catharsis in *Don't Look Up*

The Netflix-produced *Don't Look Up* (2021), a disaster film that uses a comet strike analogy to climate change, releases the pressure of critique with the catharsis of tragedy. *Don't Look Up* operates through an absurdist framework that leads to the tragic end of all life on Earth. We are invited to sneer at fatuous overlords or cry at the loss of the world where "we really had everything," as Leonardo DiCaprio's astronomer puts it. If emotions are implicit judgments of value, as Martha Nussbaum claims, both works help us to judge our current environment as fatally flawed. They also release visceral responses that find insufficient channels in disembodied social media (Nussbaum 2008, 19–85). Whatever else it is, satire is always about life in the guts.

As a satire, *Don't Look Up* is structurally more complex than a farce, like *Idiocracy*, or climate change thrillers like *The Day After Tomorrow* and *Snowpiercer*. It opens with the terrifying discovery of a comet on a collision course with Earth. The astronomers responsible, graduate student Kate Dibiasky and her mentor Dr. Randall Mindy, are not grotesque exaggerations of human frailty, but the virtuous protagonists around whom the vice organizes itself. Their discovery is dismissed and then manipulated by Meryl Streep's Trumpian President Orlean and accepted and subverted by Peter Isherwell, a creepy telecommunications magnate who hybridizes Elon Musk and Mark Zuckerberg. President Orlean terminates a mission to deflect the comet after Isherwell discovers that the comet's core is composed of the rare minerals required for cell phone manufacture. But his plan to fragment the comet and harvest the pieces fails just before the moment the comet strikes Earth, so the failure becomes an extinction-level event. What could have been a Horatian satire in which a flawed humanity muddles through becomes the last Juvenalian satire, in which irremediable vice dooms not just the wicked but every living thing. The bad guys among the global elite escape in a spaceship, only to be devoured upon landing on an Edenic planet by predators, who attack the last humans in short order. Though the wicked are finally punished, so is everyone else: the greed, pride, and hubris of the elites destroy the entire species. In fact, the audience sees the species end twice: first, with the rest of the biosphere on the ruined Earth, and again during the attack of the "Brontorocs" on the Eden world. *Don't Look Up* portrays the endgame of global capitalism, an end of all ends for the last mass extinction event. The film dramatizes the worst-case scenario of climate change that is easier to ignore because the climate crisis is a chronic rather than an acute condition. By visibly destroying the world in a one-time cataclysm, the film witnesses to the thing deniers deride: the destruction of the planet as *oikos*, as home. A planet-killer's effect cannot be dismissed as exaggeration as are the most extreme futures of climate change (Wallace-Wells 2017). The comet analogy provides a gut-punch that climate crisis stories often do not. At least some viewers have reacted in a manner associated with classical tragedy: catharsis, the collective release of pity and horror. In the film itself, Dibiasky and Mindy scream on camera to smug audiences primed for infotainment. The climate scientist Peter Kalmus, writing in *The Guardian*, relates that the moment Dibiasky screams, "Are we not being clear? We're all 100% for sure going to fucking die!" on live television is the moment he felt a connection to his lived experience (Kalmus 2021).

Nevertheless, the film critiques the assumption that humans are rational actors and that all we need to avoid disaster is a consensus about the nature of the problem. Science is not enough in a world dominated by profiteering elites. The combination of individual vice and systems of oppression finally tip the plot into tragedy, and the vivid depiction of the asteroid collision, which flings human and nonhuman debris into space, enables the final catharsis of weeping at the end we do not want to imagine. Even the mid-credits sight of Meryl Streep being eaten by a Brontoroc cannot retrieve the film for comedy, if viewers even waded through the credits to see it at all. We argue, however, that *Don't Look Up* provides a tapestry of comedic and tragic laughter, a Dickensian ghost of climates yet to come, that invites us to feel the emotions of the climate crises we have wanted to push aside.

Conclusion

We propose that the evocation of different forms of satire *inside* each work is a commentary on satire itself. That is to say, in their swings from parody to the absurd, the Horatian to the Juvenalian, these eco-satires participate in the search for the right mode in which to communicate. Rather than seeing this oscillation as failing in regard to "how hard it is to come up with something, anything, funnier or stranger or more shocking than what's already unfolding on our [current news and social media] feeds," we see it as self-consciously grappling with that "struggle to heighten the heightened" (Herman). We can't help but connect this commentary to one of the most common critiques of satire – namely, that it "doesn't really do anything." Consider comedian Kevin T. Porter's satirical tweet:

> I showed my anti-vax parents [*Don't Look Up*] and they fell to their knees, thanking ... [director] Adam McKay for showing them the error of their ways. They pledged to reduce their carbon emissions by 80% by 2024 ... joined the DSA [Democratic Socialists of America], stopped using Amazon, and are dedicating the rest of their lives to fighting climate change.

As the tweet suggests, many *Don't Look Up* viewers and critics had misplaced expectations. They failed to grasp the fact that satire denies the humanist commonplace that art makes people better.

Art can diagnose the trouble, but only people can change hearts, minds, and politics – and sometimes we refuse to do so. Art is not a silver bullet for corruption.

When it comes to satire from Black creators, scholar Danielle Fuentes Morgan seems to agree that a purely instrumentalist, as opposed to affective, approach is off-base, claiming that "inspiring knowing in-group laughter opens up Black interior space that wards off psychic, or even physical, death" (2021, 5). Hence the title of her study of African American satire, *Laughing to Keep from Dying* – a play, of course, on the phrase, "laughing to keep from crying." Fuentes Morgan offers several other takes on the effects of African American satire throughout history, aside from those aforementioned instrumentalist measures – including "demonstrat[ing] one's cleverness, feeling, and, ultimately, one's own humanity in the face of its constant denial" (13) and experiencing "the pleasure of being understood, the pleasure of defining oneself" (14). In this sense, the criticism that much satire entails simply "preaching to the choir" is moot. Preaching to the choir, as Fuentes Morgan would have it, is not frivolous but in fact necessary for the choir's survival. Moreover, we suggest that there's a crucial difference between the effects of the fictional characters we watch (such as Steele and Cooper, prior to their breakdowns) and what we as viewers experience. That is to say, there is a difference between what author and activist Barbara Ehrenreich has called "brightsiding" – an apolitical dismissal of real issues – and "laughing to keep from crying/dying." This difference between elite optimism and comedy of the oppressed produces a formal challenge for eco-satire: in the case of corruption at the scale of the planet, what happens to the traditional satiric tool of exaggeration?

Some critics had trouble identifying *Don't Look Up* as successful because Aristophanic satire depends on exaggeration at a moment when exaggerated behavior is normal (Robinson 2021). However, as Nathan J. Robinson argues, this is not "a nihilistic film about nincompoops," a film that blames the victim (Robinson). While it is possible to see the film as a comedy, not a satire, the ending makes that difficult once the tragedy becomes unavoidable. Even so, the tragic ending reinforces the film's urge to punch up, to condemn the vices of the powerful, which goes beyond the bounds of comedy. We propose that one of the formal innovations of the works we have examined is the ability to attain the ends of satire even while the strategy of exaggeration becomes less workable because of the intensity of vice (Trump) and the scale of the problem (climate crisis). Other strategies of absurdism, laughing-in-order-to-not-cry, primal screaming, and so on take center stage because and in spite of the impossibility of exaggeration at the present time. This is also a reason to resist an instrumental analysis: as the problem becomes harder to represent, the chain of causation between representation and action becomes longer. Under such conditions, the representation of the crazy-making environments creates the possibility of sanity through laughing, screaming, vulgarity, and solidarity. In *Don't Look Up*, there is certainly an urge to reform and revolution. But the strength of its catharsis leaves open the question of what to do about wickedness at the scale of nation and planet, depending on the agency of the audience to resolve the problems that satire eviscerates. Donna Lu notes the popularity of the film among activists: "the lukewarm critical reception contrasts sharply with the response from the film's allegorical heroes: climate scientists and activists," who believe the film's recognition of elite resistance to solutions outstrips its lack of programmatic answers, a lack that is traditional in satire and tragedy (Lu 2021). These forms are not about pragmatic action, but shared experiences and emotional revelation, which can be stones on the path to action. Here, we follow Cynthia Willet and Julie Willet's claim that

> [c]athartic processes [such as laughter] can … serve as … catalyst[s] for social change … We cannot heal and regenerate apart from a rechanneling of the flows of affect and power on

this biosocial field. As a biosocial event, laughter reshapes the contours of social space ... and offers ... a reimagined social life.

(2019, 12)

Modes like satire, and the cathartic laughs they usually offer, are not *sufficient* for social and political change but are nonetheless *necessary* for such change. *Don't Look Up* offers the desire to act without a manifesto. The performance of the truth channeled through ecstatic vulgarity sponsors the joy of revelation and contempt for the political machine. Joy and contempt constitute ethical clarity and a chance at moral victory. *Don't Look Up* offers a website that encourages participation in liberal democracy as a means of addressing the climate crisis. Are these limitations? Yes, but as there is no dearth of environmental activism in the Anglosphere, *Don't Look Up* favors audience autonomy over a plan that might appear to be propaganda.

As Seymour has argued, there are more potential purposes to satire than, say, changing laws and policies – or even changing hearts and minds: "a less strictly instrumentalist approach," she maintains, "allows us to imagine additional, or different, capacities for environmental art," including "bearing witness to crisis, enacting catharsis, raising activist morale, building community ... [and] modeling flexibility and creativity in the face of crisis" (7). Further, we might want to sidestep questions of "purpose" or "importance" altogether, recognizing that we actually need space for the *unimportant*, the frivolous, the play that doesn't "go anywhere" or "mean anything" – for those phenomena resist the relentless expectations for productivity, self-justification, and "use value" that in part drive environmental crisis in the first place.

Acknowledgments

Nicole wishes to thank Julia Leyda for companionship and conversations about *Sarah Cooper: Everything's Fine* in late 2020 – when we two Americans were living overseas and watching U.S. presidential election proceedings with the barely suppressed anxiety depicted in the special! Thanks also to Terri Patchen for facilitating an invaluable writing bootcamp.

Further Reading

Branch, Michael. 2014. "Are You Serious? A Modest Proposal for Environmental Humor." In *The Oxford Handbook of Ecocriticism*, ed. Greg Garrard. Oxford: Oxford University Press, 378–90.
Meeker, Joseph. 1974. *The Comedy of Survival: Studies in Literary Ecology*. New York: Scribner.
Sze, Julie. 2021. "Climate Justice, Satire, and Hothouse Earth." In *The Routledge Companion to Contemporary Art, Visual Culture, and Climate Change*, eds. T.J. Demos, Emily Eliza Scott, and Subhankar Banerjee. New York: Routledge, 173–81.
Takach, Geo. 2022. "Eco-Comedy." *Environmental Humanities* 14 (2): 371–74.
Zinoman, Jason. 2020. "What Happens When Sarah Cooper Speaks in Her Own Voice?" *The New York Times*, October 27. https://www.nytimes.com/2020/10/27/arts/television/sarah-cooper-netflix.html

References

Don't Look Up. 2021. Dir. Adam McKay. Netflix.
Fuentes Morgan, Danielle. 2021. *Laughing to Keep from Dying: African American Satire in the Twenty-First Century*. Urbana: U of Illinois Press.
Greenberg, Jonathan. 2019. *The Cambridge Introduction to Satire*. Cambridge: Cambridge UP.
Hennefeld, Maggie. 2016. "Laughter in the Age of Trump." *Flow*, December 18. https://www.flowjournal.org/2016/12/laughter-in-the-age-of-trump/

"How to Climate Change." 2020. World War Zero. September 23. https://www.youtube.com/watch?v=_XpVcXO3sYU

Kellogg, Carolyn. 2015. "Karl Taro Greenfeld on the Fiction, Grim Reality in 'The Subprimes.'" *Los Angeles Times*, June 4. https://www.latimes.com/books/jacketcopy/la-ca-jc-karl-taro-greenfeld-20150607-story.html

Kalmus, Peter. 2021. "I'm a Climate Scientist. *Don't Look Up* Captures the Madness I See Every Day." *The Guardian*: US Edition. December 29. https://www.theguardian.com/commentisfree/2021/dec/29/climate-scientist-dont-look-up-madness?

LaSalle, Mick. 2020. "Review: Sarah Cooper Invents Satire Style for an Anxiety-Ridden World in 'Everything's Fine.'" *Rolling Stone*, October 27. https://datebook.sfchronicle.com/movies-tv/review-sarah-cooper-invents-satire-style-for-an-anxiety-ridden-world-in-everythings-fine

Lu, Donna. 2021. "'It Parodies Our Inaction': *Don't Look Up*, an Allegory of the Climate Crisis, Lauded by Activists." *The Guardian*: US Edition, December 30. https://www.theguardian.com/environment/2021/dec/30/it-parodies-our-inaction-dont-look-up-an-allegory-of-the-climate-crisis-lauded-by-activists

Nussbaum, Martha. 2008. *Upheavals of Thought: The Intelligence of Emotions*. Cambridge: Cambridge UP.

Ray, Sarah Jaquette. 2021. "The Unbearable Whiteness of Climate Anxiety." *Scientific American*, March 21. https://www.scientificamerican.com/article/the-unbearable-whiteness-of-climate-anxiety/

Robinson, Nathan J. 2021. "Critics of *Don't Look Up* Are Missing the Entire Point." *Current Affairs*, December 21. Horten URL: https://www.currentaffairs.org/2021/12/critics-of-dont-look-up-are-missing-the-entire-point?

Sarah Cooper: Everything's Fine. 2020. Dir. Natasha Lyonne. Netflix.

Wallace-Wells, David. 2017. "The Uninhabitable Earth, Annotated Edition." *New York Magazine*. https://nymag.com/intelligencer/2017/07/climate-change-earth-too-hot-for-humans-annotated.html

Willet, Cynthia and Julie Willet. 2019. *Uproarious: How Feminists and Other Subversive Comics Speak Truth*. Minneapolis: University of Minnesota Press.

35
FEAR AND LOATHING IN ECOMEDIA

Channeling Fear through Horror Tropes in Invasive Species Outreach

Katrina Maggiulli

In mid-2017, media chaos erupted in the wake of the publication of David Wallace-Wells's "The Uninhabitable Earth" in *New York Magazine* (Wallace-Wells 2017).[1] The piece outlined worst-case scenarios for the aftermath of climate change, including descriptions of humans being "cooked to death from the inside and out" within hours. Some upset over the article came from scientists who saw its depictions misleading of scientific consensus (see Vincent 2017), but much of the outcry came over its overwhelming affective basis in fear (Mann, Hassol, and Toles 2017). The debate became binary: is fear or hope a better strategy? The basis of arguments one way or the other, however, were rarely supported by convincing empirical data from either well-designed survey-based studies or insights from scientific research in cognitive and behavioral psychology (Chapman, Lickel, and Markowitz 2017; Kidd, Bekessy, and Garrard 2019). However, I was interested in Wallace-Well's controversial strategy not purely based on its affect but also its engagement in genre. The success of many of the article's affective appeals seemed to lie in its redeployment of tropes from the apocalyptic genre that has nearly dominated Hollywood blockbuster film for the last 20 years.

I noticed this trend in an array of educational environmental media—rather than reinventing the wheel, these outreach materials just redeployed tropes and imagery from fictional genres such as apocalyptic film and horror that specialized in *affecting* their audiences. But what "comes with" these genre tropes when they are redeployed? While this approach may be productive for gaining audience attention (a question I do not interrogate here), I am interested in the potential unintended consequences such genre borrowing might produce. What political and cultural assumptions built into the genres themselves come along for the ride to frame audience understanding of informational content in troubling ways? For example, as Ailise Bulfin has suggested, "spectacular catastrophe scenarios, coupled with the focus on the redemptive post-catastrophe experiences of small groups of survivors, may lead to over-confident identification with the survivors, and worse still to individualistic 'prepping' responses" (Bulfin 2017, 146). If literary and cultural scholars are concerned about the "takeaways" of blockbuster genre films, what happens when those same genre tropes appear in ostensibly informational and educational media? And while these conversations are being had at an academic level as well as within media journalism, this does not mean that this critical lens is being deployed by the everyday employees of land management agencies and other environmental organizations—the group that bears the brunt of responsibility when it comes

This chapter has been made available under a CC-BY-NC-ND license.

to convincing the public to adopt environmentally friendly behaviors. The focus of this chapter is on one area of environmental communication and education that has been under scrutiny of late: invasive species management.

Much of the scrutiny on invasive species communication is due to the widespread deployment of xenophobic rhetoric in these outreach materials—where "evil" becomes synonymous with "foreign" and the public is called upon to enlist in the fight against the "invaders" (Eskridge and Alderman 2010; Subramaniam 2014). While this public scrutiny has begun productive conversations on how we talk about nonnative species,[2] the way these xenophobic frameworks appear through the redeployment of media culture objects and tropes has been less interrogated. In a playful twist on the rhetorical strategies of fear, some invasive species programming has drawn directly on the genre of fear itself, horror, to explore the "monstrosity" of invasive species through popular monster movie tropes. However, rather than resolving the problem of xenophobia, using monster movie tropes merely calls on a longer cultural history where xenophobic and problematic stereotypes are embodied in the villains of monster movies. Thus, while the xenophobia is cleverly masked by the light-hearted comedy of laughing at "bad" monster movies, the racist themes are still reproduced in the invasive species outreach media—lightly reworking rather than fundamentally altering how invasive species are depicted. In my entry into this conversation, I bring insights from media and cultural studies to bear on the question of emotional appeals in environmental communication to consider what "comes with" educational and outreach strategies that draw on popular genre tropes already rich in cultural meaning to achieve affective responses from the public. In this chapter, I will first look at the explicit deployment of the monster movie genre in United States' invasive species outreach generally and then hone my analysis to consider the affective dimensions of monstrosity in the United States Department of Agriculture (USDA) Animal & Plant Health Inspection Service (APHIS) pest education mascot "Vin Vasive."

Ecocritical Affect Theory and the Horror Genre

As is evident from the fiery fear-hope debate in climate outreach, whether emotional responses can be predicted or even well understood, they are nonetheless a fundamental component of how we engage with environmental media and the environment itself. Ecocritics of diverse media types have therefore attempted to make sense of the sensations evoked by environmental media, whether it be within the space of cinema, news media, photography, social media, or other media spaces. The study of affect and emotion is a flourishing area in film and media theory and in the past decade it has readily expanded into ecocritical media scholarship through contributions such as Adrian Ivakhiv's *Ecologies of the Moving Image: Cinema, Affect, Nature* (2013) and the collections *Moving Environments: Affect, Emotion, Ecology, and Film* (2014), edited by Alexa Weik von Mossner and *Affective Ecocriticism: Emotion, Embodiment, Environment* (2018) edited by Kyle Bladow and Jennifer Ladino. Expanding beyond a traditional discourse-based analysis, affective ecocriticism draws on work from neuroscientists, cognitive psychologists, phenomenologists, and others to recenter embodied experience and assess the role of emotion in how we engage with the environment and environmental media.

Here I follow David Ingram's approach, informed by cognitivists and phenomenologists, that distinguishes between affect and emotion while marking both as essential and interconnected areas of study. As Ingram notes, affect is "a viewer's automatic, visceral response to a film, whereas 'emotion' includes a cognitive element in addition to this bodily feeling" (Ingram 2014, 23). This distinction is important because, whether or not the viewer is *actually* frightened of the organism depicted, the species is framed through the genre of horror and it is therefore understood, cognitively, that we should assess the species through an affect of fear. This is a formal quality of the content that frames our response to the species in question. In Noël Carroll's piece "Film, Emotion, and Genre," he addresses the importance of cogitation in the production of physical emotion (or affect):

> by criterially prefocusing the film text—where the criteria in question are the ones appropriate to certain emotions—filmmakers encourage spectators to assess or to subsume the events onscreen under certain categories, namely the categories pertinent to the excitation of the relevant emotional states.
>
> (Carroll 2005, 232)

For the horror film to be successful, of course, the audience must then in turn interpret the onscreen events as intended by the filmmaker—if we aren't sufficiently convinced that a monster can cause harm to the onscreen protagonists, it will fail to produce fear—the intended emotion.

Thus, to understand the horror genre, in Carroll's framework, is to recognize both the emotions it elicits (fear and disgust) and the necessary "emotive criterions" needed to produce those emotions (harmfulness and impurity) (Carroll 2005, 228). "Criterial prefocusing" is key to my understanding of the functioning of genre here. As everyday "interpreters" of movies or even just their trailers or posters, we can easily identify an array of genres despite a lack of any formal training. Genre tropes and content, no matter where they appear, have a "prefocused" nature that tells us what to look for and how to interpret media. As Carroll notes, "once this sort of emotive focus takes control, the audience keeps surveying the image of [*insert movie monster here*] for further evidence of impurity and danger, thereby sustaining the operation of their ongoing emotional process" (Carroll 2005, 229). The prefocusing which can be produced by the presence of a familiar genre trope (for instance a monster) provides the initial "trigger" that orients viewer attention to continue looking for genre content. Thus, if an invasive species is placed in the formulaic role of the monster, the audience for that media outreach content will be "prefocused" to assess the species for impurity and danger—the "emotive criterions" for horror's emotional states of fear and disgust.

However, as some scholars of affect theory and horror have noted, while Carroll's cognitivist theory grasps *emotion* (in the sense of the cognitively translated component of affect), his work fails to account for the very somatic experience that viewing horror entails—or the actual *affect* (Hanich 2010; Aldana Reyes 2016). As Xavier Aldana Reyes points out, "it is now widely accepted that cognition is marked by psycho-motor processes that we cannot always control and which are *prior to a psychological awareness of any fact*" (Aldana Reyes 2016, 9; my emphasis). The body is therefore responding before cognitive processing occurs, suggesting that the somatic elements of affect must also be considered apart from emotions as such—however our brains choose to rationalize our responses, there is a knee-jerk response that must be evaluated perhaps separately from the emotion language with which we might choose to make sense of it. I thus look here at both the genre anchored *emotions* that are cognitively processed as well as the *affects* produced by the content that are, perhaps, pre-cognitive in nature, therefore enhancing a sense of instinctive repulsion toward invasive species.

Invasive Species Outreach and the Monster Movie Genre

Invasive species outreach material has seemingly taken particular pleasure in drawing on monster movie imagery and tropes to help garner public attention. For example, the Whatcom

County, Washington, USA Noxious Weed Board developed three monster movie "PSAs" in 2012 to spread awareness about spotted knapweed, knotweed, and aquatic weeds (WhatcomCountyGov 2012a,b,c). Each of these videos plays on the threat to a 1950s-reminiscent domestic bliss as the monstrous knotweed sends a happy couple fleeing from their home (PSA #1) and a desperate housewife screams incoherently into the phone—pleading with the police officer to "do something!" about the spotted knapweed outside her window (PSA #3). PSA #3 concludes with townsfolk gathering behind a makeshift barricade, their police chief stating, "Spotted knapweed? Not in my county." Drawing on these videos and other land management-developed content, the U.S. Fish & Wildlife Service Pacific Region Fisheries hosted an "All Tricks, No Treats" publicity campaign in October 2012 with the "MOVIE INVASION!" feature to promote invasives management, a theme they then reprised in Fall 2014 for their interactive newsletter, *Invasives Quarterly*. In the feature, they introduce their invasive species monster movie mashups by comparing their experiences with invasive species to "Alien attacks from outer space, flocks of birds that peck out your eyes, staggering zombies that never quite die" because "these all combine fear of the unknown with masses too numerous to be reckoned with" (USFWS Pacific Region Fisheries 2012). The banner for their campaign features people fleeing a Chinese mitten crab grown to monstrous proportions and the bold text "INVASION."

While certainly a playful approach to education on invasive species (likely a primary driver for the deployment of the monster movie genre in this content to begin with), there are several troubling dynamics and outcomes from the reframing of nonnative species in the role of the horror movie monster. The familiarity of the monster movie genre for the intended United States audience here will assure an immediate recognition and "criterial prefocusing" of the content, therefore ensuring the audience will be on a lookout for the additional evidence that our "monster" is harmful and impure. The genre frame of the species as monster encourages a pure assessment of it as evil, morally corrupt, or degenerate in some way—all then being cognitively processed to produce the fear and disgust emotions that align with these criteria. In this way, then, whether or not we are readily *afraid* of the species that is depicted, the framework of monster leads us to nonetheless look for evidence that would *justify fear*. These representational alignments have consequences, however. As Stacy Alaimo argues

> such representations vilify nature, justifying the slaughter of creatures we construct as repulsive. Carrollton, Texas, for instance, recently slaughtered thousands of egrets ..., calling the massacre Operation Remove Excrement. The "plot" of this incident echoes ... a slew of horror films featuring monstrous natures that must be eradicated.
> (Alaimo 2001, 280)

What is framed as monstrous is exterminated; the formulaic narrative structure of these stories dictates for us how they end.

Aside from the ethical dilemmas that have arisen over treatment and management of nonnative and invasive species,[3] another primary problem of these invasive species media is their racist and xenophobic elements. As Jeffrey Jerome Cohen attests, "One kind of difference becomes another as the normative categories of gender, sexuality, national identity, and ethnicity slide together ... abjecting from the center that which becomes the monster" (Cohen 1996, 11). In Banu Subramaniam's *Ghost Stories for Darwin*, she flags one of the key "ironies" of the era of globalization as the simultaneous opening of borders with a renewed interest in the native—a panic that stokes fears of immigrating humans and nonnative plants and animals alike

> we begin to obsess about our different natures and cultures with a fervent nationalism, stressing the need to close our borders to 'outsiders.' ... Rhetoric of 'nature out of place' is everywhere ... *We respond with xenophobic ideologies across multiple sites, trying to restore nature to its rightful place.*
>
> (Subramaniam 2014, 101; emphasis added)

Subramaniam helps gloss the cultural moment that our monstrous invasive species embody—the anxieties of "nature out of place" that draw on both cultural xenophobia as well as concern for the preservation of biodiversity. To be clear—I am *not* arguing here that particular invasive species do not have clear and documented negative impacts on certain ecosystems, as they most certainly do, I am more interested in the cascading effects that carelessness in rhetorical strategies about invasive species can have on human immigrant communities. Xenophobic ideologies, as Subramaniam asserts, are appearing "across multiple sites" as a white American majority attempts to make sense of both changing environments and diversifying communities.

In some cases, racial politics come to the forefront of these invasive species monster movie mashups. Take, for example, a poster developed by the Invasive Species Management Program at St. Mark's National Wildlife Refuge in Florida and reposted on the Illinois Invasive Species Awareness Month blog which mimics the *Creature from the Black Lagoon* (Dir. Jack Arnold) movie poster from 1954 ("Invader+from+the+Black+Lagoon.Jpg (635×660)" n.d.). In the image, the gillman[4] from the original feature film now sports air potato leaves across his shoulders and in place of the vulnerable white woman, he now clutches the state of Florida in his webbed claws. What is at stake when we depict Florida—a mostly white state with diverse immigrant-rich regions—as a vulnerable white woman at risk from invasion and attack? And while the gillman of the original film could not be considered "invasive," as he never left his native Amazonian "Black Lagoon,"[5] his original South American origins merely serve, in this new context, to underscore his role as invading aggressor—and one with a racialized undertone. In addition to this more explicit case, clear racial politics come through in the Whatcom County Noxious Weed Board PSAs, as their deployment of the white American domestic space as under threat (a clear theme from the twentieth-century American horror film) helps emphasize the xenophobia of the invasive species threat. Indeed, when the police chief stares nobly into the sun, stating "spotted knapweed? Not in my county," viewers could easily imagine a simple fill in the blank of "spotted knapweed" with any particular racial group deemed "undesirable" for the American heartland. It recalls sundown towns and other legal and social frameworks of segregation in America. In this way, then, the genre structuring (criterial prefocusing) of the invasive species content that cognitively frames the nonnative species in question through fear and disgust becomes particularly troubling when paired with nostalgic monster movie tropes that figure a threatened white American domesticity.

Vin Vasive: A Case Study in Monster Affect

But monstrosity is more than a cognitive understanding of harmfulness and impurity, it is also anchored in the shuddering, visceral *affect*—the knee-jerk response that comes before any conscious awareness of threat or disgust. The USDA APHIS' "Hungry Pests" educational mascot, Vin Vasive,

Figure 35.1 "Have We Met? I'm Your Worst Nightmare": USDA APHIS produced banner display for outreach featuring the Vin Vasive "Hungry Pests" mascot, 2012

whose character is developed in the course of several educational videos, is a paradigmatic example of affective invasive species media (Figure 35.1).[6] Vin's legibility as threatening is anchored in the visual politics of the monstrous as well as affect rendered through his audio tracks. Vin's visual monstrosity is first constructed through his creepy crawly body— a composite of thousands of individual Asian longhorn beetles, Emerald Ash Borers, Gypsy Moths, and assorted species of fruit flies, an esthetic that instills fear of the hive mind or swarm. The swarm is an unknown and perhaps unknowable form of intelligence reminiscent of the zombie horde—the only clear motivation is a believed uncontrollable desire to feed. Vin attempts to hide the expansiveness of his "family" in his sport coat, seeking to convince his audience that he and his family are just innocent travelers here to sample the local fare. At the conclusion of one video, however, they pour out of his sleeve, giving "tell" to his apparent lie regarding their modest appetites (USDA APHIS 2012).

The audience for the Vin Vasive materials is regularly instructed to stay vigilant against the devious strategies invasive pests might take to infiltrate your nation/home. It is made clear throughout the content that what appears to be one thing may indeed be another—that you should perhaps mistrust your first interpretation to better see what is lurking beneath. Vin Vasive regularly draws attention to these "flip sides." In one video, he looks at mud in truck tires, saying you might call the mud and larvae a "souvenir" but he calls it "family" (USDA APHIS 2014c). In another video, the "innocent" mail order through the internet could result in Vin himself arriving (he frames his face in an eaten-out cardboard box to underscore the "surprise") (USDA APHIS 2014b). And another begins with a beautiful "still life" of a basket of fruit. Vin tells the audience, however, that you are "looking at it all wrong"—the camera swoops around to show the backside all rotten and full of bugs, to which Vin says: "it's so much better from my perspective" (USDA APHIS 2014a). All these contrasts between the expectation of good fruit, an innocent drive in the woods, or a mail-ordered plant are followed by a close-up of Vin's face and his high-pitched cackle as he reveals the dark "truth" of the matter.

But it is the sound design of the videos that most effectively produces Vin Vasive's affect. Vin's voice is digitally altered to add slithering, whispering, and insect sounds just behind his main voice track. His movements are also marked by the clacking of wing carapaces and the gentle scrabbling of insect feet and antennae. In some videos, the use of mud as a travel vector means an addition of gelatinous sucking effects. This emphasis on the auditory aspects of "creepy crawlies" draws on evolutionarily hard-wired anxieties about insects that could cause lethal bites or stings. As Jeffrey Lockwood playfully remarks regarding the evolutionary roots of these reactions, "We reacted decisively rather than thinking, 'Skittering things are dangerous.' These inborn commands were overly inclusive for a good reason: avoiding a wad of spider-like hair on the cave floor had nominal costs, while grasping a vine-like snake in the jungle was disastrous" (Lockwood 2013, 22). The pre-cognitive nature of a body's response to the sound of insects likely bears psychological and evolutionary plausibility—a gut-deep reaction that is deployed directly by the auditory effects of the Vin Vasive videos. How we are to understand Vin as "creepy" or "bad" is thus built affectively through the visceral shuddering and "chills" derived from the sound of millions of insect feet and goopy "gross" sounds. The discomfort these sounds produce physically work to reinforce what you understand cognitively from the media's framing: invasive species are gross and dangerous (read: impure and harmful).

Future Considerations for Genre Affect in Educational Ecomedia

By drawing attention to the use of the genre of horror and the affective and cognitive productions of fear in these outreach materials, I am not arguing that affective appeals should not have a place in outreach and education. Indeed, some studies have indicated that emotional "priming" before the delivery of scientific information can in fact help an audience by offering familiar entry points into the issue (Gunther, Hild, and Bieber 2018). What I hope to stress here is not the role of emotion or affect *generally* in this outreach content, but rather how this content is transplanting *affective registers from the horror genre* specifically *onto an environmental issue*. Because this content triggers a cognitive recognition of horror genre tropes, the audience is affectively primed not through valid fear or concern about the environmental issue but rather through the emotive expectations of the horror genre. The genre tropes tell us clearly who our "villain" is and, whether laughable or not, the familiar formula serves to reinforce the monstrosity and unnaturalness of the invasive species depicted.

In this critique, I hope to underscore the high stakes for thinking through how and when suites of genre tropes, like those from horror I discuss here (though apocalyptic film is also commonly used), might be deployed in environmental communication and educational outreach media. As the "fear versus hope" debate I flagged at the beginning of this chapter attests, considering how we communicate environmental issues is more than just a matter of finding the best tools to achieve desired outcomes. Positive ends should not justify whatever means necessary because this approach tends to leave out precisely what I am interested in here: what *comes with* the strategies we use to produce certain outcomes—for much more is reproduced than is intended. The overemphasis on "success" of media communication can also lead to not only a presumption that desired outcomes or messages are universally agreed upon[7] but also might result in misguided conclusions for communication studies.[8] Assessment of environmental messaging and communication for messages *other than* desired outcomes is therefore essential for a clear understanding of both the content in question and its broader political and societal impact. To this end, I call for a more self-aware approach to environmental communication—one that is attentive to not only its goals but also self-critical of the tools it deploys to meet those goals.

Notes

1 Wallace-Wells has since expanded it into a book, *The Uninhabitable Earth: Life After Warming* (2020).
2 See, for example, Warren (2007); Keulartz and van der Weele (2008); and Larson (2008).
3 This is a rich debate with many facets that there is no room to do justice to here, but here are some readings that help frame some of the primary concerns: Lodge and Shrader-Frechette (2003); Davis et al. (2011); Hobbs et al. (2014); Munro, Steer, and Linklater (2019).
4 The gillman of *Creature from the Black Lagoon* (1954) is one of the few recognizable Hollywood monsters that regularly appears replicated in invasive species content. See, for example, the "Creature from Lower Lake" cartoon by Matt Bodkin (Bodkin 2014), as well as the PSA #2 from Whatcom County, WA on aquatic weeds (2012c).
5 Though the movie was filmed in California and the underwater scenes in Florida.
6 The Vin Vasive content includes middle school-level curricula, PowerPoint for general audiences, and an array of other materials that I do not go into detail with here. See their Hungry Pests website to explore: www.aphis.usda.gov/aphis/resources/pests-diseases/hungry-pests.
7 For an in-depth analysis of the problematic ethical dimensions of assuming invasive species management decisions are already "settled," see Maggiulli (2022).
8 For example, one study (Kohl, Collins, and Eichholz 2020) suggested "that using the metaphor 'invasive' can generate more support for action to control non-native species" therefore that "militaristic metaphoric language is viewed as applicable to the problem of non-native species issues and at least some control methods as a solution" (681). In this case, the oft-critiqued term "invasive" and militaristic metaphors are deemed acceptable based on their support for a desired *action* outcome and further consideration of fallout from the terminology was not addressed.

Further Reading

Bladow, Kyle and Jennifer Ladino, eds. 2018. *Affective Ecocriticism: Emotion, Embodiment, Environment.* Lincoln: University of Nebraska Press.
Murray, Robin L. and Joseph K. Heumann. 2016. *Monstrous Nature: Environment and Horror on the Big Screen.* Lincoln: University of Nebraska Press.
Otieno, Christine, Hans Spada, Katharina Liebler, Thomas Ludemann, Ulrich Deil, and Alexander Renkl. 2014. "Informing about Climate Change and Invasive Species: How the Presentation of Information Affects Perception of Risk, Emotions, and Learning." *Environmental Education Research* 20 (5): 612–38. https://doi.org/10.1080/13504622.2013.833589.
Tidwell, Christy and Carter Soles, eds. 2021. *Fear and Nature: Ecohorror Studies in the Anthropocene.* University Park: The Pennsylvania State University Press.
Weik von Mossner, Alexa, ed. 2014. *Moving Environments: Affect, Ecology, and Film.* Waterloo: Wilfrid Laurier University Press.

References

Alaimo, Stacy. 2001. "Discomforting Creatures: Monstrous Natures in Recent Films." In *Beyond Nature Writing: Expanding the Boundaries of Ecocriticism*, edited by Karla Armbruster and Kathleen R. Wallace, 279–96. Charlottesville: The University Press of Virginia.
Aldana Reyes, Xavier. 2016. *Horror Film and Affect: Towards a Corporeal Model of Viewership.* New York: Routledge.
Bodkin, Matt. 2014. Creature from Lower Lake. http://www.mattersnot.com/creature-from-lower-lake-yaphank/ .
Bulfin, Ailise. 2017. "Popular Culture and the 'New Human Condition': Catastrophe Narratives and Climate Change." *Global and Planetary Change* 156: 140–46. https://doi.org/10.1016/j.gloplacha.2017.03.002.
Carroll, Noël. 2005. "Film, Emotion, and Genre." In *Philosophy of Film and Motion Pictures: An Anthology*, edited by Noël Carroll and Jinhee Choi, 217–33. Williston: John Wiley & Sons, Incorporated. http://ebookcentral.proquest.com/lib/uoregon/detail.action?docID=243561.
Chapman, Daniel A., Brian Lickel, and Ezra M. Markowitz. 2017. "Reassessing Emotion in Climate Change Communication." *Nature Climate Change* 7 (12): 850–52. https://doi.org/10.1038/s41558-017-0021-9.
Cohen, Jeffrey Jerome. 1996. "Monster Culture (Seven Theses)." In *Monster Theory: Reading Culture*, edited by Jeffrey Jerome Cohen, 3–20. Minneapolis: University of Minnesota Press.
Davis, Mark A., Matthew K. Chew, Richard J. Hobbs, Ariel E. Lugo, John J. Ewel, Geerat J. Vermeij, James H. Brown, et al. 2011. "Don't Judge Species on Their Origins." *Nature* 474 (7350): 153–54. https://doi.org/10.1038/474153a.
Eskridge, Anna E., and Derek H. Alderman. 2010. "Alien Invaders, Plant Thugs, and the Southern Curse: Framing Kudzu as Environmental Other through Discourses of Fear." *Southeastern Geographer* 50 (1): 110–29.
Gunther, Kristen E., Ann L. Hild, and Stephen L. Bieber. 2018. "Natural Resource Experience Affects Engagement with Emotionally Primed Presentations of Science." *Rangeland Ecology & Management* 71: 163–70.
Hanich, Julian. 2010. *Cinematic Emotion in Horror Films and Thrillers.* New York: Routledge.
Hobbs, Richard J, Eric Higgs, Carol M Hall, Peter Bridgewater, F Stuart Chapin III, Erle C Ellis, John J Ewel, et al. 2014. "Managing the Whole Landscape: Historical, Hybrid, and Novel Ecosystems." *Frontiers in Ecology and the Environment* 12 (10): 557–64. https://doi.org/10.1890/130300.
Ingram, David. 2014. "Emotion and Affect in Eco-Films: Cognitive and Phenomenological Approaches." In *Moving Environments: Affect, Emotion, Ecology, and Film*, edited by Alexa Weik von Mossner, 23–39. Waterloo, Ontario: Wilfred Laurier University Press.
"Invader+from+the+Black+Lagoon.Jpg (635×660)." n.d. Accessed January 13, 2022. http://2.bp.blogspot.com/-QnD75szG_9w/Ua-RBHmEqKI/AAAAAAAAes/ynZvTimnndI/s1600/Invader+from+the+Black+Lagoon.jpg.
Keulartz, Jozef, and Cor van der Weele. 2008. "Framing and Reframing in Invasion Biology." *Configurations* 16 (1): 93–115.

Kidd, Lindall R., Sarah A. Bekessy, and Georgia E. Garrard. 2019. "Neither Hope nor Fear: Empirical Evidence Should Drive Biodiversity Conservation Strategies." *Trends in Ecology & Evolution* 34 (4): 278–82. https://doi.org/10.1016/j.tree.2019.01.018.

Kohl, Patrice A., Steve J. Collins, and Martin Eichholz. 2020. "Metaphor, Trust and Support for Non-Native Species Control." *Environmental Communication* 14 (5): 672–85.

Larson, Brendon M. H. 2008. "Entangled Biological, Cultural and Linguistic Origins of the War on Invasive Species." In *Sociocultural Situatedness*, edited by Roslyn M. Frank, René Dirven, Tom Ziemke, and Enrique Bernárdez, 170–95. Berlin: De Gruyter Mouton. https://doi.org/10.1515/9783110199116.

Lockwood, Jeffrey. 2013. *The Infested Mind: Why Humans Fear, Loathe, and Love Insects*. Cary, NC: Oxford University Press, Incorporated. http://ebookcentral.proquest.com/lib/uoregon/detail.action?docID=1426640.

Lodge, David M., and Kristin Shrader-Frechette. 2003. "Nonindigenous Species: Ecological Explanation, Environmental Ethics, and Public Policy." *Conservation Biology* 17 (1): 31–37.

Maggiulli, Katrina. 2022. "Teaching Invasive Species Ethically: Using Comics to Resist Metaphors of Moral Wrongdoing & Build Literacy in Environmental Ethics." *Environmental Education Research* 28 (9): 1391–1409. https://doi.org/10.1080/13504622.2022.2085247

Mann, Michael E., Susan Joy Hassol, and Tom Toles. 2017. "Doomsday Scenarios Are as Harmful as Climate Change Denial." *The Washington Post*. July 12, 2017. https://www.washingtonpost.com/opinions/doomsday-scenarios-are-as-harmful-as-climate-change-denial/2017/07/12/880ed002-6714-11e7-a1d7-9a32c91c6f40_story.html.

Munro, David, Jamie Steer, and Wayne Linklater. 2019. "On Allegations of Invasive Species Denialism." *Conservation Biology* 33 (4): 797–802. https://doi.org/10.1111/cobi.13278.

Subramaniam, Banu. 2014. *Ghost Stories for Darwin: The Science of Variation and the Politics of Diversity*. Chicago: University of Illinois Press.

USDAAPHIS, dir. 2012. *A Lot of Mouths to Feed (:60)*. https://www.youtube.com/watch?v=PRmdzi-smoY.

———, dir. 2014a. *Invasive Pests on Moving Plants & Fruit*. https://www.youtube.com/watch?v=nTFueqpY0ao.

———, dir. 2014b. *Invasive Pests on Online-Ordered Plants*. https://www.youtube.com/watch?v=nD3372BQIvc.

———, dir. 2014c. *Invasive Pests on Dirty Outdoor Gear*. https://www.youtube.com/watch?v=5XRY--DRUyI.

USFWS Pacific Region Fisheries. 2012. "Week 4-All Tricks, No Treats." *Pacific Region Fisheries Resources*. 2012. https://www.fws.gov/pacific/fisheries/aquaticnus/AIS_Week4.cfm.

Vincent, Emmanuel, ed. 2017. "Scientists explain what New York Magazine article on 'The Uninhabitable Earth' gets wrong." *Climate Feedback*, July 12, 2017. https://climatefeedback.org/evaluation/scientists-explain-what-new-york-magazine-article-on-the-uninhabitable-earth-gets-wrong-david-wallace-wells/.

Wallace-Wells, David. 2017. "The Uninhabitable Earth." *New York Magazine*, July 9, 2017. Intelligencer. https://nymag.com/intelligencer/2017/07/climate-change-earth-too-hot-for-humans.html.

Warren, Charles R. 2007. "Perspectives on the 'Alien' versus 'Native' Species Debate: A Critique of Concepts, Language and Practice." *Progress in Human Geography* 31 (4): 427–46.

WhatcomCountyGov, dir. 2012a. *Whatcom County Noxious Weed Board – PSA #1*. https://www.youtube.com/watch?v=5-jTpZw2kfY.

———, dir. 2012b. *Whatcom County Noxious Weed Board – PSA #3*. https://www.youtube.com/watch?v=NOMKwZqmfd0.

———. 2012c. *Whatcom County Noxious Weed Board – PSA #2*. https://www.youtube.com/watch?v=3eeCoCDRhkA.

36
SLOW MEDIA, ECO-MINDFULNESS, AND THE LIFEWORLD

Jennifer Rauch

Slow Media is an innovative cultural perspective that urges people to reappraise and recalibrate relationships among their media choices, personal well-being, and the natural environment. Inspired by the Slow Food movement, advocates of Slow Media began in the aughts to promote an array of creative approaches to using and not using media (Rauch 2015, 2018)—including some that would prove uniquely suited to pandemic shutdowns. Slow Media philosophy resonates with long-standing traditions of Transcendentalism, Romanticism, and Zen Buddhism as well as contemporary ideas about re-focusing one's life through "digital minimalism" (Newport 2019) and resisting the attention economy by doing "nothing" (Odell 2020). Many people who embrace such perspectives find value in the Slow identifier that connects their efforts with a global food network nurturing social and environmental sustainability.[1]

Core elements of the Slow Media value system include slowness, quality, materiality, and mindfulness. In this context, practitioners associate *slowness* with positive traits such as sustainability, strength, thoughtfulness, reflection, open-mindedness, confidence, and balance rather than negative traits like laziness, boredom, stupidity, deficiency, and inferiority (David 2015). "Slow" somewhat mislabels this temporal approach, which neither condemns hurriedness nor promotes universal sluggishness. In actuality, Slow Media encourages shifting among a wide range of speeds and finding the right tempo (*il tempo giusto*) for any given activity. Slowness and sustainability share the pursuit of paces that let people and the planet replenish themselves.

Slow practitioners value *quality* in media, which they associate with being good, durable, beautiful, authentic, healthy, pleasurable, artisanal, natural, local, organic, and sustainable. Quality means that media creators use their time to write, report, record, edit, and/or design their products more thoughtfully. Slow Journalism is an example of such quality-oriented productive activity (Gess 2012, Le Masurier 2019). Slow approaches often mean that consumers give more time and attention to using and appreciating media products. Slow Reading, a.k.a. Slow Books, and Slow Film, a.k.a. Slow Cinema, are examples of such quality-oriented consumptive activity (see MacDonald 2004, Miedama 2009 respectively). *Materiality* refers to the physical, tactile, and sensuous properties of media—to print or analog objects that engage the senses of touch and smell as well as vision and hearing. *Mindfulness* describes the ability to recognize how we cognitively, physiologically, emotionally, and sensorially interact with media as well as how media impact our perceptions of time, space, and place, i.e., our "lifeworld" (López 2020).

Slow Media practices aim to reduce not just the speed but the quantity of one's mediated experiences, as well as to transform their quality. The reductive aspect means consuming less media and decreasing time spent in mediated activities. The transformative aspect means engaging with media more slowly and mindfully, as both consumer and producer. These behaviors can significantly affect one's attention economy and sensory ecosystem in ways that encourage eco-cultural behaviors and attitudes. In contrast with ecomedia studies addressing negative environmental impacts of media use, Slow Media explores practical solutions for extricating bodies, hearts, and minds from commercially mediated scripts that promote consumption and limit eco-cultural imaginations.

This chapter examines some ways in which Slow Media cultivates an ecomedia perspective by increasing critical distance from media use and awareness of media's effects upon the lifeworld. *Lifeworld* refers to one's subjective perception of reality, including time, pace, space, and place. Individual people construct lifeworlds according to idiosyncratic circumstances alongside structural factors. Because people experience the world together and share many perceptions of reality, the lifeworld also has intersubjective, social, and collective dimensions. As we shall see, Slow Media offers strategies for resisting the attention economy, for pursuing digital minimalism, and for reconnecting our lifeworlds with physical environments in ways that bolster environmental attitudes and behaviors.

Slow Principles in Food and Media

The Slow Food movement, which spurred Slow Media, has long appreciated connections between human well-being and ecological health. The concept of "ecogastronomy" is one example. Activist Carlo Petrini helped theorize and popularize this idea in the 2007 book *Slow Food Nation*, in which he proposed the slogan "Good, Clean, Fair" to unite human and environmental concerns. As he explicates, *good* signifies qualities beneficial to the consumer's senses, health, and conscience. *Clean* conveys environmentally sustainable production such as organic ingredients and de-industrialized methods, often small-scale and local. *Fair* means made in socially sustainable ways, such as treating workers, users, and the public ethically. In ecogastronomy, the three principles are interdependent. To identify good products, a consumer must become knowledgeable about the conditions of their production: their provenance. The effort to appreciate goodness or quality in a product has sensory implications, as well as ecological ones. Our senses are enhanced when we spend more time selecting and perceiving stimuli. "To reappropriate one's senses is to reappropriate one's own life and cooperate with others in creating a better world," Petrini wrote (2007, pp. 98–99). Reasserting control over one's attention and senses is central to being mindful about the food one consumes.

And the media one consumes. Environmental sustainability was first among ten items in the "Slow Media Manifesto," an influential tract that declared "Slow Media are a contribution to sustainability" (David, Blumtritt and Kohler 2010). Other items in the manifesto included "promote monotasking," "aim at perfection," "focus on quality," "make quality palpable," and "respect users." To these authors, sustainability interweaves eco-friendly materials and processes of media production with ethical working conditions and data collection. They recommend that Slow Media be consumed with "full attention of all senses" and in "focused alertness," thus underscoring mindfulness and materiality.

My work on Slow Media—from the blog I began in 2009 to the book I published in 2018 and beyond—has described many resistant practices that not only boost awareness of an unsustainable status quo but also encourage adoption of more sustainable alternatives (Rauch 2015, 2018). In

Slow Media: Why Slow is Satisfying, Sustainable and Smart, I examined the movement's critique of global capitalist values like efficiency, industrialization, technocracy, and standardization. I documented the power of Slow Media interventions to spark new ethical sensibilities, attenuate consumer culture, minimize media spectatorship, encourage wiser use of material resources, and better synchronize personal rhythms with the natural world (2018). Here, I expand on that discussion by spotlighting the environmental awareness incipient in Slow approaches to mediated experience.

Mediating the Lifeworld

Practicing Slow Media affects the phenomenological lifeworld by changing how one perceives time, pace, space, and place. In the media-ecology tradition, the lifeworld is highly sensitive to mediated environments that both enable and constrain cognitive, sensory, and emotional experiences. For example, the transition from print to electronic media technologies violently disturbed the human sense ratio, per Marshall McLuhan. By emphasizing sight relative to hearing, print culture disrupted what he saw as the "natural" balance of senses inherent in oral, face-to-face culture. This analysis is rooted in Western, racialized assumptions about human life, according to Armond R. Towns (2022), who highlights both the utility and the limitations of McLuhan's media theories. Electronic media restored a lost balance, McLuhan believed, by stimulating multiple senses simultaneously. To him, the rise of screen culture was largely positive in terms of human senses if not hearts, minds, and bodies. However, others have seen a negative valance in this sensory realignment.

Two perspectives that illuminate how mediation can impair perceptions of physical reality come from Jerry Mander and Bill McKibben. Like McLuhan, these pre-digital analysts focused on television, although many of their insights apply equally to later screen-based media, whose lifeworld effects are likely amplified by their mobility and omnipresence. Mander described TV as a "sensory deprivation environment" that eliminates three systems (touch, smell, taste) and narrows two others (visual and auditory) (1978, p. 61). Indeed, McKibben observed, if television "is doing its job 'correctly,' we lose consciousness of our bodies" (2006, p. 189). Immersing ourselves in an on-screen world dims our awareness of proximate real-world lights, noise, stimuli, and people. Mediation also reduces formerly first-hand experiences to second-hand ones. This means other human beings are interpreting, altering, and processing reality for us (1978). Media reconstructions alter perception partly by decontextualizing information and images from their original times and places. Television, like TikTok and other small-screen media forms, "rarely provides a vista; its instinct is for the closeup," as McKibben wrote. "It chops away perspective; peripheral vision ceases to function" (2006, p. 190). Media producers often condense time in ways that skew perception—choosing unusual, fast, noisy, and exciting events that are unrepresentative of reality over routine, slow, quiet, and dull ones that are common.

Certain kinds of information, understanding, and knowledge are marginalized or misplaced as we increasingly engage with media and disengage from the physical world. Relying on televised reconstructions of reality handicaps one's understanding of, say, a marsh. "Images and words about a marsh do not convey what a marsh is," Mander said. "You must actually sense and feel what a strange, rich, unique and unhuman environment it is" (1978, pp. 278–79). That marsh is also habitat for animals, not least of which birds whose calls and songs fill the air. For his part, McKibben proposes an embodied experience not of touching mud in a marsh but of sitting "by a pond beside a hemlock tree under the sun and stars" in order to "acquire some information that would serve you well." Spending time physically surrounded by flora and fauna, air and water teaches us things that mediated experiences cannot about "the physical limits of a finite world; about sufficiency and need; about proper scale and real time; about the sensual pleasure of exertion and exposure to the elements; about the human need for community," according to McKibben (2006, p. 236). While spending time in nature is necessary to counter this loss, it is not sufficient.

These observations suggest two realms of potential action to recover missing knowledge. One involves not using media and instead seeking out unmediated, first-hand, and direct experiences. The other involves pursuing a kind of Brechtian alienation from media by continuing to use it while also resisting immersion, learning about its techniques, and widening one's perceptual environment. By doing this, audiences can achieve more self-awareness, discernment, reflection, and criticism of mediated experiences. Through mindful attitudes and practices, Slow media ecology connects media to *ecology* in its original sense, including concerns for climate change and the environment. Slow approaches manifest an ecomedia perspective that contrasts with earlier media-ecological theories, which viewed mediated experience as disconnected from material realities.

The realm of media mindfulness is, of course, the lifeworld. This is a zone where culture, materiality, and political economy intertwine—or, alternately, eco-culture, eco-materiality, and political ecology, in Antonio López's conceptualization (2020). People who partake in mindfulness exercises such as comparing experiences of a particular locale with and without media nurture their ability to "care for the living systems that they depend on and to become [more] conscious of their living habitats," he asserts (ibid.). Let's explore some ways in which Slow engagement can cultivate greater awareness of media's influences on our lifeworlds.

Time for Slow Media Perceptions

In Slow Media practice, transforming one's experience of time commonly precedes altering one's perception of space. Recognizing the finitude of time and attention, as well as material resources, is essential to Slow lifestyles. Because people have a limited amount of attention to pay to any combination of activities (including media consumption), Slow practitioners are mindful of how they spend this scarce resource. Digital detoxes, fasts, and sabbaths offer methods of reducing the quantity of one's time spent in mediated environments (see Rauch 2014). The Slow goal of using media less aligns with the ecological quest to find less consumptive ways of living. Slow principles respond to the fact that media are *finite*, that "their constituent elements – matter and energy, information and entropy, time and space, but especially the first pair – are finite resources in the closed system of planet Earth" (Cubitt 2017, p. 7). Reducing the degree of mediatization in one's lifeworld is a step toward decreasing the degree of computerization in society, which some consider a necessary precursor to decreasing planetary carbonization (Tarnoff 2019).

Through mindfulness, Slow practitioners *make* (rather than *take*) time to spend away from screen-based and otherwise-mediated activities. Doing so enhances users' awareness of time and pace, resulting in perceptions of having more time and of time moving more slowly. Many find this experience of "free," empty, or slow time pleasurable and liberating, while others find it uncomfortable, even boring—at least at first. People report that intentional media (dis)use contributes to their feeling happier, more focused, more self-aware, more creative, and more productive (Levy 2016, Moeller 2010, Rauch 2014, 2018). Intentional (dis)engagement with media helps some people realize and assert control over their own time and pace. Such practices have nurtured a counterculture that is more patient, empathetic, self-compassionate, attuned to ecological time, and resistant to domination than mainstream culture is (MacDonald 2004, Rifkin 1987, Zerubavel 1985).

Slow Media nudges people to seek out alternatives to screen culture partly by creating a temporal void. This emancipated time offers opportunities to redirect one's attention from fast-paced digital media toward slower print and analog materials as well as toward unmediated interactions in one's physical space. As Maxwell and Miller note, "re-enchantment with both low-wattage culture and nonhuman nature are prerequisites to ecologically sound uses of media" (2012, p. 7). Replacing digital media use with activities like reading printed matter or hand-writing letters affects one's perception of time (namely, by slowing it down) and one's sensory balance (by enhancing smell and touch vis-a-vis sight and sound). Analog media objects must be acquired with care, since many are manufactured or disposed of in ways harmful to the environment. The paper, printing, and publishing industries have taken a significant toll on the environment due to their reliance on chemical, mechanical, and electrical processes, including energy use (Maxwell and Miller 2012). Using Slow Media objects that are made, distributed, and shared in local communities boosts one's connection to place through engagement with record shops, thrift stores, libraries, and other physically proximate spaces.

Supplanting sedentary and homebound activities with bodily movement through one's locality, whether walking around one's neighborhood or venturing farther afield, promises a deeper sense of place. Communion with nature is a potential result—and, for many, a goal—of adopting Slow Media practices. Many people find that immersion in natural spaces provides a restorative counterbalance to digitally mediated experiences. People widely report that spending time in natural environments ameliorates a range of cognitive, emotional, and sensory conditions, including anxiety, alienation, attention deficit, aversion to nature, and addiction to technology (López 2020, Louv 2005, Rauch 2018). The fact that some people have little or no access to nature and wilderness is another political concern constraining Slow Media, as well as the broader environmental movement. The rise of attention disorders and depression has been linked to a preponderance of digital media use and an absence of nature in people's lives (Louv 2005). Slow methods of disengaging from media enhance one's mental health, biophysical (circadian) rhythms, sense of the sublime, and love for fellow animals.

Direct experience of one's physical surroundings improves awareness of how media affect the lifeworld through senses, emotions, and cognition. Beyond gaining stronger connections with the natural environment, people gain insight to their own brains, bodies, and senses through Slow methods. This includes greater awareness of the quality of one's cognitive attention/distraction and of physiological responses to media use such as holding one's breath and feeling tense (Levy 2017, Rauch 2018). Mindfulness in media use, and in other activities, stimulates the parasympathetic nervous system (PNS), which is responsible for "rest and digest" functions like slowing one's heartbeat and respiration. Slow Media prompts us to engage with complex physical senses beyond the five "basic" ones (sight, hearing, smell, touch, taste). These include *thermoception*, the ability to sense heat and cold; *equilibrioception*, the sense of bodily balance; *interoception*, the perception of sensations within the body such as heartbeat, respiration, and satiety; and *proprioception*, the perception of where body parts are and how they move in space—all of which orient us toward our physical environs.

Mindful use of print and analog objects offers a better understanding of the material properties of these media forms. Slow practitioners report having a deep appreciation for the craftsmanship, durability, and other sustainable affordances of media objects that can be reused, repaired, and repurposed over many decades and even generations (Rauch 2015, 2018). Slow Media calls attention to the rapid, planned obsolescence of digital media materials and the environmental implications of an economic system based on production, consumption, and disposal of cheap, short-lived goods. By embodying principles of design and manufacturing aimed at longevity, Slow Media forms offer alternatives to digital platforms, gadgets, and support apparati that are extracted from living systems and return unto them all too quickly. (As do print and analog media, though much more slowly.)

Slow Media and ecomedia practices alike require reclaiming control over one's own schedule, since it takes time to learn about, pursue, and achieve better habits. This brings us full circle to the "attention merchants": technologists, content managers, and advertisers driven by profit prerogatives to hack eyeballs and minds so people browse more ads, faster. Mental and physical distance from media—and sponsored content, specifically—helps build awareness of and resistance to this colonization of the lifeworld, which Habermas (1981) attributed to rich and powerful people inundating culture with their own viewpoints through advertising. Ad-saturated culture contributes to making market forces and instrumental rationality seem normal and relevant to a public that might otherwise see them as illegitimate or unjustifiable. Slow Media challenges the assumption that time spent "not producing value" is reducible to "doing nothing."

The distanciation effected by Slow Media can stimulate people to question broader ideological forces such as voracious consumerism and commercialism that gorge on our attention and our environment alike. Resistance to attention extraction can buttress other struggles against material extraction. Using media often transports us to a "present" beyond geographic place. This decontextualization nudges us to lose touch with physical locations and disrupts our ability to create and care for local communities, as Odell explicates (2020). Slow Media offers strategies for resisting the attention economy and for recontextualizing our lifeworlds.

A Slow Path to Eco-Optimism

Slow Media offers creative new narratives about how mediated and unmediated interactions can move people "from eco-pessimism to the politics of possibility" (Parham 2015, p. 1). My work complements other contributions to this volume that explore how digital immersion entangles our worldview in global capitalist concerns that are quite distant from our shared material lives (Citton); how media exploit our attention in ways that harm our perception of actual surroundings (Von Mossner); how embodied media experiences challenge dominant narratives and shape eco-cultural identities (Milstein); how "new folk" music nurtures local cultures and ecological visions (Parham); and how Slow experiences in analog film labs promote recycling as well as low-tech principles that refuse market logic (Rasmi).

Voluntary experiments in reducing screen time are one of many Slow approaches to mediated experience that are potentially transformative. The fact that some people are not adequately empowered to control their own time and pace is a political question with which sustainability advocates need to engage more deeply. Many people are "not economically or culturally positioned to claim the progressive, political, or sustainable promise of Slowness," as Sarah Sharma, director of the McLuhan Centre for Technology and Culture, has observed (2014, p. 110). Some people lack the ability to spend time in nature and to access wilderness that U.S. environmentalists and media critics often take for granted. Moving toward sustainability requires us to recognize these politics of time, to promote changing both ourselves and our institutions.

By contrast with intentional slowing, the global pandemic that began in 2020 presented an involuntary, natural experiment that generated mindful media habits, rebalanced attention economies, and re-sensitized people to physical environments. A public-health emergency compelled withdrawal from physical materials and in-person interactions, the consequence of which might be ever-more streamed content and virtual communication. Post-shutdown, challenges loom for those espousing Slow Media interactions and material objects.

At the same time, "sheltering in place" has renewed many people's engagement in unmediated, place-bound activities like making bread, walking dogs, and pulling weeds that put one's senses in more direct contact with physical materials, animal life, and the great outdoors. We might be more engaged than ever with digital platforms and networks while also more aware of the lifeworld effects of mediation. Lockdown showed humanity a tantalizing sliver of a silver lining. Some skies blued, some watered cleared, and some animals perambulated in spaces once shunned. Such resilience evokes possibilities for human habits and the natural environment to adapt in tandem—and for the better.

Note

1 I capitalize "Slow" to signal the adjective's particular meaning in the context of Slow Living, Slow Food, Slow Media, and so on.

Further Reading

Gess, Harold. "Climate Change and the Possibility of 'Slow Journalism.'" *Ecquid Novi: African Journalism Studies* 33, no. 1 (2012): 54–65. https://doi.org/10.1080/02560054.2011.636828.

Le Masurier, Megan, ed. *Slow Journalism*. Journalism Studies: Theory and Practice. London New York: Routledge, Taylor & Francis Group, 2019.

MacDonald, Scott. "Toward an Eco-Cinema." *Interdisciplinary Studies in Literature and Environment* 11, no. 2 (2004): 107–32.

Rauch, Jennifer. "Constructive Rituals of Demediatization: Spiritual, Corporeal and Mixed Metaphors in Popular Discourse about Unplugging." *Explorations in Media Ecology* 13, no. 3 (2014): 237–52. https://doi.org/10.1386/eme.13.3-4.237_1.

Rauch, Jennifer. *Slow Media: Toward a Sustainable Future*. Book, Whole. Oxford: Oxford University Press, 2018.

References

Cubitt, Sean. *Finite Media: Environmental Implications of Digital Technologies*. Durham, NC: Duke University Press, 2017.

David, Sabria. "How 'Slow' Are the Germans?" *DCore/Slow Media Institut*, October 12, 2015. http://www.dcore.de/index.php/wie-slow-sind-die-deutschen-neue-slowtypes-studie- ermoeglicht-spannende-einblicke-in-die-lebenswelt-der-digitalen-mediengesellschaft.

David, Sabria, Jorg Blumtritt, and Benedikt Kohler. "Slow Media Manifesto." *Slow-Media* (blog), January 2, 2010. http://en.slow-media.net/manifesto.

Gess, Harold. "Climate Change and the Possibility of Slow Journalism." *Ecquid Novi: African Journalism Studies* 33, no. 1 (2012): 54–65.

Habermas, Jürgen. *The Theory of Communicative Action*. Boston, MA: Beacon: 1981.

Le Masurier, Megan. *Slow Journalism*. Abingdon and New York: Routledge, 2019.

Levy, David M. *Mindful Tech: How to Bring Balance to Our Daily Lives*. New Haven, CT and London: Yale University Press, 2016.

López, Antonio. *Ecomedia Literacy: Integrating Ecology into Media Education*. New York and London: Routledge, 2020.

Louv, Richard. *Last Child in the Woods: Saving Our Children from Nature Deficit Disorder*. Chapel Hill, NC: Algonquin Books, 2005.

MacDonald, Scott. "Toward an Eco Cinema." *Interdisciplinary Studies in Literature and Environment* 11, no. 2 (Summer 2004): 107–32.

Mander, Jerry. *Four Arguments for the Elimination of Television*. New York: HarperCollins, 1978.

Maxwell, Richard, and Toby Miller. *Greening the Media*. New York: Oxford University Press, 2012.

McKibben, Bill. *The Age of Missing Information*. New York: Penguin, 2006.

McLuhan, Marshall. *Understanding Media: The Extensions of Man*. New York: McGraw-Hill, 2014.

Miedama, John. *Slow Reading*. Sacramento, CA: Litwin Books, 2009.

Moeller, Susan. "A Day without Media." International Center for Media and the Public Agenda and the University of Maryland, 2010. https://withoutmedia.wordpress.com.

Newport, Cal. *Digital Minimalism: Choosing a Focused Life in a Noisy World*. New York: Portfolio, 2019.

Odell, Jenny. *How to Do Nothing: Resisting the Attention Economy*. Brooklyn, NY and London: Melville House, 2020.

Parham, John. *Green Media and Popular Culture: An Introduction*. London: Palgrave, 2015.Petrini, Carlo. *Slow Food Nation: Why Our Food Should Be Good, Clean, Fair*. New York: Rizzoli, 2007.

Rauch, Jennifer. "Constructive Rituals of Demediatization: Spiritual, Corporeal and Mixed Metaphors in Popular Discourse about Unplugging." *Explorations in Media Ecology* 13, nos. 3–4 (2014): 231–46. https://doi.org/10.1386/eme.13.3-4.231_1.

Rauch, Jennifer. "Slow Media as Alternative Media: On the Cultural Persistence of Print and Analog Forms." In *The Routledge Companion to Alternative and Community Media*, edited by Chris Atton, 571–81. Oxford and New York: Routledge, 2015.

Rauch, Jennifer. *Slow Media: Why Slow Is Satisfying, Sustainable and Smart*. New York and Oxford: Oxford University Press, 2018.

Rifkin, Jeremy. *Time Wars: The Primary Conflict in Human History*. New York: Touchstone, 1987.

Sharma, Sarah. *In the Meantime: Temporality and Cultural Politics*. Durham, NC: Duke University Press, 2014.

Tarnoff, Ben. 2019. "To Decarbonize We Must Decomputerize: Why We Need a Luddite Revolution." September 18, 2019. *The Guardian*. https://www.theguardian.com/technology/2019/sep/17/tech-climate-change-luddites-data

Towns, Armond R. 2022. *On Black Media Philosophy*. Oakland: University of California Press.

Zerubavel, Eviatar. *Hidden Rhythms: Schedules and Calendars in Social Life*. Chicago, IL and London: University of Chicago Press, 1985.

AFTERWORD
Posthumous Ecomedia

Seán Cubitt

Ecomedia confronts, 500 years after the cataclysm unleashed by Columbus' voyage, the challenge of surviving after the worst has already happened. Reading that '252 men have more wealth than all 1 billion women and girls in Africa and Latin America and the Caribbean, combined' (Oxfam 2022: 7), it seems clear that, like the Americas in 1492, the world today is dominated by economic, political and technical systems prepared to sacrifice the planet and its human inhabitants. At this point, ecomedia is faced with the question of how to bear witness (Fuller and Goriunova 2019: xiv). A blazing forest or a failed crop used to be local events witnessed firsthand: how can we witness a cataclysm as vast as climate change? Enmeshed and dispersed in its technologies and ecologies, the human who used to witness an event is becoming posthuman. Haunted by the fear that we may be at the end of our species and of life itself, ecomedia takes up the burden of 'survivance' (Vizenor 2009): it is becoming posthumous.

Media have always encouraged posthumous survival since the Homeric epics first reached out for immortality (Arendt 2006 [1968]). Taking media to mean anything that connects us to one another, the dominant media of our time are cash and pollution. Money – inheritance for the rich, debt for the poor – outlives individuals and, as medium of devastation, will outlive our species. Plastics will infest the oceans, nuclear fuel the land, long after humanity is a memory held in recordings no-one will read or remember. These forms of connection, unlike natural ecologies, divide and destroy. They also displace in the precise sense that they are ubiquitous without belonging to any one place. Witnessing used to imply the presence of a witness at an event: we posthumans are no longer present, and events occur on scales that exceed any one witness.

Ecomedia can no longer start from assertions of the identity of a witness with the truth they want to communicate. We must instead begin in non-identity. Like Luce Irigaray's *Sex Which Is Not One* (1977), ecomedia no longer claims the One – patriarchal, colonial – as the primal object/subject. Irigaray claimed the multiplicity of femininity; almost a century earlier, the mathematical philosopher Gottlob Frege (1953 [1884]) argued that since everything that exists is identical to itself, zero, which by definition does not exist, should be defined as the non-identical. Frege went on to demonstrate that every assertion of identity and existence includes non-identity. For ecomedia, where presence and connection are ecologically and technically dispersed, every event of mediation that exists – by dint of occurring – contains in itself the reasons why it is otherwise.

Split into its elements, any ecomediation is always already 'other-wise', an ephemeral event at the crossroads of multiple, non-identical and ultimately cosmic forces.

'Ecomedia' is such a precise term it is unlikely I was the first to use it. In any case, my book with the title *EcoMedia* (Cubitt 2005) was preceded by David Ingram's *Green Screen* in 2004 and was inspired by meetings with Pat Brereton, whose *Hollywood Utopia* (2005) came out the same year, all preceded by, among others, book-length studies by Jhan Hochman (1998), Gregg Mitman (1999) and David Bousé (2000). Adrian Ivakhiv (2008) gave a thorough account of the first decade of 'eco-cinecriticism', with roots in literary studies and art history and emerging directions in feminist and decolonial work. Many of us also drew on various philosophical and political traditions including the work of the poet Hans Magnus Enzensberger (1974) and historical and political books by Murray Bookchin (1982), and Leo Marx (1964) and were influenced by contact with Indigenous ways of knowing (Barclay 2005, Smith 2005). As befitted a nascent field, referencing was eclectic but habit led to a less invigorating main activity: close readings of movies and TV shows. In 2012, Nadia Bozak and Richard Maxwell and Toby Miller brought out books addressing the production cycle. Swiftly, across digital and media and communications journals, studies of distribution, display, materials, waste and energy resources established that media ecologies were no longer metaphors but material as well as cultural processes. As we argue in the introduction to *Ecocinema Theory and Practice 2* (Rust, Monani, and Cubitt 2023), in 25 years, ecomedia has become core business for media and cultural studies, as feminism did before it.

Presence and connectivity, the global in the local, the ethical scale of encounter and the political scale of planetarity frame ecomedia today. The real abstraction of money and exchange value leaves a residue beyond the monetizable aspects of the world: an organic slurry shaped by exclusion. But since what excludes it is disconnected from exchange, the quantitative management of flow, this residue is fluidly connected, qualitatively, through gravity, sunlight, air and water, the slower forces of minerals and swifter ones of affect. Even technologically quantised, the circulation of language, images and sounds are also sensory phenomena which I cannot help but modify as they course through me. This post-personal and posthuman slurry is where, today, we speak from, as technical-ecological and therefore social beings articulated with and dispersed among the materials and energies that comprise us. It constitutes what Siobhan Angus calls a counter-archive, whose construction 'reflects a belief that, in the face of the overwhelming scale and the perceived inevitability of climate change, possible futures can be rewritten and called forward from the ruins of failed histories' (2021: 131).

Forced to face the possibility, possibly even the inevitability, of extinction (Lovink 2022), the melancholy logic of exchange claims, in the absence of both subject and species, a fantastic immortality that can be brought forward and enjoyed – now. Sharing the structure of debt, where we agree to spend the future today, this same fantasy powers both the belief that there is nothing to be done and the ideological commitment to keep destroying the planetary future in the interests of the profitable present. Here capital is not only irrational: it has sealed itself off from reality, absorbed in a terminal spiral into solipsistic derivatives producing actual money from its real absence. It gets the energy it needs for this self-obsession by withdrawing its affective connection to the world: by ceasing to be eco-technically connected with anything beyond itself. Leaving as remainder the tailings of human and physical nature, the discarded refuse is the only place its madness can be seen from.

The new aesthetic of unpredictable AI (Amoore and Piotukh 2016, Amoore 2020) – the latest iteration of glitch – mirrors the new rule of contingency in finance capital (Appadurai 2016, Ayache 2016, MacKenzie 2006). The question of what follows from the new conditions cannot be separated from the solution to the prior question: where we can witness from? We humans are excluded from the systems that exploit and govern us and therefore are becoming environmental – resources to exploit, dumps for excess product. In an era of environmental devastation and degradation, experience is also degraded; as quality (beauty, good, truth) but also in the experience of de-grading, of being put down, lowered, in the gutter. But because we are environmental externalities, we can witness, from that position, just as dispossession and marginalisation make possible the decolonial critique which so deeply inflects ecomedia. No longer from a place in a hierarchy that recognises 'me', we speak in, from and as habitats – *perspectiveless*.

Simultaneously, the consciousness that witnesses can no longer be considered unitary, since it has been ejected from the phallic regime of the corporate cyborg, and is no longer structured exclusively by phallogocentric reason but also by code, and so multiplies and proliferates its initiating non-identity. And yet, what remains of consciousness is still structured in part by language and is therefore social, and in part by mathematics and logic, a product of generations of reflections on and with the material world and so ancestral. The new ancestral and social unconscious is also structured by its distribution, no longer primarily through the senses but by transmission, specifically packet-switching under the provisions of internet and transfer-control protocols which, today, also escape conscious command, becoming themselves unconscious and therefore, beyond print/mechanical mass and network distributed subjects, *subjectless*.

Deprived of subjectivity and perspective, presence and connection, non-identical and otherwise ecomedia are indistinguishable from their technical and ecological habitat as the distinctions between human, ecology and technology vanish in a Gaussian blur. As the AIs powering future-eating financialisation colonise even the utopian 'not-yet', the question of what comes next has two distinctly answers. In one the posthuman condition presages a posthumous condition: we make culture today for generations that will never be born. Or, as Brian Massumi (2018: 40) suggests, contemporary finance capital depends on, exploits, and dictates to its externalities, the n-dimensional slurry of life, but Life will exploit that dependency: 'Life will dictate its qualities to the economy'.

The prognosis is over-optimistic but its structure is surely correct. As enclosure, colonisation brought its outside into its interior in the interests of control, but algorithmic derivatives cede control in the interests of capture, their peculiar mode of profit-taking. Command and control cannot oscillate indefinitely: both depend on growth, and though derivatives return to Marx's classic formula M-C-M' (money invested in commodities produces more money), this cycle is limited by its parallel C-M-C' (commodities generate money which generates more commodities), which demands more and more depletion of the material world. So the alternative to a posthumous culture, that may persist somehow post-mortem after extinction, is the low ambition to return to an imagined state of nature that preceded all this degradation.

Accelerationism hastening capital's demise may be no more politically sound than cheering on Gaia's revenge. Intuitively, the third alternative lies in the borders between scales, between now and a long time, between here and everywhere, that are core concerns of ecomedia. At one end we face the increasing velocity and diminishing sizes of media, from frames to pixels and, in the prototypical medium of our days, from cash transactions to the femtosecond operations of blockchain and its crises such as the 2022 collapse of the FTX exchange (Reiff 2022). On the other, the dissolving boundaries between previously human and previously non-human others open onto vistas of molecular exchange at the scales of climate and community.

Tuvalu foreign minister Simon Kofe's address to COP-26, knee-deep in the rising Pacific, is an epochal exemplar of posthumous ecomedia that rejects the eternity of growth in favour of the longevity of cultures co-dependent with their environs (ABC/Reuters 2021). Reversing Plato and the *Timaeus*, eternity is a stilled image of time. Tuvalu's COP-27 threat to live forever in exile in the Cloud (SBS 2022) is a cunning ourobouros: the Cloud itself is too dependent on the destructive exploitation of the world for profit. But Kofe has on his side the political assertion that the future is not based on the privations consequent on private property but on the commons. Profoundly anti-natural in its essence (money is unique among non-theological entities in having an essence), money pits itself against time. Time is the quality of nature that money hates most. Intuitively, again, ecomedia's next turn must be to erase the Brechtian question 'who does the future belong to?' in favour of a commons that exceeds both property and humanity, because this move alone opens up from the deep history of media (Parikka 2017) to its deep future.

References

ABC/Reuters (2021). "Tuvalu's Foreign Minister Simon Kofe Gives COP26 Speech Knee-Deep in the Sea to Show Nation on Frontline of Climate Crisis." *ABC News*. November 10. https://www.abc.net.au/news/2021-11-10/tuvalu-minister-makes-cop26-speech-from-sea/100608344

Amoore, Louise (2020). *Cloud Ethics: Algorithms and the Attributes of Ourselves and Others*. Durham, NC: Duke University Press.

Amoore, Louise and Volha Piotukh (eds) (2016). *Algorithmic Life: Calculative Devices in the Age of Big Data*. New York: Routledge.

Angus, Siobhan (2021). "Atomic Ecology." *October* 179 (Winter). 110–31

Appadurai, Arjun (2016). *Banking on Words: The Failure of Language in the Age of Derivative Finance*. Chicago, IL: University of Chicago Press.

Arendt, Hannah (2006 [1968]). "History and Nature." In *Between Past and Future: Eight Exercises in Political Thought*. Expanded edition. Introduction by Jerome Kohn. New York: Penguin. 41–63.

Ayache, Elie (2016). "On Black-Scholes." In *Derivatives and the Wealth of Society*. Edited by Benjamin Lee and Randy Martin. Chicago, IL: University of Chicago Press. 240–51.

Cubitt, Seán (2005). *EcoMedia*. Amsterdam; New York: Rodopi.

Barclay, Barry (2005). *Mana Tuturu: Maori Treasures and Intellectual Property Rights*. Auckland: Auckland University Press.

Bookchin, Murray (1982). *The Ecology of Freedom*. Palo Alto, CA: Cheshire Books.

Bousé, David (2000). *Wildlife Films*. Philadelphia: University of Pennsylvania Press.

Bozak, Nadia (2012). *The Cinematic Footprint: Lights, Camera, Natural Resources*. New Brunswick, NJ: Rutgers University Press.

Brereton, Pat (2005), *Hollywood Utopia: Ecology in Contemporary Hollywood Cinema*. London: Intellect.

Enzensberger, Hans Magnus (1974). "Critique of Political Ecology." In Translated by Stuart Hood. *New Left Review* 84, March–April. 3–31. Reprinted in Enzensberger (1988) *Dreamers of the Absolute: Essays on Ecology, Media and Power*. London: Radius. 253–295.

Frege, Gottlob (1953 [1884]). *The Foundations of Arithmetic*. Translated by J.L. Austin, second revised edition. New York: Harper.

Fuller, Matt and Olga Goriunova (2019). *Bleak Joys: Aesthetics of Eoclogy and Impossibility*. Minneapolis: University of Minnesota Press.

Hochman, Jhan (1998). *Green Cultural Studies: Nature in Film, Novel, and Theory*. Moscow: University of Idaho Press.

Ingram, David A. (2004). *Green Screen: Environmentalism and Hollywood Cinema*. Exeter: University of Exeter Press.

Irigaray, Luce (1977). *Ce sexe qui n'en est pas un*. Paris: Editions de Minuit. [Irigaray, Luce (1985). *This Sex Which Is Not One*. Translated by Catherine Porter and Caroline Burke. Ithaca, NY: Cornell University Press].

Ivakhiv, Adrian (2008). "Green Film Criticism and Its Futures." *Interdisciplinary Studies in Literature and Environment* 15(2) (Summer): 1–28.

Lovink, Geert (2022). *Extinction Internet: Our Inconvenient Truth Moment*. Amsterdam: Institute for Network Cultures. https://networkcultures.org/blog/publication/extinction-internet/

MacKenzie, Donald (2006). *An Engine, Not a Camera: How Financial Models Shape Markets*. Cambridge: MIT Press.

Marx, Leo (1964). *The Machine in the Garden: Technology and the Pastoral Ideal in America*. New York: Oxford University Press.
Massumi, Brian (2018). *99 Theses on the Revaluation of Value*. Minneapolis: University of Minnesota Press.
Maxwell, Richard and Toby Miller (2012). *Greening the Media.* Oxford: Oxford University Press.
Mitman, Gregg (1999). *Reel Nature: America's Romance with Wildlife on Film*. Cambridge: Harvard University Press.
Oxfam (2022). "Inequality Kills." Oxfam Briefing Paper, January. Oxford: Oxfam International. https://oxfamilibrary.openrepository.com/bitstream/handle/10546/621341/bp-inequality-kills-170122-en.pdf
Parikka, Jussi (2017). "Deep Times and Media Mines: A Descent into Ecological Materiality of Technology." In *General Ecology: The New Ecological Paradigm*. Edited by Eric Hörl and James Burton. London: Bloomsbury. 169–92.
Reiff, Nathan (2022). "The Collapse of FTX: What Went Wrong with the Crypto Exchange?" *Investopedia*, November 18. https://www.investopedia.com/what-went-wrong-with-ftx-6828447
Rust, Stephen, Salma Monani and Seán Cubitt (eds) (2023). "Introduction - Cut to Green: Tracking the Growth of Ecocinema Studies." In *Ecocinema Theory and Practice 2*. New York: Routledge. 1–15.
SBS (2022). "Why Tuvalu Is Building a Digital Replica of Itself in the Metaverse." *SBS News*. 16 November. https://www.sbs.com.au/news/article/why-tuvalu-is-building-a-digital-replica-of-itself-in-the-metaverse/30ictx9yl
Smith, Linda Tuhiwai (2005). *Decolonizing Methodologies: Research and Indigenous Peoples*. London: Zed Books.
Vizenor, Gerald (2009). *Native Liberty and Cultural Survivance*. Lincoln: University of Nebraska Press.

FURTHER READING

Abraham, Benjamin J. 2022. *Digital Games after Climate Change*. Cham: Palgrave Macmillan.
Alaimo, Stacy. 2016. *Exposed: Environmental Politics & Pleasures in Posthuman Times*. Minneapolis: University of Minnesota Press.
Alia, V. 2004. *Media Ethics and Social Change*. New York: Routledge.
Anderson, Alison. 2014. *Media, Environment and the Network Society*. New York: Palgrave Macmillan.
Badami, Nandita. 2021. "Let There Be Light (or in Defense of Darkness)," *The South Atlantic Quarterly* 120 (1): 51–61.
Baldé, C. P., Forti V., Gray, V., Kuehr, R., and Stegmann, P. 2018 *The Global E-Waste Monitor* 2017. Bonn/Geneva/Vienna: United Nations University, International Telecommunication Union, and International Solid Waste Association. https://ewastemonitor.info/
Basso, Keith H. 1996. *Wisdom Sits in Places: Landscape and Language Amongst the Western Apache*. Albuquerque: University of New Mexico Press.
Bayman, Louis. 2009. "Melodrama as Realism in Italian Neorealism," in *Realism and the Audiovisual Media*, edited by Lúcia Nagib and Cecilia Mello, 47–92. Basingstoke: Palgrave Macmillan.
Benjamin, Ruha. 2019. *Race after Technology*. Medford: Polity Press.
Bhandar, Brenna. 2018. *Colonial Lives of Property: Law, Land, and Racial Regimes of Property*. Durham, NC; London: Duke University Press.
Birkinbine, Benjamin J., and Dorothy Kidd. 2020. "Re-Thinking the Communication Commons," *Popular Communication* 18 (3): 152–54.
Bladow, Kyle and Jennifer Ladino, eds. 2018. *Affective Ecocriticism: Emotion, Embodiment, Environment*. Lincoln: University of Nebraska Press.
Blum, Hester. 2019. *The News at the Ends of the Earth: The Print Culture of Polar Exploration*. Durham, NC: Duke University Press.
Borunda, Stephen N. 2019. "Mapuche Cosmovision and the Cinematic Voyage: An Interview with Filmmaker Francisco Huichaqueo Pérez (English Version)," *Media+ Environment* 1 (1): 10788.
Borunda, Stephen N. 2022. "A Body Downwind of the Atomic Attack at Trinity: Mediations of Atomic Coloniality in Nuevo México," *Media+Environment* 4(1) (August). https://doi.org/10.1525/001c.36561
Boyle, James. 1996. *Shamans, Software, & Spleens, Law and the Construction of the Information Society*. Cambridge, MA: Harvard University Press.
Bozak, Nadia. 2012. *The Cinematic Footprint. Lights, Camera, Natural Resources*. New York: Routledge University Press.
Branch, Michael. 2014. "Are You Serious? A Modest Proposal for Environmental Humor," in *Oxford Handbook of Ecocriticism*, edited by Greg Garrard, 378–90. Oxford: Oxford University Press.
Bratton, Benjamin. 2015. *The Stack: On Software and Sovereignty*. Software Studies. Cambridge: MIT Press.
Bratton, Benjamin. 2019. *The Terraforming*. Moscow: Strelka Institute.

Brevini, Benedetta. 2022. *Is AI Good for the Planet?* Cambridge; Medford, MA: Polity Press.
Brevini, Benedetta. 2023. *Communication, Technology and the Environment*. Cambridge; Medford, MA: Polity Press.
Brevini, Benedetta and Graham Murdock. 2017. *Carbon Capitalism and Communication: Confronting Climate Crisis*. Cham: Palgrave.
Buck, Susan. J. 2017. *The Global Commons*. London: Routledge. https://doi.org/10.4324/9781315086415
Buckingham, David. 2019. *The Media Education Manifesto*. Cambridge; Medford, MA: Polity.
Bullard, R. 2000. *Dumping in Dixie: Race, Class, and Environmental Quality* (3rd ed.). Boulder, CO: Westview Press.
Carlson, B. and Frazer R. 2021. *Indigenous Digital Life: The Practice and Politics of Being Indigenous on Social Media*. London: Palgrave Macmillan.
Carr, J. and Milstein, T. 2021. "See Nothing but Beauty": The Shared Work of Making Anthropogenic Destruction Invisible to the Human Eye. *Geoforum* 122 (June), 183–92. https://doi.org/10.1016/j.geoforum.2021.04.013
Castro-Sotomayor, J. 2020. "Ecocultural Identities in Intercultural Encounters," in *Routledge Handbook of Ecocultural Identity*, edited by Milstein and Castro-Sotomayor, 66–85. London: Routledge.
Chan, J., Selden, M., and Ngai, P. 2020. *Dying for an iPhone: Apple, Foxconn, and The Lives of China's Workers*. Chicago, IL: Haymarket Books.
Chandler, Nahum Dimitri. 2014. *X– The Problem of the Negro as a Problem for Thought*. American Philosophy. New York: Fordham University Press.
Chang, Alenda Y. 2019. *Playing Nature: Ecology in Video Games*. Minneapolis: University of Minnesota Press.
Chang, Alenda Y., and Jeff Watson. 2022. "Steam Clouds and Game Streams: Unboxing the 'Future' of Gaming," in *The SAGE Handbook of the Digital Media Economy*, edited by Terry Flew, Jennifer Holt, and Julian Thomas, 240–59. London: Sage.
Chang, C. 2019. "The Missing View in Global Post-Secular Cinema: Crouching Tiger Hidden Dragon as a Visual Kōan/Gong'an," *Paragraph Journal*, Special Issue: "Critical Theory, Religion and Film." 42 (3): 370–86.
Cho, F. 2008. "Buddhism, Film and Religious Knowing: Challenging the Literary Approach to Film," in *Teaching Religion and* Film, edited by G. Watkins, 117–27. Oxford: Oxford University Press.
Cho, F. 2017. *Seeing Like the Buddha: Enlightenment Through Film*. Albany, NY: State University of New York.
Citton, Yves. 2017a. *The Ecology of Attention*. Cambridge: Polity.
Citton, Yves. 2017b. *Mediarchy*. Cambridge: Polity.
Clark, Timothy. 2015. *Ecocriticism on the Edge: The Anthropocene as a Threshold Concept*. London: Bloomsbury.
Coryat, Diana, Christian Leon and Noah Zweig. 2023. *Small Cinemas of the Andes: New Aesthetics, Practices and Platforms*. London; New York: Palgrave MacMillan.
Couldry, Nick and Ulises Mejias. 2019. *The Costs of Connection: How Data is Colonizing Human Life and Appropriating It for Capitalism*. Palo Alto, CA: Stanford University Press.
Cubitt, Sean. 2005. *EcoMedia*. Contemporary Cinema, 1, Book, Whole. Amsterdam; New York: Rodopi.
Cubitt, Sean. 2016. *Finite Media: Environmental Implications of Digital Technologies*. Durham, NC: Duke University Press.
Daggett, Cara New. 2019. *The Birth of Energy: Fossil Fuels, Thermodynamics, and the Politics of Work*. Durham, NC: Duke University Press.
Della Noce, Elio, and Lucas Murari. 2022. *Expanded Nature. Ecologies du cinéma expérimental*. Paris: Light Cone.
Demos, T. J. 2016. *Decolonizing Nature: Contemporary Art and the Politics of Ecology*. London: Sternberg Press.
———. 2017. *Against the Anthropocene: Visual Culture and Environment Today*. London: Sternberg Press.
Devine, Kyle. 2019. *Decomposed: The Political Ecology of Music*. Cambridge: MIT Press.
Devine, Kyle, and Alexandrine Boudreault-Fournier, eds. 2021. *Audible Infrastructures: Music, Sound, Media*. New York: Oxford University Press.
Dobrin, Sidney I. 2021. *Blue Ecocriticism and the Oceanic Imperative*. Routledge Environmental Humanities. Abingdon; New York: Routledge.

Emejulu, A. and C. McGregor. 2019. "Towards a Radical Digital Citizenship in Digital Education," *Critical Studies in Education* 60 (1): 131–47. https://doi.org/10.1080/17508487.2016.1234494

Fredericks, B. et al. 2021. "Disrupting the Colonial Algorithm: Indigenous Australia and Social Media," *Media International Australia*. https://doi.org/10.1177/1329878X211038286

Freitag, Charlotte, Mike Berners-Lee, Kelly Widdicks, Bran Knowles, Gordon S. Blair, and Adrian Friday. 2021. "The Real Climate and Transformative Impact of ICT: A Critique of Estimates, Trends, and Regulations," *Patterns* 2 (9): 100340. https://doi.org/10.1016/j.patter.2021.100340

Furuhata, Yuriko. 2022. *Climatic Media: Transpacific Experiments in Atmospheric Control*. Durham, NC: Duke University Press.

Gabrys, Jennifer. 2011. *Digital Rubbish: A Natural History of Electronics*. Ann Arbor: University of Michigan Press.

Gallese, Vittorio, and Michele Guerra. 2012. "Embodying Movies: Embodied Simulation and Film Studies," *Cinema: Journal of Philosophy and the Moving Image* 3: 183–210.

Garcia Espinosa, Julio. 1979. "For an Imperfect Cinema," *Jump Cut* 20: 14–26.

Garritano, Carmela. 2020. "Waiting on the Past: African Uranium Futures in Arlit, Deuxième Paris," *Modern Fiction Studies* 66 (1): 122–40.

Gess, Harold. 2012. "Climate Change and the Possibility of 'Slow Journalism,'" *Ecquid Novi: African Journalism Studies* 33 (1): 54–65. https://doi.org/10.1080/02560054.2011.636828

Gibson, Chris, and Andrew Warren. 2021. *The Guitar: Tracing the Grain Back to the Tree*. London; Chicago, IL: The University of Chicago Press.

Goeman, Mishuana. 2013. *Mark My Words: Native Women Mapping Our Nations*. Minneapolis: University of Minnesota Press. http://ebookcentral.proquest.com/lib/gettysburg/detail.action?docID=1362032

Gonzalez, Carmen G. 2020. "Climate Change, Race, and Migration," *Journal of Law and Political Economy* 1 (1):109–146.

Grodal, Torben. 1997. *Moving Pictures: A New Theory of Film Genres, Feelings, and Cognition*. Oxford: Clarendon Press.

Grossman, Z. and W. LaDuke. 2017. *Unlikely Alliances: Native Nations and White Communities Join to Defend Rural Lands*. Seattle, WA: University of Washington Press.

Guattari, Félix. 2000. *The Three Ecologies*, trans. by Ian Pindar and Paul Sutton. New Brunswick, NJ: Athlone Press.

Gudynas, Eduardo. 2021. *Extractivisms: Politics, Economy and Ecology*. Rugby: Fernwood.

Harney, Stefano and Fred Moten. 2021. *All Incomplete*. Wivenhoe: Minor Composition.

Harris, I. Cheryl. 1993, June. "Whiteness as Property," *Harvard Law Review*: 1707–91.

Hogan, Mél, and Asta Vonderau, eds. 2019. "The Nature of Data Centers," Special Issue. *Culture Machine* 18. https://culturemachine.net/vol-18-the-nature-of-data-centers

Hornborg, Alf. 2015. "The Political Ecology of the Technocene: Uncovering Ecologically Unequal Exchange in the World-System," in *The Anthropocene and the Global Environmental Crisis*, edited by Clive Hamilton, François Gemenne, and Christophe Bonneuil, 57–69. London; New York: Routledge.

Hu, Tung-Hui. 2016. *A Prehistory of the Cloud*. Cambridge: MIT Press.

Huhtamo, Erkki, and Jussi Parikka, eds. 2011. *Media Archaeology: Approaches, Applications, and Implications*. Berkeley: University of California Press.

Iheka, Cajetan. 2021. *African Ecomedia: Network Forms, Planetary Politics*. Durham, NC: Duke University Press.

Iheka, Cajetan. 2022. *Teaching Postcolonial Environmental Literature and Media*. New York: Modern Language Association.

Ingram, David. 2010. *The Jukebox in the Garden: Ecocriticism and American Popular Music*. Amsterdam: Rodopi.

Iqani, Mehita. 2020. *Garbage in Popular Culture: Consumption and the Aesthetics of Waste*. Albany, NY: SUNY Press.

Ivakhiv, Adrian. 2013. *Ecologies of the Moving Image: Cinema, Affect, Nature*. Kitchener-Waterloo: Wilfrid Laurier University Press.

Ivakhiv, Adrian. 2018. *Shadowing the Anthropocene: Eco-Realism for Turbulent Times*. Santa Barbara, CA: Punctum Books.

Judy, R. A. 2020. *Sentient Flesh: Thinking in Disorder, Poiēsis in Black*. Black Outdoors: Innovations in the Poetics of Study. Durham, NC: Duke University Press.

Jue, Melody. 2020. *Wild Blue Media: Thinking Through Seawater*. Elements. Durham, NC: Duke University Press.
Jue, Melody, and Rafico Ruiz. eds. 2021. *Saturation: An Elemental Politics*. Durham, NC: Duke University Press.
Kääpä, P. 2018. *Environmental Management of the Media: Industry, Policy Practice*. New York: Routledge.
Kääpä, P. and H. Vaughan. 2022. "From Content to Context (and Back Again): New Industrial Strategies for Environmental Sustainability in the Media," in *Cinema and the Public Good*, edited by Hjort, Mette and Ted Nannicelli, 308–26. Chichester: Wiley-Blackwell.
Kääpä P. and H. Vaughan. ed. 2022. *Film and Television in the Age of the Climate Emergency*. Basingstoke: Palgrave MacMillan.
Käll, Jannice. 2022. *Posthuman Property and Law: Commodification and Control through Information, Smart Spaces and Artificial Intelligence*. New York: Routledge.
Keenan, Sarah. 2019. "From Historical Chains to Derivative Futures: Title Registries as Time Machines," *Social and Cultural Geography* 20 (3), 283–303. ISSN 1464-9365.
Kellner, Douglas, and Jeff Share. 2019. *The Critical Media Literacy Guide: Engaging Media and Transforming Education*. Leiden; Boston, MA: Brill Sense.
Kidd, Dorothy. 2020. "Mobilizing with Video in the Extractive Zone," in *InsUrgent Media from the Front: A Media Activism Reader*, edited by Chris Robé and Stephen Charbonneau, 151. Indiana University Press.
Knowles, Kim. 2020. *Experimental Film and Photochemical Practices*. New York: Palgrave Macmillan.
LaDuke, W. 2017b. *The Winona LaDuke Chronicles: Stories from the Front Lines in the Battle for Environmental Justice*. Nova Scotia: Fernwood Publishing.
Lay, Samantha. 2002. *British Social Realism: From Documentary to Brit Grit*. London; New York: Wallflower, 2002.
Le Masurier, Megan, ed. 2019. *Slow Journalism*. Journalism Studies: Theory and Practice. London; New York: Routledge, Taylor & Francis Group.
Lee, Robert and Tristan Ahtone. 2020. "Land-Grab Universities," *High Country News*, March 30, 2020. https://www.hcn.org/issues/52.4/indigenous-affairs-education-land-grab-universities
Lekakis, Eleftheria J. 2022. *Consumer Activism*. London: Routledge.
Lennon, Myles. 2017. "Decolonizing Energy: Black Lives Matter and Technoscientific Expertise amid Solar Transitions," *Energy Research & Social Science* 30: 18–27.
Lippit, Akira. 2005. *Atomic Light (Shadow Optics)*. Minneapolis: University of Minnesota Press.
López, Antonio. 2021. *Ecomedia Literacy: Integrating Ecology into Media Education*. London; New York: Routledge.
MacDonald, Scott. 2004. "Toward an Eco-Cinema," *Interdisciplinary Studies in Literature and Environment* 11 (2): 107–32.
MacKenzie, Scott and Janine Marchessault. eds. 2019. *Process Cinema. Handmade Film in the Digital Age*. Montreal: McGill-Queen's University Press.
Mattern, Shannon Christine. 2017. *Code + Clay... Data + Dirt: Five Thousand Years of Urban Media*. Minneapolis; London: University of Minnesota Press.
Mattern, Shannon Christine. 2018. "Scaffolding, Hard and Soft: Media Infrastructures as Critical and Generative Structures," in *The Routledge Companion to Media Studies and Digital Humanities*, edited by Jentery Sayers, 318–26. New York; London: Routledge.
Mattern, Shannon Christine. 2019. "Networked Dream Worlds: Is 5g Solving Real, Pressing Problems or Merely Creating New Ones?" *Real Life Magazine*, July 8. https://reallifemag.com/networked-dream-worlds/
Maxwell, Richard. Ed. 2016. *The Routledge Companion to Labor and Media*. New York: Routledge.
Maxwell, Richard and Toby Miller. 2012. *Greening the Media*. New York: Oxford University Press.
Maxwell, Richard, and Toby Miller. 2020. *How Green Is Your Smartphone?* Cambridge; Medford, MA: Polity.
Maxwell, R., Raundalen, J., and Vestberg, N. L. eds. 2015. *Media and the Ecological Crisis*. London; New York: Routledge.
Meeker, Joseph. 1974. *The Comedy of Survival: Studies in Literary Ecology*. New York: Scribner.
Milstein, T. 2020. "Ecocultural Identity Boundary Patrol and Transgression," in *Routledge Handbook of Ecocultural Identity*, editor by T. Milstein and J. Castro-Sotomayor, 26–52. London; New York: Routledge. https://doi.org/10.4324/9781351068840-2
Milstein, T., and J. Castro-Sotomayor. eds. 2020. *Routledge Handbook of Ecocultural Identity*. London: Routledge. https://doi.org/10.4324/9781351068840

Mocatta, G. 2020. "When Water Is Energy: Tracing Mediatized Discourse in Chile's Mega-Hydro Debate," in *Water, Rhetoric, and Social Justice: A Critical Confluence*, editor by C. Schmitt, C. Thomas, and T. Castor, 43–62. Lanham, MD: Lexington Books.

Moradewun, Adejunmobi. 2016. "African Media Studies and Marginality at the Center," *Black Camera* 7 (2): 125–39.

Mudimbe, V. Y. 1988. *The Invention of Africa: Gnosis, Philosophy, and the Order of Knowledge*. African Systems of Thought. Bloomington: Indiana University Press.

Mukherjee, Rahul. 2020. *Radiant Infrastructures: Media, Environment, and Cultures of Uncertainty*. Durham, NC: Duke University Press.

Mullaney, Thomas S. et al. 2021. *Your Computer Is on Fire!* Cambridge: MIT Press.

Murphy, Patrick D. 2017. *The Media Commons: Globalization and Environmental Discourses*. Champaign: University of Illinois Press.

Murphy, Patrick D., and José Castro-Sotomayor. 2021. "From Limits to Ecocentric Rights and Responsibility," *Communication Theory* 31 (4): 978–1001. https://doi.org/10.1093/ct/qtaa026

Murray, Robin L. and Joseph K. Heumann. 2016. *Monstrous Nature: Environment and Horror on the Big Screen*. Lincoln: University of Nebraska Press.

Nost, Eric, and Jenny Elaine Goldstein. 2022. "A Political Ecology of Data," *Environment and Planning E: Nature and Space* 5 (1): 3–17.

Nyamnjoh, Francis B. 2011. "De-Westernizing Media Theory to Make Room for African Experience," in *Popular Media, Democracy and Development in Africa*, edited by Herman Wasserman, 19–31. London: Routledge.

Ostrom, Elinor. 2010. "Beyond Markets and States," *American Economic Review* 100: 641–72.

Otieno, Christine, Hans Spada, Katharina Liebler, Thomas Ludemann, Ulrich Deil, and Alexander Renkl. 2014. "Informing about Climate Change and Invasive Species: How the Presentation of Information Affects Perception of Risk, Emotions, and Learning," *Environmental Education Research* 20 (5): 612–38. https://doi.org/10.1080/13504622.2013.833589

Parham, John. 2016. *Green Media and Popular Culture: An Introduction*. London: Palgrave Macmillan.

Parikka, Jussi. 2015. *A Geology of Media*. Minneapolis: University of Minnesota Press.

Parks, Lisa. 2015. "Stuff You Can Kick: Toward a Theory of Media Infrastructures," in *Between Humanities and the Digital*, edited by Patrik Svensson and David Theo Goldberg, 355–73. Cambridge: MIT Press.

Parks, Lisa, and Nicole Starosielski, eds. 2015. *Signal Traffic: Critical Studies of Media Infrastructures*. Urbana: University of Illinois Press.

Pasek, Anne. 2019. "Managing Carbon and Data Flows: Fungible Forms of Mediation in the Cloud," *Culture Machine* 18 (April). http://culturemachine.net/vol-18-the-nature-of-data-centers/managing-carbon/

Pasek, Anne, Cindy Kaiying Lin, Zane Griffin Talley Cooper, and Jordan B. Kinder. 2023. *Digital Energetics*. Minneapolis: University of Minnesota Press.

Pedelty, Mark. 2011. *Ecomusicology: Rock, Folk and the Environment*. Philadelphia, PA: Temple University Press.

Peters, John Durham. 2015. *The Marvelous Clouds: Toward a Philosophy of Elemental Media*. Chicago, IL: University of Chicago Press.

Plantinga, Carl. 2009. *Moving Viewers: American Film and the Spectator Experience*. Berkeley: University of California Press.

Plath, Tara. 2020. "From Threat to Promise: Mapping Disappearance and the Production of Deterrence in the Sonora-Arizona Borderlands," *antiAtlas Journal* #4: 1–29.

Pomerance, M. 2008. *The Horse Who Drank the Sky: Film Experience Beyond Narrative and Theory*. New Brunswick, NJ: Rutgers University Press.

Powys White, K. 2018. "White Allies, Let's Be Honest About Decolonization," *Yes!* Available: https://www.yesmagazine.org/issue/decolonize/2018/04/03/white-allies-lets-be-honest-about-decolonization/. Accessed 30 Sept 2022.

Rauch, Jennifer. 2014. "Constructive Rituals of Demediatization: Spiritual, Corporeal and Mixed Metaphors in Popular Discourse about Unplugging," *Explorations in Media Ecology* 13 (3): 237–52. https://doi.org/10.1386/eme.13.3-4.237_1

Rauch, Jennifer. 2018. *Slow Media: Toward a Sustainable Future*. Book, Whole. Oxford: Oxford University Press.

Robbins, Paul. 2020. *Political Ecology: A Critical Introduction*. Third Edition. Oxford: John Wiley & Sons.

Further Reading

Rose-Redwood, Reuben, Natchee Blu Barnd, Annita Hetoevėhotohke'e Lucchesi, Sharon Dias, and Wil Patrick. 2020. "Decolonizing the Map: Recentering Indigenous Mappings," *Cartographica: The International Journal for Geographic Information and Geovisualization* 55 (3): 151–62. https://doi.org/10.3138/cart.53.3.intro

Rust, Stephen, Salma Monani, and Seán Cubitt. eds. 2022. *Ecocinema Theory and Practice 2*. New York: Routledge.

Smith, Jacob. 2015. *Eco- Sonic Media*. Berkeley: University of California Press.

Smith, Linda Tuhiwai, Eve Tuck, and K. Wayne Yang. 2019. *Indigenous and Decolonizing Studies in Education: Mapping the Long View*. Indigenous and Decolonizing Studies in Education. New York: Routledge Press.

Soper, Kate. 1995. *What Is Nature? Culture, Politics and the Non-Human*. Oxford: Blackwell.

Starosielski, Nicole. 2015. *The Undersea Network*. SST, Sign, Storage, Transmission. Durham, NC: Duke University Press.

Starosielski, Nicole. 2021. "Beyond Sun: Embedded Solarities and Agricultural Practice," *The South Atlantic Quarterly* 120 (1): 13–24.

Starosielski, Nicole. 2021. *Media Hot & Cold*. Durham, NC: Duke University Press.

Starosielski, Nicole and Janet Walker, eds. 2016. *Sustainable Media: Critical Approaches to Media and Environment*. New York; London: Routledge.

Sze, Julie. 2021. "Climate Justice, Satire, and Hothouse Earth," in *The Routledge Companion to Contemporary Art, Visual Culture, and Climate Change*, edited by T. J. Demos, Emily Eliza Scott, and Subhankar Banerjee, 173–81. New York: Routledge.

Taffel, Sy. 2019. *Digital Media Ecologies: Entanglements of Content, Code and Hardware*. New York; London: Bloomsbury.

Takach, Geo. 2022. "Eco-Comedy," *Environmental Humanities* 14 (2): 371–74.

Thouvenel, Eric and Carole Constant. 2014. *Fabrique du cinéma expérimental*. Paris: Paris Experimental.

Tidwell, Christy and Carter Soles. eds. 2021. *Fear and Nature: Ecohorror Studies in the Anthropocene*. University Park: The Pennsylvania State University Press.

Towns, Armond R. 2022. *On Black Media Philosophy*. Oakland: University of California Press.

Vaughan, H. 2019. *Hollywood's Dirtiest Secret: The Hidden Environmental Costs of the Movies*. New York: Columbia University Press.

Waldmüeller, Johannes. 2021. "The Eco-Territorial Turn in Latin America: A Conversation with Maristella Svampa," Accessed at http://www.alternautas.net/blog/2021/3/31/the-eco-territorial-turn-in-latin-america-a-conversation-with-maristella-svampa

Walker, Janet. 2018. "Media Mapping and Oil Extraction: A Louisiana Story," *NECSUS* 7 (2) (Autumn): 229–251.

Watkins G. 1999. "Seeing and Being Seen: Distinctively Filmic and Religious Elements in Film," *Journal of Religion and Film* 3 (2): October Article 5.

Weik von Mossner, Alexa, ed. 2014. *Moving Environments: Affect, Emotion, Ecology, and Film*. Waterloo: Wilfrid Laurier UP (II).

Weik von Mossner, Alexa. 2017. *Affective Ecologies: Empathy, Emotion, and Environmental Narrative*. Columbus: Ohio State UP.

Young, Rob. 2011. *Electric Eden: Unearthing Britain's Visionary Music*. London: Faber and Faber.

Yusoff, Kathryn. 2018. *A Billion Black Anthropocenes or None*. Minneapolis: Minnesota University Press.

Zacks, Jeffrey M. 2015. *Flicker: Your Brain on Movies*. Oxford: Oxford UP.

INDEX

Note: *Italic* page numbers refer to figures and page numbers followed by "n" denote endnotes.

Abbott, M.C. 301
Abdul-Kareen, Waqia 94
Aboriginal and Torres Strait Islander peoples 212–213
Abraham, Benjamin 6, 146–147
Abram, David 44–45, 234
Accenture 122
Acequia Madre, Albuquerque, New Mexico (Wittick) 73, *74*
Acosta, Alberto 247
activism: anti-imperial 75; consumer 165; Dakota Access Pipeline (DAPL) 8, 199–200; ecomedial 300; environmental 9, 55; media 200, 245, 247–249
Adamson, Natalie 155
ADM 222
Adtech 19
Aebischer, Bernard 124
Affective Ecologies: Empathy, Emotion, and Environmental Narrative (Weik von Mossner) 11
affect: affective engagement 37, 39; affective turn 1, 3–4, 29; climate anxiety 320–322; data centers 125; digital media ecologies 65; eco-affects 10–12; ecocritical affect theory 328–329; ecomedia literacy 104; ecomentia of 297–303; eco-optimism 342–343; embodied experience 305–310; monster 331–333, *332*; new materialism and film 44; phenomenological lifeworld 339–343; relational ecology 155, 157; satire 319–325; in social realism 312–317; *see also* attention

Africa: centering in ecomedia studies 67–72; e-waste collection and recycling 163–164; mining in 221
African Ecomedia: Network Forms, Planetary Media (Iheka) 4
African Ecomedia: Network Forms, Planetary Politics (Iheka) 5, 9, 67–68, 70, 72
agential realism 37, 43, 48
The Age of Stupid (Armstrong) 317
agricultural technologies 137
Ahnelt, Josephine 275
Akeley, Carl 47
Alaimo, Stacy 43, 44, 45, 330
Alderson International Mining and Manufacturing (AIMM) 288
algorithms 19, 31, 64, 101, 103, 163, 173; bias 31n2; codes 31n2; colonial 213, 215; knowledge 31n2; oppressive forces of 215; *see also* ChatGPT
Alibaba 172
All Incomplete (Moten and Harney) 301
Almendra, Vilma 246
Alphabet 19
Alvitre, Weshoyot 257
Amazon 19, 64, 103, 115, 172, 176; Alexa 172
Ambient Media: Japanese Atmospheres of Self (Roquet) 12
AMC: *The Walking Dead* 196
American Civil War 254
American War of Independence 163
Anderson, Alison 209
Anderson, Benedict 74
Android operating systems 62, 64

Index

Angerer, Marie-Luise 12
Animal Planet: *Whale Wars* 196
Ankuash, Domingo 248
Anthropocene 56, 61, 79, 286, 298, 317; racist 94; White 5
anthropocosmism 37, 41n2
anti-Western hegemony 289–290
Apex Legends tournament 150
apolitical ecologies 61–62; of digital media 59–65
Apple 19, 62, 120, 172, 223
Application-Specific Integrated Circuit (ASIC) 147
ArcGIS StoryMap 252
Are we Changing Planet Earth? 55
Arivaca Lake Reservoir 90, *90*
Arlit, Deuxième Paris 140–141
Armand, Octavio 153
Armstrong, Franny 317
Arnold, David 284n1
art 12, 47, 323–325; collapse-informatics 125; digital 187; in emergent eco-territorial media cultures 246–247; environmentalist 319; history 155; Indigenous materialist 48; music 281; *see also* Core Dump project; *Mojo: Da Floods*; photography
artificial intelligence (AI) 8, 20, 31n2, 171, 173–175; and climate emergency 175–176; and communication scholarship 175–176; as communication technologies 174–175; environmental costs of 174–175; environmental toll of 172–173; fixing the world, fixing the environment 173–174; inequality and exploitation 174–175; potentials of 173–174; *see also* ChatGPT
Asia: Asian Games 150; and digital waste 224; mining in 221
Aspire Zone Foundation 150
Association for the Study of Literature and Environment (ASLE) 2, 67
The Atlantic 55
atmospheric media 26
Atomic Garden 275
Attenborough, Sir David 51–56; blue ecomateriality 53–54; and blue mediascape 53–54
attention: collapsonaut 302–303; ecology of 11, 29; economy 101; extractivist 11; restorative 253; Slow Media 338
Australia: bluestriped blenny 51; forest fires in 283; per capita e-waste generation rates in 64; settler-colonial 212; *see also* Indigenous Australians
Avatar: The Way of Water 56, 180

Bacigalupi, Paolo 150
Baidu 172
Barad, Karen 43, 44, 46, 48
Barandiarán, Javiera 137

Barclay, Bridgitte 47
Barker, A. J. 213
Barker, Jennifer 307
Barnard, Clio 11, 312–317
Barney, Darin 141
Bateson, Gregory 37
Bayman, Louis 316
BBC 181, 183; and BAFTA 180; *The Blue Planet* 44; *Zoo Quest* 54
The Beach 182
Beach Boys 278
Bean, Anna 9, 203–209
Bean, David Z. 204
Bear, Leroy Little 43
Beck, U. 237
Becoming Animal (Davie and Mettler) 44–45
Belkhir, Lotfi 172
Belmont, Cynthia 288
Benítez, Verenice 248
Benjamin, Ruha 31n2, 212
Bezos, Jeff 64
Bhandar, Brenna 188, 190
Biden, Joe 222
A Billion Black Anthropocenes or None (Yusoff) 92
Birkinbine, Benjamin J. 197
The Birth of Energy (Daggett) 146
Blackhawk, Ned 82n3
Black Lives Matter movement 67, 302
Black media philosophy 25–26, 261–269
Black media theory 3, 4
Black Panther: Wankanda Forever 56
Bladow, Kyle 328
Bleak House (Dickens) 313
Block, Ursula 158n2
blockchain: energy-intensive 192; proof-of-work (POW) blockchain systems 147; registries 187–192; technologies 8, 187, 191
blue media ecologies 51–56; Attenborough on 53–54; blue ecomateriality 53–54; feeling blue 55–56; metaphors 52–53; outlook 56
The Blue Planet 44, 53, 55
Blue Planet II 51, 53, 55
Blum, Hester 75, 79
body/embodiment 3, 11, 29, 44, 147, 305–310
Bonnetta, Joshua 89, *89, 90*, 92, *93*, 94, 95n5, 95n7
Bookchin, Murray 346
border 73–81, 84–94
Border As Method (Neilson and Mezzadra) 84
Borunda, Stephen 94
Bousé, David 346
Boyes, Georgina 279
Boyle, James 188, 190
Bozak, Nadia 2, 6, 22, 346
Bradfield, Abraham 214
Brakhage, Stan 275

Bratton, Benjamin 27, 263, 267–268, 298
Breaking Boundaries 56
Brereton, Pat 11
Brevini, Benedetta 8, 171–173
Browne, Simone 137
Bruno, Giuliana 86
Brunton, Finn 145
Buckingham, David 100
Buddhist hermeneutics 290–292
Bulfin, Ailise 327
Burton, James 36
Büscher, Bram 30–31
Butler, Judith 302

Calarco, Matthew 41n2
Callison, Candis 253
Cameron, Courchene 210
capitalism: carbon 171–176; consumer-based 101, 165; data-driven 191; digital 64–65; extractive 244; global 323; industrial 189; neoliberal 281; print 74; racial 78; racist colonial-capitalism 161; supply chain 59; surveillance 19, 31, 101
Capitalocene 61–62, 299, 300
carbon capitalism 171–176
Carbon Capitalism and Communication: Confronting Climate Crisis (Brevini and Murdock) 8, 171–172
carbon footprints 131
Carlson, B. 213
Carolan, Michael 24
Carr, John 234, 235, 238
Carroll, Noël 329
Cartographic Cinema (Conley) 86
Casey, Edward S. 95n12
Castro-Sotomayor, José 4, 9
catharsis: in *Don't Look Up* 322–323; social 237
Cavell, Stanley 52
Chang, Alenda Y. 6, 7, 45
Chang, Chia-ju 10, 293n1
Chapman, Tracy 278
ChatGPT 19, 21, 31, 31n2
The Che Brother 286, 289, 290–292
Children of the Jaguar 248
Chile: copper and rare metals 120; transforming identity in 237–238
Chinese Environmental Humanities (Chang) 9
Chiu, Samson 290
Cho, Francisca 292
Chow, Stephen 289–290
cinema *see* film
Cinematic Footprint (Bozak) 2
Cine-Regio 182, 185
Citton, Yves 11, 29

Clark, Kate 47
Clark, Timothy 312
climate: anxiety 320–322; as game infrastructure 149–150
climate change 61, 173–174, 281, 283, 312, 315, 317; anthropogenic 149; catastrophic 65; and destruction 299–300; and digital technology 130; and geoengineering 146
Climate Change: The Facts 55
climate crisis: and communication scholarship 175–176; and pandemic 171–172; in Washington State 205–206
Climate Realism 312
cloud computing 171, 174
coal-burning power plant 234–235
code (computer) 28, 164
cognition and film 305–306
Cohen, Jeffrey Jerome 44, 330
collapsology 297; collapse informatics 124–126
collapsonaut attention 302–303
colonialism 12, 23, 61, 75, 154, 160, 188–189; data colonialism 75; and racism 163; settler 78, 200, 212; Western 262; *see also* digital colonial power; neo-colonial
The Comedy of Survival: Literary Ecology and a Play Ethic (Meeker) 319
common pool resources (CPRs) 8, 194–195, 197–201; case examples 197–200; commons in media 196–197, 200–201; communication scholarship 196–197; Dakota Oil Access Pipeline (DAPL) 199–200; Grand Ethiopian Renaissance Dam (GERD) project 198–199; and media 200–201; Standing Rock Sioux Tribe 199–200
"the commons" 20, 188, 195–196, 348; global media commons 196–197; ICT contribution to 126; in media and communication scholarship 194–201; *see also* communications commons
communication commons 197; and CPRs 200–201; and media 200–201
computer 112, 113; gaming 145, 147–148, 150; human-computer interaction 119; networks 20
Conley, Tom 86
consumerism 8, 105; global 288; hyper 175–176; voracious 342
Consumer Protection Act 221
Contagion 286, 287–289
Cooper, Sarah 12, 319, 320–322
Cooper, Zane Griffin Talley 147
Core Dump project 7; 160–165; aesthetic and political issues 164–165; Dakar 163–164; e-waste in global perspective 164–165; Kinshasa 160–162; New York City 162–163; Shenzhen 162

corporate/corporation 8; board reports 10; branding 180; gatekeepers 208; greenwashing 119; personhood 30; superorganisms 62
Correa, Rafael 247
Coryat, Diana 9–10
Costco 54
Couldry, Nick 40, 75, 197
Cousteau, Jacques 44
Covid-19 pandemic 287; mitigation efforts 181; scapegoating the "Other" in 287
Cox, Robert 4
Creative Spirits 214
Creature from the Black Lagoon 331
Crête 274
Cruz, Teddy 88
Cubitt, Seán 2–4, 6, 25, 39, 45–46, 52
curriculum development 100–101

Daggett, Cara New 146–147, 148–149
Dahr, Julia 72
Dakar: disposal 163–164; dumping 163–164; toxicity 163–164
Dakota Oil Access Pipeline (DAPL) 8, 199–200
dark ecology (Morton) 279
Dark River 11, 312–317; metonymy in 313–317; social realism in 313–317; stylistic hybridity in 313–317
da Silva, Denise Ferreira 301
data: centers 112–113; colonialism 75; -driven economy 187–192; warehouses of the Internet 112–113
David Attenborough: A Life on Our Planet 54, 55
The Day After Tomorrow 180, 322
decarbonization fallacies 120
decolonial: anti-Western hegemony 289–290; critique 347; critiques of Western modernity 3; media logic 20; methodologies 10, 252–253; strategy 213; struggles 9; theorists 23; turns 37
decolonization: of the digital 216–217; effective 217
De León, Jason 84, 91, 95n1, 95n7, 95n10
Deleuze, Gilles 24, 305
De Line, Sebastian 43
Deloria, Vine 48
DeLoughrey, Elizabeth 94, 138
dematerialization: ICT 120–121
Democracy Now! 200
Democratic Republic of Congo (DRC) 63, 120, 160, 199, 221
Destiny, Manifest 5
Devine, Kyle 45–46, 154
Dibiasky, Kate 323
DiCaprio, Leonardo 322
Dickens, Charles 313
Didur, Jill 94
DiFranco, Ani 10, 278, 280–283, 284n1

digital colonial power 212–218; colonial power, perpetuating 213–216; new digital worlds 216–217; and problematic digital worlds 213–216; self-determination of Indigenous Australians 216–217; and sovereignty 216–217
Digital Games After Climate Change (Abraham) 146
digital media: apolitical and metaphorical ecologies 61–62; environments and ecologies 60–61; political and apolitical ecologies of 59–65; political ecologies 62–65; technologies 130
Digital Media Ecologies: Entanglements of Content, Code and Hardware (Taffel) 5
digital pollution: material processes of 130–132
digital rights management (DRM) 187
Digital Rubbish (Gabrys) 6, 130
digital technologies *see* digital media; digital worlds; information and communication technologies (ICTs)
digital worlds: dismantling problematic 213–216; Indigenous Australian sovereignty 212–218; perpetuate colonial power 213–216; self-determination in 212–218
Dion, Mark 47
disaggregated footprints 111–117
discourse: academic 53; anthropocentric 234; cultural 9; Earth 196–197; environmental 3, 194; global media 165; heteronormative 23; mediatized 237; neocolonial 105; Promethean 196; "the Limits discourse" 195; universalized Anthropocene 9
displacement of saliences 298–300
Dobrin, Sidney 52
Doctor, Daisy 8
documentary: natural-history 55; South African 231; *see also* Animal Planet: Whale Wars; Arlit, Deuxième Paris; Becoming Animal; The Blue Planet; Blue Planet II; Breaking Boundaries; Children of the Jaguar; Climate Change: The Facts; David Attenborough: A Life on Our Planet; El Mar La Mar; Electronic Waste in Ghana; Life in Colour; Life on Earth; My Octopus Teacher; Our Planet: Behind the Scenes; Racing Extinction; Seaspiracy; Seven Worlds; ToxiCity; The Truth About Climate Change
Dodd-Frank Wall Street Reform 221
Don't Look Up 12, 319–320, 322–323, 325
Dorado, Gabriel 236
Dreisbach, Jeconiah Louis 9
Dryzek, John 195–196
Duarte, M. E. 217
Du Bois, W. E. B. 269

"Earth Day" 180
East India Companies 154, 157
eco-affects 10–12; *see also* affect
ecocinema: d-ecocinema 259n2; studies 2, 105
Ecocinema Theory and Practice 346
ecocritical affect theory 328–329
ecocriticism 1–2; ecocritical affect theory 328–329; empirical 30; and environmental communication 3; Euro-American orientation of 2; Indigenous 3; material 43; postcolonial 2–3
ecocultural identity 232; ecocultural identity revolution 238–239; environmental conflict 233–234; identity revolution 238–239; media and 231–239; mediacy and immediacy 233–234; mediated ecocultural identities 234–238; mediatized identities 233–234; "new public sphere" 233–234; overview 232
ecocultures 3, 4, 9–10, 29
ecofeminism 23, 46, 105, 290–292; feminist ecology 36
ecojustice (environmental justice) 6, 30, 99, 105; *see also* decolonization
ecolinguistics 3, 104
ecological esthetics 272
ecological futurabilities of experimental film labs 271–276
ecological media 134–135
ecological triad 38–40; three ecologies 2, 5, 36–38, 298, 301
Ecologies of Affect: Intensive Milieus and Contingent Encounters (Angerer) 12
Ecologies of the Moving Image: Cinema, Affect, Nature (Ivakhiv) 328
ecology 2, 24, 61; blue media 51–56; of creation and production 272; of distribution and reception 272; and environments 5, 60–61; environment *vs.* 35–36; and media 1; of mediation 39; multiple 36–38
ecomaterial thinking 154–156
EcoMedia (Cubitt) 2, 346
ecomedial counter-activism: sovereign individuals 300–302; undercommon assemblies 300–302
ecomedia literacy: curriculum development 100–101; ecomediasphere 101–103, *102*; ecomedia studies 100–101; iceberg model of systems thinking 103–105
Ecomedia Literacy: Integrating Ecology into Media Education (López) 100
ecomediality 40–41; as ontology 35–41
ecomediasphere 101–103, *102*
ecomentia: affects and saliences 298–300; collapsonaut attention 302–303; ecomedial counter-activism 300–302; mapping the mediarchy 298; performative assembly 297–303; televised catastrophe 297–303
An Ecomodernist Manifesto 173–174
eco-optimism 342–343
ecopolitical satire in Global North 319–325
Eco-Sonic Media (Smith) 12
ecosystems 20, 24, 36, 62
eco-territorial media cultures: ecomedia field, relevance to 244–245; emergent 246–247; historical and conceptual notes 245–246; media activism in Ecuador 247–249; social movements in Ecuador 247–249
eco-territorial media practices 244–250
Ecuador 247; media activism in 247–249; social movements in 247–249
edge caching 115–116
educational ecomedia: future considerations for 333–334; genre affect in 333–334
Eichberger, Ryan 217
EirGrid 120
Eisner, Elliot 253
Electric Eden (Young) 280
electronic environmentalism 130, 134–135; digital energy 132–134; digital pollution 130–132; ecological crises, monitoring/making 132–134; ecological media 134–135; media ecologies 134–135
Electronic Waste in Ghana 224
elemental media 24, 26, 28, 52, 68, 92–94
El Mar La Mar 84–94, *87*, 87–89, *89, 90*, 92, *93, 94*, 95n2, 95n11; ambulatory 91–92; film as map 88–90; navigating the desert 91–92; and "unwalling" borderzone 86–92
Elmeligi, Ahmed 172
El retumbar de las voces/The roar of our voices 249
emancipatory catastrophism 237–238
embodied experience, mediation of 305–310
embodiment 11, 29, 44, 147, 305, 309; technological 3
Emejulu, Akwugo 216
emissions/exposures 139–140
empire, naturalizing 76–79
empirical ecocriticism 30
enclosure 20, 189–190, 195, 347
energy: carbon-free 55; consumption, and pandemic 171–172; digital 132–134; ecological crises and digital energy 132–134; fossil fuel 12; green 26; grids 112; hydrocarbon 30; infrastructures 6
Energy Information Administration (EIA) 120
Energy Transfer Partners (ETP) 199
engineering: cultural 154; geo-engineering 62, 146; ICT 119, 124
engines of play 147–149
Enhoff, Beth 287–288
Enhoff, Mitch 287

environment 1, 3, 24, 27; and ecologies 60–61; and ecology 5, 60; *vs.* ecology 35–36
Environment, Media, and Popular Culture in Southeast Asia (Telles, Ryan, and Dreisbach) 9
environmental humanities 2–3, 23, 72, 94, 104, 292, 312
Environmental Management of the Media (Kääpä) 8
Environmental Media Association 180
Environmental Media Lab 28
environmental media management: environmental media production management 180–181; responsibility deficit in media content 183–184; responsibility deficit in media production 181–183
environmental media production management 180–181
Environmental Systems Research Institute (ESRI) 255
Enzensberger, Hans Magnus 346
Ericsson 142
Ernst, Wolfgang 155
Esbjorn-Hargens, Sean 41n1
Estok, Simon 11
EU Green New Deal 185
e-waste 20, 59, 64, 113, 130, 171, 175; global aesthetics 160–165; global generation of 223–225; politics of 160–165
experimental film labs: brewing images in ruins of industry 273–274; ecological futurabilities of 271–276; homemade emulsions, crafting 275; processing films 274–275
externalization 20, 31, 104
Extinction Rebellion 116, *117*
extractivism 30, 154, 201, 244, 248; audiovisual resistance to 250; capitalist 300; colonial practices of 7; postcolonial practices of 7
extractivist industry 209
ExxonMobil 175

Facebook/Meta 19, 62, 64, 120, 172, 185, 200
Fanon, Frantz 266
Farming by Irrigation in New Mexico 77
Fay, Jennifer 75, 79
feminist ecology *see* ecofeminism
feminist new materialists 43
feminist standpoint theory 103
Fenton, Will 257
Ferguson, Bob 204
fiber-optic cables 114
FIFA World Cup 149
"The 15 Most Eco-Friendly Rockers" (Coscarelli) 278
film: and cognition 305–306; and emotion 305–306; experimental film labs 271–276; and nature of human perception 305–306; new materialism on 44–45; *see also The Age of Stupid*; *Avatar: The Way of Water*; *The Beach*; *Black Panther: Wankanda*; *The Che Brother*; *Contagion*; *Creature from the Black Lagoon*; *Crête*; *Dark River*; *The Day After Tomorrow*; *Don't Look Up*; *The Fly*; *The Garden of Earthly Delights*; *Golden Chicken II*; *Hong Kong: A Winner*; *In the Earth*; *Helena from Sarayaku*; *Kawsak Sacha*; *L'amitié, ce n'est pas toujours du ski de fond*; *La Trilogie Carnassière*; *Mad Max: Fury Road*; *Syriana*; *Thank You for the Rain*; *The Thing*; *Titanic*; *Wild*
Film-Makers' Cooperative 273
Filmwerkplaatz 275, 276n4
finance/banking 30, 63, 160, 181–183, 347
Finite Media (Cubitt) 6
The Fly 45
Flynn, Elizabeth 214–215
folk: as green cultural production 278–284; and rock 279–280
Food and Wine Magazine 200
Forman, Fonna 88
Fornoff, Carolyn 9
fossil fuel 5–6, 12, 26, 59, 61, 93, 103–104, 112–114, 123–124, 141, 172, 203–204, 206, 210
Fourth Industrial Revolution 173
FoxConn 103, 222, 223; *see also* Hon Hai
Fox & Friends 321
Frammartino, Michelangelo 272
Frasher, Burton 79
Frazer Ryan 213
Fredericks, Bronwyn 213, 214, 215
Frege, Gottlob 345
Freire, Paolo 101
French, Jennifer 9
French Bibliothèque Nationale 156
Frith, Simon 282
Fuller, Matthew 24, 276n1
functional magnetic resonance imaging (fMRI) research 306

Gabrys, Jennifer 4, 6, 7, 24, 27, 29, 30, 130, 154
Gaia Foundation 45
Gallese, Vittorio 306
game infrastructure, climate as 149–150
Garcia, Edgar 75
Gärdebo, Johan 27
The Garden of Earthly Delights 275
Garrard, Greg 99
Garritano, Carmela 140
gender 99, 154, 157, 247–249, 281, 287, 330; *see also* ecofeminism
genre 11–12, 104, 248–249, 317; horror 328–329; in music 279–281, 283–284; monster movies

329–331; *see also* global pandemic films; satire; social realism
genre affect: in educational ecomedia 333–334; future considerations for 333–334
Geographic Information Systems (GIS) tools 255
geography: creative 86, 88–89; cultural 85; human 85; inhuman 85, 92–94
Gettysburg 256
Gettysburg National Military Park *254*
Ghosh, Amitav 317
The Ghost River: Rise and Fall of Conestoga (Lee Francis IV) 257
Ghost Stories for Darwin (Subramaniam) 330
Gibson, James J. 11, 312
Gilsoul, Sarah 10
Girard, René 286
Global Apollo Program 55
Global e-Sustainability Initiative (GeSI) 122
Global E-Waste Monitor 164
global greenhouse gas (GHG) emissions 116, 120, 122
globalization 1; capitalist 180; neoliberal 196
Global North 1, 12, 54, 56, 163, 244, 250, 264, 319; catharsis in *Don't Look Up* 322–323; ecopolitical satire in 319–325; Sarah Cooper and climate anxiety 320–322
global pandemic films: *The Che Brother* 290–292; *Contagion* 287–289; *Hong Kong: A Winner* 289–290; women in 287–292
Global South 1, 7, 9, 10, 12, 140, 141, 165, 224, 264
Gmail 175
Goeman, Mishuana 256
Golden Chicken II 290
Goldman Sachs 123
Gómez, Laura 81n1, 82n3
Gonzalez, Carmen 85
González, María Buey 301
Google 19, 62, 112, 120, 129, 131, 172, 185, 214, 236, 287; Deepmind 175
Google Maps 234, 239
Gouyon, Jean-Baptiste 55
governance: adaptive 194–197, 200–201; media 8, 179; neoliberal 23
gramophone disc: ecomateriality in action 156–157; ecomaterial thinking 154–156; open horizons 154–156; phonographic surfaces 153–154; poetics/politics of shellac 156–157; relational ecologies of 153–158
Grand Ethiopian Renaissance Dam (GERD) project 8, 198–201
Great Barrier Reef 51
Greenberg, Jonathan 319
green cultural production: folk as 278–284; folk rock as 278–284
Greenfeld, Karl Taro 319

greenhouse gas (GHG) emission 61, 63, 174
Greening the Media (Miller and Maxwell) 6, 9, 52
GreenQloud 185
Green Screen (Ingram) 346
greenwashing 105, 119, 124, 180, 186
Greimas, A. J. 315
Grierson, John 312
Grodal, Torben 313, 317
Gruning, Tom 281
Gualinga, Eriberto 248
The Guardian 55, 196, 323
Guattari, Félix 2, 5, 24, 36–37, 38, 271, 298, 301
Guattarian tri-ecological framework 41n2
Gudynas, Eduardo 244
Guevara, Che 290–291
Gulf War (1991) 22
Guterres, António 287
Gutiérrez, Ramón 81n2

Hadl, Gabriele 99
Hallam, Julia 314, 316
Han, Lisa 52
Handmade Film Institute 275
Hansen, Anders 4
Haraway, Donna 44, 276
Hardin, Garret 195–196
Harley, J.B. 86
Harnessing Artificial Intelligence for the Earth 173
Harney, Stefano 301
Harris, Steven 155
Hartley, Jeremy Kamal 261–269
Hawitt, Rowan Bayliss 279
Hayward, Susan 2
Hayward, Tim 314
Hearne, Joanna 259
Heart of the Well Country 79
heat and light 138–139
heating, ventilation, and air conditioning (HVAC) industry 150n1
Hecht, Gabrielle 139
Heise, Ursula K. 52, 53
Hekman, Susan 43
Helena from Sarayaku 248
Henschel, Jon Henschel 46
Hepp, Andreas 31n3, 40
Herman, David 315
Heumann, Joseph 11
Hilty, L. M. 124
HidroAysén 237
Hirst, Damien 47
History Channel: *Life After People* 196
Hobbes, Thomas 263
Hochman, Jhan 346
Hogan, Patrick Colm 306
Hollywood scapegoats 287–289
Holtmeier, Matt 41n3

Index

Hong Kong: A Winner 286, 289–291
Hon Hai 221
Hörisch, Jochen 92
Hörl, Erich 36
Horn, Eva 22
horror 328–329
Houser, Heather 76, 79
Houssami, Eyad 94
Hu, Tung-Hui 27
Huawei 142
Hugo, Pieter 67, 164
human ecology 35
humanitarian organizations 88
Hutto, Joe 41n2
hypertext transfer protocol 64

IBM 19
iceberg model of systems thinking 103–105
Iheka, Cajetan 4, 5, 9, 22, 26, 28, 30, 67–72, 75, 81, 137, 164
immediacy 233–234; and emancipatory catastrophism 237–238; living 236–237; through mediatized empathy 235–236
Immediation project 12
"imperfect ecomedia" 81
"imperfect media" 81
independent film lab movement 272–273
Indigeneity 76, 81n1, 237
Indigenous: activism 203–210, 199–200; cartographies 252–258; community media 236–237; media 236, 238, 245; ontologies 65n1; sovereignty 212–218
Indigenous Australians: Aboriginal and Torres Strait Islander peoples 212–213; new digital worlds and sovereignty 216–217; self-determination in digital worlds 212–218; self-determination of 216–217; sovereignty in digital worlds 212–218
Indigenous Digital Life (Carlson and Frazer) 213
Indigenous Knowledge Keepers 210
Indigenous Pennsylvania: Past, Present and Future 252, 255, 257–258
Indigenous Pennsylvania StoryMaps project 253, 256
IndigenousX 217
information and communication technologies (ICTs) 1, 101, 174, 176, 223; collapse informatics 124–126; contribution to commons 126; decarbonization fallacies 120; dreams of dematerialization 120–121; environmental impact of 119–126; infrastructure anticipating demand 121; prospects 123–124; rebound effects 122; rebound in global perspective 122–123; self-sustainability and computing 124; *see also* infrastructure

infrastructure 3, 6–7, 19–22, 26–30, 31n1, 39, 52, 54, 62, 64, 71, 74–75, 81, 88, 90, 99–101, 103–105, 111–117, 121, 122–125, 129–134, 146–147, 153–154, 171–173, 175, 180, 182, 184–185, 265, 273–274, 298; climate as game infrastructure 149–150: emissions and exposures 139–140; fossil fuels 200, 206, 209; radiant 137–143
Ingram, David 11, 278, 279, 280, 328, 346
Ingwerson, Moritz 94
inhuman geography 92–94
Innis, Harold 25, 73–74
Instagram 200
Integral Ecology (Esbjorn-Hargens) 41n1
Intel 222
intellectual property (IP) 173, 190; in digitally mediated spheres 190; law 189
intellectual property rights (IPRs) 188
International Energy Agency (IEA) 171
International Environmental Communication Association (IECA) 2
International Kyoto Protocol 174
internet: data centers as warehouses of 112–113; driveways of 113; exchanges 113–114; fiber-optic cables as highways of 114; Internet exchanges as transit hubs of 113–114; protocol 27, 64
Internet exchange points (IXPs) 113–114
Internet Service Providers (ISPs) 115
In the Earth 45
Invasive Species Management Program 331
invasive species outreach 329–331
iOS operating systems 64
Iqani, Mehita 6, 7
Irigaray, Luce 345
irrigation media 79–81
Is AI good for the Planet (Brevini) 171, 173
Isherwell, Peter 322
Ivakhiv, Adrian 2, 4–5, 11, 12, 27, 41n3, 45, 328, 346

Jazz Age modernity 153
Jenkins, Henry 24
Jevons paradox 113, 122
Jim Crow laws 212, 267
Johannesburg Earth Summit 297
Johnson, Samuel 319
Johnston, Trevor 316
Journal of Environmental Media 2, 28
The Journal of Media Literacy 100
Journal of Native American 253
Journal of Sustainability Education 100
Joy, Eileen A. 52, 56
Judy, R. A. 263
Jue, Melody 4, 26–27, 29, 44, 52, 53, 79, 137

Index

Kääpä, Pietari 8
Kahiu, Wanuri 67
Käll, Jannice 8
Kalmus, Peter 323
Kamal, Jeremy 10
Kaplan, E. Ann 11
Kaur, Valarie 283
Kawsak Sacha 248
Keenan, Sarah 190
Keightley, Keir 281
Keogh, Brendan 147, 148
Keola, Anysay 290
Kerridge, Richard 279–280
Keywords for Environmental Studies 21
Kichwa Sarayaku 248
Kidd, Dorothy 197, 200
Kinder, Jordan 94
Kinshasa 160–162
Kittler, Friedrich A. 25, 26, 298
Kiu-wai-Chu 67–68, 70–71
Knoetze, Francis 160, *161*
Kofe, Simon 347–348
Kong, Yani 125
Korff, Jens 214
Kunstman, Adi 1

Labayen, Miguel Fernández 88
labor 59, 62–63, 154, 220–225; child 46; digital 20, 71; exploited 8, 12
Ladino, Jennifer 328
Lambert, Michael 253, 255, 258
Lambert, Sofie 124
Lambert, Valerie 253, 258
L'amitié, ce n'est pas toujours du ski de fond 274
Land Acknowledgment initiatives: Indigenous cartographies 255–257; mapping for accountability 253–255; overview 252–253
Land Acknowledgment Statement (LAS) 252–253, 255–256
Landesman, Ohad 94
Land of Abundant Water 76
Land of Open Graves: Living and Dying on the Migrant Trail (De León) 84
Land of Sunshine 76
Lang, Herbert 81n2
Latin America: copper and rare metals in Chile 120; audiovisual resistance to extractivism 250; extractive activities in 244; Indigenous community media 236–237; media activism in Ecuador 247–249; transforming identity in Chile 237–238
The Latin American Ecocultural Reader (French and Heffes) 9
Latour, Bruno 40
La Trilogie Carnassière 275
Laughing to Keep from Dying 324

law: intellectual property (IP) 179, 187–192; biodiversity protection 246–248; in media management 181, 183–184; e-waste 224; Jim Crow 212; tribal law 204
Lawler, Robert 215
laws of thermodynamics: first law 149; second law 149
Lawson, Angelina 259
Lay, Samantha 313
Lebow, Alisa 94
Le Collectif Jeune Cinéma 273
Lee Francis IV 257
Lefebvre, Martin 314
Lekakis, Eleftheria 163
LeMenager, Stephanie 79
Lessig, Lawrence 190
LGBTQI 246–247, 249; *see also* queer
Liboiron, Max 49
Life in Colour (2021) 51, 53, 56
Life on Earth (1979) 51
Linux operating systems 64
Lioi, Anthony 12
liquified natural gas (LNG) 203–205
Lison, Andrew 147–149
living immediacy 236–237
Locke, John 263
The London Filmakers Co-op 273
López, Antonio 4, 6, 12, 67, 340
Los Angeles Times 319
Louis, Renee 253
Louisiana Purchase Exposition 75
Lowen-Trudeau, Greg 217, 253
Lowood, Henry 148
Lu, Donna 324
Luang Prabang Film Festival (LPFF) 290
Luhmann, Niklas 298

Ma, Jessica 95n1
Ma, Justin 133, 135n1
MacDonald, Scott 89
machine-to-machine (M2M) communication 27
machine-to-people (M2P) communication 27
MacKenzie, Alex 275
Maddox, Richard Leach 275
Mad Max: Fury Road 46
Maggiulli, Katrina 12
Mahākāśyapa 292
Mander, Jerry 339
Manifest Manners: Narratives of Post Indian Survivance 259n4
Manning, Erin 12
The Maori News 200
Mapping Indigenous L.A. 256
maps/mapping: for accountability 253–255; expanded cartographies 94; film as 88–90; indigenous cartographies 255–257;

the mediarchy 298; *see also Mapping Indigenous L.A.*
Marez, Curtis 75
Marks, Laura U. 6, 7, 52, 307
Marshment, Margaret 314
Martin, Noélie 10
The Marvelous Clouds: Toward a Philosophy of Elemental Media (Peters) 4
Marx, Leo 346
Massumi, Brian 347
matter 43–49
Mattern, Shannon 112, 142, 154
Maturana, Humberto 37
Maxwell, Richard 6, 9, 24, 52, 346
McGregor, Callum 216
McKay, Adam 323
McKibben, Bill 339–340
McLean, Jessica 9, 213, 216
McLuhan, Marshall 25, 52, 53, 61–62, 146, 298, 302, 339
McQuail, Denis 20
mediacy and immediacy 233–234
media-ecological registry of property rights 191–192
media ecologies 24, 134–135, 276n1, 297; of blockchain registries 187–192; and ecomedia 52
media ecosystem 24
Media+Environment article 2, 28, 253
media geology 74
medial ecology 40
medial-perceptual 38–40
media producers 233
mediated ecocultural identities 234–238; coal-burning power plant 234–235; emancipatory catastrophism 237–238; immediacy through mediatized empathy 235–236; Indigenous community media 236–237; living immediacy 236–237; *My Octopus Teacher* 235–236; transforming identity in Chile 237–238
mediation/mediatization: of embodied experience 305–310; lifeworld 339–340
mediatized empathy 235–236
medium *see* art; digital media; documentary; gramophone; ICTs; maps; music; photography; radio; smartphones; Slow Media; streaming; TV; video games
medium theory 25
Meeker, Joseph 319
Mejias, Ulises 75
Mekas, Jonas 273
mental ecology 37, 39, 298
metaphorical ecologies 61–62
metaphors 52–53
methodology 29–31, 101–105, 155, 247

metonymy in *Dark River* 313–317
#MeToo movement 183, 320
Mezzadra, Sandro 84
micro/climates of play 145–150
Microsoft 19, 172; Project Natick 149
Miessler, R.C. 259
Millennium Folk (Gruning) 281
Miller, Jocelyn 52, 99
Miller, Toby 6, 9, 24, 346
Milstein, Tema 4, 9, 99, 234
mimetic desire 286–293
Mindy, Randall 322, 323
MintGreen 150n4
Mitman, Gregg 346
Miyake, Esperanza 1
Mocatta, Gabi 9
Modern Language Association (MLA) 2
Moholy-Nagy, László 153
Mojo: Da Floods 261, *261*, 264, *265*
Monani, Salma 2–4, 10
Monbiot, George 55
monster affect 331–333, *332*
monster movie genre 329–331
Moore, Ellen E. 9, 148–149, 204–209
Moore, Jason W. 24
Mora, Anthony 81n1, 82n3
Morag, Raya 94
Mora-Kpai, Idrissou 140
Morgan, Danielle Fuentes 324
Morozov, Evgeny 173
Morrill Act 252
Morton, Timothy 279
Moschek, Wolfgang 95n4
Moten, Fred 301
Moving Environments: Affect, Emotion, Ecology, and Film (Weik von Mossner) 11, 328
Mukherjee, Rahul 6, 7, 75
Mukurtu CMS (content management system) 216
Mulvey, Peter 280
Mumford, Lewis 27
Murphy, Patrick D. 8, 196
Murray, Robin 11
Musk, Elon 322
music: gramophone 153–158; green 278–279; popular music 278–284
Myazaki, Hayao 272
My Octopus Teacher 44–45, 184, 235–236

Nadler, Anthony 24
National Aborigines and Islanders Day Observance Committee Week (NAIDOC Week) 214
Navarro, Vinicius 88, 92
Neilson, Brett 84
neo-colonial: apparatus 31; discourses 105; structure 31; *see also* colonialism

neoliberalism 23, 36, 173, 180, 196, 235, 239, 245, 281–282, 288
Netflix 19, 54, 64, 115, 176, 183, 184, 319, 320, 322; *Don't Look Up* 196; and environmental impact of edge caching 115–116; *Kingdom* 196
network: digital infrastructure 113; discourse 46; human-nonhuman 75; infrastructure 7; network exchange 111; relational 36; social 6; symbolic and material 24; traffic infrastructures 113; Wi-Fi 64
networking technology 124; *see also* infrastructure
new materialism: in ecomedia 47–48; on film 44–45
New Mexico Bureau of Immigration (NMBI) 75–79, *77, 78, 80,* 81
news 4, 19, 25; fake climate 103; literacy 100; media coverage 207–208; media ecosystem 101
Newsom, Joanna 279
Newton, Huey P. 302
Newton, Isaac 65
New York City 162–163
New York Magazine 327
New York Times 95n1, 120, 198, 200
Nicoll, Benjamin 148
Nieto-Phillips, John 81n1, 81n2
Nietzsche, Friedrich 155
"Nile Waters Agreement" 198
#NODAPL movement 200, 203, 204, 205, 206, 208
Nokia 142
#NOLNG253 movement 203, 204, 205; Anna Bean 204–209; climate crisis in Washington State 205–206; extractivist industry 209; LNG and fossil fuel projects 203–204; Water Warriors movement 206
non-Western ontologies 65n1
Nugent, Carlos 5
Nussbaum, Martha 322

Oedipus Rex (Sophocles) 288
Oguz, Zeynep 94
Olsson, Carl 301
Olympic Games 150
On Black Media Philosophy (Towns) 4, 72, 301–302
ontology 23, 43, 48, 60, 248, 282; ecomediality as 35–41
Open Educational Resource (OER) 252
Organ Pipe National Monument 89
#OscarsSoWhite 183
Ostrom, Elinor 195
O'Sullivan, Sandy 214
Our Planet: Behind the Scenes 51, 54, 55, 56

Palmer, Mark 253
pandemic: and climate crisis 171–172; and energy consumption 171–172; global pandemic media imagination 286–293; *see also* Covid-19
parasympathetic nervous system (PNS) 341
Parham, John 10
Parikka, Jussi 21, 76, 155, 271
Parks, Lisa 6, 30, 94, 112, 140
Pasek, Anne 6
The Past Didn't Go Anywhere 283
Patel, Raj 24
Pearce, Margaret 253
Pearson, Luke 217
Pedelty, Mark 280, 284
Pegatron 221–222
Peirce, C. S. 37–38
people-to-people (P2P) communication 27
perceptual ecology 39
Perec, Georges 155
Permanent Error (Hugo) 67
Peters, Benjamin 303
Peters, John Durham 4, 25–26, 39, 52, 75, 92
Petrini, Carlo 338
Petrobras 175
Philippe, Édouard 302
photography 73–74, 79, 81, 138–139, 153, 164, 222, 275, 276n4; in African ecomedia 67–69
Pickles, John 85–86
Pink, Sara 100
Pinker, Steven 174
Pisters, Patricia 41n3
Pitrou, Perig 276
planetary system 20
Planet Earth 51, 54
Planet Earth II 54
Plant Health Inspection Service (APHIS) 328
Plantin, Jean-Christophe 26
Plath, Tara 91, 94, 95n11
Plato 347
play: engines of 147–149; micro/climates of 145–150
Playing Nature (Chang) 150n2
A Play of Bodies (Keogh) 147
PlayStation 146–147
Plumwood, Val 23
Poliquin, Rachel 47
political ecologies 7–9, 29, 59–65
Politics, and the Dakota Access Pipeline (Moore) 9
Polwart, Karine 283
polyvinyl chloride (PVC) 157
Pomerance, Murray 292
Ponge, Francis 155
popular culture 2, 6, 8, 30
postcolonial: African nations 67; ecocriticism 2–3; practices of extractivism 7; "self-other"

inversion 290; strategy of self-narration 290; studies 4, 105; *see also* decolonization
Posthuman Property and Law (Käll) 8
posthumous ecomedia 345–348
Postman, Neil 24, 52, 61–62
Predpełski, Radek 125
Preist, Chris 121
Prigogine, Ilya 37
Princess Mononoke 272
production chain *see* supply chain
Program Earth: Environmental Sensing technology and the Making of a Computational Planet (Gabrys) 4
proof-of-work (POW) systems 147
propaganda 100, 103, 325
property as a registry of control 188–189
property rights: control in data-driven economy 187–192; lack of ecology 189–191; media-ecological registry of 191–192; property as a registry of control 188–189
Przedpełski, Radek 123
Psihoyos, Louis 46
Pueblo del Mediodia *see* Kichwa Sarayaku
Puget Sound Clean Air Agency 204
Puget Sound Energy LNG plant 203–204, 206
Punathambekar, Aswin 26
Pushing Past the Human in Latin American Cinema (Fornoff and Heffes) 9
Puyallup Water Warrior movement *see* #NOLNG253 movement
Puyallup Water Warriors 204, 206–207, 209

Qualcomm 222
Quanta 221
queer 302
queer ecology 23

race 76, 81n1, 85, 92, 157, 246, 261–263; *see also* Black media philosophy
Racing Extinction 46
radiant energy 137–143
radiant infrastructures 137, 142–143; emissions and exposures 139–140; infrastructural imaginaries 142; infrastructural (in)visibilities 139–140; socio-material relations 140–142
radical digital citizenship 216
radio 121, 139, 143, 156, 225, 236–237, 239n2, 247–250, 280, 298
Raghavan, Barath 133, 135n1
Rama, Angel 74
Rasmi, Jacopo 10
Rauch, Jennifer 30, 99, 100
rebound effects 122
Red Planet 257
relational ecologies of gramophone disc 153–158

renewable energy 124
Report of Doña Ana County 76
Report on Bernalillo County 76
resistance 5, 10, 92, 190, 197, 199–200, 207, 209, 213, 248, 250, 261, 342; *see* activism
responsibility deficit: in media content 183–184; in media production 181–183
Revolutionary Love 283
Reyes, Xavier Aldana 329
Reynolds, Malvina 278
#ReZpectOurWater 200
Rich, Adrienne 308
Rio Grande Project 81
Rivera, José 82n4
Robins, Ann 257
Robinson, Brett H. 135n2
Robinson, Nathan J. 324
Rogoff, Irit 85
The Rolling Stone 200, 278
Roquet, Paul 12
Ross, Andrew 2
Rousseau, Jean-Jacques 263
The Routledge Handbook of Ecocultural Identity (Milstein and Castro-Sotomayor) 4, 9
The Routledge Handbook of Environment and Communication (Hansen and Cox) 4
Roy, Elodie A. 6, 7
Royal Dutch Shell 175
Rudolph, Maya 320–321
Rust, Stephen 2–4, 5, 67, 69, 71
Ryan, John 9

sacrifice zone 20, 30, 31
Samsung Electronics 142, 222
Sanchez, Griselda 245, 250
Sarah Cooper: Everything's Fine 12, 319–322
satire: Aristophanic 324; ecopolitical 12, 319–325; Horatian 320, 322; Juvenalian 320, 322; neoclassical 320
Schaller, Robert 275
scientific ecology 39
search engine optimization (SEO) processes 215
Seaspiracy 184
Seeger, Pete 278
See No Stranger: A Memoir and Manifesto of Revolutionary Love (Kaur) 283
self-sustaining systems 124
Senier, Siobhan 256
Sense Lab 12
Sentient Flesh (Judy) 263
Sessou, Emmanuel Septime 8
settler colonialism 78, 200, 212; *see also* colonialism
Seven Worlds 55
Sex Which Is Not One (Luce Irigaray) 345
Seymour, Nicole 12, 259, 319, 325

Sharma, Sarah 342
shellac: poetics of 156–157; politics of 156–157
Shenzhen 162
Shiva, Vandana 190
Signal Traffic (Starosielski) 6
Silcox, Nicholas R. 6
Singh, Abhigyan 141
Slow Food movement 338
Slow Food Nation (Petrini) 338
Slow Media 337–343; perceptions 340–342
Slow Media: Why Slow is Satisfying, Sustainable and Smart (Rauch) 339
slow violence 12, 27, 46
smartphones 63–64, 10, 156, 163–164, 165, 172, 297; global e-waste problem 223–225; manufacturing and assembly 221–222; mining hazards and conflict minerals 220–221; subcontracting 223
Smith, Jacob 12, 154
Smith, Murray 306
Sniadecki, J.P. 86–89, *89, 90,* 92, *93,* 94, 95n5, 95n7
Snider, Dee 200
Sobchack, Vivian 307
Sobo, Elisa J. 258
social 38–40; ecology 36, 39; media 208–209
social movements in Ecuador 247–249
social realism 312–317; in *Dark River* 313–317
Society for Cinema and Media Studies (SCMS) 2
Society of Tammany 254
socio-ecological conceptions: in Indigenous cartographies 255–257; of space and time 255–257
socio-environmental systems 3
socio-political ecology 29
socio-technical environments 273
Soderbergh, Steven 287
Solar Protocol 116
Sophocles 288
Sorkin, Andrew Ross 120
sovereign individuals 300–302
Sovereign Nature Initiative 191
Spanish Empire 74
spatial documentary studies 85–86
spatiality 25, 54, 59, 84–94
Spotify 64
The Stack (Bratton) 263
Standing Rock Sioux Tribe 199–200, 204–205, 208
Starosiekski, Nicole 4, 6, 22, 26, 29, 52, 54, 94
State of the Planet 55
Steele, Andrea 320–322
Stengers, Isabelle 37
Stewart-Ambo, Theresa 258
Stiegler, Bernard 298
Strayed, Cheryl 306–307, 308–309, 310

streaming 6, 27, 52, 54, 101–102, 115–116, 121–126, 245, 247, 287; *see also* Netflix; Spotify; YouTube
Streep, Meryl 322
subcontracting 223
Subramaniam, Banu 330–331
Sullivan, Corrinne 9, 213
supply chain 9, 22, 27, 59, 62–63, 154, 182, 221–225, 273, 297
sustainable development 124
Sustainable Subsea Networks research project 114
Svampa, Maristella 244
Syriana 313
systems thinking 100–105
Szeman, Imre 141

Taffel, Sy 5
Tampa Electric Company 234
Teaching Ecocriticism and Green Cultural Studies (Garrard) 3
Telles, Jason Paolo 9
Tencent 172
Texas Instruments 222
Thank You for the Rain 72
Thibaud, Carole 275
The Thing 45
The Three Ecologies (Les Trois Écologies) (Guattari) 37
three ecologies 2, 5, 36–38, 298, 301; *see also* ecological triad
Thunberg, Greta 171
Thunig, Amy 215
Tidwell, Christy 5
TikTok 112, 120, 287, 339
Timaeus (Plato) 347
Tisch, Steve 94
Titanic 182
Todd, Zoe 48
Tola, Miriam 67, 69, 71–72
"Tormenta" 94
Toshiba Electronics 222
Towns, Armond R. 4, 10, 25, 72, 261–269, 339, 301
ToxiCity 224
"The Tragedy of the Commons" (Hardin) 195
Transmission Protocol 27, 64
Tripadvisor 234, 239
Trump, Donald 171, 319–320, 321
The Truth About Climate Change 55
TV 53–55, 100, 121, 182, 186, 207, 322, 339, 346; commercial 101
Twitter 171, 200, 214, 283

undercommon assemblies 300–302
Undercommons (Moten and Harney) 301
The Undersea Network (Starosielski) 54
Understanding the Media (McLuhan) 298

Index

Undocumented Migration Project 84
The Uninhabitable Earth: Life After Warming (Wallace-Wells) 334n1
United Kingdom (UK): Parliamentary Office of Science and Technology 135n1; per capita e-waste generation rates in 64
United Nations Environment Programme 135n2, 172
United Nations Security Council 198
United States: Army Corps of Engineers 199; Border Patrol 84, 88, 95n1; Customs and Border Protection agency 88; Department of Agriculture (USDA) 328; Environmental Protection Agency 135n4; Fish & Wildlife Service Pacific Region Fisheries 330; immigration policy 84; per capita e-waste generation rates in 64
The Unity Game Engine and the Circuits of Cultural Software (Keogh and Nicoll) 148
"Unnatural Ecologies" (Heise) 52
Urlus, Esther 275
US Academy of Motion Picture Arts and Sciences 183
U.S.-Mexico border 86, 93; ecomedia and empire in 73–81

Vallée, Jean-Marc 11, 305–310
Varela, Francesco 37
Varjacques, Leah 95n1
Vaughan, Hunter 2, 6, 8, 44, 45–46
Vaz, Ana 275
Vice 200
video games 19, 145–150
Vin Vasive 331–333, *332*
Virilio, Paul 138
visual culture 3, 68
visual ecologies 261–269
Vizenor, Gerald 259n4
Voices of the First Day: Awakening in the Aboriginal Dreamtime (Lawler) 215
von Lünen, Alexander 95n4
von Mossner, Alexa Weik 328
Voodoo (video game developer) 163

Wald, Sarah 259
Waldrop, M. Mitchell 148
Walker, Alison 307
Walker, Christopher 94
Walker, Janet 4, 5, 22, 45
Wallace-Wells, David 327, 334n1
Walmart 54
Wang, Xiaowei 189
Warren, Karen 23
The Washington Post 198
water 28, 38, 46, 52–53, 60, 62, 77–81, 92–93, 111–112, 122, 171–175, 206–209

Waterman, Ellen 207–209, 279
Water Warriors movement 206
Water Wars, in East Africa 67
Watkins, George 292
Weik von Mossner, Alexa 10–11
Weissman, Dick 279
Western colonialism 262
WhatsApp 287
Whitehead, Alfred North 29, 37
White Paper on Artificial Intelligence 173
white supremacy 48, 69
Whyte, Kyle Powys 256, 259
Wickberg, Adam 27
Wi-Fi networks 64
Wijaya, Elizabeth 41n3
Wild 305–310; material, narrative in 306–309; material in 306–309; visual strategies in 306–309
Wild Blue Media: Thinking Through Seawater (Jue) 4
Wild: From Lost to Found on the Pacific Crest Trail (Strayed) 307–308
Wildscreen Arkive 55
Willet, Cynthia 324
Willet, Julie 324
Williams, Eric 129
Williams, Peter 47–48
Williams, Raymond 23, 52
Windows operating systems 64
The Windup Girl (Bacigalupi) 150
wireless 64, 142
Wistron 221
Wittick, Ben 73, *74*, 81
women: in global pandemic films 287–292; in global pandemic media imagination 286–293; *see also* ecofeminism
World Economic Forum 173
World Energy Outlook 172
World War II 61, 157, 288
World Wildlife Fund UK (WWF) 187
Wright, Frank Lloyd 91
Wurth, Verena 5
Wynter, Sylvia 300

Yes Magazine 200
Yong, Ed 55
Young, Mary Lynn 253
Young, Neil 200, 278
Young, Phyllis 206
Young, Rob 280
Your Computer Is on Fire! 299
YouTube 172, 175, 176, 200
Yusoff, Kathryn 5, 92, 94, 95n13

Zacks, Jeffrey 305
Zenner, Christiana 94

Index

Zielinski, Siegfried 155
Ziewitz, M. 215
Zimmerman, Eric 145
Zimmerman, Michael E. 41n1
Zimmermann, Patricia 94

Zion Market Research 175
Ziser, Michael 21
Zoom 121
Zoo Quest in Colour 51, 54
Zuckerberg, Mark 64, 322

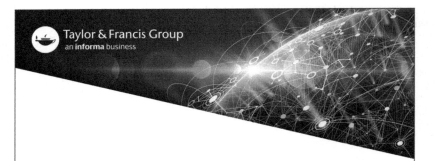